Repeated Measures ANOVA

$$SS_{TOTAL} = \sum (X - M_G)^2$$

$$SS_{TREATMENT} = \sum (M_{Group} - M_{Grand})^2(n)$$

OR

$$SS_{TREATMENT} = \sum (SS_{Means})(n)$$

$$SS_{ERROR} = ss_{Group\,1} + ss_{Group\,2} + SS_{Group\,3}$$

$$SS_{Between\,Subjects} = \sum (M_p + M_{Grand\,Person})^2(k)$$

$$df_{Total} = N - 1$$

$$df_{Treatment} = k - 1$$

$$df_{Error} = N - k$$

$$df_{BS} = n - 1$$

$$df_{WS} = df_{Error} - df_{BS}$$

$$MS_{Treatment} = \frac{SS_{TREATMENT}}{df_{Treatment}}$$

$$MS_{Error} = \frac{SS_{ERROR}}{df_{Error}}$$

$$MS_{Between\,Subjects} = \frac{SS_{BS}}{df_{BS}}$$

$$MS_{Within\,Subjects} = \frac{SS_{Within\,Subjects}}{df_{Within\,Subjects}}$$

$$F = \frac{MS_{Treatment}}{MS_{Within\,Subjects}}$$

$$\omega^2 = \frac{(k - 1)(MS_{Treatment} - MS_{Within\,Subjects})}{SS_{TOTAL} + MS_{Between\,Subjects}}$$

FORMULAS FOR CHAPTER 10

$$SS_{TOTAL} = (X - M_G)^2$$

$$SS_{Factor} = \sum (M_{Level} - M_{Grand})^2\,n$$

$$SS_{Cell} = (M_{Cell} - M_{Grand})^2 n$$

$$SS_{Group} = \sum (M_{Cell} - M_{Grand})^2 n$$

$$SS_{Interaction} = [\sum (M_{Cell} - M_{Grand})^2 n] - SS_A - SS_B$$

$$SS_{ERROR} = SS_{Cell\,1} + SS_{Cell\,2} + SS_{Cell\,3}$$

$$df_{Factor} = k - 1$$

$$df_{Interaction} = (A - 1)(B - 1)$$

$$df_{Error} = N - k$$

$$MS_{Factor} = \frac{SS_{Factor}}{df_{Factor}}$$

$$MS_{Interaction} = \frac{SS_{Interaction}}{df_{Interaction}}$$

$$MS_{Error} = $$

$$F_A = \frac{MS}{MS}$$

$$F_B = \frac{MS}{MS_{Error}}$$

$$F_{A\times B} = \frac{MS_{A\times B}}{MS_{Error}}$$

$$\omega^2 = \frac{SS_A - (df_A MS_{Error})}{SS_{TOTAL} + MS_{Error}}$$

$$\omega^2 = \frac{SS_{A\times B} - (df_{A\times B} MS_{Error})}{SS_{TOTAL} + MS_{Error}}$$

FORMULAS FOR CHAPTER 13

Correlation

$$r = \frac{s_{xy}}{s_x s_y}$$

$$SP = \sum (X - M_X)(Y - M_Y)$$

$$s_{xy} = \frac{\sum (X - M_X)(Y - M_Y)}{N - 1} \text{ OR } s_{xy} = \frac{SP}{N - 1}$$

$$r = \frac{N\sum XY - (\sum X)(\sum Y)}{\sqrt{[N\sum X^2 - (\sum X)^2][N\sum Y^2 - (\sum Y)^2]}}$$

Regression

$$Y = a + (b)(X)$$

$$b = \frac{SP}{SS_x}$$

$$a = M_Y - (b)(M_X)$$

Chi-Square

$$\mathcal{X}^2 = \sum \frac{(f_o - f_e)^2}{f_e}$$

$$V = \sqrt{\frac{\chi^2}{n(df^*)}}$$

Research Methods and Statistics

Research Methods and Statistics

Bernard C. Beins

Ithaca College

Maureen A. McCarthy

Kennesaw State University

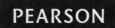

Boston   Columbus   Indianapolis   New York   San Francisco   Upper Saddle River
Amsterdam   Cape Town   Dubai   London   Madrid   Milan   Munich   Paris   Montreal   Toronto
Delhi   Mexico City   São Paulo   Sydney   Hong Kong   Seoul   Singapore   Taipei   Tokyo

Executive Editor: Stephen Frail
Editorial Assistant: Madelyn Schricker
Senior Marketing Manager: Nicole Kunzmann
Marketing Assistant: Jessica Warren
Senior Production Project Manager: Roberta Sherman
Editorial Production and Composition Service: Laserwords Maine
Manufacturing Buyer: Linda Cox
Cover Administrator: Leslie Osher

The following SPSS screen images appear courtesy of International Business Machines Corporation © 2010 International Business Machines Corporation. Images include Figures 5.3, 5.4, 5.5, 5.6, 5.7, 5.8, 5.9, 5.10, 7.13, 7.14, 7.15, 7.16, 8.5, 8.6, 8.7, 8.8, 8.9, 8.10, 8.11, 8.12, 9.11, 9.12, 9.13, 9.14, 9.15, 9.16, 10.6, 10.7, 10.8, 12.8, 12.9, 12.10, 12.11, 12.12, 12.13, 12.14, 12.15, 12.16, and Table 5.5.

Library of Congress Cataloging-in-Publication Data

Beins, Bernard.
   Research methods and statistics / Bernard C. Beins, Maureen A. McCarthy.
      p. cm.
   Includes bibliographical references and index.
   ISBN-10: 0-205-62409-X
   ISBN-13: 978-0-205-62409-6
   1. Psychology—Research—Methodology. 2. Psychometrics. I. McCarthy, Maureen A. II. Title.
   BF76.5.B4393 2012
   150.72'1—dc23

                                         2011023750

10 9 8 7 6 5 4 3 2   EBM 15 14 13 12

ISBN-10:   0-205-62409-X
ISBN-13: 978-0-205-62409-6

www.pearsonhighered.com

As always, I dedicate this book to Linda, Agatha, and Simon—my wonderful family that makes it all worthwhile.

—Barney Beins

I dedicate this book to Dennis, Mary Ann, Tom, Dan, and Brenda—as they made this work possible.

—Maureen McCarthy

CONTENTS

Preface   xv

Part I: Understanding Research   1

1 Psychology, Science, and Life   1

Why Are Research Methods Important Tools for Life?   2
Creating Knowledge   3 / Answering Important Questions   3

Why We Do Research   4
Description   4 / Explanation   5 / Prediction   6 / Control   6

What Constitutes Scientific Knowledge?   7
Science Is Objective   8 / Science Is Data Driven   9 / Science Is
Replicable and Verifiable   9 / Science Is Public   10

The Interaction of Science and Culture   10
The Government's Role in Science   11 / Cultural Values and Science   11

Scientific Literacy   13
Science and Pseudoscience   14 / Warning Signs of Bogus
Science   15 / Junk Science   18

Chapter Summary   18

Key Terms   19

Chapter Review Questions   20

Part II: The First Steps in Conducting Research   23

2 Ethics in Research   23

Unethical Research Practices—Past and Present   25
Ethical Problems in the Early Years of the Twentieth Century   25 / Ethics
and Plagiarism   27 / Current Examples of Unethical Research   28

Ethical Guidelines Created by the American Psychological Association   29
Aspirational Goals and Enforceable Rules   29 / Ethical Standards as They
Affect You   30

Legal Requirements and Ethics in Research   33
Institutional Review Boards   34

The Importance of Social Context in Deciding on Ethics in Research   **35**

Stanley Milgram's Research Project on Obedience   36   /   The Ethical
Issues   36   /   The Social Context   37

What You Need to Do if Your Research Involves Deception   **38**

Some Research Requires Deception   39   /   The Effects of Debriefing
on Research   40

Ethical Issues in Special Circumstances   **42**

Ethics in Cross-Cultural Research   42   /   Ethics in Internet
Research   42   /   Ethics in Animal Research   43

Chapter Summary   **45**

Key Terms   **46**

Chapter Review Questions   **46**

3   *Planning Research: Generating a Question*   **51**

*Where Research Ideas Begin: Everyday Observations
and Systematic Research*   **52**

Informal and Formal Sources of Ideas   53   /   The Effect of Theory   55

How Can You Develop Research Ideas?   **58**

Generating Research Hypotheses   59

The Virtual Laboratory: Research on the Internet   **59**

Internet Research   61   /   Respondent Motivation   64   /   Advantages
to Web-Based Research   64   /   Potential Problems with Web-Based
Research   65   /   The Future of the Internet in Psychology   66

Checking on Research: The Role of Replication   **66**

Don't Reinvent the Wheel: Reviewing the Literature   **68**

What Is a Literature Review?   69   /   The Effect of Peer Review
on the Research Literature   69

How to Conduct a Literature Review   **71**

Electronic Databases   71   /   Starting Your Search   71   /   Different
Sources of Information   73

How to Read a Journal Article   **74**

Understanding the Format of a Research Paper   74

Chapter Summary   **77**

Key Terms   **78**

Chapter Review Questions   **78**

4 *Practical Issues in Planning Your Research* **81**

Practical Questions in Planning Research **82**

Different Ways of Studying Behavior **83**
Measuring Complex Concepts 83 / The Importance of Culture and Context in Defining Variables 84 / Carrying Out a Literature Search 86

Conducting Your Study **87**
Determining the Research Setting 88 / Approaches to Psychological Research 88 / Selecting Research Materials and Procedures 90 / Why Methodology Is Important 92

Choosing Your Participants or Subjects **93**
The Nature of Your Participants 94 / Deciding How Many Participants to Include 94

Can Rats, Mice, and Fish Help Us Understand Humans? **96**

Probability Sampling **97**
Simple Random Sampling 98 / Systematic Sampling 98 / Stratified Random Sampling 98 / Cluster Sampling 99

Nonprobability Sampling **99**
Convenience Sampling 99 / Quota Sampling 100 / Purposive (Judgmental) Sampling 100 / Chain-Referral Sampling 100

Chapter Summary **101**

Key Terms **101**

Chapter Review Questions **102**

5 *Organizing Data with Descriptive Statistics* **105**

Using Statistics to Describe Results **106**

Descriptive Statistics **106**
Scales of Measurement 107 / Measures of Central Tendency 109 / Distributions of Scores 111 / Measures of Variability 113 / Summarizing Data 118

Computer Analysis Using SPSS **119**
Generating Descriptive Statistics 119 / Illustrating Descriptive Statistics 120

Chapter Summary **125**

Key Terms **125**

Chapter Review Questions **125**

Part III: Creating Experiments   **129**

6 *Conducting an Experiment: General Principles*   **129**

Choosing a Methodology: The Practicalities of Research   **130**

Determining the Causes of Behavior   **131**

Trying to Determine Causation in Research   131   /   Requirements for
Cause–Effect Relationships   131   /   Internal and External Validity   132

The Logic of Experimental Manipulation   **135**

Experimental Control   **136**

Threats to Internal Validity   136   /   Lack of Control in Experimental
Research: Extraneous Variables and Confounds   138

Experimenter Effects   **142**

Participant Effects   **142**

The Hawthorne Effect   143

Interaction Effects Between Experimenters and Participants   **144**

Biosocial and Psychosocial Effects   144

Realism in Research   **144**

Chapter Summary   **145**

Key Terms   **146**

Chapter Review Questions   **146**

7 *Basic Inferential Statistics*   **149**

Probability   **150**

Hypothesis Testing   **151**

Decisions in Statistical Hypothesis Testing   153   /   Normal
Distribution   156   /   Sampling Distributions   157   /
Single Sample z Test   162   /   Steps in Hypothesis Testing   164   /
Single Sample t Test   166

Computer Analysis Using SPSS   **171**

Chapter Summary   **173**

Key Terms   **173**

Chapter Review Questions   **174**

8   *Looking for Differences Between Two Treatments*   **177**

Statistical Testing for Two Independent Groups   **178**
Stating the Hypothesis   179   /   Significance Testing   180   /   Confidence Intervals   185

Statistical Testing for Related and Repeated Measures   **187**
Stating the Hypothesis   187   /   Significance Testing   188   / Confidence Intervals   190   /   Advantages of Repeated Measures Designs   192   /   Limitations of Repeated Measures Designs   195

Computer Analysis Using SPSS   **196**
Independent Samples *t* Test   196   /   Related Samples *t* Test   197

Chapter Summary   **199**

Key Terms   **200**

Chapter Review Questions   **200**

9   *Looking for Differences Among Multiple Treatments*   **203**

Statistical Testing for Multiple Treatments   **204**

Statistical Testing for Multiple Groups   **205**
Stating the Hypothesis   205   /   Significance Testing   207   /   Post Hoc Analyses   214   /   Effect Size   217   /   Computer Analysis Using SPSS   217

Statistical Testing for Repeated Measures   **220**
Stating the Hypothesis   221   /   Significance Testing   222   /   Post Hoc Analyses   227   /   Effect Size   227   /   Computer Analysis Using SPSS   228

Chapter Summary   **231**

Key Terms   **232**

Chapter Review Questions   **232**

10   *Multiple Independent Variables: Factorial Designs*   **235**

Factorial ANOVA   **236**
Stating the Hypotheses   237   /   Partitioning Variance   238

Calculating the Factorial ANOVA   **239**
TOTAL Variance   239   /   TREATMENT Variance   240   /   ERROR Variance   245   /   *F* Statistics   247   /   Determining Significance   248   /   Post Hoc Analyses   250   /   Effect Size   251

Computer Analysis Using SPSS 252

Chapter Summary 254

Key Terms 254

Chapter Review Questions 254

Part IV: Correlational and Nonexperimental Research   **257**

11 *Principles of Survey Research*   **257**

Surveys: Answering Diverse Questions 258
   Census Versus Sample 259 / Accuracy of Survey Results 260

Anonymity and Confidentiality in Survey Research 261

Selecting Your Methodology 263
   Question Types 264 / Question Content 264

Response Bias 270
   Studying Sensitive Issues 271 / Social Desirability 272 /
   Acquiescence 273 / Satisficing Versus Optimizing 273 / Minimizing
   the Occurrence of Satisficing 275

Sampling Issues 275
   Finding Hidden Populations 276

Chapter Summary 277

Key Terms 277

Chapter Review Questions 278

12 *Correlation, Regression, and Non-Parametric Tests*   **281**

Correlational Studies 282

Correlational Analyses 282
   Traditional Correlation Tests 283 / Pearson's r 284

Regression 291
   Multiple Regression 293

Chi-Square Goodness of Fit 295

Chi-Square Test of Independence 298
   Strength of Association 300

Computer Analysis Using SPSS 301
   Correlation 301 / Regression 302 / Chi-Square 302

Chapter Summary 306

Key Terms 306

Chapter Review Questions 307

13 *Research in Depth: Longitudinal and Single-Case Studies* **311**

Longitudinal Research **312**

Common Themes in Longitudinal Research 312 / Cross-Sectional Versus Longitudinal Research 313

Varieties of Longitudinal Research **314**

Trend Studies 314 / Cohort Studies 316 / Cohort Sequential Studies 317 / Panel Studies 318

Issues in Longitudinal Designs **320**

Retrospective and Prospective Studies 320 / Attrition 321

Single-Subject Experimentation **324**

Experimental Analysis of Behavior 325

Methods of Single-Case Designs **325**

Withdrawal Designs 325 / Single-Subject Randomized Controlled Trials 326 / Strengths of Single-Participant Designs 326 / Weaknesses of Single-Participant Designs 327 / Misunderstandings About Single-Case Research 327

Case Studies **328**

A Case Study with Experimental Manipulations: Tasting Pointed Chickens and Seeing Colored Numbers **329**

Chapter Summary **330**

Key Terms **330**

Chapter Review Questions **331**

Part V: Culture and Research **333**

14 *People Are Different: Considering Cultural and Individual Differences in Research* **333**

Different Cultural Perspectives **335**

What Is Culture? 335

Defining an Individual's Culture, Ethnicity, and Race **336**

Criteria for Inclusion in a Group 337 / Social Issues and Cultural Research 338

Cross-Cultural Concepts in Psychology   **339**

Are Psychological Constructs Universal?   339   /   Issues in Cross-Cultural Research   341

Is There a Biological Basis for Race?   **342**

The Criteria for Race   342   /   Current Biological Insights Regarding Race   343   /   Historical Error   343   /   Current Controversies   345

Practical Issues in Cultural Research   **345**

Lack of Appropriate Training Among Researchers   345

Why the Concepts of Culture and Ethnicity Are Essential in Research   **346**

Differences Due to Language and Thought Processes   346   /   Differences in Simple and Complex Behaviors   347   /   Is Culture-Free Theory Really Free of Culture?   348   /   Similarities and Differences within the Same Culture   348

Cultural Factors in Mental Health Research   **349**

Content Validity   349   /   Translation Problems   350   /   Cross-Cultural Norms   351   /   Cross-Cultural Diagnoses   351

Sex and Gender: Do Men and Women Come from Different Cultures?   **353**

Stereotypes and Gender-Related Performance   353

Chapter Summary   **354**

Key Terms   **355**

Chapter Review Questions   **355**

Appendix A   Writing a Research Report   359

Appendix B   Developing an Oral Presentation   387

Appendix C   Creating a Poster   389

Appendix D   Answers to Chapter Review Questions   393

Appendix E   Statistical Tables   409

References   421

Index   441

PREFACE

Students who are curious and who like solving puzzles are ideal candidates for a course in psychological research methods. We developed this book in order to meet the needs of students who are learning to think like psychologists. We assume that you have already completed at least one course in psychology and have developed an interest in the discipline, so you are ready to apply your knowledge to ask and answer questions about thought, attitude, and behavior.

We also think that you are probably uncertain about the prospect of learning about statistics and the methods of research. Throughout the book, we have tried to show how the content of this course involves tools for understanding people. What is most important is that these tools help us learn about people and other animals. So we worked to create a book that will not let you lose sight that psychologists focus on questions about what people do and why they do it.

To benefit from your course on asking and answering research questions about people, you only need to bring your sense of curiosity and a willingness to puzzle through the complexities of behavior. It is not always an easy task, but it is an interesting task. And at the end of a research project, you know something that nobody else in the world knows; you have created knowledge through your research that helps us advance, one step at a time, what we know about people.

Throughout the book, we have tried to make our writing as clear and accessible to you as possible. There are technical terms that you need to learn and understand, but we strove to minimize wording that would distract you from the points that we think you should know. As we progress through each chapter, our goal is to help you gradually build your skill set. First, we introduce basic tools for understanding research, then we show how you use those tools. At each step along the way, your knowledge will grow until, at the end of the course, you will understand the process of planning a research project, carrying it out, and then drawing conclusions about the question that interests you. And, as we mentioned before, at the end of your project, you will know something that nobody else in the world knows. You will have created a new nugget of knowledge.

In order to think like a psychologist, you have to acquire some skills that you may not already have. These skills include the ability to formulate a question that can be answered through psychological, scientific procedures; to develop a plan for arriving at a valid answer; and to draw conclusions that are sound.

You must also learn how to analyze data that you might collect to answer a research question. We explain basic statistical concepts using a clear and direct approach. We focus on helping you to understand how and why to use statistics rather than emphasizing calculations of statistics. After all, statistical software is very useful for performing the actual calculations.

As you learn the tools of research, we will show you how psychologists have studied interesting topics using those tools. Previous research is often the key to developing new projects. With the diversity of topics we provide in this book, you will be able to see the diversity of projects that psychologists undertake. We also give ideas about how to extend previous research. To help you solidify your knowledge, we have created problem sets for you to use to check your progress.

In addition, we have provided guidance for writing research reports. Psychologists typically use the style of the American Psychological Association. There are a lot of details, but we have outlined them in a way that will make it possible for you to create a report that conforms closely to APA style. Beyond the written report, we have also included ways to enhance a poster presentation of your work and an oral presentation.

The book has six sections, each with its own focus. The first section (Chapter 1) introduces you to the general principles of scientific research. The second section (Chapters 2 to 5) provides practical guidance for creating a sound research project. The third section (Chapters 6 to 10) describes how to set up experiments and analyze data to draw conclusions about behavior. The fourth section (Chapters 11 to 13) provides information about nonexperimental types of research, like surveys and case studies and ways to make sense of the data. The fifth section (Chapter 14) shows how individual and cultural differences can affect research results. This final chapter is unique to this book; most treatments of research methods do not consider the effects of culture, race, ethnicity, gender, and so forth in research. We have tried to remedy this shortcoming to account for these important issues.

In order to help instructors with their work, we have included supplements to this book. The instructors' manual includes many activities that will help students to actively engage in creating research designs and interpreting statistical analyses. Laboratory and data-collection exercises will help students understand how psychologists actually collect and analyze data. The data sets will be particularly useful for small classes that may not have enough students to generate data with sufficient power to detect real differences across groups or correlations among variables. The data sets are the result of participation of students across many semesters.

We also provide instructors with PowerPoint slides that will aid in presenting information to students in a traditional class setting or in an online format. A set of testing materials for evaluating student progress is also available to faculty. We provide questions in a variety of formats to aid instructors in designing tests that might be used in a variety of instructional formats.

We are happy to acknowledge the people who have helped us bring this project to a successful conclusion. They include a group of fastidious reviewers who provided very helpful feedback during the development of the book: Pam Ansburg, Metropolitan State College, Denver; Joan Bihun, University of Colorado, Denver; Alaina Brenick, University of Maryland; Jay Brown, Texas Wesleyan University; Stephen Burgess, Southwestern Oklahoma State University; Pamela Costa, Tacoma Community College; Alyson Froehlich, University of Utah; Don Hantula, Temple University; Constance Jones, California State University, Fresno; David Kreiner, University of Central Missouri; Marianne Lloyd, Seton Hall University; Bryan Myers, University of North Carolina, Wilmington; Katia Shkurkin, St. Martin's University; and Eric Stephens, University of the Cumberlands. We also want to thank Tim Martin and Terry Jorgensen, Kennesaw State University, and Sue Frantz, Highline Community College, for their technical help.

In addition, we appreciate the work of our editors Susan Hartman, Jeff Marshall, Stephen Frail, Roberta Sherman, and Madelyn Schricker from Pearson Education, who we could count on to help us solve problems and keep the book moving in the right direction. Our thanks also go to Karen Berry at Laserwords, who guided us through the editing details. Barney Beins recognizes that none of this would be nearly as meaningful without his wonderful family, Linda, Agatha, and Simon. Maureen McCarthy recognizes her brothers Tom and Dan McCarthy for their insights into the world of student learning.

Research Methods and Statistics

CHAPTER 1

PSYCHOLOGY, SCIENCE, AND LIFE

CHAPTER OUTLINE

WHY ARE RESEARCH METHODS IMPORTANT TOOLS FOR LIFE?
Creating Knowledge
Answering Important Questions

WHY WE DO RESEARCH
Description
Explanation
Prediction
Control

WHAT CONSTITUTES SCIENTIFIC KNOWLEDGE?
Science Is Objective
Science Is Data Driven

Science Is Replicable and Verifiable
Science Is Public

THE INTERACTION OF SCIENCE AND CULTURE
The Government's Role in Science
Cultural Values and Science

CONTROVERSY: SHOULD WOMEN SERVE AS JURORS?

SCIENTIFIC LITERACY
Science and Pseudoscience
Warning Signs of Bogus Science
Junk Science

CONTROVERSY: WHAT CAUSES AUTISM?

LEARNING OBJECTIVES

- Identify and describe the four basic goals of science.
- Explain why falsifiability is important in scientific research.
- Define the five different ways of knowing.
- Explain the advantages of using the scientific approach to knowing.
- Describe the four characteristics of scientific research.
- Explain how science is driven by government, culture, and society.
- Explain how researchers try to generalize from laboratory research to the natural world.
- Differentiate between science and pseudoscience.
- Identify the general characteristics of pseudoscience.

CHAPTER PREVIEW

You probably know a great deal about people and some interesting and important facts about psychology, but you probably know relatively little about psychological research. This book will show you how research helps you learn more about people from a psychological point of view. You can be certain of one thing: There are no simple explanations.

When you read through this chapter, you will learn that there are different ways of knowing about behavior. As a beginning psychologist, you will get a glimpse about why some types of knowledge are more useful than others. In addition, you will see that people can be resistant to changing what they believe. For instance, a lot of people believe in ESP or other paranormal phenomena, even though the scientific evidence for it just isn't there. One reason for such beliefs is that most people don't approach life the same way that scientists do, so the evidence they accept is sometimes pretty shaky.

Finally, this chapter will introduce you to some of the cautions you should be aware of when you read about psychological research in the popular media. Journalists are not scientists and scientists are not journalists, so there is a lot of potential for miscommunication between the two.

Why Are Research Methods Important Tools for Life?

The great thing about psychology is that people are both interesting and complicated, and we get to learn more about them. As you learn more, you will see that there can be a big difference between what we think we know about behavior and what is actually true. That is why you need this course.

Your course on research begins the process of learning about how psychological knowledge emerges. This knowledge can be useful when applied to people's lives. For instance, even four years after a domestic terrorist destroyed a federal building in Oklahoma City, killing 168 people, about half the survivors were still suffering from some kind of psychiatric illness (North et al., 1999). This pattern mirrors the effects of the terrorist attacks in the United States in 2001, the devastation and hurricane damage in Louisiana in 2005, and the experiences of many soldiers in combat in Iraq and Afghanistan, indicating the critical need to provide effective treatments (Humphreys, 2009).

We don't have to rely on such extreme examples of the use of psychological research. For example, scientists have suggested that some people suffer from addiction to indoor tanning (Zeller et al., 2006), with some people showing withdrawal symptoms when the researchers experimentally blocked the physiological effects of tanning (Kaur et al., 2006).

Another complex question relating to everyday life has involved something as seemingly noncontroversial as the *Baby Einstein* DVDs that purport to enhance language learning. Researchers have found that with increasing exposure to the *Baby Einstein* videos, language development actually slows down (Zimmerman, Christakis, & Meltzoff, 2007). In fact, Christakis (2009) has claimed that there is no experimental evidence indicating any advantages for language development in young infants. The developer of the videos makes the opposite claim. So how should we respond?

The only way to address such issues is to do research, which means that we need to create knowledge where it does not already exist. It might sound strange to think of "creating" knowledge, but that is exactly what happens in research. You end up with information that didn't exist before. This is one of the exciting parts of doing research: When you complete a study, you know something that nobody else in the world knows.

Creating Knowledge

In reading textbooks or journal articles, we might get the impression that we can carry out a research project and an explanation jumps clearly out of the results. In reality, there is always uncertainty in research. When we plan our investigations, we make many decisions about our procedures; when we examine our results, we usually have to puzzle through them before we are confident that we understand what we are looking at. In textbooks and journals, we only see the end product of ideas that have worked out successfully, and we do not see the twists and turns that led to those successes.

In this course, we will see that research requires imagination, creativity, and ingenuity in developing knowledge. If we want to address the question of indoor tanning addiction (or any other behavior), we need to understand how we can create knowledge, which is what a course in research methods is all about.

This course in research methods will also help you prepare for a possible future in psychology. If you attend graduate school, you will see that nearly all programs in psychology require an introductory psychology course, statistics, and research methods or experimental psychology. Most programs do not specify much more than that. Your graduate school professors want you to know how psychologists think; research-based courses provide you with this knowledge. Those professors will provide courses that will help you learn the skills appropriate for your career after you develop the basics. As a psychologist, you also need to understand the research process so you can read scientific journals, make sense of the research reports, and keep abreast of current ideas. Even if you don't choose a career as a researcher, you can still benefit from understanding research. Many jobs require knowledge of statistics and research.

In addition, every day you will be bombarded by claims that scientists have made breakthroughs in understanding various phenomena. It will be useful for you to be able to evaluate whether to believe what you hear. One of the purposes of a course in research is to help you learn how to think critically about the things people tell you. Is their research sound? Is the conclusion they draw the best one? Do they have something to gain from getting certain results? This process of critical thinking is a hallmark of science, but it is also a useful tool in everyday life.

Answering Important Questions

There are many important scientific questions in need of answers. The journal *Science* (2005) listed what some scientists see as the top 25 questions that society needs to address. At least five of these are associated with issues that psychologists can help address:

- What is the biological basis of consciousness?
- How are memories stored and retrieved?
- How did cooperative behavior evolve?
- To what extent are genetic variation and personal health linked?
- Will the world's population outstrip the world's capability to accommodate 10 billion people?

These questions deal with behavior, either directly or indirectly. As such, psychologists will need to be involved in providing portions of the answers to each of these questions.

Of the next 100 important questions, 13 are psychological and behavioral, at least in part. These questions appear in Table 1.1, along with the areas of psychology to which they relate. As you can see, regardless of your specific interest in psychology, you will be able to find important questions to answer.

TABLE 1.1   *Psychological Questions Listed Among the Top Unanswered Questions in Science (2005) Magazine and the Areas of Psychology Associated with Them*

Area of Psychology	Question
Social psychology	What are the roots of human culture?
Cognitive psychology	What are the evolutionary roots of language and music?
Biological bases of behavior/Cognitive psychology	Why do we sleep?
Personality/Learning	Why do we dream?
Biological bases of behavior	What synchronizes an organism's circadian clocks?
Comparative psychology/Learning	How do migrating organisms find their way?
Social psychology/Biological bases of behavior	What is the biological root of sexual orientation?
Abnormal psychology	What causes schizophrenia?
Developmental psychology	Why are there critical periods for language learning?
Personality theory/Biological bases of behavior	How much of personality is genetic?
Biological bases of behavior	Do pheromones influence human behavior?
Developmental psychology/Biological bases of behavior	What causes autism?
Personality theory	Is morality hardwired into the brain?

After you complete this course in research methods, you will be able to apply your new knowledge to areas outside of psychology. The research skills you pick up here will let you complete solid psychological research projects, but will also help you understand life better.

Why We Do Research

People are curious, social beings. As a result, most of us are interested in what others are up to and why. By the time you read this book, you have been observing others since childhood. You have probably become a sophisticated observer of others' behaviors and can predict pretty well how your friends will react if you act a certain way, at least some of the time. How did you gain this knowledge? Throughout your life, you have done things and then you observed the effect you had on others. Although you probably have not gone through life wearing the stereotypical white lab coat worn by some scientists, you have acted like a scientist when you discovered that "When I do this, they do that." One of the differences between scientific and nonscientific observation, though, is that scientists develop systematic plans, and we work to reduce bias in recording observations. In the end, however, curiosity and enjoyment in finding out about behavior underlies the reason why researchers do their work—they think it is fun.

As curious scientists, we generally work toward four increasingly difficult goals based on our observations: **description, explanation, prediction,** and **control of behavior.**

Description

Our tendency to act and then to observe others' reactions fulfills what seems to be a basic need for us: describing the world around us. In fact, when you can *describe* events around you, you have taken the first step in scientific discovery. In research, description involves a systematic approach to observing behavior

In your course on behavioral research, you will learn how, as scientists, we systematically begin to understand why people act as they do. The biggest difference between what you

Description—A goal of science in which behaviors are systematically and accurately characterized.

do in your everyday observations and what scientists do is that scientists pay attention to a lot of details that we normally think of as unimportant. Unlike most of us in everyday, casual observation, researchers develop a systematic plan for making objective observations so we can generate complete and accurate descriptions.

Explanation

This leads to the second goal of science, *explanation*. When we truly understand the causes of behavior, we can explain them. This is where theory comes in. A theory helps us understand behavior in a general sense. In scientific use, a theory is a general, organizing principle. When we have enough relevant information about behavior, we can develop an explanatory framework that puts all of that information into a nice, neat package—that is, into a theory.

In order to develop a theory, we look at the facts that we believe to be true and try to develop a coherent framework that links the facts to one another. The next step is to test the theory to see if it successfully predicts the results of new research. So we generate hypotheses, which are educated guesses, about behaviors, and we test those hypotheses with research. The research shows us whether our hypotheses are correct; if so, the theory receives further support.

If enough of our hypotheses support a theory, we regard it as more useful in understanding why people act in a certain way; if those hypotheses do not support the theory, we need to revise or abandon the theory. When we conduct research, we should have an open mind about an issue; we might have preconceived ideas of what to expect, but if we are wrong, we should be willing to change our beliefs. Scientists do not revise or abandon theories based on a single research study, but after enough evidence accumulates showing that a theory needs revision, then we work to determine what would constitute a better model of the behavior in question.

When we examine hypotheses, we make them objective and testable. This means that we define our terms clearly so others know how exactly what we mean, and we specify how our research will assess whether a hypothesis is valid. One of the important elements of the scientific method is **falsifiability.** That is, we will test hypotheses to see if we can prove them wrong. Scientists do not believe that you can prove that an idea or theory is absolutely true. There may be a case that you have missed that would disprove the theory. But we can see when the theory breaks down, that is, when it is falsified. The best we can do is to try to falsify the theory through continual testing. Each time we try and fail to falsify the theory, we have greater confidence in it.

For decades, people have used Freudian (psychodynamic) or behavioral theories to try to understand behavior. Both approaches have generated useful ideas about human behavior and have been accepted, at least in part, by the general public. You can see the impact of Freudian theory if you consider some of Freud's terms that have gained currency in everyday language, like repression, penis envy, or Freudian slips.

Some psychologists believe that many of Freud's ideas are not scientifically valid. In fact, when Freudian ideas have been subjected to experimentation, they often have not stood up well. In a perspective as complicated as psychodynamic theory, though, there is still disagreement about the scientific status of ideas such as unconscious processing of information, and some psychologists maintain that Freudian ideas have received support from research (Westen, 1998). Many psychologists today believe that Freud was a good observer of what people do and think but that his explanations of those behaviors were not valid.

Behavioral terms have also made their way into everyday language, as when people talk about positive or negative reinforcement. In the case of behaviorism, most psychologists

Explanation—A goal of science in which a researcher achieves awareness of why behaviors occur as they do.

Falsifiability—A characteristic of science such that any principle has to be amenable to testing to see if it is true or, more specifically, if it can be shown to be false.

affirm that it is a truly scientific approach. The ideas are objective and testable; in a wide variety of research programs, the utility of behavioral ideas has been well established. The principle of falsifiability is relevant here because theories are supposed to generate new ideas. If we can't test those ideas to see if they withstand scrutiny, the theory isn't very useful.

In research, we use hypotheses to make predictions about behavior; theories are useful for helping us explain why our predictions are accurate. As psychologists, we use theory to explain behavior. Our explanations differ from the ones we generate in everyday life in that scientific explanations involve well-specified statements of when behaviors will or will not occur.

Prediction

After you describe what people are likely to do in a certain situation, the next logical step is to expand your knowledge beyond simple description. The third step is to *predict* behavior. Suppose you tell a story. You are likely to make a prediction about how your friends will react to it. In considering whether to tell the story, you are making a prediction about their response. Every time you tell a story, you are engaging in a kind of experiment, making a prediction about the outcome. Naturally, you are sometimes wrong in your prediction because people are not easy to figure out.

Similarly, in any kind of research, scientists sometimes make poor predictions. When that happens, we try to figure out why the predictions were wrong and attempt to make better ones next time. A big difference between casual and scientific predictions is that scientists generally specify in great detail what factors lead to a given outcome. For most of us in everyday life, we have a vague notion of what behaviors to expect from others and, as a result, will accept our predictions as true if somebody behaves in ways that are roughly approximate to what we expected. There is a lot of room for error.

In our relationships with others, we find it helpful to describe and to predict their behaviors because it gives us a sense of control; we know in advance what will happen. At the same time, most of us want to know even more. We want to know *why* people act as they do. This is a difficult process because people's behaviors arise for a lot of reasons.

Control

The final step in the scientific study of behavior is *control.* Some people may ask whether it is right for us to try to control others' behaviors. Most psychologists would respond that we affect others' behaviors, just as they affect ours. It is not a matter of *should* we control behavior, but rather *how* does it happen. For example, parents try to raise children who show moral behavior. It would be reassuring to parents if they knew how to create such behavior in their children.

In order to exert control of behavior effectively, we need to understand why the behavior occurs as it does. To understand the elements of control, we need to have well formulated theories. At this point, we don't have a single theory of behavior that can capture the variety of human experience.

Psychologists with different theoretical orientations may use similar statements in describing behavior, but they will begin to diverge when making predictions, become even more different regarding explanation, and even more so with respect to control. Table 1.2 summarizes the four different goals of science and how psychologists have used them at various points in their research programs.

Prediction—A goal of science in which a researcher can specify in advance those situations in which a particular behavior will occur.

Control—A goal of science in which a researcher can manipulate variables in order to produce specific behaviors.

TABLE 1.2 *Example of the Goals of Research and How They Relate to the Development of Knowledge*

Description	One evening in 1964, a woman named Kitty Genovese was attacked and murdered while walking home from work at 3 a.m. in Queens, New York. It was originally—and mistakenly—reported that thirty-eight people saw what was happening from their apartment windows, but nobody helped; nobody even called the police.
	Two psychologists (e.g., Latané and Darley, 1970) wondered why this might happen. Their first step in understanding this phenomenon was to describe what happened. Based on descriptions of the initial event, Darley and Latané (1968) investigated some of the implications of Genovese's murder as they relate to helping behavior.
	This event was so striking that it led to an enormous amount of research and analysis (e.g., Cunningham, 1984; Takooshian & O'Connor, 1984) and stands as a prime example of research that results from something that occurs outside the laboratory. (Manning, Levine, and Collins [2007] have identified some important discrepancies between the actual events and what has been reported, but that does not detract from the important research that emerged based on what people thought had happened.) (See Cialdini, 1980, for a discussion of using naturally occurring events as a basis for behavioral research.)
Explanation	Once we can document and predict events, we can try to explain why behaviors occur. Psychologists have identified some of the underlying factors that may help us understand why people do not help others. As Darley and Latané (1968) have noted, when there are more people around, we are less likely to notice that somebody needs help and, even when we notice, we are less likely to offer aid. Part of this failure to act involves what has been called diffusion of responsibility; that is, when others are around, we can pass blame for our inaction to them, assuming less (or none) for ourselves.
Prediction	We can try to determine those conditions where helping behavior is likely to occur. Helping occurs as people try to avoid feeling guilty (Katsev et al., 1978), and helping diminishes if people have been relieved of guilt (Cialdini, Darby, & Vincent, 1973). In addition, if people believe that another individual is similar to them, they will help (Batson et al., 1981).
	Helping behavior involves complicated dynamics, so it will be difficult to identify precisely those conditions in which helping will occur, but we have identified some variables that allow us to make generally accurate predictions.
Control	Once we are confident of our predictions, we can ultimately control behavior. Behaviors in everyday life are seldom controlled by a single variable, but we can control behavior to a degree by manipulating the relevant variables.
	Programs to help poverty-stricken people often rely on guilt or empathic pleas. Depending on the particulars of the circumstances, we may help others if our mood is positive because we tend to generalize our good mood to everything around us (Clark & Teasdale, 1985); or we may help if our mood is negative, but we think that helping somebody will improve our mood (Manucia, Baumann, & Cialdini, 1984). Knowledge of these effects can help us control behaviors.

What Constitutes Scientific Knowledge?

Tenacity—The mode of accepting knowledge because one is comfortable with it and simply wants to hold onto it.

There are different paths to factual knowledge in our lives. We will see that not all roads to knowledge are equally useful. The nineteenth-century American philosopher Charles Sanders Peirce (1877) identified several ways of knowing, which he called **tenacity, authority,** the **a priori method,** and the **scientific approach.** He concluded that the best approach was the scientific one.

Authority—The mode of accepting knowledge because a person in a position of authority claims that something is true or valid.

Tenacity involves simply believing something because, based on your view of the world and your assumptions, you don't want to give up your belief. People do this all the time; you have probably discovered that it can be difficult to convince people to change their minds. However, if two people hold mutually contradictory beliefs, both cannot be true. According to Peirce, in a "saner moment," we might recognize that others have valid points, which can shake our own beliefs.

An alternative to an individual's belief in what is true, Peirce thought, could reside in what *authorities* say is true. This approach removes the burden from any single person to make decisions; instead, one would rely on an expert of some kind. Peirce talked about authorities who would force beliefs under threat of some kind of penalty, but we can generalize to any acceptance of knowledge because somebody whom we trust says something is true. As Peirce noted, though, experts with different perspectives will hold different beliefs. How is one to know which expert is actually right?

He then suggested that people might fix their knowledge based on consensus and reasoned argument, the *a priori approach.* The problem here, he wrote, was that reasons for believing something may change over time, so what was seen as true in the past may change. If we want to know universal truths, he reasoned, the most valid approach is through science, which is objective and self-correcting. Gradually, we can accumulate knowledge that is valid and discard ideas that prove to be wrong.

One of the major differences between scientific knowledge and other kinds of knowledge is that scientific work is much more systematic than casual observation. In addition, researchers abide by certain general principles in deciding what to believe. Our scientific knowledge relies on the fact that our observations are objective, data-driven, public, and potentially replicable. We will see shortly what this means, but what it all comes down to is the fact that, as scientists and as good decision makers, we need to evaluate how well research has been done. If we decide that the investigators have done everything correctly, we should be willing to change our minds about what we believe to be true, even if we don't like the truth. As it turns out, people are so complicated that a single research study will never lead to a complete change in beliefs; the process is incremental, with a series of small steps rather than a giant leap. This is why reports of *breakthroughs* are not credible—new knowledge is always the result of an accumulation of earlier research findings, no matter what you hear on the news.

Science Is Objective

What does it mean for our observations to be **objective?** One implication is that we define clearly the concepts we are dealing with. This is often easier said than done. Psychologists deal with complex and abstract concepts that are hard to measure. Nonetheless, we have to develop some way to measure these concepts in clear and systematic ways. For example, suppose we want to find out whether we respond more positively to attractive people than to others.

To answer our question, we first have to define what we mean by "attractive." The definition must be objective; that is, the definition has to be consistent, clear, and understandable, even though it may not be perfect.

Researchers have taken various routes to creating objective definitions of attractiveness. Wilson (1978) simply mentioned that "a female confederate . . . appearing either attractive or unattractive asked in a neutral manner for directions to a particular building on central campus at a large Midwestern University" (p. 313). This vague statement doesn't really tell us as much as we would like to know. We don't have a clear definition of what the researchers meant by "attractiveness." Juhnke et al. (1987) varied the attire of people who seemed to be in need of help. The researchers defined attractiveness based on clothing. Unattractive people, that is, those wearing less desirable clothing, received help, even though they did not look very attractive.

On the other hand, Bull and Stevens (1980) used helpers with either good or bad teeth. In this case, attractive was defined as having good teeth, whereas unattractive was defined as having bad teeth. In this study, it didn't matter whether a person had good teeth. People were just as likely to help those with bad teeth, although they were willing to do so for a shorter length of time.

If the different research teams did not report how they created an unattractive appearance, we would have a harder time evaluating their research and repeating it exactly as they

A priori method—The mode of accepting knowledge based on a premise that people have agreed on, followed by reasoned argument.

Scientific approach—The mode of accepting knowledge based on empirically derived data.

Objective—Measurements that are not affected by personal bias and that are well-defined and specified are considered objective.

did it. It may be very important to know what manipulation the researchers used. Differences in attractiveness due to the kinds of clothes you are wearing may not lead to the same reactions as differences due to unsightly teeth.

Interestingly, Stokes and Bikman (1974) found that people may be less willing to ask help *from* attractive people than from unattractive people. In their study, they defined attractiveness on the basis of physical appearance as rated by other people. This strategy relies on a clear and consistent method of defining attractiveness. Because attractiveness can be defined in many ways, we need to tell others what we mean when we use the term, which is what we mean by objectivity.

Science Is Data Driven

Our conclusions as scientists must also be **data driven.** This simply means that our conclusions must follow logically from our data. There may be several equally good interpretations from a single set of data. Regardless of which interpretation we choose, it has to be based on the data we collect.

To say that science is based on data is to say that it is **empirical.** Empiricism refers to the method of discovery that relies on systematic observation and data for drawing conclusions. Psychology is an empirical discipline in that knowledge is based on the results of research, that is, on data.

The critical point here is that if we are to develop a more complete and accurate understanding of the world around us, scientific knowledge based on data will, in the long run, serve us better than intuition alone. Don't discount intuition entirely; quite a few scientific insights had their beginnings in intuitions that were scientifically studied and found to be true. We just can't rely on it entirely because intuitions differ across people and may change over time.

Science Is Replicable and Verifiable

Data driven—Interpretations of research that are based on objective results of a project are considered data driven.

Our scientific knowledge has to be potentially **replicable** and **verifiable.** This means that others should have the opportunity to repeat a research project to see if the same results occur each time. Maybe the researchers who are trying to repeat the study will generate the same result; maybe they will not. We do not claim that *results* are scientific; rather, we claim that the *approach* is scientific. Any time somebody makes a claim but will not let others verify it as valid, we should be skeptical.

Empirical approach—The method of discovery that relies on systematic observation and data collection for guidance on drawing conclusions.

Why should one scientist repeat somebody else's research? As it turns out, there is a bias among journal editors to publish findings that show differences across groups and to reject studies showing no differences. So a relatively large number of research reports may describe differences that occurred accidentally. That is, groups may differ, but not for any systematic or reproducible reason. If the researcher were to repeat the study, a different result would occur.

Replicable—When scientists can recreate a previous research study, that study is replicable.

Ioannidis (2005), referring to genetic and biomedical research, noted that "there is increasing concern that in modern research, false findings may be the majority or even the vast majority of published research claims" (p. 696). His conclusion comes, in part, from a recognition that journal editors and researchers are more impressed by findings that show that something interesting occurred but not by findings that do not reveal interesting patterns. Ioannidis's speculation may be true for psychological research, just as it is for biologically based studies.

Verifiable—When scientists can reproduce a previous research study and generate the same results, it is verifiable.

Psychologists have recognized this problem for quite some time (e.g., Rosenthal, 1979). Fortunately, when a research project is repeated and when the same outcome results, our confidence in the results increases markedly (Moonesinghe, Khoury, & Janssens, 2007). The reason that replication of research is such a good idea is that it helps us weed out findings that turn out to be false and strengthen our confidence in findings that are valid.

Sometimes even when researchers follow a completely scientific path, there can be great controversy in the conclusions about what the research is telling us. For instance, in the determination of the causes of rape, there are at least two distinctly different schools of thought. One approach invokes the ideas of evolutionary psychology. The other is more socially oriented. The arguments are heated, and each camp believes that it has useful insights into the problem. Both groups have data and theory to support their ideas, although both are clearly still incomplete.

Science Is Public

When we say that our research is **public,** we mean this literally. Scientists only recognize research as valid or useful when they can scrutinize it. Generally, we accept research as valid if it has undergone **peer review.** For instance, when a psychologist completes research, the next step is often to write the results in a scientific manuscript and submit it for publication in a research journal.

The editor of the journal will send the manuscript to experts in the field for their comments. If the editor and the reviewers agree that major problems have been taken care of, the article will appear in the journal. Otherwise, the article will be rejected. Among major journals in psychology, about a quarter or fewer of all manuscripts that researchers submit are published. The process of peer review is not perfect, but it is the standard means that journal editors use to decide what research to publish in their journals. Unfortunately, there is significant disagreement among reviewers and editors about what manuscripts are published and which are rejected (Kravitz et al, 2010).

Another approach to making our research public involves submitting a proposal to a research conference for a presentation. The process for acceptance to a conference resembles that for acceptance by a journal. In some cases, researchers may initially present their ideas at a conference, then follow up with a published article.

The Interaction of Science and Culture

Public—Scientists make their research public, typically by making presentations at conferences or by publishing their work in journal articles or books.

Peer review—A process in which researchers submit their research for publication in a journal or presentation at a conference to other experts in the field who evaluate the research.

Many people undoubtedly think of science as happening in laboratories remote from the lives of real people. Nothing could be farther from the truth. Scientists live in communities and go to the same movies you do, coach their children's soccer teams, and worry about the same things that you do. Not surprisingly, culture shapes the research conducted by many scientists because our culture shapes the way we think. For example, after the terrorist attacks in the United States, some person or persons sent anthrax spores through the mail, infecting a number of people and killing some of them. This spurred increased scientific attention to anthrax.

In addition, in an energy crisis, researchers in psychology, biology, physics, and chemistry are motivated to study patterns of energy-using behavior, the development of biofuels, creation of efficient technologies, and conservation of energy. When environmental issues loom, such as the release of massive amounts of oil in the Gulf of Mexico in 2010, researchers in the natural sciences may be predisposed to focus on ecological issues, and behavioral researchers will study the impact of the crisis on people's lives and behaviors. Children will receive particular scrutiny because research has revealed their susceptibility to post-traumatic stress disorder in times of catastrophe (La Greca & Silverman, 2009; Osofsky et al., 2009). Psychologists are as much a part of the community as anyone, so it should come as no surprise that our research reflects the needs and concerns of our society.

Discussions of research ideas are also affected by social attitudes. After Thornhill and Palmer (2000) proposed evolutionary suggestions about the causes of rape in *The Sciences*, the consequent letters to the editor took an overwhelmingly negative tone (Jennings, 2000; Müller, 2000; Steinberg et al., 2000; Tang-Martínez & Mechanic, 2000).

Can it be that not a single scientist, or even any reader of *The Sciences,* supported Thornhill and Palmer's ideas? It is more likely that people have refrained from writing letters in support of the evolutionary argument because they know that a great many people will criticize them for it. We can easily imagine that fear of reprisal might lead some people to avoid conducting research in the area. As such, research that might clarify the issue may never take place because nobody is willing to pursue it.

The Government's Role in Science

Societal issues often dictate scientific research, in part because of the way money is allocated for research. The federal government funds a great deal of the research that occurs in colleges and universities, where most scientific developments occur. As such, the government plays a large role in determining what kind of research takes place. How does the government decide which areas of research should have priority in funding? Ultimately, the decision makers pay attention to issues of pressing importance to taxpayers. This view simplifies the dynamics of how federal money is allocated for research, even in the so-called pure and abstract sciences; societal demands affect the types of questions that scientists ask. If researchers do not get funding for asking one question, they will ask a different question for which they can receive financial support.

In the United States, the federal government actively directs some scientific research. For instance, the highly secretive National Security Agency employs more mathematicians than any other organization in the world (Singh, 1999). These people work on finding ways to create and break secret codes that affect political, economic, and military activities. Many mathematicians who research the use of codes do so because the government encourages it.

Further, the U.S. government has affected social research indirectly, sometimes through questionable means. Harris (1980) noted that beginning in the 1930s, the Federal Bureau of Investigation (FBI) engaged in surveillance and kept files on the American Psychological Association (APA) and the Society for the Psychological Study of Social Issues, now a division of APA. The FBI used informants who reported on colleagues. One incident that Harris cited involved an individual who informed on a colleague who had spoken out against racism at the 1969 APA convention. The result of such activities by the government, according to Harris, may have been to lead psychologists to abandon some lines of research (e.g., on racial attitudes) because they were too controversial.

Cultural Values and Science

Even when governmental interference is not an issue, there are still cultural aspects to our research. For example, some people feel strongly that a woman should remain at home raising her children rather than taking them to a daycare center while she works. An examination of the amount of research effort devoted to the effects of childcare outside the home reveals that few behavioral scientists showed much interest in the question until the past decade or so. In fact, a search through the primary psychological database on research, PsycINFO©, reveals that the first citation with the term "childcare" in an abstract occurred in 1927; for a long time, the use of that term was often associated with orphanages. In the early 1900s, the social issue of childcare was nonexistent. Work then was more likely to center around the home, and the primary caregivers, the mothers, were less likely to work outside the home than is the case today. Thus, the issue of the effects of childcare centers on the development of children was irrelevant to society.

In contemporary life, women's work has moved from inside the home to outside, and there are more single parents who must have paying jobs. The increase in research on the effects of childcare centers has become important to many people, including psychologists, spurring an increase in psychological research on the topic. The issues are complex, and different researchers have generated conflicting results, so we still see considerable controversy surrounding the topic. Until the issue is resolved, this important societal concern will receive continued attention. Social perspectives also determine what questions are not asked. In the case of childcare, the amount of research involving working fathers is scant.

Another example of the effect of culture on research involves a commonly used technique to assess attitudes and opinions. Psychologists regularly ask people to rate something

■ ■ ■ ■ ■

CONTROVERSY
Should Women Serve as Jurors?

Psychologists are affected by the times in which they work. Their research ideas reflect the social milieu. This point is important here because the research that people view as important in one time may not carry over to another era. For instance, in the first decade of the twentieth century, Hugo Münsterberg, one of the most prominent psychologists in the United States at the time, reported the results of investigations of the question of whether women show the appropriate mental processes that would allow them to take part in jury deliberations (Münsterberg, 1914).

He presented a group of men and a group of women a pair of displays that had different numbers of dots and asked them to vote on which display contained more dots. After a group debate of the issue, they voted again.

What does this simple procedure have to do with the way trials are conducted and whether women should serve as jurors during those trials? According to Münsterberg (1914), the psychologist studies "thoughts and emotions and feelings and deeds which move our social world. But . . . he must simplify them and bring them down to the most elementary situations, in which only the characteristic mental actions are left" (pp. 186–187). As a researcher, you need to simplify complex situations so you can study each important issue individually, without being affected by complicating factors. We still do this today in psychological research; in fact, scientists in every discipline do this because reality is too complex to be studied in its fullest extent in a single study.

In Münsterberg's research, at a final vote, the percentage accuracy for the men went from guessing (52%) to reasonably accurate (78%). Women, on the other hand, began at 45% correct and stayed unimproved at 45%.

Münsterberg concluded that women were too stubborn to benefit from group discussions; they would not change their minds when confronted with evidence. He asserted that the difference in the way men and women respond to debate "makes the men fit and the women unfit for the particular task which society requires from the jurymen" (p. 198). When he published his conclusions, quite a number of people argued against them, including many women.

A few years later, another psychologist, Harold Burtt (1920) conceptually replicated Münsterberg's study. Burtt asked women and men to try to detect when people were lying to them in a laboratory study involving simulated trial witnesses. The participants then discussed the veracity of the witness and decided again. Burtt found that men and women were equally proficient in their ability to use debate to arrive at reasonable conclusions.

Burtt's conclusion was that women were as suitable for jury work as men were. In fact, he reported that men were more willing to attribute lies to simulated witnesses who were actually telling the truth. Does this suggest that women are more appropriate for jury deliberation than men are? It is most likely that sex has little to do with ability to serve competently on a jury.

It is interesting and important to be aware that neither Münsterberg nor Burtt ever hinted that they should ask the question of whether men should sit on juries. This is an important fact because it reveals that the social environment influences what questions are asked as well as what questions are *not* asked. If we intend to use our research to help answer real-life problems, we need to remember that no single experiment is going to answer a complex social question, but each one provides a small part of the answer. Our decisions will be better if we base them on sound research, but we also need to remember that we have to evaluate the research to see if it adequately answers the questions we are asking.

Questions for Discussion:

Do you believe that research projects like those of Münsterberg and Burtt could potentially contribute answers to social questions? Should we conclude that women are unfit for jury duty? Your conclusions should rest on data rather than on mere opinion.

on a scale of one to seven. (Technically, this is called a Likert-type scale, named after the American psychologist Rensis Likert, who pioneered this popular technique.) The use of such a scale may not be appropriate for people in cultures different than ours because it calls for a certain mindset that others don't share with us (Carr, Munro, & Bishop, 1995). People in non-Western cultures may not think it makes sense to assess a complex concept on a simple rating scale. We tend to assume that others think as we do, but such an assumption may lead to research results that lack validity. Greater numbers of psychologists are addressing these concerns and focusing more systematically on cultural issues in research (see Beins, 2011; Matsumoto, 1994; Price & Crapo, 1999).

A person's culture determines not only what behaviors are of interest, but how those behaviors are studied. Cultural perspective also influences how scientists interpret their data. An interesting example of the way that societal topics affect research occurred as Hugo Münsterberg (1914) decided to study whether women should be allowed to participate on juries. This topic is irrelevant now, but in the early 1900s, it was controversial. Some people thought that women wouldn't do as good a job on a jury as men did. The Controversy on female jurors presents the issues, which shed light on how attitudes change as cultures change.

Scientific Literacy

Even if you don't engage in research yourself, it is important to be scientifically literate in our society. News about science abounds on the Internet, on television, and in newspapers and magazines. In addition, voters must decide about scientific issues, like whether the federal or state governments should fund stem cell research or should act to prevent possible global warming. In order to understand the issues, citizens need to understand the nature of scientific research.

Scientific literacy is a specialized form of critical thinking, which involves developing clear and specific questions, collecting and assessing relevant information, identifying important assumptions and perspectives, and generating effective solutions to problems (Scriven & Paul, 2007). These are all goals associated with conducting research.

Are people as scientifically literate as they should be? Unfortunately, research has suggested that about 28% of Americans qualify as being scientifically literate (Miller, 2007a, 2007b). This figure is low, but it actually represents progress. In the 1980s and early 1990s, only about 10% were scientifically literate.

How can you develop scientific literacy? One way to foster such literacy is to learn about and to conduct research (Beins, 2010; Holmes, 2010; Holmes, Beins, & Lynn, 2007; Macias, 2010). Knowledge of the process of doing research appears to facilitate an awareness of the scientific process. More specifically, training in psychological research prepares a person for the kind of thinking associated with scientific literacy and critical thinking as well as training in other scientific disciplines (Lehman, Lempert, & Nisbett, 1988). Similarly, taking psychology courses in general appears to be related to increased scientific literacy (Beins, 2010).

One issue that requires a high level of scientific literacy concerns the claim that mercury in vaccines causes autism. The situation is complex, but researchers have generated data to address the issue. People need to be able to weigh the evidence in a scientifically literate manner in order to draw valid conclusions. This controversy involves the intersection of scientific knowledge, public policy, and the needs of people whose lives are affected by autism. The Controversy on autism on page 17 provides a glimpse into these issues.

Science and Pseudoscience

Various people believe in phenomena that scientists reject as being invalid. For instance, many patients and some medical practitioners believe that homeopathic medicine is effective in treating physical illness. According to mainstream medical workers, homeopathy is not effective and is not even scientifically based.

Homeopathic medicines contain ingredients that have been so diluted that a dose may not even have a single molecule of the substance associated with a supposed cure. Furthermore, controlled scientific studies have demonstrated a lack of effectiveness of homeopathic treatments. The few studies that show an effect generally reveal weak effects and may be methodologically flawed. Why do such people refuse to change their beliefs about this approach? There are many reasons, but one of them is that believers do not approach homeopathy through a scientific framework. Their belief in homeopathy stems more from a reliance on tenacity or authority.

Belief in paranormal phenomena like ESP, astrology, mental telepathy, and ghosts is perhaps more prevalent in the United States than belief in homeopathy. Although scientists firmly reject the existence of such phenomena, surveys have revealed that nearly three-quarters of all Americans believe in at least some of these things (Moore, 2005). If you look at Figure 1.1, you will see the disconnect between the general public and scientists. Why do so many people lend credibility to these ideas when the majority of scientists who have studied these things have found essentially no support for them? A number of years ago the magician James Randi (whose stage name is The Amazing Randi) issued a challenge that he would award $1,000,000 to anybody who could demonstrate paranormal phenomena that he could not successfully disprove through rigorous testing. To date, nobody has been able to do so, although some people have tried.

FIGURE 1.1   *Percentage of Respondents Who Claim to Believe in Some Kind of Paranormal Phenomenon in Different Studies*

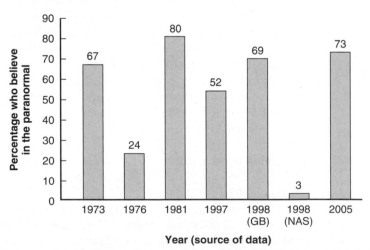

Sources: 1973 and 1998 (GB): Radford (1998), nonrandom samples from Great Britain; 1976 and 1997: Nisbet (1998), random samples from the United States; 1981: Singer and Benassi (1981), random samples from the United States; 1998 (NAS), sample of members of the National Academy of Sciences in the United States; 2005: Random sample from the United States

Most scientists reject the notion that paranormal phenomena exist. The most notable reason for scientific skepticism is that, under controlled conditions, the evidence for phenomena like ESP or mental telepathy remarkably disappear. Before we do the research, we should have an open mind about the issue, but we need to abandon such beliefs if research shows no evidence of their existence. Some recent research has made the news in this regard. Psychologist Daryl Bem (2011) made the news by publishing research that purports to demonstrate the existence of precognition. Quite a few researchers and statisticians called his methodology and his results into question. For example, Alcock (2011) pointed out that the same claims that Bem has made have occurred over the past century, and have always been shown to be invalid. We will not know how this debate ends until additional researchers attempt to replicate Bem's studies.

Another basis for rejection of paranormal phenomena is that most of the explanations offered for such events are inconsistent with the physical laws that scientists recognize. If there is no way to explain a phenomenon, scientists are reluctant to accept it as valid. So sometimes researchers have failed to accept new ideas because they could not explain those ideas. Regarding paranormal phenomena, the well-established laws of physics that have led to our current marvels of technology cannot explain something like ESP. The failure to explain how the paranormal could occur and the inability to document these phenomena in the laboratory have made scientists reluctant to embrace them.

From the viewpoint of many psychologists, the term "parapsychology" is seen as unfortunate because it links our scientifically oriented discipline with **pseudoscience.** We regard a discipline as pseudoscientific when it claims that its knowledge derives from scientific research but fails to follow the basic principles of science.

Many scientists have worked to dispel pseudoscientific myths (e.g., Radner & Radner, 1982; Zusne & Jones, 1989), as have other critical thinkers, like James Randi. There are also publications that foster critical thinking about such issues, like *The Skeptical Inquirer*. This periodical exists to examine and debunk claims of paranormal phenomena. When scrutinized, claims in favor of paranormal phenomena don't hold up well. Table 1.3 reflects some of the major characteristics of pseudoscience.

In general, pseudosciences are characterized by a reliance on flimsy and questionable evidence, a resistance to change or further development of theory, a lack of ways to test the ideas, avoidance of contradictory information, and a lack of critical thought about ways to develop the theory.

Warning Signs of Bogus Science

As a consumer of research, you can spot some of the issues associated with claims that appear to be based on science but that are not. Even if you are not knowledgeable about the technical issues associated with a scientific topic, there are some warning signs that you should be dubious about facts that others claim are true, as noted by physicist Robert Park (2003).

The first warning sign is when an investigator publicizes claims in the popular press rather than in a scientific journal. If an article appears in a journal, it will have undergone careful scrutiny by professionals in the field. Scientists are skeptical when a research claim first appears in the news because other scientists have probably not assessed its validity.

Second, when somebody claims that the scientific establishment is trying to suppress research findings, you should be careful. It may be difficult to publish radically new findings in a journal, so valid claims may need a higher standard of proof, but if the findings result from valid scientific approaches, journals will publish new work. So even though Bem's (2011) research on precognition has no known physical basis and repeats claims that have been shown

Pseudoscience—A domain of inquiry that has the superficial appearance of being scientific but that does not rely on the critical scientific principles of objectivity, verifiability, empiricism, and being public.

TABLE 1.3 *Characteristics of Pseudoscience*

General Characteristics	Example
Pseudoscientists believe that there is no more to be learned; they fail to generate testable hypotheses or to conduct objective tests of theory. There tends to be no advancement of knowledge in the field, which is resistant to change. There are few tests of previous claims.	Homeopathic medicine makes claims about cures that are not based on research. The ideas never change and believers do not conduct systematic tests that would disconfirm their ideas.
Pseudoscience is based on dogma and uncritical belief; there may be hostility in the face of counterevidence or disagreement.	Creationism is accepted by some as a matter of faith. There is no attempt to subject its tenets to scientific scrutiny. In addition, when disagreements arise, believers often show antagonism toward the individual without dealing with the evidence.
There is a suppression of or distortion of unfavorable data; selective use of data, including looking only for supportive information (confirmation bias).	People who believe that psychics can foretell the future will accept just about any statement that seems correct but will ignore errors in predictions.
Many ideas are not amenable to scientific evaluation; ideas are subjective and can't be tested objectively.	There have been claims that we have an undetectable aura surrounding us. If it is undetectable, there is to way to verify its presence.
There is an acceptance of proof with data of questionable validity; the lack of evidence is taken as support that a claim *could* be true.	Some people conclude that there is evidence for the existence of UFOs on the basis of anecdotal reports in the popular media or ancient myths. There is little or no independent evaluation of ideas, but more a reliance on questionable evidence that is not questioned.
Personal anecdotes and events that cannot be tested systematically are used to provide evidence; there is often a reliance on "experts" with no real expertise.	Anybody who claims an experience about foretelling the future or who relates a supposed experience with aliens becomes an expert whose statements are not to be questioned.
Pseudoscience involves terms that sound like scientific ideas, but the terms are not clearly defined. Often the ideas violate known scientific principles.	Varieties of extrasensory perception include phenomena like *telekinesis*, which sounds scientific. In reality, it is a poorly defined (and undocumented) notion. Paranormal phenomena do not conform to known physical laws, such as the fact that for all known forms of energy, the force exerted declines over distance, which is not the case for ESP, according to its adherents.
Pseudoscientific phenomena are "shy" or "fragile" in that they often disappear or weaken noticeably when subjected to well-designed experiments, especially with nonbelievers.	The ability to identify stimuli that are not visible is sometimes striking when two believers conduct a study; when independent scientists conduct the study, the effect is often attenuated or eliminated.
Pseudoscience involves looking for mysteries that have occurred rather than trying to generate and test explanations for the phenomena.	Sometimes people solicit incidents from people that seem unusual. For instance, mystery hunters might look for instances when a person seems to have foretold the future in a dream, ignoring the fact that if you look at enough dreams, you can find coincidental patterns that resist normal explanations.
Pseudoscientists engage in explanation by scenario. They identify a phenomenon and provide an explanation that fits the facts after they are known but doesn't provide a means for making predictions in advance.	Some years ago, Julian Jaynes suggested that, historically, the two hemispheres in the human brain were not connected as they are now. Thus, brain activity in the right hemisphere was perceived to be the voices of gods. Unfortunately for this explanation, there is no credible evidence that it is true. In fact, given what we know about evolution, there is no realistic way that our brains could have evolved as Jaynes suggested.

■ ■ ■ ■ ■

CONTROVERSY
What Causes Autism?

Children routinely receive vaccinations to prevent a variety of illnesses. So it would be ironic if vaccines were responsible for causing a disorder. Some nonscientists and physicians believe that the element mercury that manufacturers used to use as a preservative in vaccines actually causes autism (e.g., Olmstead, 2009; Tsouderos & Callahan, 2009). But when scientists have conducted research to see if there is a connection between vaccinations and autism, the results have revealed no systematic link between vaccines and autism (e.g., Baker, 2008; Heron, Golding, & ALSPAC Study Team, 2004; Schechter & Grether, 2008; Omer et al., 2009).

So where did the controversy arise? And who should we believe? The issue arose because of a confluence of several different factors (Baker, 2008).

First, the U.S. Centers for Disease Control and Prevention (CDC) recommended in 1999 that mercury-containing preservative thimerosol be removed from vaccinations because of the fear of mercury poisoning, which can cause developmental problems in fetuses and children. The CDC drew no connection between mercury and autism; in fact, no research had implicated thimerosol with any disease or health problems. The recommendation was purely preventive.

Second, around the same time, parents of children diagnosed with autism had become active in advocating for the children. These parents were reacting against hypotheses that parenting inadequacies were responsible for the onset of autism. One such hypothesis was Leo Kanner's and Bruno Bettelheim's concept that autism arose because of "refrigerator mothers" who were emotionally cold with their children (Laidler, 2004). The parents were promoting a medical model to replace the psychoanalytically based hypothesis of Kanner and Bettelheim. It was among this community of advocates that the notion of an epidemic of autism took root. Experts (e.g., Fombonne, 2001) had predicted that the increased advocacy and greater awareness of autism would lead to more diagnoses of autism, which is exactly what happened.

A third factor was the conclusion by some people that mercury in vaccines was the culprit in the supposed epidemic of autism. (It is not entirely clear if the increase of autism is due to an actual increase in incidence or to more awareness and better diagnosis.)

Prior to the recommendation to remove mercury from vaccines, nobody had associated mercury with autism. However, some people concluded that, because the CDC had recommended removal of mercury from vaccines and because there were some similarities in mercury poisoning and autistic behavior, mercury must be to blame.

A number of studies have investigated the potential mercury-autism link. What have researchers concluded? To date, there is no evidence of a causal connection between the two. In fact, the incidence of autism has increased even though mercury has disappeared from most vaccines (Schechter & Grether, 2008) and mercury levels in children with autism are no higher than those in children without autism (Hertz-Picciotto et al., 2009).

Recently, the *British Medical Journal* (now called *BMJ*) published an editorial related to the original research that linked vaccines and autism. After an extensive investigation in Great Britain, the original research was deemed fraudulent and the journal retracted it (Wakefield's article, 2011).

So why does the controversy persist? Part of the situation involves the desires of parents of children with autism to be able to place a cause for their children's problems and to prevent future occurrences. Part of the situation involves the coincidence of increased diagnoses of autism in the same time period that mercury disappeared from most vaccines. And part of the situation results from people's lack of scientific literacy in being able to evaluate scientific research and in their reliance on anecdotal information instead of systematically collected data.

---

to be invalid, the editor of the journal *Personality and Social Psychology* agreed to publish Bem's work so that it would receive scrutiny from the scientific community.

A third sign to be cautious is when a researcher's findings are difficult to detect, thus difficult to verify by an independent judge. A fourth problem appears when the only data for a discovery involve anecdotes, or stories, that other researchers cannot investigate more fully. One of the problems with anecdotes is that they can lead to powerful, emotional responses, so people are likely to accept claims about the stories as being valid. An unusual occurrence may take place, but scientists are unwilling to accept it as being real if they cannot investigate how general the phenomenon is.

A fifth warning sign is the claim by the investigator that a phenomenon is real because people have known about it for centuries. Simply because people have made claims for a long

Question for Discussion:

How do people's hopes and desires influence their willingness to examine scientific data? If there is no connection between exposure to mercury and the appearance of autism, how could you convince people who accept such a link to change their minds?

Junk science—The use of scientific research for nonscientific goals, a term with negative connotations suggesting a problem with the way scientific research is used.

time does not indicate that their claims are correct. For hundreds of years, people thought that the earth was only a few thousand years old; we know now that this claim is not true.

The next sign that you should be wary of is that the investigator worked alone and discovered an important phenomenon that nobody else had happened upon. New findings are almost invariably the result of the accumulation of ideas. Contemporary science almost involves a community of researchers or, at least, an awareness by a single researcher of the work of others.

Finally, if a researcher makes a bold claim of an entirely novel finding, the researcher must be able to propose a physical or scientific law that can account for the phenomenon. If a finding does not accord with the natural laws that scientists have established, the researcher must develop a coherent and believable explanation for the phenomenon.

Junk Science

Sometimes people, including scientists, use scientific research to promote their own causes. When they use science inappropriately, they may make claims that look good on the surface but that are really not valid. The term for such uses is called **junk science.** This term is as much a rhetorical term as a scientific one; that is, it is a term related to making arguments to support one's beliefs. A person using junk science is more interested in winning the argument than in presenting sound, valid scientific information.

Sometimes people making arguments with junk science will call upon data and research results of questionable validity. For instance, according to the Union of Concerned Scientists, people may make use of data that have not gone through peer review, meaning that experts in the field have not had the opportunity to examine the research procedures or the data. Another hallmark of junk science is the use of simple data from complex research projects to generate a solution to a complicated problem. If the problem is complicated, it is not likely that a solution will emerge based on simple data.

In other instances, people appear to refer to scientific research, but they can't actually produce examples of research to support their claims. Some scientifically based organizations work to educate the public on these empty claims. For example, Sense about Science (www.senseaboutscience.org.uk) and the Committee for Skeptical Inquiry (www.csicop.org/) devote their energy to educating the public and the media about supposedly scientific claims that don't stand up under scrutiny.

There is no clear definition of what constitutes valid science versus junk science. Sometimes it is a matter of perspective by the person using it or the person hearing it. Nonetheless, by understanding the context in which the data were generated, whether the research followed the scientific method, and the relation between the data and the question at hand, you can begin to ask the right questions about whether you are on the receiving end of real science or junk science.

Chapter Summary

Research exerts a large impact on our lives, so we are better off as citizens when we can examine research claims that people make. Knowing how to ask critical questions is also a useful skill in many other facets of our lives.

When psychologists engage in research, we do what other scientists do: We look for ways to describe behavior accurately, to establish a basis for predicting behavior, to explain why people act as they do, and ultimately to know how to control behavior. The best way to accomplish these goals is to study behavior scientifically.

Research is considered scientific when it conforms to certain game plans. Researchers strive to make objective measurements and to define precisely what they have done in their work. This allows others to evaluate the credibility of the research and to do further work to extend knowledge. After creating a research plan, psychologists collect data and draw conclusions from the data. We hope that when scientists make a claim, they can support their arguments based on objective data, not on opinion.

Another critical component of scientific research is that it must be public. The knowledge we gain in research doesn't help us advance what we know unless researchers publicize their work, usually in the form of professional papers that appear in journals or in conference presentations attended by other scientists. Only by making clear statements about what research is all about and what discoveries the scientist has made can others verify the validity of the claims made by the investigator and attempt to reproduce those results in other research projects.

We rely on the scientific approach for the study of behavior because other ways of finding out about people's thoughts, feelings, and acts are not as reliable. Sometimes we can use intuition to understand the world around us, but too often intuition leads to poor judgments. Similarly, we can ask people who are authority figures; unfortunately, they are like the rest of us—sometimes they make mistakes. We can also use logic, but all of us know that people's behaviors often don't seem to follow any logic we can detect. Finally, all of us make judgments based on our own experience. The problem with using our own experiences is that they may not reflect general principles. These other ways of understanding the world have their place, but the systematic and scientific study of behavior provides us with the best overall picture of the human condition.

As researchers investigate human behavior, they gather information and collect data. This is often the easy part. The complex part is trying to interpret what the information means. People do research for reasons that relate to their social and cultural outlook, and they interpret their results from within their own cultural framework. Sometimes people disagree vigorously on how to interpret research in all of the scientific disciplines; this reflects that science is just another type of human activity.

Finally, learning about research is one way to increase one's scientific literacy. Research promotes critical thinking about how to ask and answer questions systematically and objectively. Unfortunately, the majority of Americans show low levels of scientific literacy, which may account for acceptance by some people of certain types of pseudoscience that scientists firmly reject.

Key Terms

A priori method	Explanation	Pseudoscience
Authority	Falsifiability	Public
Control	Junk science	Replicable
Data driven	Objective	Scientific approach
Description	Peer review	Tenacity
Empirical	Prediction	Verifiable

Chapter Review Questions

Multiple Choice Questions

1. Researchers recently documented the fact that after a terrorist attack, people who refused to think about the horrible events and isolated themselves were at greater risk than others of developing post-traumatic stress disorder. This fact relates to which goal of science?
   a. control
   b. description
   c. explanation
   d. prediction

2. Researchers with different theoretical beliefs are likely to differ greatly with respect to their statements regarding the _____ of behavior.
   a. explanation
   b. testability
   c. falsifiability
   d. description

3. When colleges use high school grades and SAT or ACT scores to determine whether to admit a student, they are using the tests scores as a measure of the likelihood of student success in college. This is related to which goal of science?
   a. control
   b. description
   c. explanation
   d. prediction

4. After gaining an understanding of why behaviors occur as they do, a scientist interested in applying this knowledge would be interested in what goal of science?
   a. control
   b. description
   c. explanation
   d. prediction

5. Researchers test the strength of a theory by seeing at what point it breaks down. This activity relates to
   a. control.
   b. explanation.
   c. falsifiability.
   d. proof.

6. If a person drew a conclusion about some topic based on opinion and prior beliefs, a researcher would claim that such a conclusion was not scientific because it was not
   a. objective.
   b. intuitive.
   c. data driven.
   d. predicted.

7. A scientist who decides to repeat an experiment to see if the results are the same is interested in what characteristic of scientific knowledge?
   a. objective
   b. data driven
   c. public
   d. verifiable

8. Beliefs based on intuition or on common knowledge that people hold firmly and are simply reluctant to abandon are based on what kind of knowledge?
   a. tenacity
   b. experience
   c. authority
   d. a priori method

9. When your professor convinces you that some behavioral phenomenon is real based on knowledge of research that he has but that you didn't know about, you develop a belief system that is consistent with that information. Your beliefs are based on
   a. authority.
   b. experience.
   c. a priori method.
   d. the scientific approach.

10. One of the problems associated with knowledge based on experience is that
   a. our own experiences might not generalize to others.
   b. the use of logical deductions does not work in predicting behaviors.
   c. common knowledge might be erroneous, even if many people believe in it.
   d. experiential knowledge and scientific knowledge are usually very different from one another.

11. In planning scientific research, psychologists' choices of topics
   a. have generally been directed by theory, but seldom by cultural values.
   b. have not been influenced by the actions of the government.
   c. are most productive when they are removed from controversial topics.
   d. often reflect cultural values that they hold.

12. The effects of culture on research are reflected in the fact that
   a. the government tries to stay out of the personal choices of researchers.
   b. researchers may avoid controversial topics because of the reactions of others to their research.
   c. research methodologies in psychology tend to remain constant across virtually all societies.
   d. psychologists tend to study the same topics in the same ways across the decades.

13. Reports of scientific "breakthroughs" in the popular media
   a. let the audience know when truly revolutionary research results have been obtained.
   b. generally occur when an investigator turns toward a new area of study and manages to spot trends that others cannot.
   c. usually involve a small set of studies that an independent investigator conducts away from others in the field.
   d. are really reports of a continuous body of research that has been ongoing over a relatively long period of time.

14. A belief in parapsychology (e.g., ESP)
   a. is fairly uncommon in the general public, contrary to common belief.
   b. is typical of most scientists.
   c. has been documented in over half the general public in a number of surveys over several decades.
   d. is at the same level for scientists as it is for the general public.

15. Scientists become suspicious of scientific claims about new phenomena when the people raising the new ideas
   a. insist on publicizing their research in scientific journals instead of in the mainstream press where more people can view it.
   b. claim that the scientific establishment is actively working to suppress their new ideas.

    c. are unable to provide solid anecdotal evidence and specific examples of the phenomenon in everyday life.

    d. do not want to be limited by existing scientific data and theory in providing explanations of the phenomena.

Essay Questions

16. Identify and describe the four goals of scientific research. Include in your description how the four goals build on one another.

17. Identify and describe the five ways of knowing described by the philosopher Charles Sanders Peirce.

18. How do scientists and pseudoscientists differ with regard to the evidence that they will accept to support their ideas?

CHAPTER 2

ETHICS IN RESEARCH

CHAPTER OUTLINE

UNETHICAL RESEARCH PRACTICES—PAST AND PRESENT
Ethical Problems in the Early Years
of the Twentieth Century
Ethics and Plagiarism
Current Examples
of Unethical Research

ETHICAL GUIDELINES CREATED BY THE AMERICAN PSYCHOLOGICAL ASSOCIATION
Aspirational Goals and Enforceable Rules
Ethical Standards as They Affect You

LEGAL REQUIREMENTS AND ETHICS IN RESEARCH
Institutional Review Boards

THE IMPORTANCE OF SOCIAL CONTEXT IN DECIDING ON ETHICS IN RESEARCH
Stanley Milgram's Research Project on Obedience
The Ethical Issues
The Social Context

CONTROVERSY: DECEPTION

WHAT YOU NEED TO DO IF YOUR RESEARCH INVOLVES DECEPTION
Some Research Requires Deception
The Effects of Debriefing on Research

ETHICS ISSUES IN SPECIAL CIRCUMSTANCES
Ethics in Cross-Cultural Research
Ethics in Internet Research
Ethics in Animal Research

LEARNING OBJECTIVES

- Describe unethical historical research in the United States and in Nazi Germany.
- Describe behaviors of current researchers that violate ethics.
- Define and give examples of behaviors that constitute plagiarism.
- Identify the main reasons why researchers act unethically.
- Describe and differentiate the aspirational goals versus the ethical standards created by the American Psychological Association.
- Describe and give an example of the General Principles of ethics created by the American Psychological Association.
- Identify the General Principles of ethics created by the American Psychological Association that are associated with conducting research.
- Describe the reason for the creation of the Nuremburg Code for ethics in research.
- Explain the role of the Institutional Review Board.
- Identify the situation in which researchers do not need approval from an Institutional Review Board.

- Describe a situation in which the Institutional Review Board can hinder effective research design.
- Describe why a researcher could defend Stanley Milgram's obedience research during the time it took place but would not be appropriate today.
- Explain the concept of a cost-benefit analysis in assessing risk in research.
- Identify the criticisms leveled against Milgram's obedience research and his response to those criticisms.
- Identify criticisms associated with the use of deception in research.
- Differentiate between the different types of deception.
- Explain how researchers use debriefing, dehoaxing, and desensitization in research involving deception.
- Explain whether the debriefing process is effective in research involving deception.
- Describe the concept of ethical imperialism in research.

CHAPTER PREVIEW

Most psychological research poses little physical or psychological risk to participants or involves few serious ethical issues. Nonetheless, because some researchers in the past have conducted notorious and unethical projects, laws and guidelines have been developed for the protection of research participants. Another problem is that researchers have made up data, invented entire experiments, and misrepresented their data in published journal articles.

Researchers generally become very interested and excited in their programs of research. Sometimes this means that they focus very narrowly in their work and forget to consider the implications of what they are doing. In this chapter, you will see that investigators may get so caught up in their research that they may endanger the people who participate in their studies.

The American Psychological Association has developed a set of guidelines that has evolved over the past half century. Many researchers in disciplines other than psychology rely on these guidelines. We must also follow legal requirements that federal and state governments have enacted for the protection of human participants in research.

Students sometimes mistakenly believe that the APA approves or vetoes research. It would be impossible for any single organization to oversee as much research as psychologists conduct. Ethical supervision occurs under the oversight of Institutional Review Boards (IRBs) that evaluate proposed projects; this takes place in the colleges and universities where the research is carried out.

In discussing ethics in psychological research, the famous research of Stanley Milgram (1963) and Philip Zimbardo (1972) comes to mind. Milgram's research participants thought they were delivering electrical shocks to another person, often to the extent that the other person might have died. Zimbardo created a prison simulation that led participants, all of them students, to treat one another very brutally. This type of research is very rare in psychology, which is why the most illustrative examples of ethically controversial research occurred over 30 years ago.

We can categorize research in two groups for our discussion. In one category, involving clinically based research, the result of ignoring ethical dictates is potentially very serious. People approach clinical psychologists because of problems that need to be resolved. If clinical research involves ethical problems, those people could be seriously harmed.

Our second category involves basic research in academic settings. Most psychological research has fairly minor risk-related implications for participants. Some psychological research can involve more than minimal risk, but most psychological research on topics like learning, motivation, social processes, and attitude change would virtually never lead to long-term, highly negative outcomes, no matter how incompetent or unethical the researcher. To decide whether a project is appropriate, we conduct a cost-benefit analysis; if the risk exceeds the benefit, we should not do the research; if the benefit exceeds the risk, the research may be acceptable. Before we conduct research, we need to assess the relative risk of the research compared to the benefits for two main reasons. First, it is the ethical and moral thing to do. Second, there are legal requirements that we do it. There has been an unfortunate history of abuse on the part of researchers; some of it is due to carelessness, some due to callousness, and some due to unconscionable social and governmental policies. We hope to avoid such problems in our research.

Unethical Research Practices—Past and Present

Ethical Problems in the Early Years of the Twentieth Century

Through the past century, shameful episodes of unethical research practices have occurred, in many cases leading to extreme suffering and death. The troublesome decisions made by researchers have led to the Nuremburg Code and to the various federal laws designed to protect people. In this section, you will see examples of biomedical investigations that alerted society to the need for protection of people participating in research.

Among the most egregious examples include the investigations done by the Nazis during World War II. For example, according to Lifton (1986), the Nazi Carl Clauberg researched techniques for sterilizing women by injecting them with what was probably Formalin, which consists of formaldehyde and methanol (a kind of alcohol). Both substances are poisonous, and formaldehyde is an extreme irritant; survivors reported that the pain was excruciating. Clauberg injected this substance into the women's cervix, with the aim of destroying the fallopian tubes that are necessary for carrying an egg to the uterus for implantation. This kind of research clearly reflects a pathological society that we want to believe could not happen anywhere else.

This abuse by the Nazis is additionally horrible because Germany had an enlightened approach to research ethics prior to the Nazi takeover (López-Muñoz & Álamo, 2009). In the 1920s, for instance, German researchers approached their studies for the benefit of the patient. During the Nazi reign, however, the focus was on the benefit of the state. Research became a political and military tool.

As you will see, there have been violations in medical and psychiatric research that go beyond the bounds of good judgment and indicate a callous, sometimes horrific disregard for a person's right to be treated with dignity and fairness. The Nazis did not corner the market on such research. Beginning in the 1930s and continuing until 1972, researchers at the Tuskegee Institute in the United States purposely withheld treatment from black patients in order to study the progress of syphilis. When the study began, knowledge of the specific course of the disease and of effective treatment was minimal, but within a short period of time, the evidence was clear that lack of treatment was devastating. Syphilis can lead to blindness, organically caused psychosis, and death. The negative effects on its patients were all too clear decades before the research ceased, and the research continued after treatment with penicillin was standard practice.

The ethical issues that arose are the ones that psychological researchers must consider in planning their research, even though most psychological research is ethically trouble free and poses minimal or no risk to participants. In the Tuskegee study, however, the researchers engaged in behaviors that would not be legally permitted today. They failed to provide informed consent so the men would know that they were taking part in research and what the physical and psychological risks would be; they actively kept the men in the study from receiving effective treatment when it was available; they offered inducements to participate that the men would find hard to resist, and the men may have felt pressured to participate, which meant that participation may not have been truly voluntary; and they did not debrief the men at any point. Researchers ended up studying the men, who were never treated for the disease, for 40 years, until a Public Health Service professional, Dr. Peter Buxtun, revealed the existence of the study to the *Washington Post* in 1972. Table 2.1 details the ethical issues involved in the Tuskegee study.

A report (Research Ethics and the Medical Profession, 1996) has documented a number of problematic studies that occurred during the 1950s and 1960s in the United States. In many cases, the guidelines that had existed regarding informed consent and voluntary participation were ignored.

Examples of harmful and unethical research included cases in which researchers at the University of Cincinnati, in conjunction with the U.S. military, subjected uninformed, terminally ill cancer patients to whole-body radiation to see how it affected those people (Rothman, 1994). Further, in separate projects in the decades after World War II, researchers at the Massachusetts Institute of Technology (funded by the National Institutes of Health, The Atomic Energy Commission, and the Quaker Oats Company) and investigators at Harvard Medical School, Massachusetts General Hospital, and Boston University School of Medicine administered radioactive substances to mentally retarded children living in facilities for the developmentally disabled (ACHRE Report, n.d.). Ethical breaches in medical research continued to occur into the 1960s and 1970s such that Congress created regulations to prevent physicians from abusing their relationships with patients.

Many of the episodes of notorious research come from the 1970s or earlier. Does this mean that we have solved the problems associated with unethical research practices? Or do ethical problems continue in research programs?

Unfortunately, questionable practices still exist. For example, dozens of experiments with human participants came to a halt at Duke University Medical Center in 1999 when the federal government discovered ethical lapses in the projects involving protection of research

TABLE 2.1 *Ethical Issues Associated with the Tuskegee Study*

Ethical Problem	*Example*
Lack of informed consent	The men thought they were being treated for "bad blood," a common term at the time that referred to many possible diseases. They did not know they were participating in research, nor did they know of risks associated with their participation.
Physical and psychological harm	Lack of effective treatment led to problems caused by syphilis, including behavioral changes, blindness, psychosis, and death. They also underwent a painful spinal tap as part of the research. They agreed to be autopsied after death, which was atypical for this population. After the research became public, black people often became suspicious of any government-sponsored health programs.
Excessive inducements	The men received free transportation to the clinic, a meal when they were at the clinic, and free medical treatment for minor problems.
Lack of voluntary participation	The excessive inducement may have been hard to refuse. In addition, the men were sharecroppers who were encouraged by landowners to participate, so they may have felt social pressure to participate.
Failure to debrief	At no point in the research did the men learn about the nature or the details of the study. Such information was available only after the existence of the research was leaked to the media.

participants. One development occurred with a participant in a NASA-sponsored study who underwent testing in a chamber designed to simulate the pressure that you would feel at 30,000 feet above sea level. The man began to lose sensation in his limbs and, after treatment, became semiconscious. On the positive side of the ledger, as soon as a rare and unexpected problem occurred, the researchers terminated the study to protect a research participant; on the negative side, some ethicists questioned whether the project's risks had been adequately studied and whether the participant had received appropriate informed consent (Hilts & Stolberg, 1999).

Beyond this potentially harmful research from the past, recent investigators have engaged in potentially troublesome behaviors. In a recent survey, up to a third of respondents who had received grants from the National Institutes of Health reported engaging in some type of ethically questionable practices, including falsifying and fabricating data, plagiarism, having potentially inappropriate relationships with students or research participants, circumventing minor aspects of human-subject requirements, and others (Martinson, Anderson, & de Vries, 2005; Wadman, 2005). Sometimes researchers have even invented studies that they did not conduct (Mendoza, 2005) or add their names to reference citations, making it appear that they co-authored published papers when they had not (Case summaries, 2004).

One of the few controversies involving psychology related to a paper whose authors failed to cite important research leading to the research in question (Liston & Kagan, 2002). Kagan and Liston did not plagiarize any earlier material, they just failed to cite it. Their article was brief, limited to just 500 words, they noted, so they had to leave out a lot of important material. Nonetheless, they received criticism regarding how appropriate their behavior was (Farley, 2003).

Ethics and Plagiarism

Scientists regard plagiarism as extremely unethical. Unfortunately, there are quite a few ways to fall prey to it (Avoiding plagiarism, 2009). For example, using somebody else's words without attributing them to that person is unethical. Further, even if you take the ideas from somebody else's writing or speaking and translate those ideas into your own words, you must attribute those ideas to the person who originated them.

The issue is complicated, however. If you cite a well-known fact (e.g., humans are born without the ability to use language but learn to speak the language to which they are exposed), you don't need to provide a citation. You can assume that everybody knows that your statement is true. But if you are citing information that is not widely known (e.g., Wilhelm Wundt established the first experimental psychology laboratory in 1879), you should cite a trustworthy source to document your statement. The tricky aspect involves deciding what constitutes a "well-known fact." If you are writing for trained psychologists, most are likely to know that Wilhelm Wundt created the first psychology laboratory, so you wouldn't need to cite a source for that information. But if you are writing for students or nonpsychologists who do not know this fact, you should cite a source. Professionals urge caution and recommend citing a source if it is likely that readers will not be familiar with the topic about which you are writing (Avoiding plagiarism, 2009).

One further issue involves self-plagiarism, which is the use of your own work multiple times. So if you published a paper, as a general rule, you could not ethically use the same material in a second publication. The issue of self-plagiarism is relevant to students who do not publish their work because some sources (e.g., Avoiding plagiarism, 2009) assert that students should not hand in the same paper for more than one course. Other sources, however, do not see this dual use of a single paper as necessarily problematic (What is plagiarism?, 2010).

In the abstract, plagiarism is easy to identify. In practice, though, you have to make judgment calls. Fortunately, there are sources to which you can turn for guidance (e.g., Avoiding plagiarism, 2009; Beins & Beins, 2008; What is plagiarism?, 2010).

FIGURE 2.1 *Incidence and Types of Ethical Infractions Investigated by the U.S. Office of Research Integrity from 2001 to 2009*

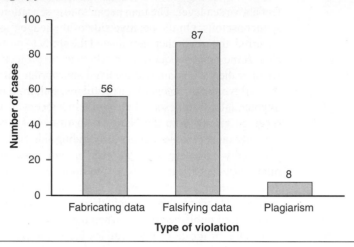

Sources: © Copyright 2010. Bernard C. Beins

Current Examples of Unethical Research

Aspirational goals— General set of ethical principles that guide psychologists in their research and other professional activities.

Ethical Standards—A set of enforceable rules created by the American Psychological Association and by legal authorities that relate to moral values of right and wrong.

Beneficence and Nonmaleficence—Acting to promote the welfare of the people a psychologists deals with (beneficence) and avoidance of harm to them (nonmaleficence).

In an attempt to monitor scientists' behaviors, the U.S. federal government's Office of Research Integrity (ORI) investigates claims of scientific misconduct in research associated with federal grants. In the period from 2001 and 2009, the office concluded that 101 researchers were guilty of misconduct related to data collection, analysis, and presentation. The number of cases identified by ORI is small and seldom involves behavioral research, but we don't know how often fraud goes undetected. According to several sources, one-third of respondents on a survey reported engaging in unethical behavior and over two-thirds said that they had observed others engaging in ethically questionable behavior (Fanelli, Innogen, & ISSTI, 2009; Martinson, Anderson, & de Vries, 2005; Wadman, 2005). Figure 2.1 shows how often the most common infractions investigated by ORI occurred from 2001 to 2009 (Handling misconduct, 2009; Office of Research Integrity Annual Report, 2001). Most cases involved falsifying or fabricating data and plagiarism, but several other severe problems also occurred. The number of infractions is greater than the number of people involved because some people violated the ethical rules in multiple ways. Some overriding causes for such behavior are financial and personal. Getting hired or promoted and getting grants often require completion of successful research. In addition, there is considerable status associated with publishing research.

Most of the research associated with such problems has been biomedical in nature. The risks associated with it may involve life and death issues. Your research in psychology is likely to have less impact. However, the behavioral research you complete also has to conform to certain ethical principles and is bound by the same laws that professional researchers must follow.

Finally, you might ask why individuals engage in these unethical behaviors. As you've just seen, receipt of money is obviously one reason. In addition, according to a researcher who has investigated why scientists cheat, there are four other, basic reasons:

- Intense pressure to publish research and to obtain grants
- Inadequate mentoring

- Some sort of mental disorder
- Scientists from outside the United States who learned standards that differ from those in the United States (Charges of fake research, 2005)

Ethical Guidelines Created by the American Psychological Association

Fidelity and Responsibility— Psychologists must act professionally in ways that support the discipline of psychology and benefit their community, especially regarding the well-being of the people with whom they interact professionally.

Researchers are not exempt from some of the same lapses in good judgment that beset the rest of us. In psychology, we are fortunate that the serious breaches of ethics are rare. Long before the general public learned of the excesses of some researchers, the American Psychological Association (APA) had formulated a set of principles that would guide psychologists in their work. Some research disciplines have yet to develop such codes (Scientists should adopt, 2007). We will discuss primarily those guidelines that relate to research, although the APA's guidelines pertain to all areas of psychological work, including therapy. The principles associated with ethics in providing psychotherapy are vitally important in the therapeutic realm, but are of less interest to us here. When the two worlds of therapy and research merge, psychologists must attend carefully to the ethical guidelines both for therapy and for research. This is an especially difficult area because it is not always clear that psychiatric patients are able to make informed decisions about participating; in part, they may be unable to understand the implications of their participation.

The first set of APA's ethical principles appeared in 1953, the most recent in 2002, with refinement in 2010. As stated in a recent version, psychologists should incorporate the rules as an integral part of their professional lives. "The development of a dynamic set of ethical standards for a psychologist's work-related conduct requires a personal commitment to a lifelong effort to act ethically" (American Psychological Association, 2002, p. 1062).

Integrity—Psychologists should promote the honest and truthful application of the discipline in science, teaching, and practice.

The General Principles espoused in the standards reflect "**aspirational goals** to guide psychologists toward the highest ideals of psychology" (p. 1061), whereas the **Ethical Standards** involve enforceable rules of conduct. When psychologists violate the ethical standards, they face possible loss of certification to work in their field of expertise. Such offenses are relatively rare and, when they occur, generally involve the areas of clinical and counseling psychology rather than research. Every year a small number of psychologists suffer such action for their violations of the ethical guidelines. Fortunately, most psychologists, like most of you, approach their work with integrity; the relatively small number who face censure are vastly outweighed by those whose work is creditable and valuable.

Justice—Psychologists must recognize the implications of their professional activity on others and strive to make the best professional judgments they can.

Aspirational Goals and Enforceable Rules

The five General Principles of the ethical guidelines appear in Table 2.2. As you look at them, you can see that the principles reflect the high moral character that we prize in people around us. In part, (a) **beneficence** and **nonmaleficence** relates to maximizing the positive outcomes of your work and minimizing the chances of harm. Psychologists must also act with (b) **fidelity** and **responsibility** in dealing with others. Psychologists should also strive for (c) **integrity** in promoting themselves and their work accurately. As psychologists, we should also aspire to (d) **justice,** recognizing our biases and the limitations to our expertise as they affect others. Finally, we need to show (e) **respect for people's rights and dignity.**

Respect for people's rights and dignity—Psychologists must recognize the dignity and value of all people and, to the fullest extent possible, eliminate biases in dealing with people.

We recognize that one of our goals is to promote human well-being. In addition, one of the critical aspects of such responsibility is that the public will lose faith in the work of psychologists and in the value of psychology if we don't act with the highest morals. The enforceable ethical standards consist of 10 categories related to different aspects of professional,

TABLE 2.2   *General Ethical Principles and Examples of Violations*

Beneficence and Nonmaleficence	A psychologist would be in dangerous territory in conducting research in which he or she has a financial interest because that interest could cloud professional judgment to the detriment of the participant and others. Further, psychologists who are aware that they are experiencing mental health problems may be acting unethically with clients if their own mental health may lead to poor judgment.
Fidelity and Responsibility	A psychologist would violate ethical principles by engaging in dual relationships with patients. One of the most notable transgressions occurs when a therapist engages in sexual relations with a person while providing therapy to that individual. Also a psychologist who knows that a colleague is engaging in unethical behavior would himself or herself be acting unethically by not taking steps to prevent further such behavior.
Integrity	Psychologists who intentionally misrepresent their research results or who falsify data are engaging in ethical misconduct because they are not striving to maximize gain to the scientific and professional community, but rather are simply trying for personal gain. In addition, psychologists who knowingly use their knowledge to mislead others, such as in courtroom testimony, are engaging in unethical conduct. In this case, they are not using their professional expertise responsibly or contributing to the welfare of society in general.
Justice	A psychologist who is not trained in the use of a test like the Minnesota Multiphasic Personality Inventory but who uses it in his or her research or with clients might be engaging in unethical behavior because the validity of test interpretations may be low.
Respect for People's Rights and Dignity	Psychologists who violate the confidentiality of their research participants act unethically. This means that if you are doing research, you may not discuss with others how a particular participant responded during a testing session. (Such a discussion could be appropriate, however, if you discuss a research session with a colleague who is also working on that project and you need to resolve a methodological problem.)

psychological work. These standards are listed in Table 2.3. Of these categories, the one that pertains most to us here involves research.

(It probably never occurred to you, but if your professors are members of the APA, they are ethically bound to educate and train you well. For example, the Ethical Principles of Psychologists [American Psychological Association, 2002] specify that psychology teachers make sure that syllabi are meaningful and that students be informed about grading procedures.)

As the ethical guidelines pertain to research, psychologists have certain responsibilities to provide research participants with informed consent, to minimize the use of deception in research, to report research results accurately, and to correct any errors in reporting. One further mandate is that researchers must be willing to share their data with other researchers, provided it does not violate the confidentiality promised to research participants.

There are a few areas that are of special relevance to researchers. You will have to consider them when you plan your own research because you must present a proposal to your school's Institutional Review Board (IRB) or to delegated representatives of that committee before you can carry out your proposed research. The committee members may approve your research as proposed, but they may require changes before you can begin. Depending on the nature of the regulations at your school, you may have to wait for a month or longer to receive permission. Your IRB will consider your research proposal based on the relevant state and federal regulations.

Ethical Standards as They Affect You

The General Principles developed by the APA cover a wide range of psychological activities (see Table 2.2). At this point in your life, many of them will be completely irrelevant to you

TABLE 2.3   *General Standards of Ethical Behavior for Psychologists*

Section 1—Resolving Ethical Issues

Psychologists need to recognize problematic ethical situations and work to resolve them on an individual level when possible. Sometimes it may be necessary to seek formal remedies to perceived unethical conduct. When there are legal issues that pose a conflict between ethical guidelines of psychologists and the law, the psychologist should work to minimize the conflict. When a conflict cannot be resolved, it may be appropriate to defer to legal authorities.

Section 2—Boundaries of Competence

Researchers, including you, may conduct research only within the boundaries of their competence. You need to pay attention to this, although most research you are likely to carry out will not be problematic. In certain circumstances, though, such as if you planned on using psychodiagnostic tests, you might be in a gray area because many such instruments require specialized training for adequate administration and interpretation. One potential problem is that you would expose your research participants to risk if you interpreted test results in a way that changed their behaviors for the worse.

Section 3—Human Relations

Psychologists must strive to minimize discrimination or harassment of people with whom they have a professional relationship. Exploitation of another by use of power or authority is unethical. For example, if a psychologist has power over others (e.g., a professor over a teaching or lab assistant, a resident assistant), he or she should take care not to coerce people when recruiting their participation for research. Psychologists should also avoid multiple relationships, one of the most egregious being sexual relationships with students or clients. Clients and research participants should also provide informed consent for research or therapy.

Section 4—Privacy and Confidentiality

You should not discuss the behavior or responses of research participants or clients with those outside your project or treatment setting if not seeking professional consultation. Your participants have a right to expect that their responses will be confidential and anonymous to the fullest extent possible.

Section 5—Advertising and Other Public Statements

Psychologists should not make fraudulent or misleading professional statements when presenting their work to the public. Nor should they misrepresent their professional expertise or credentials.

Section 6—Record Keeping and Fees

Psychologists must document their research and maintain their data so that they are available for legal or other reasons.

Section 7—Teaching, Training Supervision, Research, and Publishing

Psychologists are responsible for competent education and training of students and for accurate descriptions of education and training programs. Teachers must avoid exploiting those over whom they have authority.

Section 8—Research and Publication

With respect to research, it must be approved by an IRB. Participants should give informed consent and be debriefed (dehoaxed and desensitized). In informed consent, you have to provide them with the following information:

- the nature of the research.
- their right to decline to participate and to withdraw at any time without penalty.
- the foreseeable consequences of their participation, such as risks, discomfort, etc.

Some research projects involving anonymous questionnaires, naturalistic observation, and some archival research do not require informed consent. If you think this applies to you, you need to check with your local IRB or its representatives. Table 2.5 provides relevant information about this.

Deception in research is acceptable only if other alternatives are not available or appropriate. Presentation of results should accurately reflect the data.

Psychologists must give appropriate credit to those involved in research but should not give credit to an individual whose work on the research was minimal.

(continued)

TABLE 2.3   (*Continued*)

Sections 9 and 10—Assessment and Therapy
Psychologists must use contemporary assessment and therapeutic techniques and the psychologists must be adequately trained to use them. This complex realm is most relevant to doctoral-level psychologists who provide service to clients.

Informed consent—The process of providing to potential research participants the information they need in order to understand the nature of a research project and to be able to decide whether to participate in the project.

because you do not provide therapy for clients, engage in professional consultation, or perform psychological assessments. As a psychology student, however, you may carry out research projects, at which time the Principles will definitely apply to you. In fact, the most recent version of the ethical guidelines specifically mentions that they apply to student affiliates of APA (Ethical principles, 2002).

Your research activity may not be ethically troublesome, but you need to avoid crossing the line into the realm of unethical behavior. The major points appearing in Table 2.2 do not exhaust the Principles; they merely highlight many of the points relevant to you. You should ultimately be aware of the American Psychological Association's Code of Conduct (Ethical Principles, 2002), as well as the relevant legal considerations. You should also become familiar with the changes in ethical guidelines as they evolve.

Among the most important practical issues you will face if you conduct research are those associated with **informed consent,** that is, making sure that your participants know what they are going to do and understand the nature of the research. In addition, you must provide debriefing in which you inform participants of any deception involved in the research, called dehoaxing, and you make sure that you eliminate any potential sources of negative feelings by the participants, called desensitization. If you think that there are likely to be any long-term consequences for your participants after they complete your research, you need to engage in compensatory follow-up, which means that you arrange for those problems to be remedied. So, for example, if you carried out a study in which you manipulated a person's self-esteem, you would be ethically bound to make sure that, at the end of the study, people were feeling good about themselves and understood the nature of the study and its manipulations.

Anonymity—The practice of maintaining records so that nobody can identify which individual is associated with a certain set of data.

Confidentiality—The practice of making sure that nobody outside a research project has access to data that can be identified with a specific individual.

An additional requirement when you conduct research is that you must protect the **anonymity** and **confidentiality** of your research participants. It is desirable that, after a study is over, you cannot link people's behaviors in a research project with them personally. If there are no identifying characteristics in the data that allow you to know whose data you are examining, the data are anonymous. In some cases, you will not be able to separate a person's identity from the data. For example, if you are tracking people over time, you have to be able to link their current data with past data. In such a case, you need to make sure that nobody outside the research project has access to that information. When you do this, you are making sure that the data are confidential.

Coercion—Pressure that a potential participant feels in agreeing to take part in research.

Another ethical issue involved with interaction with participants involves **coercion.** If you were carrying out a study, you might want to solicit participation of your friends and classmates. They might not want to participate, but being your friends, they might feel social pressure. Their participation would not be truly voluntary.

Plagiarism—An ethical breach in which a person claims credit for another person's idea or research.

Finally, when you develop research ideas or when you write up a report of your project, you must avoid claiming credit that belongs to others. When an investigator asserts that he or she came up with an idea, but that idea was really developed by another person, this is **plagiarism.** It is considered a very serious breach of ethics. If an investigator has received research money from the federal government, plagiarism can lead to severe sanctions.

Legal Requirements and Ethics in Research

Nuremberg Code—A set of legal principles adopted by the international community after the Nazi atrocities in World War II to ensure fair and ethical treatment of research participants.

Shortly after World War II, the international community recognized the need for laws concerning research with people. These laws are known as the **Nuremberg Code,** named for the German city where they were developed. The 10 points of the Code appear in Table 2.4.

As you look at the Code, you might wonder why anybody had to enact such a code. All of the points seem to involve little but common sense. Unfortunately, the Nazis had victimized many people in research. The Nuremberg code formalized a set of rules that could be used by researchers with integrity when they planned their studies that involve people.

TABLE 2.4 *Ten Points of the Nuremburg Code*

Point	Comment
1. Research on humans absolutely requires informed consent.	You cannot do research on people who are not able to give voluntary, informed consent. This requires that they be sufficiently aware of their rights to be able to make a choice that is good for them. You are also not allowed to use undue influence or power you have over a person. The individual must know what risks might be involved.
2. The experiment must have the possibility of contributing to our body of knowledge.	You should not perform research that has no chance of being useful to society. This does not mean that an investigation has to produce major results, but the outcome should add to the accumulation of knowledge about human and nonhuman behavior.
3. Researchers should be informed about the topic they investigate to maximize the likelihood that the results will be useful.	Especially for biomedical research, scientists should design their research based on previous work that has been conducted using animals. In addition, the scientist must be competent enough to design a study whose results will justify the experimentation.
4. The experiment should avoid unnecessary physical and mental suffering.	Sometimes research by its nature involves discomfort of some kind (e.g., a study of sleep deprivation). Researchers should design their work to minimize the extent of the discomfort should it be necessary. Embarrassment and frustration are examples of mental suffering that might be associated with psychological research.
5. No experiment should be conducted if there is good reason to believe that death or serious injury will occur.	When an investigation involves high levels of potential risk, this restriction can be relaxed if the researchers serve as participants in this research.
6. The degree of risk must be less than the potential gain from the research.	Scientists must perform a cost-benefit analysis. If the costs exceed the potential benefits, the research is inappropriate.
7. Prior arrangements must be in place for responding to an emergency that occurs during a research project.	The investigators must make provisions for emergencies that they can reasonably foresee. Sometimes a participant may suffer harm because of an entirely unforeseen circumstance. In such a case, the researcher might not be seen as acting unethically. Points 2 and 3 relate to this—a researcher should be sufficiently well informed to know what risks are likely.
8. The investigator must have appropriate training to conduct the research.	Researchers have to know what they are doing. If a researcher fails to anticipate dangers that an expert would recognize in advance, that researcher might be judged as acting unethically. Researchers must also ensure that workers subordinate to them are qualified to carry out the tasks assigned to them.
9. Research participants must be free to terminate their involvement at any time.	When an individual has reached the point that he or she no longer feels comfortable participating in research, the person has the right to leave without penalty.
10. The experimenter must terminate a research project if he or she believes that continuing the study will lead to injury or death.	The investigator has to be aware of the dynamics of the research situation. If he or she recognizes that there is an elevated level of risk, the investigator must end the study.

In addition to the internationally recognized Nuremberg Code, the U.S. government has also passed laws to protect human subjects. These procedures were initially implemented in 1966 and have evolved over time (Reynolds, 1982).

Institutional Review Boards

Changes in the regulations appear in the *Federal Register,* which reports on congressional activities of all kinds. One of the major provisions of the federal regulations mandates an **Institutional Review Board (IRB),** a committee that consists of at least five people, including a member of the community who is not a researcher. The IRB reviews the potential risks associated with research and either approves or disapproves projects that investigators want to carry out. The official term for this group is the Institutional Review Board, but people often refer to it as the Human Subjects Committee.

Most research must receive approval from an IRB, but there are exceptions, as listed in Table 2.5. (Federal regulations stipulate that an IRB must document that research does not require formal review.) These exceptions exist because the experts who work for the government recognize that not all research carries significant risk. For example, you are allowed to conduct some survey research and simple observational research in a public area without IRB approval. The reason is that those you survey or observe do not experience greater risk because you are studying them when compared to the risks of everyday life. Survey research that probes sensitive issues may require IRB approval.

TABLE 2.5   *Types of Research Most Relevant to Psychology That Do Not Require Approval by an Institutional Review Board*

In general, research activities in which the only involvement of human subjects will be in one or more of the four following categories are exempt from review by an IRB.

(1) Research conducted in established or commonly accepted educational settings, involving normal educational practices, such as

   (i) research on regular and special education instructional strategies, or

   (ii) research on the effectiveness of or the comparison among instructional techniques, curricula, or classroom management methods.

(2) Research involving the use of educational tests, survey procedures, interview procedures or observation of public behavior. The exemption does not hold (and IRB approval is required) if

   (i) information obtained is recorded in such a manner that human subjects can be identified, directly or through identifiers linked to the subjects; and

   (ii) any disclosure of the human subjects' responses outside the research could reasonably place the subjects at risk of criminal or civil liability or be damaging to the subjects' financial standing, employability, or reputation.

(3) Research involving the use of educational tests, survey procedures, interview procedures, or observation of public behavior is exempt as listed in paragraph (2) above; in addition, research is exempt from IRB approval if:

   (i) the human subjects are elected or appointed public officials or candidates for public office, or

   (ii) federal statute(s) require(s) without exception that the confidentiality of the personally identifiable information will be maintained throughout the research and thereafter.

(4) Research involving the collection or study of existing, publicly available data, documents, records, pathological specimens, or diagnostic specimens; in addition, the research is exempt from IRB approval if the information is recorded by the investigator so that subjects cannot be identified, directly or through identifiers linked to the subjects.

Institutional Review Board (IRB)—A committee that reviews research projects to make sure that the projects are in compliance with accepted ethical guidelines. An IRB is required for every institution receiving federal funding in the United States.

One of the most important issues associated with research with people is that you need to inform them about the risks and benefits of the project. One way of recording the fact that you informed the participants and that they voluntarily agreed to take part in the study is through the informed-consent form. This form lays out the nature of the study, including potential risks for participating. Sometimes IRBs have specific formats that they want researchers to follow; in addition, institutions sponsoring research may use these forms as legal documents.

Investigators have found that research participants often cannot understand complicated informed consent forms, even when the IRBs have created the forms. Likewise, the forms that some institutions use can be very legalistic and, to a typical reader, uninformative. According to one study, the prose in the average form was between the tenth- and eleventh-grade reading level, but half of the U.S. adult population reads at the eighth-grade level or below (Paasche-Orlow, Taylor, & Barncati, 2003). This research involved medical informed consent, which is likely to be more complex and technical than behavioral research, but the important point is that research participants need to be able to understand what you are telling them in order for their consent to participate to be truly voluntary.

Ironically, Keith-Spiegel and Koocher (2005) have argued that when researchers believe that they have not received fair treatment from an IRB, they may engage in behaviors designed to deceive the IRB. The investigators may conclude that their research is truly ethical and that they need to identify ways to get around elements of the ethics review process on which the IRB treats them unfairly.

It is common to hear researchers complain about the difficulty in getting IRBs to approve research projects, but psychologists, in general, believe that their IRBs are not generally unreasonable. For instance, the majority of respondents, 62%, responded that the turnaround time between submitting a proposal and receiving a decision is reasonable. The mean time from initial submission to feedback based on revisions is a little over four weeks (Ashcraft & Krause, 2007).

There are some important questions associated with IRBs, however. For example, Sieber (2009) gave an example of student researchers who wanted to interview people living on the streets; the IRB mandated that the students tell those being interviewed that they didn't have to respond to any questions they didn't want to answer. The participants seemed to find that statement very funny because if they didn't want to answer, they weren't going to. The students believed that the street people did not take the interview seriously because of that.

Furthermore, sometimes IRBs make decisions that seem quite questionable. Ceci and Bruck (2009) reported that one of their research proposals was denied by their IRB as being potentially damaging to the children who would be participants even though the National Science Foundation (NSF) and the National Institutes of Health had reviewed the research proposal and found no problems. In fact, the NSF had even provided funding for the research. Sieber (2009) encouraged research on what behaviors by researchers might actually be risky rather than relying on intuition about it.

When considerable delays occur in IRB approval, two typical reasons are that the research involves special populations that are considered vulnerable (e.g., children) or that research protocols pose risk to participants. The experiences of all researchers are not positive, with some researchers claiming that their IRBs lack somebody with sufficient expertise about the research to come to a timely decision. However, a minority of researchers, 22%, simply agreed with the statement that, "My IRB always takes a long time, regardless of the specifics of the proposal" (Ashcraft & Krause, 2007, p. 9).

The Importance of Social Context in Deciding on Ethics in Research

Consider this: A participant volunteers to help with research. He is told that he will be in the role of the teacher, delivering electrical shocks to another person, also a volunteer, every time that person makes a mistake in a learning task. With each mistake, the strength of the shock will increase, up to a level on a panel marked "Danger: Severe Shock," followed by a mysterious higher level of shock simply labeled "XXX." The learner remarks that he has a heart condition, but the experimenter replies that it won't matter. The learner is strapped into a chair in another room and connected to the apparatus that will deliver the electrical shocks.

After the learner makes several mistakes and receives shocks, he demands to quit, but the experimenter simply says the experiment must continue. Shortly thereafter, the learner (who allegedly has a heart problem) becomes completely silent, but the researcher encourages the teacher to continue to deliver electrical shocks if the learner doesn't respond because a nonresponse is the same as a wrong answer.

Stanley Milgram's Research Project on Obedience

Suppose you were the participant. Would you continue shocking the learner? Or would you stop? If you were like the majority of people who took part in some of Stanley Milgram's (1963) experiments on conformity, you would have persisted in shocking the learner. How would you have felt afterward, knowing that you had delivered shocks to somebody with a heart condition, somebody who became utterly silent after a while, somebody you might have killed by shocking him?

(As you may already know, the victim did not receive shocks. Milgram employed deception to induce participants to feel personally involved in what they thought was a real set of conditions.)

Milgram (1974) described a variety of studies in his extensive research project that subjected his volunteers to this situation. Knowing what you know about the ethics of research, would you consider this ethical research? This experimentation has generated voluminous commentary. Some psychologists and ethicists believe that the studies were simply unethical (e.g., Baumrind, 1964). On the other hand, Milgram (1964) defended them as being within ethical boundaries. More recently, psychologists have revisited some of the issues associated with Milgram's research and its ethical dilemmas (e.g., Burger, 2009; Elms, 2009; Miller, 2009).

The Ethical Issues

What are some of the important issues to consider here? If psychologists legitimately differ in their conclusions, it is pretty certain that we are in a gray area here. You might conclude that the research was acceptable, or you might condemn it. In the end, we need to make a judgment call using the best wisdom we can muster.

An IRB decides whether any given research project would subject people to undue risk relative to possible benefits from the research. Formally, the IRB is supposed to weigh the risks (physical and psychological harm) against the benefits (increased knowledge and applications) of the research. If the risks are greater than the benefits, the research should not be done; if the benefits exceed the risks, the research can be defended on ethical grounds. This type of assessment is often known as a **cost-benefit analysis.** In essence, if the risks (costs) are great, they outweigh small and, maybe, even large benefits; as such, the researcher should not conduct the research. On the other hand, if the benefit is large, then small or maybe medium level risks are tolerable. The difficulty arises when the risks and the benefits are both high. A decision may not be easy to reach and different people may arrive at different, but legitimate conclusions.

Unfortunately, before researchers carry out their studies, nobody knows for sure what harm may occur or what benefits will actually accrue. In advance, we are talking about possibilities, not actualities. Before a study takes place, we can guess at costs and benefits, but not until after investigators complete their work can we can identify either the risk-associated problems that arose or the actual benefits of the research.

Cost-benefit analysis— An evaluation of the relative risks that research participants face in a study (the cost) relative to the potential benefit of the outcome of the research.

Criticisms of Milgram's Research.   With this uncertainty in mind, we can ask whether Milgram violated the rights of his participants. Among others, Baumrind (1964) asserted that Milgram's obedience research should not have been done. She said that the "dependent attitude" (p. 421) of the participants rendered them more susceptible to the manipulations of an authority figure, that is, the experimenter. She also named several ethical problems, asserting that Milgram did not show concern for participants' well-being, that the cost (i.e., degree of psychological distress and having been lied to) exceeded the benefits of having done the research, that the participants' long-term well-being was negatively affected, and that their attitudes toward authority figures would in the future be more negative. She also noted Milgram's statement that 14 of the 40 participants showed obvious distress and that three suffered seizures.

Baumrind (1964) did not accept Milgram's statement that the distress was momentary and that the gain in psychological knowledge outweighed the negatives: "I do regard the emotional disturbance described by Milgram as potentially harmful because it could easily effect an alteration in the subject's self-image or ability to trust adult authorities in the future" (p. 422). She also stated that Milgram's debriefing and dehoaxing processes would not have remedied the situation.

Milgram's Defense of His Research.   Not surprisingly, Milgram (1964) responded to Baumrind's criticisms. He disagreed with her assessments, saying that he tried to predict in advance how the participants would respond and had been confident that they would not engage in the shocking behavior very long. He went to great lengths, asking psychiatrists and others to estimate how often the participants were likely to engage in blind obedience. The experts thought that the overwhelming number of participants would not administer severe shocks. Thus, at the outset, Milgram firmly believed that virtually everybody would refuse to engage in extreme behavior. As a result, he felt that the risk to his participants would be minimal. As it turned out, the estimates that the experts gave were wrong—people did administer what they thought were severe electrical shocks. But it is important to note that Milgram tried to anticipate what would occur.

Milgram also noted that he debriefed and dehoaxed the participants, trying to ensure that they departed with no ill effects. Further, at his request, a psychiatrist interviewed 40 participants after a year. There seem to have been no problems at that time. In fact, Ring, Wallston, and Corey (1970) specifically examined participants' reactions to a Milgram-like study. These researchers reported that people may have felt distressed during participation, but the effects were short-lived. A large majority of the people responded that they were happy that they participated. Further, when Ring et al. debriefed their participants after using an approach like Milgram's, the level of tension by participants dropped relative to that of no debriefing.

Baumrind raised critically important points. According to the data we have, though, many or most of the problems she cited did not seem to materialize. Both Milgram's and Baumrind's predictions were off the mark. This is another good example of how experts can be wrong, and why we should not simply rely on authority for the "truth."

The Social Context

We might want to consider the social context in which Milgram did his work. His studies took place from 1960–1963, which was not long after the end of World War II. The Nazis carried out numerous experiments that no normal person could ever justify. In some very famous cases, the perpetrators of those acts claimed that they were merely following orders, that is, simply being obedient. Milgram, like many others, was greatly affected by the reports of these atrocities. In fact, when Milgram gave an overview of his research in his book *Obedience to Authority* (1974), he referred directly to the Nazi crimes in the very first paragraph of the book.

The United States, where Milgram did his research, was still in the process of recovering from the war, like citizens in many countries. In addition, people were worried about the possibility that communists would try to conquer the world, turning people into blindly obedient automatons. War was clearly on people's minds. It was reasonable that we would try to understand how seemingly normal people could commit the wartime acts of the Nazis, behaving with blind obedience. An experimental psychologist might try to reproduce the dynamics of obedience in the laboratory to find out how and why people defer to authorities. This is precisely what Stanley Milgram did.

As members of our society, we continually decide whether behaviors are acceptable. In the early years of the century, many people felt entirely comfortable discriminating against people of color in all aspects of life. Society has changed, and the number of people who agree that such discrimination is acceptable has diminished. In a similar vein, people in the post-war years may have been very comfortable with the idea of Milgram's research because the effects of blind obedience were still fresh in people's minds. Society has changed, and the number of people who would support such research has undoubtedly diminished. The question of blind obedience is no longer as relevant as it was in the aftermath of World War II. It is unlikely that an IRB would approve such research today. But in a different era, people might consider it acceptable or even desirable.

Incidentally, Milgram's application to become a member of APA was initially questioned on the basis of the ethics of his research. Ultimately, though, the organization accorded him membership, judging that he had not violated ethical guidelines in his work.

What You Need to Do if Your Research Involves Deception

For decades, deception was very prevalent in social psychological research (Adair, Dushenko, & Lindsay, 1985). This means that many psychologists have accepted it as a reality of their research. As Figure 2.2 suggests, deception may have been more routine into the 1970s compared

FIGURE 2.2   *Percentage of Studies Using Deception in a Sample of Articles from* **Journal of Personality and Social Psychology** *from 1965 to 2005*
The articles appeared in issues 1 and 6 of the journal from each year represented.

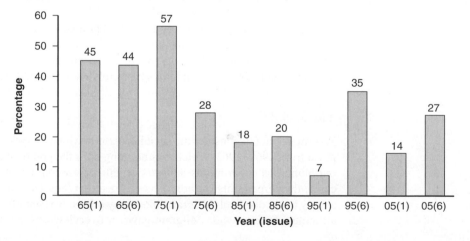

Role playing—An approach to research in which participants act as if they were participating in a study so the investigator can avoid using potentially unethical strategies that might lead to physical or psychological harm to the participants.

Naturalistic observation—A research technique in which the investigator studies behavior as it naturally occurs, without any manipulation of variables or intervention into the situation.

Simulation—An approach to research in which the investigator creates an environment similar to one of interest in order to study behaviors in a realistic way. This approach is also known as the simulated environment.

Cover story—The story a researcher creates to disguise the actual purpose of a study when deception is considered necessary to conduct a study.

Active deception—The process of misinforming a research participant about some aspect of a study so that the individual is not aware of the investigator's intent in the project.

Passive deception—The failure to provide complete information to a research participant about some aspect of a study so that the individual is not aware of the investigator's intent in the project.

to today. Nonetheless, in spite of the criticisms leveled by opponents of deception, psychological researchers have not embraced alternate methodologies like **role playing, naturalistic observation,** or **simulation.**

When many people argue against deception, they do so because they see it as immoral. In addition, a second area of concern involves the risk for participants who are deceived. In such a case, a person cannot give informed consent about his or her willingness to participate. We cannot ignore this important notion of informed consent. It is a critical component of national and international laws. Fortunately, there is good reason to believe that keeping participants ignorant of some aspects of the research has negligible effects on them in general (e.g., Bröder, 1998).

A very different type of criticism of the use of deception is that people will develop negative attitudes or suspicion toward psychology and psychological research (Orne, 1962). There is credible evidence, however, that people regard the science and practice of psychology very positively, even after learning that a researcher had deceived them (e.g., Soliday & Stanton, 1995). Christensen (1988) even reported that research participants believed that it would be undesirable if we failed to investigate important topics that might require the use of deception.

Some Research Requires Deception

The dilemma about using deception in research is that some research projects virtually require a level of deception. If you want participants to act naturally, you might have to create a **cover story** that keeps them from acting in a self-conscious manner during the study. If, after careful consideration, you conclude that you need to use deception, you must keep two points in mind.

First, you should minimize the amount of deception involved. You need to make sure that you do not withhold critical information that would make a difference in a person's decision about whether to participate in your research. Withholding too much information may mean that a person cannot give appropriate informed consent about participation because he or she cannot assess the risks. As Fisher and Fyrberg (1994) noted, we can characterize different kinds of deception, depending on the degree to which we actually provide incorrect information to participants. For example, we can distinguish between active and passive deception.

In **active deception,** you would actively mislead the participants by providing them with information that is not true. In **passive deception,** you would not actually tell a lie. Instead, you would withhold information that might give clues to the participants about the purpose of the study. That is, you give them incomplete information.

All research involves telling our volunteers less than we know. Participants would probably not be terribly interested in all the details of our research. At the same time, with passive deception, you intend to keep the participants in the dark, so your intent is clearly to deceive. One relevant question involves the extent to which you see an ethical difference between active and passive deception. This depends on your own point of view; psychologists differ in their beliefs in the matter.

Furthermore, you need to debrief your participants adequately after the session ends. There are two components to **debriefing.** One element involves **dehoaxing,** which means that you tell the individuals what you did, how you deceived them, and why it was necessary. The second element involves **desensitization,** which means that you eliminate any potential sources of negative feelings by the participants.

We have to make sure that when we explain to participants that they were deceived, the dehoaxing does not, in and of itself, lead to discomfort. Would people feel even worse knowing that they were deceived and would there be psychological risk simply because of the debriefing itself? One problem you face is that debriefing itself might lead to problems; a participant might feel worse after learning about a deception. In rare cases, one might refrain from debriefing a participant, but this should be a last resort that has received approval from an IRB.

The Effects of Debriefing on Research

Most psychologists debrief their participants immediately after a testing session concludes. Practically, this is the easiest approach. If a researcher decides to postpone the debriefing, it takes extra effort to contact the participants. One drawback to immediate debriefing is that participants might discuss the research with others. If you deceived them in order to make sure they acted naturally, there are obvious problems if your participants talk to others who later take part in your study.

How often will participants actually discuss the research with others? According to Marans (1988), of 50 participants in a debriefing-disclosure study, 10 (20%) reported discussing the experiment with other, potential participants. If 20% of participants disclose the nature of a study to others, this could pose a serious problem to the validity of research that relies on the naïveté of participants. On the other hand, Diener, Matthews, and Smith (1972) discovered that only 11 of 440 potential participants had learned about the deceptive elements of an experiment for which fellow students had volunteered. Diener et al. concluded that leakage of information is not a serious concern.

Further, Walsh (1976) reported that when researchers asked people not to disclose any information about the research, the participants refrained from discussing the study more than when such a request was not made. These results suggest that researchers must evaluate the potential problems of immediate debriefing on a study-by-study basis. If the investigator is worried that a participant might talk about the study and forewarn other potential participants of the nature of the study, the researcher might decide to defer debriefing until the end of the project. This would solve one problem: People remain naïve about the study. At the same time, this solution itself introduces a different problem, having to contact people later, which is not always easy. A new solution to the problem of delayed debriefing is some software that keeps track of participation and the email addresses of participants. As such it could be relatively easy for researchers to contact study participants for debriefing after the study ends.

Psychologists have asked the question of whether debriefing actually serves its purpose. That is, does it remove any negative responses of the participants? Although there is controversy (see Rubin, 1985), there seem to be few negative effects of deception when researchers take debriefing seriously. Gruder, Stumpfhauser, and Wyer (1977) studied the effects of feedback. These researchers provided participants with false feedback about poor performance after having taken an intelligence test. Gruder et al. wondered if there would be a difference in performance in a subsequent testing session depending on whether the participants learned about the false feedback in a debriefing session.

The results showed that when participants learned that the feedback was not accurate, their later performance on another test improved; there was no comparable trend among participants who were not debriefed. This suggests that false feedback about poor performance has a real effect on participants. On the other hand, debriefed participants were able to cast away the negative information readily. There are clear implications about the beneficial effects of debriefing and potential risks if it is not done or is not done well.

Debriefing—Informing research participants at the conclusion of a research project of the purpose of the research, including disclosure of any deception and providing an opportunity for participants to ask questions about the research.

Dehoaxing—The process of telling research participants of any deception or ruses used in a study.

Desensitization—The process of eliminating any negative aftereffects that a participant might experience after taking part in a project.

CONTROVERSY
Deception

Do you like it when people lie to you? If you do, you are probably fairly unusual. Most people are upset when others lie to them. Over the years, psychologists have used deception in their research. Do people object to being lied to in these research settings? Or do you think that people are unconcerned? The answers to these questions are difficult because there are few absolute standards.

For instance, people in different cultures may show different responses to issues like deception in research. American students are more likely to be bothered by it than are Malaysian students because of a greater tendency on the part of Malaysians to defer to the judgments of respected authorities like a researcher and to relinquish individual rights that Americans may deem more important (Bowman & Anthonysamy, 2006). So if you were interested in determining the ethics of a research project, your decision would be culturally based.

Related to cultural issues in research, the term *ethical imperialism* has appeared in the research literature. This concept refers to the idea that a researcher from one culture may try to apply his or her own ethical perspective on research participants in another culture. With the increase in cross-cultural research in psychology, this phenomenon may become much more prominent. For example, if Malaysian research participants were not bothered by some aspects of deception as Americans are, should an American researcher impose his or her ideals on them? Or if a Malaysian researcher held views that differed from those of Americans, should he apply his or her standard to the Americans?

A further question involves whether a person from one culture can truly understand the dynamics of people in another culture. Quraishi (2008) is a Muslim researcher who studied Muslim prisoners, discovering that with some Muslim prisoners, he could identify with them so that the research might have been more meaningful than if he didn't identify with them and they with him. In fact, with some Muslim populations, like Black Muslims, the cultural mismatch was notable. He used his experience with the Muslim prisoners to discuss how differences in race, ethnicity, and culture can affect the process of research.

If you were to search for published articles on ethics in psychological research, you would find that a great deal of it would relate to the use of deception. Some psychologists (e.g., Ortmann & Hertwig, 1997) have condemned the use of deception in research, calling for the outlawing of the practice, in part on purely moral grounds. In response, other psychologists have argued that moral philosophers do not agree that deception is unambiguously wrong (Korn, 1998), that the "social contract" between researchers and participants may permit behaviors that might elsewhere be considered unethical (Lawson, 1995), and that participants themselves do not condemn such an approach (Christensen, 1988).

Fisher and Fyrberg (1994) asked potential participants (i.e., college students) to evaluate research scenarios involving three types of deception: implicit deception, technical deception, and role deception. Implicit deception involves having participants complete their tasks for a purpose of which they are unaware; in this case, Fisher and Fyrberg (1994) used this type of deception to manipulate mood by means of an imagery task.

Technical deception involves misrepresentation of the use of equipment; Fisher and Fyrberg technically deprived participants by telling them that equipment had broken down when it hadn't. Finally, role deception involves misrepresenting the role of another individual in the testing session; the researchers induced participants to believe that they had damaged another person's belongings.

The results suggested that people don't see much problem with implicit deception. Ninety percent of the students participating in Fisher and Fyrberg's study thought that the benefits of the research outweighed the costs. On the other hand, just over 70 percent of the students were comfortable with technical and role deception.

It might be informative to figure out why some research situations could lead to negative reactions. Psychologists who study embarrassment note that we feel embarrassed when we think somebody may evaluate us unfavorably (Miller, 1995). If we feel that we have been fooled in the presence of someone, we might be embarrassed because we feel that the person might think less of us. Thus, in a situation like technical deception or role deception, you might be annoyed at having been deceived. On the other hand, in implicit deception, the participants may not feel they are really interacting with another during the deception, so they don't feel uncomfortable.

If participants do not particularly mind implicit deception in a research study, does that relieve psychologists of the responsibility to consider the ethics of their actions? If participants do not mind being deceived, it means that one of several issues becomes less controversial.

Fisher (2005) has proposed that we consider deception on several dimensions. Her discussion related to research with children, but the three points discussed here have validity for any project involving deception:

- Will alternative methodologies produce data of equal validity to that involve deception?
- Does deception permit the research participant to make an informed consent, thereby minimizing potential harm?
- Will debriefing eliminate the potential for risk or could it cause problems in and of itself?

(continued)

CONTROVERSY (*Continued*)

The question of using deception is complex. As Fisher and Fyrberg (1994) pointed out, participants are partners in research, not merely objects of study. As such, we have to balance the potential risks of psychological harm (e.g., embarrassment or anger at being deceived) with the potential benefits of research. We have to consider whether hiding the truth means that participants will not be able to make informed judgments about participation.

Ethical Issues in Special Circumstances

Ethics in Cross-Cultural Research

One area of ethics that does not involve issues like deception or confidentiality focuses on the implications of culturally oriented research. That is, there can be implications regarding conclusions drawn along cultural lines.

For example, psychologists should consider whether research on cultural issues could lead to stereotyping of people in various groups. Iwamasa, Larrabee, and Merritt (2000) discovered that some behaviors stereotypically associated with different ethnic or racial groups were also associated with psychological disorders. Thus, one could naively conclude that when a person from a given group exhibits a certain behavior, that behavior reflects a disorder when, in reality, it might simply be a common way of behaving within that group.

In an opposite circumstance, a psychologist who is not familiar with the behaviors in a different cultural group could observe a behavior normal in the psychologist's culture and not recognize it as symptomatic of a problem within the other culture. For instance, among the Amish, symptoms of bipolar mood disorder include giving gifts during the wrong season of the year or excessive use of public telephones (Rogler, 1999). These examples illustrate APA's aspirational principle of justice.

Another aspirational principle that is relevant in cultural research involves respecting people's rights and dignity. That is, psychologists should appreciate individual differences associated with "age, gender, gender identity, race, ethnicity, culture, national origin, religion, sexual orientation, disability, language, and socioeconomic status" (Ethical principles of psychologists, 2002, p. 1063).

Finally, among APA's enforceable ethical standards, researchers need to attend to their competence in researching complex areas involving culture and understand whether they are really able to draw appropriate conclusions. Psychologists also have an ethical responsibility to provide adequate assessments and valid interpretation of results.

Ethics in Internet Research

A new challenge that we face as researchers involves ethical issues associated with using the Internet. We are in fairly new territory with Web research. The community of psychological researchers has had a century to figure out how to complete in-person research; we have had well over a quarter of a century to come up with legally sanctioned protections for participants. Over the past decade, we have begun to learn what works and is appropriate regarding Internet research. But with Web research, some very tricky questions arise about how to deal with the issues of confidentiality and anonymity (especially regarding sensitive topics), informed consent, protecting participants from unforeseen negative consequences, debriefing them, and how to arrange compensatory follow-up if it is needed (which we may never know).

There are two main advantages of remote, online data collection with respect to ethics, according to Barchard and Williams (2008). The first is that respondents feel a sense of anonymity that leads them to be more likely to respond to sensitive questions. And, second, respondents do not feel pressure to continue their participation if they become uncomfortable for some reason.

Countering these advantages, some disadvantages also exist. First, it is not possible to know whether participants understand the informed consent process. Second, clarifying ambiguities and answering questions during debriefing are not possible. Third, the researcher does not know if a respondent is actually of a legal age to be able to participate (Barchard & Williams, 2008).

A sizable amount of Web-based research in psychology involves questionnaires. These are generally regarded as being fairly benign, so the ethical risks associated with them are minimal. An added protection for the participants is that they can quit any time they want if they feel frustrated, overwhelmed, or otherwise uncomfortable. However, suppose a researcher wants to know about serious, private issues in a person's life. Two notable concerns appear here. First, it is absolutely required that the researcher guarantee that nobody can intercept the responses of the participant. Experts in the field of ethics will have to join experts in technology in certifying secure data transfer.

Second, merely filling out a questionnaire may trigger an emotional response; if it happens in a laboratory, the researcher can try to deal with any problems and can get help for the individual if necessary. The researcher can also arrange to contact the individual at a later point to make sure that there were no lasting problems. Nobody may ever know about the unfortunate consequences for remote people who participate online. It appears that this second issue may not lead to problems because respondents may feel less pressure to complete an uncomfortable task (Barchard & Williams, 2008). Further, the response rate to sensitive questions is higher in online surveys than in mail surveys, suggesting that participants do not regularly experience discomfort in answering sensitive questions (McCabe, 2004).

The research community recognizes these concerns and has begun to address them. Major national organizations have entered the discussion. The Board of Scientific Affairs of the American Psychological Association, the American Association for the Advancement of Science, and the federal government's National Institutes of Health have worked to generate solutions to these ethical questions (Azar, 2000a).

Finally, an ethical consideration that involves researchers, not participants, has arisen. With Web research, it would be both possible and easy for an unscrupulous researcher to steal the ideas of another person (i.e., commit plagiarism), conduct a similar project, then claim priority for the ideas. Unfortunately, it could be difficult to know if somebody stole another's ideas. How could we distinguish between simultaneous discovery and chicanery (i.e., cheating)? It could be possible to determine the truth by examining the records of the researchers, but the issue is not easy and could besmirch the reputations of honest scholars.

Ethics in Animal Research

Psychologists have studied animal behavior for the past century. Much of the work has involved laboratory rats and pigeons that have learned to perform tasks in different conditions. Even though the study of animal behavior constituted one of the pillars of psychology, not all people have agreed on its value. Some have criticized animal research as being of limited applicability to human behavior and restricted mostly to one variant of one species, namely, the Norway rat (Beach, 1950). This is an important question: Can we learn about people by studying animals? The answer is definitely yes, although we cannot learn everything from animals.

A second group of people has condemned research with animals as being unethical. There are several aspects to their arguments. For instance, animal rights activists maintain that we do not have the right to keep animals in laboratory captivity. Some also believe that the animals are treated inhumanely. Over the past few decades, there has been growing sentiment against use of animals in research in society, although a majority of people still believe that if such research benefits humans, it is not unethical (see Plous, 1996a, for a discussion of these issues).

Researchers who work with animals have identified different elements of ethics in non-human animal research. Broadly speaking, the scientists have noted that investigators have to consider the ethics of fair treatment (e.g., housing and food) of the animals, the need for science to advance, and the benefit of human patients when knowledge is advanced by animal research (Ideland, 2009).

The use of animals in psychological research has diminished notably over the past several decades in the United States, Canada, and Western Europe. According to Plous (1996a), as of over a decade ago, a quarter to a third of psychology departments have either closed their animal laboratories or are giving it serious consideration. Further, there is a remarkable decrease in the number of graduate students in psychology who conduct animal research (Thomas & Blackman, 1992, cited in Plous, 1996a). This trend may continue.

Plous has found that psychologists, as a group, show overwhelming support (over 85%) for naturalistic observation, which does not involve animal confinement, somewhat less support for studies involving laboratory confinement (over 60%), and little support for research involving pain or death (17 to 34%). He has also discovered that undergraduate psychology majors are highly similar to their mentors in the attitudes they hold toward the use of animals in psychological research (Plous, 1996b). He also noted that among the general public, there is significant support for research involving rats (88%), but less for dogs (55%).

If a person's own moral principles imply that it is unethical to use animals in research, then no arguments about the benefit to people will persuade that individual to accept such research. That person has the right to hold his or her moral principles, and others must recognize that right. At the same time, the majority of Americans accept animal research as being beneficial, as long as the investigations might be beneficial to human welfare and do not expose the animals to unreasonable distress. This group also has the right to its opinion. We must rely on knowledge and common sense to make the best decision. If we are either to criticize or to defend research with animals, we need to know the truth of the animals' treatment at the hands of the scientists.

Arguments and Counterarguments.   According to Coile and Miller (1984), some animal rights activists made claims about the plight of animals in psychological experiments that would make most of us wonder if the research is justified. The claims include the idea that animals receive intense electrical shocks that they cannot escape until they lose the ability to even scream in pain, that they are deprived of food and water, and suffer until they die.

Coile and Miller discussed six points raised by the activists (Mobilization for Animals, 1984, cited in Coile & Miller, 1984). Coile and Miller's arguments are two decades old but are probably still reasonably valid, especially given the changes in the nature of psychological research away from the animal model. Coile and Miller examined the previous five years of psychological journal articles that commonly report the use of research animals, like *Journal of Experimental Psychology: Animal Behavior Processes* and *Journal of Comparative Psychology*. They only looked at psychological journals; other disciplines, like biology, also rely on animals to varying degrees.

The claims of some activists were simply wrong regarding psychological research. The alleged, intense electric shocks, severe food and water deprivation, smashing of bones and mutilation of limbs, and pain designed to make animals psychotic never appeared in research reported in the most prestigious psychology journals.

The fact that the claims about the research are false does not mean that the animals do not experience pain or distress in some studies. In fact, various experiments clearly involve discomfort, some of it intense. Research on learned helplessness, for example, involved such an approach.

Coile and Miller argued that there can be good reason for engaging in this type of research, particularly in the biomedical realm. For example, experimental animals have been used to investigate treatments for problems like living with chronic pain, cancer, and AIDS in people, but research has also benefitted both wild and domesticated animals in terms of what constitutes living areas and treatments for distemper. Researchers who seek to further our understanding of depression sometimes use electrical shock with animals in research; however, as Coile and Miller pointed out, depression can lead to suicide, which is the third leading cause of death in young adults.

Miller (1985) further amplified some of the benefits of animal research for people suffering from problems like scoliosis, enuresis (bed wetting), anorexia, loss of the use of limbs due to nerve damage, chronic pain, stress, and headaches. Many people would consider it justifiable to study animals in order to ease the plight of people suffering from such problems.

As Plous (1996a, 1996b) has found, psychologists and psychology students hold quite similar attitudes about the use of animals in research. The general public also shows sympathy toward animal research; there is widespread support regarding the use of rats in biomedical research. People do not like to see animals exposed to intense suffering or distress, though. According to the findings of Coile and Miller, psychologists do not regularly expose their research animals to the kind of treatment that people find objectionable. In some ways, however, the issue may become less pressing in psychology because the use of animals in research is on the decline.

Finally, it is important in dealing with issues of the ethics of animal research is to make sure that information advanced by those on both sides of the issue is credible. Claims that are unfounded do not help people understand problems that actually need to be addressed, so appropriate action cannot be taken.

Chapter Summary

Scientists who study people usually show consideration for the well-being of the individuals they study. After all, scientists are just like everybody else in most respects. Unfortunately, however, there have been cases in which researchers have shown a reprehensible lack of concern about the people who participate in their studies.

Probably the most notorious violators of ethics in research are the Nazi doctors who tortured people in the name of research. Unfortunately, they are not the only ones who have violated ethical standards. For instance, U.S. researchers studying men with syphilis for several decades beginning in the 1920s withheld treatment to see the course of the disease. The men thought they were receiving appropriate levels of treatment.

In order to protect human participants, the American Psychological Association was one of the first organizations to promulgate ethical standards in research. APA has developed a set of aspirational goals and enforceable rules that members of APA must follow. It is the responsibility of each researcher to be aware of these rules. Student researchers are just as responsible for ethical treatment of participants as professional researchers are.

Among psychologists, Stanley Milgram is undoubtedly the most famous person whose research was questioned on ethical grounds. He deceived his participants into thinking they were shocking another individual. The controversy over whether he should have conducted his projects persists. In the end, the decision about ethics involves complex issues that differ for each instance we consider.

After the Nazi atrocities, an international body created the Nuremburg Code, which specifies the basic rights of human participants in research. It is an internationally recognized code. In the United States, federal and state legislation similarly protects the welfare of participants. One of the newest areas that is receiving scrutiny is Web-based research. There are questions of informed consent and invasion of privacy that have yet to be addressed and resolved.

Another aspect of research ethics that has received considerable attention in the past few decades involves the treatment of animal subjects. Some people condemn any use of laboratory animals in research, regardless of the type of projects. Other people feel that if such research will ultimately benefit people, some degree of discomfort or harm is acceptable. Medical researchers are more likely to inflict pain or distress in animals; psychological research is usually more benign and may involve little, if any, discomfort for the animals. The controversial issues associated with animal rights are still an evolving field.

Key Terms

Active deception	Dehoaxing	Nonmaleficence
Anonymity	Desensitization	Nuremberg Code
Aspirational goals	Ethical Standards	Passive deception
Beneficence	Fidelity	Plagiarism
Coercion	Informed consent	Respect for people's rights and dignity
Confidentiality	Institutional Review Board (IRB)	Responsibility
Cost-benefit analysis	Integrity	Role playing
Cover story	Justice	Simulation
Debriefing	Naturalistic observation	

Chapter Review Questions

Multiple Choice Questions

1. Researchers at the University of Cincinnati wanted to investigate how much radiation military personnel could be exposed to and still function. In order to study the effects of radiation, they
   a. gave food with radioactive substances to developmentally disabled children.
   b. withheld treatment from patients who had been accidentally exposed to radiation.
   c. exposed psychiatric patients to radiation without informed consent.
   d. subjected cancer patients to whole-body radiation without informed consent.

2. In recent psychological research that has received criticism on ethical grounds, the authors (Liston & Kagan, 2002)
   a. failed to cite research by other psychologists that was important and relevant to the development of their ideas.
   b. claimed to have completed a study but they did not actually carry it out.
   c. subjected participants to high levels of pain without first obtaining informed consent.
   d. published a figure that originally came from the research of other psychologists that had appeared in a different journal.

3. According to research by the U.S. Office of Research Integrity, the single most frequently occurring ethical offenses involved
   a. not randomly assigning participants to groups.
   b. falsifying data.

   c. plagiarizing other researchers' ideas.

   d. fabricating data.

4. The enforceable rules of conduct associated with the ethical principles developed by the American Psychological Association are
   a. aspirational goals.
   b. principles of responsibility.
   c. ethical standards.
   d. ethico-legal principles.

5. A psychologist who is providing therapy for a person should not develop a close friendship with the client because such dual relationships can compromise the success of the therapy. This problem relates to which General Ethical Principle of the American Psychological Association?
   a. beneficence and nonmaleficence
   b. respect for people's rights and dignity
   c. justice
   d. fidelity and responsibility

6. In resolving ethical situations involving legal issues and confidentiality, a psychologist
   a. can never reveal what a client has revealed in a therapeutic session.
   b. may appropriately defer to legal authorities, even if involves violating confidentiality.
   c. is obligated to keep information confidential only if revealing it would cause embarrassment.
   d. is allowed to reveal confidential information only when a client gives written permission.

7. If you have deceived participants during the course of a study, you need to debrief them at the end. When you tell them about the deception, you are engaging in
   a. dehoaxing.
   b. desensitization.
   c. ethical standards.
   d. informed consent.

8. When participants in Stanley Milgram's obedience studies left the research session, they had been told that they had been deceived about the nature of the study. Because the participants might have experienced potentially serious distress after the study, Milgram arranged for visits with a psychiatrist. This process was called
   a. dehoaxing.
   b. desensitization.
   c. compensatory follow-up.
   d. informed consent.

9. The Nuremburg Code of ethics in human research arose because of the
   a. failure to provide medical treatment in the research on syphilis done at the Tuskegee Institute.
   b. addition of radioactive substances in children's food at a home for the developmentally disabled.
   c. Milgram's obedience studies.
   d. Nazi research in World War II.

10. Research may not require approval by an Institutional Review Board if
    a. it occurs in a commonly accepted educational setting and assesses instructional strategies.
    b. it involves only passive deception.
    c. a similar study has already been done elsewhere with no ethical problems.
    d. it involves studies of children.

11. Research on how people respond to informed consent forms has revealed that
    a. many Americans don't read well enough to understand what they are reading on the informed consent forms.
    b. many people do not bother to read the informed consent forms because they trust the researchers.

    c. the informed consent forms often omit information important for people to understand the research.

    d. people are often upset after learning what they will have to undergo if they participate in the research.

12. The criticism of Milgram's obedience research by psychologist Diana Baumrind (1964) included the claim that the research
    a. did not include compensatory follow-up.
    b. should have been preceded by an attempt to estimate how many participants would be willing to give high levels of shock.
    c. did not include either dehoaxing or desensitization.
    d. costs in terms of participant distress were not outweighed by the benefits.

13. Milgram's obedience research was important at the time he conducted it because
    a. behavioral theories of the time predicted one outcome but Freudian theory predicted very different outcomes.
    b. the Nazi atrocities of World War II that were based on blind obedience were still fresh in people's memories.
    c. Milgram's studies were among the first to study the effect of obedience on racist behaviors.
    d. earlier studies of obedience had erroneously predicted how people would behave under stressful conditions.

14. Milgram defended his research by pointing out that he
    a. did not intend to harm anybody and could not foresee the problems that occurred.
    b. engaged both in debriefing and in dehoaxing of participants after the study ended.
    c. paid participants well enough to overcome any discomfort they had experienced.
    d. the research was so important that it was acceptable, even if a few people were harmed.

15. Studies about participants' reactions to being deceived in research have revealed that
    a. most participants are offended when they learned that they have been lied to.
    b. deception leads participants to be skeptical or suspicious about psychological research.
    c. participants regard the science and practice of psychology positively, even after learning that they have been deceived.
    d. they agree that ethical guidelines should prohibit deception in psychological research.

16. When you decide to tell participants something false about a research session in order to mislead them, you are using
    a. naturalistic observation.
    b. role playing.
    c. active deception.
    d. dehoaxing.

17. If volunteers complete an Internet-based survey on a sensitive and potentially distressing topic, one of the ethical considerations that is hard to deal with is
    a. debriefing the participants after they complete their responses.
    b. providing any necessary compensatory follow-up.
    c. reaching people who might not take distressing topics seriously.
    d. informing the participants that they can leave the study at any time.

18. Researchers have identified advantages of online research that include
    a. lessened ethical requirements because people complete online surveys on their own.
    b. higher response rates to sensitive questions on online surveys.
    c. a reduced need to provide debriefing and clarification when people complete surveys.
    d. greater understanding by participants of informed consent issues.

19. Some psychologists have criticized research with animals on ethical grounds. They have claimed that
    a. animal research cannot be used to understand or ultimately provide the basis for control of human behavior.
    b. psychological research with animals has doubled about every 10 years.

    c. keeping animals in captivity is unethical in and of itself.
    d. moral arguments are not a sufficient basis to justify ending animal research.

20. When psychology students evaluate research with animals, students
    a. usually have very negative attitudes about the use of cats, dogs, and rats.
    b. are very similar to their faculty mentors in their attitudes toward such research.
    c. support such research for their own studies, but not for the research of others.
    d. are very likely to agree that animals are necessary for their own research.

21. When participants complete a task for a purpose of which they are unaware, the researchers are using
    a. technical deception.
    b. implicit deception.
    c. role deception.
    d. naturalistic deception.

22. Participants are often uncomfortable when they learn that a research study has involved
    a. role deception.
    b. passive deception.
    c. implicit deception.
    d. active deception.

23. If researchers provide negative, false feedback to participants, the performance of those participants may worsen. According to research, subsequent debriefing
    a. leads to improved subsequent performance compared to participants who are not debriefed.
    b. often results in anger on the part of the deceived participants.
    c. makes no difference to the participants in subsequent behavior.
    d. leads to later frustration on the part of the participants.

24. When considering the ethics of survey research, an investigator should
    a. ensure that all responses are anonymous and confidential.
    b. let respondents know from the very beginning that once they begin their participation, they need to continue with the project.
    c. remember that if the researcher makes a big point of assuring confidentiality and anonymity, it may needlessly arouse suspicions among respondents.
    d. avoid asking questions of a sensitive nature.

25. In their defense of research with animals, Coile and Miller argued that
    a. even though animals were often seriously harmed, the overall benefit to people was high enough to justify the pain.
    b. animals do not really suffer pain as intensely as people do, so the issue of pain in animal research is a minor issue.
    c. some day in the future, we will discover the benefits of research on animals, even if they have suffered.
    d. animal research is, in many cases, beneficial to animals as well as to people.

Essay Questions

26. Identify the five general principles of APA regarding ethical conduct and what behaviors they pertain to.

27. What types of research can be exempt from Institutional Review Board (IRB) consideration, according to U.S. federal law?

28. When people oppose the use of animal research, what arguments do they produce?

CHAPTER 3

PLANNING RESEARCH: GENERATING A QUESTION

CHAPTER OUTLINE

WHERE RESEARCH IDEAS BEGIN: EVERYDAY OBSERVATIONS AND SYSTEMATIC RESEARCH
Informal and Formal Sources of Ideas
The Effect of Theory

HOW CAN YOU DEVELOP RESEARCH IDEAS?
Generating Research Hypotheses

THE VIRTUAL LABORATORY: RESEARCH ON THE INTERNET
Internet Research
Respondent Motivation
Advantages to Web-Based Research
Potential Problems with Web-Based Research
The Future of the Internet in Psychology

CHECKING ON RESEARCH: THE ROLE OF REPLICATION

DON'T REINVENT THE WHEEL: REVIEWING THE LITERATURE
What Is a Literature Review?
The Effect of Peer-Review on the Research Literature

CONTROVERSY: DOES MUSIC MAKE YOU SMARTER? THE ROLE OF REPLICATION

HOW TO CONDUCT A LITERATURE REVIEW
Electronic Databases
Starting Your Search
Different Sources of Information

HOW TO READ A JOURNAL ARTICLE
Understanding the Format of a Research Paper

LEARNING OBJECTIVES

- Describe more and less formal sources of research questions
- Explain how theory leads to testable hypotheses
- Describe different approaches to generating research ideas
- Describe the advantages and limitations of Internet-based research
- Explain the benefits of replication in research
- Conduct a basic literature search using PsycINFO
- Identify the different sections of a journal article and their contents

CHAPTER PREVIEW

Research questions come from a variety of sources and motivations, most of them arising from the investigator's curiosity. At the same time, our ideas develop within a social context. The questions we consider important develop because of the combination of our personalities, our histories, what society values, and other factors that may have little to do with the scientific research question per se.

Ideas arise in different ways. Sometimes, researchers notice an event that captures their interest, and they decide to create research to study it. At other times, researchers have a specific question to address or a problem to solve that leads to a research project. In some cases, researchers develop research ideas to test theories. No matter how the idea develops, researchers have to figure out the best way to investigate their questions.

To generate good research, investigators should be aware of the work of other scientists. This allows the investigator to advance our knowledge and to avoid simply repeating what others have done. Such knowledge will also help a researcher generate new questions. Sources of information include scientific publications and presentations at research conferences. As your exposure to research expands, you will learn effective and efficient means of searching for prior work that relates to your own research question.

Electronic databases provide easy access to descriptions of research in psychology. By conducting a systematic literature review, psychologists can learn about the work of others, devise their own research questions, and ultimately publish research articles or make presentations at professional conferences.

Where Research Ideas Begin: Everyday Observations and Systematic Research

If we read journal articles or listen to psychologists give presentations of their research, we get a coherent picture of what led them to do their research, how they accomplished it, and what their results mean. The final product is a nice package whose ideas flow logically; we can see how the ideas developed and how they progressed. Researchers who communicate well can weave a good story. But where do the research ideas come from?

Why do researchers study topics ranging from thinking and problem solving to social relationships to personality development? The answer is fairly simple: The researchers are curious, and doing the research is fun. Research involves solving puzzles and getting answers, so why shouldn't it be enjoyable? Scientists like what they are doing even when they study serious and complex issues. Further, the social context of researchers' lives affect the types of questions they ask and how they ask them.

For example, people who are familiar with conventional birth control pills know that a woman takes a pill each day for three weeks out of the month. The pills in the fourth week are placebos that allow menstruation to occur. The reason for the development of this strategy is that the developer of the first birth control pill, John Rock, was a Catholic who wanted the form of contraception to be "natural," thus acceptable to his religious authorities. As such, his plan included monthly menstruation, even though it was not necessary or maybe even desirable (Gladwell, 2002). This episode provides a good example of how a researcher's religious beliefs led to his scientific approach. It would be an interesting exercise to speculate on what might have occurred if the strictures of the Catholic church had not been part of the picture. The nature of birth control may have gone through an entirely different development. In fact, the week of placebos may disappear as new contraceptive medication develops.

Let's consider an example of how simply thinking about an interesting social topic can lead to research questions. For instance, consider a topic that has captured the interest of the American public: handgun control. Some people support control; some oppose it. Using surveys, researchers have investigated how often people protect themselves with their guns.

The picture is complex, which is why there is still debate on the topic. Data collected by Kleck and Gertz (1995) suggested that Americans use their guns for self-defense about 2.5 million times a year in various emergency situations. According to Hemenway (1997), those surveys reflected overestimates of protective gun use. In this debate, there are data supporting contradictory claims. Both sides approach the research carefully and look for valid information. But the topic is very complex, and each answer to a research question raises new questions. As a result, the research on the topic continues. Because of the complexity of the issue, the data don't point to a single, clear answer regarding whether handgun ownership is, on balance, a positive or a negative phenomenon.

One of the reasons that researchers have a hard time answering questions definitively is because of their complexity. Beyond that, though, whenever you ask people for information, they may mislead you without even knowing it. People think their memories are accurate, but there are many gaps and errors in what they recall. According to Wentland and Smith (1993), people are not as accurate as you might suppose in responding to easy questions, such as whether they own an automobile, a home, a driver's license, or a library card. We should not be surprised that answers to hard questions are more problematic. It would be an interesting research project to discover the situations in which we should accept people's reports of behaviors and those situations when we should not.

In essence, any time we encounter a behavior that we do not fully understand, there is potential for a research project.

Informal and Formal Sources of Ideas

There are various ways that research ideas develop. We can characterize them on a continuum as being more or less formal. Figure 3.1 presents this continuum and the kind of question that leads to more research.

The Continuum of Research Ideas. Sometimes a research question will arise because a psychologist observes something in everyday life and decides that he or she would like to research it. The idea does not derive from theory or from previous research, only from curiosity about some behavior that takes place. This approach represents a very informal and idiosyncratic way of generating research ideas. If it weren't for the fact that the psychologist happens to notice something worth investigating in a particular situation, the research might not take place.

FIGURE 3.1 *Continuum Representing the Development of Research Ideas*

Informal			Formal
"This is interesting. I'd like to know more about it!"	"We have a problem to solve. Let's figure out the best way to do it."	"Our earlier project answered some of our questions, but there are still some unanswered questions."	"The theory says people should act this way. Let's test the theory."

One step toward the more formal or systematic end of the continuum involves solving practical problems. That is, in a particular situation, you might look around and say, "We can do this better." The next step would be to design a program to test your ideas. Psychologists who work in organizations or in industry often specialize in solving such applied problems. Their approach is not based only on personal observation and curiosity, but comes from a question that relates to the workplace. This strategy is somewhat more formal than deciding to study a behavior because it catches your eye. At the same time, it does not develop from other research or from a theory; it might be idiosyncratic to a particular time or place. The research takes place because the psychologist is in the position to solve practical problems as they arise in a particular setting.

A third point on the continuum involves researchers who evaluate the work of others or who have completed research projects. Already completed research always has some loose ends, so the investigator takes the partial answers and tries to extend our knowledge. This is a more formal approach to research because the ideas that led to a particular project are embedded within a research context and help answer a question that others are also investigating.

At the most formal end of the continuum, a research idea can develop from a well-defined theory. That is, a theory predicts certain behaviors, so the psychologist tries to see whether the behaviors follow from theoretical predictions. This approach would represent the most formal approach because theoretical expectations may dictate the nature of the research.

For example, Goldenberg et al. (1999) investigated a prediction of Terror Management Theory, that people who score high in neuroticism will have more thoughts of death than people low in neuroticism when both types of people are primed with the physical, as opposed to romantic, aspect of sex. The researchers induced research participants to think of the physical aspects of sex, then asked participants to complete word fragments like COFF_ _. The theory predicts that those high in neuroticism will complete the fragments with death-related words, whereas those low in neuroticism are less likely. (In this example, the word fragment could be completed as *COFFEE or as COFFIN.*) The results matched the prediction that Goldenberg et al. generated based on the theory.

The question to be answered in Goldenberg et al.'s research is not the result of a single, unsystematic event, but rather unfolds from a well-defined and systematic set of ideas. Most research ideas develop in the middle of the continuum. That is, old ideas lead to new ideas that we can test empirically.

According to Glueck and Jauch (1975), researchers in the natural and physical sciences tend to develop their projects based on a combination of their own insights and the results of previous research. Clark (cited in Glueck & Jauch, 1975) agreed that productive psychologists also tend to generate their research ideas based on earlier work. We see what others have done and we try to clear up the loose ends.

Glueck and Jauch (1975) found that researchers say they develop their ideas primarily on their own, followed by ideas generated on the basis of published research, then by collaboration with colleagues at other institutions.

Research ideas often arise from the personal interests of the investigators. For example, the noted psychologist Robert Sternberg became interested in issues of intelligence because of his own experience with taking tests. Sternberg, who was elected president of the American Psychological Association and has written or edited dozens of books and has authored hundreds of scientific journal articles, did not score very well on standardized intelligence tests. There is a clear discrepancy between the message given by this test scores ("he isn't very smart") and his remarkable achievements ("he is very smart"). Sternberg has spent a considerable part of his career studying the various forms intelligence can take. His research has investigated intelligence and knowledge, and how we can assess them.

The Effect of Theory

The dominant theoretical perspective affects the kind of research questions that investigators ask. We can see this pattern occurring in psychology now as it relates to animal research. From the early 1900s until well into the 1960s, psychologists studied animal behavior to help understand all behavior, including that of humans. This meant creating research questions that could be asked with nonhuman subjects.

Over the past few decades, though, there has been a notable change in the way psychologists do research. For example, in Great Britain, the amount of animal research has declined precipitously. The number of doctoral dissertations by young researchers in psychology that involve animals has declined by 62 percent over the past 25 years (Thomas & Blackman, 1992, cited in Plous, 1996a). We haven't exhausted the entire repertoire of research questions involving animals; we have just focused our attention differently.

As we have seen in the discussion of ethics in research, many people have noted that ethical concerns led them away from research with animals. There are other significant factors as well. Social forces are complex, and major changes in the way people think reflect multiple underlying causes.

Reasons for Decreases in Animal Research. Several reasons can help account for these changes. One reason is that, in general, students earning doctorates in psychology seem to be interested in different topics—those that don't involve animals.

A second possibility is that, as a society, we have become more sensitized to the ethical issues associated with animal research. Even though psychologists may support the use of animals in research, as we have seen in Chapter 2, these same psychologists may choose not to involve animals in their own professional work.

Another reason for the decline in animal research is that we have changed theoretical perspectives. For the first seven decades of the last century, the dominant paradigm was **behaviorism.** One of the fundamental tenets of behaviorism is that a few simple principles of learning and behavior can explain the behavior of virtually any organism of any species. Thus, it does not matter if you study people or rats; the specific behaviors may differ, but the principles of learning, reinforcement, and punishment hold true across species, according to the behaviorists. Thus, what is true for rat behavior should be true for human behavior.

Psychologists have expanded on this simple set of rules and have developed new ideas to explore more complex behavior and thought. Behaviorism has not been shown to be without value; indeed, its principles have led to some very useful outcomes. With the new cognitive orientation, though, psychologists have begun to ask different kinds of questions.

The Effect of the Cognitive Revolution. What does this movement away from behaviorism and animal studies mean about the nature of the research we publish? According to Robins, Gosling, and Craik (1999), the so-called "cognitive revolution" in psychology is clear from the amount of research that is cognitive in nature. According to these researchers, the percentage of articles using words related to cognition has risen dramatically since the early 1970s. As you can see in Figure 3.2, they reported that, according to a PsycINFO® search of keywords related to cognition, neuroscience, behaviorism, and psychoanalytic theory, the trend in psychology is toward the dominance of cognitive psychology, with the other approaches

Behaviorism—A theoretical approach in psychology that focused on studies of observable behaviors rather than internal, mental processes.

FIGURE 3.2 *Percentage of Articles by Decade Published in a Small Sample of Psychology Journals That Include Keywords Associated with Cognitive, Behavioral, Psychoanalytic, and Neuroscience Perspectives*

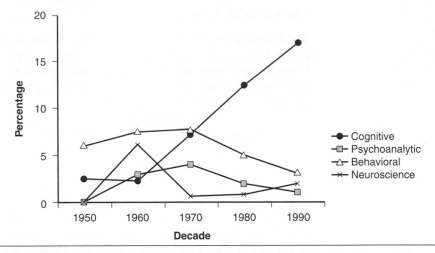

Source: Robins, R. W., Gosling, S. D., & Craik, K. H. (1999). An empirical analysis of trends in psychology. *American Psychologist, 54,* 117-128. Copyright American Psychological Association. Reprinted with permission.

falling quite short of the level of research represented by cognitive psychology. This pattern was striking when you consider the inroads that neuroscience had made in psychology up to that point. Not surprisingly, their results created some controversy. A number of psychologists criticized the validity of their methodology and their conclusions (e.g., Friman, Allen, Kerwin, & Larzelere, 2000; Martin, 2000).

In fact, using a somewhat different method of searching for research associated with the four theoretical domains, Spear (2007) found a quite different pattern, one that revealed the importance of cognitive psychology, but also of neuroscience in psychology. According to Spear, the original research focused on psychology journals that were too narrow in scope. Spear rectified that by searching in a more diverse range of journals. When he did that, the effect of neuroscience became very prominent. Behaviorism and psychoanalytic theory still appear infrequently in the research literature, however.

These two instances of research show how important methodology is in determining the results. As Figure 3.3 shows, with a narrow search of four psychology journals, Robins et al. (1999) found little presence of neuroscience; with a wider search of journals, Spear (2007) found that neuroscience is a large and growing area of psychological research.

During the past three decades, the use of behavioral terms (e.g., reinforcement, punishment, discriminative stimulus) has declined. (Even though behavioral terms have decreased in use, the principles of behaviorism still account for some of the most generally useful principles of behavior.) At the same time, the use of neuroscientific terms appears to have risen in psychology, reaching equivalence with cognition. Figure 3.3 also reveals that the interdisciplinary area of cognitive neuroscience may be on the rise. These trends allow us to make predictions about the dominant patterns of psychological research in the future.

Regardless of the particular approach, however, Rozin (2006, 2007) has described several different ways to think about developing research ideas. One approach he suggested focused on people's interests and passions rather than on negative psychological states. As he noted, important domains of most of our lives receive minimal attention from researchers.

FIGURE 3.3 *Percentage of Articles Published by Decade in a Wide Range of Psychology Journals That Include Keywords Associated with Cognitive, Behavioral, Psychoanalytic, and Neuroscience Perspectives*

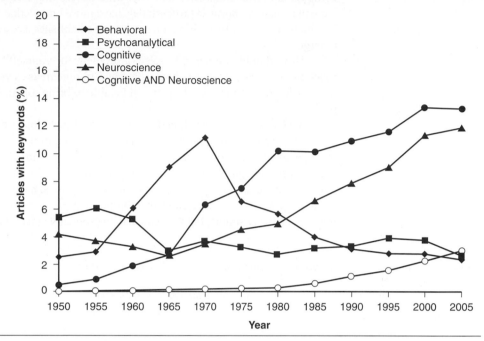

Source: Spear, J. H. (2007). Prominent schools or other active specialties? A fresh look at some trends in psychology. *Review of General Psychology, 11,* 363–380. doi:10.1037/1089-2680.11.4.363. Copyright American Psychological Association. Reprinted with permission.

There has been much more attention paid to cognitive processes and learning than to the areas that excite our interest, like eating, sports, entertainment, and politics.

There are advantages to working in an area that has not received a lot of attention by researchers. For one thing, Rozin (2007) pointed out that much less background reading is required. In addition, pilot studies are more fun to do, and there is little danger that others are doing the same study you are doing. So your work will be novel. And perhaps most important, when you do have a finding, it is likely to represent a bigger increase in the state of knowledge. Studies 1 and 2 usually add more to knowledge than Studies 1,000 and 1,001 (p. 755).

There is much research on phobias but very little on what is almost certainly a more common positive opposite, passions. Passions are strong and enduring interests and engagements with something (Wrzesniewksi, Rozin, & Bennett, 2003). Passions are important to people in their everyday lives; in spite of their importance, however, we do not know how passions develop (e.g., Deci & Ryan, 1985). An undergraduate student named Amy Wrzesniewski stimulated Rozin (2007) to collaborate on creating a scale to measure people's intrinsic interest and passion in their work (Wrzesniewski et al., 1997).

There are many interesting topics that student and professional researchers can investigate that have, so far, remained relatively untouched. Beginning with psychology's inception, it has focused on sensation, perception, learning, and other basic processes, not topics important to the quality of one's life (Rozin, 2006). Even social and personality psychologists have not devoted a lot of energy to these domains, although the emergence of positive psychology has changed that somewhat. Still a lot of interesting questions remain unasked and unanswered.

How Can You Develop Research Ideas?

Professional researchers have an easier time developing a research project than a beginning student researcher because professionals have more knowledge and a greater sense of the field in which they work. In addition, once a person establishes a research program, new ideas often emerge easily.

How should you begin to select a problem for yourself? The first step is to acquire as much knowledge as you can about as many different areas as you can. The greater your scope of knowledge, the more likely you will be able to bring together different ideas into a unique project.

McGuire (1983) developed a set of useful techniques that you could use to generate research questions. His suggestions span the continuum from very informal to very formal. At the most personal and informal level, he suggested that you introspect about your own experiences and use your thoughts to generate research questions. At the more formal level, he proposed that you can look at research in a particular area and try to adapt some of those ideas to a new area. Table 3.1 presents a list of research possibilities that you could implement; the research questions may be relatively simple, but they can lead to productive ideas. One point to remember, though,

TABLE 3.1 *Approaches to Generating Research Ideas and Some Examples of Ideas That Could Develop into Research Projects*

Types of Phenomena	*An Idea That You Could Develop*
Studying spontaneously occurring events	
Intensive case studies	Study the behavior of a friend who consistently scores well on tests. Try to find out why and see if the technique works for others.
Extrapolate from similar problems already studied	Psychologists have investigated the credibility of expert witnesses. One question that remains to be answered, though, is whether jurors respond similarly to female and male expert witnesses.
Studying the validity of everyday beliefs and when these beliefs break down	
Reverse the direction of a common-sense hypothesis	Many common sayings, like "Opposites attract," suggest behavioral hypotheses. You could investigate whether opposites really do attract by studying to see if similar people are more likely to date or form friendships.
Evaluating formal if-then statements	
Use the hypothetico-deductive method of saying that "if A is true, then B should be true"	If people are allowed to eat snacks in a situation where they can take the snacks from a single large bowl versus from multiple small bowls, they will eat less when the snack is in small bowls, consistent with the unit bias hypothesis (Geier, Rozin, & Doros, 2006).
Using previous research as a stepping stone	
Bring together areas of research that originally did not relate	Research on people with physical disabilities and research on sport and exercise psychology can come together for investigators who would like to apply knowledge on sport and exercise to a new population that has not been connected to this domain in the past (Crocker, 1993).
Tests of theory	Piagetian theory generally does not support the idea that children regress to previous levels of cognitive development; test children under difficult conditions (e.g., when they have a limited time to complete a long task) to see if they do regress.

Source: Based on McGuire, 1983.

is that if an idea is obvious to you, it may have already occurred to others, so it is worthwhile to see if another researcher has investigated the research question that occurs to you.

Generating Research Hypotheses

McGuire (1983) suggested that too many people erroneously believe that generating research questions involves creativity that cannot be taught. If this were true, highly creative individuals would use their innate gift to generate research, and for the unfortunate people with less creativity, the likelihood of engaging in good research would be low. McGuire disagreed with this pessimistic view. He proposed a set of approaches to generating research questions.

Table 3.1 illustrates that it isn't always difficult to generate research ideas. One suggestion is to evaluate commonsense ideas to see when they hold true and when they don't. You may hear that "opposites attract" as a principle of human behavior. This maxim leads to testable hypotheses. Once you define what you mean by "opposites" you can find out if we tend to select people opposite to us. You may find instead that "Birds of a feather flock together."

You could also combine previously unrelated topics. For instance, research on sports and physical disabilities don't usually fall together. You might be able to generate some interesting research projects by connecting them. It is important to remember that the more practice you get in developing ideas and the more knowledge you gain in a particular area, the easier it is to come up with new research projects.

As noted above, many of the ideas that you generate at first will probably have been studied already, so you may have to revise your initial plan. This can be a frustrating experience for students because you may not have enough background knowledge to be able to figure out how to proceed, so you feel that all the good ideas have been taken. This is where you can rely on professionals in the field (including your professor).

In making your plans, remember that you are not likely to make major breakthroughs. In reality, major changes in the way people think about an issue result from the results of many small studies that lead to a new synthesis of ideas. Similarly, some research can fall into the category of "so what?" studies (Smith, 2007) that psychologists may regard as uninteresting because the study does not really connect with other psychological ideas.

Sometimes researchers make suggestions for future projects. For instance, Goodman-Delahunty (1998) provided a set of questions of particular relevance to psychologists interested in the interface between psychology and the law.

Goodman-Delahunty reported that studies of sexual harassment typically involve college students as participants. Further, the research may not employ accurate legal definitions of sexual harassment. The mock trial transcripts are also not very complex, unlike real life. What would happen if you did a study with people from the working world? What about using more realistic scenarios? We don't know what would happen because researchers have not yet investigated these questions. Table 3.2 presents further topics for study. These examples involve psychology and the law, but you can use the same process for just about any other area of study.

You are likely to experience greater success if you pick a small research question. Even professional researchers investigate small questions, accumulating a great deal of knowledge bit by bit.

The Virtual Laboratory: Research on the Internet

Some psychological research requires specialized laboratory space and equipment. Whenever we want to measure specific behaviors or responses just as they occur, we must be in the presence of the people (or animals) we measure. It is hard to imagine that a behavioral researcher

TABLE 3.2 *Examples of Potential Research Projects on Gender and Law That Are Based on Existing Research and Legal Questions*

Current Situation: Sexual harassment creates a hostile working environment, but there are differences in people's conceptualizations of what constitutes harassment. Studies of gender differences in perception of sexual harassment are complex and inconsistent (Goodman-Delahunty, 1998).

Recommendations for Related Research:

- Do results differ when we use accurate, legal definitions of sexual harassment in research, which is not always done?
- Do simple, fictitious cases result in different outcomes than rich and complex scenarios that occur in actual legal cases?
- Do convenience samples consisting of college undergraduates produce results different from studies using other people?

Current Situation: Jurors have to evaluate the credibility and the evidence presented by expert witnesses. Are female and male experts regarded the same by different participants in trials related to battered women who kill their spouse (Schuller & Cripps, 1998)?

Recommendations for Related Research:

- What happens if we vary the sex of the expert witness as well as the nature of other testimony and evidence?
- Can we identify different mannerisms and characteristics of expert witnesses that may add or detract from their credibility and that may be confused with gender effects?
- Does gender of an expert witness make a difference in more versus less serious offenses?

Current Situation: Most sexual harassment claims are made by women against men, but on occasion, men are the victims of such harassment. Those inflicting the harassment may be either female or male, although men report fewer negative reactions to these experiences (Waldo, Berdahl, & Fitzgerald, 1998).

Recommendations for Related Research:

- Given that harassment might take different forms for female and male victims, do people show parallel criteria pertaining to women and to men?
- Can we identify whether male jurors will defer to female jurors during debate, or vice versa?
- Do juries take harassment of men as seriously as they do harassment of women? Gay men versus straight men?
- Will a jury deal with the questions of the severity of the harassment differently for men and women?

could study reinforcement or punishment without having direct contact with whomever is being observed. If developmental psychologists want to see whether an infant will cross a visual cliff, parents must bring the infant to the laboratory.

On the other hand, psychologists may be easily able to accomplish research at a distance that involves experimental manipulations or judgments of opinion and attitude. For such studies, it is common to bring participants to the laboratory for the research or to mail the materials. (Unfortunately, people often do not mail them back.) With the advent of easy access to the Internet, we no longer need to be in the physical presence of those who agree to participate in such research, and we don't need to go to the trouble and expense of mailing anything.

The concept of the laboratory is undergoing adjustment; it can be worldwide in scope. Table 3.3 presents some examples of actual Web-based research. Creative researchers should be able to use the Internet to good effect. An array of online research projects is available at http://psych.hanover.edu/Research/exponnet.html.

TABLE 3.3 *A Very Abbreviated Listing of Samples of Web-based Research Listed in 2010 at http://psych.hanover.edu/Research/exponnet.html*

Social Psychology
• Attractiveness of Faces
• Healing from the Loss of a Loved One
• In Social: Personal Judgments in Social Situations II
• In Social: Personality Judgments
• In Social: The Communication Game

Health Psychology
• Eating Disorders and Family Relationships
• Predictors of Self-Medication with Over-the-Counter Products
• Childbirth Expectations Survey
• Study on Diabetes Type I for French-Speaking People

Forensic Psychology
• Criminal Justice Survey
• Perceptions of a Sexual Assault
• Mock Juror' Perceptions
• Prostitution Attitudes Survey
• Eyewitness Recognition Study

Sexuality
• Gender Related Attitudes
• How's Your Love Life?
• Sexual Health of College Students
• Gender and Sexual Orientation Differences in Scent Preferences, Attitudes, and Behaviors
• Contact or Same-Sex Attraction: What Is Causing the Changing Climate for Gay and Lesbian Youth?

Cognition
• How Much Do You Know?
• Memories for Songs
• Decision-Making Studies
• Sequential Decision Making under Uncertainty in a Video Game
• Who Will Win—It's All about Logic

Internet Research

Some aspects of Internet research mirror those in traditional formats. For instance, changing fonts and text size, including a lot of bold and italic type, and lack of contrast between the text and the background reduce the usability of paper surveys; the pattern will likely hold true for Internet surveys. If researchers take care of these formatting considerations, computerized testing (including the Internet) may lead to comparability with other formats (Gosling et al., 2004; Vispoel, 2000).

The question is still ambiguous, however. For example, Shih and Fan (2008) found higher response rates for traditional, mailed surveys compared to Internet surveys. This finding was mitigated somewhat by the nature of the respondent. College students were more responsive to Internet surveys, whereas other groups (e.g., general consumers) were more responsive to mailed surveys. Furthermore, follow-up reminders were more useful in generating responses to mailed surveys than to Internet surveys.

Sometimes response rates are associated with the topic of the survey. For example, when Cranford et al. (2008) surveyed college students about alcohol use, response rates were higher among heavier drinkers. Not surprisingly, the demographics of the sample were also important in that white students were more likely to respond than minority students. The most common reason for not responding was that the person was too busy.

So you need to identify the population you want to sample and contact them in ways that are compatible with that group. It would be nice to know exactly who is likely to complete online surveys and experimental research. We do have a picture of who is connected to the Internet. Table 3.4 gives a breakdown of users. The incidence of Internet use in low-income households has risen in the past few years, but people in these households are connected at noticeably lower rates than people in higher-income homes. Accessibility to the Internet is also

TABLE 3.4 *Demographics of Internet Users*

Numbers reflect the percentage of each group who used the Internet in early 2007 and late 2009.

	2007 (%)	*2009 (%)*	*Difference (%)*
Total Adults	71	77	+6
Women	70	78	+8
Men	71	76	+5
Age			
18–29	87	93	+6
30–49	83	83	0
50–64	65	77	+12
65+	32	43	+11
Race/Ethnicity			
White, Non-Hispanic	73	80	+7
Black, Non-Hispanic	62	72	+9
English-speaking Hispanic	78	61	−19
Geography			
Urban	73	73	0
Suburban	73	75	−2
Rural	60	71	−9
Household Income			
Less than $30,000/yr	55	62	+7
$30,000–49,000	69	84	+15
$50,000–74,999	82	93	+11
$75,000+	93	95	+2
Educational Attainment			
Less than high school	40	37	−3
High school	61	72	+11
Some college	81	87	+6
College +	91	94	+3

Sources: Demographics of internet users (2007). Pew Internet & American Life Project, February 15–March 7, 2007 Tracking Survey Demographics of internet users (2007). http://www.pewinternet.org/trends/User_Demo_6.15.07.htm; Pew Internet & American Life Project, August 18–September 14, 2009 Tracking Survey. http://www.pewinternet.org/trends/Whos-Online.aspx. Reprinted with permission.

associated with age, race, where people live, and educational level (Demographcs of Internet Users, 2009).

Furthermore, low-income people are much more likely to have access to the Internet away from home or work (e.g., at a library) than are higher-income people who are likely to have access to computers both at home and at work (www.project.org; retrieved December 24, 2009). These differences may have a significant impact on the nature of research samples and, perhaps, research results.

Teens use the Internet much more than older adults for social networking and entertainment; adults use email, do research, and make purchases at comparable or higher levels than teens (Generational differences, 2009). Still, even among the heaviest users, young people, there may be a backlash regarding the degree to which people are willing to use their computers for less interesting (to them) applications (Vasquez, 2009).

These data have potential implications for your research. If you decide to conduct a study online, you want to maximize the return on your work and reach the people that you want to participate. What is the best way to get people to respond? This is not a question with an easy answer.

One study of Internet surveys led to minuscule response rates of 0.18 percent when notices of the survey appeared in a print magazine, requiring readers to switch to a computer to complete the survey. When a person was able to use a hyperlink to access a survey, the response rate was somewhat higher, 0.68 percent, but still extremely low. When a posting appeared in newsgroups, the response rate was estimated to be 1.68 percent. Finally, when respondents were emailed individually three times, the return rate was 31 percent, which is a respectable figure.

You can see the magnitude of the difference in Figure 3.4. Not surprisingly, persistence and a personal approach provide the best results (Schillewaert, Langerak, & Duhamel, 1998). Dillman and colleagues (2008) contacted potential respondents through telephone calls, the Internet, mail, or interactive voice response. For those who did not respond, the researchers used a different means of getting in touch (telephone or email) a second time. They found

FIGURE 3.4 *Response Rates to Online Surveys for Various Means of Contacting Potential Respondents*

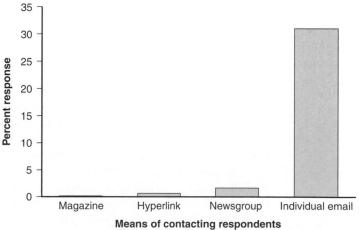

Source: Schillewaert, Langerak, & Duhamel, 1998.

that the additional contact improved response rates by over 30% in some cases, reflecting the importance of persistence in reaching your research sample.

An advantage to the email technique is that responses arrive very quickly, much more so than laboratory and mail approaches. Further, the quality of the data (i.e., how complete the responses were) seems to be comparable, regardless of the means of notifying respondents (Schillewaert et al., 1998).

Online surveys aren't noticeably worse than other approaches, and they have some practical advantages. It's not unreasonable to expect their frequency to increase as researchers become familiar with the characteristics of successful Internet surveys and the approaches that work best.

Respondent Motivation

It doesn't help a researcher if a potential respondent receives but ignores the information. For instance, over the past few decades, the response rate for surveys in general has decreased, and email surveys have lower response rates than mail and telephone surveys (Cho & LaRose, 1999).

You can try to motivate people to comply by using incentives. However, the motivating factors that work in mail surveys may not translate to the computer. Researchers have not yet determined the functional equivalents of mail incentives, which include money-in-mail surveys (Martinez-Ebers, 1997) and in face-to-face surveys (Willimack et al., 1995), and even tea bags (which don't work; Gendall, Hoek, & Brennan, 1998).

Another potential problem is that there is so much research on the Internet that it is unlikely that any single researcher's work will stand out. Scientific investigators tend to be cautious in their approaches, which includes creating credible-looking, but not flashy, Web pages. Such Web sites have a hard time competing with the more glittering marketing or entertainment pages.

Advantages to Web-Based Research

We can see four clear advantages to Web research. The first involves the amount of time required to test a single participant. In traditional research it takes a lot of time for a researcher to test people individually; the investigator needs to arrive at the testing site in advance in order to set up the experimental apparatus and materials. Then the researcher waits for the participant to show up. People do not always honor their commitments, though; they may forget where to go or when to show up. If the participant appears, the session runs its course for perhaps 15 minutes up to an hour. Then the researcher needs to collect all the data forms, informed consent forms, and put away any equipment.

For some projects, it would not be unreasonable to expect the time commitment to be an hour per person. Web-based research requires the initial time to create a Web page, but this time commitment probably would not exceed the time required to put together the in-the-lab, paper version of the study. Over time, a Web-based project could involve significantly less time per person than a laboratory-based project because there is no required laboratory setup for each new person. In fact, it can be remarkably easy to create an online survey through Web sites like SurveyMonkey (www.surveymonkey.com) or Google (www.google.com), which provides the ability to create surveys easily and to post them online with little technological knowledge.

A second advantage of Web-based research is that the investigator does not need to be available when a participant is interested in engaging in the task. The Web is open all day, every day. Data collection occurs at the convenience of the participant, not at the inconvenience of a researcher who has to set aside time from a busy schedule to be in the lab.

A third advantage of Web research is that data collection is automatic and accurate. In the traditional version of research, an investigator has to transfer information from an original data sheet to some other form so data analysis can take place. When the amount of data from a single person is large, it takes a long time to enter and record data, and there are more opportunities for error. When research occurs on the Web, the investigator can create a means by which the data are automatically transferred to a file for data analysis. The chance for error diminishes drastically.

A fourth advantage is that we can generate a sample of participants that extends beyond college students; any interested person of any age who is living anywhere in the world can take part.

Potential Problems with Web-Based Research

As you will see throughout this book, any solution to potential problems in conducting research introduces its own problems. We want to make sure that we eliminate major difficulties and that the limitations that remain are as minimal as possible. In the case of Web-based research, we eliminate the disadvantages of having to schedule participants to test in person, to code and transfer data, and so forth. At the same time, we introduce potential problems.

One concern is that, although the research can take place in the absence of the investigator, we also lose the advantage of having a person who can help a participant who is uncertain of how to proceed, who might misunderstand directions, or who might have a question. Thus, although the investigator does not have to be present (an advantage), it is also true that the researcher cannot be there (a disadvantage). The question that we need to address is whether we gain or lose more through data collection in the laboratory versus on the Web.

Second, the gain in accuracy in data collection can be offset if remote participants provide poor data. If they do not take the research seriously or if they return to the Web site for repeated testing, the quality of the data will suffer. Once again, because of the remote nature of the procedure, the investigator may never know about the problem. Fortunately, research on the quality of data collected on the Web suggests that the quality is high (Azar, 2000b; Vadillo, Bárcena, & Matute, 2006). For instance, Vadillo et al. presented their participants with a learning task that was either online or that used paper and pencil. The degree and pattern of learning were similar for both groups, leading to a sense of confidence that participants engage in the same types of behaviors and thought processes online as they do in a traditional laboratory setting.

In general, according to Krantz and Dalal (2000), the results of traditional laboratory studies with college students correspond quite closely to Web-based research, and the Internet samples are broader than the typical college student sample. This should provide some comfort to us as researchers because the behaviors of the larger group, computer users, resemble those of college students.

Third, there may be differences between computer users and the population as a whole. When we venture into the realm of online research, we can't be sure that the population of participants that we reach is always comparable to the usual samples we use. Thus, for some tasks, like Vadillo et al.'s learning task, people may learn through the same processes, regardless of who they are. So an Internet sample would reflect a typical laboratory sample. But if a study involves some topics for which different types of people show different patterns, like healthcare issues, the online population may be different from the general population.

For instance, Couper and colleagues (2006) studied an online population of older adults who provided information about their health, income, where they lived, their level of education, and so forth. These researchers discovered that less healthy, poor, and nonwhite populations were underrepresented in the online survey. If the researchers drew generalized conclusions about the health and well-being of the older population based on their online survey, those conclusions could be seriously inaccurate because of the nature of the people who have computer access and the inclination to participate in online surveys.

A fourth consideration involves the ethics of Internet research. As researchers, we need to act ethically, providing informed consent and debriefing, making sure that there is no immediate or long-term harm to participants, making sure that participants are of legal age, and so forth. When a participant is at a remote location, it may not be easy to guarantee ethical safeguards.

Finally, a fifth, fairly new concern relates to the fact that an increasing number of people access the Internet via cell phones (Mobile web audience, 2007). In fact, some segments of the population, most notably those under 35, expect advanced features, like Internet access, on their cell phones (Consumers in the 18-to-24 age segment, 2007). A survey on the small screen of a cell phone, combined with potentially slow access, might make a survey difficult to complete, leading either to nonresponse, satisficing, or acquiescence. As technology changes, the nature of these problems may change, or the problems may disappear.

The Future of the Internet in Psychology

Increasingly, psychologists are bringing research to the world at large. As we have seen, there are limitations to the kind of research that is possible, and we face new ethical concerns, but there is potential for increased contact with populations that we have previously ignored. The samples generated by Internet research will not involve random selection, which is an ideal that psychological research seldom achieves. Internet-based studies are likely to be broader than the typical, college-student samples that most research includes, even if we still don't know how well the samples represent the populations that interest us. Given the ease with which we can conduct such projects, Internet studies are almost certain to increase in size and scope.

We must remember that the research results we obtain via the Internet will only be as good as the methodology we develop. The same careful attention to detail is important for Internet research as in any other research. Once the details of the investigation are in place, there are ways to enhance the likelihood of success in a project. Table 3.5 presents some tips for creating successful Web pages for research.

Checking on Research: The Role of Replication

Validity—A property of data, concepts, or research findings whereby they are useful for measuring or understanding phenomena that they are of interest to a psychologist. Data, concepts, and research findings fall on a continuum of usefulness for a given application.

Replication—In research, the act of recreating or reproducing an earlier study to see if its results can be repeated. The replication can reproduce the original study exactly or with some modifications.

Behavior is complicated and multifaceted, so any single study cannot answer all of our questions about a topic definitively. In addition, no matter how well a researcher designs a study, problems can occur with the results. The participants might have been an unusual group or the assignment of those participants to different conditions may have led to nonequivalent groups. The wording of questions asked may have misled people. Or the selection of the variable to be measured might have been inappropriate. If any of these problems occurred, the **validity** of the results would suffer. These types of problems can and do occur; you have to learn to anticipate problems as well as possible solutions to deal with them and to recognize that you cannot eliminate them all.

This may sound like a pessimistic view, but with enough systematic research on a topic, we can identify the problems and take them into account. Ideally, researchers will replicate their research, which means to repeat the investigations to see if the same results emerge. **Replications** can take three basic different forms. In *exact replication,* a researcher repeats an earlier investigation exactly. In *replication with extension,* the experimenter asks the same question, but adds something new. The advantage of the replication with extension is that you don't spend your time merely repeating what we think might be true and that we already know; you are advancing beyond the initial knowledge. In a *conceptual replication,* the researcher attacks the same basic question, but does it from a different approach.

TABLE 3.5 *Guidelines for Creating Internet-based Research*

1. **Become familiar with related research.** You can take cues from the work others have done and avoid simply repeating research that others have already done, perhaps with a better methodology than you would have developed on your own. The methodology of online research may differ from traditional forms, so it is a good idea to see what others have done.

2. **Keep your Web page simple and informative, but attractive.** The format and information on your Web page can affect whether people begin participation in your study and whether they will complete it. Rieps (2010) has offered several helpful suggestions.
   - Try not to keep your potential participants waiting as they access lengthy Web pages.
   - Develop an attractive, professional looking site.
   - Consider presenting only one question per Web page in an online survey.
   - Give progress indicators (e.g., "You are 25% finished with the survey") for short surveys, which seem to motivate people to continue.
   - Include demographic questions (age, sex, etc.) and any incentives for participating at the beginning of the study.

3. **Follow the regulations regarding ethics in research.** The same rules and regulations about ethics in research pertain to Internet-based research. Several important points stand out; you need to check out all aspects of the approval process, however.
   - Virtually every academic institution has an Institutional Review Board (IRB) to evaluate the degree of potential risk associated with participation in your research. All research, whether by students or by professional researchers requires approval by the IRB. Most schools have a specific form to complete.
   - You need to ensure that participants understand the concept of informed consent. It will be crucial to let people know that participation is voluntary and that, by sending you their responses, they agree to let you include their responses in your analysis. You must tell them that they can terminate their participation at any time.
   - The law regards some people as unable to provide informed consent. That is, legally they are barred from volunteering to participate without approval of parents or guardians. For instance, people under the age of 18 may be legally unable to volunteer on their own. You should highlight this restriction.
   - Naturally, if there is any deception, you need to debrief your participants, but the best means of doing this is not clear at this point.

4. **Give an adequate description of your research.** It will also generate good will if you provide some means by which the participants can learn about the results of your research. You can gain cooperation from potential participants by educating them about the importance of your research. Tell them what questions you are addressing, how long their participation will take, and how you will protect their confidentiality. It would be ideal to keep their participation anonymous, so that nobody knows they took part.

5. **Check out your newly created Web site thoroughly.** If you create a Web site, you will be familiar with it, so some of the snags in using it may not be clear to you. It will help to get naive people to test your page. In addition, you can minimize problems if you check your Web page on as many different computers as possible. Not all machines display information identically; pretesting the Web pages can reduce the frustrations that your participants experience and can result in data that are more valid.

6. **Find out how to disseminate information about your study.** Several Web sites list ongoing research, and various electronic discussion groups may allow you to post announcements about your research.

Type I error—In statistics, erroneously deciding that there is a significant effect when the effect is due to measurement error.

Type II error—In statistics, erroneously failing to decide that there is a significant effect when it is obscured by measurement error.

Construct validity—The degree to which a measurement accurately measures the underlying concept that it supposed to be measured.

Replication serves several important functions. First, it can check on the reliability of research results and help us avoid seeing things that aren't there (**Type I errors**) and failing to see things that are there (**Type II errors**). That is, if an initial project erroneously suggested that some behavioral pattern was real, replications could confirm or deny that claim. Or if research seemed to indicate erroneously that some behaviors were likely, replications could show that to be false.

Second, replication can provide additional support for theories. Each replication whose results confirm a theory's predictions increases our confidence in that theory. Or replications may fail to support the predictions, which can lead to new ideas that may be better than the old ones.

A third advantage of replication is that we can increase the **construct validity** of our concepts. This means that when we are dealing with complicated and abstract concepts, such as anxiety or depression, we develop more confidence in what they involve by making diverse measurements of the same concept.

A fourth effect of replications is to help protect against fraud. If researchers who might cheat know that their work will be put to the test, they may be less likely to engage in that fraud. If they have engaged in fraud, replications can call the earlier research into question. One of the stated functions of replication is to identify whether research can withstand close scrutiny,

Even with such clear positive aspects of replication, simple replications seldom occur; replications with extension are more prevalent, but they appear in research journals with considerably less frequency than original research reports.

We can identify several reasons why researchers advocate replication but do not do it. In the end, all the reasons come down to the relative payoff for the time and energy devoted to the replication. Scientists prefer to conduct original, novel research because it generates new knowledge, for which the rewards are greater. Doing a replication is like finishing second in a race. Nobody cares about the person or remembers who it was. Familiar people in the history of psychology, like Sigmund Freud, have often worried a great deal that they would not get credit for their ideas. Outside of psychology, people are no different.

The meager reward for replications dissuades most researchers from attempting them. Ross, Hall, and Heater (1998) have identified several specific reasons for the lack of published replications in nursing and occupational therapy research. The same principles hold for all behavioral research. First, they suggest, journals are reluctant to publish replications because the results are not new. Second, researchers may be reluctant to submit replications in the first place. Third, colleagues and professors encourage original research. Fourth, funding for replication research may be very limited. Fifth, in writing up the initial research, investigators may not provide enough detail for others who want to replicate. None of these barriers is insurmountable, but they certainly need to be overcome.

A good example of how a widely publicized research project led to subsequent attempts at replication and the correction of erroneous information involves the so-called Mozart effect (Rauscher, Shaw, & Ky, 1993, 1995). Other investigators repeated the research, but were unable to generate the same results. The Controversy box on music (page 70) shows how our knowledge in this area increased as one set of research questions led to new ones.

Don't Reinvent the Wheel: Reviewing the Literature

All researchers recognize that replicating previous research is a good idea, but we also recognize that it is more useful to replicate with extension than simply to replicate. That is, it is important to develop and test new ideas as we verify the old ones. And it pays greater dividends if we can generate new knowledge in our research.

In order to maximize the gains in our research projects, it pays to know what researchers have already done. No matter what topic you choose for a research project, somebody has undoubtedly paved the way already. There is no doubt that they had to solve problems in developing a methodology that satisfied them. You do not need to repeat their mistakes. In fact, researchers consider it completely legitimate to borrow ideas from others, as long as we give appropriate credit to them and don't pass the ideas off as our own.

You are allowed to borrow somebody else's methodology for your own purposes. If it worked for them, it might work for you, and it has the advantage of having been pretested. A journal article has generally been evaluated by experts in the field and further reviewed by the journal editor. The article will not appear in print unless these experts agree that both the methodology and the ideas are sound. You can learn a lot about what to do (and what not do to) by reading the work of respected professionals.

What Is a Literature Review?

In order to find out what has been done in an area that interests you, you should conduct a **literature review.** When we talk about literature in everyday language, we generally hear about writers like Alice Walker, F. Scott Fitzgerald, Charles Dickens, and others in the pantheon of writing. People presume that any work penned by these authors is worthwhile. On the other hand, people may minimize the importance of other writers, like the horror novelist Stephen King. The enormous success of his popular and compelling work tells us that many people enjoy it. So why is his work not "literature"? In reality, it all depends on your definition of "good writing."

Among researchers, the term "literature" refers to the body of work that is considered to be of high enough quality to appear in technical journals. Psychology has its own pantheon of writers whose words (and research) have had an impact on the field. Psychology has its own versions of Stephen King as well, whose work might be considered highly valuable by one group, but minimized by another.

At the other end of the continuum are those authors who produce temporarily popular books like romance novels. These works capture an audience, but the books (and their ideas) themselves have short lives. There is a comparable group among psychologists. Radio talk show hosts like "Dr. Laura" are popular but are not taken seriously by the psychological community. Although people may ask "Dr. Laura" for advice, she is neither a psychologist nor a psychiatrist.

Literature review—An overview of published journal articles, books, and other professional work on a given topic.

When researchers prepare a literature review for a journal article or for a conference presentation, they usually discuss relevant previous studies. Because many areas of research have generated a lot of studies, authors do not present an exhaustive listing of every study that has appeared in journals or books. The amount of information would be too great. Consequently, they write about the studies that have had greatest impact on the project currently underway and about research that psychologists consider very critical in the area. Most of the research in a literature review is fairly recent, although classic and important older articles generally receive attention as well.

The Effect of Peer Review on the Research Literature

Peer review—A process in which scientific research and ideas are evaluated by experts in a field so that obvious errors or other problems can be spotted and corrected before a work is published or presented at a research conference.

As a researcher, you need to differentiate among the various levels of writing that constitute our psychological literature. This is often a judgment call, but articles that appear in **peer-reviewed** journals have been taken seriously by experts. A peer-reviewed journal publishes articles that have undergone careful scrutiny and may have been revised by the authors several times until they have eliminated any major problems. This process is a stringent one. Among the best psychology journals, the rejection rate may be around 70% or more. Thus, the editor accepts only 30% or fewer of the articles that are submitted.

One of the reasons for such a low acceptance rate is that in psychology, our ideas are very complex and abstract. We often have to develop clever operational definitions of our concepts because we cannot observe and measure them directly. It takes considerable diligence to create and conduct a well-designed study that deals with the ideas successfully. There are many ways for ambiguities and uncertainties to creep in, so reviewers and editors frequently request an author to do additional work to take care of these problems. There is another significant reason for the high rejection rate. Each journal has a set number of pages that it can publish each year. There are more pages worth of information submitted to the journal that can be printed, so some good research may be rejected. This limitation is likely to decrease as more journals adopt online-only formats.

In disciplines that are more descriptive, such as botany or other areas of biology, the acceptance rate for major journals is often much higher than in psychology. The ideas they work with are often more straightforward, so the research is easier to design. (The tools and techniques of the natural and physical sciences may be difficult to master, but so are those in the behavioral sciences. In any case, we shouldn't confuse the concepts of a science, which are the most important elements, with the tools, which are merely tools.) The differences between psychology and other disciplines in this regard do not imply that one domain is more or less important or useful; it simply means that different areas of research make different demands on researchers.

■ ■ ■ ■ ■ ■

CONTROVERSY
Does Music Make You Smarter? The Role of Replication

Does music make you smarter? A number of years ago, the public became enthralled with the idea that listening to music by Mozart could increase intelligence. Rauscher et al. (1993, 1995) reported that listening to that music could increase scores on one component of an intelligence test; the researchers determined that scores on a standardized test increased significantly, about 8 or 9 points. The implications were remarkable. People envisioned a populace that was suddenly smarter.

Other researchers were immediately interested. First, there were practical implications. Could we do something to make our children smarter? One plan proposed by the governor of Georgia was to give a tape of this music to each family of a newborn baby in the state. The payoff could be great, but so could the cost if the effect turned out to be imaginary.

A second reason for interest was that scientists were interested in finding out why intellectual functioning would improve. What was the actual cause? This is an interesting scientific question in its own right. Further, perhaps there were other, even more effective, means of enhancing thought processes.

Unfortunately, the first published report provided insufficient detail on the methodology, so it was difficult to replicate the study because the details were unavailable. The second report presented that information.

When details became available, Carstens, Haskins, & Hounshell (1995) found that listening to Mozart, compared to a silent period, had no effect on test performance. Then Newman and colleagues (1995) also reported a failure to replicate the original results. Surprisingly, they discovered that people with a preference for classical music actually showed lower test scores than others after listening to music. As the puzzle grew, Rauscher, Shaw, and Gordon (1998) proposed more arguments to support their original conclusions.

Subsequently, Steele and his colleagues extended the methodology even further. They found no Mozart effect. Subsequently, Thompson, Schellenberg, and Husain (2001) varied the types of music to which participants listened, finding that arousal levels and mood accounted for the so-called Mozart effect. Higher arousal and positive mood were associated with better test scores, not specifically having listened to Mozart.

This sequence of studies illustrates how the scientific approach, with replication, can self-correct and can lead to more complete knowledge. Although it is exciting to think that we can get smart by listening to music, it is important to know the truth—that increases in test performance are more likely to result from high levels of motivation, perhaps from positive mood, and certainly through hard work.

Since the original research and replications appeared, many psychologists have concluded that the Mozart effect may be due to relaxation rather than to the music itself.

How to Conduct a Literature Review

Researchers publish an enormous amount of research each year. In fact, there are well over a thousand journals that publish psychology-related articles. Most libraries will have no more than a tiny fraction of them on hand, so even if you wanted to browse through each one of them, you would not be able to.

So how do you find out what has appeared in print? The easiest way is to use an electronic database that lists psychological research. The most useful database for psychologists is PsycINFO®, which is published by the American Psychological Association. It references over 1,300 journals published in 25 languages, and in its most complete version, PsycINFO cites articles going back to 1887.

Electronic Databases

PsycINFO is a modern successor to Psychological Abstracts (PA), which appeared in a paper version until 2006 when they were discontinued. PsycINFO is extremely easy to use compared to PA. The basic strategy is to select a term of interest to you and to tell PsycINFO to search for published articles related to that term. There are strategies that you can use to maximize the likelihood of finding what you are seeking without also generating a long string of less relevant material. On the flip side, there are ways to expand the number of citations you generate so you can get a more complete picture of the research in an area.

Using PsycINFO is easy, but you need to learn how to do it if you want to maximize the return on your time. In the following sections, you will learn about useful strategies for searching databases. Keep in mind that we will be focusing on PsycINFO. If you use other databases, the particulars of your search may differ somewhat, but once you learn PsycINFO, you can adapt your search strategies to other databases.

Starting Your Search

A first step in searching for information is to decide on a relevant term that matches your interest. This is an important first step because it will determine the nature of the articles listed in your output.

The number of published articles listed in PsycINFO continues to increase because researchers keep publishing their work. Thus, any specific examples that appear here will become outdated over time. Nonetheless, you can get an idea of how to generate worthwhile search strategies.

Suppose that you are interested in finding out about psychological aspects of adopting children. You could type the word *adoption* and begin the search. In 2010, entering the word *adoption* resulted in a list of 27,430 references, an increase of about 3,000 in a one-year period. Obviously, it would be impossible to read every source, but you would not want to in any case because there are many citations that do not relate to your topic in the least. The reason that a search of adoption generates irrelevant references is that if you type in a word, PsycINFO will search for the word, regardless of the way that word is used.

For example, in the search for the word *adoption* in the PsycINFO listings, none of the first 30 listings dealt with adopting children. Table 3.6 gives a breakdown of the topics. PsycINFO does not know what meaning of the word *adoption* you intend without some help from you. If the article relates to adopting some strategy or plan, the database will include it, which is what happened with this search.

You can find ways to limit the search so you don't have thousands of citations, many of which are irrelevant. One of the most useful steps is to specify that the database should

TABLE 3.6 *Topics of the First 30 (of 27,430) Articles Produced by PsycINFO for* **adoption** *Anywhere in the Citation and How the Author Used the Word* **adoption** *in Those Citations*

Topic	Number of Articles
Adoption or use of some new technology	15
Adopting some strategy or procedure in a business setting	9
Adopting a procedure in neuroscience research	2
Adopting educational programs	2
Adopting an experimental methodology	1
The heritability of cognitive functioning in the elderly	1

list citations that include *adoption* as either keywords or descriptors. In a Keyword search, PsycINFO looks for the word anywhere in the record except for the references. A Descriptor search involves a search for a major topic of the entry. If you do not actively specify that you want keywords or descriptors (or in some other major field), PsycINFO will look for the word *adoption* anywhere at all. In the current search, when a keyword for the article in the search was *adoption,* the search led to 12,586 hits; for *adoption* as a descriptor, there were 2,202 hits. Twenty-nine of the first 30 of these related in some way to adoption of children; the sole exception dealt with children's rights internationally. The use of *adoption* as a descriptor led to more than a 90% reduction in the number of hits; most of the citations that were eliminated involved work that is irrelevant to adoptions.

You can further reduce the number of irrelevant citations. Table 3.7 illustrates the steps you can take to narrow your search to be more productive. One involves using the PsycINFO thesaurus to identify a narrower term than you are using; another pertains to setting limits on the search process, like a restricted range of years in which articles were published, types of

TABLE 3.7 *Examples of Strategies to Reduce the Number of Irrelevant Citations in a PsycINFO Search*

Search for References to Adoption	Strategy to Narrow the Search	Number of References
Adoption anywhere in the citation		27,430
Adoption as the Keyword of the reference	Choose "Word Appears in Keyword." (You could also select "Author" if you want to name an author who has studied adoption.)	12,586
Adoption as a Descriptor	Choose "Word Appears in Descriptors." (From this point on, change only the new search option and retain the earlier ones you selected.)	2,202
Only work published since 1980	Choose "Date Range" and indicate publication year of 1980 to the current year (or whatever time span you want).	2,037
Only work published in the English language	Choose "More Search Options" and select English as the only language.	1,921
Only work published in peer-reviewed journals	Choose "More Search Options" and select material in peer-reviewed journals. This eliminates hard-to-access material like doctoral dissertations.	1,223
Only work involving females in the adoption process	Choose "More Search Options" and select Population = Female.	444
Only work on adoption of children 12 years or younger	Choose "Set Other Limits" and select Age Group = Childhood.	178

TABLE 3.8 *Strategies for Expanding the Number of Relevant Citations in PsycINFO*

Strategy to Expand the Search	Result
Use the *Thesaurus* option and enter *Adopt**	You get a list of categories that PsycINFO uses that are related to adoption.
Use the *Index* and enter "Adopt*"' or "Adoption"	You get a dozen subject categories to search.
Example: Use the Thesaurus terms "Adopted-Children," "Adoptees," "Adoption-Child," "Interracial Adoption" and "Adoptive-Parents" connected by OR (i.e., Adopted-children OR adoptees OR adoption-child OR interracial-adoption OR adoptive-parents)	You get additional citations that relate to the Thesaurus terms and that still follow the previous limits you set.
	Using OR tells PsycINFO to access any citation that uses any of your terms. If you connected them with AND, PsycINFO would only access those citations that include all those terms at the same time, which would restrict the search greatly. In fact, a single journal article is unlikely to fall into all these categories.

studies (theoretical versus empirical), and populations (adults, children, women, men, etc.). There are quite a few ways to set limits to restrict the scope of your search. The example in Table 3.7 goes from nearly 25,000 hits down to a much more manageable 164. Of course, the final figure has some restrictions and would not include male adoptions, for example. Your narrowing of the search should meet your own particular needs.

If your search produces too few hits, there are ways of expanding it. One strategy is to insert a "wild card" in your search. For instance, in PsycINFO, you can use an asterisk (*) to expand the search. When you enter the subject of your search as adopt*, PsycINFO will look for any subject beginning with adopt, such as adopt, adoption, and adoptive. Using the wild card with *adopt** in the descriptors raises the number of hits from 2,202 to 3,695. This number is obviously more than you want to use, but using this wild card shows how the wild card can expand the number of hits.

You can also use the database's thesaurus, which tells you what terms to use when searching for a given concept. Table 3.8 gives a glimpse of the possibilities for expanding your search. By experimenting, you may be able to figure out alternate strategies for increasing the number of hits.

Different Sources of Information

Primary source—The original source of research results or theory such as a journal or book chapter.

There is a wealth of sources of information about psychological research. Some of that information is useful, some is suspect, and some is of unknown quality. When you read reports that the researchers themselves have written, you are dealing with **primary sources.** In general, if an article appears in a peer-reviewed research journal, you can have confidence that there is merit to the information in the article. There may be limitations to the work, but it is probably generally valid.

Secondary source—A source written by an author who describes somebody else's work.

Sometimes a writer will refer to the research by another psychologist, describing the methods, results, and interpretations. This type of work is a **secondary source.** The original research is likely to be valid if it appeared in a professional journal, but at this point, the new authors are giving their own interpretations of the original ideas. The secondary source is going to present a reduced version of the original, so there may be departures from what the original writers either wrote or intended. Secondary sources can be valuable, but you are not going to be getting a complete picture of the original work. At times you may need to refer to a secondary source, as when you cannot get the original, but using primary sources is preferable when possible.

Tertiary source—A source written by an author based on somebody's interpretation or original research, such that the material has undergone interpretation by two different authors in succession.

You may also see **tertiary sources.** These are descriptions of research based on somebody else's description of yet somebody else's original research. The farther you get from the original research, the more distortion you may find in the presentation of the information.

In addition to the different levels of information (primary, secondary, etc.), there are differences in the actual nature of the information you may encounter. Some sources are intended for a professional audience, such as research journals. But other sources are meant for the general public. As a rule, information in popular sources is less detailed and may be less useful for scientific purposes, although it may serve as a starting point for a review of the scientific literature.

One particularly contentious source is Wikipedia, the online encyclopedia that any person can edit (although there are some constraints on inserting new material). Many educators have a strong, negative impression of Wikipedia, suggesting that the information in it is not reliable. However, a study published in the journal *Nature* revealed that the quality of information in Wikipedia was essentially at the same level as in the highly respected *Encyclopedia Britannica*. (*Encyclopedia Britannica* disputed the findings.) It is probably safe to approach Wikipedia as a place to get some basic information, followed by the use of primary sources. The issues associated with the various sources appear in various places (e.g., Beins & Beins, 2008).

How to Read a Journal Article

When you first begin reading scientific writing, it may seem like it has been written in another language, and the organization of the information can seem convoluted. After you get used to the style of research reports, your task of reading journal articles will be easier. There is a reason for the organization of journal articles, and there is a skill involved in understanding scientific writing. Most likely, for your psychology courses, you will be reading articles written in a format often called APA style. This means that the authors have followed the guidelines set forth in the *Publication Manual of the American Psychological Association* (American Psychological Association, 2010). This style differs from others that you may have encountered, like MLA (Modern Language Association, 1995) for the humanities, or various formats for each of the scientific disciplines. APA style may seem complicated, but the primary rules are fairly easy to learn. The Publication Manual is over 250 pages long, though, so you can expect that there is a lot of detail about specific formatting and writing issues.

Understanding the Format of a Research Paper

When you pick up a research article written in APA style, you will be able to figure out very quickly where to look to find the information you seek. Writers divide their manuscripts into six sections as a rule. The actual number of sections will differ, depending on the complexity of the research report. Regardless of the exact number of sections, there are specific reasons why information appears where it does. Table 3.9 presents an overview of the different sections of a research report written in APA style and some of the questions addressed in those sections. Table 3.9 can serve as a worksheet to guide you in reading journal articles. If you write a brief answer to each of the questions in the table, you will have a pretty complete summary of the work that was done, why it was done, and what the authors think it means.

Abstract—The part of a research report that summarizes the purpose of the research, the methodology, the results of the study, and the interpretations of the research.

Abstract. In the **abstract,** the authors give an overview of the entire paper; this section is fairly short, usually 150 to 250 words. It presents a preview of the research question and hypotheses, the methodology, the results, and the discussion. The abstract is kept short so the reader can get a quick glimpse into the nature of the research.

TABLE 3.9 *Concepts That Are Clarified in the Different Sections of a Research Report*

Introduction

• What is the general topic of the research article?
• What do we know about this topic from previous research?
• What are the authors trying to demonstrate in their own research?
• What are their hypotheses?

Method

Participants—Who took part in the research?
• How many people (or animals) were studied?
• If there were nonhuman animals, what kind were they?
• If there were people, what were their characteristics (e.g., average and range of age, gender, race or ethnicity, were they volunteers or were they paid)?

Apparatus and Materials—What did the researchers need to carry out their study?
• What kind of stimuli, questions, etc. were used?
• How many different kinds of activities did participants complete?
• What instrumentation was used to present material to participants and to record their responses?

Procedure—What did the people actually do during the research session?
• After the participants began the study, what did they do?
• What did the experimenters do as they interacted with participants?

Results

• What were patterns of behaviors among participants?
• Did behaviors differ when different groups were compared?
• What types of behaviors are predictable in the different testing conditions?
• What were the results of any statistical tests?

Discussion

• What do the results mean?
• What explanations can you develop for why the participants responded as they did?
• What psychological processes help you explain participants' responses?
• What questions have not been answered fully?
• How do your results relate to the research cited in the introduction?
• How do your results relate to other kinds of research?
• What new ideas emerge that you could evaluate in a subsequent experiment?

References

• What research was cited in the research report (e.g., work published in journals or other written sources, research presentations, personal communications)?

Introduction. After the abstract comes the **introduction,** which provides background information so you can understand the purpose of the research. When the research involves specific tests of hypotheses, the authors will generally present these hypotheses here. This section also gives a general preview of how the researchers have conducted their project. The purpose of the introduction is to clarify the purpose of the study and show how relevant ideas developed in previous research. You will virtually never see a journal article that does not refer to previous research on which the current article is based.

As you read through the introduction, you will see that the first ideas are relatively broad. These ideas relate to a more general depiction of the field of interest to the researchers.

Introduction—The part of a research report that gives an overview of the field to be investigated and the investigator's hypotheses about the outcome of the research.

As the introduction progresses, the scope of the material narrows. The authors will describe and discuss in more detail the research that relates most closely to their own project. Finally, the authors will present their own ideas. They may outline how they will clarify confusions from earlier research, correct problems, and test hypotheses. By the time you finish reading the introduction, you will have a clear picture of the logic that led from the ideas of previous researchers to those of the authors.

Methods—The part of a research report that provides information about those who participated in the study, how the research was actually carried out, and the materials and apparatus used for it.

Methods.   Following the introduction is the **Methods** section. This section should allow an independent researcher to reproduce the project described in the article. The methods section contains an extreme amount of detail. Very often, students regard this section as not being very important. In some ways, you are right: without it, you can understand why the researchers conducted the study and what results occurred. In another way, though, if you do not read this section, you might miss out on important details that affected the research outcome. This section is absolutely critical for those who want to replicate the original research.

Participants—A subsection of the Methods section that details the nature of the humans or nonhumans who took part in the research. Nonhuman animals are often referred to as *Subjects* whereas humans who took part are called *Participants*.

Participants.   Writers subdivide the methods section into three or four sections. The first one, **participants,** characterizes those who took part in the study. It describes how many were there, what were their ages, racial and ethnic backgrounds, etc. This subsection provides the reader with enough information to understand if the nature of the participants may have influenced the outcome of the research in some way.

Materials and apparatus—A subsection of the Methods section that details what implements and stimuli were used to carry out the study. Sometimes the materials and apparatus appear in separate subsections.

Materials and Apparatus.   The next subsection, **materials and apparatus,** provides details about what you would need to carry out the study. Sometimes writers will create separate subsections for the materials and apparatus if there is a need.

Procedure—A subsection of the Methods section that provides extensive detail about the actual process used to carry out the study.

Procedure.   After the description of the implements of the study, the authors will describe the **procedure.** In the procedure subsection, they describe exactly what occurred during the research session. As a rule, the procedure subsection includes only what occurs during the data collection session. Based on the information in this section, an independent researcher could follow the steps that the original researchers took.

Results—The part of a research report that details the quantitative and qualitative results of an investigation, including results of statistical analyses.

Results.   After the data collection is complete, scientists typically present the outcome in a **Results** section that usually includes statistical tests. Although choosing a statistical test seems to be a pretty straightforward task, there are actually controversies in some cases about the best approach to data analysis. If you chose one approach, you might end up with one conclusion; if you took an alternate approach, your conclusion might be different. This issue has such great implications that the American Psychological Association created a task force that issued guidelines about research methodology and statistics. The task force wrote an important article that highlights some of the controversies associated with statistics (Wilkinson & the Task Force on Statistical Inference, 1999).

The results section details the outcome of the study. For example, if a researcher compares two groups, the results section tells whether they differed and by how much. The results section also presents the results of any statistical tests that the researchers conducted. This part of a research report can be very complicated because you have to translate technical materials and terminology into comprehensible English.

One way to make sure that you understand what you are reading is to keep track of the different research questions that the investigators have asked. You can do this by making note of them when you read the introduction. Then when they present the statistics, you can try to figure out the particular question that goes along with the statistic.

Discussion—The part of a research report that provides an interpretation of the results, going beyond a simple description of the results and statistical tests.

References—The part of a research report that contains complete reference information about any work cited in the research report, that is, where the work was published or presented and the source of any work that has not been published or presented.

You will also encounter figures and tables in the results section. The purpose of these graphic elements is to provide an overview when the results are complicated. By creating a figure or chart, the authors can combine a large amount of information into a single picture.

Discussion. The data do not mean anything until we, as researchers, decide what they mean. When we ask a research question, our task is to take complicated data about a question that we are the first to ask and see what the data tell us. Because nobody else has done what we have, we are the ones who have to figure out what it all means. A successful investigation generates new information that has to be interpreted and placed in the context of earlier research.

This final section involving treatment of the research ideas is the **Discussion** section, which provides closure to the project. That is, the investigators tell you what their results mean. Unlike the results section, which says what happened, the discussion tells you why it happened. Another way to characterize the distinction is that the results section provides fact, whereas the discussion section provides interpretation, explanation, and speculation. The results of a study are incontrovertible; they are what they are. What may be controversial, however, is the interpretation of the results.

At the very end of the paper, the **References** section appears. This section simply gives information on where a reader can find the ideas that others generated and that you cited in your paper.

APA style dictates a specific format for virtually any kind of reference, including references from the World Wide Web. The details are quite specific. With practice, they are not hard to master.

Sometimes authors include material in one or more appendixes at the end of the paper. The function of an appendix is to provide information that may be important for replicating a study but may not be critical to understanding the research.

Chapter Summary

Research ideas come from many different sources. Ultimately, it boils down to the fact that somebody has a question and wants to find an answer. Sometimes the source of a research project begins with an "I wonder what would happen if …" type of question. In other cases, there is a problem to be solved, and an investigator will use research skills to devise an answer that can be applied to the situation. In still other cases, a theory makes a prediction that a scientist can test through research.

Regardless of the source of ideas, the scientists who investigate them take their cues from the society around them. Scientists are members of their community and share the same attitudes and values as many others in our society. Thus, social issues are important in determining what a particular researcher will think important. This consideration is true for any scientific discipline, but it is especially true in the study of human behavior.

In our current social context, the Internet has become important in research. Psychologists are studying how to use the Internet as a research tool. A number of important issues need to be addressed before Web-based research can flourish, but scientists are working on the question.

Regardless of the topics of research or how the data are collected, we want to have confidence in the results. We want them to be meaningful. One way to ensure that scientific findings are useful is through replication, that is, repetition of the research by different investigators in different contexts. When the same results appear regularly, we can have greater confidence that our conclusions are warranted.

When you generate a research project, you can get guidance about how to conduct it by reading what others have done. This usually involves a literature review of published studies. Without such a review, you run the risk of simply repeating what others have already done. Such a replication may give you more confidence in the phenomenon you are studying, but most researchers want to include novel features in their research so they can advance the field with new knowledge. One way to increase what we know about the behaviors we study is through publication of the results in scientific journals and through presentations at research conferences.

Finally, if you conduct research, you may write it up in a formal report. You are likely to follow the style of presentation set forth in the *Publication Manual of the American Psychological Association.*

Key Terms

Abstract	Methods	Results
Behaviorism	Participants	Secondary source
Construct validity	Peer review	Tertiary source
Discussion	Primary source	Type I error
Introduction	Procedure	Type II error
Literature review	References	Validity
Materials and apparatus	Replication	

Chapter Review Questions

Multiple Choice Questions

1. When researchers develop projects to test how well competing theories predict behaviors, their ideas
   a. tend to fall more toward the formal end of the continuum of ideas.
   b. usually end up testing ideas that arise from practical issues.
   c. rely on informal and idiosyncratic approaches.
   d. seldom need to be based on previous ideas and research.

2. When scientists develop their ideas for research projects, which of the following is most often the source of their ideas?
   a. Colleagues in different departments within their own institutions
   b. Colleagues in their own department
   c. The existing research literature
   d. Discussions within their research teams

3. When the dominant theory in psychology was behaviorism, researchers
   a. used behavioral observation to study cognitive processes.
   b. believed that you could learn just about anything regarding human behavior with animal models.
   c. used neuroscientific approaches to understand brain processes that affect behavior.
   d. capitalized on the effects of the cognitive revolution to understand behaviors.

4. When you come across an interesting research idea accidentally when dealing with some other issue, your research
   a. lacks construct validity.
   b. could not undergo replication with extension.
   c. involves the use of a primary source.
   d. falls on the informal end of the research continuum.

5. If you want to discover whether "Haste Makes Waste" or "He Who Hesitates Is Lost" is a better description of the effects of human behavior, you could make an experimental test. According to McGuire's (1983) description of the development of research ideas, such an approach would involve .
   a. studying spontaneously occurring events.
   b. studying the validity of everyday beliefs and when they break down.
   c. evaluating formal if-then statements.
   d. using previous research as a stepping stone to new ideas.

6. Generating a research idea by finding an individual who acts in different or interesting ways would use which of McGuire's (1983) approaches to generating research ideas?
   a. Studying spontaneously occurring events
   b. Studying the validity of everyday beliefs and when they break down
   c. Using an intensive case study
   d. Using previous research as a stepping stone to new ideas

7. There are differences in the way we conduct laboratory and Internet-based research. The differences include the fact that
   a. actually carrying out the study on the Internet requires less time on the part of the experimenter than a laboratory study does.
   b. for Internet studies, the researcher has to be available more frequently because Internet users can access the research on the Internet just about any time of the day, so the researcher needs to be available to answer questions.
   c. laboratory research generally leads to more accurate recording of data because paper data sheets are right in front of the researcher who can enter them into a computerized database.
   d. because anybody can access the research on the Internet, an investigator can't be certain that the sample is representative of the population, whereas this isn't a problem with laboratory studies.

8. One of the problems with research on the Internet is that
   a. because many people can access the research, the samples differ from typical psychological research samples, so the results are often different.
   b. because of the remote nature of the research, the investigator might never know about problems that occur during the course of the study.
   c. the investigator usually has to commit more time for data collection than in laboratory studies.
   d. participants who have difficulty with the study are likely to contact the investigator at any time of the night or day to ask questions.

9. One practical issue in Internet-based research is that
   a. displays of the research Web page might be very different for people on different types of computers.
   b. sample sizes might become so large that the study becomes impractical to conduct.
   c. it is very difficult to create good descriptions of Internet-based research because it reaches so many people.
   d. it is almost impossible to guarantee that participation in such research will be anonymous and confidential.

10. Research on how to conduct studies on the Internet has revealed that the lowest rate of return occurs when the investigator contacts potential respondents through which of the following?
    a. Hyperlinks on Web sites
    b. Sending information to newsgroups
    c. Individual email messages
    d. Announcements of the surveys in major magazines

11. The technical differences among computers on which people complete Internet surveys
    a. are minimal with the standard Internet formatting of surveys.
    b. can lead to very different displays of the same survey.

    c. require that researchers avoid using colors that may not be the same on different computers.

    d. make constant response formats difficult to implement.

12. When a researcher repeats an earlier experiment but includes some novel elements, this process is called
    a. assessment of validity.
    b. replication with extension.
    c. conceptual replication.
    d. construct validity.

13. Replicating research so we can develop more confidence in our understanding of complex and abstract concepts helps us
    a. increase our construct validity.
    b. avoid both Type I and Type II errors.
    c. perform replication with extension.
    d. develop conceptual replication.

14. The process by which scientists try to guarantee that only high-quality research results appear in journals involves getting experts to evaluate the work, a process called
    a. construct validity.
    b. peer review.
    c. the literature review.
    d. conceptual review.

15. A literature review in a research article generally includes
    a. a listing of others' research hypotheses.
    b. a discussion of what has been written by psychologists as well as by more popular authors.
    c. the ideas that are related to the researcher's study.
    d. a discussion of research that is important but that has not yet been published.

16. If you wanted to understand the theoretical reasons that led researchers to conduct a project that appeared in an APA journal, you would read which section of their article?
    a. abstract
    b. introduction
    c. discussion
    d. references

17. The results section of an APA style report will contain
    a. information about the statistical tests used to analyze the data.
    b. a statement about the research hypotheses.
    c. the number and types of participants.
    d. an integration of the data with theory.

Essay Questions

18. Where on the continuum of formality of ideas will a beginning student's research be likely to fall? Explain your answer.

19. Explain how changes in psychology and changes in society have affected psychologists' use of animals in research.

20. Why could it be more profitable for a beginning researcher to do an exact replication, while it would be more profitable for a seasoned researcher to do a conceptual replication?

21. What are the advantages of a literature review of research related to your own investigations?

CHAPTER 4

PRACTICAL ISSUES IN PLANNING YOUR RESEARCH

CHAPTER OUTLINE

PRACTICAL QUESTIONS IN PLANNING RESEARCH

DIFFERENT WAYS OF STUDYING BEHAVIOR
Measuring Complex Concepts
The Importance of Culture and Context
    in Defining Variables
Carrying Out a Literature Search

CONDUCTING YOUR STUDY
Determining the Research Setting
Approaches to Psychological Research
Selecting Research Materials and Procedures
Why Methodology Is Important

CHOOSING YOUR PARTICIPANTS OR SUBJECTS
The Nature of Your Participants
Deciding How Many Participants to Include

CAN RATS, MICE, AND FISH HELP US UNDERSTAND HUMANS?

PROBABILITY SAMPLING
Simple Random Sampling
Systematic Sampling
Stratified Random Sampling
Cluster Sampling

NONPROBABILITY SAMPLING
Convenience Sampling
Quota Sampling
Purposive (Judgmental) Sampling
Chain-Referral Sampling

LEARNING OBJECTIVES

- Describe differences in the nature of participants in different types of research.
- Differentiate between basic (theoretical) research and applied research.
- Identify advantages and disadvantages of laboratory versus field research.
- Identify and describe the major research approaches.
- Generate examples of research using the major research approaches.
- Differentiate between populations and samples.
- Describe the issues associated with determining how many participants to include in a study.
- Identify why research with animals can help understand human behavior.

CHAPTER PREVIEW

When most students are learning about research, they typically are not aware of how many decisions are made in putting a project together. You will find that when you read a journal article, you learn only what the researchers finally did, not what they tried that didn't work. The reason for this lack of information is that journal space is in short supply. There is always more to print than the journals have space for. As a result, authors omit just about everything not entirely germane to the topic they are studying. The authors report only what was successful. If you want to plan your own research project, you can use the information in published work, but you have to fill in a lot of details on your own. You can be sure that in virtually every research program ever conducted, the researchers made choices that caused them to stop and evaluate what they were doing and make changes to improve the research design.

Some of the tasks associated with completing a study include describing in concrete terms the concepts you are interested in, figuring out how to measure them, identifying those you will test in your study, carrying out the project itself, looking at and understanding the results, then interpreting what you've discovered. If you make poor choices or conclusions at any step along the way, your research will be less meaningful than it could otherwise be.

In each case, the choices you make will each take you in a slightly different direction than some other choice. Each of these steps will involve making quite a few decisions that, you hope, will provide you with a clear answer to your original question.

Practical Questions in Planning Research

When you read about successful research projects either in a scientific journal or in a popular magazine or when you see a report on television, the reporter makes the research sound as if it were put together perfectly and that there was only one reasonable way to have conducted it. In reality, if you were to follow a research project from beginning to end, you would see that the researchers had to make a great number of decisions about the study.

We investigate concepts that are very complex and abstract. This means that we need to simplify the complex ideas so our research doesn't become unmanageable. We also have to take abstract ideas and generate concrete ways to measure them. For example, sadness is an idea that can help us understand why people act as they do. But what is sadness? It is a complex set of emotions that we don't have an easy way to measure.

If we consider the goals of science, we can see that we could try to describe what it means to be sad. To do so, we have to identify what behaviors reflect sadness. If we don't describe it well, we can't move to the more difficult goal of predicting when it will occur. How can you predict what you can't describe? Beyond that, we will not be able to understand when it occurs, or how to control it.

In other areas of science, researchers frequently engage in descriptive research. They may count the number of plants that live in a particular type of field, or the number of animals born with deformities due to the presence of toxic substances. In this research, the concepts are fairly obvious and easy to measure. In some areas, the research may require complex tools to answer the scientists' questions, but although the tools are complex, the concepts may be relatively simple. In psychology, we use tools that may be easy to develop (e.g., measuring behaviors on a scale of 1 to 10), but the concepts are complex.

Once you decide on a research question, you need to fill in the details about how you will carry out your project. This aspect of your task is not necessarily difficult, but you need to consider carefully myriad details. These details are the subject of the rest of this book.

A research project can take many different paths; you have to decide how you want yours to proceed so that you arrive at the best answer to your question.

Different Ways of Studying Behavior

If your research is going to be data-driven, you have to measure something. After you decide the topic you want to study, one of the next steps is to figure out what you will be observing. Because psychologists study complex ideas that either may not be easy to measure or may have multiple measures, the issue of measurement is critical. Consider some ways that psychologists have studied creativity.

Furnam and Nederstrom (2010) have investigated the correlation between creativity and personality among managers in the business world. Their measurement of creativity was through a test of divergent thinking, that is, a person's ability think "outside the box." In this research, the level of creativity was defined in terms of the number of outcomes that could result from situations that the researcher described to the participant. (The investigators found, among other things, that extraversion was associated with level of creativity.)

In contrast, Langer, Pirson, and Delizonna (2010) examined whether people's level of satisfaction regarding performance in a creative drawing task was affected by whether they compared their work to that of others. They measured creativity simply by asking their participants to rate their own performance on the drawing task. (One of their findings was that if people compared their work either to better or worse drawings, their satisfaction levels fell compared to the case in which they made no comparisons.)

Other researchers have defined or measured creativity according to ratings of workers by their supervisors (Baer, 2010), through student ratings of an instructor's creativity in a lecture (Milgram & Davidovich, 2010), and through a specific test of creativity (Mishra & Singh, 2010). If you designed a study of creativity, you would need to decide how you would define and measure that concept in different ways. It might make sense to use an approach that others have used, but you might want to develop one that related to the specific study you were planning.

Measuring Complex Concepts

Operational definition—A working definition of a complex or abstract idea that is based on how it is measured in a research project.

Variable—An element in a research project that, when measured, can take on more than one value.

Hypothetical construct—An idea or concept that is useful for understanding behavior, thought, and attitude but that is complex and not directly measurable.

As you plan your project, you need to translate your general ideas into concrete terms. Consider how the researchers mentioned above studied creativity. They first created an **operational definition** of the variable *creativity*. An operational definition is a way that we characterize and measure a variable. In the examples of creativity above, the operational definitions in the different research projects were self-ratings, ratings by others, or test scores. A **variable** is a concept of interest to us that can take on different values. For example, people might have low, medium, or high levels of creativity on a given task.

Operational definitions are important in psychology because we deal with concepts that are hard to define in concrete terms. Consider the concept of stress. Most people would agree that stress is a real psychological state. Unfortunately, it is completely internal, a set of feelings and responses that are hard to measure. It is a **hypothetical construct** because we are hypothesizing that it is psychologically real. In just about every area of psychology, we deal with hypothetical constructs for which we need adequate measurements and operational definitions.

If you intend to study stress, you have to figure out what observable measurements can represent this concept meaningfully. Holmes and Rahe (1967) decided they would measure stress through the amount of change a person experiences in his or her life. Think about what they had to do. They had to ask people how much change the people had experienced. This is not an easy issue. First of all, what does it mean to go through change? There are big changes and there are little changes. There are good changes and there are bad changes. What kind of change is worth mentioning? In addition, how far back should people go in their lives when they think of change? Holmes and Rahe had to answer these questions (and more) in deciding how to measure change.

They created the Social Readjustment Rating Scale (SRRS) that indicates the level of change in a person's life. For instance, the death of a spouse equaled 100 change units. An outstanding personal achievement contributed 28 change units. A change in eating habits was worth 15 change units. To identify stress, they posed 43 potential episodes reflecting some kind of change in people's lives.

Miller and Rahe (1997) updated the SRRS, finding somewhat different degrees of perceived stress in current society. For reasons we don't understand, people report that the same events today invariably generate higher levels of stress than they used to. Among the dozen events appearing in Table 4.1, only getting married failed to show an increase in stress associated with it. The researchers also found gender differences in ratings of the degree of stress of various events, a finding that did not occur in the original scale. As you can see, change can be for the better or for the worse, but it all contributes to stress. Further, it can vary depending on the cultural context.

Subsequent research has shown that SRRS scores constitute a useful predictor of number of visits and phone calls to a person's doctor, the incidence of physical symptoms with no apparent biological cause (Lynch et al., 2005), and negative outcomes like an increased likelihood of brain lesions in people with multiple sclerosis (Mohr et al., 2000) or hair loss among women (York et al., 1998). On the other hand, SRRS scores do not predict frequency or intensity of headaches, which are more predictable from the severity of a person's daily hassles (Fernandez & Sheffield, 1996).

The Importance of Culture and Context in Defining Variables

Not everybody reacts the same way to a given change; in fact, in different cultures, the same amount of change leads to quite different amounts of stress. In the United States, the death of a spouse leads to much greater relative adjustment than it does in Japan (Ornstein & Sobel,

TABLE 4.1   *Examples of Stress-Producing Life Events and Increases Over Time*

Event	Percent Increase in Stress from 1967 to 1997	Presumed Valence for Most People (Positive/Negative)
Death of a spouse	19	Negative
Jail term	22	Negative
Marriage	0	Positive
Pregnancy	65	Positive
Sex difficulties	15	Negative
Death of a close friend	89	Negative
Change in work responsibilities	48	?
Change in schools	75	?
Change in recreation	53	?
Change in sleeping habits	62	?
Change in eating habits	80	?
Christmas	250	Positive

Source: Holmes & Rahe, 1967; Miller & Rahe, 1997

1987). Likewise, people in the working world might experience stress differently than others, such as college students.

To address the differences in lifestyles of students and working adults, Renner and Mackin (1998) created a scale more suitable for many college students. The original SRRS included items involving dealing with in-laws, having mortgages, and other aspects of life that do not pertain to all students. So Renner and Mackin created a list of 51 events relevant to students. These include being raped or finding that you are HIV-positive, which have the greatest impact weight of any items on the scale; difficulty with a roommate; maintaining a steady dating relationship; getting straight As; and attending a football game. This new scale has not been evaluated for validity, but it contains items that students associate with stress.

If you were studying stress and people's responses to it, you could measure stress levels through either of these scales. Change in a person's life is not exactly the same as stress, but a score on the scale would serve as a reasonable operational definition of stress. Like any operational definition, it is not perfect, but it should work within the cultural context in which it was developed.

As a researcher, it is up to you to decide how you will define your concept. There is no perfect way; there are simply multiple ways that have their own strengths and weaknesses. Depending on the question you want to ask, you choose one over another. You could use Holmes and Rahe's scale or Renner and Mackin's to study stress, or you could find out how other researchers have decided to measure stress and adapt their strategies. In the end you have to select a method that you think will work for you.

When psychologists create experiments, one kind of variable they define is the independent variable. This is the variable that they manipulate in order to see if changes in this variable will affect behavior. Thus, if a researcher wants to see whether research participants give more help to a person with a tattoo or without a tattoo, the independent variable is presence or absence of the tattoo. In such a study, the researcher might measure how long the person provides help. Its value may change depending on whether somebody who asks for help has a tattoo; it is called the dependent variable. Strohmetz and Moore (2003) conducted this study and discovered that when the person with a tattoo was dressed in sweatshirt and jeans, that person received more help than when the person was dressed more formally.

What we need in our research are reasonable ways to measure complex concepts. Table 4.2 presents how psychologists have defined and measured some hypothctical constructs. Consider the hypothetical construct of motivation. Bell and Brady (2000) investigated the tendency of street sex workers (e.g., prostitutes) to go to health clinics depending on whether they were given motivation to do so. In this research, the investigators defined the sex workers as being motivated when they were offered monetary rewards for going to the clinic; in contrast, the researchers defined the workers as not motivated when there was no such incentive. The hypothetical construct of motivation was defined in terms of money the sex workers received. On the other hand, Novi and Meinster (2000) defined motivation in terms of the score a participant achieved on the Thematic Apperception Test, a projective test involving ambiguous pictures that an individual tries to interpret. In both research projects, these investigators were interested in motivation, but they defined motivation differently, so they measured it differently.

Sometimes, it takes some innovation to create an operational definition. For instance, Velten (1997) studied the effects of depression on behavior by inducing a mild version of depression in his research participants. His participants read a series of statements that would either elevate their moods (e.g., "If your attitude is good, then things are good, and my attitude is good.") or depress their mood (e.g., "Every now and then I feel so tired and gloomy that I'd rather just sit than do anything."). By doing this, he successfully created two groups, one that was somewhat depressed, the other more positive. Thus, people were operationally defined as

TABLE 4.2 *Examples of Operational Definitions of Hypothetical Constructs*

Independent variables (IV) reflect manipulated variables used for creating groups to compare; dependent, or measured, variables (DV) reflect variables that are either pre-existing or are the result of manipulation of the independent variable. Some variables are not amenable for use as true IVs, such as intelligence, which can't be manipulated by the experimenter.

Concept	Operational Definition and Research Topic	References
Depression	1. Score on Beck Depression Inventory (DV)–Relation between positive life events and depression 2. The mental state a person is in after reading negative or positive statements (IV)	1. Dixon & Reid (2000) 2. (a) Velten (1968); (b) Bartolic, Basso, Schefft, Glauser, &Titanic-Schefft (1999)
Intelligence	1. Score on Kaufman Assessment Battery for Children (DV)–Cognitive processing of learning-disabled children 2. Score on Raven's Progressive Matrices Test (DV)–Cognitive functioning of immigrants	1. Teeter & Smith (1989) 2. Kozulin (1999)
Happiness	1. Self-report score; amount of smiling and facial muscle activity (DV)–Happiness in people with severe depression 2. Score on Depression-Happiness Scale (DV)–(a) Subjective well-being; (b) religiosity 3. Behavioral observations of happiness (DV)–Happiness in people with profound multiple disabilities 4. Mental state of a person after listening to fearful, sad, happy, and neutral nonverbal vocalizations (IV)–Neural responses to emotional vocalizations	1. Gehricke & Shapiro (2000) 2. (a) Lewis, McCollam, & Joseph (2000); (b) French & Stephen (2000) 3. Green & Reid (1999) 4. Morris, Scott, & Dolan (1999)

Motivation	1. Score on Achievement Motives Scale (DV)–Motivation in athletes
	2. Score on Aesthetic Motivation Scale (DV)–Aesthetic motivation and sport preference
	3. Scores on Thematic Apperception Test (DV)–Peer group influence in levels of motivation
	4. Whether participants received monetary incentives (IV)–
	   (a) Enhancing attendance at clinics for street sex workers;
	   (b) time spent on different tasks in the workplace
		1. Halvari & Kjormo (2000)
		2. Wann & Wilson (1999)
		3. Novi & Meinster (2000)
		4. (a) Bell & Brady (2000);
		   (b) Matthews & Dickinson (2000)

depressed if they had read the mood-lowering statements; people were operationally defined as not depressed if they had read the mood-raising statements. (There was also a control group with neutral statements.)

Subsequently, Cronin, Fazio, and Beins (1998) used Velten's procedure to manipulate mood in a humor study. Participants in the depressed condition rated the funniness of jokes no differently than did people in the elevated mood condition. But those in the depressed laughed and smiled less than those in the elevated condition, suggesting that mood affects our mirth response, but not our ability to recognize that a joke is funny.

(Ethically, this study does not seem to pose risk and was approved by an IRB. The statements had the desired effect, but the manipulation had weak and temporary effects. In addition, seeing jokes raises a person's mood.)

Carrying Out a Literature Search

A literature search serves several particularly important purposes. First, you find the vast range of approaches that previous researchers have already used. With this knowledge, you can begin to identify the approach that might be most useful to you in answering your own question, including ideas for operational definitions. For details on conducting a successful literature search, you can revisit the process described in Chapter 3.

Second, by learning about what other researchers have discovered, you can avoid merely repeating what they have done. It is always more exciting to create a study that generates knowledge that nobody knew before you did.

Third, you can see what approach others have used and how they defined their variables. This lets you see what worked for them. When planning research, there is absolutely nothing wrong with adopting the methods that others have used. If you think back on the concept that scientific knowledge is cumulative, you will recognize that researchers expect others to follow up on their work, just as they have followed up on the work of others.

Conducting Your Study

An important choice in creating a research project concerns whether you intend to manipulate and control the situation or whether you will simply observe what occurs naturally. In experimental research, we actively manipulate what we expose the research participants to. In other research, we may not be able to manipulate variables for ethical or practical reasons.

Suppose you are studying stress. You could choose a descriptive approach in which you observed behaviors without interacting with the people you monitor. For example, you could look at behavior during stressful periods, like final exam week, compared to other less stressful times. This approach would enable you to describe stress-related behaviors that emerge during periods of differential stress.

A second method to study stress might involve administering a questionnaire that inquires about sources of stress and look at their possible effects. Miller and Rahe (1997) took the approach of developing a survey technique to study stress. They used a questionnaire to assess the amount of change in people's lives and the current levels of stress. These researchers found that apparently trivial events, even positive ones like going on vacation, contributed to overall stress levels that have an effect on one's health.

A third strategy is to identify existing stress levels in your research participants, then see how they respond to some manipulation. Some investigators (e.g., Cohen et al., 2006; Cohen, Tyrrell, & Smith, 1991) have done this. They measured participants' stress levels and then used nose drops to introduce either viruses or an inactive saline (i.e., saltwater) solution into the body and quarantined the people so they were not exposed to any other viral agents. These researchers found that people with higher levels of stress in their lives were more likely to come down with colds and, if they did, their colds were more severe. They also found that people with more positive emotional styles were less susceptible to colds.

A fourth approach would be to bring research participants to a laboratory and induce stress, but as you have learned in Chapter 2, there would be ethical questions about that strategy (just as there would be if you exposed your participants to a virus). Few researchers actively induce stress in people; if they want to control stress levels directly, they often use laboratory animals. (For an example of a study on stress and learning using animals, see Kaneto, 1997.)

The important point here is that you could study stress and its effects in a number of different ways. Each approach involves asking slightly different questions about stress and results in a slightly different portrayal of its effects. All approaches are methodologically valid and each has its own strengths and weaknesses.

Determining the Research Setting

In addition to deciding on a research question and defining our variables, we have to establish the location in which we will actually carry out the study. Some research almost by necessity requires a formal laboratory setting. If an investigation involves highly specialized equipment or a highly controlled environment, the researcher has few options other than the laboratory. For example, if you decided to study a behavior that is affected by many variables, you might want to use a laboratory to eliminate some of those variables so you can see the effect of the variables of interest to you. This approach is typical in theoretical research in which nuisance variables have large effects that can obscure small effects of an interesting variable. To study the factor that has a small effect, you need a highly controlled environment. On the other hand, if the research question involves an application relating to a particular environment like a business, you need to conduct the study in a business setting.

Another decision is whether to test people one by one or in groups. If people are tested in groups rather than individually, they might perform differently on their tasks. Social psychologists have found that people perform differently when they think others are observing them. Zajonc (1965) reported that even rats and ants work differently when in groups. If you are conducting your own study, it makes a difference whether your participants are alone or in groups, but you often do not know whether their performance changes for the better, for the worse, or in ways that are irrelevant to what you are measuring.

Very often, **applied research** takes place in a natural environment where people are acting as they normally do. **Basic (theoretical) research** is more likely to occur in a laboratory or other controlled setting. The reason for choosing a natural environment for research is that it represents the actual question you want to answer: How do people behave in a particular situation? On the other hand, when psychologists conduct theoretical research, we often want to simplify the situation so we can identify the effect of a single variable that might get lost in a complex, real-world setting.

Approaches to Psychological Research

Let's take a specific example. Suppose you wanted to see if stress level is associated with learning. Given that students report high stress levels, this could be a very important question. One decision you must make pertains to whether you would manipulate a person's stress level directly or whether you would simply measure the stress level as it naturally occurs.

If you decided not to actively manipulate a person's stress level for ethical or other reasons, you could make use of **observational research,** noting how people or animals behave in situations that are likely to lead to stress responses. By choosing simply to observe behaviors, psychologists engage in descriptive research. There are varied ways to conduct such studies. They all involve specifying particular behaviors and the situations in which they occur.

An alternative strategy would be to measure a person's existing stress level and try to relate it to some behavior. This method involves **correlational research,** which is the approach that Holmes and Rahe took in their research with the SRRS. This strategy would avoid the ethical dilemma of elevating stress, but the downside is that you wouldn't know if changes in stress actually cause changes in the amount that a person learns. Some other factor might be causing the change in stress; the amount of change might be a coincidental, nuisance variable.

Consider the situation of students who are taking classes for which they are not prepared; they might have difficulty learning the material. When they recognize that fact, it could lead to stress. There would be a relationship between stress and learning, but the causal factor is not the stress; in this example, the stress is the result.

Applied research—Research that attempts to address practical questions rather than theoretical questions.

Basic (theoretical) research—Research that tests or expands on theory, with no direct application intended.

Observational research—Investigation that relies on studying behaviors as they naturally occur, without any intervention by the researcher.

Correlational research—Investigation meant to discover whether variables covary, that is, whether there are predictable relationships among measurements of different variables.

On the other hand, people with naturally high stress levels may not learn well because they can't concentrate well. In this case there would still be a relationship between stress and learning, with the stress being the cause of poor learning.

The limitation with a correlational design is that there may be a predictable relationship between stress level and learning, but you do not know if stress affected learning, if learning affected the stress level, or if something else affected them both. If you don't actively manipulate stress levels experimentally (which could put people at risk), you can describe and maybe predict the connection between stress and learning, but you can't explain the causal mechanism.

If you actively manipulate stress to see how it affects behavior, you will be using **experimental research.** With an experiment, you control the research situation, which is clearly an advantage. In this approach, you would randomly assign participants to groups, expose them to different treatments, then see if the people in the groups behave differently from one another. In this example, you would manipulate stress level to see what effect your manipulation has on some other behavior. The measured behavior that might change depending on stress level is the amount of learning that occurs.

Sometimes you might wish to compare groups to see if they differ in their learning as a result of different levels of stress, but you use existing groups, like women and men or older and younger people. Such a design would resemble an experiment but, because people come to your experiment already belonging in a certain category, there is no real manipulation by the experimenter. We refer to such a design as a **quasi-experiment.**

You could also choose other approaches, such as a **case study,** in which you study a single individual's stress levels and the grades that person earns in classes. You can study the person in great depth over a long period of time. You end up with a lot of information about that person, which helps you put together a more complete picture of the behavior. Unfortunately, with such an approach, you do not know if this person's behavior is typical of other people. Case studies can be useful in formulating new research questions, but we have to consider whether it is prudent to use the behavior of a single individual as a model for people in general. Psychologists typically study groups rather than individuals, so case studies are relatively rare in the research literature.

The value of case studies (or case reports, as they are sometimes known) has been the subject of debate. One prestigious medical journal, *Journal of the American Medical Association,* does not publish case studies. Other journals, like the *New England Journal of Medicine* and *The Lancet* appear to regard such reports as educational or as teaching tools, not useful approaches to research.

Rare conditions may be of little use to practitioners and clinicians because of that rarity–most psychologists or medical personnel never see them. On the other hand, a report of unusual characteristics of a more frequent condition may be of greater use to practitioners.

Investigations of the frequency with which researchers cite case reports in their published studies reveal that those investigators do not cite case studies as frequently as they do other types of research. Nonetheless, a new journal, *The Journal of Medical Case Reports,* has begun publishing articles. It limits is articles to case studies (Gawrylewski, 2007).

Case Study of a Case Study: Possession by Spirits.   One such example reported on a case of possession by spirits by a young man from the country of Oman (Guenedi et al., 2009). The man's caregiver brought the man for traditional and for psychiatric treatment because he had experienced personality changes and was hallucinating. Ultimately, after a brain scan showing abnormal functioning, medication was helpful in eliminating the symptoms. Guenedi et al. noted that this case study was the first report that used neuro-imaging to connect culturally oriented behaviors associated with psychiatric diagnosis.

Experimental research—Investigation that involves manipulation and control of an independent or treatment variable with the intent of assessing whether the independent variable causes a change in the level of a dependent variable.

Quasi-experiment—A research study set up to resemble a true experiment but that does not involve random assignment of participants to a group or manipulation and control of a true independent variable, instead relying on measuring groups based on pre-existing characteristics.

Case study—An intensive, in-depth study of a single individual or a few individuals, usually without manipulation of any variables, to see how changes affect the person's behavior.

A question that remains, though, is whether the personality changes and hallucinations by this man have the same underlying neurological problems as they would in others. That is, how generalizable is this research finding? Furthermore, the man had been in an automobile accident and had suffered a head injury. Perhaps the head injury led to the abnormal behaviors in a way that was unique to that single person. In addition, it is not clear that cultural differences in and of themselves might be important in the display of symptoms. This is the dilemma associated with case studies: There are so many factors that are unique to a person that you can't say for sure that the same pattern of behaviors in another person are caused by the same things.

When we want to gather a lot of information about development over a period of time, we use **longitudinal studies.** Longitudinal research generally involves studying groups of people rather than a single individual people. This approach can require patience because observations sometimes continue for months, years, and even decades. One of its advantages is that we could see the long-term patterns of behavior that might be quite different than short-term effects.

It is even possible to study people's behaviors without ever being in contact with those people. Sometimes investigators engage in **archival research** in which they look at existing records to answer their questions. For instance, studying crime reports during periods of social unrest may provide some insights into the link between stress due to social circumstances and educational attainment.

Recently, psychologists have increased the use of **qualitative research.** This approach doesn't rely on numerical information but often uses complex description to characterize the way people respond to a situation or experience it. Analyses of behavior in qualitative studies often involve discussions of how people experience and feel about events in their lives. So a study of stress and learning with qualitative research might focus on how people react to a situation when they are trying to learn and they feel stressed.

Table 4.3 presents some of the methodologies that psychologists use to study behavior, including some of their advantages and disadvantages. These do not exhaust all possibilities, but they represent the major strategies in our research.

The approach that researchers use and the questions they ask have implications for where their work is published. As you can see in Table 4.4 on page 92, different journals show different patterns with respect to methodologies, locations of the study, and other features.

Longitudinal study—A research project in which a group of participants is observed and measured over time, sometimes over many decades.

Archival research—Investigation that relies on existing records like books or governmental statistics or other artifacts rather than on direct observation of participants.

Qualitative research—Investigation whose "data" do not consist of numerical information, but rather of narrative or textual information, often in natural settings.

Selecting Research Materials and Procedures

The details of your research include the materials and apparatus that you use to carry out your project. For example, if you are investigating the connection between stress and learning, you need to develop materials that people will try to learn; your choice of the type of stimuli (complex or abstract ideas, classroom materials, nonsense syllables, words, pictures, foreign words, etc.) may affect your outcome. For example, researchers have known since your grandparents were children that more meaningful material is easier to remember than less meaningful information (Glaze, 1928).

In connection with stress, the choice of material to be learned could be critical. For example, Gadzella, Masten, and Stacks (1998) reported that when students were stressed, they didn't think very deeply about material to be learned. As such, if you wanted to see if stress affected learning, you might get a different result by using simple versus complex material. Similarly, Heuer and colleagues (1998) found that stressors impaired the performance of more or less automatic, routine tasks, but not tasks that required more attention. Once again, your results might differ dramatically if you chose a learning task that required considerable attention.

TABLE 4.3 *Major Methodologies That Psychologists Use to Study Behavior*

Methodology	Main Characteristics	Advantages	Disadvantages
Experiments	Variables are actively manipulated and the environment is as controlled as possible	You can eliminate many extraneous factors that might influence behavior, so you can study those of interest. Consequently, you can draw conclusions about causes of behavior.	You may create an artificial environment, so people act in ways that differ from typical. Sometimes, there are ethical issues about manipulating variables.
Quasi-experiments (and ex post facto studies)	The design of the study resembles an experiment, but the variables are not manipulated. Instead, the researcher creates categories based on pre-existing characteristics of participants, like gender.	You can eliminate some of the extraneous factors that might influence behavior (but less so than in true experiments). You can also spot predictable relationships, even if you do not know the cause of behaviors.	Because you do not control potentially important variables, you cannot affirm cause-and-effect relationships.
Correlational Studies	You measure variables as they already exist, without controlling them.	You can spot predictable behavior patterns. In addition, you do not strip away complicating variables, so you can see how behavior emerges in a natural situation.	You cannot assess what variables predictably cause behaviors to occur.
Surveys, Tests, and Questionnaires	You ask for self-reported attitudes, knowledge, statements of behavior from respondents.	You can collect a significant amount of diverse information easily. In some cases, you can compare your data with established response patterns from other groups who have been studied.	You do not know how accurately or truthfully your respondents report their behaviors and attitudes. You cannot spot cause-and-effect relationships.
Case Studies	You study a single person or a few people in great depth, so you know a lot about them.	You can study people in their complexity and take their specific characteristics into account in trying to understand behavior.	You may not be able to generalize beyond the person or small group. They may not be representative of people in general.
Observational Research	You study behaviors in their natural settings without intervening (in most cases).	You can study life and behavior in its complexity.	There are so many factors that influence behavior in the natural world that you cannot be sure why people act as they do.
Longitudinal Research	You study people's behaviors over a long period of time.	You can see how behaviors change over time, particularly as an individual develops and matures.	This research may take weeks, months, or years to complete. In addition, people may change because society changes, not only because of their personal maturation.
Archival Research	You use existing records and information to help you answer your research question, even though that information was gathered for other reasons.	You can trace information historically and use multiple sources to address your research question.	The information was gathered for purposes different than yours, so the focus may be different. You also do not know how accurate the records are or what information is missing.
Qualitative Research	You study people in their natural environment and try to understand them holistically. There is reliance on descriptive rather than quantitative information.	You can gain useful insights into the complexity of people's behaviors. Very often the focus is on the meaning of text or conversation, rather than on its subcomponents.	This research often takes considerably longer than quantitative research and can involve painstaking analysis of the qualitative data. Some researchers do not like the fact that numerical analysis is not critical to this approach.

TABLE 4.4 *Differences in Research Methodologies in Psychology Journals, Based on the Listings in PsycINFO as of Early 2010*

Journal	Average Number of Participants per Study	Percentage of Different Methodologies	Percentage of Studies in Different Settings	Percentage of Articles Using Different Statistical Tests	Number of References per Article
Journal of Applied Psychology[a]	Mean = 907	59% Survey 12% Experiment 18% Archival 6% Quasi-experiment 6% Observational	53% Workplace 24% Lab/Class 18% Archive 2% Craigslist	12% ANOVA 82% Correlation 12% t-test	Mean = 79 Range = 52–125
Journal of Experimental Psychology: Applied[b]	Mean = 255	63% Experiment 25% Quasi-experiment 12% Archival	100% Laboratory/Class	57% ANOVA 12% Correlation 71% t-test 12% Other	Mean = 51 Range = 29–97
Journal of Experimental Psychology: General[c]	Mean = 156	100% Experimental	100% Laboratory	62% ANOVA 12% Correlation 75% t-test 12% Chi-square	Mean = 56 Range = 17–87
Journal of Cross-Cultural Psychology[d]	Mean = 278	60% Quasi-experiment 20% Survey 10% Meta analysis 10% Archival	30% College/School 30% Archive/Database 20% Workplace 20% Community Center	80% ANOVA 50% Correlation 10% t-test 10% Chi square	Mean = 48 Range = 8–98

[a]Volume 94(6), 2009
[b]Volume 15(4), 2009
[c]Volume 138(4), 2009
[d]Volume 40(5), 2009

Why Methodology Is Important

How you decide to test your participants is critical. For instance, psychologists have studied how easy it is to learn lists of frequently occurring words versus relatively rare words. Do you think it would be easier to remember common words or uncommon words? Some creative, excellent psychological research has revealed that more common words are remembered better. Other just as creative and excellent psychological research has shown that less common words are easier to remember.

These conflicting results do not make much sense until you know about the details of the research. There are several ways to test a person's memory. One of them is to ask the person to recall as many words from a list as possible. When we do this, people tend to recall more common words better than less common words (Wallace, Sawyer, & Robertson, 1979).

On the other hand, we could give a test of recognition memory. In this case, we would present a large group of words and ask the individual to identify which words had occurred during the learning phase of the study. Thus, the learners do not need to search through memory; they simply have to identify the words they saw before. This methodology leads to better memory for less frequent words (Underwood & Freund, 1970).

Generations of students know about the relative ease of recognition compared to recall. "College students are aware of this fact and notoriously rely on less thorough preparation for objective (multiple choice) tests than for tests which demand recall. Recognition makes no demands upon availability of items" as Deese and Hulse (1967, p. 378) noted over 40 years ago.

When you think about it, it makes sense that a recall task favors common words, whereas recognition favors less frequently occurring words. When you try to recall information, you have to search through memory for possibilities. For instance, if you can't find your keys, you may try to locate them by asking yourself where you have been. You need to generate the possibilities yourself until you identify the correct location. If you fail to think of the correct location, you will not find your keys. It would be much easier if somebody gave you a list of places you have been; all you would have to do is to select the correct one because you know the answer is in front of you.

Regarding your memory for words, you can recall more frequent words because they are easier to generate as possibilities in the first place. You have a harder time with infrequent words because you are less likely to generate them, so you aren't able to consider them as possibilities.

More recent research also shows that the nature of stimuli can be important to the way people respond to them. When research participants viewed words presented for very brief durations (i.e., one-thirtieth of a second or less), the participants were better at categorizing negative words than positive words (Nasrallah, Carmel, & Lavie, 2009). The researchers were explicitly investigating whether there would be differences between positive and negative words, but if other researchers used those stimuli for other purposes, the nature of the words might affect the outcome of the study in ways that surprised the researchers.

As these examples show, your research methodology is important to the development of your ideas. The conclusions you draw from your research result from the way you do your research. No matter what kind of research project you plan, if you overlook the importance of your methodology, you will not have a full understanding of the question you want to answer.

Choosing Your Participants or Subjects

Population—The entire set of people or data that are of interest to a researcher.

Sample—A subset of the population that is studied in a research project.

Representative sample—A subset of the population in a research project that resembles the entire population with respect to variables being measured.

Fifty years ago, psychologists studied the behaviors of rats as much as the behaviors of people. At the time, researchers felt that they could explain the behaviors of just about all animals, human or not, with a single set of behavioral principles. So it did not make much difference to them what kind of organisms they studied. We are in a different era now and we ask different questions, so we mostly study human behavior (Plous, 1996a).

The group that we are interested in understanding constitutes our **population.** It varies in different research projects. If we are interested in stress and learning in college students, then college students constitute the population. If we are interested in how the "typical" person learns, our population consists of college students and many others. If we want to study animal behavior, then a type of animal may constitute our population.

Other than in a census, we seldom have access to the entire population, and it would be too costly to observe the entire group even if we could get to them all. So we use a subset of the population, our **sample.** When the characteristics of the sample are similar to those of the population, we say we have a **representative sample.**

The decisions we make about studying people involve such questions as who we will study, how we will recruit them for our research, how many we will test, and in what conditions will be study them. We make some very practical choices. The decisions that we make depend in many cases on exactly what questions we want to ask.

The Nature of Your Participants

In general, psychologists do research with organisms that are easiest to study. Can you figure out some of the characteristics of these organisms? The typical research subject turns out to be a young, highly educated, cooperative, motivated, female, psychology student. Wouldn't you want to work with people with those characteristics? Professional researchers are like you—they want to do their work with the greatest efficiency and the least inconvenience.

Rosenthal and Rosnow (1975) investigated volunteering rates for women and men; they discovered that women tend to volunteer more than men, although the nature of the research project affects this tendency. Rosenthal and Rosnow looked at research during an era in which men were likely to outnumber women in psychology classes; the reverse is true today, so the number of female volunteers will typically outnumber the number of males by a wide margin. For very practical reasons, having access to such a population of willing volunteers (i.e., students in psychology classes) means that psychologists are going to rely on that group of people.

The good news is that when students volunteer to participate in research, they will show up and do what you tell them. The bad news is that we don't always know whether such female participants from psychology classes at a single college or university resemble the entire population. Would older people or younger people act the same way? Would men act the same way? Would less well educated people act the same way? Would people from other parts of the country act the same way? Would people of different cultures respond the same way?

We don't know the answers to these questions. So why do we continue to rely on this very restricted population? One answer is that when we study basic, theoretical processes, the exact composition of our samples may not be all that important. Another answer is because they are there. It would be more time consuming and difficult to locate a more diverse group who might not want to participate in a research study anyway. Actually, some researchers, particularly those in applied areas, often rely on quite diverse samples.

Table 4.5 presents participant characteristics typical of research in some journals and the types of research reported in those journals. As you can see, experimental work typically features students, generally undergraduates. Experimental journal articles provide very little detail about the characteristics of the participants. Traditionally, experimental psychologists assumed that we could study any population in order to understand behavior in general; they reasoned that the details of particular groups might differ, but the patterns would be valid across all of them. We now recognize that this could be a problem if we want to know about generalizing results to different populations.

Investigators studying more applied questions usually give greater detail about the people they study, including age, gender, and ethnicity. This makes sense if you consider the point of much applied research, which is to identify answers to questions related to specific situations or well-defined groups.

Deciding How Many Participants to Include

After we identify our participant population, we need to decide how many people we will study. The greater the sample size, the more time and effort it will take to complete the research. At the same time, if we test small samples, we diminish the chance of finding statistically significant results and increase the relative size of error in generalizing our results to our population. Berkowitz (1992) has commented that, in social psychology, research typically relies on sample sizes that are too small. Researchers may miss potentially important and interesting findings as a result. The larger your sample, the more likely you are to spot differences that are real, even if they are small. With smaller samples, we may detect large differences, but miss the small ones.

TABLE 4.5 *Examples of Participants Included in Different Studies in Three Major Psychology Journals*

Journal of Experimental Psychology: Applied (2000, Vol. 6, No. 1)

Topic of Research	*Description of Participants as Given in Journal Article*
Effects of characteristics of negotiators in reaching settlements in disputes	173 Undergraduates
Participants' reactions to changes in the nature of auditory displays	184 Undergraduates
Effects of verbal and spatial tasks on eye movements in driving	12 Adults with at least two years driving experience; 7 women, 5 men
Personal characteristics and completion of time-critical tasks	30 Students
Effects of sleep loss on reasoning and eyewitness identification	93 Students; 45 women, 48 men
Children's use of anatomically correct dolls in reporting genital touching in medical examinations	84 children, average age = 3 years

Journal of Experimental Psychology: General (2000, Vol. 129, No. 1)

Topic of Research	*Description of Participants as Given in Journal Article*
Backward inhibition in cognitive processing	118 Students
Memory for annoying sounds	134 Undergraduates
Personality effects, frontal lobe mechanisms, and error monitoring	42 Students
Differences in visuospatial and verbal memory	110 Undergraduates
Remembering and classifying stimuli	104 Students
Identification of visually presented stimuli	34 Students; 17 women, 17 men
Vividness of imagery and memory	112 Adults

Journal of Applied Psychology (2000, Vol. 85, No. 1)

Topic of Research	*Description of Participants as Given in Journal Article*
Nature and correlates of ethnic harassment	167 Students; 91 women, 76 men; approximately 80% Hispanic 110 School district employees; 81 women, 9 men; 50% Hispanic 295 Graduate students; 194 women, 101 men; 48% Hispanic
Identification of departure of international participants	58 International employees; 95% men 70 Workers in 40 countries; 95% men
Comparison of standardized math test results and reading accommodations	1500 Randomly sampled Kansas students
Using response times to assess guilt	72 Undergraduates
The effects of reinforcement on children's mundane and fantastic claims regarding wrongdoing	120 Children, ages 5–7
Influence of job familiarity and impression management on self-report and response time measurements	116 Undergraduates; 87% men; 84% white 198 Job applicants; 92% men, 73% white
Examination of self-reported stress among managers	841 Managers; 91% men; 96% white
Evaluating social sexual conduct at work	200 Workers recruited from newspaper ads; 100 women, 100 men; 76% white
Behaviors of female and male executives as they "climb the corporate ladder"	137 Executives; 68 women, 69 men
Group trust and workplace conflict	380 Workers; 81% men; 95% white
Comparing mechanical and computer-driven systems of creating facial composite pictures	24 Undergraduates; 75% women
Openness to change in workplace reorganization	130 Workers
Comparing different types of test items	1969 College freshmen; 915 women, 1054 men (from archival data set)

One of the other principles that should guide you in determining how many people to include in your research project involves the variability of scores across people. When you measure people, they will naturally produce different scores. Some of the discrepancy results from the fact that people differ due to intelligence, motivation, energy levels, and other personal characteristics. As a result, when you test them in a research setting, differences will emerge independent of any variables you are interested in. The greater the amount of variability among your participants to begin with, the harder it will be to spot changes in behavior due to different treatments. If you separated them into groups, they would show some differences regardless of whether you treated them differently. With groups of very different types of people, you might wind up with two groups that look very different only because the people start out different.

Consider this situation: Suppose you wanted to manipulate a variable and create a treat-ment group and a control group. You could assemble your sample and assign each person to one of the two conditions. Then you would expose one group to the treatment and leave the other group untreated. Finally, you would measure them to see if the two groups behaved differently.

If your participants were fairly similar to one another at the beginning, the effect of any treatment would be easier to spot because any differences in behavior across groups would probably be due to that treatment. On the other hand, if the people were quite different before your manipulation, you might not know if any differences between groups after the study were due to initial differences or to your manipulation.

The similarity among your participants is not the only factor influencing the sample size in your research. An additional consideration involves whether you think your manipulation will have a big or a small effect. The effect of your treatment might be real and consistent, but it might be small. For instance, if a teacher smiled at students in one class as they entered a classroom to take a test, it might relax them so their performance increased. The improvement would probably be fairly small, reflecting a small treatment effect. In order to be able to see a difference in scores because of a smiling teacher, you would need a large group of students because existing differences in learning, intelligence, motivation, and so forth would have a greater effect than the smile. Large samples are more likely in a statistical sense to let us spot small but reliable differences.

On the other hand, if the teacher announced in advance that there would be particular questions on a test, this manipulation would have a big effect. You would not need such a large sample to see the effects of the information given to the students.

If your research manipulation is likely to have a large effect, you can get away with smaller samples, especially if your participants are relatively similar to begin with. If your manipulation has only a small effect, you will need larger samples to spot differences between groups, particularly if your participants differ from one another noticeably before the experi-ment begins. You cannot always know if advance how big your effect size will be, although the more you know about the research that others have done, the better your prediction will be. You also do not know how homogeneous your samples are, but if you test college students in your research, your population is likely to be more homogeneous than the population as a whole. They are similar to one another, even if they differ from the vast array of people in general. The bottom line is to test as many people as practical so even small effects show up if they exist.

Can Rats, Mice, and Fish Help Us Understand Humans?

Psychologists have had a long tradition of studying animals and then generalizing the animal behaviors to humans. Over the years, some people have objected to characterizing people as susceptible to the same factors that affect animals. So whether studies of animals in a laboratory pertain to human behavior is an important and interesting question.

Probability sampling—
A method used in research whereby any person in the population has a specified probability of being included in the sample.

Generalization—The property of research results such that they can be seen as valid beyond the sample involved in a study to a larger population.

Continuing with the example of stress, it would be helpful if we knew more about how people exposed to chronic stress respond to it. Researchers have found that mice experiencing stressors that they cannot control (e.g., being forced to swim for 10 minutes) experience changes in the limbic system that affect the rate of extinction of conditioned fear responses. That is, they develop fear but cannot extinguish it. Additional research with animals has demonstrated that rats that experience chronic stress show less extinction of fear response than rats who are not stressed (Miracle et al., 2006; Schulz, Buddenberg, & Huston, 2007). In addition, in rats bred to show characteristics of learned helplessness, extinction of fear responses is retarded (Schulz, Buddenberg, & Huston, 2007). On the other hand, investigators have also found that some substances can foster extinction of fear responses in mice (Cai et al., 2006; Varvel et al., 2007) and fish (Barreto, Volpato, & Pottinger, 2006).

All of the research just cited involves animals. Because it would be unethical to induce chronic stress in humans or to conduct experiments that might worsen symptoms of stress, psychologists have resorted to studying stress in animals. The big question is whether what is true for rats, mice, and fish also holds true for people.

There is evidence that the same patterns of failure or success in extinguishing fear responses that occur in trout (e.g., Barreto et al., 2006), in mice (e.g., Cai et al., 2006), and in rats (e.g., Miracle et al., 2006) may be at work in people (Felmingham et al., 2007). The same kinds of processes in the brain seem to be occurring in people and in animals who experience anxiety and stress (e.g., Rauch, Shin, & Phelps, 2006). Researchers appear to have reached consensus that animal models can provide the basis for the development treatment of anxiety and stress disorders in people (Anderson & Insel, 2006).

Thus, research with animals like rodents and fish have given us clues about the development and treatment of psychiatric disorders. Such developments are important because of the high levels of stress many people experience. For instance, after the terrorist attacks in the United States in 2001, many people had significant stress reactions, even if they were not directly affected by the attacks (Melnik et al., 2002). In addition, evidence suggests that students also experienced stress reactions (MacGeorge et al., 2004). With constantly occurring stress events in contemporary life, we probably should not expect a reduction in psychological problems, particularly in light of data showing that stress and anxiety among college students at one institution increased by 73% between 1992 and 2001 (Benton et al., 2003). Researchers will undoubtedly be studying stress and its effects for a long time. It seems that we will be able to use all the help we can get from the animals studied by researchers.

Probability Sampling

Probability sampling is the gold standard of sampling. In its simplest definition, probability sampling means that everybody that you are interested in, your population, has an equal chance of participating in your study. Unfortunately, outside of some survey research, psychologists typically don't employ it because it would be very costly. If we were interested in how people in general behave, we would need to test people from every country, of all ages, with diverse backgrounds. For all of its desirability, researchers forego probability sampling in favor of less costly approaches, like the samples of college students that most research employs. The price we pay revolves around whether we can **generalize** from our sample to a larger population.

Another difficulty associated with probability sampling is that, in order to use it, we have to be able to define our population of interest. In theory, we would have to be able to list every member of the population so we could pick our participants from the list. In much of our research, it is not really clear that we could do this, even in theory.

There are four general strategies for probability sampling. They result in simple random samples, systematic samples, stratified random samples, and cluster samples.

Simple Random Sampling

Simple random sampling (SRS) involves identifying your population precisely, then identifying some probability that each person in it will appear in your sample. (We often refer to this approach just as random sampling.) In SRS, each person has an equal chance of being selected. In professionally conducted polls, the researchers use randomly selected telephone numbers, so each household with a phone has an equal chance of being called. The result is likely to be a sample that reflects the entire population.

It is important to remember that even with a random sample, you may not have a truly representative sample; sometimes pollsters get unlucky. For instance, if the voters they get in touch with are home because they are unemployed, the sample might show certain biases because such people hold different attitudes than those who are working. But the more people you call, the less likely you are to have a sample that is quite different from the whole population when you use random sampling.

Simple random sampling—A process of sampling in research that specifies that each person in a population has the same chance of being included in a sample as every other person.

Systematic Sampling

If you have a list of the entire population from which you will sample, you might decide to sample every tenth, twentieth, hundredth, etc. name after selecting a random position to start. This process will generate a **systematic sample.** Some (e.g., Judd, Smith, & Kidder, 1991) have argued that such a technique deviates from randomness because if you started with the fifth name, then went to the fifteenth, twenty-fifth, etc., then the fourteenth and sixteenth names (for example) have zero probability of being chosen. The counterargument is that empirical studies have shown the results of SRS and systematic sampling to be virtually identical, particularly if your list of people is in a random order to begin with; further, in many cases systematic sampling is simply easier to do (Babbie, 1995).

Systematic sampling—A process of sampling in which an apparently unbiased but nonrandom sample is created, such as by creating a list of every element in the population and selecting every *n*th member from the population.

Stratified Random Sampling

On occasion, you might decide that you want certain groups to be included in your sample in specific proportions. For instance, if you wanted to survey your college so that you could get responses from first-year students, sophomores, juniors, and seniors in equal proportions, you probably would not want to use SRS because you are likely to sample more first-year students because in most schools, there are more of them; the less interested or able students have not yet dropped out, as they have with upper-level students. As a result, you could employ **stratified random sampling,** in which you identify the proportion of your total sample that will have the characteristics you want.

Theoretically, stratification can be appropriate for virtually any variable you could think of. You can stratify by age, gender, socioeconomic status, education level, political affiliation, geographical location, height, weight, etc. In practice, though, some stratification is easier than others because you may not be able to identify in advance the members of your population according to some variables (e.g., height or weight) as easily as others (e.g., sex—by using the person's first name as a guide).

Stratified random sampling—A process of sampling in which groups of interest (e.g., male and female; young and old; Democratic, Republican, and Independent) are identified, then participants are selected at random from these groups.

Cluster Sampling

Finally, sometimes a strategy like simple random sampling will be impractical. For example, Burnham and colleagues (2006) sampled households in Iraq during the war there. They could not use phone or mail surveys, so they used **cluster sampling.**

They identified locations of a large number of groups (or clusters) of households. Then the researchers chose a random set of clusters and interviewed people who lived there. This is an example of research that required thinking outside the box because the people conducting the survey might well have been killed, which is why the Iraqi people who collected the data were not identified.

Nonprobability Sampling

Most psychological research does not involve probability sampling. The implication is that we often do not know to whom our research results generalize. This means that we can say that a particular result applies to students like the ones we study, but we don't know if our results also pertain to people younger or older, less or more educated, poorer or richer, etc.

Among the greatest problems with nonprobability samples is **nonsampling error.** This problem occurs when people who should be included in a sample are not. It results in a nonprobability sample that may not be representative of the population as a whole. The end result is that a researcher doesn't know to whom the survey results apply.

Cluster sampling—A process of sampling in which a number of groups (or clusters) are identified in a population, then some clusters are randomly selected for participation in a research project.

Nonsampling error—A problem in sampling that leads to a nonrepresentative sample because some members of the population are systematically excluded from participation.

Convenience sampling—A nonrandom (nonprobability) sampling technique that involves using whatever participants can conveniently be studied, also known as an accidental sample and a haphazard sample.

To ignore nonsampling error is to jeopardize the validity of a research project's results. The problem is not apparent in some research because you don't always know who you are surveying and who is being left out. For instance, in research on bulimia, investigators often study people referred from medical doctors. It turns out that, compared to bulimics in the community in general, bulimics referred for treatment by a doctor show a greater incidence of self-induced vomiting, greater likelihood of misusing laxatives, and a more severe eating disorder in general (Fairburn et al., 1996). If researchers rely on referrals from doctors, the sample will consist of people with more severe problems compared to a randomly drawn sample from the community.

The sampling approaches that psychologists use, particularly in laboratory studies, include convenience samples, quota samples, purposive (judgmental) samples, and respondent-driven (chain-referral) samples. Unfortunately, all of these approaches have limitations because of the people who do not participate in research.

Convenience Sampling

As you saw in Table 4.6, the journals of experimental psychology involve students almost exclusively. When researchers rely on such a population because it is easy or available, we refer to **convenience sampling.**

Unfortunately, in many cases, we don't really know how well our research findings generalize from our samples. At the same time, when we create experimental groups and compare them, we may not be interested in precise measurements of differences between the groups, but rather patterns of differences. For instance, Recarte and Nunes (2000) investigated how students performed in a driving task when asked to complete verbal and spatial imagery tasks. Students are probably younger, on average, than the typical driver. Do you think this would matter when we discuss the effects of verbal versus spatial thought among drivers? Students may be better or worse in their driving than older people, but will the verbal-spatial comparison differ between the two groups? When researchers conduct this type of study, they hope not.

When psychologists test theories, they may not care about the specifics of the samples they work with. In fact, in experimental journals, the researchers report very little detailed information about the participants. The philosophy is that if the theory generates certain predictions, those predictions should come true, regardless of the population tested. In the end, we have to use our best judgment when deciding how important the demographics of our samples are. Sometimes, using students is just fine; sometimes, it isn't. This is where judgment and experience become important.

Quota Sampling

Quota sampling is analogous to stratified sampling in that, in both, the researcher attempts to achieve a certain proportion of people of certain types in the final sample. Suppose an investigator wants to know if less able students differ from better students in their political beliefs.

The researcher could recruit volunteers from a class, asking the students to indicate name, contact information, and grade point average. Then the researcher could make sure that the proportion of students with low averages in the final sample matches the proportion of students below a certain grade point average in the population, with the proportion of good students in the final sample matching the proportion of better students in the population. This type of quota sampling is a variation on convenience sampling because the sample is not random.

Purposive (Judgmental) Sampling

At times, a researcher may not feel the need to have a random sample. If the investigator is interested in a particular type of person, say somebody with special expertise, the investigator may try to find as many such people as possible and study them. The result is descriptive research that may say a lot about this group of experts.

For instance, one use of purposive sampling would be to study a group of the best and the worse workers in a company. The sample would not be random, but it would give an interesting look at differences in behaviors of employees in the two extreme categories.

The problem with such a sample is the same as with any other nonprobability sample—you don't know who, beyond your sample, your results relate to. This approach is sometimes called **purposive (judgmental) sampling** because it relies on the judgment of the researcher and a specific purpose for identifying participants.

Chain-Referral Sampling

Sometimes it is difficult to make contact with some populations because they might not want to be found (e.g., drug users, sex workers, illegal immigrants). They are not likely to be conveniently listed with their phone numbers. As a result, researchers have to use creative approaches to contact them. Investigators have developed several techniques to study such groups, which are sometimes called hidden populations; the broad term for these techniques is **chain-referral** methods. As a rule, these strategies are more likely to be practical for survey and interview research than for experimental studies.

In these approaches, the researcher may use a contact in the group of interest to provide references to others who, in turn, provide other names. Another chain-referral technique involves finding where members of the group congregate, then sampling the individuals at that location. A third approach is to use a member of the group to recruit others; there may be an advantage to this technique because a known person of the group solicits participation, not an unknown and anonymous researcher. A final approach involves finding a key informant who knows the population of interest; rather than questioning members of the population, the researcher talks with a person knowledgeable about the group.

Quota sampling—A nonrandom (nonprobability) sampling technique in which subgroups, usually convenience samples, are identified and a specified number of individuals from each group are included in the research.

Purposive (judgmental) sampling—A nonrandom (nonprobability) sampling technique in which participants are selected for a study because of some desirable characteristics, like expertise in some area.

Chain-referral sampling—A nonrandom (nonprobability) sampling technique in which a research participant is selected who then identifies further participants whom he or she knows, often useful for finding hidden populations.

Chapter Summary

Once you decide the general nature of your research question, you have to make a lot of practical decisions about how exactly to conduct your study. These practical decisions can make a big difference both in the shape your research takes and the conclusions you draw. Researchers studying similar questions often take very different paths to their answers.

A good place to begin any project is through a literature search. By investigating how others have approached research like yours, you can avoid having to reinvent techniques that have already worked for others. If you find useful ways of creating and measuring variables of interest to you, it only makes good sense for you to use them if they are appropriate. This is perfectly acceptable as long as you give credit to the researchers who developed the ideas initially. In some cases, however, you might want to create different ways of approaching the question because you might not be able to find anybody else who approached your question quite the way you would like. This is an example of the kind of practical decision you will make when setting up your project.

A different decision is to identify the group of people you will study. You will have to decide how you will contact them and how to convince them to participate. Psychologists very often solicit participation from students in beginning psychology classes who receive extra credit for their participation. It can be harder to get participants from other populations. The risk in using student samples is that you are not sure that your results generalize beyond that particular type of person.

After you construct the design of your study and decide who will participate, you need to consider how exactly to measure your hypothetical constructs. This process requires you to form operational definitions of important concepts as you use them in your work. In order for you to have confidence in your measurements, those measurements need to be both reliable and valid. Reliable measurements are repeatable. That is, if measurements are taken more than once or in different ways, the results should be the same. If your measurements are valid, you will be measuring well those things that you intend to measure. In psychology, it is important to establish reliability and validity because we are often trying to assess something that is complex and abstract, something that does not lend itself to easy measurement. If our measurements are not valid, our interpretations won't be very meaningful.

Finally, it is important to remember that psychologists with different specialties will approach related questions very differently. Various areas of psychology have developed their own traditions regarding methodological approaches.

Key Terms

Applied research	Generalization	Qualitative research
Archival research	Hypothetical construct	Quasi-experiment
Basic (theoretical) research	Longitudinal study	Quota sampling
Case study	Nonsampling error	Representative sample
Chain-referral sampling	Observational research	Sample
Cluster sampling	Operational definition	Simple random sampling
Convenience sampling	Population	Stratified random sampling
Correlational research	Probability sampling	Systematic sampling
Experimental research	Purposive (judgmental) sampling	Variable

Chapter Review Questions _____

Multiple Choice Questions

1. When you complete a literature search, you can
   a. avoid engaging in replication with extension.
   b. identify the different approaches used by various researchers to address the same question.
   c. ensure that you do not use a similar means to identify and create variables.
   d. make sure that you do not use measurements that everybody else has.

2. Because psychology involves trying to understand complex and abstract concepts, researchers need to develop _____ in order to make useful measurements of those concepts.
   a. operational definitions
   b. hypothetical constructs
   c. literature searches
   d. independent variables

3. When psychologists develop their experiments, they will decide what they want to manipulate as part of the experimental procedure. The variable controlled by the experimenter is the _____ variable.
   a. hypothetical
   b. construct
   c. extraneous
   d. independent

4. When you choose your operational definitions in the research you conduct, you have to remember that
   a. there is usually a single best way to deal with complex concepts.
   b. there is usually a great deal of controversy associated with selecting an operational definition.
   c. it is important to operationally define your variable so that it is meaningful across a wide range of cultures.
   d. different operational definitions of the same concept lead to different research questions and can generate different results.

5. If psychologists want to study the interactions among children on a playground, they are likely to choose
   a. experiments.
   b. quasi-experiments.
   c. observational research.
   d. correlational research.

6. If a journal article has a title like "The relation between political beliefs and activism in students," it is likely to be
   a. observational research.
   b. correlational research.
   c. experimental research.
   d. longitudinal research.

7. If an investigator wanted to study the differences in speed of problem solving in young versus old adults, the approach is likely to be
   a. observational research.
   b. correlational research.
   c. case study research.
   d. quasi-experimental research.

8. Researchers have studied the effects of traumatic events, like experiencing devastating hurricanes, on children over an extended period of time. Such research is
   a. observational research.
   b. qualitative research.
   c. experimental research.
   d. longitudinal research.

9. The systematic elimination of extraneous variables other than those you are interested in can be eliminated in what research design?
   a. Qualitative research
   b. Correlational research
   c. Experimental research
   d. Longitudinal research

10. Research involving a single person who is studied in great depth is characteristic of
    a. survey research.
    b. longitudinal research.
    c. case studies.
    d. qualitative research.

11. If a sample in a study is generally the same as the population, we say the sample is
    a. representative.
    b. reliable.
    c. constructed.
    d. dependent.

12. When an experiment makes use of a small number of participants, the results
    a. are easier to replicate than when there are many participants.
    b. may miss potentially important findings because research with small samples is not very sensitive.
    c. make small differences easy to spot.
    d. are seldom valid.

13. It is easier to spot differences among groups when research involves small samples if
    a. the investigator uses probability sampling.
    b. the participants are homogeneous regarding the behavior to be studied.
    c. the effect sizes for the behavior to be studied are also small.
    d. the hypothetical constructs are operationally defined.

14. Research articles that appear in the *Journal of Applied Psychology* are likely to be
    a. laboratory based.
    b. experimental.
    c. basic.
    d. correlational.

15. When research uses random sampling, the samples are likely to be
    a. representative.
    b. judgmental.
    c. longitudinal.
    d. qualitative.

Essay Questions

16. Why is applied research often conducted outside a formal laboratory, whereas theoretical research generally takes place in a laboratory?

17. We hope to be able to generalize our research results to people other than those who actually participated in our research. For the typical psychology study, why is it hard to determine the people to whom our research will generalize?

CHAPTER 5

ORGANIZING DATA WITH DESCRIPTIVE STATISTICS

CHAPTER OUTLINE

USING STATISTICS TO DESCRIBE RESULTS

DESCRIPTIVE STATISTICS
  Scales of Measurement
  Measures of Central Tendency
  Distributions of Scores

  Measures of Variability
  Summarizing Data

COMPUTER ANALYSIS USING SPSS
  Generating Descriptive Statistics
  Illustrating Descriptive Statistics

LEARNING OBJECTIVES

- Describe the relationship between a population and a sample.
- Describe how parameters and statistics are related to population and sample.
- Distinguish between qualitative and quantitative variables.
- Describe the qualities of each of the scales of measurement—nominal, ordinal, interval, and ratio.
- Identify scales of measurement.
- Define, calculate, and interpret the measures of central tendency.
- Compare and contrast and apply the usefulness of central tendency measures.
- Identify applications of measures of central tendency.
- Describe measures of variability.
- Describe how kurtosis affects the distribution.
- Use measures of central tendency and variability to summarize results of descriptive data.
- Use graphical measures (i.e., bar graph and histogram) to illustrate results of descriptive analyses.

CHAPTER PREVIEW

You already know that planning your study is the most difficult and time-consuming phase of the research process. You must come up with a question about a phenomenon you are interested in, and then devise a method for investigating the question. As part of the planning process, you must also consider how you are collecting information. You must be able to quantify what you are doing and what will happen in the study in a way that provides quantifiable characteristics.

In addition to quantifying what you are doing within the study, it is important that you describe the participants in your study.

Researchers describe who participated and what happened in the study by using statistics. A *statistic* provides a quantitative measure for a *sample* or a subset of a population. A *parameter* is very similar to a statistic except that a parameter refers to some value in the *population*. We usually use statistics to describe results from our studies because we conduct research with samples of people.

We can quantify information by using one of two types of statistics, descriptive or inferential measures. Inferential statistics depend on probabilities, and we use them to test hypotheses. Descriptive statistics allow us to summarize information so that readers can quickly understand the outcomes of our study. In this chapter we will discuss how descriptive statistics are derived and how you might use them in your research.

Using Statistics to Describe Results

Popular media frequently report interesting statistics about a host of events or perceptions. For example, we often read reports about the percentages of people who belong to a political party or the average number of auto accidents that occur annually. Statistics, such as those published in the media, are usually presented as a way of describing interesting facts and figures. When we describe demographic characteristics, behaviors, or outcomes of a study, we are using a particular type of statistic called **descriptive statistics.**

The earliest known use of descriptive statistics occurred in 1662 when John Graunt published *Observations on Bills of Mortalities* in London, England. In this work, he summarized and reported information about the people who died from the plague (Stigler, 1986). Although these descriptive statistics relay information about a morbid topic, demographic information about the people who died from the plague is important for understanding the epidemiology of the disease.

Our current method of collecting data about disease is managed by the U.S. Census and Centers for Disease Control and Prevention (CDC). The staff of the CDC collects descriptive information, or statistics, about many aspects of our lives and then summarize data to provide the public with information about many aspects of public health. For example, the leading cause of death in 2003 was heart disease (www.cdc.gov/nchs/). Although it may not be immediately apparent why psychologists would be interested in this statistic, psychological health can be a factor in heart disease, so these data are an important source for investigations into behavioral health. Similarly, the National Center for Health Statistics, located within the CDC, provides additional data describing behaviors that might contribute to our overall health. These data can also be a valuable source of information for psychologists who want to investigate psychological factors that affect health.

Descriptive Statistics

Descriptive statistics—A tool to help us understand information that we generate and help us to organize large amounts of information in a succinct manner.

We have already discussed the importance of planning (Chapter 3) how we will collect data and gather information. In addition to planning for data collection, we need to organize data using common scientific language. Scientific language includes information about the research method and a description of quantifiable, that is, numerical, information. In other words, we must have a common way of communicating the outcomes of our research. Generally, we use descriptive statistics to convey results from our studies in two ways. First, we describe information about the people who participated in the study. Sample characteristics usually include information about the number of participants and their race, gender, and age. Additional relevant demographic variables are sometimes included. For example, if you are studying children, then it might be useful to report the grade level of the children who participated in the study.

Descriptive statistics are also used to report the outcomes of a study. So, in the case of survey research, we use descriptive statistics to convey quantifiable data that reflect participants' thoughts about a topic or variable of interest. Similarly, in an experimental study, we use descriptive statistics to convey information about the outcomes of the study, or the quantifiable data from the dependent variable. For example, Ginger VanVolkinburg (1998), an undergraduate student attending Missouri Southern College, conducted research to investigate how server posture, specifically, the effect of greeting a customer at eye level, might affect size of tips. She recorded the size of tips left by customers for two different conditions (i.e., servers who stand and servers that greet customers at eye level). In her study, she used descriptive statistics to provide the reader with information about her results; specifically, she used descriptive statistics to report the amount of money (i.e., tip) left by customers in both conditions.

Before we explain specific descriptive statistics, we should consider the different types of data that researchers use. There are different types of data, and we use them in different ways and the underlying properties of the data restrict the types of descriptive statistics that we can use.

Scales of Measurement

The highly respected psychophysicist S. S. Stevens (1951) argued that the numerical information provided by the data we collect depends on the type of measurements we make. Some data are relatively crude, providing information about categories in which observations fall. Other data are more mathematically sophisticated, permitting more complex algebraic manipulation.

As such, Stevens reasoned, some data are appropriate for a given psychological test, but other data are not. Even though there are compelling reasons to believe that Stevens overstated his case greatly, his arguments have had significant impact on the way psychologists organize and analyze data (Gaito, 1980; Lord, 1953; Velleman & Wilkinson, 1993). Nonetheless, controversies and misunderstandings about the issues Stevens raised still persist.

Selection of an appropriate descriptive statistic requires an understanding of the mathematical properties of the information that is being reported. For example, the nature of demographic information about age or about gender is fundamentally different because these variables are derived from two different scales of measurement. Let's begin by considering the most basic **scale of measurement,** categorizing people into different groups.

Scales of measurement—Classification of numerical values on the basis of permissible mathematical functions.

Nominal Scales. Stevens (1951) identified four different levels or scales of measurement—nominal, ordinal, interval, and ratio, with increasing levels of sophistication. *Nominal scales* involve information that is categorical. In other words, the data do not possess an underlying hierarchy that would suggest one category could be placed higher than another category. So, when we are describing a sample of participants in a research study, we generally recognize that people can be classified into one of two sexes, female and male (although there is some argument on that count, too; Fausto-Sterling, 1993). When we categorize people or things, we are engaging in the simplest form of measurement. As we conclude that one person is female and another is male, we are measuring them on a **nominal scale.**

Nominal scale—Allows for classification or categorization of data. A nominal scale uses labels, rather than numbers.

In our earlier example from the Van Volkinburg (1998) study, she used a nominal scale to describe participants by providing the number of men and women servers. Thus, there is not an inherent ranking of these two categories. Nominal scales are useful and appropriate for reporting categorical data; such scales impose limits on the types of descriptive measures that are reported. Nominal data are *qualitative.* In other words we compute the frequency. So, although we can tally the number of men and women in each category, it would not make sense to compute an average for the categories.

Ordinal Scales.   When our measurements do fall on a number line, we are dealing more quantitatively, not just categorically. Data on an **ordinal scale** suggest a hierarchy or a ranking of information that provides a greater level of mathematical sophistication than data on a nominal scale. Ordinal data allow us to indicate that one person or a person's score is higher than another. However, an ordinal scale does not allow us to examine the actual amount of difference between people. As such, we cannot conduct some of the basic mathematical operations, limiting the descriptive statistics we can use with the data.

For example, *US News and World Report* produces an annual ranking of colleges. These rankings indicate a hierarchy or listing of colleges on the basis of criteria that are defined by the publishers of the magazine. Because the data are ranked, there is no way to know how much difference in quality exists between the colleges. In other words, the reader cannot assume equal differences between sets of schools that are separated by the same number of ranks. The difference between the first and second schools may not be the same as the difference between the ninth and tenth schools. We can only deduce that one school is ranked higher than another school.

Interval Scales.   We can go beyond ranking and indicate an amount of difference between two measurements. When we use such measurement, and when the measurement system has an absolute zero (i.e., it will not permit negative numbers), we have a *ratio scale.* However, if the zero point on the scale is arbitrary (i.e., it will allow negative numbers), we have an **interval scale.** When data inherently possess equal intervals across numerical values, the data fall at least on an interval scale of measurement. Equal intervals mean that the distance between 10 and 20 is equivalent to the distance between 40 and 50. As you have seen, on ordinal scales, equal separation by rank does not necessarily mean that the actual differences are equal.

As an example, researchers often report interval-level data when the dependent variable is a number derived from self-report surveys. So, if people report their feeling of anger on a continuum from 1 to 7, the difference between ratings of 1 and 2 should be the same as the difference between ratings of 6 and 7, in other words, the difference of 1. When people report feelings on a continuum, sometimes called the Likert scale, the values reflect an interval scale of measurement. At the same time, the lowest rating does not necessarily reflect a complete absence of anger, in other words, the measurement is not on a ratio scale, which must have a real zero point. We can argue that self-report for any characteristic can not be explicitly measured on an ordinal, interval, or ratio scale. For example, can we really state that the difference in the amount of anger between a rating of 1 and 2 is the same as the difference between 6 and 7? Even scientists (Hays, 1988; Nunnally, 1978) do not always agree with the underlying scale of measurement for many self-report instruments. More importantly, we must consider the application of the information and whether the presumed scale of measurement makes sense. Scientists generally accept self-report Likert scores as interval scales of measurement.

Ratio Scales.   The ratio level scale includes the properties of equal intervals between numerical values, with an additional, distinguishing feature of a ratio level of measurement being the inclusion of an absolute zero. An absolute zero simply means that if a zero is used in calculation of the statistic, then there is an absence of that particular variable. For example, returning to the example about tipping behavior, when considering the tip that the server received, a value of zero would indicate that the server did not receive any money. Thus, size of tip, as a measure of the dependent variable, is reported on a true ratio scale.

Ordinal scale—Allows for information to be placed in a hierarchy, but does not assume equal distances between values.

Interval scale—Contains mathematical properties that suggest equal intervals between values.

TABLE 5.1 *Scales of Measurement*

	Examples
Nominal	Automobile brand, shirt manufacturer, rat strain, gender, blood type
Ordinal	Class rank, placement in a road race, rank classification (i.e., average, above average), military rank, letter grades
Interval	Fahrenheit temperature scale, Likert-type scales, intelligence test scores
Ratio	Height, weight, time that it takes to finish a race, miles per hour, distance traveled.

A **ratio scale** also allows a researcher to describe data as a proportion. So, a tip of $4.00 is twice as large as a tip of $2.00, or a two-to-one ratio. Ratio scales provide the widest range of flexibility in terms of reporting descriptive statistics. From a mathematical standpoint, with a ratio scale, scores retain the original properties of measurement when transformed to a new unit of measurement. For example, regardless of how the tips were reported (e.g., pennies, nickels, or dimes), the ratio would remain constant. By using a ratio scale we can compare a $2.00 tip with a $1.00 tip. The larger tip is twice as big as the smaller one. It would still be twice as big if we transformed it to pennies (200 versus 100) or to a percentage of the bill (20% versus 10%). The stability of the ratio is a characteristic of a ratio scale; it does not hold for scores on an interval scale.

Scales of measurement provide a framework for understanding how data may differ with respect to underlying mathematical properties. Additional examples of scales of measurement are provided in Table 5.1.

However, it is important to note that psychology is a neoteric, or young, science and that measurement of human behavior is still not well understood. Hence, it is not always possible to clearly label data on a particular scale. Furthermore, it is also not the case that discriminating across those scales is all that important. It is more important to relate quantitative information back to the variable of interest (Howell, 2007). In other words, reporting descriptive statistics in a meaningful way (e.g., twice the amount of money) helps to convey important outcomes from a research study. However, when scales of measurement are influential in our use of specific statistics, we will highlight important distinctions.

Measures of Central Tendency

Scientists have suggested that physical and psychological characteristics fall within a normal distribution. **Measures of central tendency** allow us to consider where in the distribution typical values fall relative to the larger group of people. Psychologists generally use three different measures of central tendency to identify what they consider average or typical scores in a distribution—*mode, median,* and *mean.* Each of these measures is easily derived from statistical software. Nevertheless, we will illustrate the mathematical calculations of these statistics so that the underlying meaning of central tendency is clear.

Measures of central tendency and variability form the basis for more complex statistics, including statistical tests. A thorough understanding of these descriptive statistics will be essential to our later discussion about inferential statistics. Researchers regard all of the measures of central tendency as averages, although in everyday use, most people use the word *average* to refer to the mean. In addition to an average, two additional measures of central tendency are available for describing how scores are grouped near the middle of the distribution.

Mode. Organizing and summarizing data helps a reader to quickly understand information about a sample or the outcomes from an empirically based study. The simplest and

Ratio scale—Scale where data possess equal intervals between values and an absolute zero.

Measures of central tendency—Provides a mathematical index of how scores are grouped around the middle of the distribution. There are three measures of central tendency (Mode, Median, Mean).

easiest measure of central tendency is the **mode**—the most frequently occurring score in a distribution. Used infrequently, the mode is helpful when describing peaks in a distribution. Although we refer to the most frequently occurring score as the mode, it is also possible to obtain more than one mode. Two modes would yield a **bimodal distribution,** and several modes, result in a **multimodal distribution** of scores. For example, if we were to consider a distribution of ages for students enrolled in a course much like this one, we might discover the following range of ages.

$$18, 18, 19, 20, 20, 20, 20, 22, 23, 40$$

The mode typically requires no mathematical calculation, and in this distribution the mode would be 20. In other words, four students reported that they were 20 years of age. The mode conveys the least sophisticated measure of central tendency. The mode can be reported regardless of the scale of measurement (i.e., nominal, ordinal, interval, ratio).

Median.   The **median** (*Mdn*) is the halfway point in the distribution. Although the definition of the median seems simple, it is important to remember that you must organize each of the values in increasing order of magnitude before calculating the median. If we are using a small number of values, calculation of the median is relatively simple. We can easily rank the scores and examine the distribution for the center point. When a distribution contains an odd number of scores, the *Mdn* is simply the middle value in the list of scores. With even numbers of scores, it may be necessary to calculate a median value, or midpoint between two scores. For example, using a distribution of 10 age scores, we could count upwards five values or downward five values. In either case, we would discover that the halfway point falls between two occurrences of age 20.

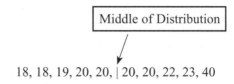

When the midpoint or the median falls between two scores, a *Mdn* can be calculated by adding the two middle scores together and then dividing by 2. In this case the *Mdn* will still be 20 years of age. However, if the two values are different, the median may reflect a fractional value. Researchers used to employ a more sophisticated calculation, or interpolation, when tied scores were present at the median point. Statistical software now quickly generates exact median values for large data sets, so a more thorough presentation of interpolation is not necessary. The important thing to understand is that the median reflects the halfway point in any distribution, or the 50th %.

It is important to note that the median is a useful measure of central tendency in specific circumstances. Three conditions suggest use of a median as the preferred measure of central tendency if a distribution contains at least one extreme score, sometimes called an outlier, if the scores are ordinal in nature, or if the distribution is skewed.

Mean.   The **mean,** as a measure of central tendency, is used frequently when researchers report both demographic characteristics of participants and measures of the dependent variable. Quite simply, the mean is what most people think of as the average; you add up the values and divide by the number of values you added. Statistical notation for calculation of the mean employs the use of a summation sign ($\sum$), a symbol that represents each value in

Mode—The most frequently occurring score in a distribution.

Bimodal distribution— A distribution that contains two modes.

Multimodal distribution—Contains more than two modes; in other words, the most frequently occurring score occurs at several points in the distribution.

Median (*Mdn***)**—The halfway point in a distribution.

Mean (*M***)**—The arithmetic average of a distribution of scores.

the distribution (X), a symbol that indicates the total number of scores in the distribution (N), and a symbol to represent the Mean (M or $\overline{X}$).

$$M = \frac{\sum X}{N} \quad \text{OR} \quad \overline{X} = \frac{\sum X}{N}$$

Using this formula, we can easily derive a mean or average from the data we presented above. The first step in this process is to add or sum all of the ages or values ($\sum X = 220$) in our sample. In order to complete the calculation, we simply divide by the total number of individuals in our sample ($N = 10$). This calculation is illustrated below.

$$M = \frac{220}{10}$$

Using data from our distribution of ages, we find that the mean for the distribution is 22. A summary of the measures of central tendency for these data would be correctly reported as follows:

$$Mode = 20$$
$$Mdn = 20$$
$$M = 22$$

Note that there are conventions in using APA style to correctly report statistical values. The *Publication Manual of the American Psychological Association* (2010) defines explicit rules for scientific writing, including detailed descriptions of how statistics should appear in research. In this case, the statistical notation is reported in an italic font as specified by the APA Publication Manual.

We have illustrated calculation of a simple mean value. In addition to a simple mean, statisticians use a multitude of other averages (e.g., geometric and harmonic means) but we will only discuss use of the simple mean because this is the measure of central tendency that is most common.

We have described calculation of the mean for a sample, the ages of people taking a statistics course. Most often we have only a sample, but the sample is derived from a larger population of individuals. In this example, the population might be all students taking statistics at a particular college. Notation for a population mean (μ), pronounced "mew," uses a Greek symbol. (The symbol for population mean is not reported in italic font.) We use M to report the mean of our sample rather than population mean symbol (μ). The μ symbol is not typically used to report a mean because we don't often have access to an entire population. Population mean will be discussed further in Chapter 7 when we provide information about calculating inferential statistics.

Distributions of Scores

We have described how to derive measures of central tendency, or values that describe a central point within a set of scores. Quite often measures of central tendency are considered within the context of a normal distribution. Most of the data in a normal distribution are grouped near the center of the bell-shaped curve, and very few data points are located near the ends, or tails of the distribution. This **normal**, or Gaussian, **distribution** is predicated on the theoretical notion that scores are distributed according to a probability model (Hays, 1988). Theoretically, this distribution suggests that a large percentage of individuals are normal, or that most of these data fall within a central range of scores, and very few people

Normal distribution— A theoretical distribution of scores associated with percentiles reflected in the population.

fall at the extreme ends of the distribution. For example, average height for women is 64 inches (Ogden et al., 2004) or 5 feet 4 inches tall. Because height is normally distributed, most women are close to average height, with the largest percentage of women ranging in height between approximately 60 to 68 inches. Extremely tall or short women (i.e., seven feet or four feet tall) are relatively unusual, so in a normal distribution, only a small percentage of women would be in the tail of the distribution.

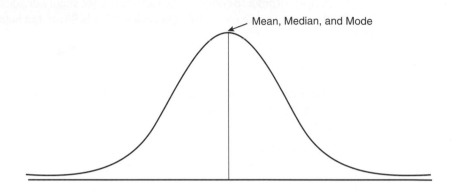

Mean, Median, and Mode

The normal distribution possesses specific characteristics. First, the shape of the distribution is always symmetrical. Second, the mean, median, and mode are located at the exact midpoint of the curve. Because the area underneath the curve contains 100% of the population, we can use the normal distribution to convey information about relative placement of a score. For example, because the median splits a distribution exactly in half, and we know that the median, mean, and mode are located in the middle of a normal distribution, we can easily see that this point breaks the distribution into two equal amounts, 50%, as the figure shows.

The normal distribution also provides a mechanism for locating scores at specific locations within the distribution—percentile placements. Returning to our census data describing heights for women, most women would be placed near the middle of the distribution, and only a few women (very tall or very short) would be located near the ends of the distribution. Although the normal distribution provides a helpful way of comparing relative height, the distribution is also important as a basis for more complex statistical analyses. We will describe the normal curve in more detail when we discuss the logic of probability and statistical testing (Chapter 7).

Not all distributions are normal. Sometimes we obtain a set of scores that are unusual and that would not allow us to use the assumptions underlying the normal distribution. When the three measures of central tendency do not match up in the center of the distribution we have a *skewed* distribution. Distributions can be skewed in one of two directions (positive or negative). Labeling of these distributions refers to the tails of the distribution. A **positively skewed** distribution suggests that most of the scores are grouped at the lower end of the distribution and the tail is pointed in the positive direction. If we collect a sample of women who are unusually short, we would obtain a positively skewed distribution because the majority of the women would be grouped at the lower end of the distribution. A **negatively skewed** distribution includes scores that are concentrated at the high end of the distribution and the tail is pointed in a negative direction. In this instance, we might have an unusually tall group of women.

Skewed distributions indicate that a large percentage of scores are grouped together at one end of the distribution. This unusual arrangement changes the placement of measures of

Positively skewed—A distribution with unusual variability. Most of the data are grouped at the lower end of the distribution and one outlier is typically contained at the upper end of the distribution. The tail of the distribution points in a positive direction.

Negatively skewed—A distribution with unusual variability. Most of the data are grouped at the upper end of the distribution and one outlier is typically contained at the lower end of the distribution. The tail of the distribution points in a negative direction.

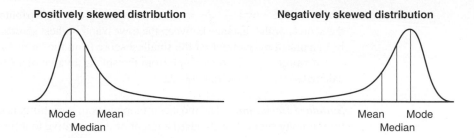

central tendency. In a positively skewed distribution, the mean is located closest to the tail and may provide an artificially high measure of central tendency. Skewed distributions are non-normal and the mean ceases to be useful as a measure of a typical score. As illustrated in the figure above, the median is located closer to the peak of the distribution. The median actually offers a more useful measure of central tendency as it reflects the midpoint or 50th % for the distribution. In a positively skewed distribution, the mode is the lowest value of the three measures of central tendency, and is located at the highest point in the curve. So, when a distribution is positively skewed (many low values), the measures of central tendency are distributed such that the mode is the lowest value, followed by the median, and finally the highest reported value of the mean.

Measures of central tendency are distributed in a similar manner for the negatively skewed distribution. However, the values associated with the measures of central tendency are exactly the reverse of the positively skewed distribution. Again, the mean is located nearest the tail and the mode is the highest point in the curve, but the mean in a negatively skewed distribution is the lowest reported measure of central tendency. Similarly the median and mode reflect increasingly higher values.

A normal distribution is shaped like a bell, with measures of central tendency grouped together near the middle of the curve. These measures of central tendency are slightly offset in skewed distributions, yet they still provide important descriptive information about the central area in the distribution. Although useful, measures of central tendency alone do provide a complete picture of the data. In addition to measures of central tendency, we must consider the spread, or the relative location of scores as indexed by measures of variability. Measures of variability are based on the normal distribution or theoretical distribution generated by an equation. When we use numbers from actual research, distributions are never perfectly normal, although they tend to be close to it. Nevertheless, as we discuss measures of variability, we can generally use the normal distribution as a model for understanding variability.

Measures of Variability

Measures of variability—Provides a mathematical index of how spread out the scores are around the mean. There are three measures of variability (Range, Variance, Standard Deviation).

A description of how data fall relative to typical scores in a distribution provides a necessary, but incomplete, understanding of the larger picture. Sometimes data are grouped closely together. For example, if we obtain a sample of college students, it is quite likely that age will range from 18 to 22 years. In other words, the ages or data do not span a very large range of values. Alternatively, if we obtained ages from a group of people attending an exercise class offered at a local gym, the ages of those individuals may be much more diverse or spread out. In order to illustrate the complete picture, it would be necessary to report an index, or some value, that reflects this difference in the distribution of scores. Scientists have created several **measures of variability** to help describe how scores are distributed, including the range, variance, and standard deviation.

Range.   The simplest way to describe how scores are distributed is to consider the range of the scores, or the distance between the lowest and highest scores. In fact, this single value can be calculated by subtracting the smallest score from the largest score is a descriptive statistic called **range.** So, if scores range from the smallest value of 18 to the largest value of 40, the calculated value of the range is 22.

Standard Deviation.   The most common index of variability is the **standard deviation.** This terminology suggests a standard amount or unit, relative to a fixed point. Indeed the standard deviation is an index of variability that reflects a fixed distance from the mean of the distribution, the distance a typical score falls from the mean. To fully understand how the standard deviation contributes to the description of the variability of the data, we will need to explain how to derive this value. Using our original data set from the statistics class, we already know the average value, or $M = 22$.

$$18, 18, 19, 20, 20, 20, 20, 22, 23, 40$$

These data also appear to be closely grouped together. It would be much more efficient to be able to report a single value that reflects how closely to the mean the numbers of the distribution tend to be. Therefore, our first step in calculating a standard deviation will be to subtract the mean from each of the values in the distribution to obtain a *deviation score,* reflecting the deviation of that score from the mean (see Table 5.2).

Range—The difference between the highest and lowest scores in the distribution.

What is wrong with simply calculating an average distance from the mean of the distribution, or an average deviation score? Conceptually, this is exactly what we hope to do. Unfortunately, an examination of these data reveals that the sum of these values $\sum(X - M)$ equals 0. Therefore, this average does not provide us with a very meaningful measure of variability. Summing the deviation scores will *always* produce a zero value because distances from the mean vary equally above the mean and below the mean. Therefore, it will be necessary to apply a mathematical transformation that will allow for calculation of the standard deviation, or a standardized value, an index of variability around the mean.

Standard deviation—An index of variability or standard distance from the mean, as reported in raw score values.

The second step in calculating the standard deviation is to square each of the deviation scores. Squaring each of these values (deviation scores) produces only positive values and

TABLE 5.2   *Deviation Scores*

X	M	X − M
18	22	−4
18	22	−4
19	22	−3
20	22	−2
20	22	−2
20	22	−2
20	22	−2
22	22	0
23	22	1
40	22	18
		$\sum = 0$

the sum of the squared values is called the sum of squares (*SS*). The conceptual formula for calculating the *SS* is as follows:

$$SS = \sum(X - M)^2$$

An alternative computational formula is illustrated in the following box.

Computational Sum of Squares Calculation

The sum of squares (*SS*) allows us to obtain an overall measure of how far scores deviate from the mean. In other words the *SS* captures all of the variability among scores. We can calculate the *SS* by subtracting the mean from each individual value, squaring the deviations, and summing the values. However, subtracting the mean from each score can be difficult and has the potential for more error. Rather than using subtraction, we can use an alternate formula for calculating the *SS*. The computational *SS* formula is as follows:

$$SS = \sum X^2 - \frac{(\sum X)^2}{N}$$

It is quite simple to calculate the *SS* using this formula.

X	X²
18	324
18	324
19	361
20	400
20	400
20	400
20	400
22	484
23	529
40	1600
$\sum X = 220$	$\sum X^2 = 5222$

Hence, the equivalent *SS* calculation is:

$$SS = \sum X^2 - \frac{(\sum X)^2}{N}$$

$$SS = 5222 - \frac{(220)^2}{10}$$

$$SS = 5222 - \frac{48400}{10}$$

$$SS = 5222 - 4840$$

$$SS = 382$$

You will notice that this calculation yields a value that is identical to that of our earlier calculation (*SS* = 382). We will use this computational version of the sum of squares formula in our subsequent analyses.

We can now use these positive scores for the next step in calculating the standard or typical distance of scores that scores vary from the mean (see Table 5.3).

Transformation of the deviation score, squaring each of the deviation values, eliminates the negative values that prevented us from deriving the standard deviation, or index of variability from the mean. So, the next step is to obtain an average from these transformed scores. The squared values are added and the summed value is referred to as the *sum of the squares* or *SS*; $\sum(X - M)^2 = 382$.

We are attempting to derive an index of variability that quickly conveys information about the spread of scores around the central point in the distribution, therefore, our next step in the process will be to derive an average from the sum of the squares value;

TABLE 5.3 *Calculating SS*

X	M	X − M	(X − M)²
18	22	−4	16
18	22	−4	16
19	22	−3	9
20	22	−2	4
20	22	−2	4
20	22	−2	4
20	22	−2	4
22	22	0	0
23	22	1	1
40	22	18	324
			SS = 382

$s^2 = \dfrac{\sum(X - M)^2}{N} = 38.2$.* This value ($s^2 = 38.2$) is an average, but it is not the standard deviation. Instead, this value is the average of the sum of the squares, and this average is labeled in specific statistical terminology as the **variance** or s^2.

In other words, the variance is the average of the sum of squares. The variance then, serves as an intermediate step toward calculation of the standard deviation.

One final step remains for calculation of the standard deviation. Because we squared each of the deviation scores, the square effect must now be removed. In order to remove this effect, it is necessary to apply the square root to the average of the sum of the squares, or variance. In other words we apply the square root to remove the earlier squaring of values.

Application of this step is as follows:

$$SD = \sqrt{\dfrac{\sum(X - M)^2}{N}} = \sqrt{38.2} = 6.18$$

or

$$SD = 6.18$$

Variance—Average of squared deviations from the mean.

Our calculated standard deviation provides an easily interpretable index or average amount of distance from the center of the distribution of scores. We know that not every score falls at the mean. The value of the standard deviation here suggests that, on average, the typical discrepancy between a given score and the mean is about 6.18.

---

*When calculating variance for a *population*, N is the denominator. Calculation for the *sample* variance uses degrees of freedom for the denominator ($N - 1$). A truly unbiased estimate of the population standard deviation would require use of Hays (1988, pp. 203–204) classic formula: $E(\sigma) = \left[1 + \dfrac{1}{4(N - 1)} \right] s$ and this calculation is beyond the scope of this text. We use N as the denominator for calculation of variance and standard deviation when reporting descriptive statistics from our study. SPSS uses $N - 1$ as the denominator to calculate variance and standard deviation. You will find a slight difference in your calculations and those of SPSS.

If we obtained another sample in which the ages of people were different, it is quite possible that we would have a wider range of scores and a larger standard deviation. For example, if we collected the ages from people enrolled in an evening section, or online section of this course, it is quite likely that there would be more diversity in the ages of the people taking the class. We can use the following data to calculate a standard deviation that reflects the wider range of scores (see Table 5.4).

$$18, 20, 22, 30, 35, 40, 40, 50, 55, 60$$

Calculation of the standard deviation for these data is illustrated below.

$$SS = \sum (X - M)^2 = 1968$$

$$s^2 = \frac{\sum (X - M)^2}{N} = 196.8$$

$$SD = \sqrt{\frac{\sum (X - M)^2}{N}} = 14.03$$

The calculated value of the standard deviation ($SD = 14.03$) indicates that the scores in this distribution are, in general, further apart. On average, scores, or the ages of the participants, deviate approximately 14 points from the mean. A quick visual inspection of the actual ages in the sample reveals that these data are more spread out than the scores from the first set of data ($SD = 6.18$).

The standard deviation, the standard index of variability, is calculated from a sample of scores and we use SD as the statistical notation for reporting. As noted earlier, statistical measures for a population, or **parameters,** are reported using Greek symbols. Sigma (σ) is the notation for a population standard deviation. Because the standard deviation is the square root of the variance, the population variance would simply be sigma squared, or σ^2.

Parameter—A statistical measure used to describe a population.

The standard deviation is the most common measure of variability reported in journal articles. One reason for the frequent use of the standard deviation is that standard deviation

TABLE 5.4 *Calculating SS*

X	M	X − M	(X − M)²
18	37	−19	361
20	37	−17	289
22	37	−15	225
30	37	−7	49
35	37	−2	4
40	37	3	9
40	37	3	9
50	37	13	169
55	37	18	324
60	37	23	529
			$\sum = 1968$

FIGURE 5.1   *Normal Curve*

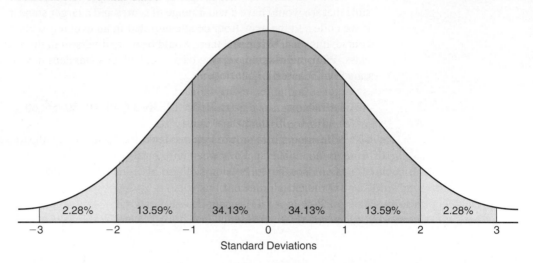

units are associated with particular points on a normal distribution. Each standard deviation point is linked to a particular percentile within the normal distribution.

As illustrated in Figure 5.1, the standard deviation units break the distribution into defined sections. Most of the scores in any normal distribution will fall between one standard deviation above and below the mean, and this percentage will be approximately 68% of the population. These percentages remain constant as long as we are referencing a normal distribution and it allows for researchers to use a common metric to convey information about the index of variability.

Earlier, we described distributions that were unusual because the measures of central tendency were not located in the middle of the distribution, resulting in skewed distributions. Unusual variability in data can also produce unusual or non-normal distributions. The distribution cannot only be skewed, but the shape can be very peaked or very flat and this characteristic is labeled kurtosis. When a distribution is normally distributed, the curve would be described as *mesokurtotic* as illustrated in Figure 5.2. If the standard deviation is small, or the scores are very close together, the distribution will appear peaked. This type of distribution is *leptokurtotic*. When the standard deviation is large, or the scores are very spread out, the distribution would be flatter or *platykurtotic*.

Summarizing Data

Descriptions of data include measures of central tendency *and* measures of variability. Selection of the appropriate descriptive measures requires careful consideration of the nature of the data. In other words, it is important to consider the scale used to derive each of the individual

FIGURE 5.2   *Kurtosis*

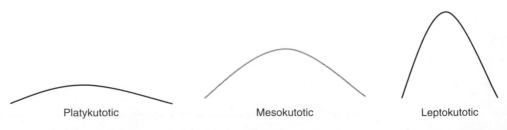

Platykutotic   Mesokutotic   Leptokutotic

scores and how to communicate the information in a clear and concise manner. Descriptive statistics are used to describe participants in a research study and to report the outcomes of the study by reporting summary information about the dependent variable. Measures of central tendency and variability together provide a complete picture or the data. In our examples, we calculated measures of central tendency and variance for the ages of people in two different samples. Because data (i.e., age) are on a ratio scale we report the mean and standard deviation as the respective measures of central tendency and variability. Thus, an example or description of these groups using data about ages is provided below.

> Twenty participants were recruited from two different classes, a daytime college statistics course ($n = 10$) and night class ($n = 10$). Six of the participants were men and 14 of the participants were women. The average age for students enrolled in the day class was 22 ($SD = 6.18$), and for the night class the average age was 37 ($SD = 14.02$).

Use of appropriate reporting style is critical when conveying scientific findings. The *Publication Manual of the American Psychological Association* (2010) provides rules for writing scientifically. Hence, it is not permissible to begin a sentence by using a figure to express an amount, so we used the word "twenty" instead of the value "20" in the example above. We reference the total number of people contained in the sample as *N,* and subsets of the larger sample are referenced by using a lowercase *n.* We also use typical conventions to report measures of central tendency and variability. For example, whenever a mean value is reported, the standard deviation should also be reported as is illustrated in the example above. Combining this information provides a more comprehensive picture of the data. One final note about statistical reporting: Statistical symbols (e.g., *n, SD*) should be reported in italic.

Computer Analysis Using SPSS

We explained how measures of central tendency and variability are calculated; however, statistical software packages produce these measures very quickly. It would not be efficient to regularly calculate these values manually for large data sets. Throughout this text we will be describing how to use Statistical Package for Social Sciences, or SPSS, to illustrate analyze quickly, and report data.

Generating Descriptive Statistics

After entering your data into the spreadsheet section of SPSS, it is easy to get descriptive statistics. We may enter all of our data into a single spreadsheet. However, if we want to generate descriptive statistics for two groups that are contained in a single sample of data, we need to specify that we want two sets of descriptive statistics. Using our example data, we need to split the data file, and then perform the descriptive data analysis. To split a file:

Click on data.
Split file.
A dialogue box will appear.
Select the variable designating the two groups.

In our example, we are splitting the file based on day or night classes, and this variable is labeled class. The steps for this process are illustrated in Figure 5.3.

FIGURE 5.3   *Generating Descriptive Statistics*

Splitting a file	Dialogue Box	Basic descriptive statistics

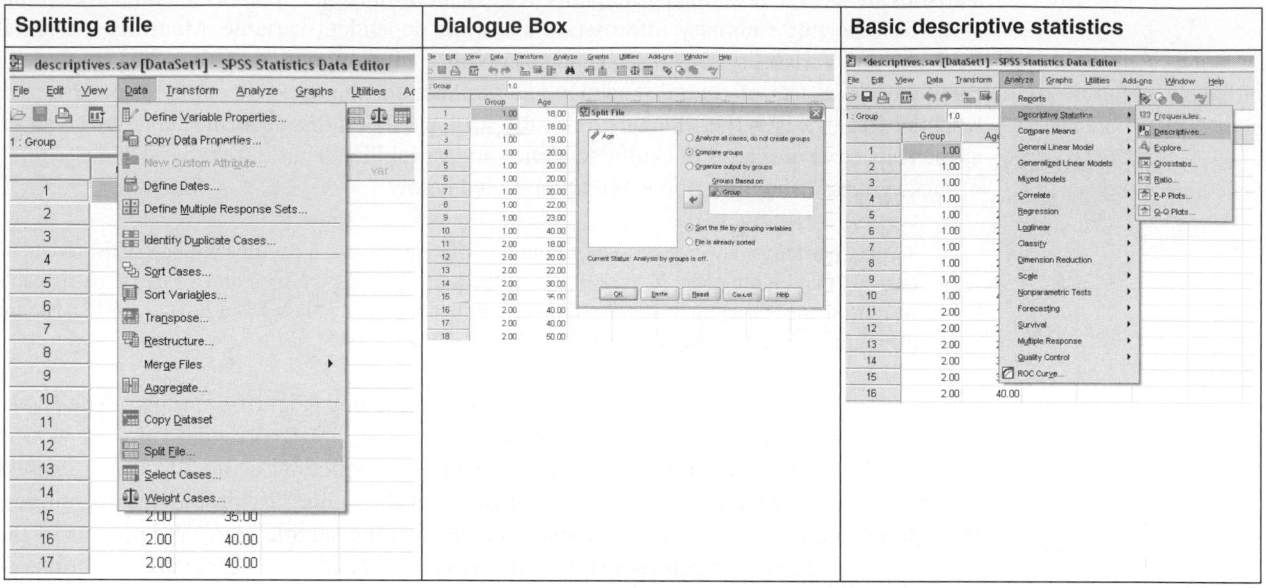

You can obtain basic descriptive statistics (i.e., Mean, Standard Deviation) using the analysis function as illustrated above. SPSS will quickly produce common measures of central tendency and variability (see Table 5.5).

If a more complete set of descriptive statistics is desired, the *explore* function should be used as illustrated in Figure 5.4. This function produces the median value and additional descriptive information about the distribution.

Illustrating Descriptive Statistics

Charts and graphs are frequently used to illustrate descriptive information about participants or the dependent variable. Selection of a graphing format is dependent on the type of data collected. Two broad categories of data should be considered. *Discrete* or categorical data classify participants into distinct or separate groups. Examples of discrete data typically used to describe participants include gender and race. *Continuous* data suggests an underlying continuity of numerical values. Examples of continuous descriptive data include such variables as age.

TABLE 5.5   *SPSS Data Output*

Descriptive Statistics						
	Class	*N*	*Minimum*	*Maximum*	*Mean*	*Std. Deviation*
Day Class	Age	10	18.00	40.00	22.0000	6.51494
	Valid N (listwise)	10				
Night Class	Age	10	18.00	60.00	37.0000	14.78738
	Valid N (listwise)	10				

FIGURE 5.4   *Producing Expanded Descriptive Statistics*

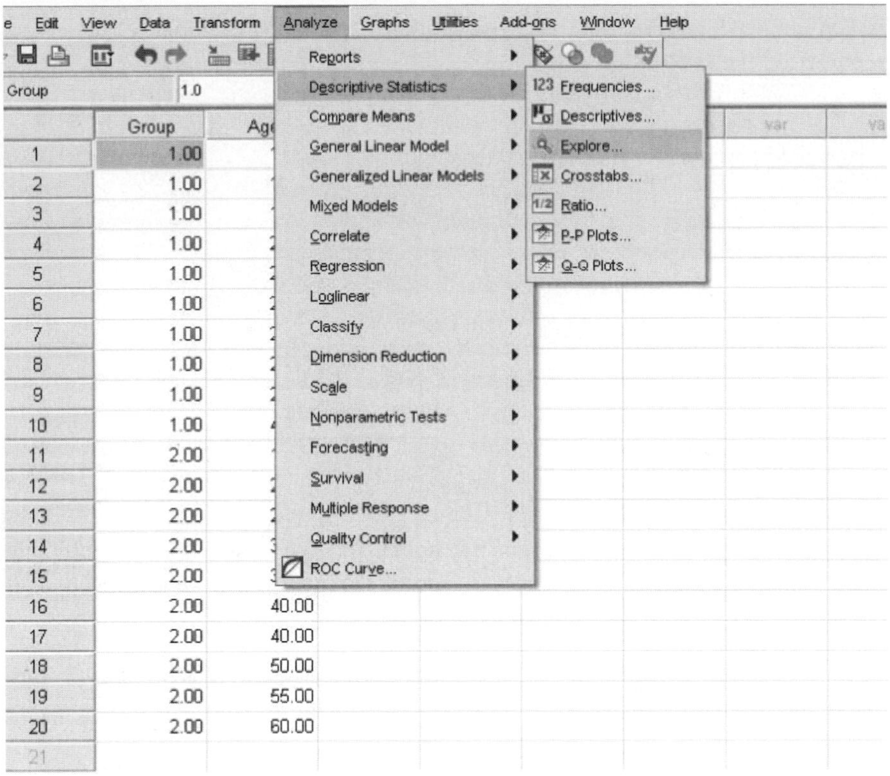

Bar Chart.   If we consider the sample of participants from the statistics course, we may wish to illustrate the number of men and women participating in our study. A categorical variable, such as gender, would allow us to use a bar chart or a pie chart. SPSS produces charts and graphs under the graphing function. Steps for producing a bar chart are illustrated in Figure 5.5. First select the graphing function, then select the simple bar chart and when the dialogue box appears, select gender as the variable of interest.

The bar graph clearly illustrates the disparate number of men and women participants. A bar chart and histogram orient graphs using an *x* and *y* axis. The *y* axis is used to illustrate frequency, or the number of participants possessing a particular characteristic. Note this bar chart reflects the total number of participants (see Figure 5.6).

If we wish to examine the number of men and women in each class, we can use the Crosstabs function to produce a bar chart that illustrates gender within each class. Steps for producing a bar chart reflecting both of these variables are illustrated in Figure 5.7.

Histogram.   Age is a continuous variable and requires use of a histogram instead of a bar or pie chart. Although a histogram displays data using bars, the bars in a histogram touch each other, suggesting the continuous nature of the data displayed. Therefore, to produce an illustration of ages for all of participants (not just one of the classes) we would use the graphing function (Figure 5.8) to produce a histogram whenever we have a variable that is continuous.

FIGURE 5.5 *Producing a Bar Chart*

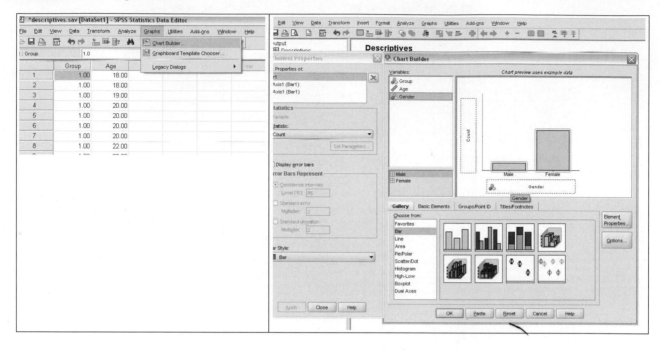

FIGURE 5.6 *Bar Chart of Gender Variable*

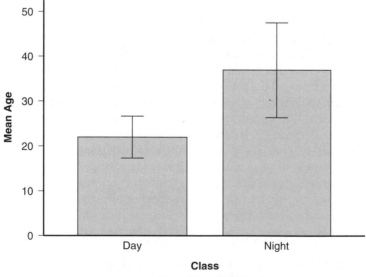

FIGURE 5.7 *Steps for Producing Gender by Class Bar Chart*

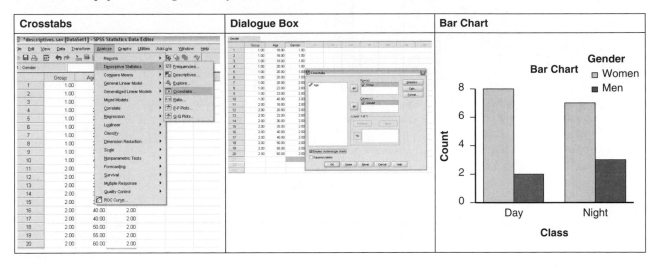

FIGURE 5.8 *Producing a Histogram*

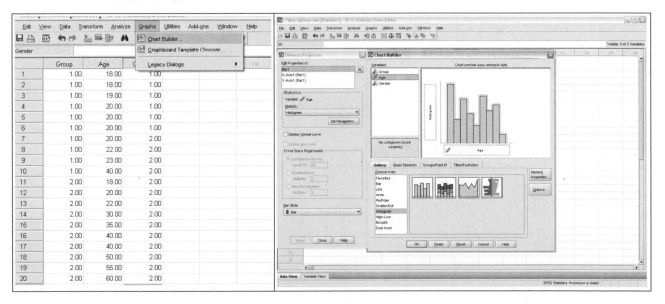

FIGURE 5.9 *Histogram of Age Variable*

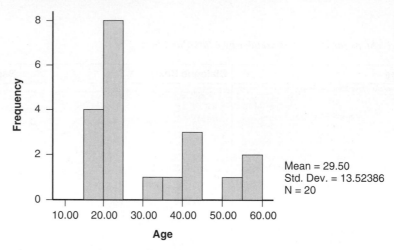

The histogram illustrating the ages of participants appears in Figure 5.9.

A frequency polygon differs from a histogram only in the presentation of data. Rather than displaying data in the form of bars, the frequency polygon (Figure 5.10) illustrates data in a line format. To produce a frequency polygon, select line from the graphing function.

When graphing data to illustrate demographic variables, we use information or data about the frequency of the values. As we indicated at the beginning of this chapter, descriptive statistics can be used to provide information about demographic characteristics of the sample. The frequency polygon and histogram allow you to illustrate characteristics of the people who participate in your study.

Descriptive statistics can also be used to describe the outcome of a study. For example, if we wanted to try to improve grades in a statistics class, we might implement a special intervention or tutoring program for one of our courses. The intervention would be the independent

FIGURE 5.10 *Frequency Polygon for Age*

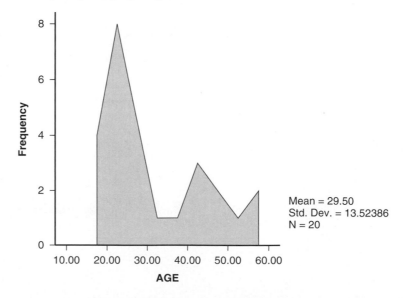

variable. In order to measure the effect of the tutoring program, we might examine the grades from this class. Grades, in this case, would be a measure of the outcome of the tutoring program, or dependent variable. In order to plot the outcome of this study, you would need to illustrate the independent variable and the dependent variable. Researchers use graphs to illustrate the effects of the independent variable (tutoring) on the dependent variable (grades). Fortunately, deciding how to plot the independent and dependent variables follows a specific set of rules. The independent variable is placed on the *x* axis or the horizontal line. The dependent variable is located on the *y* axis and in this case is the average grade earned by students in each of the groups.

Chapter Summary

When we plan our research, we need to carefully consider exactly how we want to measure or quantify the information we are most interested in discovering. We may want to know how we can earn the largest amount of money through tips, or we might want to know which intervention is most effective. The only way to fully understand these outcomes is to assign a numerical value, or quantify this information. Although we don't often reference the term **descriptive statistics,** we quantify many aspects of our world using descriptive statistics every day. For example, we are bombarded with information about buying trends, political polls and frequency of common behaviors. These statistics are descriptive and easily accessible to most of the general population.

In this chapter we provided a thorough explanation of statistics that are typically used to describe the outcomes of research and common phenomena reported in the media. The only real difference between the statistics in this chapter and those in the media is that we described how these statistics are calculated. Descriptive statistics serve as a common language among researchers. Understanding these statistics will allow you to comprehend reporting of both primary and secondary research.

Key Terms

Bimodal distribution	Mode	Positively skewed
Descriptive statistics	Multimodal distribution	Range
Interval scale	Negatively skewed	Ratio scale
Mean	Nominal scale	Scales of measurement
Measures of central tendency	Normal distribution	Standard deviation
Measures of variability	Ordinal scale	Variance
Median	Parameter	

Chapter Review Questions

Multiple Choice Questions

1. Media reports of race results often list the first three people to finish the race. Data reported in this format use which of the following scales?
   a. Nominal
   b. Ordinal
   c. Interval
   d. Ratio

2. Sometimes the media also report the finishing times for racers. Data reported in this format use which of the following scales?
   a. Nominal
   b. Ordinal
   c. Interval
   d. Ratio

3. An undergraduate research team collected demographic data to describe their sample. They reported ethnicity of the participants. Data are reported using which of the following scales?
   a. Nominal
   b. Ordinal
   c. Interval
   d. Ratio

4. Researchers collected data designed to describe annual salary information for teachers. Most of the data were similar, but one of the salaries was a significant outlier. Which of the following measures of central tendency is most appropriate for reporting the data?
   a. Mean
   b. Median
   c. Standard Deviation
   d. Variance

5. When data are reported using the ordinal scale, which of the following measures of central tendency is most appropriate?
   a. Mean
   b. Median
   c. Variance
   d. Standard Deviation

6. What is the median for the following data: 5, 4, 6, 8, 2?
   a. 2
   b. 4
   c. 5
   d. 6

7. What is the mean for the following set of data: 5, 4, 6, 8, 2?
   a. 3
   b. 4
   c. 5
   d. 6

8. Which of the following provides an index of variability around the mean of the distribution?
   a. Range
   b. Standard Deviation
   c. Variance
   d. Median Split

9. The variance is a measure of:
   a. an index of variability around the mean.
   b. an approximate average of the sum of the squares.
   c. a range of scores.
   d. central tendency.

10. A leptokurtotic curve indicates which of the following?
    a. A large standard deviation
    b. A medium standard deviation

c. A small standard deviation
d. A large range

Essay Questions

11. VanVolkinburg (1998) wanted to find a way to increase tips for servers at restaurants. Which scale of measurement did she use to report the outcome of her study?

12. VanVolinburg (1998) also reported information about the participants in her study. What scale of measurement is used for reporting gender? What scale of measurement is used for reporting age?

13. Which measure of central tendency is most appropriate for reporting ages of participants?

14. Which demographic characteristic would most appropriately use the mode as a measure of central tendency?

15. If the ages for participants are skewed, which measure of central tendency would be most appropriate?

16. A researcher reported that the mean or average age of participants was 22 and the standard deviation was 2. The youngest participant was 18 and the oldest participant was 28. Use this information to describe the distribution of ages.

17. If the range of ages was 40 (instead of 10), but the standard deviation remained constant, how would you describe the distribution?

Practice Exercises

18. Students reported their age as a demographic variable when they agreed to participate in a research study. Identify the scale of measurement and calculate the respective measures of central tendency and the requisite measures of variability. The data appear below:

    39, 27, 21, 21, 23, 21, 22, 21, 22, 20

19. Two sets of data are contained in the table below. The group data simply identify the treatment group. The DV data reflect the level of perceived guilt on a Likert scale. Specify the scale of measurement for each variable. Report the group and DV data using the appropriate descriptive statistics.

Group	DV
1	2
3	4
2	5
1	4
1	3
2	4
1	3
3	6
3	3
2	5

20. Use the data from question 19 to construct a bar graph for the group variable.

21. Use the data from question 19 to construct a frequency polygon for the DV.

22. Using the data, describe the measures of variability. Explain the relationship between the variables using the range and standard deviation.

Variable 1	Variable 2
6	18
3	21
2	21
6	21
3	19
6	19
4	21
3	22
6	19
3	19

CONDUCTING AN EXPERIMENT: GENERAL PRINCIPLES

CHAPTER OUTLINE

CHOOSING A METHODOLOGY: THE PRACTICALITIES OF RESEARCH

DETERMINING THE CAUSES OF BEHAVIOR
Trying to Determine Causation in Research
Requirements for Cause–Effect Relationships
Internal and External Validity

THE LOGIC OF EXPERIMENTAL MANIPULATION

EXPERIMENTAL CONTROL
Threats to Internal Validity
Lack of Control in Experimental Research: Extraneous
Variables and Confounds

CONTROVERSY: DO WOMEN FEAR SUCCESS?

EXPERIMENTER EFFECTS

PARTICIPANT EFFECTS
The Hawthorne Effect

INTERACTION EFFECTS BETWEEN EXPERIMENTERS AND PARTICIPANTS
Biosocial and Psychosocial Effects

REALISM IN RESEARCH

LEARNING OBJECTIVES

■ Differentiate experimental from nonexperimental research design.

■ Identify the three criteria for establishing cause-and-effect relations.

■ Define the concept of causal ambiguity.

■ Differentiate experimental, control, and placebo groups.

■ Describe special ethical considerations in research in clinical psychology and medicine.

■ Explain the concept of measurement error.

■ Identify and explain the different types of reliability.

■ Identify and explain the different types of validity.

■ Explain why validity implies reliability, but reliability does not imply validity.

■ Describe the process and purpose of random assignment of participants to groups.

CHAPTER PREVIEW

If you want to study behavior, it is useful to be able to describe and predict behavior, but it will be more satisfying to know why people act the way they do. It is relatively easy to observe different kinds of behavior and, from there, to make predictions about other behaviors. Most of us have a general sense of how people are going to act in certain circumstances (although we are fooled often enough). The next goal in psychology is to understand the causes of behavior.

In research, we choose experimental designs when we want to discover causation. Descriptive approaches can be quite useful for making predictions about behavior, but they do not inform us about the underlying reasons for those behaviors.

In the simplest experiment, the researcher creates a treatment group that will be compared to an untreated, or control, group. If the two groups start equal but end up different, we presume that the treatment made a difference. In practice, most studies employ more than two groups, but the logic is the same regardless of the number of groups.

Complications arise in any research project because small details of the research situation often have effects on participants' behaviors that we don't anticipate or even recognize. Further, because an experimental session involves an interaction between people—an experimenter and a participant—social effects can contribute to changes in behavior.

Choosing a Methodology: The Practicalities of Research

In psychology, the word **experiment** has a specific meaning. It refers to a research design in which the investigator actively manipulates and controls variables. Scientists regard experimental methods of research as the gold standard against which we compare other approaches because experiments let us determine what causes behavior, leading to the ultimate scientific goal—control. In general, researchers often prefer experiments over other methods such as surveys, observational studies, or other descriptive and correlational approaches even though studies that describe and predict behaviors provide important information about thought and behavior.

It is important to understand the difference between an experiment and other ways of carrying out a research project. It can be confusing sometimes because in everyday language people often refer to any data collection project as an experiment. In fact, until the middle of the 1900s, psychologists, like other scientists, referred to any research project as an experiment. Since then, however, psychologists have used the term in a specific way.

An experiment is a methodology in which a researcher controls variables systematically. As researchers alter the level, intensity, frequency, or duration of a variable, they examine any resulting change in behavior in the person or animal being studied. As such, research is experimental only when the investigator has control over the variable that might affect a behavior. By controlling and manipulating variables systematically, we can determine which variables influence behaviors that we are studying.

Experiment—A research project in which the investigator creates initially equivalent groups, systematically manipulates an independent variable, and compares the groups to see if the independent variable affected the subsequent behavior.

Given that we recognize the advantage of the experimental approach, we still value nonexperimental approaches because of their strengths. For example, suppose we wanted to know whether the amount of sleep a pregnant woman gets affects a baby's weight at birth. It would be unethical to force a woman to get a certain number of hours of sleep each night. It would also be impossible to do. You can't force people to sleep. In addition, in the course of living a life, people don't always stick to the same schedule every day. There are too many inconsistencies in people's lives to permit strict control over sleeping schedules.

An investigator who wanted to see the relation between amount of sleep women get and their newborn babies' weights would have two basic options: to experiment with nonhuman animals or to use a nonexperimental method.

In some areas of psychology, the experimental approach predominates. In other domains, researchers choose other methods. In the end, the choice of research strategies depends on the practicalities of the project. Sometimes experiments are possible and feasible, sometimes they are possible but not realistic. Sometimes they are simply impossible. Psychologists have to use good judgment and creativity in deciding what will work best in their research.

Determining the Causes of Behavior

Describing behavior is fairly easy. Predicting behavior is usually more difficult. Understanding exactly why people act as they do and controlling behavior is fiendishly difficult, especially because our ideas of causation may be affected by our favored theory or our cultural perspective. Nonetheless, one of the ultimate goals of most sciences is to be able to exert control over events in our world.

Trying to Determine Causation in Research

Research psychologists who want to know what factors lead to a certain behavior follow a logical plan in the experiments they devise. The details of different studies vary widely, but the underlying concept is consistently very simple. In the simplest situation, we identify a factor that, when present, affects the way a person acts (or increases the probability of a certain behavior) but that, when absent, results in the person's acting differently.

For instance, we know that depressed people have typically experienced more stressful, negative life events than nondepressed people. Positive life events may lessen depression that already exists (Dixon & Reid, 2000). This fact may be quite relevant to you because college students seem particularly prone to stress and to symptoms of depression (Affsprung, 1998; Benton et al., 2003; Shannon, Neibling, & Heckert, 1999).

Could we find out if positive experiences would make a difference in level of depression? We might expose depressed students to different levels of positive feedback. If those who received the most feedback showed lower levels of depression, we could conclude that more positive feedback causes lower levels of depression.

Covariance rule—One of the criteria for assessing causation such that a causal variable must covary systematically with the variable it is assumed to cause.

Temporal precedence rule—One of the criteria for assessing causation such that the variable assumed to have a causal effect must precede the effect it is supposed to cause, that is, the cause must come before the effect.

Requirements for Cause–Effect Relationships

In simple terms, if three particular conditions are met, we conclude that a variable has a causal effect. The first condition for claiming causation involves the **covariance rule.** That is, two variables need to be correlated (i.e., to vary together in predictable ways—to covary) so you can predict the level of one variable given the level of the other. In the example of depression, you can predict the degree of depression from the number of positive life events. More positive life events are correlated with lower levels of depression (Dixon & Reid, 2000).

Knowing that the two variables are correlated does not establish causation. As virtually all statistics students learn, correlation does not equal causation. But you need correlation if there is to be causation; correlation is one requirement for determining causation, even though it is not sufficient by itself. As Dixon and Reid pointed out, depression could be a causal variable, not the effect. People who were depressed might have sought out fewer positive situations.

In order to determine causation, we need to satisfy two other conditions. A second critical element is the **temporal precedence rule;** that is, the cause has to precede the effect. This makes sense based on our everyday experience. An effect occurs only after something else causes it to occur.

If covariance and temporal precedence hold, we need to meet one further criterion. We have to rule out other causal variables, satisfying the **internal validity rule.** Some unknown factor may be affecting the depression and also the number of positive life events. For instance, perhaps a person finds himself or herself socially isolated. This might cause depression; it might also cause a person to have fewer positive life events. Thus, it could be the social isolation that actually influences the degree of depression as well as the number of positive life events.

Establishing internal validity is extremely difficult because our behaviors are influenced by multiple factors. Even in a well-controlled experiment, it is not unusual for participants to be affected in ways the experimenter doesn't know. Later in the chapter, you will see how some of these extraneous variables affect our research.

In summary, the only time we are safe in determining a causal relationship between two variables is when (a) two variables covary, (b) the causal variable precedes the effect, and (c) we can rule out any other variables that could affect the two variables in question. Unless these three criteria are met, we are in a state of **causal ambiguity.**

Internal and External Validity

Internal Validity.   Two concepts of importance in interpreting the results of research are internal validity and external validity. When research shows **internal validity,** it means that your research design is well structured: You started your project with groups that were comparable with respect to the behavior you are measuring, eliminated nuisance variables, manipulated a variable effectively, held everything but the experimental treatments constant across your groups, and measured your participants' behaviors accurately on another variable.

In establishing internal validity, the chief means that scientists use to create comparable groups in an experiment is to use random assignment of participants to groups. Random assignment means that any single individual can end up in any group in the experiment and that the individual is placed in the group on the basis of some objective and unbiased strategy. No approach to assignment guarantees that in a single experiment, the groups to be compared would have equivalent scores on the DV at the start of the study. Sometimes an experimenter is simply beset by bad luck. But, in the long run, **random assignment** is an effective way to create equivalent groups.

You can randomly assign participants to groups by using a random number table. Figure 6.1 illustrates how you could assign 10 people to two groups on a random basis. In this case, if you took numbers from a random number table and used them to assign people to conditions, you could match the random numbers to people based on the order in which they arrived at the lab, alphabetically, by height, by IQ score, by grade point average, or by any other means. As long as one of the lists is random, the grouping is random.

Random assignment of participants to groups keeps us from introducing systematic bias into the process of creating groups. Consequently, we can have confidence that any group differences after a treatment are due to the treatment, not to pre-existing differences. This produces a greater level of internal validity. Across many experiments, this process is the most valuable in creating groups that don't differ systematically at the start. In any given experiment, you might be the victim of bad luck, so that all the smart, tall, nervous, friendly, etc. people are in one group instead of being evenly distributed across conditions. Unfortunately, there is nothing you can do about it. You have to decide on a process of randomization (random number table, drawing names out of a hat, rolling dice, etc.), then

(text continues on p. 134)

Internal validity rule— One of the criteria for assessing causation such that the variable assumed to be causal must be the most plausible cause, with other competing variables ruled out as the cause.

Causal ambiguity—The situation of uncertainty that results when a researcher cannot identify a single logical and plausible variable as being the cause of some behavior, ruling out other possible causal variables.

Internal validity—The degree to which an experiment is designed so that a causal relationship between the independent and dependent variable is demonstrated without interference by extraneous variables.

Random assignment— The process of assigning participants in an experiment to groups on a random basis in order to maximize the likelihood of creating comparable groups.

FIGURE 6.1   *Steps to Take to Randomly Assign Participants to Groups in an Example with 10 People Taking Part*

1. Go through a random number table and write down the numbers from 1 to N (or whatever your sample size is) in the order in which they occur in the table. In this example, we will move down the columns, choosing the first two digits of the column in each block of numbers. The critical numbers are in bold for this example.
2. Create a list of your participants. (The actual order of listing of participants isn't critical here; any ordering will do–alphabetical, in order of arrival to the lab, etc.)
3. Pair each person with the random numbers as they occur.
4. Put each person paired with an odd number into Group 1 and each person paired with an even number into Group 2.

EXAMPLE

Part of a Random Number Table

91477	29697	90242	59885	**07**839
09496	48263	55662	34601	56490
03549	90503	41995	**06**394	61978
19981	55031	34220	48623	53407
51444	89292	**10**273	90035	**04**758
66281	**05**254	35219	96901	38055
08461	61412	53378	13522	80778
36070	12377	52392	67053	49965
28751	**01**486	54443	01873	**02**586
64061	22061	10746	84070	71531

The first number, 91, is bigger than our sample size of 10, so we ignore it. The second number, 09, is odd, so the first person on the list goes into group 1. The next number, 03, is odd, so the second person also goes into group 1. The next three numbers are greater than 10, so we ignore them. Then we see 08, an even number, so that person goes into group 2. We continue to go down the list until our 10 participants are in their assigned groups.

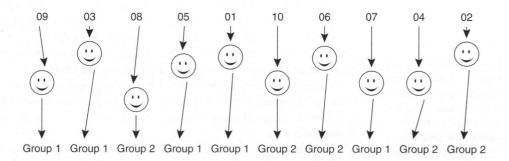

follow it and live with the results. In the long run, random grouping of participants will lead to the most valid results.

External Validity. In order to have **external validity,** your experiment has to be meaningful in a context outside of your laboratory with people (or animals) other than the ones who took part in your study. In other words, would your findings be replicable in another setting with different participants and at a different time? In addition to random assignment, there is another randomization process sometimes used in research. In some research, mostly surveys, investigators make use of random selection. When researchers use this technique, it means that everybody in the population has a specified probability of being included in the research.

The goal of random selection is to increase the representativeness of the sample. With random selection, a scientist can have confidence that the sample used in the research is generally similar to the population as a whole. If your sample is like the population, you can conclude that the results from your sample will be similar to what would happen if you measured the entire population. When you can generalize beyond your sample, your results show external validity.

So random assignment relates to internal validity, the degree to which an experiment is structured so that its results can be interpreted unambiguously, and random selection relates to external validity, the degree to which the experiment pertains to those other than the participants in the study. In experimental research, it is typical to have random assignment of participants to groups, but not to have random selection because most experiments use convenience samples, usually college students.

In some cases, using college students will lead to low levels of external validity. On the other hand, college students are people, and you are interested in people. In many ways, they are going to be like other older and younger people who come from the same socioeconomic and ethnic groups. As such, their behaviors during experiments might very well reflect the behaviors of others from the same background.

If you use nonhuman animals in your research, you are likely to use rats, mice, or pigeons. Historically, psychologists who studied learning processes used rats or pigeons; researchers studying genetics have used mice. These creatures are very different from other animals; they have been bred for laboratories and are likely to be more docile than rats that you might see in the wild. Domesticated mice, for instance, are larger than wild mice and reach sexual maturity quicker. But domesticated mice are physically weaker and have poorer vision than their wild counterparts. And laboratory mice, like all domesticated animals, show more chromosomal breakage than wild animals (Austad, 2002). So there are differences between laboratory animals and wild animals and people, but research with lab animals has still provided a lot of useful information about other animals and about people.

For example, in considering psychological problems, researchers have discovered that an alteration to the same gene in mice and in people leads to similar anxiety-related behaviors (Soliman et al., 2010). Among others findings, the researchers reported that the same genetic alteration in mice and people leads to more difficulty in eliminating conditioned fear. The investigators concluded that laboratory animals can make a useful model in studying anxiety. Obviously, mice lead different kinds of life than people do, but we might be able to learn about causes of and treatments for anxiety by studying the lab mice.

Can you generalize from white lab rats, from pigeons, or from mice to other rats, pigeons, and mice? to other animals? to people? These are not questions that are always easily answered. You have to use good judgment and expert opinion, plus a lot of caution, when you generalize across species.

In any case, Mook (1983) has suggested that asking about the generalizability of research results may not really be the best question to ask. He proposed that we may want to test a set

External validity—The property of data such that research results apply to people and situations beyond the particular sample of individuals observed in a single research setting.

of ideas or a theory in the lab. For purposes of testing a theory, internal validity is critical, but external validity (and generalization) isn't relevant.

To illustrate his point, Mook used Harry Harlow's classic studies of young monkeys that could turn in a time of distress to either a soft and cuddly, artificial "mother" or an uncomfortable, wire "mother" from which the monkey got its milk (from a baby bottle). Drive-reduction theory would lead to the prediction that the animal would turn to the wire mother. Harlow tested this assumption and found that, in times of distress, the monkey preferred warm and cuddly.

The experimental setup was very artificial. The monkeys were probably not representative of baby monkeys in general; after all, they had been raised in a laboratory. They were certainly not like people.

The important issue here is that Harlow's results further weakened a dying theory and helped replace it with a different theory. In some ways, it doesn't matter, Mook explained, whether the results would generalize to people. The critical issue in some cases is development of ideas to test a theory.

The Logic of Experimental Manipulation

The logic of an experiment is simple, even for complex studies. Most psychological experiments involve comparison of more than two groups, but describing research with two groups involves the same logic. So we'll start with a discussion of research with two sets of people (or other animals). If you understand the idea here, you can understand the structure of any experiment.

The basic idea of our simple, hypothetical experiment is this: You start with two groups that are the same, then you do something to one group that you don't do to the other. The group that experiences the manipulation is called the **experimental group;** the group that doesn't is called the **control group.** (In medical research, this approach is called a randomized clinical trial, or RCT, and may use a control group called the **placebo group** if it receives a sham, or fake, treatment.) If the two groups behave differently afterward, whatever you did to the experimental group must have caused the change. The scheme for the simplest experimental design appears in Figure 6.2.

If you understand the logic of this approach, you can comprehend more complex designs. Experimental designs usually involve multiple groups that receive different experimental manipulations; most of the time there is no control group as such. Rather, each group receives a different treatment. The simple questions that would allow us to create meaningful two-group studies have often been answered; we need to create more complex designs in order to advance

Experimental group— The group (or groups) in an experiment that receives a treatment that might affect the behavior of the individuals in that group.

Control group—The group in an experiment that receives either no treatment or a standard treatment with which new treatments are compared.

Placebo group—In medical research, the comparison group in an experiment that receives what appears to be a treatment, but which actually has no effect, providing a comparison with an intervention that is being evaluated.

FIGURE 6.2 *Logic of an Experiment*

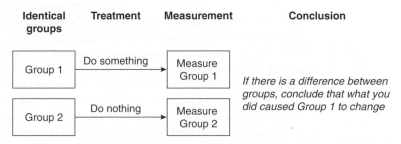

If there is a difference between groups, conclude that what you did caused Group 1 to change

our knowledge. In this chapter, you will learn about the principles and the practicalities of each component of the logic presented in Figure 6.2.

Experimental Control

If you keep the basics of experimental research in mind, it becomes apparent why it is critical to control the research environment very carefully. The essence of good experimental research is the control that an investigator has over the situation and the people in it. When researchers create a solid experiment, they minimize the presence of factors other than the treatment variable that affect participants' behaviors and are able to measure a meaningful outcome.

It is easy to specify on paper that you are going to manipulate a variable and measure the effect on a person's behavior. But it is safe to say that most experiments involve problems and surprises that the researcher has not anticipated. People may stop paying attention to their task, they forget instructions, they fail to show up for a lab session that requires group participation, equipment breaks down, and so on.

The problem is that surprises can arise at many different points during an experiment. We are people, and people make mistakes. In addition, we live in an imperfect world where unexpected things happen. For one thing, try as we might to create comparable groups, we are not always able to do so. When we administer the experimental treatments, initial differences between people in different groups that we might not know about may affect the participants' behaviors.

Further, researchers may inadvertently treat people differently, leading to changes in behavior that have nothing to do with the treatment variable. Furthermore, when we measure the outcome, we can make mistakes in recording the data, or we might use a behavior that is not a very good measurement of what we are interested in. Finally, when we analyze the results of the research, we might use a statistical approach that is not the best one available, and we might interpret it incompletely or inaccurately. Even though life tends to throw us curve balls, there are steps we can take to maximize the likelihood that research results will be meaningful and accurate.

Threats to Internal Validity

The internal validity of a research project is critical to the level of confidence you have in your conclusions. The greater the internal validity, the more you can have faith that you know what factors cause an individual to act in a certain way.

The major threats to internal validity were initially elucidated by Campbell and Stanley (1966). Researchers now recognize that we have to take these potential problems very seriously. These threats are particularly troublesome when a research design uses repeated measures and nonequivalent groups. Such problems are common in applied research that takes place outside of the laboratory, but we can't ignore them in laboratory-based studies.

The reason that non-laboratory studies are more prone to these problems than other research is because we generally have less control over the research setting outside the lab. When we conduct theoretical or applied research in a laboratory, we can simplify the environment to include only a few major variables so that if the groups then behave differently, we assume that a variable or a combination of variables that we manipulated had an effect.

If you create a study in a retail establishment, the company still wants to make money, so you have to work around the business that takes place. As such, you make compromises and conduct your study differently than if you could manipulate the situation to your liking.

Threats Associated with Participants. Several of the threats to internal validity pertain to the characteristics of the research sample. The first threat involves **selection.** Whenever we design a study that does not involve random selection and assignment of participants to groups, the selection threat may be a problem. This threat reflects the fact that if we compare two groups with predetermined characteristics, the groups may not start out the same. Differences other than the independent variable may cause differences in the dependent variable.

For example, Bell and colleagues (2000) noted that a lot of research has found that women suffer sports injuries at a higher rate than men. Conclusions have been drawn about the various reasons why the female body is more prone to injury. However, Bell et al. discovered that initial fitness levels among army inductees was more predictive of future injury than sex was. If so, injuries among women athletes might be reduced through increased fitness training. You can see here one of the threats to internal validity. When you cannot assign people to groups randomly, you are never sure that you have comparable people in each condition. In studying the incidence of injury to female and male athletes, as Bell et al. (2000) did, differences may emerge because of initial differences in fitness across groups.

A second threat to internal validity is **maturation.** People change the way they act for a lot of reasons. If you study individuals over time, they may not be the same at the end as they were at the start. Their behavior with respect to your DV might change because of the changes in the participants, not because of your IV.

Maturation is more clearly a problem if you study children over time because they mature physically and psychologically in dramatic ways. But maturation can also come into play with adults. They may not change physically in obvious ways over a short period, but they can change psychologically. In this case, maturation does not only mean maturation of the kind from infancy to older childhood to adolescence; it means any physical or psychological changes, including fatigue, boredom, having learned about the study, etc.

A third threat, **attrition** (also called subject mortality), can affect your results. If you test people over time, some may not return for later tests. You can't be sure that the people who drop out are like the ones that remain when it comes to your DV. For instance, if you are studying the development of skill over time, the participants who are progressing slowly may drop out, leaving you only with those people who are competent. Any conclusions you draw about your research will thus be based on a sample consisting of more proficient people.

The issue is not attrition in and of itself. Rather, problems arise because of nonrandom attrition. That is, the participants in one group who drop out may exhibit different characteristics from those who remain, or those who drop out of one group may have different characteristics from those who drop out in a different group. In either case, groups may look like they differ because of the IV; in reality, groups may differ because of the effect of those who left the study.

A fourth threat to validity is **history.** Events during the course of a study may affect one group and not another. Even if you started with randomly assigned groups, this could happen. But if you are conducting a study with two different groups, like young people versus old people, one group may be affected by some event outside your research so their behaviors change. If you concluded that your IV is the reason for the differences across groups, you would be victimized by the history threat.

Threats Associated with Measurement. A fifth threat to internal validity is **instrumentation.** This means that there is a problem in the way you measure your dependent variable over time. If you asked different questions to a group in the initial and final research sessions, your data would not be comparable because changing the questions might lead your participants to interpret them differently. Another situation in which instrumentation could be a problem would be if you used two different people to collect data at the beginning and at the end of the

---

Selection threat—A threat to the internal validity of a study such that groups to be compared differ before being exposed to different experimental treatments, so any differences after treatment could be due to the initial differences rather than to the independent variable.

Maturation threat—A threat to the internal validity of a study due to short- or long-term changes in a participant because of psychological changes like boredom, fatigue, etc. or because of physical maturation.

Attrition (mortality) threat—A threat to the internal validity of a study when participants drop out of a study, leading to a change in the nature of the sample.

History threat—A threat to the internal validity of a study that results when some event outside the research project affects participants systematically.

Instrumentation threat—A threat to the internal validity of a study that results from changes in the way the dependent variable is measured, due to factors like poor calibration of mechanical equipment or changes in the way researchers record subjective observations.

project; the second set of data collectors might introduce changes in the research environment, leading to changes in the way participants respond.

The instrumentation threat could also come into play if you were measuring behaviors with mechanical instruments. Sometimes these instruments need calibration or readjustment; if you don't do that, two measurements that should be the same could be different because of the machinery you are using.

A sixth threat to internal validity is **testing.** Sometimes, initial testing of your participants can sensitize them to the reasons for your research. As a result, they may act differently because they know too much about the nature of your research question, and it biases their responses.

A seventh threat to internal validity is **statistical regression.** A researcher might want to compare good and poor students who are admitted to a special program. In order to make the groups seem equivalent, the researcher might study students from the special program and students not in the program who have comparable test scores at the start of the project. This strategy would involve the poorest students from the higher-level group and the best students from the lower-level group. This would mean that the two groups would seem equivalent to begin with.

Unfortunately, the better students who score low in their group may really be typical students who, for no systematic reason, fell at the low end of the distribution. Similarly, the poorer students at the top of their group may not be all that different from their peers; they just scored higher, also for unknown reasons.

We know that such error, on average, is zero. So, in later testing, these better students' scores are likely to be closer to the mean of their group than they were on the initial testing. The poorer students' scores also go back where they belong, toward the low end of the scale.

This means that, even if no research were done, the average scores of the two groups would quite likely be different on the retest even if there were no independent variable at all. Such a phenomenon is very real. It is sometimes called regression to the mean.

When researchers attempt to match participants in nonequivalent groups, there is a high likelihood of statistical regression. Consequently, if you are not going to randomly assign matched pairs to the different treatment conditions, you probably should not use matching as a strategy to equate groups because statistical regression can obscure the effects of your treatment.

These threats to internal validity, which are summarized in Table 6.1, reduce our confidence in the conclusions we draw about our results. A critical assessment of a study's research design, attention to other researchers' methodologies, and use of a variety of different procedures can lead to a greater level of confidence.

Lack of Control in Experimental Research: Extraneous Variables and Confounds

When you think of all the factors that can influence people's behaviors, you can appreciate how hard it can be to control all the variables that might influence the behavior you want to observe and measure. Factors other than your intended treatment that affect the outcome are called **extraneous variables.** They are variables that make unambiguous interpretation of your results impossible: You don't know if your results are due to the effect of an independent variable or to the extraneous variable.

One particular type of extraneous variable is called a **confound.** A confounding variable systematically affects participants in one group differently than it affects those in other groups. As a result, when groups differ at the end of a study, it may be because a confounding variable, not the treatment variable, affected one group. If researchers aren't aware of the confound, they may attribute differences to the treatment.

Testing threat—A threat to the internal validity of a study that results when participants' behavior changes as a function of having been tested previously.

Statistical regression threat—A threat to the internal validity of a study that results when participants are categorized or selected for research participation on the basis of an initial observation that involves significant measurement error that is not likely to repeat itself on later measurements, giving the false impression that change is due to a treatment when it is really due to the difference in measurement error.

Extraneous variable—A variable that is not of interest to a researcher and that may not be known by the researcher that affects the dependent variable in an experiment, erroneously making it seem that the independent variable is having an effect on the dependent variable.

Confound—A variable that is not controlled by an experimenter but that has a systematic effect on a behavior in at least one group in an experiment.

TABLE 6.1 *Major Threats to the Internal Validity of a Research Project*

Threat	*Description*
Selection	When participants are not randomly assigned to conditions, groups to be compared may differ before the experimental treatment is applied. Any difference between groups may be due to initial differences, not the treatment.
Maturation	In the short term, people become fatigued or bored, or they may learn how to perform better with practice on a task, so behaviors may differ due to changes in psychological states. In the long term, people change physical and psychologically; such changes may affect behavior, not a treatment.
Attrition (Mortality)	When researchers monitor participants over time, some participants may leave a study. If people with certain characteristics drop out, there may be a biasing effect so that the remaining sample contains people who are very different from the original sample. Differences in behaviors may not be due to the research variables.
History	An event may occur outside the study during the course of a research project that leads to a change in behavior. If one group is differentially affected, it may appear that a treatment was responsible for the differences between groups when, in fact, it was a particular event that influenced one of the groups.
Instrumentation	If the way a researcher measures the DV varies over time due to changes in equipment or to changes in subjective judgments by the researcher, differences in measurements may have nothing to do with the research variables.
Testing	When people go through a research protocol multiple times, they may change their behaviors because they are sensitized to the testing situation itself.
Statistical regression	When people exhibit extreme scores on an initial test, one of the reasons for the extreme score may random error. On a subsequent test, that random component of the score is no longer so prominent and the person's score regresses, that is, moves back toward the average of the group.

A confound may also obscure real differences between groups by raising or lowering the scores in a group affected by that confound. A group that might ordinarily perform poorly on a task could, because of a confound, show high scores. That group might then have an average that is not much different from a group that is really more proficient. As a researcher, you would conclude that your treatment did not make a difference when it really did. The problem is that the confound helped the poorer group, obscuring a real effect of the treatment. Thus, extraneous variables can erase the difference between two groups that should differ. Or extraneous variables can make a difference appear where none should be.

One example of published research illustrates how even experienced researchers rely on public scrutiny of their work in spotting extraneous variables. Such scrutiny leads to advances in knowledge that go beyond the original study. Quinn and colleagues (1999) investigated whether using night lights for children under the age of 2 years will lead them to become nearsighted (myopic) later. Previously, scientists studying chickens noted that the birds developed visual problems if they did not experience a period of darkness each day. These researchers wondered whether nearsightedness in people might be related to the incidence of light throughout the day and night.

The results were shocking. When children had slept with their rooms illuminated, the incidence of myopia was very high, with 45% of the children nearsighted, compared to only 10% of the children who did not have a night light. The researchers knew that their findings were preliminary and, given the correlational nature of the data, not appropriate for cause–effect analysis. Still, the findings were intriguing and Quinn et al. offered their results to the research community.

Subsequently, researchers have been able to identify some potential extraneous variables at work here. First, it may be that parents with myopia, which they can pass on to their children, may prefer to have night lights so they themselves can see when they enter their infant's room at night. (Stone noted that their preliminary analysis of parental vision did not reveal problems for the research.)

Second, the study was done in an eye clinic, which makes it likely that the children who were studied did not reflect children in general. Characteristics of the sample other than whether they had night lights may have affected the results.

Third, the study relied on parental memory from an average of six years before the study. Such memories are notoriously unreliable. It could be that parents with poor vision simply remember about night lights, which help them see, whereas parents with normal vision might be less attuned to such memories.

Subsequent to the publication of the Quinn et al. research, other research provided reassurance that nighttime illumination would not cause myopia (Gwiazda et al., 2000; Zadnik et al., 2000). In some studies, we may not be able to spot confounds and extraneous variables based on research reports. Fortunately, in the Quinn et al. work, because they provided enough detail about their methodology, others could continue to investigate their ideas.

Problems may also arise because research is a human enterprise. If there are two groups to be compared and if a researcher acts differently toward the people (or animals) in each group, the resulting behaviors may be different because of the way the participants were treated rather than because of the IV.

Rosenthal and Fode (1966) first demonstrated that visual and verbal cues by an experimenter have an effect on participant behavior. Most researchers are aware that they may have an effect on the way experimental participants act. At the same time, the cues may be so subtle that the researchers (or their assistants) don't know what changes they are causing in participant behaviors. The effect is large enough to raise the success rate in making predictions about some behaviors from about 35% to 65% (Rosenthal, 2003).

Consider the effect of small wording changes on behavior. Elizabeth Loftus was among the first researchers to document the effect of "leading questions," that is, wording that may lead a respondent in a particular direction. Experimenters can unknowingly use leading questions or other wording that affects the way participants behave. Loftus (1975) showed her participants a film clip of an automobile accident, then asked them one of two questions:

1. How fast was Car A going when it ran the stop sign? or
2. How fast was Car A going when it turned right?

A final question asked "Did you see a stop sign for Car A?" When participants had been asked Question 1, they were significantly more likely to respond that they had seen a stop sign. When the experimenter planted the seed of a memory, participants nourished that memory and began to believe in it. There actually was a stop sign in the film clip. Nonetheless, it was clear that the change in wording affected how people responded to later questions. There has subsequently been ample research demonstrating that false memories can be planted successfully (e.g., Loftus, 1997; Mazzoni & Loftus, 1998) and that slight changes in wording or even simply exposing a person to an idea can change later responses (Loftus, 2003). These effects are very important for you to understand because even a small change in communication can have a significant impact on a person's response and memory, unbeknownst to the researcher.

An additional source of extraneous influences in an experiment can be the stimulus materials. When investigators change materials across different groups, subtle differences in the nature of the materials can make a notable difference in the outcome of the research.

Sometimes we are able to spot confounds and sources of error in research, but it is possible that we may not recognize that research has subtle problems that lead to poor conclusions. One area of research that has been beset by a potentially very important confound involves whether women show fear of success (FOS). Psychologists have identified FOS in women with a variety of tasks. Over two decades after the initial research appeared, though, some hidden problems became apparent, as described in the controversy on FOS.

Fortunately, scientific research is done so that problems can be corrected. As a result, we have overcome one stumbling block in studying FOS. It is clear now that FOS is not a function of sex alone, as you can see in controversy on fear of success.

The problem with extraneous variables and confounds is that no experiment has complete control over what a participant experiences in the lab or over any of the participant's life experiences. If you set up an experiment as outlined in Figure 6.1, there are many variables other than the IV that could affect the outcome of your project. Conducting a sound study requires attention to detail and a good grasp of how researchers in the past have overcome the problems they faced.

CONTROVERSY
Do Women Fear Success?

Research across the past 40 years has suggested that women fear success. A typical experimental strategy was to give participants an essay to read and then to ask them to write about it. Horner (1968, cited in Kasof, 1993) gave male participants a story in which the main character was a man; female participants read stories in which the main character was a woman. A critical sentence in the essay was "After first-term finals, John (Anne) finds himself (herself) at the top of his (her) medical school class." Horner reported that women wrote more negative essays, which the researcher interpreted to indicate that women were more fearful of success than men were. Subsequent to this research, investigators studied such topics as sex discrimination, sex stereotypes, and fear of success by altering experimental stimuli for women and men by changing the name of the protagonist in a story.

We could debate Horner's original interpretation about women's fear of success, but there was a fundamental problem with the fear of success research that lay hidden for two decades. According to Kasof (1993), the names of the characters in the experimental stimuli were not comparable across sexes.

The tendency among researchers was to use male and female versions of a name, such as John and Joan or Christopher and Christine. Kasof reported that, in as many as 96% of the studies, the female names tended to be more old-fashioned, connoted lower intelligence, and were associated with being less attractive compared to male names.

As Kasof pointed out, dependent variables in sexism studies often relate to intellectual competence (e.g., who is more competent, John or Joan). Some names are associated with lower intelligence, even though we know that how smart you are has nothing to do with what your parents named you.

In recent decades, the attractiveness of the names seems to be more nearly equal. Not surprisingly, during this period researchers have learned that fear of success has little to do with sex per se and more to do with whether a woman holds a traditional view of sex roles (Basha & Ushasree, 1999; Krishnan & Sweeney, 1998; Kumari, 1995) and careers (Hay & Bakken, 1991) and whether she is gifted (Hay & Bakken, 1991). There also seems to be an intergenerational effect such that children of parents with fear of failure tend to show such fear themselves (Elliott & Thrash, 2004). More recently, researchers have reported that women can have lower FOS than men (Mandel, 2007) and that women engage in self-handicapping, which can lead to failure, less than men and view it negatively (McCrea, Hirt, & Milner, 2008).

In addition, women who are concerned about being evaluated negatively because they are "too successful" may show higher levels of fear of success. But it's not that they actually fear success; they are just sensitive to social evaluation (Exline & Lobel, 1999). Further, being a successful woman entails taking risks, and women may be less likely to engage in risky social behavior (Byrnes, Miller, & Schafer, 1999).

Sometimes, apparently small changes in the way an experiment is set up (e.g., the stimulus names) introduce extraneous variables that can be more important than the IV. Now that we are aware of the effect of stimulus names, we may be able to identify more precisely who fears success. Sometimes it can be men (Rothman, 1996).

Experimenter Effects

One source of difficulty in research involves experimenter bias, the tendency for the researcher to influence a participant's behavior in a certain direction. If the experimenter thinks that one group will perform better on a task than another, the investigator may inadvertently lead the participants to act in the expected way.

How often do researchers engage in such behavior? It is hard to tell, although when surveyors were studied to see how often they departed from the directions they were supposed to follow in administering questionnaires, the results showed that there were notable deviations from the standardized protocol (Kiecker & Nelson, 1996).

One of the most common departures involved rephrasing or rewording a question; the interviewers reported that, on average, they had done this about 18% of the times in their last hundred sessions. (The standard deviation was 27.2 percent, indicating that some interviewers may have changed the wording around half the time.)

These data suggest that, in an attempt to be helpful or to clarify a question, the surveyors regularly rephrased questionnaire items. Given the results of extensive research like Loftus's (1975, 1997), the changes in wording may very well have affected the survey results. We don't know how often comparable behaviors occur in experiments or how big the effects might be, but the survey results suggest that researchers deviate from their directions regularly.

Interestingly, Kiecker and Nelson (1996) reported that surveyors rarely fabricated an interview that never took place. Thus, even though their behaviors could have changed people's responses, we can infer that they were trying to be helpful to the respondents. Unfortunately, even apparently small changes in the way researchers administer their studies can affect the outcomes.

Participant Effects

The majority of psychological research with people involves college students. Students generally have some very desirable characteristics, three of which are a high degree of education, a willingness to cooperate, and a high level of motivation. These are helpful traits most of the time. Unfortunately, in the context of an experiment, they might pose some problems.

It isn't unusual for a student who participates in a study to try to figure out what the experimenter "wants." This can be a problem because the experimenter really wants the person to act naturally.

How might we keep participants from reliably picking up on clues? One means is to use automated operations whenever possible. If the participant reads the instructions, then carries out a task on a computer, there is less risk that the experimenter will influence the person's behavior.

Cover story—A fictitious story developed by a researcher to disguise the true purpose of a study from the participants.

A second strategy is to use a convincing **cover story.** This is a story about the study that either conveys the actual purpose of the study or successfully hides the true nature of the research. Some people object to deceptive cover stories, but others have argued that the nature and level of the deception is trivial. If you carry out your own research projects, you will have to decide on your own whether deception is warranted and appropriate.

Blind study—A research design in which the investigator, the participants, or both are not aware of the treatment that a participant is receiving.

Another solution is to use a **blind study.** In such an approach, the participants do not know the group to which they have been assigned. Thus, it will be harder for participants to know what treatment they receive, so they are less likely to try to conform to expectations, even if they know the general nature of the study.

When either the participants or the researchers do not know to which group the participants are assigned, we call it a **single blind study.** When the participants in different groups are blind, which is how single blind studies usually proceed, they don't have systematically different expectations that they might try to fulfill. When the investigators who actually conduct the study are blind to which group a person is in, it keeps a researcher from unintentionally giving clues to a participant. When neither the investigator nor the patient knows which group the patient has been assigned to, it is called a **double blind study.**

The Hawthorne Effect

When people change their behavior because they know they are being observed in a scientific study, the results can lack validity. The behaviors are due to the motivation rather than to the IV. This phenomenon is often referred to the **Hawthorne effect.** (Ironically, the participants after whom the Hawthorne effect was named were probably not beset by the effect; Adair, 1984; Bramel & Friend, 1981.)

In addition to the Hawthorne effect, a commonly described participant effect involves **demand characteristics.** When participants actively try to figure out the purpose of the study and act in ways they think are helpful, they are said to be showing demand characteristics. It should come as no surprise that people are active participants in a research setting; they try to figure things out, just as they do in any other aspect of their lives.

One compelling example of a situation involving demand characteristics was provided by Orne and Scheibe (1962). These researchers told individual participants that they might experience sensory deprivation and negative psychological effects while sitting in a room. When the researchers included a "panic button," the participants tended to panic because they thought it would be an appropriate response in that situation. When there was no panic button, the participants experienced no particular adverse effects. The inference we can draw here is that when the participants concluded that a highly negative psychological condition would emerge, they complied with that expectation. When the expectation wasn't there, neither was the negative response.

Another source of bias associated with participants is **evaluation apprehension.** This bias arises because people think others are going to evaluate their behaviors. As a result, the participants are on their best behavior. This is something we do all the time. Many people will litter as they walk or drive down the street, but not if they think somebody (even a stranger) is going to see them and, presumably, evaluate their littering behavior negatively.

This evaluation apprehension is not always so benign. Researchers have shown that when people begin thinking about stereotypes applied to them, their behavior changes. Thus, women may perform less well on mathematics tests because women "aren't supposed" to be good at math (McGlone & Aronson, 2007; Spencer, Steele, & Quinn, 1999), African Americans may perform less well on academic tests because blacks "aren't supposed" to be as strong academically as whites (Steele & Aronson, 1995), and poor people "aren't supposed" to be as proficient as rich people (Croizet & Claire, 1998).

Laboratory studies have generated the stereotype effect for people from different cultural backgrounds, including Italian (Muzzatti & Agnolik 2007), German (Keller, 2007), French (Croizet & Claire, 1998), Chinese (Lee & Ottati, 1995), and Canadian (Walsh, Hickey, & Duffy, 1999). Fortunately, though, appropriate messages can mitigate it (McGlone & Aronson, 2007).

Surprisingly, even groups of people who are demonstrably proficient in an area can suffer from stereotype threat. Aronson et al. (1999) showed that math-proficient white males could be induced to perform more poorly than expected on a test of math skills if they were compared to a group that is expected to perform even better than they, namely, Asians.

Single blind study—A research design in which either the investigator or the participant is not aware of the treatment a participant is receiving.

Double blind study—A research design in which neither the investigator nor the participant is aware of the treatment being applied.

Hawthorne effect—The tendency of participants to act differently from normal in a research study because they know they are being observed.

Demand characteristics—The tendency on the part of a research participant to act differently from normal after picking up clues as to the apparent purpose of the study.

Evaluation apprehension—The tendency to feel inadequate or to experience unease when one is being observed.

Some researchers have questioned the external validity of stereotype threat in applied settings. Kirnan and colleagues (2009) studied a potential workplace situation involving stereotype threat and supplemented that research with laboratory studies. They found minimal support for it as described by Steele and Aronson (1995). This is a good example of research in which external validity might be an important issue.

Interaction Effects Between Experimenters and Participants

Biosocial and Psychosocial Effects

Experimenter bias—The tendency of researchers to subtly and inadvertently affect the behaviors of participants in a study, obscuring the true effect (or lack thereof) of the independent variable.

Biosocial effect—The type of experimenter bias in which characteristics of the researcher like age, sex, or race affect the behavior of the participant.

Psychosocial effect—The type of experimenter bias in which attitudes of the researcher affect the behavior of the participant.

Research projects are social affairs. This may not be obvious at first glance, but whenever you get people together, they have social interactions of various kinds. However, when you are carrying out a research project, you don't want either experimenters or participants to communicate in ways that will compromise the study.

In a research setting, behaviors that we generally take for granted as normal (and maybe even desirable) become problematic. Consider the following situation: A college student agrees to participate in an experiment and, when arriving there, finds a very attractive experimenter. Isn't it reasonable to suppose that the student will act differently than if the experimenter weren't good looking? From the student's point of view, this is a great opportunity to show intelligence, motivation, creativity, humor, etc. In other words, the research project is a social affair.

Just as the experimenter and the participant bring their own individual predispositions to the lab, they bring their own interactive, social tendencies. Research results are affected not only by **experimenter bias** and participant bias, but also by interactions between experimenter and participant.

If a participant responds to some "natural" characteristic of the researcher, we may have a distortion of experimental results due to a **biosocial effect.** For instance, if the experimenter seems too young to be credible, the participant may not take research seriously. Or if the participant is overweight, the experimenter may be abrupt and not be as patient in giving directions. Other examples of factors that could induce biosocial effects could include race, ethnicity, nationality, and religion. Obviously, these are not strictly biological characteristics, as the term "biosocial" implies. Nonetheless, these characteristics all pertain to what people may see as fundamental about another individual.

A different, but related, bias involves **psychosocial effects.** This type of bias involves psychological characteristics, like personality or mood. Researchers with different personality characteristics act differently toward participants. For instance, researchers high in the need for social approval smile more and act more friendly toward participants than those lower in this need (Rosnow & Rosenthal, 1997).

It is clear that the way an experimenter interacts with a participant can affect the outcome of a study (Rosenthal & Fode, 1966). For instance, Malmo, Boag, and Smith (1957, cited in Rosnow & Rosenthal, 1997) found that when an experimenter was having a bad day, participants' heart rates were higher compared to when the experimenter was having a good day.

Realism in Research

A potential weakness of the experimental approach is that it is usually a stripped-down version of reality. In an effort to create groups that are virtually identical except for differences on one dimension, scientists try to simplify the experimental setting so that anything that will get in the way of a clear conclusion is eliminated.

Mundane realism—The characteristic of a research setting such that it resembles the kind of situation that a participant would encounter in life.

Experimental realism—The characteristic of a research setting such that the person participating in a study experiences the psychological state that the research is trying to induce, even if the research setting is artificial, like a laboratory.

When we use simple laboratory situations for our research, the result is often a reduction in mundane realism. When a situation has **mundane realism,** it resembles the normal environment you live in on an everyday basis. If you have ever volunteered to participate in a laboratory study, you probably saw pretty quickly that the environment was different from what you encounter normally.

The low level of mundane realism sometimes makes researchers wonder if their experimental results are applicable to normal human interaction. The simple version of reality in a laboratory can give us useful information about human behavior if the tasks of the participants have experimental realism. This type of realism relates to whether the participants engage in their tasks seriously.

An example of a series of studies that has little mundane realism is Stanley Milgram's obedience studies. He asked people to shock others if they made a mistake in a learning task in a laboratory. This is not something that most of us will ever do in our lives. As such, the mundane realism is fairly low. On the other hand, the research participants acted like they were very engaged in the task, showing nervousness and extreme discomfort in many cases. This behavior suggests a high level of experimental realism. When research shows good **experimental realism,** the research results may pertain to the real-world behaviors the researcher is investigating.

The critical element regarding realism is that we want our research participants to be in the psychological state of interest to us. The nature of the setting, whether it is a laboratory or not, may not be relevant. We are more interested in whether the person is engaged in the task in the way that will provide insights into behaviors and emotions we are studying.

Chapter Summary

The single most important advantage associated with experiments is that they allow you to determine the causes of behavior. Not only can you predict the behaviors, but you can also control them.

The basic idea behind the experiment is that you start with two groups that are equivalent and apply a treatment to one of them. If differences appear after you do that, you can assume that your treatment made a difference.

If life were this simple, we would not need to pay as close attention to the details of research as we must. Characteristics of experiments, participants, and the context of the research can all affect the outcome of a research project in subtle but important ways. For instance, extraneous variables that you don't know about can affect the DV, so you mistakenly think that your IV is responsible for differences across groups. One particular type of extraneous variable is the confounding variable, which affects at least one group in systematic ways.

It is also important to remember that experiments involve social interactions among experimenters and participants. These interactions can affect the outcome of research in predictable ways, although the problem is that researchers are often not aware of these effects in their own studies.

When we are able to control for outside factors that affect the behavior of research participants, we can maximize the internal validity of our studies. Sometimes we are more concerned with internal validity, that is, the structure of the experiment itself. At other times, though, we are more concerned with external validity, the extent to which our results make sense outside the confines of our own research setting.

Key Terms

Attrition threat	Experiment	Maturation threat
Biosocial effect	Experimental realism	Mundane realism
Blind study	Experimental group	Placebo group
Causal ambiguity	Experimenter bias	Psychosocial effect
Confound	External validity	Random assignment
Control group	Extraneous variable	Selection threat
Covariance rule	Hawthorne effect	Single blind study
Cover story	History threat	Statistical regression threat
Demand characteristics	Instrumentation threat	Temporal precedence rule
Double blind study	Internal validity	Testing threat
Evaluation apprehension	Internal validity rule	

Chapter Review Questions

Multiple Choice Questions

1. The research approach that involves changing the level, intensity, frequency, or duration of an independent variable is
   a. correlational.
   b. observational.
   c. experimental.
   d. validational.

2. Psychologists have speculated that having more acquaintances leads to better health. Research has supported this connection. Which principle of causation is met in this relation between acquaintances and health?
   a. Internal validity rule
   b. Covariance rule
   c. Causal ambiguity rule
   d. Temporal precedence rule

3. If we want to conclude that a given variable has a causal relation with a second variable, we have to be able to rule out other possible causal variables. The principle of causation involved here is the
   a. covariance rule.
   b. internal validity rule.
   c. causal ambiguity rule.
   d. temporal precedence rule.

4. In a research project, a group that experiences the manipulated independent variables is called the
   a. independent group.
   b. experimental group.
   c. control group.
   d. placebo group.

5. Researchers have discovered that children experiencing Attention Deficit Hyperactivity Disorder (ADHD) show improvements if they attend classes on involving behavioral and social skills, compared to a group of ADHD children who did not attend the classes. The group of children who attended the classes constitute the
   a. experimental group.
   b. independent group.
   c. control group.
   d. placebo group.

6. In medical research, groups sometimes undergo an experience that resembles the experimental manipulation but does not actually involve that manipulation. Such a group is called the
   a. independent group.
   b. experimental group.
   c. control group.
   d. placebo group.

7. Extraneous variables
   a. tend to be problems in single blind studies, but not double blind studies.
   b. tend to reduce the degree of external validity in a study.
   c. can be avoided through random sampling.
   d. can sometimes be dealt with by using control groups.

8. A group of researchers discovered that people who slept with night lights as children were more likely to be nearsighted than were children who did not have night lights. In the end, the night lights didn't seem to be the cause; rather, parental nearsightedness was. Parental vision, which affected the DV, not the night lights, reflected the presence of
   a. a single blind design.
   b. a confound.
   c. lack of mundane realism.
   d. lack of experimental realism.

9. In a double blind study, an experimenter cannot influence participants' behaviors differently across groups. As such, we should expect that there will be little
   a. Hawthorne effect.
   b. external invalidity.
   c. placebo effect.
   d. experimenter bias.

10. If a researcher deceives a participant by telling the individual that a study is about one thing, but it is really about something else, the researcher is using
    a. a double blind study.
    b. a cover story.
    c. experimental realism.
    d. demand characteristics.

11. When a researcher sets up a study so that the participants do not know to what condition they have been assigned, we refer to this design as
    a. a blind study.
    b. a cover story design.
    c. a control design.
    d. an externally valid design.

12. People often change their behavior when they know they are being observed in a scientific study, a phenomenon called
    a. mundane realism.
    b. experimental realism.
    c. the Hawthorne effect.
    d. external validation.

13. When psychologists Orne and Scheibe gave research participants a "panic button" in the event that they began to experience negative psychological effects while sitting in a room, the participants showed panic responses. When there was no mention of a panic button, the participants experienced no negative effects. Orne and Scheibe were documenting the existence of
    a. experimenter bias.
    b. mundane realism.
    c. demand characteristics.
    d. evaluation apprehension.

14. Participants sometimes act differently than normal in a research project because of the race or ethnicity of the experimenter. This change in behavior occurs because of what psychologists call
    a. psychosocial effects.
    b. biosocial effects.
    c. stereotype effects.
    d. experimenter bias effects.

15. Initial studies of fear of success included descriptions of fictitious characters with corresponding male and female names, like John and Joan, who were engaged in activities that could lead to success. The researchers did not realize that
    a. research participants tended to relate those names to actual people they knew.
    b. women were seen as being high in fear of success but were really high in expectation of failure.
    c. the names used as stimuli in the research were associated with different levels of achievement, with female names being associated with less success.
    d. over time, fear of success became less meaningful among men but not among women.

16. When laboratory research settings are created to resemble the real-life situations they are investigating, the effect is to lead to
    a. the Hawthorne effect.
    b. causal ambiguity.
    c. random selection.
    d. mundane realism.

Essay Questions

17. Why is research involving already existing groups rather than randomly assigned groups prone to the effects of extraneous variables?

18. Explain how demand characteristics and evaluation apprehension affect participant behavior in research.

- - - - -

CHAPTER 7

BASIC INFERENTIAL STATISTICS

CHAPTER OUTLINE

PROBABILITY

HYPOTHESIS TESTING
  Decisions in Statistical Hypothesis Testing
  Normal Distribution
  Sampling Distributions

Single Sample *z* Test
Steps in Hypothesis Testing
Single Sample *t* Test

COMPUTER ANALYSIS USING SPSS

LEARNING OBJECTIVES

- Distinguish between the uses of descriptive and inferential statistical procedures.
- Define inferential statistics.
- Explain the meaning of statistical significance.
- Define Type I error.
- Define Type II error.
- Define statistical power.
- Describe the relationship between standard deviation and the normal distribution.
- Explain how the *z* score is related to the normal distribution.
- Describe how a *z* score differs from a *z* test.
- Define the standard error of the mean (*SEM*).
- Describe the role of sampling distributions in hypothesis testing.
- Explain the difference between standard deviation (*SD*) and standard error of the mean (*SEM*).
- Explain the difference between a *z* score and a *z* test.
- List the steps in hypothesis testing.
- Explain effect size.
- Describe when to use a *t* test.

CHAPTER PREVIEW

In the previous chapter we provided an overview of basic experimental designs that allow us to establish cause-and-effect relationships. One reason that we can claim a cause-and-effect relationship is that we use random assignment when conducting experimental studies. We also rely upon statistical assumptions when deriving statements of cause and effect. In this chapter we will discuss the statistical assumptions and applications that allow us to make statistical claims about cause and effect. In particular, we will discuss the theory of probability and how it applies to statistical hypothesis testing. We will also discuss effect sizes that we use to describe meaningful differences that occur as a result of an IV.

We begin with an explanation of probability as applied to individual circumstances. Probability, or the likelihood of a particular outcome, is present in our daily lives. We extend our explanation of individual probability to statistical samples, which provides us with the foundation for hypothesis testing. Using the theory of probability, we describe how to use samples to test hypotheses and generalize the results back to the larger population—in other words, we describe basic inferential techniques. In this chapter we also describe two inferential techniques, the single sample z test, and the single sample t test, and we provide examples of how they might be used with experimental designs. Finally, we provide instructions for using SPSS to conduct the statistical tests described in this chapter.

Probability

Almost every day we make decisions based on an implicit set of assumptions about the likelihood of an event's occurring. We might consider the possibility of winning the lottery, and we might even anticipate what we would do with all the money if we win.

What is the likelihood that you will win the lottery? The real likelihood of winning is based on the theory of probability. Although the likelihood of winning the megaball lottery is extremely remote (i.e., 1 in 175,711,536), many people continue to play the lottery each day in hope that they will be the lucky winner.

We stand a much better chance of winning a prize in virtually any other contest. For example, door prizes are frequently offered as an incentive for attendance at an event. Imagine that a door prize is awarded for every day that you attend class. How likely is it that you will win the prize? This all depends on how many people are in class. If the class is large, perhaps 25 people attend; your chances of winning are only one in 25 or approximately 4%. Similarly, if very few people attend ($N = 4$), then your chances of winning increase to one in four or 25%. In each case your chance, or probability of winning, is dependent upon how many people are in class, or the ratio of prizes to people. We calculate probability by using a ratio. In this example, we simply divide the number of door prizes by the number of people attending. This calculation provides us with a probability of winning. This ratio is another way to describe probability, and we use probability every day to inform our choices.

Calculation of probability rests on underlying mathematical assumptions, or properties of distributions. Although there are many different theoretical distributions, most of our statistical tests are based on the *normal distribution*. The normal distribution makes the assumption that we are using a large number of scores so it is symmetrical; the mean, median, and mode are located exactly at the center of the distribution (Hays, 1988), and each point in the normal distribution is associated with a specific probability value. The normal curve is continuous, so each point has an infinitely small (i.e., zero) probability. Only ranges of scores are associated with non-zero probabilities. For discrete distributions we can use specific points on the curve and we use the normal distribution to specify probability, which ranges from 0 to 100%.

The normal distribution can be used for calculating the probability of winning the attendance prize. But what if we are interested in calculating the probability of the same person winning multiple times? If the same person receives the attendance prize many times (an unlikely event), we might begin to suspect that the drawing is rigged. We might even conclude that this unusual occurrence is not likely to happen if the drawing is fair. **Inferential statistics** are based on estimating the likelihood of just such an unlikely event.

We use the theory of probability to make scientific or statistical decisions. In other words, inferential statistics use likelihood, or probability, as a method for assessing whether an event is common or unusual. In psychological science we use the probability model to test a sample and to make generalizations back to a larger population.

Hypothesis Testing

Early mathematicians used the theory of probability to create today's common application of hypothesis testing (Salsburg, 2001). Almost every day we hypothesize or consider the probability of an event. For example, we might want to use operant conditioning to modify the behavior of the family pet. Really, we are training people (not dogs) to use principles of operant conditioning with their pets. To test the efficacy of this method, we might hypothesize that continuous positive reinforcement (i.e., a dog treat) will result in changing Fido's actions, or, more specifically, teaching Fido to sit. Ideally, we want our hypothesis, commonly referred to as a **research hypothesis** or **alternative hypothesis,** to be true. From a practical standpoint we use the research hypothesis to describe our ideas in writing.

However, we actually use two types of hypotheses when we apply the probability model. A second hypothesis not typically articulated, is the null hypothesis, and it serves as the underlying assumption of statistical testing. Remember that probability theory relies upon the occurrence of unusual events. When we conduct hypothesis testing, we specify a point at which we believe that an outcome is so unlikely that it probably belongs to a population other than the one we were originally working with. Because hypothesis testing is based on probabilities, not certainties, we can never be certain that our findings are in fact true. Instead, we rely on a preponderance of evidence. If we replicate results that are unlikely, we have additional evidence of an effect. Thus, scientists do not prove events; instead we collect evidence of a phenomenon. So, if we repeatedly obtain unusual outcomes, we likely conclude that there is something, usually a condition of an independent variable (IV), producing these outcomes. Statistically speaking, we set up a contingency commonly referred to as the **null hypothesis.** The null hypothesis is merely a statement that a treatment has *no* effect.

Using our dog training example, the null hypothesis is that positive reinforcement will *not* change Fido's actions. This statement, that no effect will be present, is used only for the purpose of applying statistical probability. The null hypothesis is not typically used when writing a manuscript, and we are seldom really interested in it. Instead, we state the null hypothesis only for the purpose of using a statistical test.

The alternative and null hypotheses can be written using the following statistical notation:

Alternative Hypothesis	$H_1: \mu_1 \neq \mu_2$
Null Hypothesis	$H_0: \mu_1 = \mu_2$

When using statistical notation to write an alternative hypothesis ($H_1: \mu_1 \neq \mu_2$) we indicate that the two population means are not equal. Remember, we state the alternative hypothesis to

---

Inferential statistics—Using a sample to calculate probability of an event and to generalize the likelihood of the event back to the larger population.

Alternative (Research) hypothesis (H_1)—A statement about the anticipated relationship between the IV and the DV.

Null hypothesis (H_0)—A statistical hypothesis that posits there is no relationship between the IV and DV.

reflect what we are hoping to find. Similarly, the null hypothesis (H_0: $\mu_1 = \mu_2$) indicates that the population means are equal, and it is used as the basis for statistical testing.

Conceptually, we only use the null hypothesis to conduct inferential statistics. Let's consider an experiment with two different groups. We ask one group of people to train their dog using principles of operant conditioning, and a second group (the control group) does not use a specific training program. Specifying our alternative hypothesis, we hope that the two groups perform differently. In other words, we hypothesize the dogs in the operant conditioning group will sit more often than the dogs in the group not using a training program.

Our null hypothesis, simply stated, is that the groups will not differ. In other words, dogs in the operant conditioning group will not sit more often than those in the non-treatment group.

In order to test this hypothesis, we establish a threshold for rejecting the null (H_0) or statistical hypothesis. Ideally, we *want* to reject the null hypothesis. Rejecting the null hypothesis suggests that our operant conditioning group and the non-treatment group are probably different, or that the training probably worked. We use the theory of probability in deciding whether to reject the null hypothesis and to assert that an effect is present. We need to decide what criterion we will use in our definition of an unlikely event. For this, we determine a threshold for rejecting the null hypothesis by specifying a probability value. This threshold of probability is called alpha and we usually set alpha $= .05$. Alpha (α) is a probability based on the normal distribution. In other words, there is only a 5% chance (i.e., alpha) that we declared a statistically significant difference when one was not present. In our dog training example, we reject the null hypothesis anytime we obtain a statistic that is located in the very small probability area of the distribution (that is, when the number of times the dogs sit exceeds what we expect to observe if the treatment was not effective).

How do we choose alpha? We want to be relatively confident when we reject the null hypothesis or declare a significant difference between two means. Therefore, we usually set the criterion conservatively so that we don't make too many mistakes. Setting the threshold for rejection is analogous to setting the detection level for a metal detector in an airport. We don't want the metal detector to sound an alarm at the mere presence of a single ounce of metal because it does not necessarily mean that we are carrying contraband. Instead, we calibrate the metal detector to sound whenever the metal reaches a particular threshold (perhaps several ounces of metal), one that is likely to reflect the presence of a weapon or another prohibited device.

Using this threshold, when we reject the null hypothesis (sound the alarm), leading us to conclude that the results are statistically significant, we are simply saying that based on our sample data, these results are unlikely if our IV had no effect (or if there is no metal present). In other words, in all probability, when we compare the mean of a control group with the mean of a group that received a treatment, it is unlikely that the two sample means for these groups reflect the same population means. It appears as though the treatment group mean is disparate enough from the control group mean for us to infer that the two means came from different populations; the two populations are different with respect to the dependent variable. Conversely, a non-significant difference indicates that the scores of the treatment group may have come from the same population with respect to the dependent variable; we can't reject the null hypothesis.

Remember, when we reject a null hypothesis, we are making a decision based on probability. We could also decide *not* to reject the null or statistical hypothesis. In other words, our metal detector does not sound an alarm because the metal was not detected. Not rejecting the null hypothesis simply means that our data, or calculated statistic, did not fall beyond the threshold for rejection (alpha). In terms of probability, we did not obtain results that allow us to confidently state that our means were different enough to conclude that it is unlikely that they came from the same population. As such, we would conclude that there were not differences between the sample means. Similarly, if the metal detector does not sound, we conclude that a person is not carrying contraband.

When using hypothesis testing we make a decision to either reject or not reject the null hypothesis. In other words, we may or may not detect the presence of an effect. It is important to note that we don't use the terminology "accept the null hypothesis" because we aren't trying to say that there is no effect when we test a treatment. Rather, we are looking for enough of a change in the data to move past the predetermined threshold of probability. Yet, even when we make this decision, we can be wrong.

Decisions in Statistical Hypothesis Testing

As we have already discussed, we make one of two decisions when we test a statistical or null hypothesis: (a) reject the null hypothesis or, (b) not reject the null hypothesis. However, in either case, we can make a mistake. How do these mistakes happen? Remember, hypothesis testing is based on the probability model. Probability estimates contain some amount of error.

Amount of error is related to our sample size. Smaller samples yield larger error and larger samples contain less error. Unfortunately, no matter how large our sample is, there is always going to be some error. Therefore, we can never be certain about the outcomes unless we actually measure every person in the population.

Rejecting the Null Hypothesis.   Determining whether we are correct in our decision to reject a null hypothesis requires that we know the *actual state of affairs*. In reality, we do not know definitively if a treatment has a real effect because we are always working with samples. Whenever we use a sample, we are dealing with a subset, or probability of an outcome, so we must allow for the possibility that our sample may not accurately reflect what is true in the population. In other words, when we use inferential statistics, we make our decisions based on the likelihood of an event, or the theory of probability. That is, we don't have enough information to know for certain, so we make our best guess (based on a sample), and our best guess is based on probability.

When we make a decision to reject the null hypothesis, we assert that our results are unlikely to occur if the treatment had no effect. Yet, this decision can be either correct or incorrect.

If we make a mistake and conclude that the treatment had an effect, when in reality it did not have an effect, we have committed a **Type I error.** A Type I error, or a false positive, is usually labeled as alpha ($\alpha = .05$). Alpha is the predetermined region of rejection that we selected, and alpha is the probability or likelihood that we obtained a false positive. So, if we consider our example of the metal detector, if the detector sounds an alarm when there is no weapon, the mistake is equivalent to a Type I error. Despite the "statistically significant" outcome, the theory of probability allows for the possibility that there is a real difference or that the sample data reflect a difference that really is not accurate (Type I error).

As illustrated in Figure 7.1, using the theory of probability, if we obtain a statistic that is beyond the alpha level ($\alpha = .05$), we make a decision that the obtained statistic is unlikely and that the calculated statistic is statistically significant. However, there is always the possibility that we detected an effect when an effect was not really there. In other words, there is the possibility that we are simply wrong! For example, a few high scores in the treatment group might have occurred by accident, so the mean is higher, and we mistakenly conclude that the treatment had an effect.

Type I error (alpha)—A false positive; detecting a difference when a difference does not actually exist.

If we make a Type I error, then we make a decision that there is an effect, but in reality we are wrong because an actual effect is not present. In the case of our operant conditioning example, we find that the operant conditioning class had an effect, but if we were to test the

FIGURE 7.1   *Type I Error*

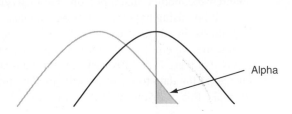

entire population, the effect would not really be present. Or, in the case of our metal detector, we may obtain a false positive or detect metal indicative of contraband, when none is present. However, if we reject the null hypothesis and we are correct, an effect is present, we make a correct decision. The likelihood of correctly detecting an effect is termed *power.*

   Power is the probability that our decision to reject the null hypothesis is correct. Power is the likelihood that we will accurately detect an effect (Murphy & Myors, 2005). As indicated in Figure 7.2 power is one of four possible outcomes that can occur when we conduct hypothesis testing.

Not Rejecting the Null Hypothesis.   When we make a decision *not* to reject the null hypothesis, we assert that our results are inconclusive, and we decide that our treatment probably did *not* have an effect. At the very least, we conclude that we do not have enough information to make a decision that there is an effect. Again, as indicated in Figure 7.2, this decision (not rejecting the null hypothesis) can be either correct or incorrect. We are correct in choosing *not* to reject the null hypothesis if there is no effect. In other words if the sample statistic does not fall beyond the level of alpha and we conclude that no effect is present, this decision is accurate if the treatment, in reality, did not have an effect. For example, if the dogs in the treatment group didn't learn to sit, then we correctly conclude that the operant conditioning treatment is not effective. Similarly, if we use the metal detector and correctly conclude that contraband is not present because the alarm did not sound, then we are correctly choosing not to reject the null hypothesis.

   However, our decision that there was *not* an effect can still be wrong. If the operant conditioning is in reality effective, but our group of dogs simply did not learn to sit, then we failed to detect the effect. Similarly, if we consider our metal detector example, this means that we did not detect metal, when in fact a person is carrying contraband. This type of an error, a **Type II error**, is defined as not rejecting the null hypothesis when we should have, that is, when the hypothesis is really false. In this case, it means that we did not detect a statistically significant difference when one was present.

Power—The likelihood that we will accurately detect an effect.

Type II error (beta)—A false negative; not detecting a difference when an actual difference is present.

FIGURE 7.2   *Hypothesis Testing Mode*

		True State of Affairs	
		No Effect	*Effect*
	Reject H_0	Type I Error α	Correct Decision (Power)
Decision	*Do Not Reject H_0*	Correct Decision	Type II Error β

FIGURE 7.3 *Hypothesis Testing Decisions*

True State of Affairs

		No Effect	*Effect*
	Reject H_0	Type I Error False Positive	Power Correct Detection of Effect
Decision	*Do Not Reject H_0*	Correct Decision Absence of Effect	Type II Error False Negative

Another way to describe a Type II error is as a false negative. A Type II error or beta (β) is not rejecting the null hypothesis when the null hypothesis is false. If we know the true state of affairs, we would also know that we erroneously concluded that there was not an effect, when an effect was actually present. Type II error is illustrated as a false negative in Figure 7.3.

A Type II error may occur because power (correctly detecting a real effect) is low. Power is influenced by several factors. One way to increase power is to increase *sensitivity of measurement.* If we use an instrument that is sensitive to changes in the DV, we are more likely to accurately detect an effect. For example, airport workers can calibrate a metal detector to be more or less sensitive. Our decision about the sensitivity level of the metal detector may result in one of two errors. The detector might sound too frequently, indicating false positives or the presence of contraband when none is present. Alternatively, the metal detector might not go off when it should, a false negative, and weapons are missed. Our decisions are affected by the sensitivity of the machine.

A second way to increase power is to increase the number of people or, in the case of our dog training example, the number of dogs in our sample. If we *increase the size of the sample,* we decrease the size of the error in our calculations. In our dog training example, we would increase the number of dogs (and their owners) participating in the operant conditioning treatment. In our metal detector example, we would calibrate the device by using many people. Remember, increasing sample size decreases error, so a decrease in the error, or the standard error of the mean (*SEM*), increases our ability to accurately detect an effect. What is the best way to decrease *SEM*? As illustrated in Figure 7.4, increasing sample size, *N*, decreases error, and increases power.

Power is also affected by effect size. **Effect size** reflects the estimated standardized difference between two means. Much like alpha, we typically specify effect size. For example, we might set the metal detector for an effect size of one ounce. In other words, we are suggesting that a one ounce increment of metal is an important minimum level. Effect size is usually reported as a standardized difference, or if we are conducting a correlation analysis, a standardized amount of shared variability. However, it is difficult to change

Effect size—Degree or magnitude of difference between treatment means.

FIGURE 7.4 *Change in Power Due to Sample Size*

N = 10   N = 50

FIGURE 7.5 *Change in Power Due to Effect Size*

FIGURE 7.5 *Change in Power Due to Effect Size*

the effect size in order to increase power. We simply specify the amount of effect that we consider to be important. Figure 7.5 illustrates how power changes based on effect size. In other words, if we believe a treatment has a very small effect, it will be difficult to detect a change in the DV. Hence, a small effect size results in lower power. A large effect size suggests that the standardized difference between means is bigger, and this increases the calculated value of power.

Normal Distribution

Earlier we described a normal distribution that comprises scores from a large number of individuals. The standardized normal distribution, sometimes called the *z* distribution, is particularly helpful because scores are associated with standard areas within the normal distribution. Most of the scores in a normal distribution are grouped near the middle of the distribution and very few scores are located in the two ends of the distribution. Because the normal distribution is broken down into standard areas, it is convenient to calculate percentiles. So, we can use the normal distribution to determine the percentage of people who are located above or below any given point. These percentages serve as estimates of probability.

As illustrated in Figure 7.6, we can see that most of the data are located near the center of the distribution. A standard percentage of the distribution is contained in the area between the mean and one standard deviation away from the mean. The actual amount of area is .3413 or approximately 34% of the distribution is located between the mean and the first standard

FIGURE 7.6 *Normal Distribution*

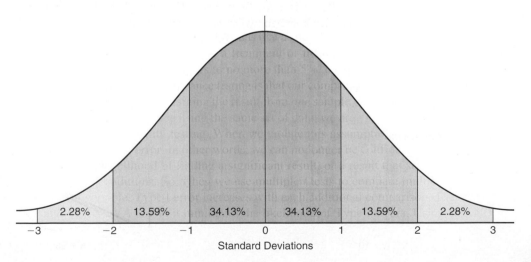

FIGURE 7.7 *Standard Deviation*

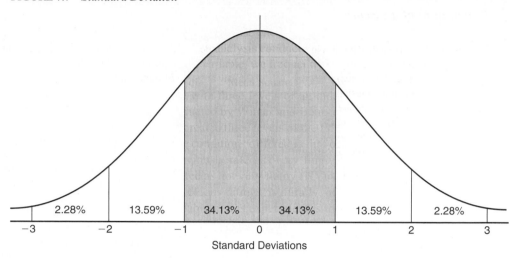

deviation. The normal curve is symmetrical, so the same proportion of the distribution is located between the mean and one standard deviation below the mean. "Therefore, if we are using a normal distribution, as illustrated in Figure 7.7, approximately 68% of the data are always located between one standard deviation above and below the mean."

You will notice that as we move further away from the middle of the distribution, the area under the curve becomes smaller. This smaller area corresponds to a lower percentage of the distribution and lower probability. Exact probability values have been calculated for each point in the normal distribution, and the probabilities are conveniently reported in the unit normal table that we will discuss later. In order to calculate an exact probability for an individual score, we must first calculate a z score (see the box on p. 158).

Once we calculate the z score, we can use it to compare an individual score to a population mean. In other words, we can gauge how likely or common a particular score is in the population. Remember, this calculation can only be applied if the distribution is normal.

How do we know that data conform to this normal distribution? First, we must understand that the normal (Gaussian) distribution is based on theory. *Theory* is simply an overriding explanation that unites and explains facts in a coherent framework. Sir Ronald Fisher was a geneticist who believed that theoretically, human characteristics are normally distributed. Therefore, if we accept the theory underlying the normal distribution, and Fisher's assertion about human characteristics, we can use the normal distribution to estimate the likelihood of many different things. Calculation of the probability of an event is simply an application of this theory, or the use of inferential techniques. However, before we can proceed with our discussion of inferential statistics, we must consider how we collect data.

Sampling Distributions

Sampling forms the basis for all inferential testing. We sample or collect data on a dependent variable and then we compare the sample data to the theoretical population distribution. Much as we use probability to calculate our possibility of winning a door prize, we can calculate the probability that our sample comes from the larger population. This idea of comparing a sample mean to a population mean forms the basis of hypothesis testing, but in order to understand hypothesis testing, we must consider many types of sampling distributions.

Calculation of a z Score

We can use the normal distribution to calculate the percentile ranking for an individual score. If we randomly select a man who is 6'2" tall (i.e., 74 inches), we can use a statistical formula to determine how unusual he is compared to the larger population. In order to compare the height of this man to that of the larger population, we must standardize the score. This *z* score formula allows us to take any raw score and convert it to a *z* score or standard score. The *z* score formula is:

$$z = \frac{X - \mu}{\sigma}$$

Where:

X = individual score
μ = population mean
σ = population standard deviation

In order to calculate the *z* score, we must know the population mean and standard deviation. The Centers for Disease Control and Prevention (CDC) maintain population data for height and other demographic characteristics. Average height for a man is approximately 70 inches with a standard

deviation of approximately 2.5 inches. We can use these data to calculate the *z* score for the man who is 6'2" or 74 inches tall.

$$z = \frac{74 - 70}{2.5} = 1.6$$

Our first step is to find the difference between the population and sample means. The difference is divided by the standard deviation to produce a *z* score. Once we obtain a *z* score, we can use it to determine a percentile ranking. The *z* Table or Unit Normal Table (Table E.1) shows *z* scores ranging from 0 to 4.00. We can associate each score with percentiles. The *z* score of 1.6 corresponds to a tabled value of .9452 or the 95th percentile. A more detailed explanation of the unit normal table is described later in the chapter.

The *z* score is standardized; this means that it possesses constant properties; the mean is always 0 and the standard deviation is always 1. Because the *z* score is based on the standard normal distribution, we can always derive a percentile ranking from a calculated *z* score when the raw scores are normally distributed.

What are **sampling distributions?** When we collect data from a group of people who we think represent the larger population, we might want to compare the mean of that sample or group to the population mean. In making this comparison, we are theoretically using all samples of a particular size (e.g., $N = 5$) and considering where our sample falls with respect to the *population of means*. Therefore, instead of using the normal distribution to estimate the likelihood of obtaining an individual score as compared to the population mean, we use the normal distribution to estimate the likelihood of obtaining a sample mean value as compared to the population of mean values. In other words, a sampling distribution contains many samples instead of only individual scores. Use of a sampling distribution allows us to apply the principles of probability to a sample rather than to an individual. These probability estimates help us determine if a sample mean is highly unlikely. Using probability to estimate the likelihood of a sample mean is another way to say that we are using inferential statistics, and we use inferential techniques to test hypotheses.

When we use a normal distribution, we rely on the mathematical assumptions that allow us to take samples and draw conclusions or calculate probabilities. However, not all distributions are normal. How can we calculate probabilities from samples if the data are not normally distributed? One answer to this question is to obtain reasonably large samples. If we use large samples, we can then rely on another mathematical assumption, the central limit theorem. The central limit theorem states that as our sample gets larger, the sampling distribution will be approximately normal (Hays, 1988).

The central limit theorem shows that as the sample size gets larger, the shape of the distribution approaches normality and variability can be standardized, that is, represented by the standard normal distribution. Recall that we discussed variance (s^2) and standard deviation (*SD*) as ways to describe variability within a sample. Variance is simply the unstandardized (i.e., raw score) version of the average squared difference between individual scores and the

Sampling distribution— Distribution of means for a particular sample size.

mean. The standard deviation is the standardized difference between the mean and an individual score. A standardized measure allows us to communicate using a common metric. In other words, when we use the standard deviation, we have the benefit of knowing that the mean is always equal to 0 and the standard deviation is always 1.

The central limit theorem also allows us to assume that with a large enough sample, we can use the normal distribution to calculate probability estimates. In addition to having a standard way of describing variability, the central limit theorem allows us to break the distribution into standard increments or percentiles. We can convert any sample mean into a standard score and place it within the normal distribution. Thus, we can calculate probabilities, or the likelihood of an event within a population, even when we don't have all of the data. Very simply, if the sample size is large enough, we can use the normal distribution to obtain probabilities.

Theoretically, each sampling distribution (not a distribution of individual scores, but rather a distribution of means) contains all possible samples for a particular sample size. For example, if we specify a sample size of five, our sampling distribution comprises all possible *samples* of five scores. If you take the average of all possible combinations of sample means (for a particular sample size), the obtained value equals the population mean or μ. We use the assumptions of normality and large sample size to calculate percentiles for sample means based on the population mean.

Standard Error of the Mean.   We use sampling distributions as a basis for determining the probability, or likelihood, of obtaining a particular effect. However, before we can proceed with using sampling distributions to determine probability, we must understand how variability works in a sampling distribution. Recall that we use the standard deviation as an index of variability for individual scores. That is, we figure out how many standard deviations from the mean a particular raw score falls, then we use the normal distribution to determine the percentile ranking for that score.

We use the standard deviation for calculating percentile rankings for individual scores, but we need to use a slightly different measure of variability for sampling distributions. When we use sampling distributions, instead of individual scores, we need a measure of variability that is comparable to the standard deviation. Indeed, the **Standard Error of the Mean (*SEM*)** provides an index of the variability of sampling means instead of individual scores. The *SEM* allows us to estimate a range of expected differences between a sample mean and a population mean. We can use the Standard Error of the Mean to calculate the percentile for a mean value, rather than an individual score.

For a moment, let's consider an *individual score.* We can use the standard deviation to describe how far an individual's score is from the mean. The standard deviation is used to calculate a *z* score, which, when used with the unit normal table, allows us to identify the percentile of the individual score.

If we use the same principle, but instead substitute the sample *mean* value, we can derive a percentile for the mean instead of the individual score. In this case, rather than working with the spread of individual scores, we are working with a *set of means*. We figure out how the means of similar samples are likely to be distributed, and then we compute how far our mean (M) is from the mean of all the means (μ), as shown in Figure 7.8. When we are working with our sample mean, our computation is based on how many standard errors of the mean units our sample mean is from the population mean. In other words, rather than using standard deviation units to describe variability of an individual score, we use the standard error of the mean (*SEM*) to describe how far a sample mean is from a population mean.

Standard error of the mean (*SEM*)—An index of variability for the means of the population distribution.

Let's compare the *standard deviation* for an individual, to the standard error of the mean for a sample. If we consider the individual score, using the mean and standard deviation from our earlier example, we know that the average height is 70 inches and the standard deviation is 2.5 inches. Whenever we know the mean and standard deviation, we can easily transform

FIGURE 7.8   *Sampling Distribution*

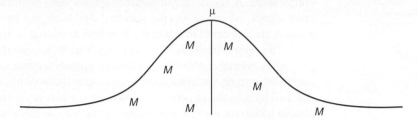

any raw score into a *z* score and ultimately, a percentile. For example, if we want to determine a percentile for a raw score value of 72.5, we simply calculate the *z* score value ($z = 1$) and use the unit normal table to identify the percentile.

$$z = \frac{X - \mu}{SD} = \frac{72.5 - 70}{2.5} = 1$$

A *z* score of 1 is located one standard deviation above the mean and corresponds to the 84th percentile of the curve.

It is easy to see how we use the standard deviation in the *z* formula to derive a percentile for an individual score. Much like using the standard deviation to calculate a *z* score for a single value, we can calculate the standard error of the mean (instead of the standard deviation) to determine the percentile of a sample mean rather than an individual score. Although the standard deviation and standard error of the mean are labeled differently, they retain the same percentile rankings contained in the normal distribution. In other words, we use standard deviation units for individual scores and standard error of the mean units for samples.

Calculation of Standard Error of the Mean   Recall that calculation of the standard deviation (*SD*) for an individual score is simply an index of variability, or standard distance from the mean. The standard error of the mean (*SEM*) is also an index of variability, but instead of individual scores we are using mean scores. Because we are using a distribution of means, rather than individual scores, we need to use the *SEM* instead of the standard deviation. Figure 7.9 illustrates the comparison of standard deviation to standard error of the mean.

The *SEM* provides us with a standard estimate of how much we can expect each sample mean to deviate from the population mean. The *SEM* is also an indication of how much inaccuracy is present in our observations. The *SEM* is very similar to a standard deviation. To calculate

FIGURE 7.9   *Distributions*

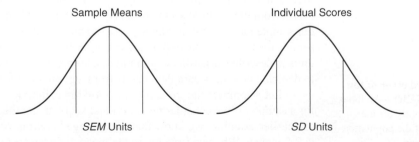

the *SEM,* simply divide the standard deviation by the square root of the sample size. In other words, the *SEM* is related to the size of the sample. In practice, we use the following formula.

$$SEM \text{ or } \sigma_M = \frac{\sigma}{\sqrt{N}}$$

Earlier we used $M = 70$ and $SD = 2.5$ to calculate an *individual z* score. Using this same information, we can perform a similar calculation for a mean score. However, instead of using the standard deviation to calculate the *z* score, we must use the *SEM.*

The *SEM* is affected by the size of the sample. Let's examine how sample size might affect our accuracy of estimating average height. The average height for 20-year-old men is 70 inches, and the corresponding population standard deviation is approximately 2.5 inches (CDC, 2007). Our first step in calculating the *z* score for a sample of 25 young men is to derive the *SEM* (σ_M) for the sample:

$$\sigma_M = \frac{\sigma}{\sqrt{N}} = \frac{2.5}{\sqrt{25}} = \frac{2.5}{5} = .5$$

Where:

σ = standard deviation
N = sample size

Our calculated *SEM* (σ_M) is .5 or $^1/_2$ an inch. In other words, with samples of $N = 25$, we can anticipate a .5 inch increment for each standard unit from the population mean. If we calculate a *z* score for the sample, rather than the individual score, the standard unit for the sample or *SEM* is .5 instead of the standard unit (*SD*) for the individual score of 2.5. As you can see in Figure 7.10, using the *SEM* allows us to determine the percentile for a sample mean, rather than an individual score.

FIGURE 7.10 *Variability*

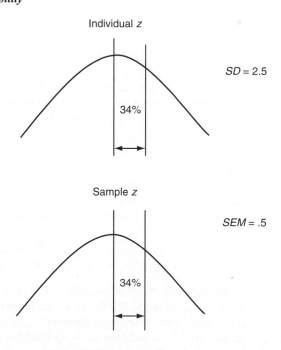

Single Sample z Test

We can use the normal distribution and the theory of probability to compare a sample mean to a population mean. A single sample z test is used when we know both the population mean (μ) and the population standard deviation (σ). Examples of data that can be used with the single sample z test include IQ scores, GREs, SATs, height, and weight. The single sample z test allows us to compare a sample mean to the known population mean.

Let's consider an example using GRE scores. If we are interested in testing whether a GRE preparation course is useful, we can compare the average GRE score from students completing the prep course to the GRE population mean, or average score from the standardized test. We can use the z test because we know the population mean and standard deviation. The GRE population mean ($\mu = 500$) and standard deviation ($\sigma = 100$) are considered to be standard scores. We rely on the probability model to determine if our sample mean, or students taking the prep course, is significantly different from the population mean.

Suppose we offer the preparation course to 25 students and find that after completing the course, the sample mean score is 540. Is a 40 point difference big enough that we believe that if we did the study again, we would get a similarly large difference? In other words, could we have obtained this difference on the basis of chance alone? There are really two important questions: (a) Is the difference statistically significant and (b) is the difference meaningful? Let us begin by examining the likelihood or probability that the change in this score is statistically significant.

Significance Testing.   The z *test* (not a z score) allows us to compare a sample mean to a population mean for the purpose of determining the likelihood that the sample mean comes from the same population. If the two means are far enough apart, we make a decision about the probability of this occurrence. So, in our GRE example we use the following formula to make this comparison:

$$z = \frac{M - \mu}{\sigma_M}$$

As you can see from the z formula, we need to calculate the standard error of the mean (σ_M) before we can compute the value of z. Remember, the *SEM* is related to sample size. An important assumption of the underlying probability model is that our estimates become more accurate as we increase sample size. Therefore, if we select sample sizes that are larger, we reduce the size of our standard error and increase accuracy. We want less error! In other words, the larger the sample, the more likely the sample mean accurately represents our population mean. So, if the sample is large, we reduce the size of the *SEM* or error.

You will notice that the *SEM* functions not only as the divisor, but it is also really an index of error. In other words, if we increase sample size, the *SEM* becomes smaller. However, if the difference between the means ($M - \mu$) remains the same, and the *SEM* or error, is reduced, we obtain a larger z score. We typically want to decrease error, obtain larger z values, and find a statistically significant difference between the sample and population means.

$$\sigma_M = \frac{\sigma}{\sqrt{N}} = \frac{100}{\sqrt{25}} = \frac{100}{5} = 20$$

Using our standard deviation ($SD = 100$) and sample size ($N = 25$), we can obtain a standard error of the mean (*SEM*). Based on the normal distribution, our estimation of the population mean gets better with larger samples because the mean of our sample, which we might use to estimate the population mean, is likely to be closer to the population mean when we use large samples. The important point is that we are trying to estimate something; larger sample sizes lead to smaller *SEMs,* therefore, our sample mean is likely to be closer to the actual population mean.

Let's calculate the *z* test for the sample of 25 students completing the GRE prep course. Our *SEM* or calculated index of error is 20 points. The difference between the students taking the prep course and the population mean ($M - \mu$ or 540–500) is 40 points. We use these values to calculate the ratio, or probability, that is associated with the difference between the students in the GRE prep course relative to the GRE population mean.

$$z = \frac{M - \mu}{\sigma_M} = \frac{540 - 500}{20} = \frac{40}{20} = 2.0$$

Our *z* test yields a z value of 2.0. What does this z value really indicate? Does this value suggest that the mean GRE score of students in the GRE prep course is likely to be reflective of the original population mean? Or, does the difference between the sample and population mean suggest, or infer, a difference that is likely to have occurred because of the preparation course?

In order to answer this question we compare our calculated *z* test value to a *z* table of probabilities. The *z* table or Unit Normal Table (Table E.1) lists all values of *z* between 0

Using the Unit Normal Table (Table E.1)

The normal distribution possesses special properties that allow us to ascertain percentiles. The *z* Table or Unit Normal Table provides cumulative probabilities associated with each calculated *z* score.

The Unit Normal Table contains three columns. Column A lists *z* scores ranging from 0 (μ) to 4.00. Although it is possible to obtain a *z* score larger than 4.00, the unit normal table only ranges to $z = 4.00$ because the percentiles associated with values larger than 4.00 are extremely small; *z* scores this large occur very rarely.

Column B contains proportions of the distribution contained in the body. This means that Column B contains the proportion, or percentage, of the normal distribution falling below the associated *z* score. In other words, the *z* table breaks the normal distribution into proportions, and the proportion located on one side of the *z* score (body) is the percentage of the distribution falling below a *z* score; and the proportion located on the other side of the *z* score (tail) is the percentage of the normal distribution falling above this value. Column C contains the percentage of the normal distribution falling above the *z* score, or the tail of the distribution.

A *z* score of 0 is equivalent to the midpoint of the distribution, thus the proportion of the distribution in the body is .5000 or 50%. A *z* score of 0 is synonymous with the 50th percentile and breaks the distribution in half. Similarly, a $z = 1.65$ is associated with a proportion of the body equal to .9505 (Column B) or 95% of the distribution. In other words, a $z = 1.65$ is located at the 95th percentile. Column C contains the remaining proportion of the distribution or tail. So, Column C lists the proportion of the distribution above the $z = 1.65$ as .0495 or, with rounding, 5%.

Because the distribution is symmetrical, the unit normal table provides us with only half of the values contained in the distribution, the positive half. We don't need the entire table because the information is identical for both sides of the distribution. In other words, positive and negative *z* values are associated with related probability values. If we simply obtain the information associated with positive values, we can use the same information to derive the probability values for negative *z* scores. For example, if we obtain a *z* value of 2.0, the unit normal table reports that .9772 or approximately 98% of the distribution is located below the point of $z = 2.0$ and .0228 or 2% of the distribution is located above this point. In other words, a value of 2.0 corresponds to the 98th percentile. If however, our z value is -2.0 instead of 2.0, we apply the principle of symmetry and find that the -2.0 value corresponds to the 2nd percentile.

z score	Proportion in body	Proportion in tail
0	0.5000	0.5000
0.01	0.5040	0.4960
0.02	0.5080	0.4920
0.03	0.5120	0.4880
0.04	0.5160	0.4840
0.05	0.5199	0.4801
0.06	0.5239	0.4761

and 4.00 with the associated percentages that we referenced earlier. This table allows us to determine the percentile associated with a z score. For example, if we obtain a z value of 1.65, this value corresponds to the 95th percentile. In other words, approximately 5% of the distribution lies beyond the z score of 1.65. Therefore, if we use the table to determine the percentile for our calculated $z = 2.0$, we find that approximately 2% of the distribution is located beyond this point. In other words, if we use the z test to compare the sample mean ($M = 540$) to the average GRE score ($\mu = 500$), we find that if we were to take repeated samples of 25 people from the population, we would end up with a mean as high as 540 only about 2% of the time.

How often would such a group that had not taken a preparation course have a mean as high as 540? According to our calculations, this would occur only about 2% of the time. That is, 98% of the time, such a group would have a mean score below 540. As such, it is reasonable to conclude that a mean of 540 is unusual enough that we should conclude that the GRE preparation group is not like the original population. In other words, our group comes from a different population, a population that scores higher than 500.

Steps in Hypothesis Testing

Earlier, we described the process for comparing a sample of students who completed a GRE preparation course to the population, or standard scores for the GRE. The z test is a single sample inferential technique that allows us to compare a single sample mean to the population mean when we are working with standardized values. From a practical standpoint, we do not use single sample tests very often. We use the z test primarily to illustrate the concept of hypothesis testing. The z test not only allows us to use probability to test the hypothesis, but it also provides us with a direct measure of effect size. Regardless of the statistical test that we might use, we follow the same basic procedures for hypothesis testing. We typically take four steps in the process.

1. *State the hypotheses.* Earlier we distinguished between the research (H_1) and the null hypothesis (H_0). Using the research hypothesis, we hypothesize that our sample of students participating in the GRE preparation course is likely to have higher scores. Because we are using an inferential technique to test this hypothesis, we also state a null or statistical hypothesis. Remember, although we don't typically use this hypothesis when writing results, we must specify this hypothesis for the purpose of statistical testing. In this case, we state that there would be no difference between the sample and population mean GRE score. Another way to state this is:

$$H_0: \mu_{GREPREP} = \mu_{GRE}$$

This statistical hypothesis provides the basis for testing whether our GRE preparation course results in an effect that is statistically unlikely to occur in the absence of a treatment.

2. *Set alpha.* Earlier, we indicated that we set alpha to reflect the point at which we conclude that the results are unlikely to occur if the treatment did not have an effect. When we test hypotheses, we must specify what we consider to be an unlikely outcome. In other words, we specify when the sample is so unlikely that we no longer believe that the treatment was ineffective. As you already know, scientists typically use the conventional value of .05 or $\alpha = .05$. Researchers almost always use what we call a *two-tailed hypothesis test.* For this reason, we will not discuss one-tailed hypothesis testing in this text. It is sufficient to know that when using a two-tailed test, the 5%, or alpha, is split between the two tails of the distribution. Our alpha level is therefore derived by obtaining the z-score associated with 2.5% (.025) of each tail or $z = 1.96$. If we obtain a sample mean located in this alpha area, then we conclude that our sample is unlikely (only a 5% chance) to be a part of the larger untreated population of GRE scores.

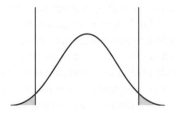

3. *Calculate the statistic.* We specify our hypothesis and alpha level prior to calculating a statistic. In our example, we calculate the single sample test or z test to determine if the GRE preparation course affected the GRE scores. If we conclude that the result is statistically unlikely, and we reject the statistical hypothesis, then our research hypothesis is true and the course affected the scores. How do we make this determination? We compare our calculated z score to the tabled z score. If our calculated z score is larger than the specified alpha value ($z = 1.96$) located in the table, we conclude that our calculated value is unlikely to have occurred if the GRE preparation group, or sample, was from the same group as the original population, and that our findings are statistically significant. However, statistical significance does not always mean that the effect is practically significant. It is possible to find a statistically unlikely occurrence or statistical significance that is not meaningfully different. For example, how much change in a GRE score would be necessary in order for you to consider the improvement in the score to be meaningful? Is a 10-point change helpful? Or would we expect a 50-point difference in our score? In order to fully understand what amount of change is meaningful, we specify an *effect size.*

4. *Calculate and report effect size. Effect size* reflects the estimated standardized difference between two means. In this case we are comparing a sample mean from students completing a preparation course to the overall population mean of GRE scores. We can also find the effect size when we compare two or more sample means. Effect size is usually reported as a standardized difference or a standardized amount of shared variability. In this example, we are working with standard scores, so the calculated z score is our measure of effect size. We calculated a $z = 2.00$. This suggests the sample of students taking the GRE preparation course performed two standard deviations above the population mean. An effect size of two standard deviations is considered to be large.

The steps for conducting a hypothesis test produce a test statistic (z value), a corresponding probability value, and an effect size. We obtain the probability value by using the calculated z (or as we will see shortly, a t statistic) to obtain the probability value from the respective statistical table. We report each of these values as a way of scientifically communicating our results. We will use these same steps for subsequent inferential tests.

Effect Size. Although we know that the obtained sample mean is unlikely to occur in a population whose mean is 500, our second question is perhaps even more important. Is the obtained sample mean for the students taking the GRE prep course meaningfully different from the population mean GRE score? In order to answer this question, we need to calculate an effect size. *Effect size,* as we discussed previously, is simply the standardized difference between the sample and population mean. In this example we can think of the unstandardized effect size as the 40 point difference between $\mu = 500$ and $M = 540$. However, if we use raw scores to report effect size, it is often difficult to communicate meaningful results when we use different measures. Therefore, effect size is a standardized index and in this example, it conveys the difference between the group taking the GRE prep course and the population mean for GRE scores. In order to report this difference, we simply standardize, or translate, the raw score into a standard score.

In general, we can think of effect size as a standardized difference between one mean and another. For example, a z score is a standardized value. When we communicate using a z score, we can easily transform any z score into a percentile. Similarly, if we transform raw scores into a standardized effect size, we can easily communicate, using a common metric, the amount of change. In this example, effect size is the standardized difference between the population mean ($\mu = 500$) and the sample mean ($M = 540$). The z value is already a standardized difference between means (Grissom & Kim, 2005), so it provides us with a direct measure of effect size. Hence, our z score of 2.0, located at the 98th percentile, suggests that, as a group, the students taking the GRE prep course outscored the general population by 98%. That is, if we studied groups of 25 students who did not take a GRE preparation course, most of the time the mean for a group would be around 500. (Remember, the z score is a standardized value. Because it is standardized, the mean for a z score is always equal to 0 and the standard deviation is always equal to 1.)

Is this a meaningful difference? The large effect size suggests that the difference is meaningful. We can also use pragmatic criteria to determine whether an effect is meaningful. For example, does the cost of the change in the GRE score justify the cost of the GRE preparation course? Deriving meaning from the effect size is sometimes a researcher's decision.

We will discuss additional standardized measures of effect size throughout this text. The APA (2010) recommends that effect size should almost always be reported because it offers important information about the applicability of differences between means.

Single Sample *t* Test

Previously, we described how we might use a z test to compare a sample mean to the population mean. Using the inferential process, if we find a large difference, we are likely to infer that our sample is not reflective of the original population, in other words, our sample differs such that it probably belongs to a different population. Think of this as implying two different populations exist, one whose members average about 500 and another whose numbers average somewhere around 540. In our earlier example, we concluded that the mean GRE score for students taking the preparatory course ($M = 540$) belonged to a distribution that was different from the original group ($\mu = 500$). In other words, the prep group belongs to a different population—a population of people participating in preparation courses.

We can only use the z test if we know the population mean and standard deviation. GRE scores are standardized; in other words, they are based on a large number of scores, and therefore we know the mean and standard deviation. In this example we were able to compare GRE scores to the normal distribution, but we usually do not know the parameters (i.e., population mean and standard deviation) associated with a characteristic that we are interested in examining. For example, perhaps we are interested in examining opinions about a political candidate. We can use a Likert scale ranging from 1 (*Disapproval*) to 5 (*Approval*) to obtain a rating of the candidate. With this type of scale, we don't usually know the population mean and standard deviation; we don't know the average approval rating of the candidate. Instead, we define the population mean as equal to 3 because this is a neutral value indicating ambivalence.

If we collect data from a group of individuals, we can generate a sample mean approval rating and compare this to the defined neutral rating or population mean. We can also calculate an estimate of the standard deviation.

It might also be helpful to conduct an inferential test to determine if the approval rating is significantly different from a neutral value. We define 3 as our population mean because it represents the average value, which is a state of ambivalence. Although we don't have a predefined population mean as we do with standardized scores (e.g., GRE, IQ), we specify the population mean as the midpoint in the Likert scale. In other words, we want to compare the average reported approval rating to the specified neutral value or population mean for the Likert scale.

This opinion questionnaire is not a standardized measure, so we cannot assume the distribution is normal. We also do not know the standard deviation. Because we cannot assume that the data are normally distributed, we must use a different sampling distribution to make our comparison. A t distribution is one such sampling distribution that is quite similar to the normal distribution. We can use the t distribution with small samples whose scores resemble normal distributions, but that aren't quite normal.

Earlier, we used a z test to compare a sample mean to a population mean. On the basis of this calculation, we inferred that our sample was different from the population. We made this determination on the basis of a ratio. In other words, we compared the actual difference between the sample and population means ($M - \mu$) to the amount of error (σ_M) present in the data.

As a reminder, error is related to the size of the standard deviation and sample size. Standard deviation is an index of the amount of variability in the scores. We cannot change the standard deviation, but we can change the size of the sample. Remember, if we increase sample size, we decrease the size of the error. The *SEM* is calculated by dividing standard deviation by the square root of the sample size. So, as we increase sample size, we necessarily decrease the error in our sample. This holds true for both the z test and the t test.

The distinction between the error term that we use in a z test and the error term that we use to calculate the t test is extremely important. When we calculate error in the z test, we make this calculation based on a known population standard deviation. However, when calculating the t test, we do not know the population standard deviation. Instead, we must use an *estimated* standard deviation for our calculation of the t test. Because our standard deviation is estimated, it is probably not as accurate. In other words, our estimated standard deviation introduces an additional element of inaccuracy. So, rather than using the sample size (N) to calculate the *SEM,* we use an adjusted sample size ($N - 1$) to calculate an *estimated* standard error of the mean.

$$\sigma_M = \frac{\sigma}{\sqrt{N}}$$

$$s_M = \frac{s}{\sqrt{N}}$$

But wait! The calculation for the standard error of the mean appears to be almost identical to that of the estimated standard error of the mean. How do these two equations really differ?

In order to find the difference between these two formulas we must go back to our formulas for standard deviation. The standard deviation provides an average distance of how likely a given score is to fall from the mean. As illustrated below, we calculate the standard deviation for a standardized normal distribution by using N, but for a sample (estimated) standard deviation we must use $N - 1$, called **degrees of freedom** (Hays, 1988). Quite simply,

Degrees of freedom (*df*)—The number of values that are free to vary when using an inferential statistic.

degrees of freedom are calculated whenever we conduct an inferential statistical test. Degrees of freedom (*df*) refer to a complicated assumption underlying our ability to take results from a sample and estimate parameters of a population. When we use a *t* test, our degrees of freedom, or number of scores that vary, increase as a function of sample size. Hence, when we estimate a sample *SEM* (s_M), we use the $N - 1$ calculation to obtain the standard deviation as illustrated below:

$$\sigma = \sqrt{\frac{\sum (X - M)^2}{N}}$$

$$s = \sqrt{\frac{\sum (X - M)^2}{N - 1}}$$

So, the degrees of freedom are taken into account when we calculate the standard deviation before we calculate the standard error of the mean.

Earlier we relied upon the underlying assumptions of the *z* distribution to derive probability estimates. When we use a *t* test, we rely upon assumptions of the *t* distribution to derive our estimated probability. The *t* distribution, or more accurately, the family of *t* distributions, is based upon the size of the sample. So, if we obtain a very large sample, the *t* distribution mirrors the normal, or *z*, distribution. As illustrated in Figure 7.11, when the sample becomes large enough, the *t* distribution approximates the normal distribution.

Using the *t* formula, although similar to the *z* formula, allows us to compare a single sample to a population for which we do not know the standard deviation.

$$t = \frac{M - \mu}{s_M}$$

If we return to our example of voter opinions, we can use the single sample *t* test to examine approval ratings for a political candidate. The population mean (μ) that we specified is the neutral value (3) from the Likert scale. The sample mean ($M = 4$) comes from our data in Table 7.1. We will need to compare this neutral value ($M = 3$) to the value in the sample data ($M = 4$) obtained from our voters. Thus, we compare the population mean of 3 to the sample mean of 4 to ascertain if the voters express a statistically significant variation in approval rating.

FIGURE 7.11   *Normal and t Distributions*

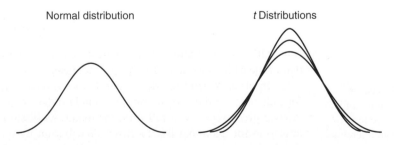

Normal distribution   *t* Distributions

TABLE 7.1 *Opinion Data*

Opinion
2
4
5
3
5
4
3
5
5
4
$\sum X = 40$

In order to complete the *t* test calculation, we must begin by calculating basic descriptive statistics; the mean and the standard deviation.

Step 1: Using the *M* for this set of scores ($M = 4$), we may now calculate the standard deviation for this sample of scores.

$$s = \sqrt{\frac{\sum (X - M)^2}{N - 1}} = \sqrt{\frac{10}{9}} = \sqrt{1.22} = 1.05$$

Remember, the standard deviation calculation employs the $N - 1$ or degrees of freedom formula in the denominator. Note that we are now using our degrees of freedom ($N - 1$) because we are calculating a *sample* standard deviation.

Step 2: We can use the *standard deviation* to perform our second step, calculating the estimated standard error of the mean (s_M).

$$s_M = \frac{s}{\sqrt{N}} = \frac{1.05}{\sqrt{10}} = \frac{1.05}{3.16} = .33$$

Step 3: Finally, we complete calculation of the single sample *t* test using our estimated standard error of the mean and the difference between means.

$$t = \frac{M - \mu}{s_M} = \frac{4 - 3}{.33} = \frac{1}{.33} = 3.03$$

Our calculated *t* test value, or ratio of the difference between means (which equals 1.00) and the estimated error (which is 0.33), is 3.03. Is this a statistically significant outcome? In order to determine if this calculated value is significant, we need to compare this value to another table, the *t* Distribution Table (Table E.2). We use $df = 9$ to find the tabled *t* value because $N - 1 = 9$ in this example. If we use an alpha level of .05 and our degrees of freedom ($df = 9$), we find that the tabled value is 2.262. This means that our calculated *t* test value needs to be larger than 2.262 to be considered statistically significant. As illustrated in Figure 7.12, our calculated value of 3.03 is

FIGURE 7.12   *Rejecting the Null Hypothesis*

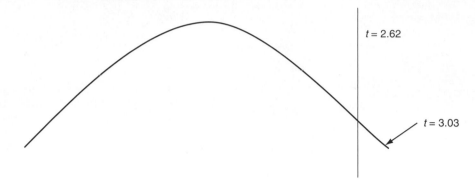

$t = 2.62$

$t = 3.03$

larger than 2.262, so we conclude that the results are statistically significant. Another, less technical way of saying this is that we have enough evidence to conclude that our group of 10 people departs from a neutral rating of the candidate.

Using the t *Distribution Table*

The *t* Distribution Table provides probabilities associated with each calculated *t* value. The *t* distribution is symmetrical; therefore, the tabled probabilities listed can be used with either positive or negative *t* values.

Each statistical table is structured differently, and the *t* table is no exception. Across the top of the *t* table we find five probability values, or alpha levels. Most often we use the 0.05 probability column. Remember we specify a desired alpha level (Type I error rate), and we use the probability

values specified by the table to determine if our calculated *t* value is unlikely. In other words, the values listed in each of the columns are a *t* value or point at which the specified probability region begins.

We use degrees of freedom (*df*) to find the *t* value. In our example, we obtained opinions from 10 people. Our degrees of freedom are related to the number of people in a sample. In the case of the single sample *t* test, degrees of freedom are calculated using $N - 1$.

TABLE E.2   *Significance values for the t distribution.*

Computed values of t are significant if they are larger than the critical value in the table.

α Levels for Directional (One-Tailed) Tests				
.05	.025	.01	.005	.0005
α Levels for Nondirectional (Two-Tailed) Tests				
df	.10	.05	.02	.01	.001
1	6.314	12.706	31.821	63.657	636.619
2	2.920	4.303	6.965	9.925	31.598
3	2.353	3.182	4.541	5.841	12.924
4	2.132	2.776	3.747	4.604	8.610
5	2.015	2.571	3.365	4.032	6.869

Reporting Results. How do we report the results of our calculated *t* test? For every statistical technique, we use a corresponding scientific writing style to report our results. It is important to write clearly. One way to ensure clarity is to write your results without reference to the statistics and to add the statistical information after clearly writing the prose. For example, you might begin with the following paragraph:

> Ten people responded to an inquiry about their approval rating of a political candidate. We obtained equal proportions of men and women. Respondents rated the candidate on a Likert scale ranging from 1 (*Disapproval*) to 5 (*Approval*). A rating of 3 indicated a neutral opinion. We compared the average rating to the neutral value in order to determine if our participants differed significantly from the average. Respondents generally expressed approval of the candidates. The average approval rating was not significantly different from average.

The paragraph conveys information that allows us to understand the results. Using the appropriate format, we simply add the statistical information:

> Ten people responded to an approval rating of a political candidate. We obtained equal proportions of men ($n = 5$) and women ($n = 5$). Respondents rated the candidate on a Likert scale ranging from 1 (*Disapproval*) to 5 (*Approval*). A rating of 3 indicated a neutral opinion. We compared the average rating to the neutral value in order to determine if our participants differed significantly from the average. Respondents generally expressed approval ($M = 4, SD = 1.05$) of the candidates. The average approval rating was significantly different from average, $t(9) = 3.03, p < .05$.

In this example we used the single sample *t* test to examine whether an opinion was different from a neutral value. The actual difference between the neutral value and the sample mean is compared to the amount of error. In other words, we calculate a ratio to determine if the opinion is likely different from a neutral value.

Computer Analysis Using SPSS

In this chapter we provided an overview of statistical hypothesis testing and an explanation of the single sample *t* test. We don't often conduct a single sample test however, if you wish to use SPSS to conduct a single sample t test, you will need to perform the following steps.

Using our hypothetical data from the survey above we employ the analyze function to initiate the single sample *t* test. As illustrated in Figure 7.13 on page 172, select Compare Means, and then select the One-Sample T test.

After selecting the One-Sample T test, you must use the dialogue box to select the variable that you wish to analyze. In this case we are using the "opinion" variable as illustrated in Figure 7.14.

Clicking on "OK" generates output for the single sample *t* test. SPSS generates descriptive statistics for the variable. As illustrated in Figure 7.15, we know that the average approval rating was 4 ($SD = 1.05$). The statistically significant results, $t(9) = 3.00, p = .01$, of the single sample *t* test are reflected in the SPSS output in Figure 7.16. Notice that we obtain an exact probability level when we use an SPSS, so it is not necessary to use a statistical table to determine if a calculated *t* value is significant, and we can report an exact probability or *p* value.

FIGURE 7.13 *Select Statistic*

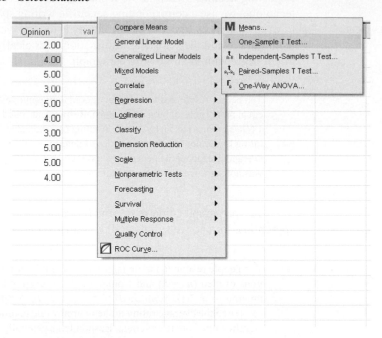

FIGURE 7.14 *Selecting the Variable*

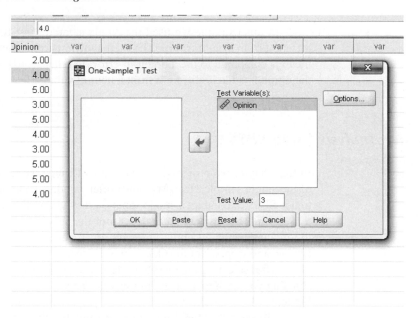

FIGURE 7.15 *Descriptive Statistics*

One-Sample Statistics

	N	Mean	Std. Deviation	Std. Error Mean
Opinion	10	4.0000	1.05409	.33333

FIGURE 7.16   *Single Sample t Test*

One-Sample Test

	Test Value = 3				95% Confidence Interval of the Difference	
	t	df	Sig. (2-tailed)	Mean Difference	Lower	Upper
Opinion	3.000	9	.015	1.00000	.2459	1.7541

Chapter Summary

This chapter contains some of the most complex information in this book. Much of what we discussed is abstract and theoretical, and this contributes to the complexity. Nevertheless, you may want to regularly refer to this chapter because it provides the foundation for inferential or statistical testing.

Statistical tests are based on the theory of probability. We apply the theory of probability to determine if an event is likely. If we find an unlikely event, we pay attention. Unlikely occurrences might reflect the presence of an aberration in the situation, or in the case of an experiment, a change or effect from an IV.

We use probability in a very specific way when conducting hypotheses tests. In essence, we compare the values from our sample to our population value. If we discover that our sample statistic (i.e., sample mean) is located very far from our population parameter (i.e., population mean), we conclude that our sample is different from our original population. Usually, this is a good thing. If our means are different, we infer that the treatment, or independent variable, had an effect and we infer, or consider, the effect of the treatment for a population of individuals that might receive the treatment.

In addition to determining the likelihood of an event, we are even more interested in the amount of change present in a study. Effect size, or the amount of the change in the dependent variable, is calculated for each inferential test. Effect size is reported as a standardized difference between means or a measure of relationship between the independent and dependent variables. In either case, effect size offers us a tangible measure of what is occurring in our experimental study.

Single sample inferential tests, the *t* test and the *z* test, allow us to compare the sample mean to a population mean. In reality, these tests are not often used because they reflect use of a single sample design, but they serve as a useful foundation for understanding inferential testing. Usually, we prefer to have at least two groups (treatment and control) for comparison. Two groups allow us to use random assignment, thus strengthening our ability to make cause-and-effect assertions. Despite the drawbacks of using a single sample design, sometimes these are the only options available, particularly when conducting applied research. Single sample tests allow us to determine whether an outcome is statistically unusual, and it allows us to determine the amount of difference between the population and sample means.

Key Terms

Alternative (Research) hypothesis (H_1)
Degrees of freedom
Effect size
Inferential statistics

Null hypothesis (H_0)
Power
Sampling distribution
Standard error of the mean (*SEM*)

Type I error (alpha)
Type II error (beta)

Chapter Review Questions

Multiple Choice Questions

1. Jane recently attended a geocaching event with 100 people and was entered in a door prize raffle. What is the likelihood that Jane will win the door prize?
   a. 1%
   b. 5%
   c. 10%
   d. 11%

2. Dr. Marek constructed a hypothesis and set limits so that she would minimize the likelihood of obtaining a false positive. Which of the following steps did she take to minimize the false positive?
   a. Set a low alpha level (.01)
   b. Set a high alpha level (.10)
   c. Specified a small effect size
   d. Stated only an alternative hypothesis

3. A researcher discovered that the technology for detecting possible tumors had a high false positive rate. In statistical terms, how would you describe this problem?
   a. Type I error
   b. Type II error
   c. Power
   d. Standard Error of the Mean

4. Several confounding variables interfered with a researcher's ability to detect a treatment effect, resulting in an unusually low rejection rate of the null hypothesis. Which of the following is most likely present in this study?
   a. Type I Error
   b. Type II Error
   c. Correctly rejecting H_0
   d. Correctly not rejecting H_0

5. A well-documented treatment was replicated and found to have an effect in improving depression. What is the most likely outcome reflected in these results?
   a. Type I Error
   b. Type II Error
   c. Correctly rejecting H_0
   d. Correctly not rejecting H_0

6. In a normal distribution, what percentage of the population falls at or below a $z = 1.25$?
   a. 11%
   b. 39%
   c. 89%
   d. 34%

7. In a normal distribution, what percentage of the population falls at or above $z = -2.15$?
   a. 2%
   b. 98%
   c. 48%
   d. 34%

8. A raw score of $X = 25$, $\mu = 27$, and $\sigma = 2$ will yield which of the following z scores?
   a. -10
   b. 10
   c. 1
   d. -1

9. A raw score of $X = 23$, $\mu = 25$, $\sigma = 10$, from a sample of $N = 100$, will yield which of the following z test values?
   a. -1
   b. -2
   c. -2.25
   d. -1.25

10. With an $X = 47$, $M = 45$, $SD = 5$ and $N = 25$, calculate the t test value.
    a. 1.25
    b. 1.50
    c. 2.00
    d. 2.25

Essay Questions

11. Describe how the standard error of the mean compares to the standard deviation.

12. Describe the relationship between standard error of the mean and sample size.

13. Using a standard deviation of 10, calculate the *SEM* for a sample size of 100. Then using the same standard deviation, calculate the *SEM* for a sample size of 25. Explain the difference between the two *SEM*s.

14. Explain how the z score compares to the z test.

15. Describe the information contained in the unit normal table. How do you use the unit normal table to describe a sample?

16. Describe and provide an example of a desirable effect size.

17. How does the single sample z test compare to the single sample t test?

18. How do we use the t table to describe the results of our single sample t test?

19. Athletes are often tested for use of performance-enhancing substances. If we consider this testing in the context of hypothesis testing, given what you know about possible outcomes of these tests, consider which error would be most desirable. Provide a rationale for why you would opt for a Type I or Type II error.

20. Identify the steps you would take to increase power in a simple experiment.

Practice Exercises

21. Kyle obtained an IQ score of 112 ($\mu = 100$, $\sigma = 15$). Calculate the z score associated with Kyle's IQ score. Calculate the z score for Jeremy with an IQ of 88.

22. What is the percentile ranking for an individual with a $z = 1.89$.

23. Several different samples of children were tested. Using the same μ and σ provided above, calculate the z score for each of the samples with a mean IQ score of 110.

    a. Sample size 10

    b. Sample size 30

    c. Sample size 40

Explain how the sample z scores differ from the individual z score. Explain the difference in scores between the sample sizes of 10 and 40.

24. What is the likelihood that a sample of 50 people had an average IQ score of at least 110? What is the likelihood that a sample of 25 people had an average IQ score of 110 or higher?

25. A sample of 25 students is selected from a population with a $\mu = 35$. The students participated in an awareness program and they were tested for an increase in knowledge after the program. The mean increased to 40, with a $SD = 10$. Is the outcome statistically significant?

CHAPTER 8

LOOKING FOR DIFFERENCES BETWEEN TWO TREATMENTS

CHAPTER OUTLINE

STATISTICAL TESTING FOR TWO INDEPENDENT GROUPS
Stating the Hypothesis
Significance Testing
Confidence Intervals

STATISTICAL TESTING FOR RELATED AND REPEATED MEASURES
Stating the Hypothesis
Significance Testing

Confidence Intervals
Advantages of Repeated Measures Designs
Limitations of Repeated Measures Designs

COMPUTER ANALYSIS USING SPSS
Independent Samples *t* test
Related Samples *t* Test

LEARNING OBJECTIVES

- Describe the difference between an independent samples and a repeated measures design.
- Explain the basic ratio for calculating tests of statistical significance.
- Write a null hypothesis for two groups.
- Write an alternative hypothesis for two groups.
- Explain how to perform a calculation of an independent samples *t* test.
- Explain the purpose of standard error of the difference between two means.
- Explain the purpose of confidence intervals in hypothesis testing.
- List the assumptions for an independent samples *t* test.
- Identify small, medium, and large effect sizes.
- Explain the standard error of the difference score.
- Explain the advantages associated with a repeated measures design.
- Describe limitations associated with repeated measures designs.

CHAPTER PREVIEW

In the previous chapter we provided an overview of probability theory and statistical hypothesis testing. We can use statistical tests when we conduct experimental studies. Statistical tests are one part of applying experimental methods that allow researchers to establish a cause-and-effect relationship between an independent variable and a dependent variable. Experimental designs employ **random assignment,** which allows us to establish cause-and-effect relationships. Random assignment ensures that each person has an equal chance of ending up in a group on the basis of an objective placement. In the simplest experiment, the researcher compares a treated group (experimental) to a control (nontreated) group. This simple two-group design, or independent measures design, allows the researcher to compare two different levels of the independent variable using two different groups of people.

Instead of using two different groups, we can also design an experiment using only one group and ask participants to engage in both the treatment and control conditions of the study. In this case, we are still testing two levels of the independent variable, but we are using one group of people and asking them to participate in both conditions. The repeated measures design, using one group of people in both conditions, allows us to test the effect of the two levels of the independent variable using only one group of people. In each of these instances we are using two levels of a single independent variable, and we are measuring a single dependent variable. In the first case, we are using an independent samples design or a two-group design, and in the second instance we are using a related-samples or repeated measures design.

In many research studies, we use several different levels of the independent variable. For example, we might test the effect of three different amounts of caffeine. The simplest design employs only two levels of the independent variable. In this chapter, we will describe how to use inferential statistics to test differences between only two levels of the independent variable. The independent samples *t* test is used to test differences between two groups. The related samples or repeated measures *t* test is used to detect differences when one group of participants experiences both levels of treatment.

Statistical Testing for Two Independent Groups

Let's begin by considering the conditions under which we might use the independent samples (two groups) *t* test. For example, we might want to examine treatment efficacy for people who are depressed. If we are using a two-group experimental design, then we need to randomly assign participants (people who are depressed) to a treatment or a control condition. However, with this design, only one group of participants receives treatment. How might we ethically conduct such a study?

One possibility is to conduct our study on a college campus. College and university counseling centers treat large numbers of students for a variety of psychological stressors. Unfortunately, it is not always possible for students to obtain an appointment immediately. Because some students are often placed on a waiting list, researchers frequently use this existing constraint in the design of their studies (cf., Tolin et al., 2004). So, one way that we can design a study is to create two groups—one group receives treatment immediately and a second control group does not immediately receive treatment, but are placed on a waiting list. As students request services, they are randomly assigned to counseling (treatment condition) or to a control group (waiting list).

In this example, there are two levels of the independent variable (i.e., treatment and no treatment). The dependent variable or efficacy of treatment is measured through self-report. At the conclusion of the study, students in both the treatment and control groups report their

Random assignment— Ensures that each person has an equal chance of ending up in a group on the basis of an objective placement.

level of depression using a simple Likert scale or a standardized measure of depression (e.g., Beck Depression Inventory-II).

In our example we are using two *different* or independent groups of students. This type of experimental design allows us to use the independent groups t test to determine whether the levels of depression between the two groups differ. Our data, or the DV, are the depression scores from each of the groups. We use the t test to determine if the average or mean depression score for the two groups is measurably different. In other words, we are interested in determining if there is a statistically significant difference in depression scores at the end of the study. To determine statistical significance, we must compare the difference between groups to the error, or variability, within the groups. In other words, we calculate a ratio using the mean difference between the two groups as the numerator and the variability within the groups (error) as the denominator. As with any inferential test, we begin by stating a statistical hypothesis.

Stating the Hypothesis

Earlier we discussed the difference between an alternative and null hypothesis. Recall that the null hypothesis is merely a theoretical statement that we use to posit there are no differences between the two groups. We make this statement only for the purpose of establishing a contingency for conducting the statistical test. We aren't hoping for the null result; instead, we use the null hypothesis as the theoretical foundation for conducting the statistical test. The statistical or null hypothesis for the independent samples t test specifies that the two group means do not differ. The statistical notation for the null hypothesis is:

$$H_0: \mu_1 = \mu_2$$

You may have noticed that we state the hypothesis by using population means. But wait, we are using samples in our study! We always use samples to test a hypothesis. The purpose of inferential statistics is to test a sample and then to generalize results back to a population. Therefore, we state the theoretical or null hypothesis in terms of the population means because our null hypothesis refers to the population. In the end, we use the results from the sample to generalize back to the population.

When using statistical notation to state the null hypothesis, the subscripts refer to each of the population means. In the notation above, we are hypothesizing no differences between the two populations. In other words, if we consider the two conditions for treatment of depression, the null hypothesis states that there are no differences between the treatment and control conditions. When we conduct an independent samples t test, we are comparing two different samples to see if they reliably differ from one another. In other words, is the difference between the two groups large enough to convince us that if we repeated our data collection, we would end up with similar results a second time? After all, we are relying on the theory of probability to make our decision about the likelihood that the sample belongs to the population.

Although we are using the theory of probability as the basis for our statistical test, we use actual sample data to conduct our test. In other words, we calculate the likelihood that the two group means are significantly different. How important is it for you to calculate a t test by hand? Most often we use statistical software packages to produce a t value and to tell us if the value is statistically significant. Directions for using SPSS to conduct the t test are provided at the end of this chapter. Although we don't usually calculate the t test by hand, it is important to understand how these values are derived. Therefore, we will explain how a t value is calculated and how we use the t value to determine statistical significance and effect size.

Significance Testing

Whenever we use the theory of probability to conduct an inferential statistical test, we compare our calculated value to a tabled value in a specific distribution. We use the *t* distribution when we conduct a *t* test (i.e., single sample, independent samples, or related samples). The *t* distribution is similar to the normal distribution. To be exact, we are using a set of *t* distributions. The family of *t* distributions is similar to the normal distribution when we use large samples. However, in order to be accurate, we use a *t* table instead of a unit normal table (*z* table) when we calculate a *t* test.

As we mentioned earlier, a statistical test employs a ratio of differences between groups over error within groups. Therefore, a *t* value is simply the ratio of the differences between the two groups divided by the variability within the groups. We compare the actual difference between the hypothesized mean values to the error variance contained in the sample. So, when we compare two different groups, we are calculating the ratio of the actual difference between sample means divided by the error contained in both samples.

$$t = \frac{Actual\ Variance}{Error\ Variance}$$

Another way to think about this ratio is that we are comparing the difference between the two treatment means to the individual variability that exists among the students.

Calculating an Independent Samples t Test   Let's consider some hypothetical data that could have been generated from our study designed to measure treatment efficacy. In our two group design, we randomly assign participants to one of two groups, or one of the two levels of the independent variable. After six weeks (i.e., therapy or control), we might ask participants to complete the Beck Depression Inventory-II (BDI-II) as a measure of the dependent variable. [The BDI-II is a widely used measure of depression. Scores for the BDI-II range from 0 (not depressed) to 63 (severely depressed).] The BDI-II scores or measure of the dependent variable are contained in Table 8.1. We can use these scores to determine if there is a statistically significant difference between the two treatment groups. Our first step in calculating the statistical test is to calculate the average depression score for each group.

TABLE 8.1   *BDI-II Scores*

Control	*Treatment*
50	30
55	35
45	25
40	32
45	28
50	33
51	27
59	30
55	35
50	25
$\sum X_1 = 500$	$\sum X_2 = 300$
$M_1 = 50$	$M_2 = 30$

Step 1: *Calculate the means for each treatment.* We begin with the calculation of the difference in mean scores ($M_1 - M_2$) for the two groups. Remember these scores are self-reported levels of depression representing the dependent variable. The difference between the treatment and control groups appears to be substantial. This difference (20 points), the numerator, is the actual difference between treatment means and is the first step in our calculation of the independent samples *t* test.

$$t = \frac{M_1 - M_2}{\sqrt{\dfrac{s_p^2}{n_1} + \dfrac{s_p^2}{n_2}}} = \frac{20}{\sqrt{\dfrac{s_p^2}{n_1} + \dfrac{s_p^2}{n_2}}}$$

Step 2: *Calculate the estimated standard error of the difference between means.* Our second step in calculating the *t* statistic is to obtain the error or an estimated standard error to use as the denominator of our ratio. The error is simply the variability among the depression scores. In other words, differences between individuals that are not the result of treatment reflect error. In our earlier calculation of the estimated standard error for the *single-sample t test,* we used the estimated *standard deviation* to obtain the estimated *standard error.* As a reminder, the formula for the single-sample estimated standard error of the mean is:

$$s_m = \frac{s}{\sqrt{N}} \quad \text{OR} \quad \sqrt{\frac{s^2}{N}}$$

This formula for calculating the standard error for the single sample *t* test provides us with an index of variability that is based on the sample size (rather than individual scores). Recall that as sample size increases, the error decreases. This same axiom holds true for the independent samples *t* test.

Just as we calculated a standard error for a single sample *t* test, we perform a similar calculation to obtain a standard error of the mean for the **independent samples *t* test.** However, when we conduct an independent samples *t* test, we actually have two different groups and we also have two measures of variability. We must therefore combine the variance from within each group to derive the *standard error of the difference between two means.* The formula for calculating standard error of the difference between means ($s_{M_1 - M_2}$) is:

$$s_{M_1 - M_2} = \sqrt{\frac{s_p^2}{n_1} + \frac{s_p^2}{n_2}}$$

Independent samples *t* test—A parametric inferential statistical test used to test differences between two groups. The test uses a ratio of difference between means to difference within groups (error).

Pooled variance— Contains all of the variability present among participants.

Although the formula appears daunting, we are really just calculating another form of variability. Our first step in calculating the standard error of the difference between the two means ($s_{M_1 - M_2}$), is to calculate the **pooled variance** (s_p^2). The pooled variance combines the variability that occurs within each of the groups and is the first indicator of the amount of error present in the analysis. For example, if the scores within each group are widely different from one another, these large differences contribute to a larger standard error of the difference between two means and to the overall error. Remember, the larger the error, the smaller the calculated *t* value, and the less likely that the calculated value will be significant.

So, before we can proceed further we need to obtain the pooled or combined variance (s_p^2). In general, variability is calculated by dividing the sum of

TABLE 8.2 *BDI-II Scores and Squared Values*

Control	X_1^2	Treatment	X_2^2
50	2500	30	900
55	3025	35	1225
45	2025	25	625
40	1600	32	1024
45	2025	28	784
50	2500	33	1089
51	2601	27	729
59	3481	30	900
55	3025	35	1225
50	2500	25	625
$\sum X_1 = 500$	$\sum X_1^2 = 25282$	$\sum X_2 = 300$	$\sum X_2^2 = 9126$
$M_1 = 50$		$M_2 = 30$	

the squares (SS) by degrees of freedom (df). We calculated variance for individual scores as the intermediate step toward calculation of the standard deviation. Similarly, when we calculate the pooled variance, we must combine the overall SS and df as our first step toward calculation of the pooled variance. Hence, the formula for the pooled variance (s_p^2) is:

$$s_p^2 = \frac{SS_1 + SS_2}{df_1 + df_2}$$

Using the data from our hypothetical study, we independently calculate the SS for each of our groups as illustrated in Table 8.2.

The most efficient way to obtain each SS is to use the computational formula to calculate the SS for each group as shown below:

$$SS = \sum X^2 - \frac{(\sum X)^2}{N}$$

$$SS_1 = 25282 - \frac{250000}{10} = 25282 - 25000 = 282$$

$$SS_2 = 9126 - \frac{90000}{10} = 9126 - 9000 = 126$$

We now use the SS values to calculate our combined or pooled variance.

$$s_p^2 = \frac{SS_1 + SS_2}{df_1 + df_2} = \frac{282 + 126}{9 + 9} = \frac{408}{18} = 22.67$$

The pooled variance is the first step toward calculating the standard error of the difference scores or the denominator for the t test. After we calculate our pooled variance (s_p^2), we can use the pooled variance to obtain the standard error of the difference between two means, or the denominator for the independent samples t test.

Because the pooled variance combines the sum of the squares for both groups, we arrive at a single pooled variance value. We complete our calculation of the standard error of the mean difference scores by taking sample size into account. *Remember to divide the pooled variance (s_p^2) by the df before adding the two values together.* So, using the single pooled variance value (s_p^2), we divide the pooled variance by each of the sample sizes (n_1 and n_2). We complete the calculation of the standard error of the difference scores by taking the square root as illustrated below.

$$s_{M_1 - M_2} = \sqrt{\frac{s_p^2}{n_1} + \frac{s_p^2}{n_2}} = \sqrt{\frac{22.67}{10} + \frac{22.67}{10}} = \sqrt{2.27 + 2.27} = \sqrt{4.54} = 2.13$$

Step 3: Divide mean difference by estimated standard error of the difference scores to obtain t. Our final step in calculating the independent samples *t* test is to obtain the ratio of the mean difference (between groups) to error variance.

$$t = \frac{Mean\ Difference}{Error\ Variance}$$

In our study of treatment for depression, we calculate the ratio of the difference between two means divided by the error present within the study.

$$t = \frac{M_1 - M_2}{\sqrt{\frac{s_p^2}{n_1} + \frac{s_p^2}{n_2}}} = \frac{50 - 30}{2.13} = \frac{20}{2.13} = 9.39$$

We can see that the difference between mean depression scores is 20 points, compared to the error variance of 2.13 points. In other words, the difference between groups is much greater than the variability within groups. Fortunately, this completes our calculation of the *t* test for independent samples or a test that allows us to compare sample means from two groups.

Is this calculated value really unlikely? In other words, when considered in the context of the null hypothesis, is the difference likely due to chance? To answer this question, we need to compare the calculated value above to the tabled value from our *t* table. The *t* table contains values associated with probabilities that are routinely used to determine statistical significance.

However, before we can compare our calculated value to the tabled value, we need to calculate degrees of freedom. Fortunately, we already took one step toward calculating degrees of freedom (*df*) when we calculated pooled variance. Degrees of freedom reflect the number of scores that are free to vary. For each of the groups we have one predefined score that must be held constant. Using our degrees of freedom from the calculation of pooled variance we find that:

$$df = (n_1 - 1) + (n_2 - 1) \quad OR \quad df = (n_1 + n_2) - 2$$
$$df = (10 - 1) + (10 - 1) \quad OR \quad df = (10 + 10) - 2$$

So, for our study, the degrees of freedom are equal to 18.

Using our degrees of freedom along with our alpha level of .05, we refer to our Table E.2, and we find that the tabled value is 2.101. This tabled value is the point at which we reject the null hypothesis. As illustrated in Figure 8.1, if we compare the tabled value ($t = 2.101$) to our calculated value ($t = 9.39$), we find that because our calculated value exceeds our tabled value, the results are statistically unlikely to occur by chance alone and we deem these results statistically significant.

FIGURE 8.1   *Rejecting the Null Hypothesis*

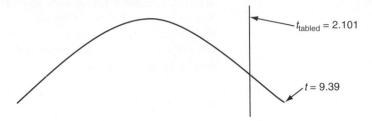

APA style guidelines specify how statistical results are reported. An example of how to report results is detailed in the box below.

Writing Results

Regardless of the outcome, it is important to report results using the appropriate scientific format. In this case, we found statistically significant results and one way to report results is as follows:

> After six weeks, we compared the self-reported levels of depression (BDI-II) for the treatment and control groups. Average levels of depression for the control group were higher ($M_1 = 50, SD = 5.59$) than those of the treatment group ($M_2 = 30, SD = 3.74$). We found that these results were statistically significant, $t(18) = 9.39, p < .05$.

You will notice that results are written in a direct manner. So, if you were to remove the numerical values, you would be able to understand the outcome of the study even without the statistical values. One way to ensure that you are writing your results correctly is to read through your results without the numbers. If your description makes sense, you have communicated well.

Assumptions of Parametric Tests   With all *parametric* inferential tests we must understand that the veracity of our findings is based on underlying assumptions about the population. The assumptions for the independent samples *t* test are the following:

- The data used to measure the DV are interval or ratio level.
- The underlying populations for each group are normally distributed.
- The variances for the populations are roughly equivalent (homogeneity of variance).

In order to use the *t* test, data must be interval or ratio level; otherwise, we should use a nonparametric statistical test (e.g., chi-square test). The second two assumptions are important, but they are somewhat negotiable. For example, as long as we have reasonably large sample sizes, we don't have to worry too much about the distribution being normal. The second assumption, that variances in the two populations are equal, is a bit more troublesome. (The *Hartley F Max* test is used to determine if the assumption for homogeneity of variance is met. You may wish to consult an advanced statistics text if you are interested in this statistical test.) As long as the variances are relatively similar, we can have confidence in our results. This is particularly important when we consider using unequal sample sizes. Most often, we do end up with unequal sample sizes due to participant mortality. Even if we use unequal sample sizes, if our variances are relatively similar, we can be confident in the robustness of our statistical test (Hays, 1988).

Confidence Intervals

In our example, we conducted a statistical test to determine if our treatment (or nontreatment) resulted in a change in the level of depression. We used an inferential statistic to determine if our results were statistically significant. Inferential techniques were developed so that we could use a smaller number of individuals (as our sample), rather than an entire population, to test the effects of our IV. In conducting our t test, we used a parametric inferential test statistic to compare two sample means, and we want to generalize these results back to the populations of interest. However, when we generalize these results back to the population we will still have some error present in our generalization. In order to account for the error, we make our estimates using a **confidence interval** that is based on the estimated error that is present in our statistic.

In our study of treatment efficacy, we found a statistically significant difference in reported levels of depression between the treatment and control groups. In fact, we found that the mean difference in depression scores was 20 points!

$$M_1 - M_2 = Difference$$
$$50 - 30 = 20$$

Using the inferential data from our samples, we might be tempted to report that, when generalized to the population, the treatment will produce an average decline in depression of 20 points. However, we must consider the error that is present when we use a sample rather than a population. Instead of reporting a single value, or point estimate, we are much better off reporting a possible range of values. In other words, if we generalize the results of our sample back to the population, we can estimate the likely decline in depression within a range of scores.

The confidence interval, or range of scores, is derived by considering the error, or amount of variability within each of the samples, that is present in the data. For example, we might want to report a confidence interval (CI) that spans one standard deviation on either side of the mean difference. One standard deviation on either side of the mean captures approximately 68% of the population. Remember, we found that the mean difference between groups was 20 points. We can use the standard error from our calculated t test to derive this estimated range of scores.

$$CI = (M_1 - M_2) \pm s_{M_1-M_2}$$
$$CI = 20 \pm 2.13$$
$$CI = 20 + 2.13 = 22.13 \quad \text{and} \quad CI = 20 - 2.13 = 17.87$$

Our confidence interval of one standard deviation on each side of the mean ($M = 20$) suggests that 68% of the time the average decline in depression scores will range between 17.87 and 22.13. Although this provides us with a one standard deviation confidence interval, most often the reported confidence is not one standard deviation, but instead it is an interval of 95%. You will also notice that in most statistical software packages, the default confidence interval is 95%. So, how do we obtain this value? We can use the t table to identify the middle 95% of the distribution. We already know this value because it is the tabled value that we used to determine the threshold for statistical significance ($t_{tabled} = 2.101$). Using this value we can derive a 95% CI for our average decline in depression scores.

$$CI = (M_1 - M_2) \pm (t_{tabled})s_{M_1-M_2}$$
$$CI = 20 \pm (2.101)2.13$$
$$CI = 20 - 4.475 = 15.525 \quad \text{and} \quad CI = 20 + 4.475 = 24.475$$

Confidence interval— The estimated range of error associated with treatment effect.

So, when generalizing the results of this study, or inferring back to the population, we can estimate that 95% of the time, depression scores will decline between 15.52 and 24.47 points.

Effect Size. Determining statistical significance is only one way to evaluate differences between the two groups. In addition to determining the likelihood that a treatment works, we might want to consider the magnitude of the treatment effect. *Effect size* provides a standardized estimate of the magnitude or the amount of the effect of the independent variable.

One common estimate of effect size is the *standardized difference* between two means, commonly referred to as **Cohen's *d*.** We use Cohen's *d* as a measure of effect size when we have a two-group design. In essence, we simply find the difference between the means of the two groups (experimental and control) and divide by the standard deviation to produce a standard estimate of the effect of the IV:

$$d = \frac{M_1 - M_2}{s_p}$$

Where:

Experimental Group Mean $= M_1$
Control Group Mean $= M_2$
Pooled Standard Deviation $= s_p$

Calculation of effect size is relatively straightforward because we already calculated most of these values for the independent samples *t* test. The difference between means is identical to the numerator for the *t* test, and in this instance the value is $20 (50 - 30 = 20)$. We also calculated a pooled variance (not a pooled standard deviation). However, we can easily obtain the pooled standard deviation by taking the square root of the pooled variance.

$$s_p^2 = 22.67$$
$$\sqrt{s_p^2} = 4.76$$

Using both our difference between means and our pooled standard deviation, Cohen's *d*, or standardized difference between two means, is:

$$d = \frac{M_1 - M_2}{s_p}$$

$$d = \frac{20}{4.76} = 4.20$$

How do we interpret the effect size or magnitude of change in depressions scores?

Interpreting Effect Size *Effect size* can be defined as the standardized difference between two means. In other words, effect size, much like a standard deviation, allows us to compare results across studies. Cohen's *d* is very similar to a standard deviation. If we find a $d = 1.00$, then the means differ by one standard deviation. Therefore, we can easily calculate the standardized *d* for any study, thus allowing us to compare results across studies.

How do we know what value constitutes a large effect size? Considerable debate surrounding the magnitude of effect size has ensued in recent years. Generally, researchers (Cohen, 1988; Murphy & Myors, 2004) have defined effect size as small ($d = .20$), medium ($d = .50$), or large ($d = .80$). Each of these values is interpreted as a standardized value that can be interpreted much like a standard deviation. So, our calculated effect size, $d = 4.20$, is actually quite large. In other words, groups are separated by 4.20 standard deviations. It is important to report effect size whenever you write the results of a study as illustrated below:

Cohen's *d*—A standardized measure of effect size.

After six weeks, we compared the self-reported levels of depression (BDI-II) for the treatment and control groups. Average levels of depression for the control group were higher ($M_1 = 50$, $SD = 5.6$) than those of the treatment group ($M_2 = 30$, $SD = 3.74$). We found that these results were statistically significant and the effect was quite large, $t(18) = 9.39$, $p < .05$, $d = 4.20$.

We used the independent samples t test, an inferential technique, to determine if the difference between the treatment and control groups was statistically significant. In other words, were the differences between the two groups likely to have occurred by chance? Based on our calculations, we rejected the null hypothesis and reported that the differences were not likely the result of chance. We also calculated the magnitude of the difference between means and found that the standardized difference (effect size) between the two means was large. Is this difference meaningful? Although the standardized effect size is considered large, the answer to this question can only be determined by the researchers. In other words, a meaningful difference is dependent on the context of the study and in this case, we would probably consider this large reduction in depression scores to be meaningful.

Statistical Testing for Related and Repeated Measures

Our independent samples t test involved a comparison of two groups of depressed students—one group that received treatment and control group that did not receive treatment. It is also possible to design the study with only one group of participants who undergo both levels of the IV (i.e., treatment and no treatment). In a repeated measures design we obtain two measures of the DV (e.g., Beck Depression Inventory-II) from the same participants. For example, rather than assigning participants to one of two groups, we might wait-list all of our participants and obtain a measure of their depression. We would then provide them with treatment and measure their level of depression after the final psychotherapy session. In this case, we are obtaining two measures of reported levels of depression, one before treatment and one after treatment. Because we are using a repeated measures design, we use a **repeated measures t test** to evaluate the outcomes of this study.

Much like the independent samples t test, we determine statistical significance by comparing the ratio of the mean difference between scores (before and after treatment) to the error or variability within the scores. Remember we are using the same participants and measuring them twice. Because the participants act as their own control, we don't have to worry about the variability within each group. When we use a repeated-measures t test, we actually reduce our sampling error (Hays, 1988) because our denominator or error becomes smaller. We can easily illustrate this reduction in error by using the data from our earlier example. Rather than treating these data as coming from two different groups, the data are derived from the same individuals, but at two different points in time.

Stating the Hypothesis

Repeated measures t test—An inferential parametric test for differences between two levels of an independent variable using one group of participants.

The statistical or null hypothesis for the related samples t test specifies that the pre- and posttest scores or "difference scores" do not differ. The statistical notation for the null hypothesis is:

$$H_0 : \mu_D = 0$$

The statistical notation above indicates that the population mean difference score (μ_D) is equivalent to 0. In other words, there are no differences between the pre- and posttest measures.

Significance Testing

Much like an independent samples *t* test, the repeated samples analysis compares the actual difference between scores, or the difference score (*D*), to the error present within the data. We derive the difference score by subtracting the posttest score from the pretest score.

$$D = X_1 - X_2$$

The average difference score (M_D) is a reflection of the average amount of change between the pretest and posttest measures of depression.

The variability among the scores constitutes error, and the estimated standard error of the sample mean difference score (s_{M_D}) reflects this value. In other words, any preexisting differences among the participants are classified as error.

The ratio of the difference between treatments divided by the variability among participants is the formula that we use to calculate the repeated measures *t* test. Again, we undertake a series of steps to calculate a related samples *t* test using the following formula:

$$t = \frac{M_D}{s_{M_D}}$$

Step 1: Calculate the mean difference score. In our previous analysis using two groups we compared BDI-II scores of participants who had been assigned to two different treatment conditions. Instead of using data from two different groups, in a repeated measures analysis we use data from *two different points in time*. Participants are measured before treatment and after treatment. Using the same data from our previous example, as illustrated in Table 8.3, we can calculate a repeated measures *t* test. [Remember scores for the BDI-II range from 0 (not depressed) to 63 (severely depressed).] Our first step is to calculate a difference score for each of the participants.

Mean difference score— In a repeated measures design, the mean difference score represents the average amount of change between the two conditions.

The difference score is simply the difference between the pretest and the posttest measure of depression ($D = X_1 - X_2$).

We can now calculate the mean difference score as the overall measure of treatment variability. The **mean difference score** (M_D) reflects the average amount of change in depression scores between the first and second measurements.

TABLE 8.3 *BDI-II Scores Repeated Measures*

Pretest	Posttest	Difference (D)	D^2
50	30	20	400
55	35	20	400
45	25	20	400
40	32	8	64
45	28	17	289
50	33	17	289
51	27	24	576
59	30	29	841
55	35	20	400
50	25	25	625
		$\sum D = 200$	$\sum D^2 = 4284$
		$M_D = 20$	

Step 2: *Calculate the standard error of the mean difference score.* Our second step in calculating the repeated measures t statistic is to obtain an **estimated standard error of the mean difference score** (s_{M_D}), or the denominator for our t test.

$$s_{M_D} = \sqrt{\frac{s_D^2}{n}}$$

First, we need to calculate the estimated variance (s_D^2) of the difference scores. Substituting the difference scores for the raw scores, we can use a variation of our original sum of squares and variance formulas to calculate the variance for the difference scores.

$$SS = \sum D^2 - \frac{(\sum D)^2}{n}$$

We begin by calculating the sum of the squares for the difference scores:

$$SS = \sum D^2 - \frac{(\sum D)^2}{n} = 4284 - \frac{(200)^2}{10} = 4284 - \frac{40000}{10}$$
$$= 4284 - 4000 = 284$$

We now use the SS to calculate the estimated variance of the difference scores (s_D^2):

$$s_D^2 = \frac{SS}{n-1}$$

$$s_D^2 = \frac{SS}{n-1} = \frac{284}{10-1} = \frac{284}{9} = 31.56$$

We now use the estimated variance of the difference scores to calculate the estimated standard error of the difference scores (s_{M_D}):

$$s_{M_D} = \sqrt{\frac{s_D^2}{n}} = \sqrt{\frac{31.55}{10}} = \sqrt{3.15} = 1.78$$

Step 3: *Calculate the repeated measures t test.* Now we have both elements needed to calculate the ratio of actual difference between scores (M_D) to the estimated error or variability within scores (s_{M_D}).

$$t = \frac{M_D}{s_{M_D}} = \frac{20}{1.78} = 11.24$$

When we complete the t test calculation, we find that the calculated t value is ($t = 11.24$) relatively large.

Estimated standard error of the mean (S_{M_D}) difference score—An index of variability associated with differences between participants. The estimated standard error of the mean difference score is the error term for calculated the independent samples t test.

However, we need to consider the likelihood of obtaining this ratio and compare this calculated value to the value from our t table. In order to make this comparison, we need to calculate degrees of freedom. Our formula for calculating degrees of freedom for the related-samples t test is as follows:

$$df = n - 1 = 10 - 1 = 9$$

For our hypothetical study the degrees of freedom are equal to 9. The tabled value with an alpha level of .05 is 2.262.

As illustrated in Figure 8.2, we compare the tabled value ($t = 2.262$) to the calculated value ($t = 11.24$) and find that because our calculated value exceeds our tabled value, the results are unlikely to occur by chance and we deem these results statistically significant.

FIGURE 8.2   *Rejecting the Null Hypothesis*

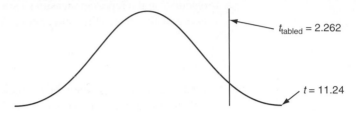

We use the calculated results to report the outcome of the study. An example is contained in the box below.

Writing Results

Similar to the results for the independent samples *t* test, we strive for clarity in reporting the results of our statistical analysis for the repeated measures *t* test.

After six weeks, we compared the self-reported levels of depression (BDI-II)

before and after treatment. We saw an average decline of 20 points in the self-reported levels of depression as measured by the BDI-II. This decline in reported levels of depression was statistically significant, $t(9) = 11.24, p < .05$.

Inferential techniques were developed so that we could use a smaller number of individuals or a sample, rather than an entire population. A repeated measures *t* test is similar to the independent measures test in that it is a parametric inferential test statistic that is used to compare two sample means, and we use the results of this test to generalize back to the population of interest. When we generalize these results from a sample back to a population, we always have some error present in our generalization. Therefore, mean estimates using a confidence interval that is based on the estimated standard error helps to account for the error present in our statistic.

Confidence Intervals

In our example, participants' depression scores declined an average of 20 points after they received treatment. Using the data from our sample, we might be tempted to report that when generalized to the population, the difference between pre- and posttest measures of depression will be 20 points. Again, we must consider error that is present when we use a sample. Instead of reporting this single value, or point estimate, we are much better off reporting a possible range of values. In other words, if we generalize the results of our sample back to the population, we can estimate the likely decline in depression within a range of scores.

We can derive the range of scores or confidence interval (*CI*) from the standard error of estimate used to calculate our *t* test.

$$CI = (M_D) \pm s_{M_D}$$
$$CI = 20 \pm 1.78$$
$$CI = 20 - 1.78 = 18.22 \quad \text{and} \quad CI = 20 + 1.78 = 21.78$$

In this case our confidence interval of one standard deviation on each side of the mean ($M = 20$) suggesting that 68% of the time the average decline in depression scores will range between 18.22 and 21.78.

Notice that the range of scores for the repeated measures *t* test is actually smaller than that of the independent measures *t* test. The error term is smaller because each person acts as his or her own control so we actually have a more accurate measure of treatment efficacy. In order to obtain the 95% confidence interval, we would again use the tabled critical value associated with the *t* test. We already know this value because it is the tabled value that we used to determine the threshold for statistical significance ($t = 2.262$). Using this value, we can derive a 95% *CI* for our average decline in depression scores.

$$CI = (M_D) \pm (t)s_{M_D}$$
$$CI = 20 \pm (2.262)1.78$$
$$CI = 20 + 4.03 = 24.03 \quad \text{and} \quad CI = 20 - 4.03 = 15.97$$

When generalizing our results, or inferring back to the population, we can estimate that 95% of the time, depression scores will decline between 15.97 and 24.03 points.

Effect Size. Earlier we defined effect size as the magnitude of the treatment effect. Cohen's *d* is a standardized way of reporting the size of the treatment effect or the *standardized difference score*. This standardized score allows us to report the difference that occurs between the first and second measures of the dependent variable using a common metric. When calculating effect size (*d*) for a repeated measures *t* test, we simply divide the mean difference score (M_D) by the standard deviation (s_D).

$$d = \frac{M_D}{s_D}$$

Where:

M_D = mean difference score
s_D = standard deviation of the difference scores

Again, this calculation is relatively simple because these values are already available to us. The mean difference score, calculated earlier, was 20. The standard deviation ($s_D = 5.62$) is derived by taking the square root of the estimated variance ($s_D^2 = 31.55$). Cohen's *d* or the standardized effect size for the difference scores is:

$$d = \frac{M_D}{s_D}$$

$$d = \frac{20}{5.62} = 3.56$$

Interpreting Effect Size Our measure of effect size is simply the standardized amount of difference that occurs between the pre- and posttest measurement of depression. Again, the standardized measure of change allows us to compare results across studies. The general parameters for small ($d = .20$), medium ($d = .50$), or large ($d = .80$) effect sizes are the same as those that we used with the independent measures *t* test. Although the effect size for the repeated measures example is smaller ($d = 3.56$) than the independent measures test ($d = 4.20$), because it exceeds the general parameter $d = .80$, we classify this effect size as large. Similar to the results for the independent samples *t* test, we include the effect size in the reported results.

Example Results

After six weeks, we compared the self-reported levels of depression (BDI-II) before and after treatment. We saw an average decline of 20 points in the self-reported levels of depression as measured by the BDI-II. This decline in reported levels of depression was statistically significant, $t(9) = 11.24, p < .05, d = 3.56$.

Advantages of Repeated Measures Designs

Researchers frequently use repeated measures designs because they are efficient and the advantages usually outweigh the disadvantages. There are several advantages associated with repeated measures designs, some purely practical, and others statistical. You can identify clear advantages with repeated measures designs, but you have to consider whether this approach is best for your particular research. In many cases, repeated measures are very helpful, but there are some situations where they will be inappropriate.

One advantage of using a repeated measures design is that you might be able to increase the amount of data that you are able to collect without a marked increase in time and effort. If, for example, your design involves three treatment conditions and you want to test 50 people in each group, using an independent subjects design would require 150 participants. By using a repeated measures design you could test 50 people in each condition, but get the benefits of using 150 people simply by testing the participants in each condition. Table 8.4 illustrates the comparison of the independent versus repeated measures design.

In some studies you may gain a great deal of extra information with repeated measures. For instance, if you want to know whether people remember a list of words better under a fast versus slow condition, you could use a repeated measures design, with each participant learning the words in each condition. If the experiment takes 45 minutes with one condition, it might only take an additional 15 minutes to add a second condition. You would save time because there would be no additional need to set up the second condition because the participant is already ready to go. In this case, although the experiment with two conditions would take 33% longer, you would get 100% more data.

In addition to creating a more efficient design for the researcher, a repeated measures design can be more efficient for the participants. This advantage is particularly important when the group that you want to test is rare (e.g., airline pilots) because you might not be able to find very many of people to participate in your study. By using a repeated measures study, you can reduce the likelihood of running out of participants. On the other hand, if you have access to plenty of participants, you may not gain much from a repeated measures approach. For example, if your testing sessions require a lot of time and effort, it might be better not to use a repeated measures design because your participants might become fatigued or bored after finishing only one condition. Testing them in a second condition might be a problem.

A second advantage to using a repeated measures design is that you may have greater confidence in the validity of your data. Psychologists have found that people have unique perspectives, so they may respond to a given question from very different vantage points. Sometimes participants in different groups approach the same task very differently. Their behaviors

TABLE 8.4   *Comparison of Independent and Related Samples Designs*

Example of how repeated measures lead to greater amounts of data without increases in the number of participants in a hypothetical design.

Number of Participants Required for an Independent Samples Design

Group A	*Group B*	*Group C*	*Total Number of Participants*
Participants$_{1-50}$	Participants$_{51-100}$	Participants$_{101-150}$	$N = 150$

Number of Participants Required for a Repeated Measures Design

Condition A	*Condition B*	*Condition C*	*Total Number of Participants*
Participants$_{1-50}$	Participants$_{1-50}$	Participants$_{1-50}$	$N = 50$

may look as if the IV made a difference when the participants' varied perspectives are causing the changes. A repeated measures approach can remedy this problem.

One clever experiment reveals how personal context can create this type of problem. Birnbaum (1999) recruited participants via the Internet, asking them to serve in a "1-minute judgment study." Participants were asked to "judge, how large is the number 9" or ". . . the number 221." A rating of 1 reflected "very, very small" whereas a 10 reflected "very, very large."

Figure 8.3 reflects the participants' judgments. Surprisingly, the results showed that people believe that 9 is larger than 221. If you were to accept this result uncritically, you would believe that people think that a small number is bigger than a big number.

What is going on? Most likely, according to Birnbaum, people in the "Judge 9 Group" were comparing 9 to single-digit numbers or to small numbers in general; in that context, 9 is pretty large. Whereas, the participants in the "Judge 221 Group" were comparing it to much larger triple-digit numbers, so it seemed relatively small (Figure 8.4).

When you ask people to provide different ratings, you need to make sure that they are using the same context. Thus, for this judgment task, you could provide context in the form of an anchor for the participants; that is, you could say that for this judgment, 1 would be considered *very, very small* and 1000 would be considered *very, very large*. Would this solve the problem? According to Birnbaum (1974), even when you do this, participants rate smaller numbers as being bigger than larger ones. Participants rated 450 as larger than 550 when he provided the anchors. The implications from Birnbaum's findings is that for subjective judgments, like providing ratings when there are no objective guidelines for responses, it may be a good idea to use repeated measures for the research design. With repeated measures, it's the same person being measured in each condition, so changes in behavior are more likely to be due to the IV than to differing perspectives. This problem of different contexts occurs only for subjective judgments. If the measures are objective (e.g., number of tasks completed) context is less likely to be influenced by individual perspective.

FIGURE 8.3   ***The Surprising Results of the Study in which Participants Rated the Size of "9"***
and "221" on a Scale of 1 (very, very small) to 10 (very, very large)
The study involved independent assignment to conditions rather than repeated measures. That is, different people judged the size of 9 and of 221.

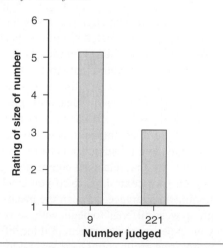

FIGURE 8.4 *Relative Ratings Can Be Misleading When Based on Subjective Criteria*
A value like 9 might seem big in comparison with small numbers, and 221 might seem small in comparison to big numbers.

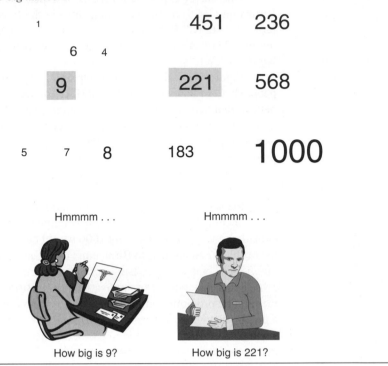

Source: M. H. Birnbaum. (1999). How to show that 9 > 221: Collect judgments in a between-subjects design. *Psychological Methods, 4,* 243–249. Copyright © 1999 American Psychological Association. Used with permission.

Sometimes it simply makes sense to use repeated measures. For instance, Leirer, Yesavage, and Morrow (1991) investigated the effects of marijuana use in airline pilots over a 48-hour period. The researchers legally obtained marijuana and administered controlled doses to pilots who engaged in simulated flights. The investigators were interested in how long marijuana affected the pilots' performance and whether the pilots were aware of any effects of the marijuana on their behaviors.

They discovered that most of the pilots experienced residual effects of marijuana after 24 hours, but they typically were not aware of the effects. You could conduct this research without using repeated measures, but there were clear advantages to following the same individuals as the marijuana leaves their systems.

A third advantage to using repeated measures designs is that, in general, your groups are equivalent at the outset because they are the same people in each group. One commonly used phrase that relates to comparable groups is that we say that the participants are serving as their own control group. If you have two different groups of participants and you end up finding a difference between the means of the two groups, it may be that the people in each group were different to begin with, so you don't know if the difference between means reflects your experimental treatment or if the differences simply existed prior to the treatment; in other words, one group could have several high scores and the other group several low scores.

With a repeated measures design, the participants may differ greatly from one another. However, differences between participants may not be a problem because you are comparing a single person in one condition with his or her performance in another condition. In other words, if an individual within a condition is different from another person, because we are comparing scores of the same person, we do not need to worry about the differences between people.

Matching designs are related to repeated measures designs, in that, they maintain some of the advantages associated with reducing overall statistical error. If you were going to investigate how long it takes for people to interact with a single stranger versus a group of strangers, you might initially measure your participants' levels of introversion and extroversion because these characteristics might affect the experiment. You could then match two people (**matched pairs**) on the basis of their introversion-extroversion scores. Participants with similar scores could then be assigned to each of the conditions.

A second type of matched design is created when we use **natural pairs.** This could involve twins, siblings, or other pairs (e.g., partners) that share a variable that is important in the research. You can see how repeated measures and matching are conceptually related; the big difference is that in repeated measures, the participant is identical in all conditions, whereas with matching, there is similarity across conditions, but the match is imperfect. Although matching offers the advantage of reducing error, matching is cumbersome and is not used as frequently as we might desire.

Limitations of Repeated Measures Designs

Some research projects do not lend themselves to repeated measures designs, and some variables make repeated measures impossible. If you conduct a study in which you compare people according to a participant variable, that is, according to an existing personal characteristic, you will not be able to use repeated measurements. So, if you want to compare the study habits of high-achieving students and low-achieving students, it would be impossible to use repeated measures because each student would fall into only one category.

Another consideration when testing one person repeatedly is that, if you test participants over time, you have a big investment in each participant. If the person fails to return, you have committed time and effort that will not be repaid. The loss is less of a problem with nonrepeated or independent samples designs because you don't count on extended participation from anyone.

Using a repeated measures design may simply be impractical. For example, suppose you want to see whether young adults and older adults could complete a learning task with equal speed. Although a repeated measures design offers statistical advantages, it is simply unrealistic to test participants as young adults, wait 50 years, and test them again when they are older adults. You generally can't use repeated measures when you examine pre-existing characteristics, such as sex, political affiliation (e.g., Democrat versus Republican), religious affiliation (e.g., Protestant, Catholic, Jewish, Muslim), sexuality (e.g., homosexual, heterosexual). People are what they are.

In a repeated measures design the mere exposure of the participant to multiple conditions may result in complications generally considered to be **carry-over effects. Sequence effects** in testing are said to occur when different treatment sequences (e.g., A-B-C versus C-B-A) lead to different outcomes. Sequence effects occur when one treatment influences performance on a later treatment. If a particular treatment, no matter where in the sequence of treatments it occurs, affects performance in subsequent conditions, this would involve sequence effects.

Order effects, which are progressive effects of testing when an individual is tested repeatedly, are also problematic in a repeated measures design. Fatigue that sets in after repeated testing is an example of an order effect. In other words, order effects are cumulative.

When sequence or order effects are likely, researchers often use **counterbalancing** to avoid mistaking these effects for actual treatment effects. If you created a project with two conditions, A and B, you would want to test some participants in the AB order and other participants in the BA order. If you had three conditions A, B, and C, you could order them ABC, ACB, BAC, BCA, CAB, and CBA if you wanted to use all possible orderings. This approach reflects complete counterbalancing because you use all possible orders.

Matched pairs—In a repeated measures design, participants are matched on a variable of interest and then assigned to treatment conditions.

Natural pairs—A special case of matched pairs in which related participants (e.g., twins) are treated as a pair and assigned to treatment conditions.

Carry-over effects—Confounds introduced into a repeated measures design due to exposure to multiple treatment conditions.

Sequence effects—The result of multiple or repeated measurements of individuals in different experimental conditions such that they behave differently on later measurements as a result of having undergone the earlier measurements.

Order effects—The result of multiple or repeated measurements of individuals in different experimental conditions such that a particular behavior changes depending on which condition it follows.

Counterbalancing—The changing of the order of conditions across individuals to avoid contamination of data because of systematic sequence or order effects.

As you add conditions, the number of orderings grows quickly and requires that you test a large number of participants. Thus, with three conditions you have six orders; with four conditions, it grows to 24, and with more conditions, the number of orders increases exponentially. Normally, you would test multiple participants in each order; so if you had four conditions (i.e., 24 orders) and if you wanted to include three participants in each condition, you would need to test 72 people. Fortunately, there is no need to use complete counterbalancing. Partial counterbalancing, using a subset of orders, can help keep experiments manageable.

Computer Analysis Using SPSS

In this chapter we described how you might use an experimental design to investigate differences between two levels of an independent variable. You can use a *t* statistic to test for differences between the levels of treatment using an independent or related samples test.

Independent Samples *t* Test

The most important part of performing an independent samples *t* test is setting up the data correctly. We begin by setting up our data correctly. Create a column for the dependent variable and create a variable for specifying the group, or level of the independent variable.

The first step in actually performing the independent samples *t* test is to select the test from the Analyze menu as illustrated in Figure 8.5. If you use an independent measures design, then you need to use an Independent Samples *t* Test as illustrated in Figure 8.5.

FIGURE 8.5 *Performing an Independent Samples t Test*

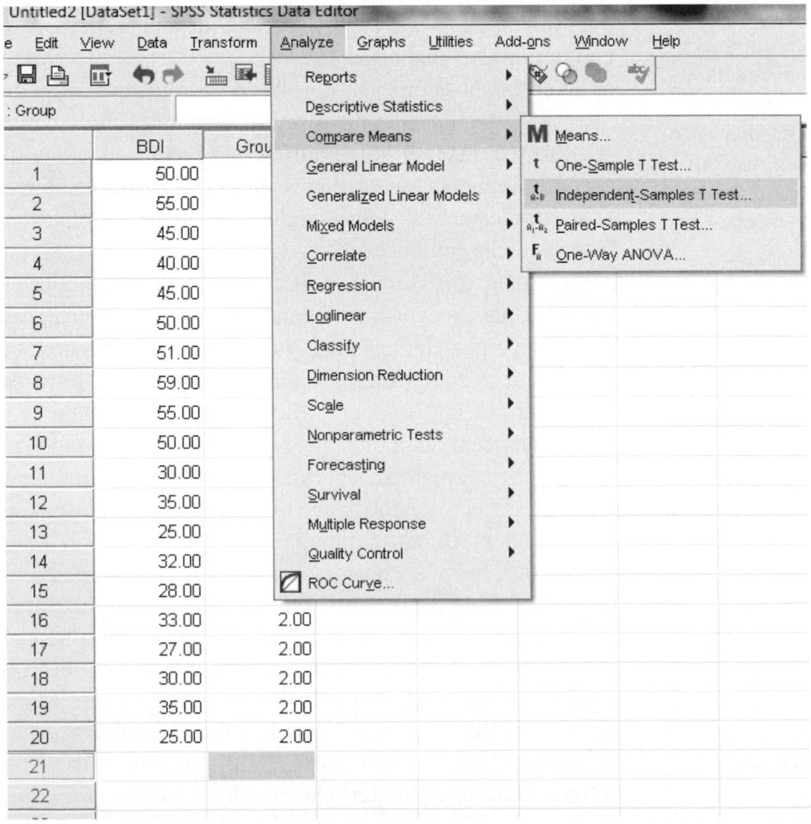

FIGURE 8.6 *Specifying Variables*

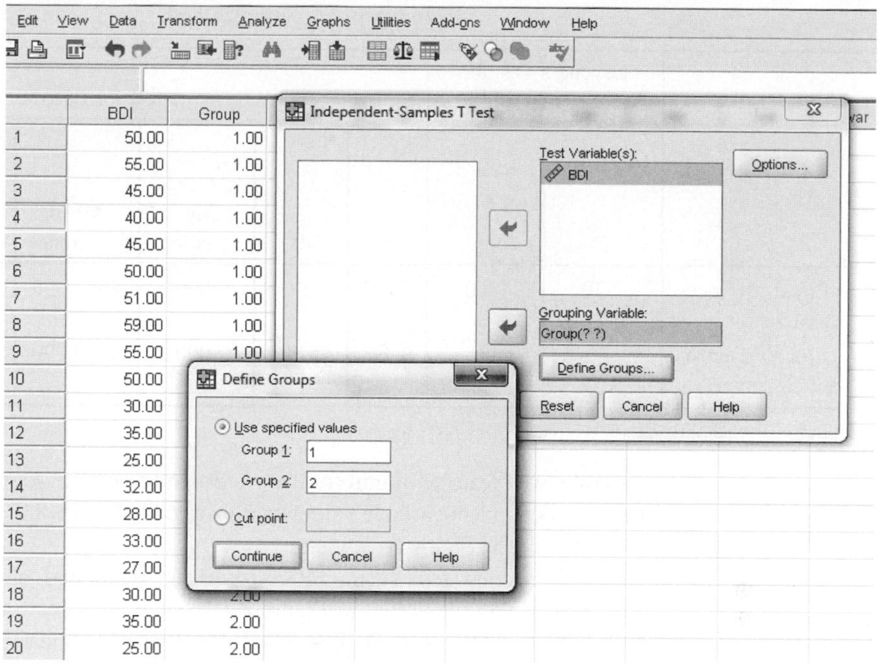

After selecting the test for independent samples, the dialogue box requires us to specify the independent and dependent variables. As illustrated in Figure 8.6, we must also specify the values for our groups (i.e., levels of the independent variable) at this time. Because we are working with only two groups, and we coded the groups as 1 and 2 when we entered the data, we define the groups using values 1 and 2.

We can now run the independent samples *t* test. SPSS quickly produces output in the form of descriptive statistics as illustrated in Figure 8.7. A quick review of the output reveals that we can quickly find the mean and standard deviation for each of the groups from our earlier example.

The second important set of output is the independent sample test as illustrated in Figure 8.8. The data that are important for our purposes are the *t*, *df*, and *Sig.* columns. The statistically significant results, $t(18) = 9.39$, $p < .001$, are reflected in the SPSS output in Figure 8.8. Notice that we obtain an exact probability level when we use an SPSS. Because the significance value is truncated in this analysis ($p = .000$), we use the default ($p < .001$) to report level of significance because we know that the calculated value at least reaches the .001 level (Davenport & Shannon, 2001).

Related Samples *t* Test

We need to set up our data differently when we perform a related samples *t* test. Instead of creating one column for the independent variable and a second column for the independent

FIGURE 8.7 *Descriptive Statistics*

Group Statistics

	Treatment	N	Mean	Std. Deviation	Std. Error Mean
BDI-II	Control	10	50.0000	5.59762	1.77012
	Treatment	10	30.0000	3.74166	1.18322

FIGURE 8.8 *Independent Samples* t *Test Output*

Independent Samples Test

		Levene's Test for Equality of Variances		t-test for Equality of Means						
									95% Confidence Interval of the Difference	
		F	Sig.	t	df	Sig. (2-tailed)	Mean Difference	Std. Error Difference	Lower	Upper
BDI-II	Equal variances assumed	.570	.460	9.393	18	.000	20.00000	2.12916	15.52680	24.47320
	Equal variances not assumed			9.393	15.704	.000	20.00000	2.12916	15.47946	24.52054

variable, we create a column for the pretest and a column for the posttest. In this case, we enter only the dependent variable values as illustrated in Figure 8.9. We then select the Paired-Sample test from the SPSS analysis menu.

The second step in using SPSS to perform the related samples *t* test is to select the variables for analysis. As illustrated in Figure 8.10, when we select our variables, SPSS automatically performs the analysis using those variables (Pretest-Posttest).

Similar to our output from the single sample *t* test, the related samples output includes descriptive data for the pretest and posttest measures (Figure 8.11). These data reflect the average values and standard deviations for each condition.

Our statistical test is reported in the Paired Samples Test portion in our output. In Figure 8.12, we find that the calculated *t* value is consistent with our earlier calculations, $t(9) = 11.26, p < .001$. Again, because the significance value is truncated in this analysis ($p = .000$), we use the default ($p < .001$) to report level of significance.

FIGURE 8.9 *Related Samples Data Format*

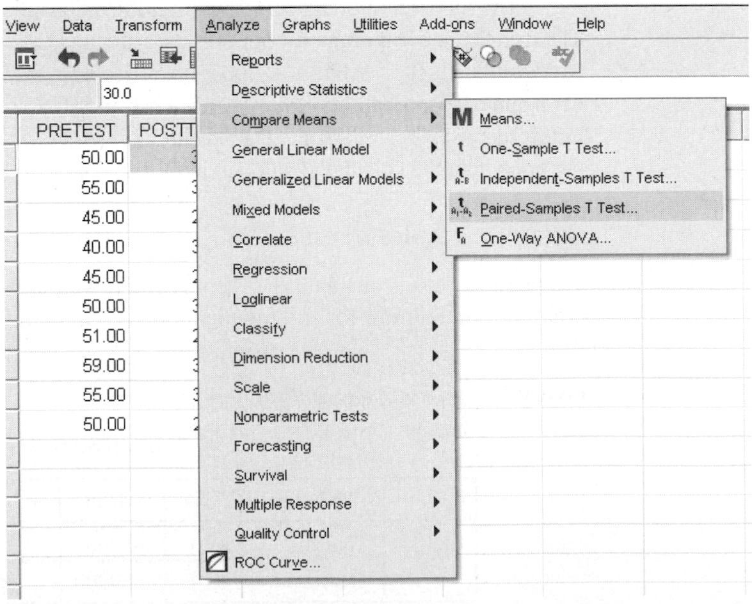

FIGURE 8.10 *Related Samples* **t** *Test*

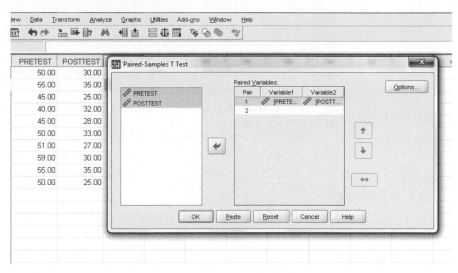

FIGURE 8.11 *Descriptive Statistics for Related Samples* **t** *Test*

Paired Samples Statistics

		Mean	N	Std. Deviation	Std. Error Mean
Pair 1	Pretest	50.0000	10	5.59762	1.77012
	Posttest	30.0000	10	3.74166	1.18322

FIGURE 8.12 *Repeated Measures* **t** *Test Output*

Paired Samples Test

		Paired Differences							
					95% Confidence Interval of the Difference				
		Mean	Std. Deviation	Std. Error Mean	Lower	Upper	t	df	Sig. (2-tailed)
Pair 1	Pretest - Posttest	20.00000	5.61743	1.77639	15.98153	24.01847	11.259	9	.000

Chapter Summary

In this chapter we provided an example of how to use experimental design with two levels of an independent variable. In our example we created two conditions (IV) for treating depression (DV). The two conditions (i.e., treatment and wait list) were applied using an independent samples design and a repeated measures design.

With the two-group design we explained how the independent samples *t* test is used to test for statistical significance. In addition to testing for significance, we described how the difference between means serves an estimate of the difference between groups resulting from the treatment.

We described how to derive a standardized measure of effect by calculating an effect size or Cohen's *d.* Effect size is a standardized measure of differences between the two groups, and using a standardized measure allows us to compare effects across studies.

In our second analysis, we described how a treatment can be tested with one group of people using a repeated measures design. In a repeated measures design, the participants experience each of the treatment conditions, thus reducing the amount of error present in the statistical analysis. In this chapter we provided an example of how to use the repeated measures *t* test. We also described how the standard error of the difference score can be used to estimate the difference in treatment. We also illustrated how to calculate a confidence interval, or estimated range of difference likely to occur as a result of the experimental treatment. Finally, we explained how to derive a standardized measure of effect size, or Cohen's *d* for a repeated measures test.

We introduced both the independent and repeated measures tests for two groups. As we noted earlier, random assignment to treatments allows us to establish a cause-and-effect relationship between the independent and dependent variables. An independent measures analysis entails assigning participants to one of two different treatment conditions.

In a repeated measures experiment, we use the same participants in each of the conditions. A repeated measures design offers several advantages including the need for fewer participants, increased validity, and greater statistical power. Repeated measures designs also include some limitations including the possibility for carry-over effects. Ultimately, the choice between independent and repeated measures designs is dependent upon weighing the advantages and disadvantages of the design within the context of the experiment.

Key Terms

Carry-over effects	Estimated standard error of the mean	Order effects
Cohen's *d*	difference score	Pooled variance
Confidence interval	Matched pairs designs	Random assignment
Counterbalancing	Mean difference score	Repeated measures *t* test
Independent samples *t* test	Natural pairs	Sequence effects

Chapter Review Questions

Multiple Choice Questions

1. One group of participants memorized a list of words in an environment with a high level of ambient noise. A second group memorized the list in a low noise condition. The number of correctly identified words are as follows:

Noise	Silent
6	10
4	3
5	6
4	4
3	7

What type of statistic should be used to analyze these data?
a. *t* test for single sample
b. *t* test for repeated measures

   c. *t* test for independent groups

   d. *z* test for single sample

2. Which of the following values reflects the between treatment variance in this study?

   a. $S_{M_1-M_2}$

   b. $M_1 - M_2$

   c. M_D

   d. s_D

3. Which of the following values reflects the correct calculated statistic for the data?

   a. 2.96

   b. 2.65

   c. 2.92

   d. 2.52

4. Which of the following tabled values indicates statistical significance at the .05 level?

   a. 2.306

   b. 2.896

   c. 1.960

   d. 1.397

5. Identify the correct degrees of freedom for these data.

   a. $df = 10$

   b. $df = 9$

   c. $df = 8$

   d. $df = 7$

6. Participants listened to a lecture ($N = 10$) on good sleep hygiene. They then attended a second lecture on sleep hygiene that included PowerPoint slides. At the end of each presentation they completed a 20 item quiz about the material. What type of statistic should be used to analyze these data?

   a. Independent samples *t* test

   b. Repeated measures *t* test

   c. Single sample *t* test

   d. Single sample *z*

7. Which of the following values reflects the error variance in this study?

   a. $s_{M_1-M_2}$

   b. $M_1 - M_2$

   c. M_D

   d. (s_{M_D})

8. Which of the following values reflects the actual difference in treatments?

   a. $s_{M_1-M_2}$

   b. $M_1 - M_2$

   c. (s_{M_D})

   d. M_D

9. Identify the correct degrees of freedom for these data.

   a. $df = 6$

   b. $df = 7$

   c. $df = 8$

   d. $df = 9$

10. What is the tabled *t* value for rejection of the null hypothesis at the .05 level with these data?

   a. 1.833

   b. 1.960

   c. 2.262

   d. 3.250

Essay Questions

11. Use your own words to describe the *t* test ratio.

12. How are the standard error of the difference between two means and the standard error of the mean difference scores similar?

13. How does the repeated-measures *t* test differ from the independent samples *t* test?

14. Describe the purpose for reporting confidence intervals with your results.

15. Why is the estimated standard error of the mean difference score smaller for the repeated measures *t* test?

16. If we ask participants to provide subjective ratings of satisfaction with the quality of the food at two different campus locations, why can a repeated measures design be more useful than an independent samples design?

17. Describe one group on your campus for which matching could be particularly useful in setting up a study. Why would they be appropriate?

18. Can you think of a study you could do on your fellow students for which matching would be helpful if you could generate good matches? Why would matching be useful in your example?

19. Why is it impossible to carry out a repeated measures experiment when you are studying participant variables?

20. What is the difference between sequence and order effects? Give an example of each.

Practice Exercises

21. A psychologist is testing the effectiveness of two weight loss programs. She randomly assigns 20 participants to either the Euell Gibbons Pine Needle Diet or the Beins Basketball regimen. At the conclusion of the study, the participants in the EG group lost an average of 2 pounds and the BB group lost an average of 5 pounds. Which inferential test would be used to test for statistically significant differences between the treatments?

22. Using the following data, determine if the average weight loss for the two groups differs significantly.

Euell Gibbons	Beins Basketball
$n = 10$	$n = 10$
$M = 2$	$M = 5$
$SS = 12$	$SS = 22$

23. A psychologist developed a study to test the effectiveness of a new memory technique. He presented words to a sample of 25 participants and then tested their recall. He then trained them using the Beck Confirmation Bias Memory technique and he again tested their recall for words. Which inferential technique would you use to test whether the Beck Confirmation Bias Memory technique is effective?

24. Using the following data determine if the Beck Confirmation Bias Memory technique is effective. The data for this study are: $M_D = 3, s_D^2 = 2, N = 10$.

25. Calculate and explain effect size for the memory study.

CHAPTER 9

LOOKING FOR DIFFERENCES AMONG MULTIPLE TREATMENTS

CHAPTER OUTLINE

STATISTICAL TESTING FOR MULTIPLE TREATMENTS

STATISTICAL TESTING FOR MULTIPLE GROUPS
Stating the Hypothesis
Significance Testing
Post Hoc Analyses
Effect Size
Computer Analysis Using SPSS

STATISTICAL TESTING FOR REPEATED MEASURES
Stating the Hypothesis
Significance Testing
Post Hoc Analyses
Effect Size
Computer Analysis Using SPSS

LEARNING OUTCOMES

- Explain when it is appropriate to use an ANOVA.
- Distinguish a Between Groups ANOVA from a Repeated Measures ANOVA
- Explain the assumptions of the ANOVA.
- Identify the basic components of variability in the ANOVA.
- Explain the ratio used to obtain an F statistic.
- Explain the difference between an independent samples and repeated measures ANOVA.
- Identify the basic components of variability in the repeated measures ANOVA.
- Identify and explain post hoc analyses.
- Identify and explain measures of effect size for an ANOVA.
- Write an example results section reporting results of a repeated measures ANOVA.

CHAPTER PREVIEW

In the previous chapters we introduced probability as the foundation for testing differences between two treatments. We then described how the independent t test allows us to determine if statistically significant differences are present between two groups receiving two different levels of an IV. Similarly, the repeated measures t test allows us to use a more sensitive analysis to examine differences in treatments using one group of subjects who experience both conditions. In this chapter we expand the probability model for testing statistical significance to include more than two levels of the IV. We explain how we can use an Analysis of Variance (ANOVA) to test for statistical significance when we have more than two groups or when participants experience more than two treatment conditions.

A between groups ANOVA is an inferential test of probability that we can use with one independent variable having more than two levels. In addition to determining whether groups differ as a function of the level of the independent variable, we must conduct additional statistical tests to determine where, exactly, the differences exist. We conduct post hoc analyses to isolate specific differences when we have more than two groups. We also derive an overall measure of effect size as an estimate of the strength of the treatment effect.

In most ways, a repeated measures ANOVA is much like the between groups ANOVA. The difference between these two inferential statistical tests is whether different groups receive the levels of the independent variable, or if one group of participants experiences all of the conditions, or levels, of the independent variable. The repeated measures ANOVA is more sensitive to detecting a statistically significant outcome because there is less error. So, when we find a statistically significant outcome, we also conduct post hoc analyses and calculate a measure of effect size.

Statistical Testing for Multiple Treatments

Thus far, our discussion of statistical analyses has been limited to comparing two levels of an independent variable. In the previous chapter, we used an example comparing two treatments for depression (i.e., treatment and control group), and we measured the effectiveness of the treatment using the Beck Depression Inventory (BDI-II). However, we frequently encounter research questions that include more than two levels of treatment. If we have three or more levels of an independent variable, we still use a test of statistical significance to determine if differences between treatments are statistically significant. When results of a statistical test are significant, we conclude that the differences between treatments are unlikely to have occurred by chance. Remember, statistical significance is determined by calculating a ratio of variance between treatments (treatment variance) to variance within treatments (error variance). Earlier we used the *t* test to calculate this ratio for two groups. The Analysis of Variance, commonly referred to as **ANOVA**, allows us to calculate a ratio of treatment to error variance for more than two groups.

Why not just use the *t* test when we have multiple groups? After all, we are using the same basic logic to calculate statistical significance. One of the problems with using a *t* test for more than two levels of an IV is that repeated use of the *t* test may increase the likelihood of Type I error. Remember, a Type I error means that a statistically significant difference occurred by chance, rather than as a result of a treatment or the independent variable. Researchers typically want to limit Type I errors to no more than 5%, or an alpha level of .05. One of the assumptions of statistical significance testing is that our comparison of the calculated statistic is based on the probability of obtaining the result from *one* sample of data. If we calculate several tests of statistical significance using the same set of data, we are violating the assumption that we are using for probability testing. When we violate this assumption, we are increasing the likelihood of a Type I error. In other words, we can no longer be confident that our results are limited to a 5% likelihood of finding a significant result, or a result that suggests real differences between conditions. So, when we use multiple *t* tests to compare multiple levels of an independent variable, Type I error increases with each additional comparison. The advantage of using the ANOVA is that it minimizes the likelihood of Type I errors. Using an ANOVA allows us to test multiple levels of the independent variable using one overall test for significance, rather than conducting multiple *t* tests with an increased likelihood of a Type I error.

ANOVA—A family of statistical tests that compares group means to assess whether differences across means are reliable.

Statistical Testing for Multiple Groups

Depending on the research design, we may use one of several different ANOVAs. The simplest ANOVA is a one-way ANOVA, or an analysis conducted with only one independent variable. Although we have one independent variable, we frequently have multiple levels or conditions of the independent variable.

Let's consider an example with three levels of an independent variable. Our example is based on a study that was conducted by Wimer and Beins (2000), except they used a much larger sample. Wimer and Beins created three levels of the IV or groups and asked participants to rate the funniness of jokes. The conditions differed in that one group was told that they were about to see jokes that were previously rated as very funny (VF), a second group was told that the jokes were previously rated as not very funny (NVF), and a control condition did not receive any information about previous ratings. Naturally, all the jokes were constant across conditions. The independent variable in this experiment is the type of framing, or priming of participants, and the dependent variable is the funniness rating of the jokes. In this case, we have one independent variable with three levels. Because the three levels of the independent variable involved different people in each group we use a one-way **between groups ANOVA**. If instead we conducted the study so that the same people experienced all three conditions, we would use a one-way repeated measures ANOVA.

Stating the Hypothesis

When we conduct research, we are looking for differences, so we expect to find that participants rate the jokes differently based on the information they were provided. In other words, our alternative hypothesis is that instructions will affect the funniness rating of the joke.

$$H_1 : \mu_1 \neq \mu_2 \neq \mu_3$$

Because we wish to test the probability that the instructions affect ratings, we also need to state a null hypothesis for the purpose of statistical analysis.

$$H_0 : \mu_1 = \mu_2 = \mu_3$$

The null hypothesis simply reflects the statistical statement that the population means for each of the three conditions are equal. Remember, we don't actually refer to the null hypothesis when writing the results of the study. The null hypothesis exists only for the purpose of conducting the statistical analysis.

Assumptions of ANOVA.   With an ANOVA, rather than comparing two treatments means, we are now comparing three or more treatment means. Nevertheless, we are using the same basic ratio to make the comparison. We are interested in whether the difference between the treatment means is larger than the differences that exist within the groups, or error.

$$ANOVA = \frac{Treatment\ Variance}{Error\ Variance}$$

Between groups ANOVA—An ANOVA in which a single individual does not provide data for more than one condition or group.

You will notice that we are calculating the ratio of the variance that is present between treatments versus the variance that is present within treatments, or individual differences among participants. If the calculated ratio is large, then the treatment effect is large compared to measurement error, and we conclude that the treatment likely made a difference and that there is a statistically significant outcome.

Before we examine the formula used to calculate the ANOVA, it is interesting to consider how the ANOVA became such a widely used statistical test. The ANOVA is named for Ronald Aylmer Fisher, who suggested that probability is at the heart of calculating a good inferential statistic (Salsburg, 2001). Because Dr. Fisher is credited with having advanced the ANOVA, the **F statistic** was named in honor of Sir Ronald Fisher.

It is important to note that there are several assumptions that must be met if we arc to be confident in the accuracy of our results. First, and foremost, the dependent variable must be measured at an interval or ratio level. Assuming that we are measuring the dependent variable using the appropriate scale of measurement, we turn to the more complicated assumptions.

Homogeneity of variance is the assumption that variability across the treatment conditions will be similar. We usually think about variance using the standard deviation. In other words, we want the standard deviation for each of the conditions to be similar. Although we typically think about variability using the standard deviation metric, the homogeneity of variance assumption is tested statistically, so we use statistical notation in the form of variance to ensure that we meet this assumption.

$$\sigma_1^2 = \sigma_2^2 = \sigma_3^2$$

In other words, we *want* the variances to be similar! In our example of rating jokes in the three conditions, we want a similar distribution of the variances across ratings of the three different conditions as illustrated in Figure 9.1 below.

If the ratings across conditions possessed different variances, then the distributions would appear very different, as illustrated in Figure 9.2. The kurtosis or relative size of curve would change with the size of the standard deviation (Figure 9.2).

F statistic—Ratio of Treatment to Error variance used to detect statistical significance.

We typically use the **Hartley F-Max test** to determine if we meet the homogeneity of variance assumption. However, rather than trying to find differences between groups, we actually want the opposite outcome. In other words, we don't want to find differences in the variances across groups when we are applying the *F*-Max test, so we want results of the test to be non-significant.

A second test of homogeneity of variance is Levene's test. Many statistical software packages automatically produce **Levene's Test of Equality of Variances** with the ANOVA output. When we interpret Levene's test, we do not want to reject the null hypothesis, so we hope for a non-significant result. In other words, we want the *p* value to be larger, rather than smaller, than .05.

Homogeneity of variance—The assumption that groups contain similar variances.

Two tests, the Hartley *F*-Max and Levene's Test of Equality of Variances, can be used to test the homogeneity of variance assumption. We are searching for non-significant differences in the variances of the groups. Although we prefer to meet the assumption of homogeneity of variance, the ANOVA is relatively robust to violations of this assumption (Howell, 2007).

Hartley *F*-Max test—Test of homogeneity of variance.

Another assumption underlying the ANOVA is the presumption that scores are *normally distributed*. If we consider the illustrations of the distributions in Figure 9.1, we expect to find that the distributions generally appear normal, or we violate the normality assumption. Because we are referencing the variance in each of the distributions, and variance within the distribution represents error, the assumption of normality really suggests that we want the error to be normally distributed. However, as with the assumption of homogeneity of variance, violations of the normality of variance, within reason, are not cause for too much concern.

Levene's Test of Equality of Variances—Test of homogeneity of variance.

FIGURE 9.1   *Homogeneity of Variance*

FIGURE 9.2 *Heterogeneity of Variance*

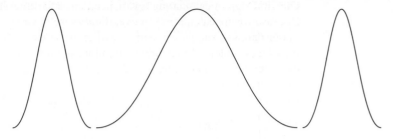

The third statistical assumption, *independence of observations,* is much more susceptible to violations. Statistical significance is calculated by deriving the ratio of treatment to error variance (Howell, 2007), so we must ensure or assume that the observations, or data, in each of the treatment conditions are independent. In other words, we must be sure that participants are assigned to only one of the conditions. Having checked our data to ensure that we have met all of the assumptions for the ANOVA, we can proceed to examine the variance that is present in the data.

Significance Testing

We will use the following data to illustrate how an ANOVA is used to partition, or separate, the overall variance into variance associated with the treatment and that of error. Using the scenario that Wimer and Beins (2008) provided as an example (Table 9.1), we can imagine that data in each of the three groups (i.e., very funny, not very funny, control) reflect funniness ratings of jokes. Ratings of funniness range from 1 (*not funny*) to 7 (*very funny*).

So, the average rating for jokes in the VF condition is highest ($M_1 = 6$), followed by the control condition ($M_2 = 4$), and the lowest rating occurring in the NVF group ($M_3 = 2$). It is useful to consider how each of the group means differs from the overall or grand mean ($M_G = 4$).

Although the average rating provides us with preliminary insight into how the conditions might affect perceptions of funniness, we need to consider the variability that is present across all of the conditions. The probability model serves as the basis for conducting an analysis of the variability that is present in data, or ANOVA. We are interested in three measures of variability—total variance, error variance, and variance between groups. Our first step in examining variability is to derive an overall measure of the variance present in the data. In other words, we combine all of the data into one large group and we calculate the TOTAL variance as the first step in performing an analysis of variance.

TABLE 9.1 *Funniness Ratings*

Very Funny (VF)	Not Very Funny (NVF)	Control
7	1	4
5	4	6
6	1	2
5	1	3
7	3	5
$\sum X = 30$	$\sum X = 10$	$\sum X = 20$
$M_1 = 6$	$M_2 = 2$	$M_3 = 4$

TOTAL Variance. Let's consider the very basic calculation of variance from Chapter 5. Our first step in calculating a variance is to determine how far each score is from the mean. Because we are calculating an overall measure of variance, we must combine all of the scores in our data set, and as we learned earlier, we must employ an intermediate step, or calculate the sum of squares (*SS*) in preparation for calculation of the **TOTAL variance.** As a reminder, the formula for calculating the *SS* is:

$$SS_{TOTAL} = \sum (X - M_G)^2$$

The SS_{TOTAL} allows us to derive an overall difference or sum of how far each score deviates from the mean. However, we really want to obtain an average, or an index of how far each score typically varies from the mean. As we learned in Chapter 5, to obtain the variance, or an approximation of an average deviation from the mean, we simply divide the *SS* by $N - 1$.

$$s^2 = \frac{SS_{TOTAL}}{N - 1} \quad s^2 = \frac{SS_{TOTAL}}{df_{total}}$$

TOTAL Variance—
Variability between all dependent variable data.

The denominator $(N - 1)$ reflects degrees of freedom (*df*) for the total variance present in our data. As a reminder, *df* are the number of scores that are free to vary. Because we are using a sample, rather than a population, we lose one degree of freedom in the overall measure of variance, so the number of scores that are free to vary is $N - 1$. Degrees of freedom are divided into the sum of squares to obtain the total variability present among all of the scores in our study. Using our example, we begin by calculating total *SS* by first combining the data from all three conditions, then calculating an overall or grand mean ($M_G = 4$). We then use the overall mean to calculate the SS_{TOTAL} for the combined data set (see Table 9.2).

TABLE 9.2 *Sum of Squares TOTAL*

X	$X - M$	$(X - M_G)^2$	
7	$7 - 4 = 3$	9	
5	$5 - 4 = 1$	1	
6	$6 - 4 = 2$	4	$SS_{Treatment_1} = 24$
5	$5 - 4 = 1$	1	
7	$7 - 4 = 3$	9	
1	$1 - 4 = -3$	9	
4	$4 - 4 = 0$	0	
1	$1 - 4 = -3$	9	$SS_{Treatment_2} = 28$
1	$1 - 4 = -3$	9	
3	$3 - 4 = -1$	1	
4	$4 - 4 = 0$	0	
6	$6 - 4 = 2$	4	
2	$2 - 4 = -2$	4	$SS_{Treatment_3} = 10$
3	$3 - 4 = -1$	1	
5	$5 - 4 = 1$	1	
$\sum X_G = 60$		$SS = \sum (X - M_G)^2 = 62$	
$M_{Grand} = 4$			

Using all of the data, the SS_{TOTAL} is 62. We can now quickly derive a measure of variance for the entire set of data by dividing by *df:*

$$s^2 \text{ or } MS_{TOTAL} = \frac{SS_{TOTAL}}{N-1} \quad s^2 = \frac{SS_{TOTAL}}{df_{total}} \quad s^2 = \frac{62}{14} = 4.43$$

Our calculated variance ($s^2 = 4.43$) gives us an indication of how much variability is present in the full set of data. However, this calculation is only the first step in deriving an *F* statistic, or ANOVA. To actually calculate the *F* statistic, we must obtain the ratio of treatment variance to error variance, so we need to partition the TOTAL variance into Treatment and Error variance. A **Source Table** is typically used to keep track of the elements of variance. In other words, the Source Table provides a quick reference for the *sources* of variance present within our data.

Thus far, we have calculated several elements for the Source Table. We already calculated the TOTAL Sum of Squares ($SS_{TOTAL} = 62$) and the degrees of freedom ($df_{total} = 14$). These values are contained in Table 9.3. We also calculated the variance for the total set of scores ($s^2 = 4.43$). Note that the variance is located in the mean square (*MS*) column of the table. The *MS* is essentially the average of the sum of squares, in other words, *MS* is an average amount of variability. Although we included the *MS* TOTAL in our source table for the purpose of illustration, it is typically not necessary to derive the TOTAL *MS* when calculating the *F* statistic.

TREATMENT Variance. We obtained an index of the total amount of variability present in our data, but our goal is to derive a ratio of the **TREATMENT variance** to Error variance. Another way to think about the *F* ratio is that we are comparing the amount of variability that is present *between* groups to the amount of variability that is present *within* groups. The variability that is present between the groups reflects the effect of the treatments, whereas the variability within the groups reflects individual differences among individuals in a single treatment, or error variance.

We can isolate the amount of variability that is attributable to the treatment, or to the level of the IV, by calculating a variance that reflects differences between the means of the groups. When we calculated the total variance, we divided the SS_{TOTAL} by df_{Total} to obtain an average amount of variability for all of our data. We now need to calculate a Sum of Squares value and *df* that can be used to calculate the average amount of variance between treatments, or treatment variance (see Table 9.4).

It is possible to calculate *SS* treatment by comparing the means of each treatment group (i.e., $M_1 = 6$, $M_2 = 2$, $M_3 = 4$) to the overall or Grand Mean ($M_G = 4$). Using our standard *SS* formula, we subtract the Grand Mean from each of the sample means, and square the resulting deviations scores (see Table 9.5).

Because each of these *SS* calculations is conducted with a Mean (*M*) value for each treatment, rather than an individual score (*X*), we need to multiply our sum of the squared deviation scores by *n* to account for the total number of people in the study. The lower case *n* signifies that we are using the treatment sample size, rather than the overall sample size (*N*).

Source Table—A table of values that contains the elements for calculating an ANOVA.

TREATMENT variance—Variance associated with the Mean differences between treatments.

TABLE 9.3 *Source Table*

Source of Variation	SS	df	MS	F
TREATMENT				
ERROR				
TOTAL	62	14	4.43	

TABLE 9.4 *Sum of Squares TREATMENT*

X

7
5
6 VF
5
7

$$(M_1 - M_G)^2(n) = SS_{TREATMENT_1}$$

$M_1 = 6$ $\qquad (6 - 4)^2(5) = 20$

$\sum X_1 = 30$

1
4
1 NVF
1
3

$$(M_2 - M_G)^2(n) = SS_{TREATMENT_2}$$

$M_2 = 2$ $\qquad (2 - 4)^2(5) = 20$

$\sum X_2 = 10$

4
6
2 Control
3
5

$$(M_3 - M_G)^2(n) = SS_{TREATMENT_3}$$

$M_3 = 4$ $\qquad (4 - 4)^2(5) = 0$

$\sum X_3 = 20$

$$SS_{Treatment} = \sum (M_{group} - M_{Grand})^2(n)$$

$$SS_{Treatment} = 20 + 20 + 0 = 40$$

Thus, for studies in which the number of participants in each group is equal (here, $n = 5$) the $SS_{TREATMENT}$ is:

$$SS_{Treatment} = \sum (SS_{Means})(n)$$

$$SS_{Treatment} = (8)(5) = 40$$

Although this calculation of the TREATMENT SS is intuitive, most of the time we don't end up with equal sample sizes for each of our groups, so this method of calculation is not always possible. Sometimes people drop out of our study, or some unforeseen circumstance may

TABLE 9.5 SS_{Means}

M	$(M - M_G)$	$(M - M_G)^2$
6	$6 - 4 = 2$	4
2	$2 - 4 = 2$	4
4	$4 - 4 = 0$	0
	$\sum (M - M_G)^2 = 8$	

produce data that can't be used. Because we can't guarantee equal samples sizes, we employ a less intuitive method of calculating the *SS* treatment.

Recall that the treatment variance reflects the effect of the IV for each of the conditions present in our study. To derive our treatment variance, we compare the Mean from each treatment group to the overall Mean of our data ($M_G = 4$). On a scale of 1 to 7, a score of 4 is the midpoint on our rating scale. The average funniness rating across all of our conditions is 4. However, a visual inspection of our data suggests that the overall or Grand Mean ($M_G = 4$) does not capture the differences between treatment groups. When participants were told that a joke was very funny, they tended to rate the funniness of the joke higher ($M_1 = 6$). Participants who were told that a joke was not very funny rated the jokes lower ($M_2 = 2$), and the control group, like the overall group, rated the jokes at the midpoint of the scale ($M_3 = 4$). The $SS_{TREATMENT}$ is calculated for each of the groups in the study and then summed to derive an overall TREATMENT *SS*. The formula for calculating each treatment *SS* is:

$$SS_{TREATMENT} = \sum (M_{Group} - M_{Grand})^2(n)$$

OR

$$SS_{TREATMENT} = \sum (SS_{Means})(n)$$

Our first step in calculating the $SS_{TREATMENT}$ is to calculate the difference between each group mean and the total, or Grand Mean. We then multiply by the respective *n* as follows:

$$
\begin{aligned}
\text{VF} &= (6 - 4)^2(5) = 20 \\
\text{NVF} &= (2 - 4)^2(5) = 20 \\
\text{Control} &= (4 - 4)^2(5) = 0
\end{aligned}
$$

These values are summed to obtain the $SS_{TREATMENT}$.

$$SS_{TREATMENT} = 20 + 20 + 0 = 40$$

Using this formula we are able to account for different sample sizes in each group. To obtain the variance associated with the treatment, we divide the $SS_{TREATMENT}$ by degrees of freedom associated with the treatment. Degrees of freedom for treatment are calculated by subtracting 1 from the total number of treatment conditions. The number of treatments is specified using *k* as the notation. So, in this example, $df_{Treatment} = k - 1$.

$$df_{Treatment} = 3 - 1 = 2$$

Thus far, we have calculated two of the components necessary for deriving an index of treatment variance: $SS_{TREATMENT} = 40$ and $df_{Treatment} = 2$. To keep track of our calculations, we place these values in our Source Table (Figure 9.3). Much like our calculation of a variance for the TOTAL, we can easily use these values to calculate a variance for the TREATMENT. Remember, the variance is reported as the Mean Square (*MS*) or, the approximate average of the *SS*.

ERROR variance— Variability between individuals participating in the same condition. Error variance is the denominator used in calculating the ANOVA.

$$MS_{TREATMENT} = \frac{SS_{TREATMENT}}{df_{Treatment}} = \frac{40}{2} = 20$$

ERROR Variance.   **ERROR variance** is the final source of variability that we need to derive when calculating an ANOVA or *F* test. It would actually be quite simple to obtain our

FIGURE 9.3 *Source Table*

Source of Variation	SS	df	MS	F
TREATMENT	40	2	20	
ERROR				
TOTAL	62	14		

respective error values (i.e., *SS* and *df*) using the Source Table. Because TOTAL variance is the sum of both Treatment and Error variance, we need only subtract the TREATMENT *SS* and *df* to derive the respective Error terms. Using the source table we find:

$$SS_{ERROR} = SS_{TOTAL} - SS_{TREATMENT} = 62 - 40 = 22$$

AND

$$df_{Error} = df_{Total} - df_{Treatment} = 14 - 2 = 12$$

Although this method of calculation for the Error terms is efficient, it is instructive to consider how these values are derived within the context of the ANOVA. Therefore, let's consider how we might derive the error terms in the absence of the TOTAL *SS* and *df*.

Recall that error is reflected in the differences among people within each treatment group. Therefore, we are interested in calculating the amount of variance that constitutes error, or the amount of variability *within* each treatment condition. Comparable to our calculations of the total and between *SS*, we need to calculate a *SS* for the Error (SS_{ERROR}) and *df* for the Error (df_{Error}). As illustrated in Table 9.6, if we treat each group as an independent source of error variance, we begin by calculating the *SS* for each of the groups.

To complete the calculation for SS_{ERROR}, we merely add the sum of the squares that we derived for each of the groups.

$$SS_{ERROR} = SS_1 + SS_2 + SS_3$$
$$SS_{ERROR} = 4 + 8 + 10 = 22$$

To complete the calculation of error variance or MS_{ERROR}, we must calculate the *df*s associated with the error or within-subjects variance. We lose one degree of freedom for each of the groups. Thus, degrees of freedom error is calculated by subtracting one degree of freedom from each *n*. A simpler method for calculated df_{Error} is to subtract the number of groups from the overall sample size.

$$df_{Error} = N - k$$
$$df_{Error} = 15 - 3 = 12$$

Note that both of the methods for calculating *df* lead to identical values. In this example our df_{Error} are equal to 12. Dividing SS_{ERROR} by df_{Error} allows us to obtain the amount of variance associated with the error, or MS_{ERROR}. Inserting the SS_{ERROR}, df_{Error}, and MS_{ERROR} into the Source Table provides all of the necessary information for calculation of the ANOVA or *F* statistic (Figure 9.4).

F Statistic.   The ANOVA is used to partition the total amount of variability (i.e., differences between treatments and differences within treatments) so that we can derive a ratio of explained to error variance. We have already calculated the variance (*MS* or s^2), or an index of the amount

TABLE 9.6 *Sum of Squares ERROR*

X		$X - M$	$(X - M)^2$
7		$7 - 6 = 1$	1
5		$5 - 6 = -1$	1
6	VF	$6 - 6 = 0$	0
5		$5 - 6 = -1$	1
7		$7 - 6 = 1$	1
$M_1 = 6$			$\sum(X - M_1)^2 = 4$
$\sum X_1 = 30$			
1		$1 - 2 = -1$	1
4		$4 - 2 = 2$	4
1	NVF	$1 - 2 = -1$	1
1		$1 - 2 = -1$	1
3		$3 - 2 = 1$	1
$M_2 = 2$			$\sum(X - M_2)^2 = 8$
$\sum X_2 = 10$			
4		$4 - 4 = 0$	0
6		$6 - 4 = 2$	4
2	Control	$2 - 4 = -2$	4
3		$3 - 4 = -1$	1
5		$5 - 4 = 1$	1
$M_3 = 4$			$\sum(X - M_3)^2 = 10$
$\sum X_3 = 20$			

of variability that is present between the three treatment conditions. The variance is reported as the $MS_{TREATMENT}$ in the Source Table. Similarly, we derived an index of variability (MS_{ERROR}) for the error, or differences among people, within each of the treatments. When we test for statistical significance, we are merely comparing the amount of variability present between treatments to the variance within treatments.

$$ANOVA = \frac{Treatment\ Variance}{Error\ Variance}$$

Thus, we can now use the information in the Source Table to derive the F statistic. The $MS_{TREATMENT}$ is divided by MS_{ERROR} to obtain the F value.

$$F = \frac{MS_{Treatment}}{MS_{Error}} = \frac{20}{1.83} = 10.93$$

FIGURE 9.4 *Source Table*

Source of Variation	SS	df	MS	F
TREATMENT	40	2	20	10.93
ERROR	22	12	1.83	
TOTAL	62	14		

As with the t test, we compare the calculated F statistic to a table of values from an F distribution, or the F table. Because we used two variances (i.e., treatment and error) to calculate our F statistic, we have two measures of df. Therefore, we use both the treatment df and the error df to obtain the tabled F value, or the value that is used for comparison to the calculated F statistic. As illustrated in the example table, we use df from the numerator ($df = 2$), or the treatment variance, and the df from the denominator ($df = 12$), or the error variance, to enter the table and find the appropriate tabled value. In our example, we compare the calculated F value of 10.83 to the tabled F value of 3.88. We also use the dfs to report the outcome of the ANOVA as $F(2,12) = 10.83, p < .05$. Because our calculated value is larger than our tabled value, we conclude that our results are statistically significant. In other words, we reject the null or statistical hypothesis.

Significance Values for the Analysis of Variance (F Test)

Degrees of freedom for treatments (df$_{between}$) appear in the left column. Degrees of freedom for the error term (df$_{within}$ or df$_{error}$) are across the top. Computed values of F are significant if they are larger than the critical value in the table.

Values for $\alpha = .05$ are in normal Roman type
Values for $\alpha = .01$ are in bold type
Values for $\alpha = 0.001$ are in italics

DF FOR THE NUMERATOR
(DF$_{BETWEEN}$ OR DF$_{TREATMENT}$)

		1	2	3	4	5	6	8	12	24
DF for the denominator										
(DF$_{WITHIN}$ OR DF$_{ERROR}$)										
11	$\alpha = .05$	4.84	3.98	3.59	3.36	3.20	3.09	2.95	2.79	2.61
	$\alpha = .01$	**9.65**	**7.20**	**6.22**	**5.67**	**5.32**	**5.07**	**4.74**	**4.40**	**4.02**
	$\alpha = .001$	*19.69*	*13.81*	*11.56*	*10.35*	*9.58*	*9.05*	*8.35*	*7.63*	*6.85*
12	$\alpha = .05$	4.75	3.88	3.49	3.26	3.11	3.00	2.85	2.69	2.50
	$\alpha = .01$	**9.33**	**6.93**	**5.95**	**5.41**	**5.06**	**4.82**	**4.50**	**4.16**	**3.78**
	$\alpha = .001$	*18.64*	*12.97*	*10.80*	*9.63*	*8.89*	*8.38*	*7.71*	*7.00*	*6.25*

Recall that we are trying to obtain a very large difference between groups and a small difference within groups so that we obtain a large F, or a value that is statistically significant. In other words, we want to maximize the difference attributable to the treatment, and minimize the difference in error.

So, if we obtain a large difference between groups, relative to the variability within the groups, we conclude that our results are statistically significant. At this point, we know only that there are differences between the levels of the independent variable. However, we do not know exactly where those differences lie. If we compare the means of the groups, we can anticipate where the differences might be. However, to determine if the differences between means are statistically significant, we must conduct a post hoc, or subsequent, analysis to determine which of the differences between treatments are significant.

Post Hoc Analyses

Recall that our rationale for using an ANOVA, rather than multiple t tests, is that we want to control for Type I error. Remember that if we simply conduct multiple t tests, we cannot be confident that our specified level of Type I error is accurate. In other words, if we conduct multiple t tests, our likelihood of concluding that we have a reliable difference is actually higher than our stated alpha.

Using an ANOVA allows us to test for statistically significant differences among multiple conditions while holding alpha constant. However, to determine which of individual treatments differ, we must conduct a **post hoc test**. A post hoc (after the fact) test is performed after we find a significant *F* test, or overall difference among means. The post hoc test is a second level of analysis that allows us to test for differences between pairs of conditions. Using our jokes example, it is possible to make three pairwise comparisons:

Comparison 1: NVF versus VF
Comparison 2: VF versus Control
Comparison 3: NVF versus Control

Notice that with three levels of the IV, only three comparisons are possible. As the number of conditions increase, the numbers of comparisons increase exponentially, so the process can become quite complicated. [Statistical software packages quickly produce post hoc analyses, so we don't usually calculate them by hand.] For example, if we use four levels of the IV, six comparisons are possible. As the number of comparisons increase, the likelihood of a Type I error also increases.

So, how do we test differences between groups, while at the same time controlling for Type I error? Statisticians have developed more than a dozen post hoc analyses that help to control for both types of error (Type I and II), differences in sample sizes, differences in types of treatments, and several other factors that may influence error (Field, 2009).

The Tukey post hoc test, also referred to as the Honestly Significant Difference (*HSD*) test, offers good protection against Type I error. The *HSD* is widely used; however, the *HSD* requires equal sample sizes.[1] Realistically, we often experience participant mortality so we frequently end up with unequal sample sizes. Despite these limitations, many researchers use the *HSD* as a post hoc test because it is efficient.

Tukey **HSD.**   Following the overall significance or *F* test, we move to a more detailed level of comparison. A post hoc analysis allows us to compare only two conditions at a time. With the Tukey post hoc analysis, we essentially derive a minimum mean difference value. In other words, when we compare any two conditions, we calculate the smallest possible significant difference between the means. If our difference between the means exceeds our honestly significance difference (*HSD*), then we conclude that the differences between conditions are statistically significant.

The **Tukey *HSD*** is calculated using information from our ANOVA Source Table along with the *q* statistic derived from the *q* table (Appendix E). The formula for calculating the minimum mean difference between means is:

$$HSD = q\sqrt{\frac{MS_{ERROR}}{n}}$$

Post hoc test—A comparison of differences across levels of an independent variable conducted after an initial data analysis.

Our first step in calculating the *HSD* is to use the data from the ANOVA Source Table to derive an average that reflects the amount of error present across all conditions. Remember the MS_{ERROR} reflects the proportion of error variance present in the data and *n* is the number of people in each condition.

$$HSD = q\sqrt{\frac{1.83}{5}} = q\sqrt{.366}$$

Tukey *HSD*—A test of pairwise comparisons conducted after obtaining a statistically significant *F* test.

---

[1]Small differences in sample sizes can be accounted for by using the harmonic mean: $\tilde{n} = \dfrac{k}{\Sigma\frac{1}{n}}$ (Winer, Brown, & Michels, 1991).

We need to obtain the *q,* or studentized range statistic from the *q* table (Table E.4) to complete the calculation of our Tukey *HSD* statistic. We use the number of treatments (*k*), an alpha (α = .05), and df_{Error} to obtain *q*. With three conditions or treatments, an alpha of .05, and *df* = 12, the *q* = 3.77. Thus,

$$HSD = 3.77\sqrt{.366} = (3.77)(.60) = 2.26$$

In other words, we use the *HSD* = 2.26 to determine the minimum amount of difference that must be present between treatment means. Let's return to our pairwise comparisons:

$$\begin{aligned} \text{VF versus NVF} \quad &= M_1 - M_2 = 6 - 2 = 4 \\ \text{VF versus Control} \quad &= M_1 - M_3 = 6 - 4 = 2 \\ \text{NVF versus Control} &= M_2 - M_3 = 4 - 2 = 2 \end{aligned}$$

The largest difference between means ($M_1 - M_2 = 6 - 2 = 4$) is present between the VF and NVF conditions. If we compare the four-point difference to our calculated *HSD* of 2.26, we conclude that there is a statistically significant difference in the funniness ratings between the VF and NVF ($M_1 - M_2 = 4$) conditions because our difference between means exceeds the *HSD* value of 2.26. The mean difference in the two remaining comparisons is two points. Comparing the mean difference of 2 to the *HSD* of 2.26, we conclude that funniness ratings for these comparisons are not significantly different. The *HSD* test supports the hypothesis that priming influences the ratings of jokes as we expected.

Scheffé Test.   A second, more versatile and statistically conservative post hoc test, the Scheffé, is useful as an all-purpose test for comparison of means, or all possible comparisons (Hays, 1988; Winer, Brown, & Michels, 1991). One additional advantage of using the Scheffé is that we aren't constrained by a need for equal sample sizes. The Tukey *HSD* allows us to use information from the Source Table to derive minimum mean difference to determine statistical significance. We use intermediate calculations from our ANOVA to derive a new *F* statistic to calculate the **Scheffé test**.

As you recall, the *F* statistic that we calculate for the overall ANOVA is a ratio of Treatment to Error variance. With the Scheffé, we calculate a similar ratio. Instead of using the full amount of Treatment variance from the overall *F* statistic, we calculate a new Treatment variance for each pairwise comparison. Recall that the formula for Treatment variance is:

$$MS_{Treatment} = \frac{SS_{TREATMENT}}{df_{Treatment}}$$

Returning to our example, if we wish to compare the VF condition with the NVF condition, we need to calculate the new $MS_{TREATMENT}$ using the *SS* from only these two conditions. Table 9.2 provides us with the *SS* for each of the treatment conditions. So, if we compare the VF condition to the NVF condition we calculate a new variance for this pairwise comparison.

$$MS_{Treatment} = \frac{SS_{TREATMENT}}{df_{treatment}} = \frac{24 + 28}{2} = \frac{52}{2} = 26$$

One way that the Scheffé uses a conservative determination of statistical significance is, in part, to retain the *df* from the overall *F* statistic. The pairwise $MS_{TREATMENT}$ is used to calculate the new *F* statistic.

$$F = \frac{MS_{TREATMENT}}{MS_{Error}} = \frac{26}{1.83} = 14.21$$

Scheffé test—A test of pairwise comparisons conducted after obtaining a statistically significant *F* test.

We find that the pairwise calculated value, $F(2,12) = 14.21$, exceeds our original tabled *F* value, $F(2,12) = 3.88$; therefore, the difference between the VF and NVF conditions is statistically significant.

Similar calculations are conducted for each of the pairwise comparisons of interest. As we saw with the Tukey *HSD,* only one of the comparisons is statistically significant. It is now time to turn our attention to the final calculation for reporting the outcomes of an ANOVA.

Effect Size

Recall that effect size is an estimate of the proportion of variability explained by the independent variable, that is, the strength of association (Grissom & Kim, 2005). Much like the post hoc analyses, statisticians offer many options for reporting effect size. **Omega squared** (ω^2) is a very accurate but complicated estimate of effect size. A more conceptually direct measure of effect size is **eta squared** (η^2). For our purposes, it is probably easier to consider eta squared as an all-purpose method of reporting effect size.

Simply stated, eta squared provides an estimate of the proportion of variability that is attributable to the IV. To obtain this estimate we use the *SS* values that are already available in the Source Table.

$$\eta^2 = \frac{SS_{Treatment}}{SS_{Total}}$$

Working with our example we find:

$$\eta^2 = \frac{40}{62} = .65$$

Calculation of eta squared produces a value of .65. How should we interpret this value? Eta squared is a proportion or percentage of variance accounted for by the IV, therefore in our joke study we are accounting for approximately 65% of the variance.

Writing Results

Reporting results of an ANOVA requires more detail than what is reported for a *t* test. We begin by reporting whether the overall *F* is significant. The next step is to report outcomes of the significance tests for the pairwise comparisons. Recall that post hoc tests provide the information for the pairwise comparisons. Along with reporting statistical significance, we report descriptive data for each of the conditions. Finally, a measure of effect size is reported. Using our data from the funniness study, we provide an example of how to report results.

Participants rated jokes in accord with the information provided about prior ratings. We found statistically significant differences between treatment conditions $F(2, 12) = 10.93, p < .05, \eta^2 = .65$. Participants in the very funny (VF) condition rated funniness more highly ($M = 6, SD = 1$) than participants in the NVF condition ($M = 2, SD = 1.41$). According to the Tukey *HSD,* the two extreme conditions differ significantly from the neutral condition ($p < .001$), whereas the funniness ratings of the participants in the two moderate groups (VF and control, NVF and control) do not differ significantly ($p > .05$).

Omega squared— Measure of effect size representing the proportion of accounted for variance.

Eta squared—Measure of effect size representing the proportion of accounted for variance.

Computer Analysis Using SPSS

When we wish to investigate differences between more than two levels of an independent variable, we use the ANOVA. We can use SPSS to run either a between groups ANOVA or a repeated measures analysis. Let's begin with how to use SPSS to conduct the between groups ANOVA.

Data for an ANOVA are set up much like the independent *t* test. One column contains the dependent variable data and the second column is used to designate the group or level of

FIGURE 9.5   *Independent Samples ANOVA*

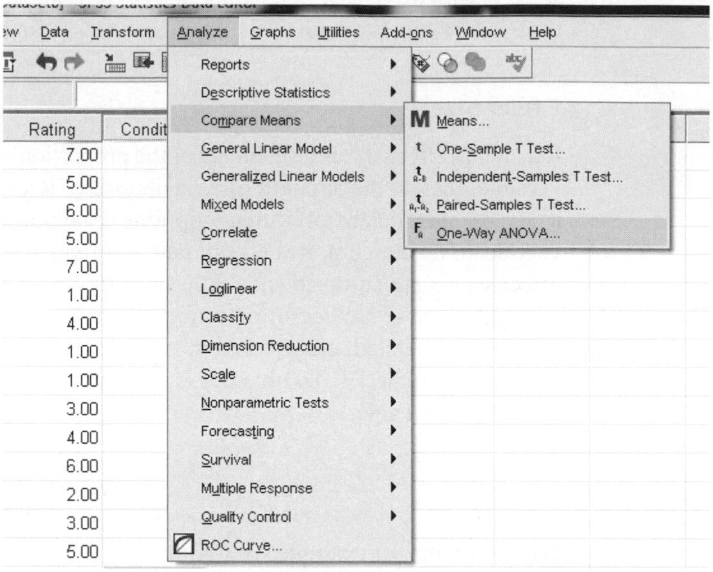

the IV. The first step in conducting the ANOVA is to select the appropriate statistical analysis as illustrated in Figure 9.5.

After selecting the One-Way ANOVA, the dialogue box requires us to specify the dependent variable and a factor. As illustrated in Figure 9.6, the dependent variable is Funny and the factor is the independent variable or group. We must also specify the values for our groups (i.e., levels of the independent variable) at this time. We are working with three groups, so we coded the groups using 1, 2, and 3 when we entered the data, and we define the values for groups 1, 2, and 3.

FIGURE 9.6   *Specifying Variables*

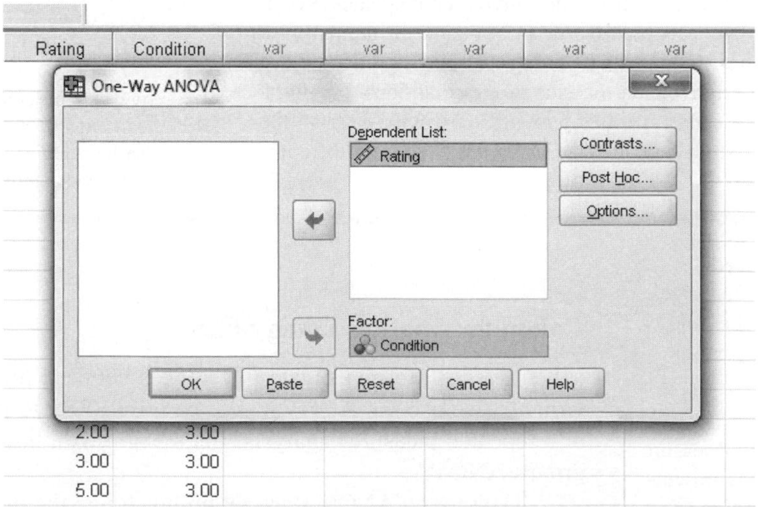

FIGURE 9.7 *Post Hoc Analyses*

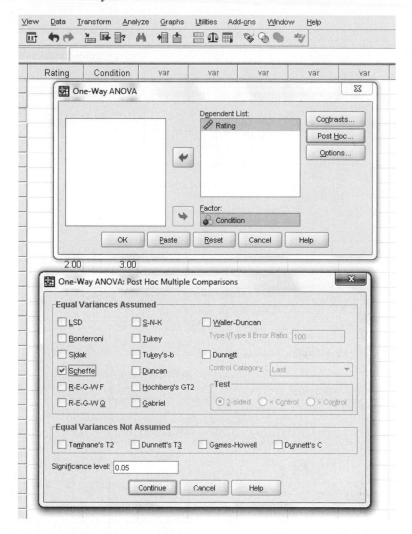

Our next step is to specify the post hoc test, and select options that will produce the desired output from the analysis. In Figure 9.7 you will notice that we selected the Scheffé post hoc test. From the Options tab we requested descriptive statistics for each of the groups. Clicking the "OK" tab will produce the ANOVA output.

The output includes descriptive data for each of the groups as illustrated in Figure 9.8. If you compare the output from SPSS to the calculated values from our example, you will find that the data are identical.

Similarly, Figure 9.9 is the source table produced by SPSS. These values are also approximately the same as those illustrated in our example above.

Finally, post hoc analyses are contained in the multiple comparisons table as illustrated in Figure 9.10. Significance is denoted by the asterisk. Regardless of the post hoc test selected (i.e., Scheffe or Tukey *HSD*), the Very Funny (VF) and Not Very Funny (NVF) conditions are the only statistically significant outcomes.

FIGURE 9.8   *Descriptive Statistics*

Descriptives

Funny

	N	Mean	Std. Deviation	Std. Error	95% Confidence Interval for Mean		Minimum	Maximum
					Lower Bound	Upper Bound		
1.00	5	6.0000	1.00000	.44721	4.7583	7.2417	5.00	7.00
2.00	5	2.0000	1.41421	.63246	.2440	3.7560	1.00	4.00
3.00	5	4.0000	1.58114	.70711	2.0368	5.9632	2.00	6.00
Total	15	4.0000	2.10442	.54336	2.8346	5.1654	1.00	7.00

FIGURE 9.9   *Source Table*

ANOVA

Funny

	Sum of Squares	df	Mean Square	F	Sig.
Between Groups	40.000	2	20.000	10.909	.002
Within Groups	22.000	12	1.833		
Total	62.000	14			

FIGURE 9.10   *Post Hoc Output*

Multiple Comparisons

Dependent Variable: Funny

	(I) Group	(J) Group	Mean Difference (I-J)	Std. Error	Sig.	95% Confidence Interval	
						Lower Bound	Upper Bound
Tukey HSD	VF	NVF	4.00000*	.85635	.001	1.7154	6.2846
		Control	2.00000	.85635	.089	−.2846	4.2846
	NVF	VF	−4.00000*	.85635	.001	−6.2846	−1.7154
		Control	−2.00000	.85635	.089	−4.2846	.2846
	Control	VF	−2.00000	.85635	.089	−4.2846	.2846
		NVF	2.00000	.85635	.089	−.2846	4.2846
Scheffe	VF	NVF	4.00000*	.85635	.002	1.6129	6.3871
		Control	2.00000	.85635	.106	−.3871	4.3871
	NVF	VF	−4.00000*	.85635	.002	−6.3871	−1.6129
		Control	−2.00000	.85635	.106	−4.3871	.3871
	Control	VF	−2.00000	.85635	.106	−4.3871	.3871
		NVF	2.00000	.85635	.106	−.3871	4.3871

*The mean difference is significant at the .05 level.

Statistical Testing for Repeated Measures

The one-way ANOVA is used to examine differences between multiple levels of one independent variable. Wimer and Beins (2008) used three different groups to examine the effects of priming on funniness of cartoons. Because priming (IV) included three levels, and three groups of different people participated, the between groups ANOVA was used to test for statistical differences between treatments.

It is also possible to create a similar study with three levels of treatment using one set of participants. In other words, each person would experience each of the three treatment conditions. As we indicated in Chapter 7, repeated measures experiments are useful because they involve fewer participants. However, we must also balance the advantages of the repeated measures design against the potential disadvantages (e.g., carryover effects, order effects) of asking participants to experience each of the conditions.

Our funniness study involved priming participants, or telling them about the jokes they were about to hear. It would be difficult to conduct this study using a repeated measures design because of the potential problems with carryover effects. For example, participants are likely to catch on when they are told first that the jokes are funny, and then that the jokes are not very funny. Because our funniness scenario does not work well for illustrating the repeated measures ANOVA, we will use a different scenario to illustrate how to perform a **repeated measures ANOVA**.

Let's consider an example from cognitive psychology. Cognitive psychologists frequently use repeated measures designs in their research. For example, participants might be asked to view a set of words, then listen to the same set of words, and finally, both view and listen to the same set of words. Ultimately, participants are asked to recall the words at the conclusion of each of the treatments. This memory task involves asking participants to indicate the words that were present in each of the conditions. Thus, the number of correct responses is recorded for each condition. Because participants serve as their own control, the repeated measures design is actually more statistically sensitive. To help us understand the increased sensitivity, or reduction in overall error, we will use the same data from the between groups ANOVA for our repeated measures ANOVA. The difference is that we will consider the data in the context of the new example.

Stating the Hypothesis

Much like our between groups ANOVA, we begin with a statement of the hypothesis. We anticipate that the number of words that participants remember will differ across conditions. So, our alternative or research hypothesis indicates that the treatment means across conditions are different.

$$H_1 : \mu_1 \neq \mu_2 \neq \mu_3$$

To test the probability that memory for words differs across conditions we need to state the hypothesis statistically:

$$H_0 : \mu_1 = \mu_2 = \mu_3$$

Again, the null hypothesis simply reflects the statement that the population means for each of the three conditions are equal.

Assumptions of Repeated Measures ANOVA. The repeated measures ANOVA is similar to the independent samples ANOVA because we use an F ratio to determine if the treatment variance is statistically significant.

$$ANOVA = \frac{Treatment\ Variance}{Error\ Variance}$$

Repeated measures ANOVA—An ANOVA in which the same individuals provide data in more than one treatment.

Although the ratio of treatment to error variance appears to be identical to the one-way ANOVA, an important distinction is present when we are conducting a repeated measures ANOVA. Our error variance is actually smaller because we are using a repeated measures design. Because participants act as their own control, we can remove the variability associated with an individual participant from the error variance. Again, if the calculated *F* ratio is large, then we conclude that the treatment likely made a difference and that there is a statistically significant outcome.

Earlier we indicated that the ANOVA requires us to meet several assumptions. When using the repeated measures ANOVA we still need to ensure that the *homogeneity of variance* and *normality* assumptions are met.[2] However, we cannot use the independence assumption because we are, in fact, using the same participants across treatments. In other words, we *do not* want our observations to be independent. Using the same participants across conditions allows us to extract some of the error because the participants act as their own controls. The effect of having different people in the different groups can be removed because we have the same people across conditions; consequently, these same differences can be removed from the error term of repeated measures ANOVA, and we have a more sensitive statistical test.

Significance Testing

We will use the following data to illustrate how an ANOVA is used to partition, or separate, the variance into respective treatment and error variance when calculating a repeated measures ANOVA. Recall that earlier we used these data to calculate a between groups ANOVA. We are using these same data for our repeated measures ANOVA, but with a different scenario. Instead of using the funniness scenario, imagine that individuals are presented with words using different modalities (i.e., Visual, Auditory, and Visual + Auditory). As a measure of the dependent variable, participants are asked to recall the words that were presented under each of the conditions. Therefore, the data in Table 9.7 reflect the number of words that each participant recalled correctly (ranging from 1–7).

So, the average number of words recalled under the visual condition is much higher ($M_1 = 6$) than the auditory condition ($M_2 = 2$). The average number of words recalled under the combined condition resides somewhere in the middle ($M_3 = 4$). These data are identical to the data that we derived for the between groups ANOVA. However, instead of 15 participants, the data reflect values for only five people across each of the three conditions.

TOTAL Variance.   Recall that as with the between treatments ANOVA, TOTAL variance reflects the combined variability of our data. As a reminder, the formula for calculating the *SS* is:

$$SS_{TOTAL} = \sum (X - M_G)^2$$

TABLE 9.7 *Word Recall*

Participant	Visual (V)	Auditory (A)	Visual + Auditory (VA)
1	7	1	4
2	5	4	6
3	6	1	2
4	5	1	3
5	7	3	5
	$\sum X = 30$	$\sum X = 10$	$\sum X = 20$
	$M_1 = 6$	$M_2 = 2$	$M_3 = 4$

---

[2]Technically, an additional assumption of sphericity (Mauchly's test) should also be met when conducting a repeated measures ANOVA. This assumption is beyond the scope of this text, and readers are referred to Winer, Brown, and Michels (1991) for additional information.

The SS_{TOTAL} allows us to derive an overall difference or sum of how far each score deviates from the mean.

Partitioning TREATMENT Variance. A repeated measures ANOVA uses the same ratio of Treatment to Error variance to derive the F statistic. Because we are using the same ratio of Treatment to Error variance, we must begin by calculating the variance associated with the treatment. Using data from our previous example, we calculate the Treatment and Error variance just like we did before. Let's begin with calculating the Treatment variance. Recall that the SS formula for Treatment variance is:

$$SS_{TREATMENT} = \sum (M_{Group} - M_{Grand})^2(n)$$

OR

$$SS_{TREATMENT} = \sum (SS_{Means})(n)$$

So, using the means from the treatment conditions ($n = 5$), we obtain exactly the same treatment SS as with the between groups ANOVA.

$$SS_{Treatment} = (8)(5) = 40$$

To complete our calculation of treatment variance ($MS_{Treatment}$), we divide the $SS_{TREATMENT}$ by $df_{Treatment}$.

$$MS_{Treatment} = \frac{SS_{Treatment}}{df_{Treatment}} = \frac{40}{2} = 20$$

We use the Treatment or explained variance as the numerator for our F statistic.

ERROR Variance. The repeated measures test differs from the between groups ANOVA in the amount of Error variance that is present in the F ratio. We begin with the same Error variance ($SS_{ERROR} = 22$), but because each participant acts as his or her own control, we can reduce the Error variance by removing the variance attributed to individual differences of the participants. In other words, we further split the Error variance into a portion of variance that is attributable to treatment and a portion that reflects error. This change in the Error variance is reflected in a new version of the Source Table. As you can see in Table 9.8, we include our original values along with the additional space for calculating the new Error variance.

It is important to note that these values are identical to the values that we derived for the between groups ANOVA. In other words, at this point all sources of variance within the table remain the same.

In the between groups ANOVA, we calculated treatment variance by calculating the overall difference between the treatment means and the grand mean. When we calculated Error

TABLE 9.8 *Source Table Repeated Measures*

Source of Variation	SS	df	MS	F
TREATMENT	40	2	20	
ERROR	22	12	1.83	
Between Subjects				
Within Subjects				
TOTAL	62	14	4.43	

TABLE 9.9   *Word Recall*

Participant	Visual (V)	Auditory (A)	Visual + Auditory (VA)	Mean Participant Score (M_P)
1	7	1	4	4
2	5	4	6	5
3	6	1	2	3
4	5	1	3	3
5	7	3	5	5
	$\sum X_1 = 30$	$\sum X_2 = 10$	$\sum X_3 = 20$	$\sum M_P = 20$
	$M_1 = 6$	$M_2 = 2$	$M_3 = 4$	$M_P = 4$

variance, we began by calculating the SS for each of the treatment conditions, and then we summed the values to obtain the overall Error variance.

In the repeated measures ANOVA, we want to remove variance that can be attributed to the level of the independent variable from the overall Error variance. Therefore, in the repeated measures ANOVA, we calculate an additional value that is associated with Treatment or explained variance.

The Between Subjects variance (MS_{BS}) is an additional measure of explained variance. In other words, we begin by deriving an overall measure of differences between treatments for each of the participants. Let's consider our new version of the data in Table 9.9. As we indicated earlier, we have only five people participating in each of the three treatment conditions. Our first step in calculating the new Between Subjects score is to derive a mean participant score that reflects the average change across conditions. We hope to find larger mean differences because a large mean participant score is a reflection of bigger differences between treatments.

To obtain the Between Subjects variance, we use a formula that is almost identical to the Treatment variance. As a reminder, the $SS_{TREATMENT}$ formula is:

$$SS_{Treatment} = \sum (M_{group} - M_{Grand})^2 n$$

The formula for calculating $SS_{Between\ Subjects}$ or SS_{BS} is:

$$SS_{Between\ Subjects} = \sum (M_P - M_{Grand})^2 k$$

It should be evident that these formulas are similar. The primary difference is the substitution of the Mean Participant Score for the Mean Group score. The second difference involves multiplying by the number of treatments (k) instead of the number of people (n). [The notation for number of people in a repeated measures ANOVA is n rather than N.]

As illustrated in Table 9.10, we can derive the new $SS_{Between\ Subjects}$ value as the intermediate step for calculating the additional explained variance term.

The degrees of freedom associated with the between subjects SS is based upon the number of participants. Therefore, df_{BS} is:

$$df_{BS} = n - 1$$

So, our example degrees of freedom for the between subjects are:

$$df_{BS} = 5 - 1 = 4$$

TABLE 9.10 $SS_{Between\ Subjects}$

Mean Participant Score (M_P)	$M_P - M_G$	$(M_P - M_G)^2$	$(M_P - M_G)^2 k$
4	$4 - 4 = 0$	0	0
5	$5 - 4 = 1$	1	3
3	$3 - 4 = -1$	1	3
3	$3 - 4 = -1$	1	3
5	$5 - 4 = 1$	1	3
			$\sum (M_P - M_G)^2 k = 12$

We can quickly derive the variance (MS_{BS}) for the between subjects component of the ANOVA using the familiar mean square formula:

$$MS_{Between\ Subjects} = \frac{SS_{BS}}{df_{bs}}$$

$$MS_{Between\ Subjects} = \frac{12}{4} = 3$$

The Between Subjects variance is a measure of the amount of difference between treatments. Because we are using a repeated measures design, we can rely on participants to act as their own control, thus, the difference between treatments can be attributed to the IV. In other words, we move the between treatment variance to the numerator, or explained variance in our F ratio.

Source Table Formulas for Repeated Measures ANOVA

The repeated measures formulas differ slightly from the independent samples ANOVA. So, the following table provides a summary of the formulas that are used to calculate a Repeated Measures ANOVA.

Source of Variation	SS	df	MS	F
TREATMENT	$\sum (SS_{Means})(n)$	$k - 1$	$\dfrac{SS_{TREATMENT}}{df_{treatment}}$	$F = \dfrac{MS_{Treatment}}{MS_{Within\ Subjects}}$
ERROR	$SS_{TOTAL} - SS_{TREATMENT}$	$N - k$	$\dfrac{SS_{ERROR}}{df_{Error}}$	
BS	$\sum (M_P - M_{Grand})^2 k$	$n - 1$	$\dfrac{SS_{BS}}{df_{BS}}$	
WS	$SS_{Error} - SS_{within\ subject}$	$df_{Error} - df_{BS}$	$\dfrac{SS_{within\ subjects}}{df_{within\ subjects}}$	
TOTAL	$SS_{Treatment} + SS_{error}$	$N - 1$		

Where:

N = number of observations
n = number of people
k = number of conditions

TABLE 9.11   *Source Table*

Source of Variation	SS	df	MS	F
TREATMENT	40	2	20	16
ERROR	22	12	1.83	
Between Subjects	12	4	3	
Within Subjects	10	8	1.25	
TOTAL	62	14		

Combined Treatment Variance

One final step remains—calculation of the Error variance. The new Error variance, or Within Subjects variance, is derived from the residual (left over) variability present in the data. To fully understand how the Error or residual variance is derived, we need to return to the initial calculation of the sum of the squares. Our first step in calculating the respective variances was to separate the Treatment ($SS_{Treatment} = 40$) from the Error ($SS_{Error} = 22$) sum of the squares. The repeated measures design allows us to reduce the error term in our analysis. So, our next step was to remove an additional increment of explained variability ($SS_{Between\ Subjects} = 12$). Thus, our remaining Error (Within Subjects) is reflected in what remains after we subtract the Between Subjects sum of the squares from the initial Error sum of the squares. To obtain the sum of the squares that we will use for the Error variance, we merely subtract the Between Subjects SS from the Error SS.

$$SS_{Error} - SS_{Between\ Subjects} = SS_{Within\ Subjects}$$

In other words, our Within Subjects SS is now used to calculate the error variance present in the design as indicated in Table 9.11.

Remember that mean square (MS) is the variance. To obtain the MS or Error variance for this repeated measures design, we must use the appropriate degrees of freedom. Again, we simply subtract the Between Subjects df from the Error df to obtain the Within Subjects df. So, our final step in calculating the $MS_{Within\ Subjects}$ is:

$$MS_{Within\ Subjects} = \frac{SS_{Within\ Subjects}}{df_{within\ subjects}} = \frac{10}{8} = 1.25$$

We now have the both the Treatment ($MS_{TREATMENT}$) and Error variance ($MS_{Within\ Subjects}$) to calculate the F statistic.

F Statistic.   We now use the new error term ($MS_{Within\ Subjects}$) to obtain our final F statistic. As a reminder, the F statistic is the ratio of treatment or explained variance to error variance.

$$F = \frac{Treatment\ Variance}{Error\ Variance}$$

So, using our new error variance ($MS_{Within\ Subjects}$), we calculate the new F statistic:

$$F = \frac{MS_{Treatment}}{MS_{Within\ Subjects}} = \frac{20}{1.25} = 16$$

Is this new F value statistically significant? Because the repeated measures design is more sensitive, we can reasonably assume that this new F value is significant because the F value in the original, independent groups analysis was significant. However, we should also apply the same steps that we used with the between groups ANOVA to determine significance by using the F table. As illustrated earlier we use df from the numerator (2), or the Treatment variance, and the df from the denominator (8), or the Error variance to find the appropriate tabled value. The respective degrees of freedom are used to obtain the tabled values for the F test. In our example, we compare the calculated F value of 16 to the tabled F value of 4.46.

We also use the *df*s to report the outcome of the ANOVA as $F(2, 8) = 16, p < .05$. Because our calculated value (16) is larger than our tabled value (4.46), we conclude that our results are statistically significant. In other words, we reject the null hypothesis.

Post Hoc Analyses

When we explained the Between Groups ANOVA at the beginning of the chapter, we found that the omnibus or overall ANOVA allows us to test for statistically significant differences among multiple conditions while holding alpha constant. However, to determine which of individual treatments differ, we suggested using a post hoc test. Remember, the post hoc test is a second level of analysis that allows us to test for differences between treatment conditions.

Post hoc analyses for Repeated Measures ANOVA are similar to post hoc tests for the Between Groups ANOVA. To determine which of the treatment conditions are statistically significant, you can use the Tukey *HSD* or the Scheffé test that we described earlier. Statistical packages also generate a host of additional post hoc tests that might be appropriate for reporting results.

Effect Size

Effect size is an estimate of the proportion of variability explained by the independent variable (Grissom & Kim, 2005). Another way to think about effect size is as an estimate of a percentage of variance in the DV that is accounted for by the IV. Again, we use eta squared (η^2) as our estimate of the effect of the IV.

Simply stated, eta squared provides an estimate of the proportion of variability that is attributable to the IV. A second, and more sensitive, measure of effect size is the omega squared (ω^2). To obtain an estimate of effect size for a Repeated Measures ANOVA, we again return to our Source Table. To calculate the effect size, or ω^2, we use the following formula:

$$\omega^2 = \frac{(k - 1)(MS_{Treatment} - MS_{Within\ Subjects})}{SS_{TOTAL} + MS_{Between\ Subjects}}$$

Working with our example we find:

$$\omega^2 = \frac{(2)(20 - 1.25)}{62 + 3} = \frac{37.5}{65} = .58$$

So, approximately 58% of the variance in the dependent variable is accounted for by the level of the independent variable. In other words, 58% of the variability in recall can be accounted for by type of modality. You can see that the effect size here is larger than that for

---

Writing Results

We report a Repeated Measures ANOVA in much the same way as that of an independent samples ANOVA. We begin by reporting the results of the overall ANOVA or *F* test. The next step is to report the outcomes of the significance tests for the pairwise comparisons. Along with reporting statistical significance, we report descriptive data for each of the conditions. Finally, a measure of effect size is reported. Using our data from the cognition study we provide an example of how to report results below:

Words were presented to participants using three different modalities. First, words were presented visually, followed by an auditory presentation, and finally a combination of the modalities. Results of the overall ANOVA indicate that presentation modality affected the number of words correctly recalled, $F(2, 8) = 16, p < .05, \omega^2 = .58$.

When words were presented visually, participants recalled more words ($M = 6, SD = 1$) than when words were presented aloud ($M = 2, SD = 1.41$) at a statistically significant level. Difference in modality accounted for approximately 58% of the variability in recall.

the independent groups example. The effect is larger because we accounted for error associated with individual people and removed it from our calculation here.

The Repeated Measures ANOVA, much like the Between Groups ANOVA, separates the variability of the data into variance that is associated with the treatment and variance that is associated with error. The advantage of using the Repeated Measures ANOVA is that we are able to extract some of the Error variability, thus allowing us to remove some of the overall error in testing statistical probability.

Computer Analysis Using SPSS

Conducting a repeated measures ANOVA using SPSS is slightly more difficult than comparing means when we have a between groups design. When running a Repeated Measures ANOVA we begin by recording data in a repeated measures format.

Rather than creating one column for the IV and one for the DV, we create a data file that contains DV measures for each of the conditions in our study. Using our example, we create columns for the Visual, Auditory, and the combined Visual Auditory condition.

To conduct a repeated measures analysis you must select the general linear model, then repeated measures, from the Analyze menu as illustrated in Figure 9.11.

A dialogue box will require entry of a variable name and the number of levels of treatment as illustrated in Figure 9.12.

A second dialogue box requires entry of the variable names as illustrated in Figure 9.13. Each of the conditions will be entered as a within subjects variable.

It is now time to run the analysis. At this point you will be provided with yet another dialogue box with many different options. We suggest selecting a plot to help interpret the outcome. We also suggest selecting descriptive statistics from the Options tab as illustrated in Figure 9.14.

Interpreting the output requires a bit more understanding. Descriptive statistics are contained in the output, and reporting these results parallels that of the Between Groups ANOVA. Barring any serious violations of the assumption of homogeneity, an overall F value can be obtained from the Tests of Within-Subjects Effects table as illustrated in Figure 9.15.

FIGURE 9.11   *Selecting Repeated Measures*

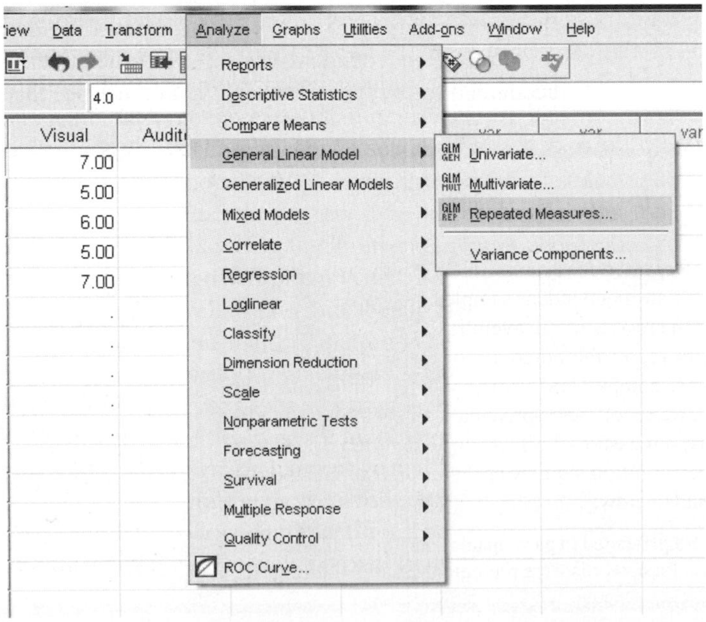

FIGURE 9.12 *Specifying Levels*

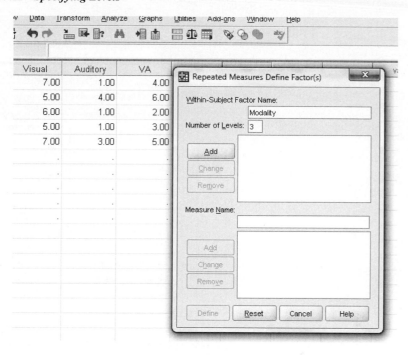

FIGURE 9.13 *Specifying Comparisons*

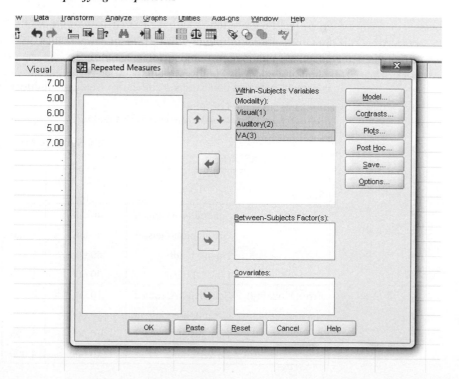

FIGURE 9.14 *Selecting Descriptive Statistics from the Options Tab*

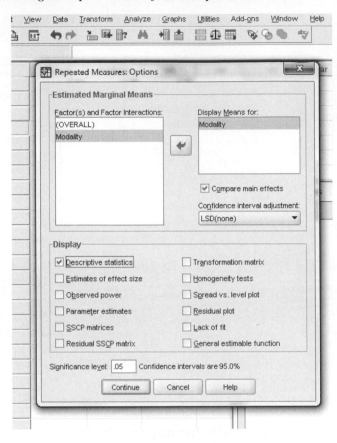

In this case, the ANOVA is statistically significant, $F(2, 8) = 16, p = .002$, so we can move forward to determine where pairwise comparisons are significant, as illustrated in Figure 9.16.

Similar to the results of the between groups analysis, we see that a significant difference is present between conditions 1 and 2, or visual and auditory presentations of the words.

FIGURE 9.15 *Repeated Measures ANOVA Output*

Tests of Within-Subjects Effects

Measure: MEASURE_1

Source		Type III Sum of Squares	df	Mean Square	F	Sig.
Modality	Sphericity Assumed	40.000	2	20.000	16.000	.002
	Greenhouse-Geisser	40.000	1.220	32.800	16.000	.010
	Huynh-Feldt	40.000	1.474	27.143	16.000	.005
	Lower-bound	40.000	1.000	40.000	16.000	.016
Error(Modality)	Sphericity Assumed	10.000	8	1.250		
	Greenhouse-Geisser	10.000	5.895	1.696		
	Huynh-Feldt	10.000	5.895	1.696		
	Lower-bound	10.000	4.000	2.500		

FIGURE 9.16 *Post Hoc Analyses*

Pairwise Comparisons

Measure: MEASURE_1

(I) Modality	(J) Modality	Mean Difference (I-J)	Std. Error	Sig.[a]	95% Confidence Interval for Difference[a]	
					Lower Bound	Upper Bound
1	2	4.000*	.837	.009	1.677	6.323
	3	2.000	.837	.075	−.323	4.323
2	1	−4.000*	.837	.009	−6.323	−1.677
	3	−2.000*	.316	.003	−2.878	−1.122
3	1	−2.000	.837	.075	−4.323	.323
	2	2.000*	.316	.003	1.122	2.878

Based on estimated marginal means.

*The mean difference is significant at the .05 level.

[a]Adjustment for multiple comparisons: Least Significant Difference (equivalent to no adjustments).

Chapter Summary

In this chapter, we extended our discussion of testing one independent variable. When we exceed two levels or conditions, we employ the ANOVA, or *F* statistic, to ensure that we do not exceed our stated alpha level. In other words, using the ANOVA allows us to have confidence that we are not increasing the Type I error rate.

Depending on the type of design, we use either a Between Groups ANOVA or a Repeated Measures ANOVA. When we assign different people to multiple groups, we use a Between Groups ANOVA to examine the effects of the IV. The ANOVA is a ratio of the differences between the groups (Mean differences) to differences within groups. The *F* statistic reflects this ratio. So, if differences between groups are large in comparison to differences among individuals within groups, we conclude that the treatment had an effect on the DV.

Upon completing the overall ANOVA, we typically try to determine which groups differ by conducting pairwise comparisons. Using a post hoc test, we compare two groups at a time. We introduced two possible post hoc tests, the Tukey *HSD* and the Scheffé. Both tests protect the overall Type I error rate.

We also introduced a new measure of effect size. Recall that effect size is a standardized measure of the treatment effect. So, eta squared reflects the percentage of variance that is explained by the treatment.

Our second type of design, the repeated measures design, employs the Repeated Measures ANOVA as the test for significance. Because subjects participate in each of the treatment conditions, they act as their own control, thus minimizing error. The reduction in overall statistical error is reflected in the *F* statistic. When we use the Repeated Measures ANOVA, we reduce Error variance. Between Subjects variance becomes explained variance. Thus, the Repeated Measures ANOVA is a more sensitive statistical test.

As with the Between Groups ANOVA, we conduct post hoc analyses for the Repeated Measures ANOVA. We also calculate effect size to determine the amount of variance explained by the treatment, or IV. We introduced a more conservative estimate of effect size, omega squared, for use with the Repeated Measures ANOVA.

In this chapter we presented a comprehensive explanation of the two types of one-way ANOVAs. We use the Between Groups ANOVA to test for differences between treatments with participants are assigned to different groups. We use the Repeated Measures ANOVA when one group participates in each of the treatment conditions.

Key Terms

ANOVA
Between groups ANOVA
Error variance
Eta squared
F statistic
Hartley F-Max test

Homogeneity of variance
Levene's Test of Equality of Variances
Omega squared
Post hoc test
Repeated measures ANOVA
Scheffé test

Source Table
Total variance
Treatment variance
Tukey *HSD*

Chapter Review Questions

Multiple Choice Questions

1. Which of the following reflects the null hypothesis for a between groups ANOVA with four treatments?
   a. $\mu_1 = \mu_2 = \mu_3$
   b. $\mu_1 \neq \mu_2 \neq \mu_3$
   c. $\mu_1 = \mu_2 = \mu_3 = \mu_4$
   d. $\mu_1 \neq \mu_2 \neq \mu_3 \neq \mu_4$

2. Which of the following outcomes is desirable when testing data to meet the assumptions for an ANOVA?
   a. Reject Levene's Test for Equality of Variances
   b. Do not reject Levene's Test for Equality of Variances
   c. Reject the Hartley F Max Test
   d. Reject the calculated F Test

3. With a sample of $N = 40$ and $k = 4$, what are the Total df for a between subjects ANOVA?
   a. 40
   b. 39
   c. 38
   d. 37

4. With a sample of $N = 40$ and $k = 4$, what are the Treatment df for a between subjects ANOVA?
   a. 1
   b. 2
   c. 3
   d. 4

5. With a sample of $N = 40$ and $k = 4$, what are the Treatment df for a between subjects ANOVA?
   a. 36
   b. 37
   c. 39
   d. 40

6. How many treatment conditions were present in a between groups ANOVA with the following results: $F(4, 20) = 18.23, p < .05$?
   a. 5
   b. 4
   c. 3
   d. 2

7. How many participants were in the between groups study: $F(4, 20) = 18.23, p < .05$?
   a. 26
   b. 25
   c. 24
   d. 23

8. What should the respective degrees of freedom be for reporting a repeated measures ANOVA with four treatments and 10 people?
   a. 3, 36
   b. 4, 9
   c. 3, 27
   d. 4, 39

9. For a repeated measures ANOVA with three treatments and 20 people, what are the degrees of freedom between subjects?
   a. 9
   b. 19
   c. 38
   d. 59

10. What are the correct degrees of freedom for reporting a repeated measures ANOVA with three treatments and 20 people?
    a. 3, 38
    b. 2, 19
    c. 2, 59
    d. 3, 38

Essay Questions

11. Explain how the sources of variability contribute to the F ratio.

12. Explain the relationship between Treatment and Error variance.

13. Describe the conditions that would prevent you from meeting the homogeneity of variance assumption.

14. Explain why we use treatment and error degrees of freedom when reporting the results of the F statistic.

15. Explain the purpose of eta squared.

16. How does the Repeated Measures ANOVA differ from the Between Groups ANOVA?

17. Why is the Repeated Measures ANOVA more sensitive to treatment effects?

18. What are the drawbacks of using the Repeated Measures ANOVA?

Practice Exercises

19. Psychologists designed a study to test for the effects of rewards on learning. Participants ($N = 40$) were randomly assigned to one of four treatment conditions. Learning was measured using a memory test. Results of the experiment:

Group	Treatment	Mean
Group 1	No Reward	$M = 5$
Group 2	Reward of $1.00	$M = 7$
Group 3	Reward of $10.00	$M = 9$
Group 4	Reward of $25.00	$M = 12$

Complete the Source Table and determine if the F test is significant.

Source of Variation	SS	df	MS	F
TREATMENT			10	
ERROR			.5	
TOTAL				

Compute the Tukey *HSD* post-test and determine which pairwise comparisons are significant. Graph the results.

20. Psychologists designed a study to test the effect of stereotyping on memory. Retired adults ($N = 40$) participated in three different conditions. In the first condition, participants were not giving any priming (control). In the second condition, participants were provided with a cartoon that contained negative stereotypes about aging. In the third condition, participants were primed with a cartoon that contained positive stereotypes of aging. Following each of the priming conditions, participants were asked to report the number of words that they recalled. Results are as follows:

Group	Treatment	Mean
Condition 1	Control	$M = 5$
Condition 2	Negative Stimulus	$M = 7$
Condition 3	Positive Stimulus	$M = 9$

Complete the Source Table and determine if the *F* test is significant.

Source of Variation	SS	df	MS	F
TREATMENT			20	
ERROR		117	1.83	
Between Subjects			3	
Within Subjects			1.25	
TOTAL	62	119		

Graph the results.

21. Using the Source Table below, determine the number of treatments and number of participants in the study. Determine whether the *F* value is significant and report using appropriate statistical format.

Source of Variation	SS	df	MS	F
TREATMENT	60	3	20	
ERROR	230	46	5	
TOTAL	290	49		

22. Using the Source Table below, determine the number of treatments, number of participants, and number of observations in the study. Determine whether the *F* value is significant and report using appropriate statistical format.

Source of Variation	SS	df	MS	F
TREATMENT	30	3	10	
ERROR	29.28	16	1.83	
Between Subjects	12	4	3	
Within Subjects	15	12	1.25	
TOTAL	32.28	19		

23. Using the following results, determine how many treatments and participants were used in the independent samples study.

$$F(4, 24) = 4.6, p < .05.$$

CHAPTER 10

MULTIPLE INDEPENDENT VARIABLES: FACTORIAL DESIGNS

CHAPTER OUTLINE

FACTORIAL ANOVA
  Stating the Hypothesis
  Partitioning Variance

CALCULATING THE FACTORIAL ANOVA
  Total Variance
  Treatment Variance

  Error Variance
  F Statistics
  Determining Significance
  Post Hoc Analyses
  Effect Size

COMPUTER ANALYSIS USING SPSS

LEARNING OBJECTIVES

- Explain when it is appropriate to use a factorial design.
- Identify the minimum number of variables present in a factorial design.
- Describe the advantages of using a factorial design.
- Explain the assumptions of the factorial ANOVA.
- Define main effects in the context of a factorial ANOVA.
- Explain interaction effects for a factorial ANOVA.
- Identify the basic components of variability in the factorial ANOVA.
- Explain how components of variability are used to determine statistical significance.
- Identify and explain measures of effect size for a factorial ANOVA.
- Write an example results section reporting results of a factorial ANOVA.

CHAPTER PREVIEW

The simplest experiments involve manipulation of one independent variable to determine the effects on the dependent variable. In this chapter, we expand the possibilities for testing experimental conditions by adding a second independent variable. When we use more than one independent variable, we use an expanded ANOVA model for statistical analysis.

Researchers frequently manipulate more than one independent variable in a single experiment. The advantage of a multifactor study (more than one IV) is that we can get a better look at the complex interplay of variables that affect behavior. After all, we are complex, and our behavior is often the result of more than one factor or variable.

In this chapter, we introduce the factorial design. We use two independent variables to illustrate potential interaction effects and we describe how to interpret results of the factorial ANOVA to fully understand the effects of the IVs.

Factorial ANOVA

Expanding on the one-way design, we can manipulate more than one IV in a single experiment. When we have more than one IV, we use a **factorial ANOVA** for statistical analysis. The advantage to using more than one IV is that you can get a more detailed picture of behavior because you are measuring more complex conditions.

One reason for using multiple IVs is that many psychological questions are too complicated to answer using a single independent variable. Another reason for using more than one IV is that we gain twice as much information from a two-factor study as in a one-factor study. And, even better, we may not need to devote twice the time and energy to get this information because we examine multiple IVs simultaneously.

When we use multiple IVs, each level of one variable is represented at every level of the other variables—the approach is referred to as a factorial design. What do we mean by a **factorial** (or **crossed**) **design**? If there are two variables, one IV with two levels, and a second IV with three levels, we would end up with six different conditions. In other words, each level of the first IV is present in each level of the second IV. The number of conditions, or factors, is derived by multiplying the number of levels of the first IV by the number of levels of the second IV (i.e., $2 \times 3 = 6$). As illustrated below, three IVs produce a three-dimensional model. Each variable is multiplied to derive the total number of conditions. So, if we add a third variable to a study, we have:

$$2 \times 3 \times 2 = 12 \text{ conditions}$$

IV (2 levels) $\times$ IV (3 levels) $\times$ IV (2 levels)

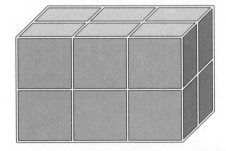

Factorial ANOVA—
An experimental design where more than one independent variable is manipulated.

Factorial (crossed) design—Each level of one independent variable is represented in each level of a second independent variable.

The equation indicates that we are using three IVs ($2 \times 3 \times 2$). There are two levels for two different IVs, and one IV with three levels; so 12 conditions are present. It is always possible to add yet another IV with multiple levels and greatly expand the model. Theoretically, the number of factors you can study is unlimited. Realistically, though, you won't encounter more than four IVs except in extremely rare cases. For clarity, we won't expand beyond two IVs in this chapter.

FIGURE 10.1 *Factorial ANOVA with Completely Crossed Design*

Type of Voice

		Voiced	*Unvoiced*
Gender	*Male*	Male/Voiced $N = 5$ Men using a voiced laugh	Male/Unvoiced $N = 5$ Men using an unvoiced laugh
	Female	Female/Voiced $N = 5$ Women using a voiced laugh	Female/Unvoiced $N = 5$ Women using an unvoiced laugh

Stating the Hypotheses

Hypothesis testing with a one-way ANOVA is used to test for differences between the means of multiple levels of a single independent variable. When we add a second independent variable, we not only have a more efficient design, but we must consider additional hypotheses. So, let's consider an example with two independent variables.

Bachorowski and Owren (2001) were interested in how the sound of laughter might influence desirability for meeting a person. They conducted an experimental study using two IVs. Gender, the first IV, consisted of two levels, male and female. The second IV was type of laughter and they used two types, or levels, of laughter. The "voiced" laugh was "harmonically rich" (p. 253), and sounded like genuine laughter. The "unvoiced" laugh included "grunt-, cackle-, and snortlike sounds" (p. 253). Participants rated desirability of meeting the person based on the laughter that they heard.

Bachorowski and Owren used recorded "voiced" and "unvoiced" laughter from both male and female actors. Four different recordings (i.e., Male/Voiced, Male/Unvoiced, Female/ Voiced, Female/Unvoiced), reflecting the four different conditions, were produced. So, in this completely crossed design, we can test the effects of both independent variables (i.e., gender and type of voice) simultaneously as illustrated in Figure 10.1.

The simultaneous testing of the two IVs allows us to test four different conditions. Each condition contains either men or women and one type of voice. So, in our example we test for differences between Male Voiced and Unvoiced laugher, while at the same time testing for Female Voiced and Unvoiced laugher. In other words, we test the hypothesis that desirability differs based on gender and type of voice. Stating the hypothesis with both IVs allows us to examine the data to determine if there is an **interaction** among the IVs that might influence desirability of meeting a person (DV). An interaction occurs when the level of one independent variable is affected by the level of a second IV. In other words, the two variables, considered together, produce a combination of effects that is not predictable from either one alone.

In addition to hypothesizing a difference among the four different treatment conditions, we can also state hypotheses for each of the IVs separately. For example, we can hypothesize that desirability of the laugh differs based on whether the voice is male or female. We can also hypothesize that desirability differs on the basis of whether the laughter is voiced or unvoiced. We are using two separate hypotheses, referred to as **main effects.**

Each of the hypotheses can be tested using the ANOVA statistic. In each instance, we will calculate a ratio of Treatment variance compared to Error variance. The factorial ANOVA is valuable because it allows us to test for an interaction effect and main effects for each of the IVs simultaneously.

Assumptions of the Factorial ANOVA.   The ANOVA employs the basic statistical ratio that we have been using to conduct our inferential statistical tests. In other words, we are simply

Interaction effects—The simultaneous effects of multiple independent variables on a dependent variable.

Main effects—The effects of a single independent variable on a dependent variable.

calculating a ratio of Treatment to Error variance. We compare the difference between the treatment means to the differences that exist within groups, or error.

$$ANOVA = \frac{Treatment\ Variance}{Error\ Variance}$$

If the calculated ratio is large, then we conclude that the combination of treatments or a particular treatment likely made a difference and that there is a statistically significant outcome.

As with a single factor ANOVA, several underlying assumptions must be met when conducting a factorial ANOVA. Measurement of the DV must employ an interval or ratio scale. The first assumption is that variability is relatively similar across conditions. We test for **homogeneity of variance**, or the assumption that variance across the multiple treatment conditions is similar. As with the one-way ANOVA, we use the Hartley *F*-Max test to determine if we meet the homogeneity of variance assumption. Levene's Test of Equality of Variances is often used as an alternative test because we can quickly derive the test when we use SPSS. Using either test, we are looking for a non-significant outcome so that we meet the homogeneity of variance assumption.

We typically check to ensure that the distribution in each of the conditions is normal. In other words we need to meet the assumption of *normality*. And in a Factorial ANOVA, or a completely crossed design, we must ensure that our *observations are independent*. Generally, if we meet the homogeneity of variance assumption, we probably have met the normality assumption. The independence of observations assumption can be easily addressed when we design the study. Each person in the study should participate in only one of the conditions. If we are careful to ensure that participants are randomly assigned to *only* one condition, we can be confident that we have met the independence assumption. Howell (2007) suggests that the statistical model is strong, and we can have confidence in our statistical results even if we violate these assumptions (i.e., equal variances and normality).

Partitioning Variance

Let's consider the following set of data as we illustrate how a factorial ANOVA is used to test two IVs simultaneously. Using the scenario that Bachorowski and Owren (2001) provided, the following data might be similar to those contained in their study. Consistent with our assumptions, rating the desirability of the laughter is an interval measure of the DV, and our hypothetical data are contained in Table 10.1.

You will also notice that the means for each variable (Main Effects) are listed on the outside of Table 10.1 ($M_{Male} = 4$, $M_{Female} = 6$, $M_{Voiced} = 4$, $M_{Unvoiced} = 6$). We derive an *F* ratio for each of the main effects (i.e., the two IVs individually).

These data also include means for each of the four treatment groups or cells ($M_1 = 5$, $M_2 = 3$, $M_3 = 3$, $M_4 = 9$). In other words, we simultaneously compare two IVs, in this case gender and voice, and we derive an *F* value to determine if an interaction effect is present.

So, we actually derive three *F* ratios (two main effects and one interaction effect) because we are testing three hypotheses. Our first hypothesis is that desirability of laughter changes based on how it is voiced (Main Effect). The second hypothesis is that desirability of laughter will change based on whether the voice is male or female (Main Effect). And our third hypothesis is that desirability of laughter will change based on the gender and type of voice used to express the laughter (Interaction Effect).

Homogeneity of variance—Variance across groups is similar.

TABLE 10.1 *Gender by Voice Data*

Gender		Type of Voice		
		Voiced	**Unvoiced**	
	Male	7	1	
		5	4	
		3	4	$M_{Male} = 4$
		3	3	
		7	3	
Gender		$M_1 = 5$	$M_2 = 3$	
		4	8	
		1	10	
	Female	2	10	$M_{Female} = 6$
		3	9	
		5	8	
		$M_3 = 3$	$M_4 = 9$	
		$M_{Voiced} = 4$	$M_{Unvoiced} = 6$	

Calculating the Factorial ANOVA

Our first step in testing these hypotheses is to calculate variances. Remember, calculating variances is also the first step in constructing our Source Table for the factorial ANOVA. Let's begin by calculating an overall measure of the variance.

TOTAL Variance

Although we don't actually calculate a total variance for the Source Table, we do calculate variances for the Treatment ($MS_{Treatment}$) effects and Error (MS_{Error}). However, we do calculate a total SS that reflects all of the variability present in the data. We use all of the data when we obtain the total SS.

Much as we did in the one-way ANOVA, we combine all of the scores to calculate the sum of squares (SS) for the Total variance. The formula for calculating the total SS is identical to the formula that we used with the one-way ANOVA:

$$SS_{TOTAL} = \sum (X - M_G)^2$$

Using the data from our example, we calculate total SS by first combining the data from all four conditions. The first step in the process is to calculate an overall mean or grand mean ($M_G = 5$). We then use the Grand mean to calculate the SS_{TOTAL} for the combined data set ($SS_{TOTAL} = 156$) as illustrated in Table 10.2.

The total SS gives us a general indication of the total amount of variability present in our data. To actually calculate the F statistic, we need to calculate the ratio of Treatment variance to Error variance, so, much like the one-way ANOVA, we partition the TOTAL variance into Treatment and Error variance.

TABLE 10.2 *Sum of Squares Total*

X	$X - M_G$	$(X - M_G)^2$	
7	$7 - 5 = 2$	4	
5	$5 - 5 = 0$	0	
3	$3 - 5 = -2$	4	$SS_{Treatment_1} = 16$
3	$3 - 5 = -2$	4	
7	$7 - 5 = 2$	4	
1	$1 - 5 = -4$	16	
4	$4 - 5 = -1$	1	
4	$4 - 5 = -1$	1	$SS_{Treatment_2} = 26$
3	$3 - 5 = -2$	4	
3	$3 - 5 = -2$	4	
4	$4 - 5 = -1$	1	
1	$1 - 5 = -4$	16	
2	$2 - 5 = -3$	9	$SS_{Treatment_3} = 30$
3	$3 - 5 = -2$	4	
5	$5 - 5 = 0$	0	
8	$8 - 5 = 3$	9	
10	$10 - 5 = 5$	25	
10	$10 - 5 = 5$	25	$SS_{Treatment_4} = 84$
9	$9 - 5 = 4$	16	
8	$8 - 5 = 3$	9	

$$\sum X_G = 100 \qquad\qquad SS_{TOTAL} = (X - M_G)^2 = 156$$
$$M_{Grand} = 5$$

TREATMENT Variance

With the factorial ANOVA, we break out the Treatment variance even further. In other words, because we now have more than one independent variable, we need to separate the treatment into variability associated with each of the IVs. In this example, we have two IVs. So, we obtain measures of variability for each of the IVs (i.e., gender and laughter) and for the combined effect of the IVs, or the interaction. Thus, we partition Treatment variance into three values associated with each of the treatments.

Our goal is to calculate a ratio of the Treatment variance to Error variance for each of our three hypotheses. Our first step is to independently calculate the treatment sum of the squares for each of the IVs. Recall that to obtain variance we begin by calculating the *SS*, then we divide by *df*.

Gender. Let's begin by examining just one of the IVs (gender), one of the two main effects, as illustrated in Table 10.3. Main effects refer to the effect of an independent variable by itself. So, in this example, we have two main effects, gender and voice.

We use the treatment *SS* formula that we used with the one-way ANOVA. The main effect SS treatment formula is:

$$SS_{Factor} = \sum (M_{Level} - M_{Grand})^2 n$$

$$SS_{Variable1} = \sum (M_{Level} - M_{Grand})^2 n$$

TABLE 10.3 *Gender*

	Gender		
	Voiced	**Unvoiced**	
	7	1	
	5	4	
Male	3	4	$M_{Male} = 4$
	3	3	
	7	3	
	4	8	
	1	10	
Female	2	10	$M_{Female} = 6$
	3	9	
	5	8	

So, we begin by calculating *SS* for gender. We subtract the Grand Mean (M_G) from the mean for each level of one IV (Factor A). So, if we are calculating the SS for gender, we subtract the Grand Mean (M_G) from Mean for male (M_{Male}), and the Mean for female (M_{Female}) as a first step in the process.

$$SS_{Male} = (M_{Male} - M_G)^2 n$$
$$(4 - 5)^2 10 = 10$$
$$SS_{Female} = (M_{Female} - M_G)^2 n$$
$$(6 - 5)^2 10 = 10$$

We then square the result and multiply by the number of men ($n = 10$) or women ($n = 10$) in the study. In this case, we are deriving the SS_{Factor} for the IV gender (Factor A).

The *SS* value for gender is obtained by summing the two sum of the squares, so $SS_{Gender} = 20$.

$$SS_{Factor} = SS_{Male} + SS_{Female}$$
$$10 + 10 = 20$$

We complete our calculation of variance (*MS*) for the IV gender using degrees of freedom. In other words, we divide the SS_{Gender} by degrees of freedom associated with gender. Degrees of freedom for treatment are calculated by subtracting 1 from the total number of conditions (*k*). So,

$$df_{Gender} = k - 1$$
$$df_{Gender} = 2 - 1 = 1$$

We begin constructing our Source Table by placing our *SS* and *df* into the appropriate cells as illustrated in Table 10.4. Notice that our Source Table now contains separate treatment values for each IV and the Interaction (A × B).

We complete the calculation of the variance (*MS*) for gender by dividing the *SS* by *df*.

$$MS_{Gender} = \frac{SS_{Gender}}{df_{Gender}} = \frac{20}{1} = 20$$

TABLE 10.4   *Partial Source Table*

Source of Variation	SS	df	MS	F
TREATMENT				
Factor A (Gender)	20	1	20	
Factor B (Voice)	20	1	20	
A × B				
ERROR				
TOTAL	156	19		

Voice.   The second main effect, or IV (Factor B), is type of voice. Quite simply, we calculate the *SS* for voice in much the same way as for gender. As illustrated in Table 10.5, we examine the effects of voice alone (i.e., voiced and unvoiced). In other words, we look only at how people responded to the type of voice without considering whether the voice was male or female.

When we calculated the *SS* for gender, we subtracted the Grand Mean (M_G) from the mean for males ($M_{Male} - M_G$) and females ($M_{Female} - M_G$).

Similarly, we subtract the Grand Mean (M_G) from each of the means of the voice conditions before multiplying by the *n,* as illustrated below.

$$SS_{Voiced} = (M_{Voiced} - M_G)^2 n$$
$$(4 - 5)^2 10 = 10$$
$$SS_{Unvoiced} = (M_{Unvoiced} - M_G)^2 n$$
$$(6 - 5)^2 10 = 10$$

Again, to obtain the *SS* associated with the IV of voice, we sum these two calculated *SS* values.

$$SS_{Factor} = SS_{Voiced} + SS_{Unvoiced}$$
$$10 + 10 = 20$$

TABLE 10.5   *Voice*

	Type of Voice	
	Voiced	**Unvoiced**
Male	7	1
	5	4
	3	4
	3	3
	7	3
	4	8
	1	10
Female	2	10
	3	9
	5	8
	$M_{Voiced} = 4$	$M_{Unvoiced} = 6$

We use the SS_{Factor} values and df_{Factor} to calculate variance (MS) for voice. Degrees of freedom for the voice treatment are calculated by subtracting 1 from the total number of conditions (k) as we did before. So, once again, $df_{Voice} = k - 1$, or $df_{Voice} = 2 - 1 = 1$. We complete the calculation of MS for voice just like we did for gender.

$$MS_{Voice} = \frac{SS_{Voice}}{df_{Voice}} = \frac{20}{1} = 20$$

Gender by Voice Interaction. We just calculated the treatment sum of squares (SS) and degrees of freedom (df) for our variables of gender and voice independently. Our next step is to calculate a treatment sum of squares (and df) for the combination, or interaction, of the two variables (A $\times$ B) together. We use the same basic sum of squares formula:

$$SS_{Cell} = (M_{Cell} - M_{Grand})^2 n$$

However, rather than using the row means (Gender), or the column means (Voice), we use the means from each of the cells or groups. As illustrated in Table 10.6, the first cell contains desirability ratings for a male voiced laugh ($M_1 = 5$).

To obtain the SS for the interaction effect (i.e., Gender $\times$ Voice) we use the basic formula for calculating Treatment SS for each of the four conditions.

$$SS_{MaleVoiced} = (M_{MaleVoiced} - M_{Grand})^2 n$$
$$(5 - 5)^2 5 = 0$$
$$SS_{MaleUnvoiced} = (M_{MaleUnvoiced} - M_{Grand})^2 n$$
$$(3 - 5)^2 5 = 20$$
$$SS_{FemaleVoiced} = (M_{FemaleVoiced} - M_{Grand})^2 n$$
$$(3 - 5)^2 5 = 20$$
$$SS_{FemaleUnvoiced} = (M_{FemaleUnvoiced} - M_{Grand})^2 n$$
$$(9 - 5)^2 5 = 80$$

TABLE 10.6 Gender $\times$ Voice Interaction

		Type of Voice	
		Voiced	**Unvoiced**
		7	1
		5	4
	Male	3	4
		3	3
		7	3
Gender		$M_1 = 5$	$M_2 = 3$
		4	8
		1	10
	Female	2	10
		3	9
		5	8
		$M_3 = 3$	$M_4 = 9$

Summing the individual treatment sum of squares we find:

$$SS_{Group} = \sum (M_{Cell} - M_{Grand})^2 n$$
$$SS_{Group} = 0 + 20 + 20 + 80 = 120$$

However, our calculations for the interaction effect are not complete until we remove the independent contributions of the main effects (i.e., gender and voice). The complete formula for the *SS* interaction is:

$$SS_{Interaction} = \left[\sum (M_{Cell} - M_{Grand})^2 n \right] - SS_A - SS_B$$

We find:

$$SS_{Interaction} = [120] - 20 - 20 = 80$$

We can now enter our interaction Sum of Squares ($SS_{Interaction} = 80$) into our Source Table (Table 10.7).

The variance associated with the interaction effect is simply the $SS_{Interaction}$ divided by $df_{Interaction}$. So, we need to calculate new *df* for the interaction effect. To obtain the interaction *df*, we simply multiply the *df* for the main effects:

$$df_{Interaction} = (A - 1)(B - 1)$$
$$df_{Interaction} = (2 - 1)(2 - 1) = 1 \times 1 = 1$$

So, our *df* for the interaction effect is 1.

We now use the values in Table 10.7 (*SS* and *df*) to obtain variances, or Mean Squares, for each of the treatments.

$$MS_{Interaction} = \frac{SS_{Interaction}}{df_{interaction}}$$

Using our variance or *MS* ratio, and the respective *SS* and *df,* we derive each of our mean squares.

$$MS_A = \frac{SS_A}{df_A} = \frac{20}{1} = 20$$

$$MS_B = \frac{SS_B}{df_B} = \frac{20}{1} = 20$$

TABLE 10.7 *Source Table*

Source of Variation	*SS*	*df*	*MS*	*F*
TREATMENT	120			
Factor A (Gender)	20	1	20	
Factor B (Voice)	20	1	20	
A × B	80	1	80	
ERROR				
TOTAL	156	19		

$$MS_{A \times B} = \frac{SS_{A \times B}}{df_{A \times B}} = \frac{80}{1} = 80$$

So, we now have variances for the effect of Gender ($MS_A = 20$), the effect of Voice ($MS_B = 20$), and the combined effects of voice and gender ($MS_{A \times B} = 80$). We can now turn our attention to the next step in completing the factorial ANOVA—calculation of a single error term.

ERROR Variance

We have one final measure of variability that we need to calculate before we can complete our factorial ANOVA. Error variance, or the variability within each cell, is the final source of variance.

Recall that error is reflected in the differences among people *within* each treatment group. Therefore, we are interested in calculating the amount of variance that constitutes error, or the amount of variability *within* each treatment condition. Variability within a cell is called error because, theoretically, scores for people getting the same treatment should be the same. But in real life, people differ, due to variables that we do not control, which is why we call any deviation within a treatment, error.

Table 10.8 contains the data from each of the four groups, or combinations of the two independent variables.

So, the first set of data reflects the desirability rating for the male voiced condition. If we treat each group as an independent source of Error variance, we begin by calculating the *SS* for each of the groups.

$$\sum(X - M_1)^2 = 16$$
$$\sum(X - M_2)^2 = 6$$
$$\sum(X - M_3)^2 = 10$$
$$\sum(X - M_4)^2 = 4$$

After calculating *SS* for each of the groups, we simply add the *SS* to obtain SS_{Error}.

$$SS_{ERROR} = SS_{Cell1} + SS_{Cell2} + SS_{Cell3} + SS_{Cell4}$$
$$SS_{ERROR} = 16 + 6 + 10 + 4 = 36$$

We now have our *SS* value, but our ultimate goal is to obtain an index of error, or Error variance. So, we must calculate the *df*s associated with the Error or Within Groups variance to complete the calculation of Error variance or MS_{Error}. Remember, we lose one degree of freedom for each of the groups. The formula for calculating *df* for the error is:

$$df_{Error} = \sum n - 1$$

So, we subtract one degree of freedom from each *n*. We then add these degrees of freedom to obtain df_{Error}.

A simpler method for calculated df_{Error} is to subtract the number of groups (*k*) from the overall sample size. In this example our df_{Error} is equal to 16.

$$df_{Error} = N - k$$
$$df_{Error} = 20 - 4 = 16$$

TABLE 10.8 *Sum of Squares ERROR*

X		X − M	(X − [M])²
7		7 − 5 = 2	4
5		5 − 5 = 0	0
3	Male/Voiced	3 − 5 = −2	4
3		3 − 5 = −2	4
7		7 − 5 = 2	4
$M_1 = 5$			$\sum(X − M_1)^2 = 16$
$\sum X_1 = 25$			
1		1 − 3 = −2	4
4		4 − 3 = 1	1
4	Male/Unvoiced	4 − 3 = 1	1
3		3 − 3 = 0	0
3		3 − 3 = 0	0
$M_2 = 3$			$\sum(X − M_2)^2 = 6$
$\sum X_2 = 15$			
4		4 − 3 = 1	1
1		1 − 3 = −2	4
2	Female/Voiced	2 − 3 = −1	1
3		3 − 3 = 0	0
5		5 − 3 = 2	4
$M_3 = 3$			$\sum(X − M_2)^2 = 10$
$\sum X_3 = 15$			
8		8 − 9 = −1	1
10		10 − 9 = 1	1
10	Female/Unvoiced	10 − 9 = 1	1
9		9 − 9 = 0	0
8		8 − 9 = −1	1
$M_4 = 9$			$\sum(X − M_4)^2 = 4$
$\sum X_4 = 45$			

Now that we have both the SS_{Error} and df_{Error}, we can take the next step and calculate the variance associated with error. We simply divide SS_{Error} by df_{Error} so that we can obtain the amount of variance associated with the error, or MS_{Error}.

$$MS_{Error} = \frac{SS_{Error}}{df_{Error}}$$

$$MS_{Error} = \frac{36}{16} = 2.25$$

We now have all of the necessary measures of variance for calculating our respective *F* values as illustrated in Table 10.9.

It is important to note that the Total values in the table are always summative. Note that the *SS* for Treatment is the sum of the two main effects and the interaction effect. So, one way

TABLE 10.9 *Source Table*

Source of Variation	SS	df	MS	F
TREATMENT	120			
Factor A (Gender)	20	1	20	
Factor B (Voice)	20	1	20	
A × B	80	1	80	
ERROR	36	16	2.25	
TOTAL	156	19		

to check the accuracy of your calculations is to make sure that the *SS* and *df* values add up to the Total values that we calculated earlier.

F Statistics

As with the one-way ANOVA, we partition the total amount of variability into differences between treatments and variability within treatments (or error). With the factorial ANOVA, we are testing the effects of more than one IV. So, we test for the effect of each IV independently (Main Effects), and we test for the combined effects (Interaction), or the interaction of the IVs.

In our example, we have two independent variables, so we test two main effects (i.e., gender, voice), and we test for the interaction (i.e., gender and voice combined). In other words, we are interested in testing for patterns of means on one variable depending on the value of the other independent variable. When we test these combinations of effects, we are in essence, testing the interaction of the IVs.

A factorial design is generally a more efficient approach to testing the effects of multiple independent variables on a single dependent variable. As we just saw, a factorial ANOVA yields multiple *F* values. In other words, we derive multiple measures of treatment variance ($MS_{Treatment}$); one for each main effect, and one for the combination of the IVs, or the interaction effect. However, we need only derive one measure of Error variance (MS_{Error}) for the entire analysis. Using the constant Error variance term, we test for statistical significance by comparing the amount of variability present between treatments (i.e., main effects and interaction effect) to the variance within treatments.

$$ANOVA = \frac{Treatment\ Variance}{Error\ Variance} = \frac{MS_{Treatment}}{MS_{Error}}$$

We can now use the information from the Source Table to complete the calculation of the three *F* statistics for our example. The $MS_{Treatment}$ for each of the main effects and the interaction effect is divided by MS_{Error} to obtain the *F* values.

$$F_A = \frac{MS_A}{MS_{Error}} = \frac{20}{2.25} = 8.89$$

$$F_B = \frac{MS_B}{MS_{Error}} = \frac{20}{2.25} = 8.89$$

$$F_{A \times B} = \frac{MS_{A \times B}}{MS_{Error}} = \frac{80}{2.25} = 35.56$$

TABLE 10.10 *Source Table*

Source of Variation	SS	df	MS	F
TREATMENT	120			
Factor A (Gender)	20	1	20	8.89
Factor B (Voice)	20	1	20	8.89
A × B	80	1	80	35.56
ERROR	36	16	2.25	
TOTAL	156	19		

We place these *F* values in Table 10.10.

Determining Significance

Our final step is to determine if our calculated *F* values are statistically significant. After completing the calculations for our three statistical tests (i.e., two main effects and one interaction effect), we compare our calculated *F* values to the tabled *F* values. Recall that we use the numerator (1) and denominator *df*s (16), to find the appropriate tabled values.

Significance Values for the Analysis of Variance (F Test)

Degrees of freedom for treatments (df$_{between}$) appear in the left column. Degrees of freedom for the error term (df$_{within}$ or df$_{error}$) are across the top. Computed values of *F* are significant if they are larger than the critical value in the table.

Values for α = .05 are in normal Roman type
Values for α = .01 are in bold type
Values for α = 0.001 are in italics

DF FOR THE NUMERATOR
(**DF**$_{BETWEEN}$ OR **DF**$_{TREATMENT}$)

		1	2	3	4	5	6	8	12	24
DF FOR THE DENOMINATOR (**DF**$_{WITHIN}$ OR **DF**$_{ERROR}$)										
15	α = .05	4.54	3.68	3.26	3.06	2.90	2.79	2.64	2.48	2.29
	α = .01	**8.68**	**6.36**	**5.42**	**4.89**	**4.56**	**4.32**	**4.00**	**3.67**	**3.29**
	α = .001	*16.59*	*11.34*	*9.34*	*8.25*	*7.57*	*7.09*	*6.47*	*5.81*	*5.10*
16	α = .05	4.49	3.63	3.24	3.01	2.85	2.74	2.59	2.42	2.24
	α = .01	**8.53**	**6.23**	**5.29**	**4.77**	**4.44**	**4.20**	**3.89**	**3.55**	**3.18**
	α = .001	*16.12*	*10.97*	*9.00*	*7.94*	*7.27*	*6.81*	*6.19*	*5.55*	*4.85*

Interaction Effect. Beginning with the interaction effect, we compare the calculated *F* value of 35.56 to the tabled *F* value of 4.49 to determine if our calculated statistic is statistically significant. Because our calculated value of 35.56 is larger than the table value of 4.49, we reject the null hypothesis and conclude that the interaction effect is statistically significant as illustrated in Figure 10.2.

FIGURE 10.2 *Determining Significance*

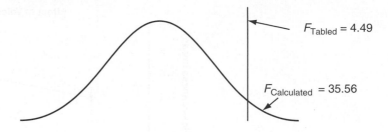

$F_{\text{Tabled}} = 4.49$

$F_{\text{Calculated}} = 35.56$

We conduct the same inspection with each of the main effects. In our example, we need only compare the F value for gender (8.89) to the tabled F value (4.49) to determine if gender is statistically significant. Similarly, the calculated F value for type of voice is 8.89, so the main effect for voice is also significant.

We generally interpret a statistically significant interaction effect first. Why? As we indicated at the beginning of this chapter, one of the advantages to using a factorial design is efficiency. So, the interaction reflects the combined effect of the IVs contained in the design. In our example, the interaction of gender and voice on the rating of pleasantness of laugh is statistically significant, $F(1, 16) = 35.56, p < .05$. This statistically significant outcome suggests that the pleasantness rating changes as a function of the combination of the two independent variables. In other words, the gender of the person producing the laugh in combination with the type of laugh affects the pleasantness rating of the laugh. So, a male voiced laugh is rated more highly than a male unvoiced laugh. In contrast, the female unvoiced laugh is rated more highly than the male unvoiced laugh. In other words, type of voice combined with gender affects the rating of pleasantness. An interaction is best conveyed as a graph as illustrated in Figure 10.3. The DV, pleasantness rating, is reflected on the Y axis. The IV of Gender is represented on the X axis, and Voice is represented by each of the lines contained in the graph. The interaction is illustrated by the crossing of the lines in the graph.

Main Effects. If we consider the respective IVs individually, we find interesting results. Type of voice produces statistically significant results, $F(1, 16) = 8.89, p < .05$. The IV of voice (with both levels) is what we refer to as a main effect, or an effect of a single IV. If we

FIGURE 10.3 *Interaction Effect*

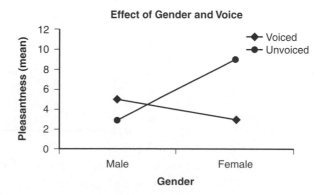

Effect of Gender and Voice

FIGURE 10.4 *Main Effect for Voice*

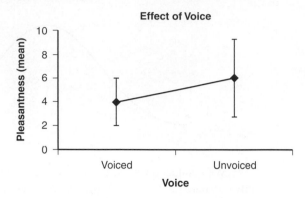

had conducted the study using only one IV, we would have concluded that type of voice had an effect on pleasantness rating, as illustrated in Figure 10.4.

Gender, as a variable by itself, is also statistically significant, $F(1, 16) = 8.89, p < .05$. In other words, participants rated pleasantness of voice differently depending on whether the voice was male or female as illustrated in Figure 10.5.

Although we found significant results for the main effects (i.e., gender and voice), these results may not tell the full story. More importantly, the factorial ANOVA allows us to test for effects of both variables simultaneously. We often find that the combination of the IVs produces a unique effect that is not present when the variables are examined independently.

Post Hoc Analyses

An ANOVA allows us to test for statistically significant differences among multiple conditions while holding alpha constant. When conducting a factorial ANOVA, we are particularly interested in examining interaction effects. So, if the IVs interact, the DV is affected by the combination of levels of the IVs. When we find an interaction, additional statistical post hoc analyses are unnecessary. In other words, one level of the IV changes as a function of the level of the second IV. Therefore, we interpret the results using the cell means.

FIGURE 10.5 *Main Effect for Gender*

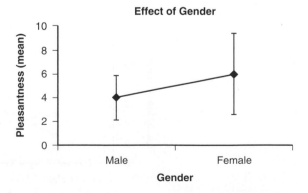

We use the standard post hoc analyses when we wish to examine a main effect with more than two levels of an IV. Our 2 × 2 ANOVA contains only two levels of each IV, so effects are clearly evident, and an additional post hoc analysis is unnecessary. However, if more than three levels of an IV are present, an additional post hoc analysis is conducted to determine which of the levels of the IV differ. Recall that the Tukey *HSD* and the Scheffé post hoc analyses are appropriate analyses to further investigate where among the levels of an IV a statistically significant difference is present.

Effect Size

We used a simple calculation of effect size, eta squared (η^2), for the one-way ANOVA. However, with the factorial ANOVA, we use a slightly more complicated measure of effect size to estimate the proportion of variability explained by the interaction of the independent variables and each IV individually. Omega squared (ω^2) is a very accurate estimate of effect size. We calculate three different measures of effect size—each provide the proportion of variability associated with the respective effects. The general formula for effect size is:

$$\omega^2 = \frac{variance_A}{variance_{Total}}$$

We begin with calculating effect size for the interaction, or the proportion of variance explained by the interaction.

$$\omega^2 = \frac{variance_{A \times B}}{variance_{Total}} = \frac{SS_{A \times B} - (df_{A \times B}MS_{Error})}{SS_{TOTAL} + MS_{Error}}$$

Using the formula for omega squared, we find:

$$\omega^2 = \frac{80 - (1 * 2.25)}{156 + 2.25} = \frac{77.75}{158.25} = .49$$

Thus, the effect size, or proportion of explained variance that can be attributed to the gender by voice interaction, is approximately 49%. Explaining 49% of variability is a relatively large effect size.

We found that the main effects, gender and voice, were also statistically significant. So, we use the same basic formula to calculate effect size for the main effects:

$$\omega^2 = \frac{SS_A - (df_A MS_{Error})}{SS_{TOTAL} + MS_{Error}}$$

Thus:

$$\omega^2 = \frac{20 - (1 * 2.25)}{156 + 2.25} = \frac{17.75}{158.25} = .11$$

A much smaller proportion of the variability (11%) is explained by effect of gender and voice alone. Indeed, using two independent variables, and investigating the interaction effect, increases the proportion of explained variability quite a bit.

Writing Results

Reporting results of a two-way ANOVA is more involved than for the one-way ANOVA. We report results of the interaction and the respective main effects, together with the requisite estimates of effect size. Using the voice and gender data, we provide an example of how to report results below.

> We tested two independent variables, gender and voice, in this study. Participants heard either a male or female laugh that was either voiced or unvoiced. Participants in each of the four conditions indicated the desirability of the laugh. We found a statistically significant interaction between gender and voice, $F(1, 16) = 35.56, p < .05, \omega^2 = .49$. In the voiced condition, the male voice ($M = 5.0, SD = 2.0$) was rated more highly than the female voice ($M = 3.0, SD = 1.22$). However, in the unvoiced condition, the male voice ($M = 3.0, SD = 1.58$) was rated as less desirable than the female voice ($M = 9.0, SD = 1.00$).
>
> The main effect for gender was also statistically significant, $F(1, 16) = 8.89, p < .05, \omega^2 = .11$. The female voice ($M = 6, SD = 3.33$) was rated more highly than the male voice ($M = 4, SD = 2.00$). Similarly, the main effect for voice was statistically significant, $F(1, 16) = 8.89, p < .05, \omega^2 = .11$. The unvoiced condition ($M = 6, SD = 3.39$) was rated more highly than the voiced condition ($M = 4, SD = 1.89$).

Computer Analysis Using SPSS

Data for a factorial ANOVA are set up much like the one-way ANOVA. One column contains the dependent variable data. Additional columns are used to designate the appropriate level of the IV. So, using our example, we have a column for type of voice and a column for gender.

The first step in conducting the ANOVA is to select the appropriate statistical analysis as illustrated in Figure 10.6. It is important to note that a factorial ANOVA is produced using the Univariate function in SPSS.

FIGURE 10.6   *Specifying the Analysis*

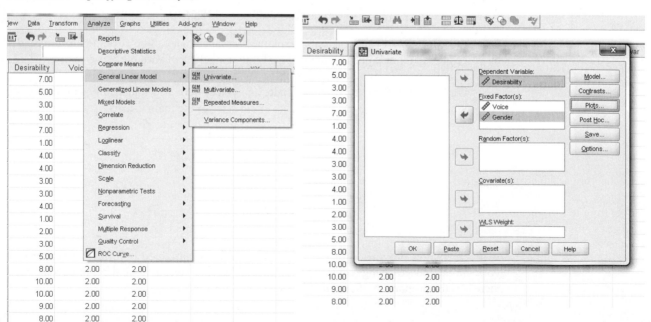

FIGURE 10.7 *Factorial Output*

Tests of Between-Subjects Effects

Dependent Variable: Desirability

Source	Type III Sum of Squares	df	Mean Square	F	Sig.	Partial Eta Squared
Corrected Model	120.000[a]	3	40.000	17.778	.000	.769
Intercept	500.000	1	500.000	222.222	.000	.933
Gender	20.000	1	20.000	8.889	.009	.357
Voice	20.000	1	20.000	8.889	.009	.357
Gender * Voice	80.000	1	80.000	35.556	.000	.690
Error	36.000	16	2.250			
Total	656.000	20				
Corrected Total	156.000	19				

[a]R Squared = .769 (Adjusted R Squared = .726)

After selecting the Univariate ANOVA, the dialogue box requires us to specify the dependent variable and fixed factors. As illustrated in Figure 10.6, the dependent variable is Pleasantness and the independent variables (fixed factors) are Gender and Laughter. It is also helpful to specify the plots and descriptive statistics necessary for reporting results of the analysis.

The output in Figure 10.7 includes results of the ANOVA for all three tests: the interaction and the main effect for each variable (gender and voice).

We find that the *SS, df, MS,* and *F* values match our hand-calculated values. The exact level of significance also appears.

SPSS output also includes descriptive statistics necessary for reporting the results of a statistically significant interaction and main effects as indicated in Figure 10.8.

FIGURE 10.8 *Descriptive Statistics*

Descriptive Statistics

Dependent Variable: Desirability

Gender	Voice	Mean	Std. Deviation	N
Male	Voiced	5.0000	2.00000	5
	Unvoiced	3.0000	1.58114	5
	Total	4.0000	2.00000	10
Female	Voiced	3.0000	1.22474	5
	Unvoiced	9.0000	1.00000	5
	Total	6.0000	3.33333	10
Total	Voiced	4.0000	1.88562	10
	Unvoiced	6.0000	3.39935	10
	Total	5.0000	2.86540	20

Chapter Summary

In this chapter, we introduced experimental designs that use more than one independent variable. The factorial design includes more than one independent variable with multiple conditions for each variable. One of the advantages of using a factorial design is that it allows us to test more than one independent variable at a time.

We described how to perform a factorial Analysis of Variance, or a factorial ANOVA, to test for statistical differences with more than one independent variable. Not only can we detect differences among treatment levels for each independent variable (main effects), but we also found that the factorial ANOVA allows us to detect the effects of the variables combined (interaction effects). A statistical interaction occurs when one level of one independent variable is affected by the level of a second independent variable.

We explained how the factorial ANOVA is used to mathematically derive the *F* ratio for each of the treatment effects (i.e., main effects and interaction effects). Using our calculated variances, we use the ratio of Treatment variance to Error variance to determine if a treatment is statistically significant. With the factorial ANOVA, we applied the *F* ratio to each independent variable and to the combination of independent variables, or the interaction. We also learned how these variances are represented in the Source Table. More importantly, we identified the elements of the table that are important for discerning statistically significant outcomes.

In addition to explaining sources of variance for each of the factorial ANOVA analysis, we described how the results of the analyses are graphed and reported. We found that graphing the results is particularly useful when an interaction is present among the variables.

Finally, we introduced omega squared (ω^2) as the standardized measure of effect size for a factorial ANOVA. Omega squared provides an estimate of the percentage of variability that is explained for each of the independent variables and for the interaction effect.

Key Terms

Factorial ANOVA

Factorial (crossed) designs

Homogeneity of variance

Interaction effects

Main effects

Chapter Review Questions

Multiple Choice Questions

1. How many variables are present in a 2 × 4 factorial design?
   a. 2
   b. 4
   c. 6
   d. 8

2. How many conditions are present in a 3 × 4 factorial design?
   a. 3
   b. 4
   c. 6
   d. 12

3. How many F ratios are calculated for a two-factor ANOVA?
   a. One interaction and one main effect
   b. One interaction and two main effects
   c. Two main effects
   d. One interaction

4. What are the degrees of freedom associated with each of the main effects in a 2 × 2 factorial ANOVA?
   a. 1
   b. 2
   c. 3
   d. 4

5. How many degrees of freedom are associated with the interaction effect in a 3 × 2 ANOVA?
   a. 2
   b. 3
   c. 4
   d. 6

6. Results from a two-way ANOVA produced the following cell means reflecting level of impairment when testing the effects of alcohol and caffeine. Alcohol with Caffeine ($M = 10$); Alcohol without Caffeine ($M = 10$); No Alcohol and Caffeine ($M = 5$); No Alcohol and no Caffeine ($M = 6$). The interaction effect was not statistically significant. Which of the following explanations reflects the outcome from this study?
   a. Alcohol did not significantly impair performance.
   b. Caffeine did not significantly impair performance.
   c. Alcohol did not combine with caffeine to significantly impair performance.
   d. Alcohol combined with caffeine significantly impaired performance.

7. Results from a two-way ANOVA produced the following factor means reflecting level of impairment: Alcohol ($M = 10$); No Alcohol ($M = 6$). The main effect for alcohol was statistically significant. Which of the following explanations reflects the outcome of this study?
   a. Alcohol did not significantly impair performance.
   b. Alcohol significantly impaired performance.
   c. Alcohol did not combine with caffeine to significantly impair performance.
   d. Alcohol combined with caffeine significantly impaired performance.

8. A psychologist conducted a study ($N = 80$) to compare type talk therapy to a no treatment condition. A second variable involved drug treatment (drugs and no drugs). The $MS_{A \times B}$ value for the interaction effect was 30 and the MS_{Error} was 5. Which of the following values reflects the F tabled for testing this effect at an alpha of .05?
   a. $F = 3.13$
   b. $F = 2.96$
   c. $F = 1.96$
   d. $F = 3.98$

9. A psychologist conducted a study ($N = 80$) to compare type talk therapy to a no treatment condition. A second variable involved drug treatment (drugs and no drugs). The $MS_{A \times B}$ value for the interaction effect was 30 and the MS_{Error} was 5. Which of the following values reflects the F calculated value for testing this effect at an alpha of .05?
   a. 3
   b. 5
   c. 6
   d. 8

10. Calculate the MS_{Error} for a study with $N = 50$, $k = 3$, and $SS = 50$.
    a. 2.50
    b. 3.00
    c. 1.06
    d. 16.60

Essay Questions

11. Describe how a factorial ANOVA differs from a one-way ANOVA.

12. Describe how to calculate the number of treatment conditions present in a factorial ANOVA.

13. How many variables are present in a $2 \times 3 \times 3$ design? How many levels of each independent variable are present? How many conditions are present?

14. What are the advantages of using a factorial design?

15. Describe how to determine if the calculated F values are statistically significant in a factorial ANOVA.

Practice Exercises

16. How many treatment conditions are present in a $3 \times 3 \times 2$ design?

17. How many levels are there in the second independent variable for the $2 \times 3 \times 4$ factorial design?

18. In a 2×2 factorial ANOVA the following data are reported. For each of the factors determine if a calculated $F = 5.63$, $df_{Factor\ A} = 1$, $df_{Factor\ B} = 1$, and $df_{Error} = 20$ is statistically significant. How many people participated in the study?

19. Complete the missing values in the following Source Table. How many participants were in this study?

Source of Variation	SS	df	MS	F
TREATMENT	50			
Factor A (Gender)		1	10	4.00
Factor B (Voice)		1		4.00
A × B		1	40	16.00
ERROR	40	16	2.50	
TOTAL	90	19		

20. Report the results for each of the statistical analysis from the Source Table above.

21. Calculate omega squared (ω^2) for the interaction effect in the Source Table above.

CHAPTER 11

PRINCIPLES OF SURVEY RESEARCH

CHAPTER OUTLINE

SURVEYS: ANSWERING DIVERSE QUESTIONS
  Census Versus Sample
  Accuracy of Survey Results

ANONYMITY AND CONFIDENTIALITY IN SURVEY RESEARCH

SELECTING YOUR METHODOLOGY
  Question Types
  Question Content

RESPONSE BIAS
  Studying Sensitive Issues
  Social Desirability
  Acquiescence
  Satisficing Versus Optimizing
  Minimizing the Occurrence of Satisficing

SAMPLING ISSUES
  Finding Hidden Populations

LEARNING OBJECTIVES

- Describe the problems with early surveys of U.S. presidential elections in 1936 and 1948.
- Differentiate the characteristics of scientific survey research and junk mail surveys.
- Explain the difference between a census and a sample.
- Describe the degree of accuracy of national political polls.
- Describe the controversy associated with statistical sampling to improve census results.
- Identify the ethical issues associated with survey research.
- Describe the concept of the sampling frame.
- Identify cultural issues associated with survey research.
- Define and explain the difference between open-ended and closed-ended questions.
- Explain the advantages and the disadvantages of open-ended and closed-ended questions.
- Identify four potentially problematic issues associated with surveys involving memories for past behaviors.
- Identify the seven potentially problematic issues associated with surveys involving attitudes.
- Identify six strategies that will help avoid problems in creating memory questions in survey research.
- Identify the methodological issues that need to be addressed in survey research on adolescent smoking.

- Describe the issues associated with survey research on sensitive issues.
- Describe the two types of social desirability bias.
- Identify strategies to overcome potential social desirability bias.
- Describe the problem of acquiescence in survey research.
- Differentiate the concepts of optimizing and satisficing in survey research.
- Describe the problem of self-selected samples.
- Identify four strategies for finding so-called hidden populations in survey research.

CHAPTER PREVIEW

Asking questions in survey research is an important aspect of research methodology. Surveys have become a fixture in modern life, with professional pollsters examining details of our lives and social scientists uncovering trends in attitudes and patterns of behavior. Most surveys rely on samples rather than on an exhaustive questioning of the entire population, which is a census.

Surveyors can choose from among different question types and content. The construction of the questions is probably the hardest part of a project because the form of a question influences responses, depending on the wording. So researchers need to take great care in creating questions in their survey research. In addition, respondents don't want to be seen in unfavorable light, so they may alter responses to make themselves look good and may tailor their answers to meet what they think are the expectations of the researcher. Fortunately, there are ways to avoid pitfalls in asking questions.

Finally, survey researchers prefer probability samples, and are wary of self-selected, convenience samples that do not represent the entire population. Researchers continue to develop new sampling strategies to overcome potential problems in current strategies.

Surveys: Answering Diverse Questions

We tend to take questionnaires for granted today, but they are really a relatively recent form of data collection. Late in the nineteenth century, G. Stanley Hall and psychologists in his laboratory made extensive use of questionnaires to study children's thought processes.

The first two listings of attitude research in the PsycINFO database were published in *The American Journal of Psychology* and *Proceedings of the Society for Psychical Research,* which is now considered a nonscientific journal. Both deal with belief in life after death.

Beginning a little over half a century ago, investigators began developing the theory and techniques of survey research. Surveys took place that increased our information base on various topics, but by today's standards they were methodologically suspect. For instance, in 1936, the now defunct magazine *Literary Digest* confidently, but inaccurately, predicted that Franklin Roosevelt would lose the U.S. presidential election in a landslide. This may be the most famous error in the history of research. The problem was that the editors of that magazine used a sampling method that led to an unrepresentative picture of the voting population.

A little more than a decade later, a newspaper proclaimed just as confidently but just as inaccurately that Thomas Dewey had defeated Harry Truman in the 1948 presidential election. The problem there was that in the forecasting, George Gallup had used quota sampling (Moore, 1992), which as a type of convenience sampling is prone to error in depicting the population as a whole.

Today's researchers can also make mistakes, as they did in the 2000 presidential election when they declared that Al Gore won the state of Florida. In spite of this recent major mistake, which occurred because the election was so close, current survey techniques provide very useful information most of the time. After all, in the 2000 presidential election, the pollsters called 49 of the 50 states correctly.

The implication here is that using samples to understand populations can lead to mistakes because we are using incomplete information to draw conclusions, but if researchers use proper techniques, the number of misjudgments and the magnitude of error are small.

Surveys are one of the most widely used forms of research. When a company considers developing a new product, it hires survey marketing researchers to find out whether the product could compete in the marketplace. When politicians want to know what the voters think, surveys are the best way to find out. When social researchers want to know about behaviors and attitudes, they often design surveys.

Just as survey researchers want you to complete their questionnaires, retailers who send out junk mail disguised as scientific surveys want to capture your attention. And just as researchers have evaluated different strategies to increase response rates, marketers have also addressed that issue (Headden, 1997). It turns out that many of the same tactics that work for scientific surveys lead to greater responsiveness by consumers.

Researchers and junk mailers both try to get your attention. Their goals differ, however. Researchers want information, junk mailers want your money. By considering the content and purposes of surveys, you may be able to spot those associated with research and those with money-making intent. As you can see in Table 11.1, research surveys tend to be personally directed and involve fewer gimmicks.

We see so many questionnaires in all facets of our lives that we often do not realize how difficult it is to create a valid survey instrument. Over the past half century, researchers have spent considerable energy trying to find out what works best and what pitfalls to avoid.

Census Versus Sample

Survey—A research method in which an investigator asks questions of a respondent.

When researchers conduct survey research, they must decide whether to contact everybody in the population of interest or to sample a subset. Probably the most famous example of the former in the United States is the census. The constitution of the United States mandates a decennial **census,** that is, a complete counting of everybody living in the country every 10 years. The basic purpose of the census is to inform the Congress about how many people live in each state so there can be proportional representation in the House of Representatives. There are also other uses for the results, like figuring out where the population is growing so adequate highways can be built or where to build hospitals to meet the needs of an aging populace.

Census—Data collection that includes every member of a population of interest.

Although everybody agrees that the census is necessary, we must face the fact that it is very costly. The 2010 census had a price tag of just about $13 billion, or about $45 to count

TABLE 11.1   *Characteristics Differentiating Survey Research and Junk Mail That Simulates Survey Designs*

Researchers	*Junk Mailers*
Letters addressed to a specific person	Letters addressed to a specific person after an individual responds to an initial, less personal mailing
Real signatures at the end of the letter	Fake handwritten notes and fake signatures
Monetary incentives	Gifts like decorative stamps or offers of free gifts
Sincere statements of appreciation	Appeals to fear, greed, guilt, and exclusivity; association with high-status individuals or organizations
Distinctive envelopes and surveys	Envelopes that appear to be from the government

each person, according to *USA Today* (2010 census, 2008), up from $7 billion, or about $25 per head, in 2000. Mailing a census form to every household in the country alone is an enormous expense; when people don't reply, a personal follow-up takes place, which is also expensive. We also know that many people are missed in the census, particularly people who have no fixed address, people from countries where they may have had an appropriate fear of the government, and others. In addition, some people are counted twice, like those who own multiple homes. The process of counting every resident is not easy, cheap, or completely accurate.

The census has never been perfect, beginning with the first one in 1790. Even with our increasing technical sophistication, the accuracy of the census is probably worse than it used to be. As you can see in the Controversy on the U.S. census, there are scientific ways to reduce the error, but they face political obstacles.

One difference between the Census Bureau and most other researchers is that, generally, researchers are content to survey a portion of the population, that is, a sample, rather than take a census. A relatively small percentage of the population is needed to get a fairly accurate picture of the group you want to describe.

Accuracy of Survey Results

How accurate are surveys that professional researchers conduct? When it comes to scientific research, we generally don't know. But we can look at the surveys whose accuracy has been assessed: polls for political elections. Researchers who are conducting scientific surveys often use the same methodologies that political pollsters do, so if the political surveys are accurate, it is likely that scientific surveys are, too.

So let's take a look at political surveys on a national level. There are about 100 million potential voters in the United States. It would make no sense to try to ask each of them about their views; it would take too long and cost too much money. If you wanted to characterize 100 million possible voters with reasonable accuracy, how many would you have to sample? Typically, political polls sample about 1,000 people; ranging from 700 or 800 to perhaps 1,500. These numbers reflect about .001 percent of the voting population.

How accurate are these polls? After every election, the vote count provides a test. In the 2008 U.S. presidential election, the predictions of percentage vote for the winner in eight major final pre-election polls differed from the actual vote by an average of less than one percent (Silver, 2008), a figure similar to those in 2004 and 2000 (Election polls, 2011; High accuracy found, 2001). Polls for the 2004 election were the most accurate to that time (Traugott, 2005), and the most recent election seems just as accurate. The polls are not error-free, but they are pretty impressive, especially when you consider the modest sample sizes.

When you sample a subset of the population, you can count on getting some differences between what your sample is like and what the population is like. If you have a small sample, a few unusual people can distort your results; if you have a large sample, those same unusual people don't make much of a difference.

This means that you can get a pretty good picture of your population by sampling a relatively small number of people. As you increase your sample size, the accuracy of your information grows, but for a population as large as 100 million voters, once you reach a sample size of about 1,000, your accuracy doesn't grow very much for each new person you sample. As a result, it doesn't pay to increase your sample size above a certain point if you are not going to increase the sample greatly.

Population—A set consisting of every person or data point that would be of interest to a researcher.

If the **population** from which you want to sample is relatively small, you might need a larger proportion in order to end up with accurate results, but the actual number will not be all that large.

CONTROVERSY
The U.S. Census

It would be natural to think that if the government used a census to count everybody in the country, we would know how many people reside in our land. In truth, the census never achieves the ideal of counting everybody. In fact, in the first set of mail returns for the 2000 census, about two out of every five households failed to return the form, in spite of the fact that it is required by law. Consequently, the Census Bureau dispatched over half a million workers to follow up the nonresponses.

The incomplete count is nothing new. According to Anderson and Fienberg (2000), none of the 22 census counts done since the inception of the United States has actually found everybody, even with the current $13 billion price tag.

One of the most contentious debates about the 2000 census was whether the Bureau would be able to use statistical sampling to estimate the number of people who had not responded. According to every panel of statisticians commissioned by the National Research Council, statistical sampling would at least partially remedy the undercounts, even if some error remained in the count. Some statisticians did not favor statistical sampling, but they were in the minority.

As a group, Republicans opposed correcting the undercount with statistical sampling, whereas the Democrats favored it. The Supreme Court ruled that the sample data could not be used for apportionment of seats to the House of Representatives but could be used for all other purposes.

The undercount is greater for minority populations, so areas with larger numbers of minorities appear to have smaller populations than they actually do. The result of the Supreme Court's decision will be to reduce congressional representation of those areas.

Political considerations are nothing new in the census. In 1920, Congressional Republicans refused to recognize the results because potential changes in reapportionment would not favor them. As a result, they continued to use results of the 1910 census, even though it did not accurately represent the country. Finally, in 1929, Republican President Herbert Hoover resolved the impasse as he pressured members of his party to pass a census bill for the 1930 count. By doing this, Hoover averted a constitutional crisis.

What all this means is that simply counting people in this country involves error. The statistical, scientifically based methods designed to eliminate some of the error are affected by social and political considerations. Once again, we see that scientific research is affected by the same factors as every other aspect of our lives.

Anonymity and Confidentiality in Survey Research

All research carries the requirement of ethical behavior on the part of the investigator. With regard to survey research, we have to pay attention to two critical, related considerations—anonymity and confidentiality. It is standard practice to completely guarantee both the anonymity and confidentiality of responses. This means that nobody who is not part of the research will have access to information about whether an individual participates or what his or her responses might have been.

If a researcher is tracking whether people have responded and wants to send a reminder to those who have not completed a survey, some kind of identification is necessary. In the rare event that an investigator needs to keep identification information over a long period of time, the data cannot be anonymous. There is nothing wrong with such procedures in and of themselves, although at the end of the project, the researcher should destroy any information that could link a respondent with participation in the study.

When researchers cannot guarantee anonymity, they can at least assure respondents that participation will be kept confidential. Confidentiality means that nobody will be able to connect a given person with participation in a study. This is typically assured by reporting the data only in aggregate, that is, in a summarized form so that nobody can tell who responded in one way or another. For surveys that ask sensitive questions, you must provide such assurances because your respondents will either decline to respond or will not tell the whole truth.

The situation is complex because, with sensitive questions, anonymity may be a critical issue. For example, when Lavender and Anderson (2009) studied behaviors associated with eating disorders (extreme dieting, purging, investment in body weight and shape, fear of weight gain, and the belief that others worry about their weight), they discovered that their respondents reported a higher incidence of problematic behaviors when the respondents were more confident that their responses were truly anonymous. The effect was more pronounced with questions associated with more undesirable behaviors, suggesting that the quality of data may be lower when respondents are responding to very sensitive questions and are not completely sure that their responses are anonymous.

Ironically, if you make a big point of assuring confidentiality and anonymity, it may arouse suspicions in those you survey (Singer, Von Thurn, & Miller, 1995). In a situation involving mundane questions, it might be more reasonable to play down the confidentiality and anonymity aspects because they may distract a participant from the real purpose of the study.

A further ethical constraint is that your respondents must know that they do not have to participate in your research and that they can terminate their responses at any time, without any penalty. This constitutes voluntary participation. If you stand over their shoulder or are even in their presence, you may be influencing a person's behavior; your respondent may feel compelled to enter answers because you are watching. You may be acting unethically and unprofessionally. You may also pay a price in the data. People may not respond honestly.

You can see in Table 11.2 the professional code developed by the Marketing Research Association regarding Internet research (Use of the Internet, 2000). As you can see, these principles are generally similar to those developed by APA but with a focus on Internet research. This code provides good guidance about ethical behavior in survey research. Naturally, you would want to follow APA's ethics code and state and federal laws as well.

TABLE 11.2   *Ethical Guidelines Regarding Internet Research as Developed by the Council for Marketing and Opinion Research*

Ethical Principle	*Concerns Regarding Violations of the Principle*
Participation must be voluntary and researchers must avoid deception	If respondents are made to believe that the survey relates to some topic but it really relates to a different topic, the person cannot truly give informed consent because the person does not really know what he or she is responding to.
Researcher's identity should be made available to respondents	Without knowledge of who is conducting the research, the respondent cannot find out about the person or organization in order to freely decide about participating.
A respondent's anonymity must be respected	It is a violation of ethical principles of professional researchers if a respondent's contact information is sold to others.
Privacy policies need to be available online and should be clear and understandable	The research organization must disclose how it will use the data provided by respondents; failure to do so is an ethical violation.
Security of the data is essential	Any information provided by respondents could be redirected to people who are not connected to the research project in which the respondent has agreed to participate.
Reliability and validity of findings should be public	Researchers who make their research public should not make deceptive statements about their findings or make generalizations that go beyond what the data permit.
Research with minors should follow the principles of the Children's Online Privacy Protection Act	Parental consent is absolutely required, and children's identities must be held in strictest confidence.
Additional e-mail should not be sent to respondents if they do not want to receive it	Solicitations or other intrusions are inappropriate for people who choose not to have further contact with the research organization.

Selecting Your Methodology

Most research projects begin with a general question that needs an answer. After that, practical issues arise. In the case of surveys, the critical issues include identifying the sampling frame. The **sampling frame** is the entire list of elements from which the sample is drawn. In psychological research, we seldom have a list of all possible respondents; in fact, we usually do not even have any way to detail the population of interest to us. Nonetheless, any survey research that we conduct should begin with an identification of the source of our respondents that will lead to our actual sample.

We decide the specific means of constituting a sample. This step is critical if we are interested in drawing conclusions that generalize beyond our sampling frame. Researchers who conduct surveys prefer to use probability samples. If the process is done properly, researchers can be confident that the sample is likely to represent the entire population.

Researchers also spend considerable time developing the questions. Creating survey questions seems as if it should be easy, but is probably the most difficult part of survey research and requires the greatest creativity and insight. And it takes on even greater importance when the sampling frame contains people of diverse backgrounds. For example, investigators studied the effect of wording of questions on the Center for Epidemiologic Studies Depression Scale (CES-D) and found notable differences among Mexican Americans, black Americans, and white Americans due simply to differences in the way the items are structured. Mexican Americans were more likely to endorse a greater number of depressive items compared to white and black Americans (Kim, Chiriboga, & Jang, 2009).

And as Chen (2008) noted, there are four general issues associated with making comparisons across cultures, including problems with translation from one language to another, the possibility that an item does not really measure the same construct in different cultures, varying response styles across cultures, and issues of social desirability. Oyserman, Coon, and Kemmelmeier (2002) pointed out, for instance, that people from cultures that are high both in collectivistic and individualistic tendencies often use more extreme ratings on a Likert-type scale than do people from cultures low in those tendencies.

Further complicating the picture is that people may respond to items differently depending on their degree of acculturation into a new culture. In assessing depression, Chiriboga, Jang, Banks, and Kim (2007) reported that elderly Mexican Americans showed different patterns of responses depending on the degree to which they were proficient in English, the language in which they were tested. In such groups, it is likely that language skills will affect most research results involving verbal responses.

Another important issue that has gained in importance in the past decade is the use of computers to collect self-reported data. Switching from paper and pencil to a computer might seem like a minor issue, but there is no guarantee that people will respond the same way for both. (You can refer to Chapter 6 for guidance regarding online data collection.) Fortunately, for many measurements, respondents have shown comparable behavior (e.g., Vispoel, 2000) although there can be some differences. For instance, Heerwegh (2009) found that nonresponse to items was greater for Web-based surveys, but social desirability bias was less, although the differences were quite small. Further, having multiple items on a screen shortens the length of the interview, but respondents may have a less positive response to the session than with fewer items per screen (Toepoel, Das, & Van Soest, 2009). Any time you change methodologies, you don't know if the new and the old means will result in the same outcome until you research the question. There seems to be reason to be optimistic that computerized data collection will lead to results that are as valid as those in traditional methods.

Throughout the entire process of survey research, the investigators must make a series of very practical decisions so that at the end they can have confidence in the conclusions they

Sampling frame—A subset of a population from which a sample is actually selected.

draw. The discoveries in such research are only as good as the practical decisions the researchers make: Your question type has to meet your needs, the way you word your questions should not distort the responses, and the format of your instrument has to promote people's willingness to complete the task. If you meet these criteria, the quality of your data can be high.

One practical example of the difficulty in answering even a simple question involves the determination of how many adolescents in the United States smoke. A generally accepted answer based on survey research is about 4 million, but this number can be deceiving because the definition of "smoking" makes a big difference in the number that you accept as valid. The Controversy on adolescent smoking at the end of this section illustrates this problem.

Question Types

In terms of question and response structure, there are two main types of survey items: **open-ended questions,** which allow respondents to generate an answer without limitations regarding length or content, and **closed-ended questions,** which require respondents to select from a set of answers already provided. Each type has its own advantages and disadvantages. Table 11.3 shows how a researcher might develop different types of questions to investigate a topic.

If you answered an open-ended question about drinking alcohol, as illustrated in Table 11.3, you could discuss many different aspects of drinking behavior. You would determine what you thought was important and what was irrelevant, then respond accordingly. The advantage of such questions is that they provide a rich body of information. The disadvantage is that they can be harder to categorize, sort, and summarize because the responses can go in any direction the participant wants to take them. If the sample size is large, it may take a long time to describe and interpret the collection of very diverse responses. In addition, the respondent might fail to mention some elements of a response that the researcher was very interested in.

On the other hand, researchers can use closed-ended questions. These items do not permit free responding. There is a set of responses from which to choose, such as *yes–no* or *strongly agree/somewhat agree/somewhat disagree/strongly disagree.* The information provided by such questions is not as rich as with open-ended questions, but these questions are much quicker and easier to score and summarize. Further, with closed-ended questions, the investigator can make sure that the respondent has the chance to answer questions of critical importance to the research project. For example, if the investigator wants to know whether teenagers drink alone or with others, the closed-ended question may provide that information from every respondent. Few people may address that issue in the open-ended question.

Although research has shown that both types of question format lead to answers of comparable validity, since the 1940s, researchers have preferred closed-ended questions because such a format lends itself to easier scoring.

However, recent evaluation of closed-ended questions has revealed some of their limitations. For instance, if people can choose from among answers prepared by the surveyor or can generate their own, they will often pick one of the surveyor's responses, even if they could provide their own, better answer (Krosnick, 1999). One reason is that people generally don't want to work any harder than they have to; it is easier to select a response that somebody else provides than to work to find your own. This phenomenon of selecting the first acceptable answer, even if it is not the best, is called **satisficing.**

Question Content

The structure and wording of survey items pose challenges for people who create surveys. Slightly different wording can lead to very different responses; consequently, researchers may end up with conclusions that vary considerably from those that they would have made with slightly different survey questions.

Open-ended question— In survey research, a question that respondents answer using their own words, unconstrained by choices provided by the researcher.

Closed-ended question— In survey research, a question that contains a set of answers that a respondent chooses.

Satisficing—The tendency of respondents to be satisfied with the first acceptable response to a question or on a task, even if it is not the best response.

TABLE 11.3 *Examples of Questions in Open- Versus Closed-Ended Formats That Relate to the Same General Topic, Alcohol Consumption*

OPEN-ENDED QUESTION:

Describe the situations in which you consume alcoholic beverages and what you drink.

CLOSED-ENDED QUESTIONS:

1. On how many days per week do you consume alcohol?
☐ None
☐ 1–2 times per week
☐ 3–4 times per week
☐ 5 or more times per week

2. When you drink alcoholic beverages, what do you drink most frequently?
☐ I do not drink alcoholic beverages
☐ Beer
☐ Wine
☐ Liquor (Gin, Vodka, Scotch, Bourbon)

3. Which of the following statements describes the most likely situation when you drink alcoholic beverages?
☐ I do not drink alcoholic beverages
☐ I am alone
☐ I am with one other person
☐ I am in a small group (2 to 5 people)
☐ I am in a larger group (6 or more people)

4. Do you think it is easier, no different, or harder for teenagers to obtain alcohol compared to 10 years ago?
☐ Easier
☐ No different
☐ Harder

5. The minimum legal age for drinking alcoholic beverages in the United is 21 years. Do you agree with the statement, "The minimum legal age for drinking should remain at 21 years"?
☐ Strongly Agree
☐ Agree
☐ Disagree
☐ Strongly Disagree
☐ No Opinion

It is also critical to understand how different types of questions lead to variable responses. A key difference among questions involves what the researcher is trying to measure. In general, we can divide the purpose of the questions into three domains: measures of memory and behavior, measures of attitude and opinion, and demographics.

Memory Questions. Most of the time in our lives, when we converse with people, we assume that they are telling us the truth. This is usually a reasonable assumption. The same is probably true regarding answers on a questionnaire. At the same time, we all know that we don't always tell the whole truth, and sometimes we lie outright. This pattern is also true for responses to surveys.

People may not be lying when they misreport their behaviors. They may not know the answer to a question, but they give it their best guess (maybe a bad one), trying to be helpful. When you want people to tell you how often they have engaged in mundane behaviors that don't stand out in memory, they are prone to significant error (Rockwood, Sangster, & Dillman, 1997). For example, for many students, it would be difficult to answer precisely the question, "How often in the past two months have you eaten pizza?" The episodes individually do not stand out in memory because they are so normal. Thus, it may be difficult to come up with an accurate response.

Researchers often ask respondents to answer questions that require the person to remember something. For instance, Kleck and Gertz (1995) wanted to know the extent to which people report having protected themselves with handguns against burglars. Their analysis revealed 2.5 million instances of such protection, implying that handguns in such situations exert a positive effect. Hemenway (1997) argued that the problem with Kleck and Gertz's data is that more people claim to have protected themselves with guns during burglaries than were actually burglarized.

Hemenway argued that whenever you ask a sample to remember relatively rare events of any kind, a small increase in false positives (i.e., saying something happened when it did not) leads to an inappropriately large estimate when you generalize to the population.

Hemenway's point about the reporting of rare events was reinforced by further research. Cook and Ludwig (1998) noted that reports of defensive gun use (DGU) in studies with relatively small samples suggest greater rates of DGU than are likely to be true. This doesn't mean that there is not significant defensive gun use, only that we may not know how often it occurs. Considering less controversial topics, Wentland and Smith (1993) noted that people have trouble with remembering if they have a library card.

We can identify four particularly troublesome problems associated with memory questions. First, people use different strategies to recall events from the recent past and distant past in some cases. When Winkielman, Knäuper, and Schwarz (1998) inquired of people how often they have been angry either in the last week versus in the last year, the respondents interpreted the meaning of the question differently. In the *Last Week* group, participants decided that the surveyor wanted a report of minor irritations, whereas the *Last Year* group focused on major irritations.

A second source of problems is that, when a question involves a time span (e.g., "How many times in the last year have you . . ."), people may engage in a memory phenomenon called **telescoping.** When you look through a telescope, distant objects do not seem as far away as they really are; similarly, when people try to remember events from the past, things that happened a long time ago tend to be remembered as having happened more recently than they actually did.

A third difficulty is that the nature of previous questions affects the responses to later ones. People want to appear consistent in their responses, so they may use previous answers to help them form responses to new questions. If their initial responses are inaccurate, later ones may distort the truth. Todorov (2000) discovered that people reported different levels of vision problems in a health survey depending on what questions had been asked just before a critical question.

A fourth concern involves the nature of alternatives presented in a closed-ended question. Schwarz (1999) and others have reported that the scale of alternatives can make a big difference in a person's response.

For example, Schwarz and colleagues (1985) asked people how much daily television they watched. Respondents saw one of two scales for their response. One set of options provided response options in half-hour increments starting at zero (0 to .5, .5 to 1, 1.5 to 2, 2 to 2.5, and 2.5 or more); this was the low-frequency condition. A different set of respondents

Telescoping—A phenomenon of memory in which events that occurred in the distant past are remembered as having occurred more recently than they actually did.

saw options that began at 2.5 hours; that is, the lowest response category was 2.5 to 3 hours. This was the high-frequency condition. Over a third of those who answered using the high-frequency scale replied that they watched television more than two and a half hours a day. Less than half that number using the low-frequency scale reported such television watching.

Why would there be such a discrepancy? For the high-frequency television watching scale, respondents are likely to conclude that the surveyor is asking a reasonable question and that numbers in the middle of the scale are typical. Accordingly, if they think they watch a "normal" amount of television, their answers will gravitate toward the numbers that are in the middle of this scale, which are relatively high.

People responding to the low-frequency scale expressed a belief that the typical person watched 2.7 hours of television a day, whereas those responding on the high-frequency scale suggested that the typical person watched 3.2 hours. Clearly, the participants were using the scale for information about what is "typical."

Obviously, the problem with this type of question is that, as a researcher, your confidence in your data decreases. Do the respondents watch a lot of television or not? Unfortunately, the wording of a question can leave you with considerable uncertainty. Sometimes you should simply ask a direct question to get the best answer. On the other hand, a direct question may tax a person's memory too greatly. You should rely on pretesting your questions, on your best judgment, and on the strategies that successful researchers before you have employed. As noted earlier, writing questions is the most difficult aspect of survey research.

Table 11.4 provides some guidelines that survey researchers have made about asking questions when you want people to recall something. You will notice that some of the points

TABLE 11.4 *Elements for Constructing Survey Questions Involving Respondents' Memory*

Guideline	Comment
Do not ask for details of mundane activities that are beyond a person's ability to remember (e.g., "How many people are usually in the library when you study there?").	Some people are better at remembering details than others are; asking for too much recall of detail may lead some groups to produce low-quality data based on faulty estimates.
If possible, when you ask people how frequently they have engaged in a behavior, request the respondent to provide as specific a number as possible.	If you give respondents a series of alternatives to choose from, the scale you use will influence the answer to this question and possibly to others.
If you need to ask about specific periods of time, make sure that the respondent can accurately gauge behaviors in the time frame you specify.	People are better at the recent past than the distant past. Further, respondents are more accurate for behaviors they engage in on a regular schedule.
Avoid questions that have vague quantifiers (e.g., "rarely" or "sometimes"); instead, use more specific quantifiers (e.g., "twice a week").	Vague quantifiers like "frequently" differ depending on the person and on the event being judged. For example, "frequent headaches" means something different than "frequent brushing of teeth."
Avoid questions that require overspecific quantifiers (e.g., "How many times have you eaten at a restaurant in the past year?"); instead give ranges (e.g., "0–1 times," "2–3 times," etc.).	When people engage in commonplace activities on an irregular basis, precise estimates are little more than guesses.
Do not ask questions using words that might distract the respondent (e.g., offensive or inflammatory words).	Respondents may use negative or emotionally charged words as a cue to how often they should report a behavior, trying to avoid a negative evaluation of such behavior.

seem to contradict one another. For example, one element says to ask for specific information and another says not to. When you are preparing survey questions, you need to make decisions about each question in the context in which it is asked. Sometimes you will want to ask specific questions, sometimes you will not.

Understanding the people you query and the behaviors you want to assess is critical to developing a useful survey. Pilot testing can help you decide if you have made good decisions. One noted expert once reported generating 41 different versions of a question before he arrived at one he considered "passable" (Payne, 1951, cited in Dillman, 2000).

Attitude Questions.   People have attitudes on many different issues, and they are often willing to share them. But asking about attitudes is difficult. There are seven major concerns that researchers have to ponder.

One prime concern with questions about attitudes, just as with memory questions, is the wording of the item. For example, emotionally laden terms can result in answers that are more likely to be responses to the wording than to the meaning of the question. For instance, a question that refers to sexual material as "hard-core pornography" is likely to elicit negative responses because of the attitude to the words, even if those words do not describe that sexual material very well.

Professional researchers are likely to be sensitive to the biasing factor of the words they use, but sometimes the effects are subtle. Rasinski (1989) pointed out that people voiced less support for "welfare" for the poor than they did for "assistance to the poor."

A second variable that can affect responses is the order of the questions. The attitudes that people report are highly context-dependent. That is, they feel one way when thinking about certain things, but they feel another way when thinking about other things. Memories and feelings about a topic that always surface when a respondent addresses some topic are **chronically accessible.** This means that respondents call some information to mind very readily; this information will affect their responses. Other memories and feelings might be **temporarily accessible.** This information also affects responses, but only if it has been recently brought into awareness, as by an earlier question on the survey.

Such accessibility may explain why, in nationwide polls, people generally claim that their own school systems are doing a good job, but that the nation's schools as a whole are not doing well (e.g., Satisfaction with local schools, 2005). When events in educational settings are especially troubling, news reports highlight the problem. So people compare their own schools with the negative reports and conclude that their own system is just fine. It makes you wonder: If just about all respondents report that their own schools are doing a good job, where are the problematic schools?

A third feature that guides participants' responses is their perceptions of the purpose of the interview or questionnaire. In one study, participants completed a questionnaire that had printed on the top "Institute for Social Research," whereas others saw "Institute for Personality Research." The responses of the two groups differed, with the first group concentrating on social variables in their answers and the second group concentrating on personality issues (Norenzayan & Schwarz, 1999).

A fourth possible variable influencing the expression of attitudes is the sensitivity of the issue being investigated. People may be reluctant to admit to drunken driving, illegal drug use, some sexual behaviors, or other such behaviors. There are two likely sources of invalidity for analysis of responses to these items. One source is nonresponse. That is, people simply ignore the question. The problem is that if too many people fail to answer the item, you may have problems with the representativeness of the answers you actually get. A second likely source of invalidity is simple lying.

A fifth factor that may come into play in personal interviews is the nature of the person doing the questioning. Finkel, Guterbok, and Borg (1991) discovered that white respondents were more likely to express support for a black candidate when an interviewer was black rather

Chronically accessible information—Memories that are available for retrieval at any time.

Temporarily accessible information—Memories that are available for retrieval only when cued by exposure to information that cues those memories.

than white. A surprising element here is that the interview was over the telephone. You can imagine that a face-to-face interview could lead to an even greater response bias.

In considering a sixth possible source of problems with the quality of data, it is important to distinguish between attitudes and opinions that people already have as opposed to attitudes that they create when a researcher asks them a question. Some people might not actually have an opinion on some topic until the surveyor asks them about it. They then construct one. Sometimes people even report attitudes on fictional topics.

Why would somebody state an attitude about a fictional topic? People might want to look thoughtful and would feel foolish about saying they don't know about a topic that they think they should. Another reason for making up an opinion is that respondents assume that the surveyor is asking a reasonable question, so they draw from their knowledge of apparently related topics and give an answer that would be consistent with their attitudes in general (Schwarz, 1999).

Researchers have discovered that when people have pre-existing attitudes, their response times to a question are shorter than when the respondent is creating an attitude to report (Powell & Fazio, 1984). Thus, if researchers are worried about differentiating between existing and newly created attitudes, keeping track of response times might be a useful strategy. Some online software permits such timing of individual responses.

A seventh concern about obtaining high-quality data with attitudinal questions is that people may hold a positive or a negative attitude about some topic, but it is not always clear how deeply they hold that attitude. Thus, a lot of people may favor gun control laws, but they might not hold that conviction deeply enough to write a letter to their political representatives. There may be fewer people who oppose such laws, but they may be more committed to act on their beliefs. These seven concerns are summarized in Table 11.5.

TABLE 11.5 *Seven Major Concerns About Surveys That Investigate Respondents' Attitudes*

Concern	*Reason for Concern*
Wording of the question	Wording that predisposes a respondent to answer in a particular way (e.g., an item that is emotionally loaded) does not give valid information about an attitude because the person is responding on the basis of wording.
Order of the question	Early questions may prime a respondent to think about issues in a given way or may bring information into memory so that it affects responses to a later question.
Perceived purpose of the survey	Respondents may interpret the meaning of questions differently, depending on what they believe is the underlying purpose of the survey.
Sensitivity of the issue being investigated	People may alter their responses or simply lie when asked about issues that might be embarrassing or otherwise make the respondent uncomfortable. Respondents may also omit answers to such questions.
The nature of the surveyor	People may respond more frankly to a researcher who is similar to them, particularly when the survey involves sensitive issues.
Respondents may not have pre-existing attitudes about a topic	Sometimes people are not aware of the issues being surveyed, so they don't have attitudes about them. They may make up their attitudes on the spot, sometimes on the basis of previous questions and their responses to them.
Surveys may not reveal the intensity with which a respondent holds an attitude	We can identify the extent of agreement with an issue, but we don't know the depth of feeling or commitment associated with that issue.

CONTROVERSY
Adolescent Smoking

The U.S. government regularly conducts surveys on health-related matters. The National Household Survey on Drug Abuse specifically investigates the use of various legal and illegal drugs. Based on the results of such surveys, various prominent people (e.g., then-President Bill Clinton, the Secretary of Health and Human Services, and the Surgeon General) publicly stated that four million adolescents (aged 12–17) smoked (Kovar, 2000).

This figure may be alarming and, if true, signals potentially serious health issues. In order to figure out what to do about such apparently prevalent smoking behavior, we need to understand what the data really signify. What constitutes an "adolescent"? What do we mean when we say that a person is a "smoker"?

An adolescent is somebody from age 12 to 17. This span covers a large range of development, though. A 12-year-old is very different from a 17-year-old on many behavioral, physical, and psychological dimensions. As it turns out, very few 12-year-olds smoke, so to believe that 12-year-olds are being lured into smoking is not accurate. Most of the smoking occurs toward the top of the age range.

When it came to defining a smoker in the survey, anybody who had had even one puff within the past 30 days was considered a smoker. One puff on one day is very different from a pack-a-day smoker.

About 25% of the adolescent smokers were heavy smokers. The survey defined "heavy" as indicating that the person smoked 10 cigarettes a day or more for over 20 days in the past month.

Of the middle group of smokers (41% of adolescents), most used one to five cigarettes on the days when they smoked, and they smoked relatively infrequently.

The results also revealed that 31% of the "smokers" had less than one cigarette when they did smoke. Smoking less than a cigarette in many cases meant sharing a single cigarette with friends in a social situation.

What do these data tell us? The sad news is that the heavy smokers are probably already addicted in adolescence; many report smoking more than they really want to. The better news is that about two in five of these teen smokers have had less than half a pack of cigarettes in their entire lifetime and are unlikely to become addicted. The data also reveal that smoking is pretty rare among the youngest adolescents.

The survey results can provide useful information about smoking and health policies, but the simple claim that 4 million adolescents smoke hides the truth that few of the younger adolescents smoke and that a large percentage of this group experimented irregularly. Unfortunately, by age 17, addiction has occurred in more adolescents than we would like. Knowing the complete picture, which means understanding the definitions used in the survey, will allow us to generate public health policies that do what we want them to.

Response Bias

Response bias—A tendency for a respondent to answer in predictable ways, independent of the question content, such as always agreeing with a statement or always providing high or low ratings on a Likert scale.

Surveyors have long known that people may hesitate to tell you the truth when they fear a negative reaction to their answers. This should come as no surprise; as social beings, we all consider how much to reveal to another person, whether we are talking to a friend or to a stranger. As long as people think that they are going to be evaluated, they will tailor their responses in a survey.

Sometimes respondents show certain patterns in their answers, regardless of the content of the question. One person may be likely to agree with questions most of the time; another person might be likely to disagree most of the time. When people engage in such patterns of behavior, they are showing **response bias.**

Researchers are now developing models that are helping us understand the nature of people's response tendencies. For example, Shulruf, Hattie, and Dixon (2008) created a five-stage model of how people comprehend and respond to survey questions. In this model, respondents are seen as progressing through the following steps: (a) understanding the question, (b) establishing the context, (c) retrieving available information about related behaviors, (d) integrating information and assessing impression management, and (e) evaluating all the information and aligning it with the available range of responses.

As you can see, the process of answering a question may take considerable mental processing. A person needs to understand the question itself, figure out how it relates to the current situation, then decide what to reveal to the researcher. A respondent could provide data of low quality if there is a problem in any of the stages.

Shulruf et al. (2008) described the various stages of the process during which response biases may arise. You will read about these response biases shortly. They speculated that social desirability biases arise in stages 3 and 4 and that acquiescence appears in stage 5. The tendency to respond either with extreme or with neutral values on a scale also arises in stage 5. The decision to choose an easy answer (as opposed to one that requires some thought) might be associated with stage 1.

Studying Sensitive Issues

Sometimes the best way to get information from people is simply to ask them. Surprisingly, many people are willing to give researchers reports of intimate details of their lives.

Researchers have developed varied techniques designed to result in meaningful results. One approach is simply to guarantee anonymity to respondents. In many cases, this promise will suffice; naturally, it relies on trust between the researcher and the respondent. Dillman (2000) illustrated an effective method that allows a researcher to know whether an individual has returned a mail questionnaire while maintaining anonymity. He has sent postcards to the potential respondents that they complete and return separately from the questionnaire itself.

Thus, the researcher knows if somebody has returned the questionnaire, but there is no way to identify which survey is associated with any single individual. The advantage to this approach is that it allows the surveyor to contact people who have not returned the postcards, reminding them to complete the survey.

Researchers have documented the fact that, in some cases, it does not make much of a difference whether people complete questionnaires anonymously or not. Clients at a substance abuse clinic responded to questions about their satisfaction and their motivation related to the treatment program. The clients generated the same patterns of response across three administrations of the same questionnaire; one administration was anonymous, whereas for the other two, the clients gave the survey directly to a therapist (Leonhard et al., 1997).

There are ways to maximize accurate response rates, however. For example, recent research by the U.S. government investigated the incidence of sexual behavior by young people. The methodology involved face-to-face surveys. To ensure the highest level of responses, the surveyor was always a middle-aged woman because research has shown that respondents feel most at ease answering sensitive questions when the surveyor is such a person (Chandra, Mosher, Copen, & Sionean, 2011; Shute, 2011).

Does Mode of Data Collection Affect Responses? Researchers used to be concerned that telephone interviews may not generate high-quality data. However, this issue has been put to rest because studies have shown that telephone surveys are highly effective when done properly. Johnson and colleagues (2000) found that when respondents think that an interviewer is different from them, they are less forthcoming in reporting drug use in a telephone survey. However, a respondent talking to somebody of the same relative age, gender, race, and educational level may be more likely to report sensitive behaviors than when the interviewer is seen as different.

In a comparison of telephone and other survey techniques, McAuliffe et al. (1998) reported that researchers can get very high-quality data with telephone surveys, even when the topic involves an issue like substance abuse. After studying the advantages and disadvantages of telephone compared to other survey types, they suggested that telephone surveys can be as useful as any other mode.

A more recent issue has focused on the quality of data collected via the Internet. Fortunately, researchers have found fairly regularly that computer-based data collection is as good as in-person data collection. For example, in research on sexual behavior and drug use, respondents are willing to give such information to researchers. Fortunately, the results on in-person surveys were comparable to those on the Internet (McMorris et al., 2009). In other research on such issues as birth control use, Internet surveys provided the same quality of data as traditional paper-and-pencil surveys (Uriell & Dudley, 2009).

Given the potential savings in cost and time of research with Internet-based research, this mode of data collection is likely to be increasingly attractive to psychologists.

Social Desirability

In an attempt to look good (or to avoid looking bad), people do not always tell the truth. Researchers have written extensively about this problem, referred to as **social desirability bias.** It can take two forms. One is **impression management,** which involves active deception by respondents to keep the researcher from forming a negative impression of them. A second component of social desirability bias is **self-deception positivity,** which occurs when people do not consciously give inappropriate responses but, rather, give a generally honest but overly positive self-report. Both types of response bias pose problems for the researcher, even though the bias occurs for different reasons.

One domain that has received considerable attention regarding social desirability bias is self-concept and its relation to sex differences. The stereotypical belief is that women are more likely to excel in verbal and artistic areas, whereas men are more proficient in math and physical domains. In some research, female and male students report such differences in expertise on questionnaires even when performance is comparable across groups. The gender differences in beliefs seemed to occur because of impression management, the intentional form of social desirability bias, suggesting that differences in self-concept across sexes may occur because of a desire to report conformity to the stereotype (Vispoel & Forte Fast, 2000).

Researchers have found socially desirable responses to be problematic in a number of different domains, including marketing (King & Bruner, 2000), self-concept (Vispoel & Forte Fast, 2000), sexual behavior (Meston et al., 1998), mathematics ability (Zettle & Houghton, 1998), attendance at religious service (Presser & Stinson, 1998), and personality reports (Francis & Jackson, 1998).

How can you deal with social desirability bias? Enlightening respondents about the existence of such response biases can help (Hong & Chiu, 1991). Another strategy is to create forced choice questions so that respondents must select from among a number of equally attractive or unattractive choices (Ray, 1990).

Another approach to reducing social desirability bias is to give both sides of an attitude in the question stem. This technique may keep the respondent from concluding that the surveyor is giving his or her own opinion in a question, leading the respondent to acquiesce. Table 11.6 gives an example of how to present both sides of an issue in the question.

Finally, some researchers (e.g., Krosnick, 1999) believe that social desirability may not occur to the extent that other researchers claim. For instance, when people complete surveys on voting behavior, the percentage of respondents who report voting in the most recent election exceeds the proportion of the population that actually did. Researchers have interpreted this discrepancy to reflect social desirability bias by participants.

Newer research, however, suggests two alternate interpretations. First, people who vote are more likely to respond to surveys than those who don't vote. So the discrepancy in percentages who say they voted and who actually did may reflect a bias in the survey sample, not social desirability bias. A second interpretation is that people with a habit of voting and who

Social desirability bias—The tendency of respondents to answer questions in ways that generate a positive impression of themselves.

Impression management—A form of social desirability bias in which respondents actively deceive a researcher in order to generate a positive impression of themselves in the researcher's eyes.

Self-deception positivity—A form of social desirability bias in which respondents provide generally honest, but overly optimistic, information about themselves that generates a positive impression of them.

TABLE 11.6 *Representing Both Sides of an Issue in a Potential Survey Question and How to Reduce the Likelihood of Response Bias to It*

Poor Item: **To what extent do you agree that the Statistics course should be eliminated as a required course for a Psychology major?**

___ Strongly agree
___ Somewhat agree
___ Somewhat disagree
___ Strongly disagree

Problem: Only one side of the issue (i.e., eliminating Statistics) is represented. A respondent might think that the interviewer is stating his or her own opinion and might consequently give an "agree" reply, acquiescing with the interviewer.

Better Item: **Do you think that the Statistics course should be eliminated as part of the Psychology major or do you think that the Statistics course should be kept as part of the Psychology major?**

___ Eliminate the Statistics course
___ Keep the Statistics course
___ No Opinion

Note: The "No Opinion" option should be at the end rather than between the other two options so that the respondent does not confuse it with a neutral response.

---

did not vote in the most recent election may think (erroneously), "I always vote, so I must have voted in the most recent election." This type of response indicates a memory problem, not a social desirability bias. As a result, the individual's other answers may be valid responses, not attempts to look good.

Acquiescence

When somebody asks you, "How are you?" your tendency is probably to respond that you are just fine, thanks. In general conversation, our tendency is to provide responses that are in line with others' expectations. As a rule, when people ask, "How are you?" they are really only extending a greeting. Most of the time, they don't expect (or even want) a litany of your woes.

A related dynamic can occur with surveys. Sometimes it is just easier to respond "yes" or to agree with a question. So that's what respondents may do, engaging in **acquiescence**, the tendency to agree with the assertion of a question, regardless of what it is. When the same question appears in two forms on a survey (e.g., "I enjoy socializing" and "I don't enjoy socializing"), respondents often agree with both, even though the people are directly contradicting themselves (Krosnick, 1999).

Krosnick (1999) described several explanations for people's tendency to acquiesce. One reason has to do with personality characteristics. Some people's personalities simply predispose them to want to agree with an assertion. Another explanation is that respondents often view surveyors as having higher status, so they feel compelled to agree with an assertion that the surveyor presents because we are "supposed to" agree with our superiors. Acquiescence can also be explained through the concept of satisficing, which we encounter below.

Acquiescence—In survey research, the tendency to agree with the assertion of a question, regardless of its content.

Satisficing Versus Optimizing

Optimizing—The tendency of respondents to search for the best response to a question.

In survey research, participants often spend time deciding on responses to a question. When they try to generate the best answers, they are engaging in **optimizing.** With memory questions, an attempt to optimize can involve trying to balance two conflicting concepts. Respondents want to provide good information, and they want to give the most precise answer they can. There is a trade-off here, however. Attempts at greater precision may actually be associated with less accuracy because people may start filling in details erroneously when trying to be too specific (Ackerman & Goldsmith, 2008). That is, people are working very hard and end up trying to provide details that are beyond what they can realistically give.

On the other hand, sometimes people are responding to a difficult question. They might spend a few moments trying to conjure up the answer and as soon as they identify a possibility, they go for that answer without considering other possibilities, a process called *satisficing,* which means that survey respondents choose the first answer that is acceptable to them, even if it isn't the best answer.

This tactic occurs regularly when people answer survey questions. Respondents don't have the same commitment to a project that the researchers do. So when respondents have to work hard to come up with a response, they often decide to reply with the first thing that sounds plausible to them or with an easy answer. Obviously, what works for the respondent can be a problem for the researcher.

According to Krosnick (1999), satisficing is likely to occur for any of three general reasons: (a) high task difficulty, (b) lower respondent ability, and (c) low respondent motivation. The mode of survey research is also relevant in the occurrence of satisficing. Research has shown that phone interviews lead to more satisficing, as well as less trust by a respondent, and a greater feeling that the survey is taking too long (even though it may be shorter than a similar face-to-face interview).

Why would a survey question pose difficulties? Understanding a question and responding to it is actually a complex process. First, respondents must work to understand the point of the question. Although this seems to be pretty straightforward, people answer the same question in various ways depending on what they think the researcher is looking for.

Second, respondents have to search through memory to find relevant information. We know that the context in which a question is asked affects a person's response. Regarding surveys, it may be hard for somebody to remember events being probed in the context of the research setting because those events are neither chronically nor temporarily accessible.

A third task required of a respondent for generating good answers to survey questions is organizing everything that has been recalled. For complex surveys, there may be a lot to keep track of. The need to keep track of information is difficult for any mode of administering a survey, but phone surveys may be problematic in this regard because of limitations of short-term memory. People may respond to the most recent alternatives because they remember them, and satisficing may also occur (Brewer et al., 2004).

Finally, in order to generate a high-quality response to a question, a person must choose from among the alternatives presented on a questionnaire. When people listen to an interviewer give a series of alternatives, there can be a tendency to select the later alternatives because they are easier to remember. When a questionnaire is on paper, there is a tendency for a respondent to pay more attention to the first alternatives (Krosnick, 1999).

If a person's cognitive processes fail at any step in this chain of events, a respondent will provide lower-quality information. Given the complexity of understanding a question and producing a response, it should be no surprise to learn that respondents engage in satisficing. They simply don't want to work any harder than they have to.

A related factor that leads to satisficing is the participant's level of ability. Researchers have discovered that respondents with lower ability levels tend to satisfice because they are unable to generate high-quality responses. So they go with the first reasonable reply that they encounter.

Further, after the participant has answered a few questions, the motivation to respond may decrease. You may have participated in a psychology experiment either as a requirement

Nondifferentiation—The tendency of respondents to give the same answer to questions, regardless of content.

Self-selected sample—In survey research, a non-random, biased sampling technique in which people choose to participate in the research rather than being selected by the investigator.

for a course or for extra credit. Many students in such situations are in a hurry to complete this activity, so they are often less motivated to spend time on a response or to think deeply about a question. Many people have the same experience, engaging in satisficing as a result.

Minimizing the Occurrence of Satisficing

There will probably always be tension between the desires of the respondent and the needs of the researcher. If you conduct survey research, you will want to encourage people to optimize. How can you do this?

One way to minimize the possibility of satisficing is to create survey questions that are easily understood. In addition, when you ask people to remember events, it may help to ask several related questions so the information is more accessible. People may generate more accurate responses when the surveyor encourages them to remember events related to or close in time to the critical event, rendering obscure memories temporarily accessible.

Another path to reducing the incidence of satisficing is for the researcher to consider using ranking a group of items rather than rating them individually because if a respondent has to rank different options, the person has to consider them all. Asking respondents to use a rating scale may lead them to identify a point on the scale and generally to respond with that value (e.g., giving a rating of 3 on a scale of 1 to 5) on virtually every item. This way of responding is called **nondifferentiation** because people fail to provide different responses across questions. Unfortunately, if there are many items to rank, the process may become tedious, so ranking can be a good strategy if there are not many options.

Some researchers have suggested that you can reduce the probability of acquiescence and satisficing by not giving respondents a "No Opinion" option (O'Muircheartaigh, Krosnick, & Helic, 2000). The logic is that if you want participants to think about their responses and give high-quality answers, you should not allow them to say "No Opinion." Other investigators have suggested just the opposite, that a "No Opinion" option does not lead to more valid data (Krosnick et al., 2002).

As you can see, it isn't clear whether it is a good idea to give people a choice to say they have no opinion or are neutral about an issue. Sometimes people really are neutral, but sometimes they take the "No Opinion" option as an opportunity not to think about an issue. The research against including the "No Opinion" option indicates that people may use that option inappropriately when they are low in cognitive skills and motivation (Krosnick et al., 2002); that is, they may be satisficing. The research favoring a "No Opinion" option might be more relevant regarding acquiescence than satisficing; people may not acquiesce any more just because they have a "No Opinion" option.

Finally, if you can keep your respondents motivated, such as by establishing a positive atmosphere and by making sure they know that their answers are important, you may be able to decrease satisficing.

Sampling Issues

Most psychological research involves students, groups of people who are easily available, which is why this approach involves what is called a convenience sample. However, there are drawbacks with this approach. If you are interested in claiming that your research results are typical of people, you have to make sure that the people you study are typical of people in general.

Popular surveys rely on **self-selected samples.** These are groups of people who volunteer to participate without having been contacted by the researchers. They may see a notice on the

Internet, for example, and decide it would be interesting to participate. Or they may be willing to call a 900 number, which costs them money, in order to express their opinion. Or they may respond to a talk show host. The types of people who engage in this responding are different from the population as a whole. In fact, professional researchers regard such polls as entirely nonscientific, therefore useless in telling us what the population thinks about a topic. Some investigators refer to such polls by the derogatory acronym SLOP (i.e., SeLf-selected Opinion Poll; Horvitz et al., 1995).

Finding Hidden Populations

Hidden population—Population of interest that is hard to study because the people in those groups are engaged in activities that may be embarrassing or illegal (e.g., drug users), so they do not want to be recognized as members of that population.

In survey research, some groups of people are difficult to study because they don't want to be found. For instance, people who engage in illegal or embarrassing activities are often reluctant to admit it publicly. Such groups are referred to as **hidden populations.** Two characteristics typify hidden populations: First, it is impossible to establish who constitutes the population and, second, there are strong privacy issues associated with the groups (Heckathorn, 1997).

If we want to find out about such groups, we can't use probability samples because probability samples require that we be able to identify the entire pool of possible respondents. So researchers have to make compromises in collecting data. Researchers studying hidden populations have turned to a class of techniques called **chain-referral methods.**

Chain-referral methods—A set of sampling techniques that relies on people who know about a population or are members of that population to gain access to information about the group.

One chain-referral method for contacting respondents involves **snowball sampling,** which relies on the fact that an individual from a hidden population is likely to know others from that group. The volunteer identifies a certain number of people that the researcher will contact; the researcher will then ask each of these second-stage individuals to provide the names of yet others. The process continues through as many stages as the researchers determine desirable.

Kaplan, Korf, and Sterk (1987) studied heroin use among addicts in the Netherlands. They identified a single user and asked for names of others who fit their target categories, either prostitutes or foreigners. These referrals then identified others, and so on. Kaplan et al. found it easier to find subsequent groups of prostitutes than foreigners, reflecting the fact that some populations are more hidden than others.

Snowball sampling—A chain-referral sampling technique in which one person from a population of interest identifies another person from that population to a researcher who contacts that second person, then that new individual refers yet another person, for as many stages as desired by the researcher.

Snowball samples often contain more cooperative volunteers who have a large social network and are not considered random samples. They are a variation on convenience samples, so it is not always clear to whom the researchers can generalize their findings.

A second approach to contacting respondents from hidden populations is to use **key informant sampling.** This technique relies on information from knowledgeable individuals rather than from members of the target population itself.

For example, a researcher might contact social workers to get information about patterns of sexual behavior in the population the social workers serves. Key informant sampling may reduce the respondent's reluctance to report unusual behaviors, but it may introduce the biases of that individual and is based on the limited number of people the social worker sees.

A third approach is **targeted sampling.** With this technique, researchers work in advance to identify their population as well as possible, then to find out the different places that attract the widest range of people from that population. The results will only be as good as the researcher's knowledge of where to find members of the target population.

Key informant sampling—A sampling technique that relies on getting information from people who know about a population of interest rather than from members of that population themselves.

Heckathorn (1997) has developed a new approach called **respondent-driven sampling.** In this approach, researchers use two types of incentives to attract participants. Primary incentives are offered to individuals; one such incentive may be money. The difference between this technique and other chain-referral methods involves the presence of a secondary reward for getting others to join. When a participant identifies a potential candidate for the research, that participant uses peer pressure and social approval to induce a new person to join the project.

Targeted sampling—A sampling technique that relies on finding locations that attract members of the population of interest and getting information from these people at such locations.

Respondent-driven sampling—A sampling technique in which a researcher uses a member of the population of interest to actively recruit others, often with some incentive like money for engaging in this recruiting.

That is, the researcher doesn't actively recruit the next person; that task is performed by the first participant.

The result is that people participate not only for material reward but also because of a personal relationship. According to Heckathorn, the fact that people volunteer because of their acquaintances rather than being sought out directly by a researcher is important. Some hidden populations are subject to legal prosecution, so it would be undesirable for members of the population to reveal the names of others. In respondent-driven sampling, people self-identify. This means that if they worry about admitting to engaging in illegal behavior, they do not need to come forth. Heckathorn has demonstrated that samples based on respondent-driven sampling seem to be diverse and unbiased.

The choice of which chain-referral methods to use depends on the practical issues involved in the particular study. If the population is very closed, respondent-driven samples may be necessary. On the other hand, if the population is only somewhat hidden, snowball sampling might be adequate. For example, Frank and Snijders (1994) were able to use snowball sampling in their study of heroin use in the Netherlands because heroin use is more open there.

Chapter Summary

Professional surveyors and pollsters have developed techniques that allow researchers to use small samples to make accurate predictions and descriptions of a larger population. As a result, the more economic practice of sampling typically means that researchers don't need a census.

The most common technique in scientific survey research is the telephone survey. For most questions, people who are available by phone adequately represent the entire population. Researchers who use probability sampling can generate a good picture of the population with a relatively small set of responses.

Researchers also have to painstakingly create survey questions that lead to valid responses. This is often the most difficult part of conducting good survey research. Whether you are asking for attitudes or for people to remember past behaviors, subtle differences in the way questions are worded and presented can make a notable difference in the responses that a person makes.

Sometimes different respondents interpret the same question in different ways. They may also show response biases that will either make them look better or make it easier for them to complete a questionnaire without really thinking about the issues at hand. Researchers must work hard to overcome these tendencies on the part of respondents.

Finally, some populations don't want to be found, like those involved in criminal activity or other undesirable or embarrassing behaviors. Investigators have developed techniques designed to make contact with these hidden populations. The samples may not be probability samples, but they often provide useful information.

Key Terms

Acquiescence	Closed-ended question	Nondifferentiation
Census	Hidden population	Open-ended question
Chain-referral methods	Impression management	Optimizing
Chronically accessible information	Key informant sampling	Population

Respondent-driven sampling
Response bias
Sampling frame
Satisficing

Self-deception positivity
Self-selected sample
Snowball sampling
Social desirability bias

Survey
Targeted sampling
Telescoping
Temporarily accessible information

Chapter Review Questions

Multiple Choice Questions

1. Psychologists typically do not use a census in their research because
   a. a census often leads to telescoping of responses.
   b. census responses often result in nondifferentiation.
   c. respondent-driven sampling leads to better generalization.
   d. a census is generally too costly.

2. Researchers have greatest confidence in being able to generalize the results of research based on
   a. sampling frames.
   b. surveys.
   c. probability samples.
   d. randomly selected questions.

3. On the United States census that everybody has to complete, people identify their racial/ethnic status by selecting from among options provided on the form. This type of a question is
   a. a closed-ended question.
   b. almost always responded to accurately.
   c. part of the sampling frame.
   d. used because respondents are from a self-selected sample.

4. Researchers may avoid open-ended items on questionnaires because such items
   a. are not very scientific.
   b. permit too limited a range of responses.
   c. can result in responses that are difficult to code and categorize.
   d. generally provide details about behaviors but not the context in which they occur.

5. One of the difficulties surveying people about rare events is that
   a. those events are likely to involve sensitive issues that people are reluctant to discuss.
   b. a small increase in the rate of false positives leads to a very large, inaccurate estimate when generalized to the population.
   c. people have very different attitudes about rare events, so accurate responses are hard to get.
   d. people are likely to show high levels of acquiescence about such items.

6. By the time a person is near the end of a questionnaire, the responses
   a. have probably shifted from optimizing to acquiescence.
   b. will no longer show telescoping.
   c. will be affected by how the respondent answered earlier questions.
   d. will show high levels of self-deception positivity.

7. When people are able to retrieve information from memory only after being primed by an earlier question on the topic, we say that the memory is
   a. targeted.
   b. nondifferentiated.
   c. temporarily accessible.
   d. respondent driven.

8. When respondents make up an attitude on the spot while answering a question,
   a. the researcher can find out by asking the respondent to answer the question again.
   b. the respondents respond more quickly when they have a pre-existing attitude.
   c. they usually claim to hold that attitude firmly and deeply.
   d. they may engage in impression management tactics.

9. Sometimes, respondents engage in active deception to keep the researcher from forming a negative image of the respondent. This behavior is called
   a. self-deception positivity.
   b. impression management.
   c. acquiescence.
   d. satisficing.

10. Research has revealed that we can reduce social desirability bias by
    a. telling respondents that we will be able to detect false responses on their part.
    b. avoiding forced choice responses and creating open-ended questions instead.
    c. educating respondents about social desirability bias.
    d. presenting only one side of an issue in a given question so respondents cannot focus on only the positive response.

11. When a person responds the same way to just about every item on a rating scale, this respondent is engaging in
    a. nondifferentiation.
    b. telescoping.
    c. acquiescence.
    d. satisficing.

12. It could be useful to know about illegal immigrants and how they live, but such people are reluctant to participate in anything they think might be associated with the government. These immigrants constitute a
    a. sampling frame.
    b. chronically inaccessible, self-selected sample.
    c. hidden population.
    d. nondifferentiated sample.

13. Researchers sometimes use a member of a hidden population to provide names of other members of that population to recruit participants in research. The resulting sample would involve
    a. chain-referral method.
    b. sampling frame.
    c. probability sample.
    d. self-selected sampling.

14. When researchers try to contact members of hidden populations by finding out where such people congregate, the sampling technique they are using is
    a. key informant sampling.
    b. snowball sampling.
    c. targeted sampling.
    d. probability sampling.

Essay Questions

15. Why do open-ended questions provide more information to survey researchers than closed-ended questions? What drawbacks are associated with open-ended questions?

16. Identify the seven major problems associated with survey questions about attitudes.

17. Why does the research on how many adolescents smoke reflect the difficulty in creating good survey research?

18. What two characteristics typify hidden populations?

CHAPTER 12

CORRELATION, REGRESSION, AND NON-PARAMETRIC TESTS

CHAPTER OUTLINE

CORRELATIONAL STUDIES

CORRELATIONAL ANALYSES
Traditional Correlation Tests
Pearson's r

REGRESSION
Multiple Regression

CHI-SQUARE GOODNESS OF FIT

CHI-SQUARE TEST OF INDEPENDENCE
Strength of Association

COMPUTER ANALYSIS USING SPSS
Correlation
Regression
Chi-Square

LEARNING OBJECTIVES

- Explain the purpose and appropriate use of correlation.
- Explain how to derive the correlation ratio.
- Explain the magnitude and direction of the correlation coefficient.
- Explain factors that affect the correlation.
- Define strength of association.
- Explain the purpose of regression.
- Distinguish the Chi-Square Goodness-of-Fit test from the Chi-Square Test of Independence.
- Describe the purpose of using the Chi-Square Goodness-of-Fit test.
- Describe the purpose of using the Chi-Square Test of Independence.
- Explain the distinction between parametric and non-parametric tests.

CHAPTER PREVIEW

In the previous chapter we offered an introduction to survey research. Quite often, data from surveys are analyzed using correlations or non-parametric techniques. We now consider how to analyze the information obtained from surveys using correlation, regression, and Chi-Square techniques.

Psychologists frequently use correlational approaches to investigate the relationships among variables when experimental approaches are not feasible. Correlational studies permit us to find relationships between variables. The simplest correlational technique involves a relationship

Bivariate correlation—
A correlational analysis relating to only two variables.

between two variables, or a **bivariate correlation.** Researchers typically employ the well-known Pearson product-moment correlation in such circumstances. We can also use the correlation coefficient to develop a regression equation that can be used to *predict* behavior. A regression or prediction equation is based on the mathematical relationship between variables, and it can aid in prediction of events. Survey data are often used to predict future outcomes or behavior.

Quite often when we conduct a survey, we are interested in examining whether our sample, or respondents, accurately reflects the population. In other words, we must ensure that demographic characteristics of our sample are similar to that of our population. For example, if we conduct a survey of Psi Chi members, we will want to be sure that our results are generalizable to the larger population of Psi Chi members. In order to generalize our survey results to the larger group of Psi Chi members, we will need to make sure that our sample is comparable to the full membership of Psi Chi. For example, we will need to compare the number of women in our sample to that of the population. We can use a non-parametric technique—Chi-Square (*Chi* sounds like *sky* with the *s* missing) *goodness-of-fit test*—to test this comparison.

In this chapter, we also introduce a second type of Chi-Square analysis, or the *test of independence,* is used when we wish to determine if two variables are independent. For instance, is there independence between the numbers of women versus the number of men majoring in psychology versus chemistry? In other words, is gender related to choice of major, or are these variables unrelated or independent? We can use a second type of Chi-Square, or a contingency test, to examine this relationship. In both cases, the test of independence and the contingency test, we use nominal, or categorical, data to conduct these analyses. In this chapter you will learn about the statistics that you can use to investigate relations between variables, discrepancies among variables, and independence of variables.

Correlational Studies

Psychologists, like most scientists, search for explanations. Although it can be an elusive goal, we want to know why people behave in a particular way. In some cases, we are not able to identify the variables that effect behavior directly, but we can find patterns and relationships that make behavior predictable. A correlation allows us to gauge the strength of connection between two things.

Sometimes we are interested in behaviors or variables that would be impractical or unethical to manipulate directly. Because we can not manipulate these conditions, we do the next best thing—we watch how things occur, or we ask people to report information in a survey, and we see if we can connect the information. It is important to note that relations between variables only reflect a mathematical relationship. Because we are not actively manipulating conditions, we cannot establish a definitive cause for the behavior, only that a behavior is predictable in some certain circumstances. For example, we might discover that there is a correlation between the number of drinking establishments and the number of churches in Atlanta, GA. Are these two things related? Yes. Is there a causal relationship? It is unlikely that attending church and drinking are related in any causal way. However, as we will learn, another variable might actually produce this correlation. In fact, we have found that as the population of a city increases, so does the number of bars and churches. The increase in population or third variable is actually the explanation for the correlation.

Correlational Analyses

Correlational analyses are not the same as correlational studies. A correlational analysis uses correlations as a statistical approach, but if the research design is experimental, we can draw causal conclusions. This is easy to grasp by considering a hypothetical two-group study. If we create two groups, randomly assign participants to the two groups, and apply a treatment to only one of the groups, we have a basic experiment. If the two groups differ at the end of the experiment, we assume the treatment made the difference.

The normal approach to data analysis with such a design is to compute a *t*-test, which lets us know if the groups differ reliably. However, we could legitimately compute a correlation coefficient. It would tell us almost exactly what the *t* test does. If you look at Figure 12.1, you will find that these tests are comparable.

It is important to remember that the research design, not the statistical test, determines the type of conclusion you can draw. If you employ a correlational study, doing a statistical test does not allow you to assess causation; similarly, if you use an experimental design, doing a correlational analysis does not keep you from drawing causal conclusions.

Traditional Correlation Tests

Linear relationship— A correlational value indicating that two variables either increase or decrease in a linear fashion.

The first correlation coefficients were invented about a century ago; we now call them bivariate correlations. They involved two (bi-) variables. Typically, when you read about correlations, they are likely to involve the Pearson product-moment correlation, also called the Pearson's *r*, or sometimes simply *r*. We use Pearson's correlation whenever our data are derived from an interval- or ratio-level scale. The Pearson *r* is useful for assessing the degree to which scores on two different variables have a linear relationship. We use the term **linear relationship** when the pattern of relations between two variables result in a pattern, that when plotted, result

FIGURE 12.1 *Comparability of Correlation and Experimental Analyses*

Suppose you have two groups with 10 participants in each. Let's label them simply Group 1 and Group 2.

| Group 1 | 6 | 8 | 7 | 5 | 6 | 9 | 7 | 4 | 8 | 9 |
| Group 2 | 5 | 6 | 3 | 7 | 2 | 3 | 1 | 5 | 4 | 5 |

If you compute a *t*-test for independent samples, you get: $t(18) = -3.55, p = .002$
You can rearrange the data, as follows, showing each score next to its appropriate group:

| Score | 6 | 8 | 7 | 5 | 6 | 9 | 7 | 4 | 8 | 9 | 5 | 6 | 3 | 7 | 2 | 3 | 1 | 5 | 4 | 5 |
| Group | 1 | 1 | 1 | 1 | 1 | 1 | 1 | 1 | 1 | 1 | 2 | 2 | 2 | 2 | 2 | 2 | 2 | 2 | 2 | 2 |

Now we can compute the familiar Pearson *r* on the two variables, Score and Group. (When one variable is ordinal, interval, or ratio, and the second variable is dichotomous (i.e., it can take one of two values), the Pearson *r* is called a point-biserial correlation.) When we do this, we get: $r(18) = -.642, p = .002$. The next step in a correlational analysis is to see if the correlation is significant, for which we use a *t*-test with the following formula:

$$t = \frac{r\sqrt{N-2}}{\sqrt{1-r^2}}$$

$$t = \frac{(-.642)(4.243)}{.767} = -3.55$$

If you notice, the value of *t* is the same as when you completed your *t*-test. In other words, the analyses from the correlational and experimental approaches provide the same information.

in a line. For example, there is a linear relation between frequency of parents spanking their children and children's antisocial behavior; more spanking is associated with higher rates of antisocial behavior (Straus, Sugarman, & Giles-Sims, 1997). Figure 12.2 illustrates the linear relationship between spanking and antisocial behavior.

Alternative bivariate correlations can be used when our data are not derived from interval or ratio scales. Since Karl Pearson invented the correlation coefficient, there have been important extensions to it. Other widely used bivariate correlations are the Spearman correlation for ranked data, the phi (Φ) coefficient for relating two dichotomous variables, or the point-biserial correlation for relating a dichotomous and continuous variable. These are alternative applications to Pearson's original correlation. You can compute these three statistics using the formula for Pearson's *r*. The main differences between Pearson's *r* and the alternate formulas are beyond our considerations (Howell, 2007). Although it is quite simple to derive each of these correlations using statistical software, we will now turn to an explanation of each of these statistical analyses.

Pearson's *r*

Does media violence promote violent behavior? Earlier we presented information that suggested there is a mathematical relationship, or correlation, between watching violence and engaging in violence. How did researchers derive this information?

Scharrer (2001) examined this relationship of media violence and self-reported acts of violence. Although she did not use a correlational analysis to come to this conclusion, we can develop our own operational definitions of variables to illustrate how we might use a correlation to investigate the relationship. Our first step in understanding how to calculate a correlation is to label the two variables involved in the study. Media violence, our hypothesized independent variable, is labeled as *X*. We might operationalize media violence as the number of hours of violent television a person views weekly. We might quantify the hypothesized dependent variable, labeled *Y*, as a score that comes from a hostility questionnaire.

FIGURE 12.2   *Correlation Between Behavior and Spanking*

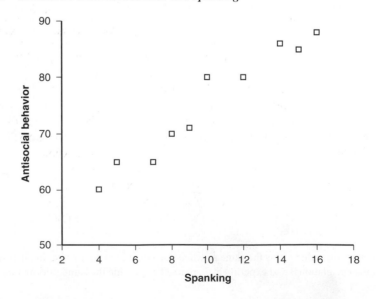

TABLE 12.1 *Example Data*

X	Y
10	80
12	80
15	85
4	60
7	65
9	71
8	70
16	88
14	86
5	65

In order to calculate the relationship between these two variables, we would need to obtain a measure of X (number of hours of violent television) and Y (questionnaire score) for each of the participants in our study. It is important to note that we obtain two measures from *each* individual. For example, in Table 12.1 we can see that the first person reported watching 10 hours of television shows classified as violent. The participant also completed a hostility questionnaire and obtained a value of 80 on the hostility scale.

Calculation of the Pearson r entails use of the fundamental element of variability or, in statistical terms, variance. As a reminder, variability is present in virtually any set of scores. Variance is a single value that allows for the statistical reporting of the amount of variability that is present in the set of scores. Earlier, when we calculated standard deviation, we were essentially examining variability of scores, yet we used standard deviation to communicate an index of variability in a way that is understandable or standard, across contexts. In other words, we used standard deviation to communicate a standard measure of variability regardless of whether we are talking about media violence, height, weight, or anger. When we calculate r, we are really using a ratio to compare the variance within each variable (i.e., variance)—to the variance with another variable (i.e., covariance).

$$r = \frac{covariance_{xy}}{(variance_x)(varaiance_y)}$$

In order to understand the correlation we will first review variance and standard deviation.

As you will recall, variance provides a statistical measure of the amount of variability among scores in a distribution or an index of variability around the mean. The first step in obtaining this measure of variability is to calculate how far each score is from the mean, or, said another way; obtain a set of deviation scores. Earlier, when we calculated variance, we began by calculating the S*um of the Squares* or $SS = \sum(X - M)^2$. In this case, we derive a deviation value for each score in the distribution. Recall that if we were to simply add the deviation scores, we would naturally obtain a value of 0 because each score is merely the calculated distance from the mean. Because adding these scores will not produce the desired measure of variability, we must square each deviation score, and then add the scores in order to obtain the variance (s^2) for a distribution. As we indicated earlier, the squaring effect must be removed in order to obtain a measure of the standard deviation (s or SD). Standard deviations, as measures of variance, are calculated for each of the variables—television (X) and hostility (Y). We will use the standard deviations for both variables in our calculation of correlation.

A correlation is simply a ratio. One general formula for correlation (r) is:

$$r = \frac{s_{xy}}{s_x s_y}$$

We already know how to calculate the standard deviations contained in this formula. In the denominator, the *standard deviation* ($s_x = 4.16$) for the number of hours of television watched (X) is multiplied by the *standard deviation* ($s_y = 10.03$) for the distribution of hostility scores (Y). This denominator (standard deviations for television and hostility) contains the individual variability of each of the variables independently.

We need only learn one new concept in order to obtain a correlation. *Covariance* (s_{xy}) is the index of shared variability between scores. In other words, covariance is how the scores change together. Remember, variability is derived by calculating how far each score, in the distribution, is located from the mean. Therefore, we first need to calculate the deviation score for each value in our distribution. We can then calculate the covariance, or numerator, for our equation above.

The respective deviation scores appear in columns two and four of Table 12.2. Our first step toward calculation of a covariance is to use these deviation scores to calculate the *sum of the cross products*. The sum of the cross products formula is

$$SP = \sum (X - M_X)(Y - M_Y)$$

As illustrated, we simply multiply each deviation score for number of hours of television ($X - M_X$) by each deviation score for hostility ($Y - M_Y$). These scores are then summed to yield the *SP*.

We complete our calculation of covariance much as we did for variance. We divide the sum of the cross products (SP) by $N - 1$. Thus, the covariance formula is:

$$s_{xy} = \frac{\sum (X - M_X)(Y - M_Y)}{N - 1} \quad \textbf{OR} \quad s_{xy} = \frac{SP}{N - 1}$$

Using values from the Table 12.2:

$$s_{xy} = \frac{SP}{N - 1} = \frac{366}{9} = 40.67$$

TABLE 12.2 *Sum of Cross Products (SP)*

X	$(X - M_X)$	Y	$(Y - M_Y)$	$(X - M_X)(Y - M_Y)$
10	0	80	5	0
12	2	80	5	10
15	5	85	10	50
4	−6	60	−15	90
7	−3	65	−10	30
9	−1	71	−4	4
8	−2	70	−5	10
16	6	88	13	78
14	4	86	11	44
5	−5	65	−10	50
$\sum X = 100$		$\sum Y = 750$		$SP = 366$
$M_X = 10$		$M_Y = 75$		

Our final step in calculating the correlation coefficient is illustrated below.

$$r = \frac{s_{xy}}{s_x s_y} = \frac{40.67}{(4.16)(10.03)} = \frac{40.67}{41.72} = .97$$

Using this set of formulas can be cumbersome. Although we could calculate the standard deviations for each variable along with the sum of the cross products as illustrated above, a simpler computational formula is usually applied if a correlation is manually calculated. We can also compute the correlation using the following raw score formula:

$$r = \frac{N \sum XY - (\sum X)(\sum Y)}{\sqrt{[N \sum X^2 - (\sum X)^2][N \sum Y^2 - (\sum Y)^2]}}$$

We don't often perform manual calculations of the correlation coefficient. Yet, it is important to understand the elements that comprise a correlation coefficient. A correlation coefficient is a succinct way to communicate information about the relatedness of data. Simply stated, we use a ratio to compare individual variability of scores to variability that is shared among two variables. In other words, a correlation coefficient provides an index of relationship between two variables.

Factors Affecting the Size of Correlations. Although we can calculate a correlation coefficient to determine if two variables are related, we can sometimes derive the wrong conclusions from our analyses. Occasionally, we erroneously conclude that there is not a relationship between variables, when, in fact, a relationship does exist. An error can occur for several reasons. First, we might underestimate the relationship between two variables because we obtain one or two very unusual cases. For example, it is possible to obtain a case in which someone watched very little television, yet expressed high levels of hostility. This unusual case is classified as an **outlier** and is illustrated in Figure 12.3.

Outlier—A value that is highly disparate from the larger data set.

FIGURE 12.3 *Outlier*

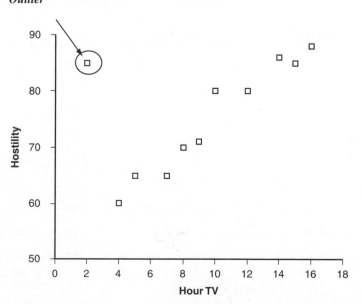

In addition to the possibility of having an outlier artificially reduce the size of our correlation, we can experience a second problem. Despite our best efforts to obtain a representative sample of the population, it is always possible that we might obtain an unusual group of participants. Even though there may be a legitimate relationship between the two variables, we may compute a lower correlation because we don't have access to the entire population.

For example, if you plotted the association between GRE scores and grades for an entire group of graduate students, you may not find a linear relationship. You might also be tempted to conclude that GRE scores are not related to success in graduate school. Figure 12.4(a) illustrates the erroneous absence of correlation. However, if we examine Figure 12.4(b), it is clear that a strong positive correlation is present between GRE scores and GPA in graduate school. Why is this contradiction present? In the first case, we see only a subset of the students who took the GRE. In other words, we do not detect a correlation because we are restricting the range of people in our sample. In this case, the data reflect only those students actually admitted to graduate school. If we were to examine the entire range of people taking the GRE test, we might discover that many of the people taking the GRE did not go to graduate school and therefore do not have a reported graduate school GPA. This example should clearly illustrate how a **restriction of range** can lead to an erroneous conclusion.

Important Attributes of Correlations. We have described the process for obtaining the Pearson correlation coefficient. As an index of relatedness, the correlation provides us with a rich set of information. Before we consider the utility of the correlation, we want to emphasize that a correlation is *only* a mathematical index of relationship. A correlation *does not* allow us to establish causes for these relationships.

Size of Correlation When interpreting a correlation, we must consider the size, direction, and significance of the correlation. A correlation coefficient ranges in value from 0 to 1.00. How would you go about assessing life satisfaction? If we consider Lang and Heckhausen's (2001) approach, they simply asked their participants three questions:

Restriction of range— Analysis using a limited range of data.

- How satisfied are you with your current life?
- How satisfied are you with the meaning and purpose in your current life?
- How do you evaluate your life in general?

FIGURE 12.4 *Scatterplots*

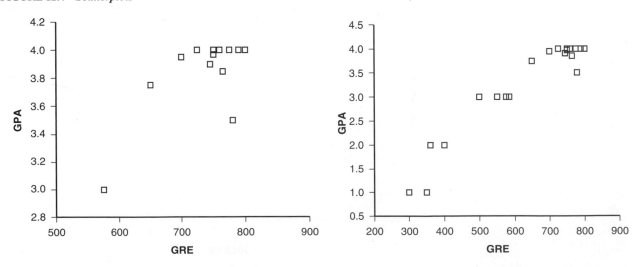

The participants answered each of these questions on a Likert scale that ranged from 1 (*very unpleasant*) to 7 (*very pleasant*). Respondents with high scores had more positive feelings about their lives than people with low scores. As noted below, the small, and in this case, nonsignificant correlation implies that knowing somebody's age would not lead to accurate estimates of life satisfaction, nor would knowing the degree of life satisfaction, give you any information about the person's age. Remember a correlation is simply an index of relationship.

High values, for example .90, suggest a strong relationship between the two variables. What happens if we see a very similar high correlation (−.90), except that the value is negative? Is the correlation equally strong? The answer, of course, is yes. We will now turn to a discussion of directionality of the relationship.

Direction of Relationship   Correlations can be either positive or negative. Perfect positive correlations have a value of +1.00; perfect negative correlations have a value of −1.00. Sometimes correlations are so close to zero (e.g., .08) that we conclude that the two variables have little or no bearing on one another. For instance, Lang and Heckhausen (2001) discovered that life satisfaction and age are not correlated. The value of their correlation coefficient was .05. This value is so close to zero that, among their participants who ranged in age from 20 to around 70, age did not help to predict how satisfied they are with their lives. In another analysis by Lang and Heckhausen, perceived control over life is positively correlated with life satisfaction. This means that, in general, the more control people have felt in their lives, the more satisfied they were. We can plot this positive relationship using a graphing procedure called a scatterplot. In this example, when we see a high score on the X axis (control over life), we can anticipate a similarly high score on the Y axis (happiness). An example of this **positive correlation** is illustrated in Figure 12.5. You will notice that each case is represented within the graph. Each dot is the intersection of the score on the control scale with the score on the happiness scale.

A **negative correlation** arises when the value of one of the two variables being correlated gets larger, while the value of the other variable gets smaller. Lang and Heckhausen observed a negative correlation between the number of negative events in people's lives

Positive correlation— A mathematical relationship that reflects an increase in two variables.

Negative correlation—A mathematical relationship that indicates that an increase in one variable is associated with a decrease in the second variable.

FIGURE 12.5   *Strong Positive Correlation (r = .97)*

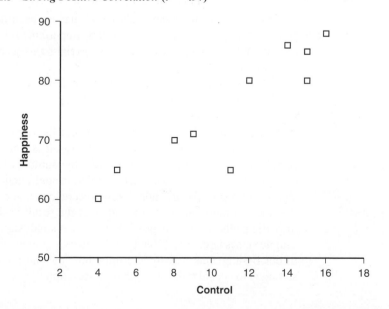

FIGURE 12.6 *Strong Negative Correlation ($r = -.90$)*

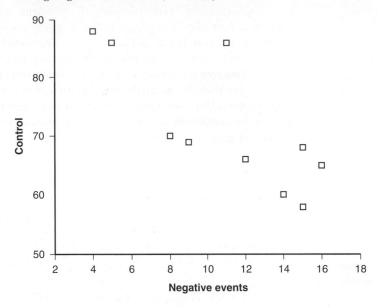

(e.g., having a small accident) and their perception of control. When people experience many negative events, they are likely to feel lower levels of control. This negative correlation can also be illustrated with a scatterplot. You will notice in Figure 12.6 that as the number of negative events in a person's life increase, the level of perceived control decreases.

Correlations can be either positive or negative. We began this section with a discussion of a very strong positive correlation ($r = .97$). It should now be clear that whether the correlation is positive or negative, the correlation is very strong. The strength of the correlation is reflected in both scatterplots. The correlations depicted in Figures 12.5 and 12.6 are both very strong, and the strength of the correlation is illustrated by the close proximity of the data points.

Significance   In our examples above we suggest that large correlations are important. Is it also possible that a small correlation could be important? It is possible for a small correlation to be important, but it is also possible for a correlation to be statistically significant, yet practically unimportant.

When we calculate a correlation, we derive an index of relationship. As with any statistical technique, it is possible to obtain a spurious value that may not accurately reflect the degree of relatedness between two variables. Statistical significance testing is designed to help us determine if our calculated statistic is likely to occur. If we calculate a highly unusual result, we are likely to conclude that the result is statistically significant. In the case of the correlation coefficient, we must consider the number of people in our study, the desired level of significance, and the calculated correlation coefficient to determine if we have a statistically significant result. We are more likely to conclude that a correlation is significant if it is large. We are also more likely to conclude that the result is significant if we have a larger sample of participants. Thus, it is possible to have a small significant correlation (e.g., .1638) if the sample size is large (see Table E.5). Of more importance is the practical or applied significance of our finding. One way to determine how meaningful our correlation may be in an applied setting is to consider the strength of association.

Strength of Association   A strong correlation merely provides us with a magnitude of relationship. Although scientists have a common language that allows us to recognize the size of a correlation, it is often helpful to have a more common way to communicate the results of our studies to people who may not be scientists. One way to communicate our results is to use a common metric that is familiar to scientists and non-scientists alike. We can use a percentage to communicate the strength of connectedness or association between two variables.

The **coefficient of determination** (r^2) is simply the squared correlation coefficient. Reporting the coefficient of determination is valuable for two reasons. First, this value represents the percentage of explained variance between two variables, and this is easily understood by most people. Second, the coefficient of determination is also a very important statistical value, or one measure of *effect size*. The *Publication Manual of the American Psychological Association* (2010) guidelines now suggest that every study should report effect sizes, or the magnitude of an effect. The coefficient of determination is just one measure of effect size and it is most appropriate when using a correlational technique.

If we return to our first example in which we found a strong correlation between the number of hours of television viewing (X) and feelings of hostility (Y), we discovered a strong correlation between these two variables ($r = .97$). A calculation of the coefficient of determination suggests that the large percentage ($r^2 = .94$) of variance in feelings of hostility is accounted by number of hours of television viewing. To correctly report the results of any study, refer to the *Publication Manual of the American Psychological Association* (2010). The authors suggest that you should include enough information to fully inform people who are reading your study. The following narrative reflects the results of our example.

> We found a statistically significant correlation between the number of hours of television viewed and feelings of hostility, $r = .97, p < .001$. The measure of effect size ($r^2 = .94$) indicates that 94% of the variability feelings of hostility can be explained by number of hours of television viewed.

In addition to presenting data in this format, we frequently see an entire correlation matrix reported in many studies. In either case, you should present your results in the most accessible and accurate way possible.

Regression

Coefficient of determination—Percent of variance explained by relationship between two variables.

Earlier we suggested that a correlation could be used to predict behavior. A regression equation is the formula that allows us to predict behavior on the basis of information from another variable. In our example of media violence and feelings of hostility, we can use a regression formula to predict feelings of hostility on the basis of number of hours of television watched.

The simplest form of regression includes only two variables (X and Y). To derive a regression equation, we must first establish a relationship between two variables. It is the correlation that serves as our basis for prediction. As illustrated earlier, a scatterplot allows us to use two scores to locate a person within a quadrant. If we obtain a correlation, we will discover that the data form a linear pattern as illustrated in Figure 12.7. It is relatively easy to plot a line amid this pattern of data, and this line is called the **line of best fit.** We then use this line of best fit to predict scores in the future. Quite simply, the line of best fit is the mathematical formula for a line, or the formula for predicting Y from X.

Line of best fit—This line is plotted to reflect the best prediction of a variable.

$$Y = a + (b)(X)$$

FIGURE 12.7   *Line of Best Fit*

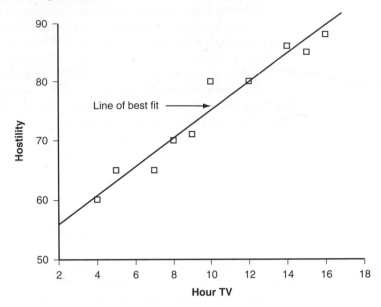

If you remember your basic algebra class, you may recall the formula for a straight line. Because we are creating this linear formula in the context of a quadrant, we must establish the point at which the line crosses the Y axis, the y-intercept, or (a). Beta (b) is the predicted change in Y that will occur as a function of X. This simple formula lets you plot a straight line on a graph such that for every increase of 1 unit on X, you get a particular increase on the Y variable. So, if $b = 2$, every increase in X leads to an increase of 2 on Y.

Returning to our example using TV and scores on a hostility questionnaire, we discovered a strong positive correlation ($r = .97$). We can use these data to create a regression equation that can be used to predict scores on a measure of hostility (Y). We will only need to calculate two new values for our regression equation, a (the y-intercept) and b (beta).

We must first calculate b in order to derive our regression equation. Beta is the mathematical equivalent to *slope* or the steepness of the line. In other words, for every change in X, you can expect a fixed amount of change in Y. Calculation of b is relatively straightforward:

$$b = \frac{SP}{SS_x}$$

If we refer to our earlier data, we can use the sum of the cross products that we calculated for the correlation. Sum of the Squares for X is also available from our earlier calculations.

$$b = \frac{SP}{SS_x} \qquad b = \frac{366}{156} = 2.35$$

Our resulting b (beta) indicates that for every additional hour of television viewed, we can expect a 2.35 point increase in scores on our measure of hostility.

Calculation of the y-intercept is also quite simple:

$$a = M_Y - (b)(M_X)$$
$$a = 75 - (2.35)(10) = 51.5$$

We use the means for X and Y, along with the b, to derive the point at which the line of best fit crosses the Y axis. As illustrated in Figure 12.7, the line of best fit crosses the Y axis at 51.5. We can use this equation to calculate any number of predictions for hostility scores on the basis of the number of hours of television viewed.

$$Y = 51.5 + (2.35)(X)$$

For example, if we want to predict the hostility score for someone who watches 7 hours of television, we simply insert $X = 7$ into our equation. Using our regression equation, we predict a hostility score of $Y = 67.95$.

$$67.95 = 51.5 + (2.35)(7)$$

Multiple Regression

A regression formula is very useful for predicting behaviors, future performance in a variety of areas, and even how long we will live. It is also possible to use a slightly more complex regression formula in which we include additional predictor variables. In *multiple regression,* you can predict a Y score using several criteria. You can compute multiple regression by hand, but it will take a while and won't be much fun. Fortunately, most statistical packages will do it for you. For example, the equation for two predictor variables would be as follows:

$$Y = a + b_1X_1 + b_2X_2$$

which tells you that the Y score you are trying to predict, the criterion variable, will be a function of the score on the first predictor variable, X_1, and the slope associated with it, b_1, plus the score on the second predictor variable, X_2, times the slope for the second predictor variable b_2. The formula may look intimidating, but the logic is the same as for the simple, one-variable equation: given the value of your X variables, you can generate a prediction of Y.

As an example of how psychologists use multiple regression, let's consider the psychological construct of resilience. Resilience is generally considered to be the presence of effective function in adverse situations. Todd and Worell (2000) used multiple regression to identify the conditions associated with psychological resilience in low-income, African American women.

There is a demonstrable association between poverty and mental health. Poorer people are more likely to be beset by psychological and adjustment problems. Nonetheless, many poor people show resilience, demonstrating effective functioning in stressful circumstances. What differentiates these people from those who aren't resilient?

Todd and Worell speculated that a number of different factors could be important. The factors appear in Table 12.3 and include whether people have a social support system in place, whether there are problematic people in their lives, and so on. In advance, it wasn't clear which of them might be reliably associated with resilience, so the investigators examined them all. They determined a Total Resilience score by summing the scores on four subscales of the *Scales of Psychological Well-Being* (Ryff, 1989). They also interviewed the participants in order to rate them on the possible predictor variables.

As you can see in the table, all of their factors seem logical. Most people would probably say that your ability to cope with adversity is going to be related to the amount of support you have, the different types of support available, the number and type of problems, and so on. The reason for conducting this research was to find out if the variables really are associated with resilience.

Using multiple regression, Todd and Worell found that the Number of Problematic Others (NPO) and the degree to which the women socially compared (SC) themselves to others who were worse off predicted resilience.

TABLE 12.3 *Predictor and Criterion Variables Used to Study African American Women and the Way the Variables Were Defined by the Researchers*

Predictor Variables	Definition
Number of Social Supports	The number of different supportive functions performed by others
Number of Social Problems	The number of different types of problems caused by others
Number of Supporting Others	The number of people available to provide support, excluding participants' children
Number of Problematic Others	The number of different people who cause problems
Frequency of Downward Social Comparisons	The degree to which the participants compared themselves to those who were either better off or worse off (on a 5-point scale of "not at all" to "most of the time")
Consequences of Downward Social Comparisons	How well the participants said they fared in social comparisons of others (on a 5-point scale of "much worse" to "much better")
General Self-Efficacy	Score on the 17-item Self-Efficacy Scale (Sherer et al., 1982)
Criterion Variable	
Total Resilience	Total of Self-Acceptance, Autonomy, Purpose in Life, and Personal Growth subscales of the *Scales of Psychological Well-Being* (Ryff, 1989)

Surprisingly, these two variables predicted resilience better than the amount of social support a person has. This is not to say that social support is irrelevant to coping; what the results suggested is that the best predictors were how many people in the participants' lives were troublesome (most frequently friends and their children's father) and the degree to which they thought they were better off than others. These two variables accounted for almost half of the variance in resilience.

This means that, even though differences in the ability to "bounce back" could be associated with countless factors, half of the differences among participants' psychological resilience was predictable from two variables. By knowing their scores on these two variables, you can get a pretty good idea of how well people cope with the adversity in their lives.

The two most important predictor variables fit in the regression equation as shown below. In much research, the investigators often do not worry about the y-intercept because they are typically more interested in generating the best values for the slopes and then seeing how much variability the variables account for. The standardized regression equation with the variables of Number of Problematic Others (NPO) and Consequences of Downward Social Comparison (SC) was:

$$\text{Resilience}(Y) = (-.30)(\text{NPO}) + (.35)(\text{SC})$$

This equation tells you that as the number of problematic friends increases, resilience is going to go down; the negative correlation ($-.30$) tells you this. At the same time, if they compare themselves more favorably to others (and the rating on the 5-point scale goes up), so does their resilience; the positive correlation (.35) tells you this. So this equation tells you that the participants who were most resilient had fewer troublesome acquaintances and relatives and felt that they were better off than others.

Multiple regression has some important constraints. Specifically, it is unsuitable for long-term, multiple repeated observations. In addition, it can only take a single dependent variable. A third limitation is that we can use it only when we have actually measured a given variable. If we group several related variables together to create a new, combined variable, we can't use multiple regression.

Keep in mind that these approaches are correlational. Using the resilience research as an example, convincing people that others are worse off may not cause the greater resilience. Higher levels of resilience may be the cause of favorable downward comparison, not the effect. We are simply looking at successful predictions here.

Chi-Square Goodness of Fit

Whenever we conduct research, whether we use a survey or an experimental study, it is important to examine the demographic characteristics of our sample. In order for the results of our study to be meaningful, we want to ensure that the sample is similar to the population (generalizable), or group to whom we want to apply or generalize the results. We should collect basic demographics (i.e., gender, age, race), and in some instances, we collect additional relevant data (e.g., year in school). These data allow us to describe the people participating in our study.

Collecting basic demographic information is only the first step in determining whether our results are generalizable. We need to compare the demographics of our sample to the overall population. For example, if our population contains 60% women and 40% men, then we want to obtain similar proportions in our sample. Fortunately, the **Chi-Square Goodness-of-Fit** test allows us to compare the proportionality of our sample to the population. In other words, we can compare the gender distribution in our sample (observed) to that of the larger population (expected) to determine if our sample is comparable to the population.

We frequently use the *Chi-Square Goodness-of-Fit* test to compare the sample to the population. However, there is a second Chi-Square test. Pearson's Chi-Square statistic refers to both the *Goodness-of-Fit* test and the *Test of Independence*. Both of these tests are **non-parametric** analyses. What is a non-parametric test? A non-parametric statistic is used when data are derived from a specific Chi-Square distribution (Kirk, 1999). We also use non-parametric techniques whenever we do not have data that is on an interval or ratio scale of measurement. If we wish to compare how proportions of men and women in our sample compare to the actual proportion in our population, our data are *nominal,* and we use the Pearson's *Chi-Square Goodness-of-Fit* to test this comparison.

Let us consider gender as a demographic variable in our study of television viewing and levels of hostility. If you begin with the assumption that the population is equally distributed with 50% men and 50% women, you can compare your sample, in terms of gender, to the larger population. In our previous example (Table 12.1) we obtained data from a sample of 10 people. If you assume that you have an equal number of men in women in the population, five men and five women should be contained in the sample. These expected values are derived by calculating the percentage for the anticipated proportion. In this example, you simply multiply the percentage (50%) by the number of people in our sample to obtain the expected frequency (f_e).

Chi-Square Goodness-of-Fit test—Non-parametric statistic using nominal data to compare proportions.

$$f_e = (N)(\text{Expected Proportion}) \qquad f_e = (10)(.50) = 5$$

The expected frequencies are compared to the actual or observed number of men and women obtained in your sample. What if we obtained a sample with three men and seven women? Would our observed proportions be similar to the expected proportions? To test this comparison we use the *Chi-Square Goodness-of-Fit* test.

Non-parametric test—A statistical method used when data are nominal or ordinal, or when the data are not normally distributed.

$$\chi^2 = \sum \frac{(f_o - f_e)^2}{f_e}$$

We can use our calculated expected frequencies ($f_e = 5$) and compare them to the actual number of men and women (observed) in our study.

$$\chi^2 = \sum \frac{(f_o - f_e)^2}{f_e} = \frac{(3-5)^2}{5} + \frac{(7-5)^2}{5} = \frac{4}{5} + \frac{4}{5} = 1.6$$

Chi-Square statistics involve squaring the numerator and therefore will always result in a positive value. We must now compare our calculated value to the Chi-Square distribution of values in order to determine if our proportion of men and women are significantly different from our larger distribution. Before we refer to the distribution located in Table E.6, we need additional information. First, we need to calculate degrees of freedom (*df*). Degrees of freedom are calculated for all inferential statistical tests. A more thorough explanation of degrees of freedom was offered in Chapter 7. For our purposes of comparing proportions, degrees of freedom are calculated by subtracting one from the number of categories. In our example, we are using two categories (i.e., men and women), therefore

$$df = C - 1 = 2 - 1 = 1$$

Where C = number of categories

We also need to specify an alpha level in order to use Table E.6. A conventional, or common level is alpha = .05. We can now compare our calculated $\chi^2 = 1.6$ to the value in the Chi-Square distribution table. The critical value, located in Table E.6 using $df = 1$ and $\alpha = .05$, is $\chi^2 = 3.84$. If we compare this tabled or critical value to our calculated value, $\chi^2 = 1.6$, we find that our calculated value is smaller. Because our value is smaller, we can conclude that our sample is not significantly different from our larger population.

In our previous example, we assumed that men and women were equally distributed in the population, and this served as our premise for calculating expected frequencies. What if we want to examine frequencies when proportions are not equal? For instance, U.S. census data indicate that in the U.S. population, race is not equally proportioned. If we classify people into three broad categories, we find the following distribution (Table 12.4).

We can compare our data to the U.S. Census data using the proportions above. For example, suppose we conduct a survey of voters in order to ascertain their political views. It will be important to obtain a sample that mirrors the larger population of Americans. Therefore, we will want to compare the number of people in each category of race in our sample to that of the U.S. Census. You might be wondering how we can do this if we don't have expected frequencies. Remember, we can calculate expected frequencies from percentages. If we ask 100 voters to participate in our survey, we can calculate the expected number of people who should be into each category,

$$f_e = (N)(\text{Expected Proportion})$$
$$f_e = (100)(.75) = 75$$

TABLE 12.4   *Percentages for Variable Race*

White	*African American*	*Other*
75%	12%	13%

TABLE 12.5 *Expected Frequencies for Variable Race*

White	African American	Other
60	20	20

$$f_e = (100)(.12) = 12$$
$$f_e = (100)(.13) = 13$$

Now, suppose we obtained the following data (Table 12.5).

Our sample data are not exactly the same as the data that would be expected based on the U.S. Census. Are our data significantly different from the population? In order to determine if our sample mirrors that of our population, we conduct the Chi-Square Goodness-of-Fit test.

$$\chi^2 = \sum \frac{(f_o - f_e)^2}{f_e} = \frac{(60 - 75)^2}{75} + \frac{(20 - 12)^2}{12} - \frac{(20 - 13)^2}{13}$$
$$= \frac{225}{75} + \frac{64}{12} + \frac{49}{13}$$
$$= 3 + 5.33 + 3.77$$
$$= 12.1$$

We must now compare our calculated $\chi^2 = 12.1$ to the tabled Chi-Square value in order to determine if our sample is significantly different from our population. Referring to Table E.6, we use $df = 2$ and $\alpha = .05$ and we find that the value listed in the table is $\chi^2 = 5.991$. Hence, our calculated value is larger. If our calculated value is larger, as is the case in our example, we find that our sample is not representative of the population.

Writing Results

Results of our analysis may read as follows:

Our sample of participants included 100 people who agreed to respond to our survey about political opinions. Sixty of our participants were white, 20 reported being African American, and 20 indicated a race of "Other." We compared our sample to data from the U.S. Census to determine if our sample adequately represented the larger U.S. population. Unfortunately, we found that our distribution of race was not comparable to that of the population, $\chi^2(2, N = 100) = 12.1, p < .01$.

This example uses the Goodness-of-Fit test to compare the proportions of race in a sample (observed) to the proportions in the population (expected). We can also use the Goodness-of-Fit test whenever we wish to compare proportions in categories on a single variable. For example, we can test whether recidivism rates differ with respect to religious preference. In this case, we compare the number of people from each religious affiliation who return to prison. Although we can test the hypothesis that recidivism rates differ by religious affiliation, we cannot establish a cause-and-effect relationship on the basis of a statistic. Instead, we must examine the design of the study.

Chi-Square Test of Independence

At the beginning of this chapter, we introduced two types of Chi-Square analyses—the Goodness-of-Fit test and the Test of Independence. Both tests are non-parametric and both use nominal (categorical) data. We use the Chi-Square *Goodness-of-Fit* test when we want to examine the proportions of one variable. The **Chi-Square Test of Independence** is used when we want to determine if two (or more) variables are independent. These tests are similar in that we test whether we can make accurate predictions about the number of observed events relative to expected events. The Test of Independence is used when we have two (or more) categorical variables from which we make predictions.

Let's examine how we can use the Chi-Square Test of Independence to make predictions. Jenni and Jenni (1976) observed college students carrying their books on campus and noted students differed in how they held them. They decided to investigate whether book carrying was associated with gender. One category of carrying books was across the front of the body with one or both arms wrapped around the books; a second category was for the books to be held more toward the side, pinched from above or supported from below by the hand and/or arm. The two categorical, or nominal variables in this study were book carrying and gender.

Jenni and Jenni conducted their observational research by recording data from several hundred college students. If you conducted this study with a smaller number of students, you might obtain data that is similar to our fictitious data below. Because the data in this study were nominal (i.e., categorical frequency data) we will use the *Chi-Square Test of Independence* to determine if gender (one variable) and method of carrying textbooks (second variable) are related. Data in Table 12.6 reflect the observations that might have been made if we repeated the study today. This particular table is known as a contingency table, and it is used anytime we classify two or more variables. In the first cell, three males were observed carrying books in the front position.

Calculation of the Chi-Square Test of Independence is similar to the Chi-Square Goodness-of-Fit test, in that we are using nominal data in both cases. The Test of Independence differs from the goodness-of-fit test because we use two variables, and we investigate whether a relationship exists between those two variables. Nevertheless, the formula for both of these analyses is the same:

$$\chi^2 = \sum \frac{(f_o - f_e)^2}{f_e}$$

Although the formula is identical to that of the Goodness-of-Fit test, calculation of expected frequencies is slightly more complex. You will notice that in Table 12.6 we have row and column totals. We use these totals in our calculations of expected frequencies. We calculate expected frequencies by multiplying the respective row total by the column total for each cell and then dividing that value by the total number of people in the entire study. We must

Chi-Square Test of Independence—A non-parametric test used to compare proportions across two variables.

TABLE 12.6   *Observed Frequencies*

	Front	*Side*	*Column Total*
Men	3	23	26
Women	21	5	26
Row Total	24	28	52

calculate expected frequencies for each of the cells. A simple formula for calculating expected frequencies is:

$$f_e = \frac{(Row_{total})(Column_{total})}{N}$$

We can use this formula to calculate each of the four expected frequencies. *A note of caution:* You should avoid computing the Chi-Square analysis when a large percentage of your *expected* values are smaller than five (Siegel & Castellan, 1988). We can occasionally violate this requirement as long as the number of such expectations is fewer than 20% of the total number of cells (Howell, 2007). In this case, we would not want to compute the Chi-Square if we calculate an expected frequency that is less than five for more than one cell. Expected frequencies for each of the cells are:

$$\text{Men carrying books in front } f_e = \frac{(24)(26)}{52} = \frac{624}{52} = 12$$

$$\text{Men carrying books on side } f_e = \frac{(28)(26)}{52} = \frac{728}{52} = 14$$

$$\text{Women carrying books in front } f_e = \frac{(24)(26)}{52} = \frac{624}{52} = 12$$

$$\text{Women carrying books on side } f_e = \frac{(28)(26)}{52} = \frac{728}{52} = 14$$

Notice, we do not have any expected frequencies fewer than five (i.e., 12, 14, 12, 14), so we have not violated the prerequisite for using the Chi-Square. We can place our expected frequencies, as noted in parentheses, in the contingency table to aid in our calculation of the Chi-Square. We use data collected from our sample to generate expected frequencies. Our expected frequencies reflect the number of observations we would anticipate, or expect, in each cell if the two variables were not related (Table 12.7).

We can complete the calculation of the Chi-Square using our original formula:

$$\chi^2 = \sum \frac{(f_o - f_e)^2}{f_e}$$

$$\chi^2 = \frac{(3 - 12)^2}{12} + \frac{(23 - 14)^2}{14} + \frac{(21 - 12)^2}{12} + \frac{(5 - 14)^2}{14}$$

$$\chi^2 = \frac{(-9)^2}{12} + \frac{(9)^2}{14} + \frac{(9)^2}{12} + \frac{(-9)^2}{14}$$

$$\chi^2 = \frac{81}{12} + \frac{81}{14} + \frac{81}{12} + \frac{81}{14}$$

$$\chi^2 = 6.75 + 5.79 + 6.75 + 5.79$$

$$\chi^2 = 25.08$$

TABLE 12.7 *Observed and Expected Frequencies*

	Front	*Side*	*Column Total*
Men	3*(12)*	23*(14)*	26
Women	21*(12)*	5*(14)*	26
Row Total	24	28	52

We must now take the final step to determine if there is a relationship between gender and the way people carry books. First, we need to calculate degrees of freedom. Because we have two variables, our formula for degrees of freedom must include both variables. The formula for degrees of freedom for a Chi-Square Test of Independence is as follows:

$$df = (R - 1)(C - 1)$$

The *R* represents the number of rows and *C* represents the number of columns. In this example we find

$$df = (2 - 1)(2 - 1) = 1$$

Earlier, we used degrees of freedom to enter the Chi-Square table and determine if the calculated Chi-Square was meaningful. We need to use Table E.6 again. However, we will interpret our answer a bit differently. When we conducted the Chi-Square *Goodness-of-Fit* we were hopeful that our outcome would *not* be statistically significant. In that case, a statistically significant outcome would suggest that our sample was not reflective of the larger population. In this case, we are hoping for the opposite outcome. We want our calculated value to be larger than the value in Table E.6. If this is the case, then we conclude that there is a relationship between our two variables. Again, we refer to the table with $df = 1$ and $\alpha = .05$ and we find the value of 3.841. Our calculated $\chi^2 = 25.08$ exceeds the tabled or critical value of 3.841. Therefore, we find our result to be statistically significant and conclude that there is a relationship between gender and the way people carry their textbooks.

Writing Results

An example of how we might report this finding follows:

> We conducted a Chi-Square Test of Independence to investigate the relationship between gender and method of carrying textbooks. We found that there is a statistically significant relationship between gender and the way in which people carry their books, $\chi^2(1, N = 52) = 25.08, p < .05$. Our data suggest that women are more likely to carry their books in front, while men are more likely to carry their books at their side.

We used an example of observational research to illustrate how you might use the Chi-Square Test of Independence to examine a relationship between two variables. Remember, we use the Chi-Square with frequency or categorical data. Although the Chi-Square is a non-parametric test, it is an important method for analysis of nominal data.

Strength of Association

We conducted the Chi-Square Test of Independence and found a statistically significant relationship. In other words, the likelihood of this relationship occurring by chance would be unusual. Merely finding a relationship is only the first step. In our discussion of correlation, we indicated that it is important to examine the amount of relationship, or strength of association (or effect size) between the two variables. The phi coefficient is a measure of association typically used when we have a 2 × 2 matrix. A second, and perhaps more general, measure of strength of association or effect size for the Chi-Square is **Cramer's *V*.**

Cramer's *V*—Measure of effect size that ranges between 0 and 1.

$$V = \sqrt{\frac{\chi^2}{n(df^*)}}$$

Only one new element is present in this formula. A special designation for degrees of freedom (df^*) merely requires that we use the smaller of the $(R - 1)$ or $(C - 1)$ calculations. In our example, the degrees of freedom are 1.

$$V = \sqrt{\frac{\chi^2}{n(df^*)}}$$

$$V = \sqrt{\frac{25.08}{52(1)}} = \sqrt{.48} = .69$$

Cramer's V ranges from 0 to 1, with larger values indicating a stronger relationship between two variables. We can interpret Cramer's V much like a correlation coefficient; larger values suggest a stronger relationship.

Computer Analysis Using SPSS

We illustrated how correlation and regression provide statistical evidence of a relationship between variables. We can use SPSS to quickly produce correlations, regression coefficients, and Chi-Square analyses.

Correlation

We begin by selecting the Correlate and Bivariate options as illustrated in Figure 12.8.

A dialogue box allows us to select the variables for the correlation analysis as illustrated in Figure 12.9.

FIGURE 12.8   *Selecting the Correlation*

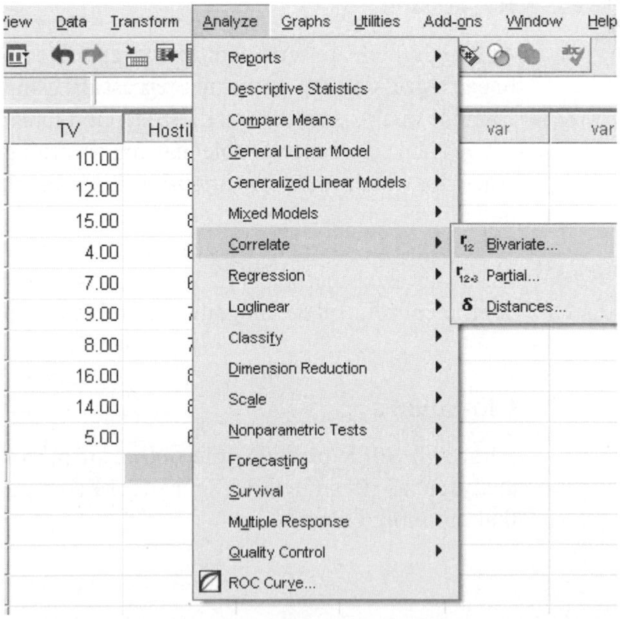

FIGURE 12.9   *Selecting Variables*

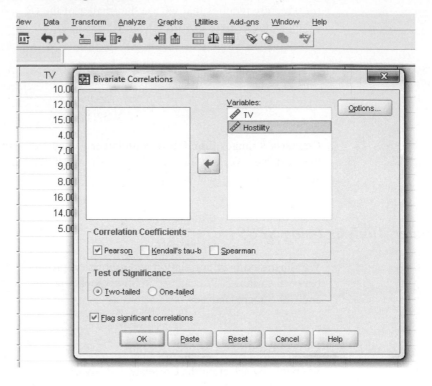

SPSS produces descriptive statistics and the correlation coefficient. A test of significance is also produced as illustrated in Figure 12.10.

Regression

Although there are several different regression models, in this chapter we described only the linear regression. To perform a regression using SPSS, select the Linear Regression options from the analysis options as illustrated in Figure 12.11.

Then select the variable that you are trying to predict and place it in the dependent box. Place the variable that you are using to predict the outcome into the independent box as illustrated in Figure 12.12.

SPSS produces the regression data in a table format. As illustrated in Figure 12.13, the unstandardized coefficient (2.346) reflects the raw score beta weight, whereas the standardized coefficient reflects the magnitude of relationship.

Chi-Square

Although SPSS provides the option of performing a Chi-Square in the non-parametric analyses, as illustrated in Figure 12.14 (see page 305), the crosstabs option provides data that are more complete.

FIGURE 12.10   *Correlation Output*

Descriptive Statistics

	Mean	**Std. Deviation**	**N**
TV	10.0000	4.16333	10
VIOLENCE	75.0000	10.03328	10

Correlations

		TV	**Violence**
TV	Pearson Correlation	1	.974[**]
	Sig. (2-tailed)		.000
	N	10	10
VIOLENCE	Pearson Correlation	.974[**]	1
	Sig. (2-tailed)	.000	
	N	10	10

[**]Correlation is significant at the 0.01 level (2-tailed).

FIGURE 12.11   *Selecting Regression*

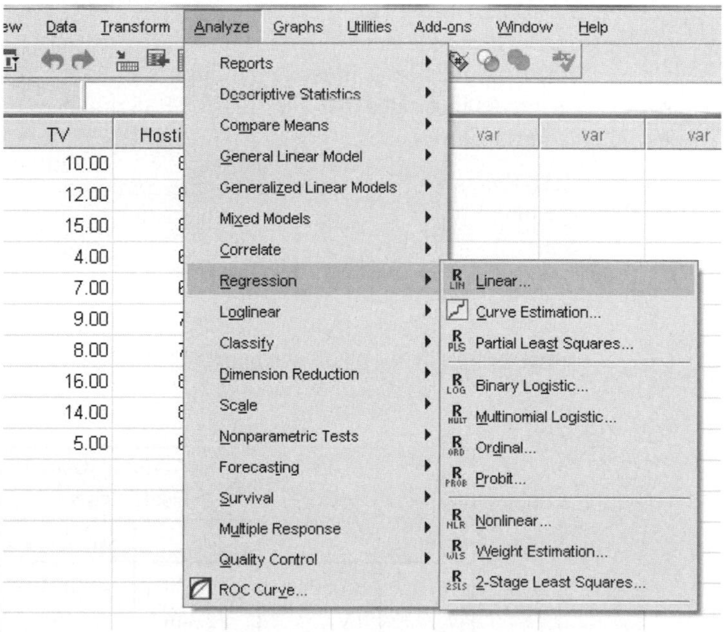

FIGURE 12.12 *Selecting Variables*

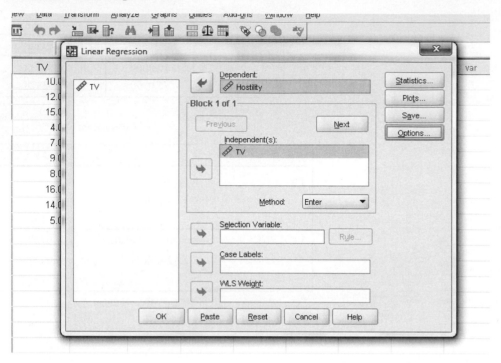

From the descriptive menu, select Crosstabs, then select the variables of interest from the dialogue box as illustrated in Figure 12.15.

As illustrated in Figure 12.16, SPSS produces the Pearson Chi-Square, as well as several additional measures.

FIGURE 12.13 *Regression Output*

Coefficients[a]

Model		Unstandardized Coefficients		Standardized Coefficients	t	Sig.
		B	Std. Error	Beta		
1	(Constant)	51.538	2.093		24.620	.000
	TV	2.346	.195	.974	12.050	.000

[a]Dependent Variable: VIOLENCE

FIGURE 12.14   *Selecting Crosstabs*

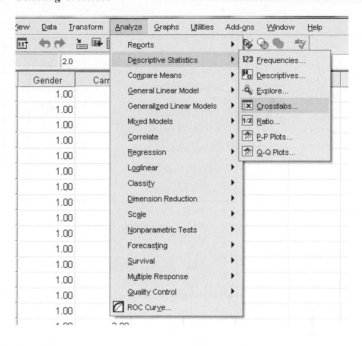

FIGURE 12.15   *Selecting Variables*

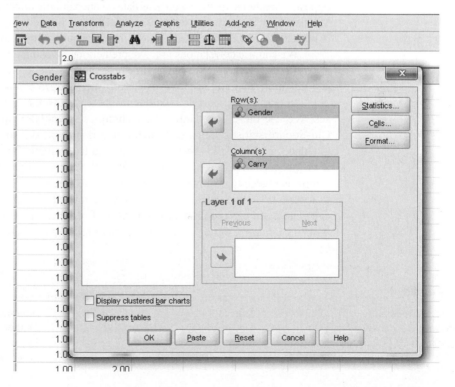

FIGURE 12.16   *Chi-Square Output*

Chi-Square Tests

	Value	df	Asymp. Sig. (2-sided)	Exact Sig. (2-sided)	Exact Sig. (1-sided)
Pearson Chi-Square	25.071[b]	1	.000		
Continuity Correction[a]	22.363	1	.000		
Likelihood Ratio	27.726	1	.000		
Fisher's Exact Test				.000	.000
Linear-by-Linear Association	24.589	1	.000		
N of Valid Cases	52				

[a]Computed only for a 2 × 2 table
[b]0 cells (.0%) have expected count less than 5. The minimum expected count is 12.00.

Chapter Summary

In this chapter, we discussed four statistics commonly used to examine survey data and observational research. Correlational techniques allow us to examine relationships between variables. Size of correlation provides us with an index or size of relationship between two variables. A positive correlation indicates that the variables covary in the same direction. In other words, as one variable increases, so does the second variable. A negative correlation indicates that the variables covary in opposite directions. In other words, as data on one variable increase, the second variable decreases. We also discussed how to interpret a correlation coefficient using the coefficient of determination. A percentage of variance is reflected in the coefficient of determination.

We can use correlations to make predictions by using a regression equation. After finding a significant correlation, we can use a regression equation to predict future outcomes. The regression equation is ubiquitous. Regressions are often used to predict future grades or even, life span.

In addition to correlational techniques, we discussed two types of Chi-Square analyses. We use these non-parametric techniques to analyze categorical or nominal data. The Chi-Square statistic helps us to determine if proportions are comparable. The Chi-Square Goodness-of-Fit test is most frequently used to evaluate the representativeness of a sample. If the proportions are roughly equivalent to the overall population, then we conclude that our sample is indeed representative of the population. We use the Chi-Square Test of Independence to determine if two categorical variables are related. Much like the correlation, we can also calculate a strength of association measure for either of the Chi-Square tests. We discussed how to calculate Cramer's V as a measure of relatedness between the two variables.

Key Terms

Bivariate correlation
Chi-Square Goodness-of-Fit (χ^2)
Chi-Square Test of Independence (χ^2)
Coefficient of determination (r^2)

Cramer's V
Line of best fit
Linear relationship
Negative correlation

Non-parametric tests
Outlier
Positive correlation
Restriction of range

Chapter Review Questions

Multiple Choice Questions

1. Which of the following values reflects the strongest correlation?
   a. $r = .80$
   b. $r = .90$
   c. $r = -.80$
   d. $r = -.90$

2. What is the value for the coefficient of determination for $r = -.70$?
   a. .70
   b. $-.70$
   c. .49
   d. $-.49$

3. Which of the following values reflects the slope of a line in a regression equation?
   a. $a = 1.0$
   b. $b = 2.0$
   c. $X = 5$
   d. $Y = 10$

4. Results from a survey suggest that as gas prices increase, miles traveled decreases. Which of the following values most likely reflects this strong correlation?
   a. $r = .60$
   b. $r = .90$
   c. $r = -.60$
   d. $r = -.90$

5. How is an outlier likely to effect a correlation?
   a. The correlation will remain the same.
   b. The size of the correlation will increase.
   c. The size of the correlation will decrease.
   d. The correlation will be negative instead of positive.

6. What is the f_e value when conducting a Chi-Square Goodness-of-Fit test for a sample of 100 people classified into one of four categories?
   a. 20
   b. 25
   c. 30
   d. 35

7. If a researcher classifies men and women as owning either a sedan, truck, SUV, or motorcycle, what type of test will help to determine if patterns of ownership vary by gender?
   a. Correlation
   b. Regression
   c. Chi-Square Goodness-of-Fit
   d. Chi-Square Test of Independence

8. A researcher classifies men and women as owning either a sedan, truck, SUV, or motorcycle. What is the tabled value that will allow the researcher to reject the null hypothesis at the .05 level?
   a. 3.84
   b. 5.99
   c. 7.81
   d. 9.49

9. How many f_e values need to be calculated for a 3×4 Chi-Square Test of Independence?
   a. 3
   b. 4
   c. 6
   d. 12

10. For a 3×4 Chi-Square Test of Independence sample, $\chi^2(6, N = 100) = 25.00$, what is the Cramer's V value?
   a. 1.2
   b. .50
   c. .35
   d. .74

Essay Questions

11. Explain how a correlational study differs from a correlational analysis.

12. How do the types of correlations (i.e., Pearson's, Phi, Spearman) differ?

13. What information does the correlation coefficient provide about a study?

14. Why can't we make causal statements when using a correlation?

15. Describe a situation in which variables would be negatively correlated.

16. What are some of the factors affecting a correlation?

17. What is the purpose of regression?

18. How would we use a regression equation to predict behavior? Be specific.

19. Under what conditions would you use a Chi-Square analysis?

20. How do the Chi-Square Goodness-of-Fit and Test of Independence differ?

Practice Exercises

21. Using the following data, calculate the Pearson correlation coefficient and coefficient of determination.

X	Y
10	8
12	6
15	4
14	3
20	2
9	18
8	17
16	1
14	2
5	12

22. Using the data from the previous question, produce a scatterplot and interpret the correlation.

23. Using the following data, derive a regression equation. Predict the Y value when X = 5.

X	Y
10	8
12	6
15	4
14	3
20	2
9	18
8	17
16	1
14	2
5	12

24. Assuming that there is an equal proportion of students in each class, determine whether the sample data below are significantly different.

Freshman	Sophomore	Junior	Senior
10	40	15	35

25. Calculate the Chi-Square Test of Significance using the following data.

	Smile	Frown	Column Total
Men	10	15	25
Women	22	3	25
Row Total	32	18	50

CHAPTER 13

RESEARCH IN DEPTH: LONGITUDINAL AND SINGLE-CASE STUDIES

CHAPTER OUTLINE

LONGITUDINAL RESEARCH
Common Themes in Longitudinal Research
Cross-Sectional Versus Longitudinal Research

VARIETIES OF LONGITUDINAL RESEARCH
Trend Studies
Cohort Studies
Cohort Sequential Studies
Panel Studies

CONTROVERSY ON STUDENT ACHIEVEMENT

ISSUES IN LONGITUDINAL DESIGNS
Retrospective and Prospective Studies
Attrition

SINGLE-SUBJECT EXPERIMENTATION
Experimental Analysis of Behavior

METHODS OF SINGLE-CASE DESIGNS
Withdrawal Designs
Single-Subject Randomized Controlled Trials
Strengths of Single-Participant Designs
Weaknesses of Single-Participant Designs
Misunderstandings About Single-Case Research

CASE STUDIES

A CASE STUDY WITH EXPERIMENTAL MANIPULATIONS: TASTING POINTED CHICKENS AND SEEING COLORED NUMBERS

LEARNING OBJECTIVES

- Identify the three possible reasons that people change psychologically over time.
- Differentiate between longitudinal and cross-sectional research.
- Describe the concept of cohort effects.
- Differentiate trend studies, cohort studies, cohort-sequential studies, and panel studies.
- Differentiate prospective and retrospective research designs in longitudinal research.
- Describe how attrition can affect the outcome of longitudinal research.
- Describe and differentiate withdrawal design, ABAB design, multiple baseline design, and single-subject randomized control trial.
- Identify the strengths and weaknesses of single-participant designs.
- Identify four common misconceptions among researchers about single-participant experiments.
- Differentiate case studies and single-participant experiments.
- Identify the strength and weaknesses of case study designs.

CHAPTER PREVIEW

In this chapter we will cover some techniques that deal with different types of research questions than we have encountered previously. The approaches here are typically employed by researchers with questions that involve in-depth study of people.

Each of these domains has developed its own traditions that sometimes differ from the ones we have already covered. This research may also answer different types of questions. Both of them have added to our understanding of behavior.

Psychologists who study development across time make use of longitudinal research. In this field, we have to deal with change over a long period, sometimes years and decades. As a result, there are special considerations to ponder. When our studies are temporally compact and can be created and completed within a matter of weeks, we think differently from when our studies will not be over for a very long time.

A second specialized research design involves single-participant research. In applied fields, particularly in psychotherapeutic settings, and in theoretical work, we may be interested in studying a single individual in depth. We can do so in a quantitative way, with N of 1 randomized clinical trials and experimental analysis of behavior that often entails animal research. We can also use the relatively rare case study approach that tends to be more qualitative.

Longitudinal Research

If you observe people long enough, you will see that they change in predictable ways. Sometimes the changes take place fairly quickly. Infants 1 year old are very different than they were even a month or two before. College students become much more sophisticated thinkers between the start of their college careers and their graduation. More mature adults show consistent developmental changes as they progress from being the "young-old," the "old," and finally, the "old-old."

Psychologists have developed techniques to study people at different stages in their lives. One such approach is called longitudinal research. In psychology, **longitudinal research** refers to the study of individuals over time, often using repeated measurements. It is similar in many ways to the other methods you know about, but there are also some elements that are unique because of the time span of such projects.

Within psychology, developmental psychologists make greatest use of longitudinal research. A developmental psychologist, or developmentalist, is interested in the nature and causes of change. Developmentalists may specialize in a particular part of the lifespan, including infant years, adolescence, early adulthood, or old age. Just as psychologists who study children may limit their focus to infancy, the toddler period, or some other preadolescent time, psychologists specializing in the elderly (who may be called gerontologists) sometimes focus on one of the specific categories of old age.

Common Themes in Longitudinal Research

Longitudinal research— A design in which an investigator studies the same people or the same population (but different individuals) over time, sometimes across decades.

When researchers study change over either a short or a long time span, they investigate the psychological and physiological causes of development. We can conveniently categorize the sources of difference among people into three general groups. First, some researchers may focus on genetic differences that underlie behavior. Scientists recognize that genetic factors can affect behaviors that psychologists study, but the extent to which genes control behavior is overwhelmed by other factors. Genetic factors may explain up to 25% of the variability in cognitive ability across different people, but much less for personality characteristics (Schaie,

2000). These figures suggest that the vast majority of individual differences arise from causes other than genetics.

A second potential cause for individual differences is environmental. Thus, a person's education, family structure, socialization, and access to good nutrition and healthcare have an effect on behavior and attitudes. Not surprisingly, these situational factors are important for the emergence of most of the variability in behavior. Another environmental (i.e., social) aspect of change involves cohort effects, that is, the effects of one's peers, that begin to exert pronounced consequences beginning with school years, but less so during infancy and toddlerhood.

Research on environmental causes of change is complex because it is virtually impossible to identify all of the individual factors that affect even the simplest of behaviors. Further, almost all longitudinal research is descriptive, not experimental. That is, the investigators do not manipulate independent variables in a controlled setting. Rather, they follow the course of a person's life over some time span and try to isolate important variables associated with behavior. This correlational approach allows us to spot relationships among variables, but not causes.

A third domain involves the interaction between genetics and environment. The reason for complexity here is that we still have a very incomplete knowledge base related to how genes and the environment interact for different people. For some behaviors, we will probably ultimately conclude that a complete understanding requires knowledge both of genetic and of environmental factors, particularly for some psychological disorders.

Many of the underlying research concerns are similar, regardless of time of life studied. We have to pay attention to the sample and whether it represents the population we are interested in. We also have to minimize the threats to internal and external validity. In this section, you will see how psychologists plan longitudinal research so that it is maximally informative.

Cross-Sectional Versus Longitudinal Research

When we discuss contemporary research, it is easy to assume that psychologists have always used the methods we now use. In reality, research strategies have to be invented. Normally, we persist in using the approach with which we are most comfortable. It is likely to be the approach that our peers and contemporaries use. That is why so many research reports describe similar methods.

On the other hand, when we become aware of the limitations of the dominant strategies, we work to overcome them. It isn't always clear how to fix the problems. It takes a lot of thought and testing to determine how to replace a current method with a valid new approach. When somebody develops a new strategy, it might be "obvious" that it is appropriate, but until we create a new blueprint, it really isn't all that obvious.

Psychologists who study developmental processes have developed increasingly useful strategies. Initially, the approach to developmental questions, particularly for studying aging, did not include longitudinal research. Instead, researchers used **cross-sectional research** (Schaie, 2000). From the beginning of the 1900s and for the subsequent several decades, if investigators wanted to know how younger and older adults differed in their intellectual functioning, they would locate two samples, one younger and one older, and assess differences in their abilities.

Cross-sectional research—A design in which an investigator studies groups differing on some characteristic (e.g., age) at the same time, in contrast to a longitudinal approach that studies the same individuals over time.

Although cross-sectional studies dominated, not all psychologists used them exclusively. Lewis Terman's longitudinal study of gifted people from childhood into old age is a case in point. The research began in the 1920s, when cross-sectional studies were the norm. (The vast majority of experimental research still employs cross-sectional research.)

Although a cross-sectional plan seemed like a reasonable approach for the first three decades of the twentieth century, after a while some cracks appeared in the foundation. For instance, researchers discovered that they could not replicate the well-documented decline in cognitive functioning across the lifespan that early cross-sectional studies reported (e.g., Jones & Conrad, 1933). Gradually through the 1930s, longitudinal studies became more common.

Researchers began to realize that in a nonequivalent groups design that investigates groups of people who grew up in different eras, the participants differed in more than just age. They experienced life from a different viewpoint, and may have had different opportunities for education and healthcare. Any of these factors (or countless others) could affect mental abilities; age might be important but it might also be irrelevant.

Differences between groups that result from participants having had quite different life experiences are called **cohort effects.** A cohort is a population whose members have some specific characteristic in common, like a birth cohort, a group of people born about the same time. A cohort doesn't have to rely on age; studying psychology majors as compared to other majors will also involve cohorts.

Once researchers accepted the notion of studying the same people over time, investigators often used two-point studies, with researchers observing their participants twice. Such studies were useful, but they were not perfect. One of the problems with two-point studies is statistical regression, sometimes called regression to the mean. It refers to the fact that when people are measured and show extreme scores, they often have less extreme scores the next time. In many cases, the extreme scores included a large amount of measurement error that is unlikely to occur in subsequent measurements. So when changes in scores occur, the result might be meaningless in a developmental sense.

Further, some variables that researchers measure show different results in cross-sectional and longitudinal studies, with longitudinal studies sometimes failing to replicate cross-sectional studies and sometimes showing greater differences (Schaie, 1992).

The methodological innovation that has allowed greater understanding of the developmental process is the longitudinal approach. Once psychologists recognized the realities of cohort effects, they began to study the same individuals across time. This strategy removes some of the difficulties associated with cross-sectional research.

Varieties of Longitudinal Research

Cohort effects—Differences across age groups having to do with characteristics of the era in which a person grew up rather than to age effects specifically.

Researchers generally categorize longitudinal research according to the way participants are selected for a study. In some longitudinal research, the measurements at each time interval involve the same people. In other designs, the measurements include different people across time. Psychological research is more likely to include the same people in each observation frame. Other research may sample from a population without concerns as to whether the same individuals are included. Such studies often involve large, perhaps national, samples.

Another way to categorize psychological studies may involve questionnaires or direct observation of behaviors and frequently involve panel studies, which are described below. Sociologists and medical researchers are often more likely to make use of trend and cohort studies, which are often much larger in scope than those done by psychologists who have direct contact with participants.

Trend study—A variety of longitudinal research in which an investigator samples randomly from a generally defined population over time, with different individuals constituting each sample.

Trend Studies

When investigators assess a general population across time, they sometimes sample randomly at each data-collection point. Depending on the nature of the study, this approach can result in a completely different sample each time. This total replacement of participants is characteristic of **trend studies.**

One example of a trend study involves the prevalence of suicidal thoughts in young people. Late adolescence and young adulthood seem like precarious times for youth in the United States. One manifestation of the problem is suicides on college campuses. Such tragedies are in the news all too frequently.

One report noted that six students at New York University had committed suicide within a one-year period (Caruso, 2004). In other well-publicized news, three Massachusetts students (at MIT, Harvard, and the University of Massachusetts at Amherst) died during a single week in 1998 amid suspicion that the deaths were suicides, according to a story in the *Christian Science Monitor* (April 7, 1998). MIT and Harvard lead the nation in student suicides, as noted in the University of Illinois's *Daily Illini* (February 14, 2001). As of several years ago, Penn State suffered an average of two student suicides a year, according to its online student newspaper, *The Digital Collegian* (July 24, 1997). When such deaths occur, college administrators and faculty ponder what they can do to keep students from feeling the despair that leads them to take their lives.

How to establish programs for suicide prevention is not an easy task because the incidence of suicide attempts differs across groups. For instance, among American Indians, about 20% of deaths among adolescents aged 15 to 19 are due to suicide, whereas it is significantly lower among Asian Americans (Goldston et al., 2008). And just as the incidence of suicide attempts differs across ethnic groups, as you can see in Figure 13.1, so do the factors associated with vulnerability to or protection from suicide.

The effects of culture are not surprising, given that other researchers have documented different patterns in a wide variety of European countries (da Veiga & Saraiva, 2003). For these countries, the patterns over time tend to be stable, suggesting that the structure of the cultures may be responsible.

Any suicide is a calamity for the friends and family of the victim, but we don't know whether suicide rates are going up or down, or staying the same. Colleges only began keeping track of suicides in 1990. Ironically, given the media attention when suicides occur on campuses, the suicide rate among students is half the rate of others the same age. Over the past decades, suicides among the young have increased dramatically, though.

We can figure the suicide rate among students, but how many students actually think about suicide? Fortunately, researchers in Vermont, in an attempt to anticipate and prevent problems in that state, have collected data from middle- and high-school students over time that

FIGURE 13.1   *Incidence of Suicide Deaths in Different Ethnic Groups in the United States (Goldston, Molock, Whitbeck, Murakami, Zayas, & Hall, 2008)*

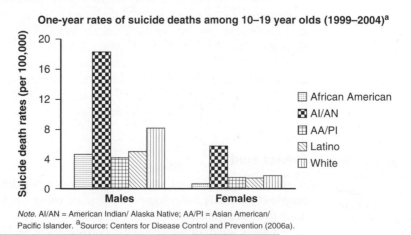

Note. AI/AN = American Indian/ Alaska Native; AA/PI = Asian American/ Pacific Islander. [a]Source: Centers for Disease Control and Prevention (2006a).

FIGURE 13.2 *Incidence of Suicide Ideation and Attempts Among Students in Vermont*
In 1995, over one in five students made a plan for suicide, while decreasing numbers attempted suicide or required medical attention after an attempt. *Made Plan* = Actually made a plan to commit suicide; *Attempted* = Carried out a suicide attempt; *Medical* = Carried out an attempt that required medical intervention.

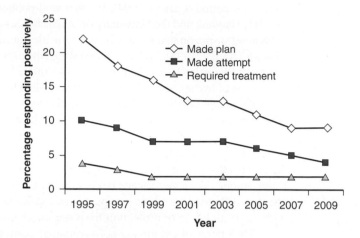

may shed light on the question. This data set can form a trend study sampled from the state's population of high-school students every two years since the mid-1990s.

The percentage of students who have had suicidal ideation (i.e., thoughts of suicide) in the 12 months prior to the survey was alarmingly high, 28%, in 1995; furthermore, among girls, 30% seriously thought of suicide in 1997. Figure 13.2 shows the extent to which students made plans, attempted suicide, and required medical attention. Fortunately, even though a large percentage of students thought about suicide, many fewer youths made plans or attempted suicide (Vermont Youth Risk Behavior Survey: Statewide Report, 1995, 1997, 1999, 2001, 2003, 2005, 2009).

The results of this trend study suggested that we cannot ignore the problems of the young. In fact, David Satcher, former Surgeon General of the United States, has declared that suicide is a public health crisis. College officials have begun to pay significant attention to ways of preventing student deaths.

Another type of trend study might, in repeated assessments, include some of the same participants. If we were interested in the extent to which eighth-grade teachers include novels in their reading assignments, we could sample from that population of teachers periodically. Some teachers might appear in both samples. As long as the sample is large, though, the instances of such overlap will be minimal. In any case, if the sampling is random, we will likely generate a representative sample each time, regardless of the degree of overlap among participants.

Trend studies typically involve applied research. They may be associated with long-term changes associated with critical societal issues, like suicide.

Cohort Studies

Cohort study—A variety of longitudinal research in which an investigator samples randomly from a population selected because of a specific characteristic, often age.

When researchers study a specific, well-defined population over time but sample different people at each data collection point, they are using a **cohort study.** (Trend studies examine more general populations.)

One of the most well-known cohort studies is the Nurses Health Study, which began in 1976. It involves about 122,000 nurses from the original cohort, followed by a new generation of nurses in 1989. (This research design is known in the medical field as an observational epidemiology study.) The project began in order to study the long-term effects of using oral contraceptives. Every two years, cohort members receive a survey with questions about health-related topics. At the request of the participants, the investigators began adding questions on a variety of topics, like smoking, nutrition, and quality-of-life issues. The researchers even collected toenail clippings so they could identify minerals in food that the participants ate.

Psychologists do not use trend studies or cohort studies very extensively. These approaches are more within the province of medical research. Psychologists can benefit from the data, though. It is not unusual for researchers to make their large data sets available to others. Thus, when there is a large database that extends across years or decades, psychologists can identify questions of interest and see how respondents have answered. For instance, the Nurses Health Study includes quality of life information that might help us answer behavioral and attitudinal questions.

Cohort Sequential Studies

If you wanted to compare people of different ages, you could use a cross-sectional design wherein you select samples of such individuals and investigate differences that might exist between them. The problem in interpretation, as mentioned before, is that the people have different life experiences because of the particular environment in which they grew up. You may not be able to attribute differences to age alone.

One solution to this problem is the **cohort sequential design,** also known as the cross-sequential design. This technique involves measuring samples of people at a selected age and testing them on a regular basis. In this approach, you study people of a given age, for example, 60 years old, and then study them again at some later point, like when they are 67. During the second test, you could also investigate a new group of 60-year-olds.

This gives you the opportunity to test 60-year-olds from slightly different eras to see if there is something special about being 60. You can also see how people change over time. The cohort sequential design mixes the cross-sectional approach with the longitudinal. The strength of the cohort sequential design is that it can help you spot changes due to age as well as to differences in the environment in which people develop.

A classic example of this research began in the 1950s by Warner Schaie. He selected a group of elderly people and tested them on their cognitive ability every seven years. At the second testing phase, he assessed the original group but also included a new group of people that he tested every seven years. This second group was as old when tested as the first group was at its initial testing. Then, at the third testing phase, he included a new group that was as old as his first group at their initial testing. So he started with a group of 60-year-olds. Seven years later, he tested these people who were now 67 and began assessment of a new group of 60-year-olds. After another seven years, he brought in a new group of 60-year-olds to compare with the second group, now aged 67, and the first group, now aged 74.

Cohort sequential design—A variety of longitudinal research in which an investigator repeatedly measures a cohort group (e.g., people 60 years of age) over time, adding a new cohort (e.g., new 60-year-olds) in each wave in order to differentiate between cohort effects and age effects.

Over four decades, he tested different groups at the same age in their lives but who grew up in different times. He was able to spot changes in their behavior as they aged and was also able to look for differences that might be attributable to cohort effects.

People performed very differently depending on when they were born. Earlier birthdates were associated with poorer performance for the same age. When people born in 1896 were tested at age 60, their performance was clearly lower than the cohorts from all other birth years when those cohorts were tested at age 60. In fact, with each successive cohort, performance at age 60 was higher than that of the previous cohort.

Thus, there is nothing special about the absolute test scores at age 60 (or at any other age); it is more reasonable to believe that having been born later led to different experiences, perhaps involving education, nutrition, healthcare, etc. that would be important in development and maintenance of their cognitive skill.

Bray and colleagues (2001) used this design to study alcohol use in children over a three-year period. In the first year, one cohort was in the sixth grade, the second cohort was in the seventh grade, and the third cohort was in the eighth grade. In the second year, the previous sixth graders were now in the seventh grade, so their alcohol use could be compared with that of the children who had been in the seventh grade the year before (and who were now in the eighth grade). In the third year, the original sixth graders were in the eighth grade, so their drinking could be compared to those children who were in the eighth grade in the first year of the study. Their results appear in Figure 13.3. Although the research lasted three years, the investigators ended up with data on children as young as sixth grade and as old as tenth grade, a five-year span. You can see the similarities in patterns of data for the different cohorts.

Other researchers have also used this approach to study alcohol use in children. For example, Duncan, Duncan, and Strycker (2005) studied even younger children (i.e., fourth graders). Drinking had already begun by some children that young.

Panel Studies

Another general category of longitudinal studies is the **panel study.** In this design, the same participants are followed throughout the course of the study. The most famous study of people throughout their lifespan was initiated by Lewis Terman in the 1920s. When he began, he didn't suspect that it would become a lifelong enterprise for him. At his death in 1956, the research was still going strong. In fact, his successors have kept it alive into its ninth decade.

Terman was born in Indiana in 1877 but moved to Los Angeles after contracting tuberculosis. (Ironically, the relocation was for the clean air that he could expect in Los Angeles at that

Panel study—A variety of longitudinal research in which an investigator studies the same individuals over time.

FIGURE 13.3 *Example of a Cohort-Sequential Analysis of Alcohol Use by Children*
The researchers studied children for the same three-year period. One cohort was in the sixth grade at the start of the research, the second cohort was in the seventh grade, and the third cohort was in the eighth grade. The results reflect an increase in alcohol use as the children get older, with similar but not identical patterns across the three years.

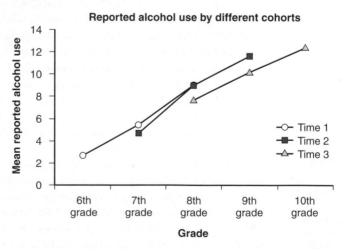

Source: Bray, J. H., Adams, G. J., Getz, J. G., & Baer, P. E. (2001). Developmental, family, and ethnic in influences on adolescent alcohol usage: A growth curve approach. *Journal of Family Psychology, 15,* 301–314. Copyright 2001 by the American Psychological Association. Adapted with permission.

CONTROVERSY
Student Achievement

Each generation of parents seems to be worried that their children are not learning as much in school as they did when they were students. It doesn't matter that the parents of the current group of parents had the same worry, as did each previous generation before them. It is an empirical question as to whether current students are less capable than previous students; that is, we can use data to answer the question.

The National Assessment of Educational Progress (NAEP) project is an example of a trend study. Since 1971, students at grades 4, 8, and 12 have been tested in a variety of subject areas, such as reading, mathematics, and science. The results are often called the "nation's report card."

In Figure 13.4, you can see how 17-year-olds (i.e., twelfth-grade high-school students) have fared in their reading since 1971. In spite of complaints about how students cannot read as well as they used to, it is pretty clear that student scores remained relatively stable over three decades. Since 1973, math scores have actually increased (Rampey, Dion, & Donahue, 2009).

At each NAEP testing, there will be a different set of students because when the test is administered every two or three years, the students in the twelfth grade will have changed. The samples used in NAEP can be considered to involve different cohorts in one sense because the actual participants differ each time, but they involve the same cohort in the sense that they sample twelfth graders each time. (The unfortunate student who is in the twelfth grade for three years and is selected to participate in two tests is rare and unlikely to be sampled more than once.)

What do these numbers say about the current generation of students? Should we believe the comments people make about how deficient students are today? The answer is that, although the situation in some schools, some neighborhoods, and some states is in dire need of remedy, the picture is not all that bleak. There is certainly room for improvement, but it appears that we are no worse off now than we were in the 1970s.

FIGURE 13.4 *Reading Scores by Gender on the National Assessment of Educational Progress (NAEP) Test for Students 17 Years of Age Since 1971*
The assessment uses a random sample of students at each data collection point so there is little or no overlap among participants. This is an example of a trend study.

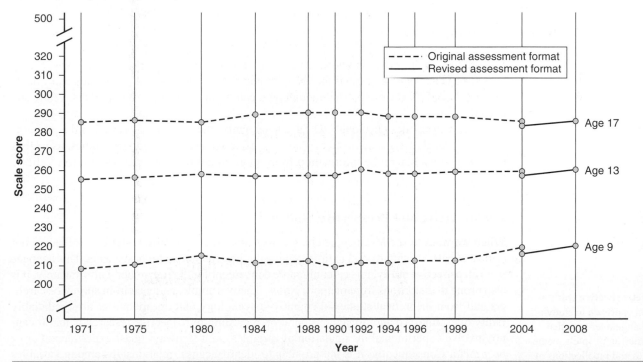

time.) While teaching there, he identified 1,528 children with IQ scores over 135 and compared them to a comparable group of unselected children, a typical cross-sectional approach. Many writers have detailed the research (e.g., Holahan & Sears, 1995) but, in essence, the gifted children and adolescents matured into adults who tended to be happy, healthy, successful, and productive.

A more typical example of a longitudinal study involved a project that investigated the effects of bullying on young teenagers. This project lasted through one school year and into a second (Bond et al., 2001). Investigators have documented that being bullied is strongly associated with depression (Hawker & Boulton, 2000). Unfortunately, the cross-sectional studies comparing depression in bullied and non-bullied groups do not allow assessment of causality because these nonequivalent control groups' designs are correlational. One remedy is to engage in a prospective study in which individuals are monitored over a period of time; this approach contrasts with retrospective studies in which people must recall events from the past.

Bond and colleagues (2001) examined bullying among high-school students in Australia in three waves, that is, at three data collection points. They administered questionnaires to 2,680 students, twice in grade 8 and once in grade 9. The investigators found that recurrent victimization like being teased or excluded, having rumors spread about them, and being physically threatened predicted depression for girls, but not for boys.

One tentative conclusion was that being bullied might cause depression. The researchers noted that previous depression did not predict being bullied; that is, depressed students were not singled out for bullying because they appeared fragile or vulnerable. Students with no sign of depression who were bullied subsequently showed depression, so bullying might be a causal agent. However, as with most longitudinal research, this project was correlational. Longitudinal studies that involve manipulated independent variables are relatively rare in psychology.

Issues in Longitudinal Designs

Longitudinal designs have provided us with a wealth of information about the ways we develop over time. They can be adapted for use with populations ranging from neonates and infants to the very old. If you are patient enough, you can monitor changes over months, years, and even decades.

As with any design, though, we have to recognize the weaknesses as well as the strengths of this approach. Researchers have discovered effective uses of long-term studies, as well as those situations where the information from longitudinal research may have lower validity than desirable.

Retrospective and Prospective Studies

When we want to see how people change over time, it is generally easier to ask them about critical events at a single point in time, relying on their memories for past events. This happens in a **retrospective study.** It is certainly more convenient for the researcher. Unfortunately, it is also prone to distortions from memory lapses. There is ample evidence from survey researchers and from theoretical studies in cognitive psychology that our memories are predictably faulty over time. An additional consideration regarding retrospective research is that it cannot involve experimental manipulation of variables, so it is always quasi-experimental or *ex post facto.* Consequently, it is not possible to identify causal relationships among variables with confidence.

Retrospective study— An approach to studying change over time that relies on people's memories and recollections of the past.

It is clear that we have trouble with mundane information. For instance, Wentland and Smith (1993) found that a significant percentage of people have a hard time remembering if they have a library card. As an example of faulty memories for major events, Cannell, Fisher, and Bakker (1965, cited in Judd, Smith, & Kidder, 1991) demonstrated that people erred in determining how many times they had been hospitalized in the past year.

We are also likely to reconstruct details of the past, in effect creating memories that fit the overall structure of what we are trying to recall. We don't do this intentionally, but it happens just the same. In longitudinal research, we shouldn't expect people to show high levels of mnemonic accuracy for remote events, even for significant events. This is particularly true when we ask children about their behavior. Furthermore, asking their parents does not lead to greater accuracy.

The alternative to a retrospective study is a **prospective study.** In this approach, researchers identify the participants they want to observe and follow them forward in time. Sometimes this is relatively easy, as in Bond et al.'s (2001) study of bullying behavior. They identified their population, created a sample, and questioned them while the events of interest were likely to be fresh in memory.

Other prospective studies rely on some event whose impact the researchers want to assess. Researchers sometimes initiate research when something of interest happens in society. For instance, Hurricane Andrew hit Florida in 1992, causing massive damage and suffering. A team of psychologists used that event to study the course of posttraumatic stress in children.

La Greca and colleagues (1996) studied 442 elementary-school children after the hurricane. The investigators administered the Posttraumatic Stress Disorder Reaction Index for Children (RI), the Hurricane-Related Traumatic Experiences (HURTE) measure, the Social Support Scale for Children (SSSC), the Kidcope survey, and the Life Event Schedule (LES). Measurements were obtained three, seven, and 10 months after the hurricane. They found that 12% of the children experienced severe to very severe levels of posttraumatic stress disorder (PTSD) at 10 months.

You can see that it would be nearly impossible to obtain valid data with a retrospective study of the effects of the hurricane. You can't go back in time to administer the RI (or any of the other scales). It is also unreasonable to think that the children could reconstruct their reactions from seven or 10 months previously. In order to know how feelings and emotions change over time, the only viable approach is prospective.

As in the latter example, the decision to use a prospective or a retrospective design is sometimes not under the control of the researcher. Prospective research is possible when the investigators identify a question and have a group that they can follow into the future. Retrospective research is called for when the answer to a research question lies, at least in part, in what has already happened.

Attrition

The single largest methodological concern in longitudinal studies is the fact that some people will stop participating. In and of itself, the loss of data reduces the amount of information that you have for drawing conclusions, but if your sample is sufficiently large to begin with, the loss of a small amount of data may not be problematic. The study of bullying by Bond et al. (2001) began with 2,680 students, but by the end of their data collection, only 2,365 remained. Still, that is a significant sample; the loss of over 300 participants is notable but may not affect the power of statistical analysis.

The biggest issue associated with this loss of participants, known as attrition, is that you don't always know whether those who disappear differ from those who remain. (If this phenomenon sounds familiar, it is because you encountered it in the context of experimental

Prospective study—An approach to studying change over time that identifies research participants at the beginning of the project who are followed throughout the course of the research.

research, where it is sometimes called subject or participant mortality.) Bond et al. (2001) reported that the attrition rate in their bullying study was higher for boys than for girls. They also noted in their results that boys showed a lower incidence of depression associated with bullying in boys. Could it be that a significant proportion of the boys who left the study experienced depression from bullying?

Further, attrition was greater for students with single-parent families. Is it possible, or even likely, that students in such circumstances are more susceptible to depression? Without being able to ask them, we don't know. Thus, the conclusion by the researchers that boys experience less depression may have been biased to reflect the remaining participants, who could very well differ from those who departed.

Sometimes it is hard to anticipate whether attrition will affect outcomes, but the concern is real. For example, McCoy et al. (2009) reported that in a year-long study of alcohol use among college freshmen, the students who dropped out of the study were systematically different from those who remained. The students who left the study reported heavier drinking, more drunkenness, getting into a greater number of fights, and higher levels of smoking than those who participated in the study to the end. Previous work revealed that heavier drinkers had lower high-school GPAs, which may also be related to the research findings (Paschall & Freisthler, 2003).

The nature of the samples is extremely important in this kind of research because of the different patterns of alcohol use by students of different ethnicity and race. For example, Paschall, Bersamin, and Flewelling (2005) reported that white students showed a much higher incidence of heavy drinking (44.9% of those responding) than did Hispanic students (30.0%), Asian students (22.4%), and black students (under 14.1%). The incidence of attrition is also of interest; in the Paschall et al. study, the attrition rate was higher among black students than for other groups and that nondrinkers were more likely to leave the study than were drinkers.

In a study of nonstudents, Hayslip, McCoy-Roberts, and Pavur (1998–99) investigated in a three-year study how well adults cope after the death of a loved one. They reported, first of all, that attrition at six months was associated with an active decision by the respondent to leave the study, whereas at three years, the researchers had simply lost track of the individuals, some of whom might have participated if found.

The investigators also discovered that attrition did not seem to affect the nature of the results of their research on the effects of the death of a spouse. The results and conclusions would have been pretty much the same regardless of whether those who left had been included.

On the other hand, Hayslip et al. (1998–99) noted that those who had suffered a nonconjugal loss (i.e., somebody other than a husband or wife) and who dropped out were younger, less active in their coping, were in better health, and were less lonely at the beginning of the study. The researchers pointed out poorer psychological recovery after the death of a spouse or other loved one is associated with younger age, poorer health, and more loneliness. Given that nonconjugal dropouts were younger, they might be expected to show poorer outcomes. Their attrition might affect conclusions greatly because those remaining in the sample were the types of people you would expect to do well. Thus, typical outcomes would appear rosier because of those who had left and were not included in the data.

Dropouts were also in better health and less lonely, factors associated with better psychological outcomes. If your study experienced attrition by those who were healthy and not lonely, you would lose people who typically recover well. As a result, your sample would look bleak, not because people can't recover from bereavement, but because the people who agree to be studied are likely to have worse outcomes than those who leave.

Hayslip et al. (1998–99) concluded that we need to be very sensitive to the nature of those who leave longitudinal projects. There is a realistic chance that dropouts lead to biased results, therefore less valid conclusions. Given the potential importance of attrition, it is common for researchers to report the degree of attrition in their reports. This information can help readers gain a sense of how confident they should be in the results. The reality of longitudinal research is that you can count on losing people. An important question is whether those who leave a study differ in relevant ways from those who remain.

When La Greca and her colleagues (1996) studied students over 10 months who suffered through Hurricane Andrew, they recorded the dropouts, documented the reasons for the attrition, and formally compared participants and non-participants. Figure 13.5 displays the percentage of the initial 568 students in the Hurricane Andrew study who departed and the general reason for having done so. As you can see, over 8% had departed by seven months and a total of about 22% by 10 months. These attrition figures are not unusual for such research.

Fortunately, La Greca et al. discovered that those who dropped out did not differ from those who remained in terms of grade, gender, ethnicity, or initial symptoms of PTSD. It is likely that the students who participated throughout the study were representative of the entire set of 568 who began the project.

Even though the research by La Greca et al. did not seem affected by attrition, it remains a serious issue. In a study of attrition during treatment after Hurricane Katrina in 2005, Wang et al. (2007) found that 49% of those who had serious mental health issues dropped out of treatment. The risk factors for attrition included being of minority ethnicity and never having been married. If these patterns hold for research, the representativeness of a final sample might be questionable.

We have found ways to reduce the attrition rates, although they are not without cost. The tactics involve a commitment of time and expense on the researcher's part.

For example, Wutzke and colleagues (2000) studied a group of 554 Australians who engaged in heavy drinking. The project extended for 10 years, a period of time that generally leads to notable attrition among highly educated and cooperative participants and extremely high levels among people with substance abuse problems. At the end of their 10 years, Wutzke

FIGURE 13.5 *Reason for Nonparticipation in the Hurricane Andrew Study of Posttraumatic Stress Disorder (PTSD)*
The researchers documented the reasons for nonparticipation and compared those who left the study with those who remained. Of the initial 568 elementary-school students, just over 22% dropped out of the study for reasons that were sometimes clear (e.g., they had moved) or vague (e.g., they had simply declined). Those who participated did not differ from those who dropped out (LaGreca et al., 1996).

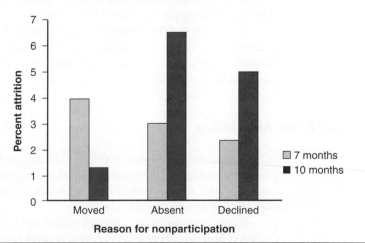

TABLE 13.1 *Steps Taken by Researchers to Decrease Attrition of Participants in a Longitudinal Study Involving Heavy Drinkers (Wutzke et al., 2000)*

Preparation

- Ensuring that dates of birth and middle names were collected (to make later tracing easier)
- Identifying a contact person who lived at a different address
- Maintaining contact throughout the project with such mailings as birthday cards or regular newsletters

Persistence

- Beginning a trace of the person as soon as contact is lost
- Making multiple phone calls to set up appointments for interviews
- Showing willingness to conduct interviews at times and locations convenient for the respondent
- Providing incentives to offset the inconvenience of participation

et al. randomly sampled and reviewed 20% ($n = 109$) of the records to see how well contact had been maintained. Surprisingly, 72.5% of the 109 people had been successfully located for the study; over 78% of the total group of 554 had been located.

The researchers had prepared well and worked diligently throughout the study to keep in touch with the participants. They enhanced their success by taking a number of steps as they initiated their project and as they conducted it. Table 13.1 presents their strategies to avoid losing track of people and maintaining the participants' motivation to continue in the project. Some of these steps are seemingly obvious, like getting participants' full names and people related to them; others are less obvious, like maintaining participants' motivation by sending birthday cards. As obvious as they might be, researchers have not always carried them out. These steps are very relevant for studies of a large and heterogeneous population.

Finally, when you are studying older people, an additional reason for attrition is likely, namely, the death of the participant. In the study begun by Terman in 1921, there has been considerable attrition, as you might expect. However, in the 35th year of the study (1955), over 88% of the women and over 87% of the men remained in the project.

When Terman died in 1956, the attrition rate increased, possibly because the participants had felt a very strong personal connection with him. Between 1955 and 1960, the number who actively declined to participate exceeded the total attrition since 1921 (Holahan & Sears, 1995). Since 1972, attrition has been more likely due to death than to a choice to drop out. Remarkably, only 8% of the women and 6% of the men have been "lost," the researchers term for loss of contact because they can't find the person.

It is ironic that the exceedingly low attrition in the Terman study is fairly unimportant in some ways. The sample he chose in 1921 wasn't representative either of the population generally or of gifted children specifically. As a result, we don't know exactly to whom we can generalize the results of the research.

Single-Subject Experimentation

In the past century, psychologists have developed the tradition of conducting studies with groups of participants, ignoring the behavior of single individuals. As a discipline, psychology was not always oriented toward this approach. In the early years of psychology, researchers often studied a single person intensively.

Experimentalists and clinicians shared this methodology. Freud used single-participant studies in his clinical work, as did John Watson (e.g., Little Albert) in his research on learning. Then in the early decades of the twentieth century, experimental psychologists gravitated toward the study of groups. Single-subject experimental research did not return until the middle of the century. When it was resurrected, researchers often conducted long-term studies of single subjects, often rats and pigeons. The research reports were largely devoid of statistical analysis; visual displays of data replaced statistics. The behaviorists who resurrected single-subject research believed that enough data over many experimental trials would reveal important patterns of behavior, so statistical treatment wasn't necessary. Today, single-subject studies with people tend to involve those with psychological problems.

Experimental Analysis of Behavior

The experimental analysis of behavior reflects a unique tradition in research. It arose from the behaviorist tradition and had significant focus on the study of reinforcement contingencies. Because one of the major tenets of behaviorism was that we can discover general principles and laws of behavior, researchers believed that studies with large numbers of subjects were not only unnecessary, but also undesirable. By using many subjects and averaging the data on their performance, the behaviorists thought that we would lose sight of critical individual details.

Consequently, the tradition of using one or a few subjects emerged. Psychologists who engage in the experimental analysis of behavior often still rely on single subjects or perhaps small groups and may rely on visual presentation of results rather than on complex statistical analysis. These researchers are not immune to psychological culture, though, so even these psychologists have altered their traditions somewhat, using some statistical analysis to help them understand their research results.

Within the realm of experimental analysis of behavior, two distinct paths have developed. Some experimenters rely on studies of animal behavior; their work is largely theoretical. When researchers use experimental analysis of behavior, their projects sometimes focus on theory, but sometimes the projects involve applications. Their investigations often involve people in clinical settings and tend to be less theoretical, although clearly based on behavioral theory. The experimental analysis of behavior is likely to be highly objective and quantitative.

Methods of Single-Case Designs

Withdrawal design—A research method in which an investigator observes a baseline of behavior, applies a treatment, and assesses any behavioral change, then removes or withdraws the treatment to see the degree to which the behavior reverts to baseline levels.

Studies with single individuals, whether human or nonhuman, do not differ in concept from many of the other approaches we have already covered. The biggest difference involves the number of people or animals tested, not necessarily the methodology. In fact, this difference in the number of participants is not necessary; single-case research can involve multiple cases. The researchers are likely to report on them individually, though. Case studies can involve controlled observations, like experiments. They can also rely on questionnaires and naturalistic observation.

Another difference between single-case analyses and group analyses is that single-case research involves continuous monitoring of behavior over time. In this sense it resembles time-series or longitudinal designs more than the typical cross-sectional design.

Withdrawal Designs

ABA design—A type of withdrawal design in which a treatment is applied only once, then withdrawn.

Single-case research can take many different forms. The general process involves assessing the behavior or behaviors of interest to monitor the baseline rate of the behaviors. Then a treatment begins. After that, different designs lead to different steps.

One design, the **withdrawal design,** entails a baseline phase, a treatment phase, then a return to a baseline phase. It is represented as an **ABA design** because researchers refer to the baseline period with the letter A and the treatment with the letter B. If treatment is effective, a simple withdrawal design should document that there is movement toward the desired outcome during the treatment phase. In medical or psychiatric research that assesses whether a drug stabilizes a person's condition, a return of the symptoms to the original level when the treatment is withdrawn may be entirely predictable, even desirable for assessing the effectiveness of a treatment. This design is most useful when researchers expect that after a treatment is removed, the original pattern of behavior will recur. In such a case, the ABA design permits the researchers to identify cause and effect relationships.

A return to baseline in such a medical study would indicate that the medication is working as it should. If the condition did not return to baseline levels when the medication was removed, the investigator might not be sure that the medication made a difference. Some alternate explanation might be better.

In much psychological research, it isn't clear what will happen in the second baseline phase. After a behavioral treatment phase ends, we hope that the desired behavior change is going to persist. So in the second baseline phase, we hope there isn't a return to the first level. In some cases, though, research has shown that people's fear responses may return when the person is exposed to the fear-producing context and even to new contexts (Neumann & Kitlertsirivatana, 2010).

In order to strengthen the internal validity of single-case research, investigators sometimes withdraw a treatment to see if a person's condition worsens, then they introduce a second baseline phase, followed by a reintroduction of the treatment, creating an **ABAB design.**

The basic ABAB design has many variations. Sometimes researchers want to assess different treatments, so after baseline phases, they introduce different treatments. If there are two different treatments, we represent the design as AB_1AB_2.

Single-Subject Randomized Controlled Trials

In medical or clinical research, large-scale studies may not be feasible. When an investigator wants to assess treatment with a single person, one option is the **N of 1 Randomized Clinical Trial (RCT).** In this approach, the researcher studies the effect of treatment on a single individual by exposing the individual to a treatment and a placebo in random order over time (e.g., ABBABAABBAB). Both the clinician and the patient are blind as to the treatment at any given time. Because neither the clinician nor the patient is aware of whether a treatment or a placebo phase is underway, there won't be any experimenter effects or demand characteristics. Any changes in the patient are likely to be due to the effectiveness of the treatment rather than to some extraneous variable.

This approach makes sense only when several criteria are met. First, the patient's problem must be chronic but relatively stable. If the symptoms are too variable or time-limited, it is difficult to attribute any changes to the treatment. Second, the treatment (usually a drug in this kind of study) should have a rapid effect and also a rapid cessation of effect. This criterion is important because the researcher doesn't want to have carryover effects that can interfere with conclusions about the effectiveness of the different approaches. Finally, there needs to be a clear and objective outcome that can be measured reliably (Cook, 1996).

Strengths of Single-Participant Designs

Just like any other method of research, single-case studies help fill in the gap in our knowledge of behavior. These approaches have some notable strengths. First, one of the most pronounced advantages is the amount of detail reported about a person. Entire books can be (and have been) written about exceptional people.

ABAB design—A type of withdrawal design that uses a baseline period followed by application of a treatment, the withdrawal of the treatment (as in an ABA design), and re-application of the treatment.

N of 1 Randomized Clinical Trial (RCT)—A research design involving the study of a single person over multiple trials, with trials involving application of the treatment and trials with no application of the treatment occurring in random order.

These designs are time and labor intensive; you can easily see why an investigator might limit the research to a single person. The amount of detail to sort through would be overwhelming if the researcher studied many people. The researcher would also have a harder time sorting out the relevant detail from the irrelevant if multiple people were involved.

Second, case studies and single-case experiments are also useful when we want to investigate rare phenomena. Researchers may not be able to locate a large group of individuals if the phenomena of interest seldom occur.

A third strength of single-case studies relates to creating and evaluating research hypotheses. We can use the results of single-participant studies to generate hypotheses that can be tested with larger numbers of people. Single-case studies can also test hypotheses based on existing theory.

A further advantage of single-case studies is that they provide help in developing and assessing therapeutic or intervention techniques. The causes of psychological difficulties in clients and patients may be unique to each person. As a result, using large numbers of research participants may actually obscure the effectiveness of a therapeutic technique that might be helpful for a particular person.

Whenever we want to know about behaviors that are particular to a single person, single-case designs can be highly beneficial. In addition to the realm of clinical psychology, single-case research can be important in areas like sports psychology (Hrycaiko & Martin, 1999). In clinical psychology, the aim is to improve a person's psychological state; in sports psychology, the goal is to enhance performance. In both cases, there are likely to be individual characteristics that are critical to change; group research would probably not be optimal in either field.

Weaknesses of Single-Participant Designs

Probably the biggest limitation of single-subject studies involves the question of external validity. In one sense, they have a high degree of external validity; case studies typically do not use controlled, laboratory manipulations as experiments do. There is generally nothing artificial about them. Thus, the studies tell us about a person in his or her natural environment.

Another component of external validity is relevant here, though. We cannot be sure that conclusions based on a single person will generalize to anybody else. In fact, because this research often involves rare phenomena, it is not clear that there are many others to whom we would be able to generalize. The results might pertain to only one person.

In addition to questions of external validity, we are also faced with potential problems with internal validity. Causal conclusions about the person's behaviors are risky if there is no controlled manipulation of variables in the research.

Misunderstandings About Single-Case Research

Single-case research is fairly rare in psychological and psychiatric research. There are several possible reasons.

First, the tradition in psychology is cross-sectional research involving comparisons between groups. Most training in graduate programs therefore focuses on research with groups rather than with individuals. For many researchers, single-case studies don't look like normal, psychological research, and the psychologists may not be well versed in the details of single-case approaches.

Second, researchers may confuse the relative subjectivity of some case-study approaches and the relative objectivity of single-subject experiments that are highly controlled. Furthermore, most psychologists and other researchers have little training in qualitative approaches. A qualitative study can provide a lot of information about behavior, but it is likely to be different information from that produced in a quantitative study. In other words, psychologists like research involving numbers and quantitative analysis.

Third, some researchers believe that the levels of internal and external validity are low in single-participant research. There is some truth to this claim, but the same can be said for cross-sectional designs. Most behavioral research involves convenience samples, so concerns about generalizability (i.e., external validity) exist for all types of data collection. Further, given that much experimentation occurs in laboratories, the question of external validity arises again. The issue of internal validity may be notable in case studies, but is less relevant for N of 1 RCT studies. Experiments with a single case may have levels of internal validity that are as high as in cross-sectional research.

Fourth, some researchers claim that the data analysis in single-case research is too subjective. It is true that there will be some subjectivity when an investigator works with subjective phenomena, like emotional states. But this is no different than with cross-sectional research. For researchers interested in the experimental analysis of behavior, they may avoid statistical analyses, but when the data are objective and when objective criteria for drawing conclusions are set ahead of time, data analysis is simply different, not necessarily less valid.

Case Studies

Case studies are investigations that focus on a single individual (occasionally a few people) in great detail. Historically, case studies did not include controlled observations, and took place in the context of psychotherapy (Kazdin, 1998). In contemporary applications, though, investigators make use of interventions and control (e.g., Cytowic, 1993; Mills, Boteler, & Oliver, 1999).

This approach to research is often seen as having more problems than other techniques. In fact, even though a new journal has appeared that deals only with case studies), some journals do not accept them as research papers. In other journals, case studies are for teaching purposes rather than research questions (Gawrylewski, 2007). Questions of causation, generalizability, and interpretation biases are among the most notable concerns. In addition, in the psychological and medical literature, case studies play a small role in research.

In case studies, it is hard to see what factors lead to certain behaviors and which are merely correlated with those behaviors. In essence, there is the problem of too many rival hypotheses and no way to see which ones are best. A second caution about case studies concerns whether we can generalize from a particular patient or client to others.

An additional concern about single-case research in general is interpretive. That is, what does the information mean? It is possible for researchers to ignore viable explanations for behaviors because those explanations do not fit with their theoretical position. This is not an attempt to deceive. Rather, it is a natural inclination on our part to accept information that supports what we believe and to ignore information that doesn't. The problem is exacerbated by the fact that studies of a single person often rely on clinical judgment and subjectivity that another person may not be able to replicate objectively.

Case study—A research design involving the in-depth study of one or a few people, historically with no manipulation of variables, although such manipulations can occur in contemporary designs.

Because of these problems, case studies are fairly rare in the research literature. At the same time, it is easy to see why clinicians use this approach. People with ailments that are interesting (in the research sense) are likely to be rare, at least when they first appear. As a case in point, AIDS was initially a puzzle to the medical community; young, healthy people were contracting unusual, fatal diseases for no apparent reason. Initial research could only involve case studies because there were so few instances.

When the numbers began to grow, preliminary studies showed patterns. Initially, physicians thought that the disease was limited to gay men, which accounts for its initial label,

Gay Related Immune Deficiency (GRID). Without continued research with larger numbers of people, it would have been impossible to understand the nature of what was ultimately renamed AIDS. But the initial case studies provided critical clues to the disease.

Within psychology, case studies can give us a lot of compelling information about individual people. The clinical researcher can then try to understand an individual's behavior by fitting a large number of puzzle pieces together. For example, how would you react if somebody told you that he knew that the food being cooked for dinner wasn't done yet because "there aren't enough points on the chicken"? Is this the utterance of a delusional person? What do "points" have to do with how well done a chicken is? You can see how an interesting case study shed light on the perceptions of the man for whom flavors had shapes (Cytowic, 1993), shapes that were as real to him as the flavor of chicken is to us.

Researchers have estimated that as few as one person in about 100,000 has such experiences, known as synesthesia (Cytowic, 1997), although some have produced higher estimates of one person in 2,000 (Baron-Cohen et al., 1996). Obviously, if you wanted to study synesthesia, you would have a hard time finding a group to study. Case studies make the most sense. You can see in the next section how Cytowic used a case study to investigate a synesthete he met.

A Case Study with Experimental Manipulations: Tasting Pointed Chickens and Seeing Colored Numbers

When somebody scratches his or her fingernails on a blackboard, the sound can send shudders down our spines, even though we have not been touched. This effect is an analogue to that of people who experience synesthesia, or the mixing of different sensory modalities. This mixing is so bizarre from our perspectives that descriptions sound like they are coming from delusional people.

Should we believe people who claim that the sound of a pager causes them to see "blinding red jaggers" or that the poison strychnine and angel food cake have the same "pink smell" (Cytowic, 1993, p. 48). Or that the number 257 induces "a swirl that consists of yellowish orange as the dominant color, green as the next most dominant, and lastly there is a small amount of pink" (Mills, Botcler, & Oliver, 1999, p. 183)?

Synesthesia can take many different forms. In the case of the man Cytowic studied, flavors had shapes. The most famous synesthete in the psychological literature experienced shapes and colors when he heard words; for him, a particular tone looked like fireworks tinged with a pink-red hue, an unpleasant taste, and was rough enough to hurt your hand (Luria, 1968).

In another documented case, the synesthete converted visually presented numbers to colors, but also experienced synesthesia to spoken numbers, music, voices, emotions, smells, and foods (Mills, Boteler, & Oliver, 1999). When she saw a written number, she perceived different colors in front of her eyes. For example, a 1 was white, 2 was yellowish orange, 5 was kelly green, 7 was pink. Each of the single digits had its own, consistent color. Multiple-digit numbers combined colors, with the color associated with the first digit predominating.

Synesthetes respond to the world in ways that are very consistent for them, even if they are strange to us. This is an ideal situation for a case study. Cytowic (1993) met a synesthete, Michael, and spent an extended period studying his perceptions. Cytowic became aware of how special this person was when the synesthete didn't want to serve the chicken he was cooking yet because it was "round," without enough "points." He also reported being able to smell a tree that nobody else could, and it wasn't because their noses were stuffed. He was able to look at a tree and smell it because his brain processed its visual components and sent information to the part of his brain that dealt with smell.

Over the course of two years, Cytowic exposed Michael to different manipulations to see how he reacted. During the development of the case study, Michael reported that quinine, a bitter liquid, felt like polished wood, whereas another liquid had "the springy consistency of a mushroom, almost round, . . . but I feel bumps and can stick my fingers into little holes in the surface" (Cytowic, 1993, p. 64).

The functioning of the brain is complex in synesthesia, as it is for everything else, but Cytowic used the results of his study with Michael to discover some important elements of the phenomenon. He presented various liquids to see what shapes and colors they generated. He also investigated the effects of amphetamines and alcohol on synesthesia; amphetamines blocked synesthesia whereas alcohol enhanced it. Cytowic also injected radioactive gas to identify the parts of the brain involved in synesthesia; he found that during synesthesia, there was minimal blood flow to Michael's cortex. At the same time, blood flow to the emotional center of the brain, the limbic system, increased greatly.

Cytowic provided an extended case study of the experiences of the synesthete and wound up with a description not only of Michael's feelings and perceptions but also of patterns of brain activity. Such research is only possible in single-subject research.

Chapter Summary

Psychologists have created specialized approaches to research to answer questions about behavior when traditional experiments may not suffice. Developmental psychologists use longitudinal approaches to study how people change over time. Some longitudinal research in psychology has continued for over 80 years. With research like this, the investigators have to contend with considerably different issues than they do in typical, short-term cross-sectional experiments. Psychologists have developed a variety of methods to maximize the validity of the information obtained in these long-range projects.

Longitudinal projects often involve studying the same people over time. For example, Terman's multi-decade study followed a set of people identified in childhood as gifted throughout their lives. Sometimes, researchers investigate groups whose members change over time. The National Assessment of Educational Progress studies twelfth graders across time, so there is a new group of students for each phase of the research. Other research follows the same people over time, but also brings new people into the study at regular intervals.

Sometimes researchers study the same individual over time, concentrating on one person (or a few) rather than on a group. Like longitudinal studies, single-case studies involve observing the same person over time, with multiple repeated measures. Depending on the specific research question, investigators might introduce a treatment, then withdraw it, sometimes multiple times. Psychologists are often not well trained in the use of single case designs, one of the reasons that this approach is relatively rare in psychology.

Key Terms

ABA design	Cohort study	Prospective study
ABAB design	Cross-sectional research	Retrospective study
Case study	Longitudinal research	Trend studies
Cohort effects	N of 1 Randomized Clinical Trial (RCT)	Withdrawal design
Cohort sequential design	Panel study	

Chapter Review Questions

Multiple Choice Questions

1. Lewis Terman's study of gifted children that continued to follow them through adulthood and into old age constitutes
   a. multiple baseline research.
   b. cross-sectional research.
   c. trend research.
   d. longitudinal research.

2. A researcher who wants to know if elderly people are more health conscious than younger people could study a group of elderly people and a group of young people to assess any differences. Such an approach would involve
   a. multiple baseline research.
   b. cohort research.
   c. longitudinal research.
   d. cross-sectional research.

3. To avoid cohort effects, researchers can
   a. conduct cross-sectional studies.
   b. use multiple baseline studies.
   c. make use of panel studies.
   d. conduct retrospective studies.

4. To find out if using night-lights affected the development of nearsightedness, a group of researchers asked parents whether their teenaged children had slept with night-lights on as infants. This research illustrates a
   a. retrospective design.
   b. cohort design.
   c. cross-sectional design.
   d. longitudinal design.

5. The single largest methodological concern in longitudinal studies is
   a. cohort effects.
   b. attrition.
   c. trend effects.
   d. retrospective errors.

6. Wutzke et al. (2000) studied ways to reduce attrition in longitudinal research on heavy drinkers. They found that they could reduce attrition by
   a. promising the participants total confidentiality and anonymity in their participation.
   b. increasing internal motivation rather than relying on incentives to the participants.
   c. maintaining a strict policy of participation in order to establish routines for participation.
   d. maintaining contact throughout the project by sending birthday cards or regular newsletters.

7. Studies in the experimental analysis of behavior rely on
   a. case studies.
   b. cohort-sequential studies.
   c. trend studies.
   d. single-subject studies.

8. An ABA design would not be useful in research if
   a. a treatment had a permanent effect.
   b. a researcher expected a high level of attrition.
   c. the research is prospective.
   d. participants form a cohort.

9. Single-subject research that involves a series of measurements of a dependent variable during periods when a treatment is applied and also when the treatment is not given could be classified as
   a. an N of 1 randomized clinical trial.
   b. a multiple baseline design.
   c. a trend study.
   d. a panel study.

10. The most notable weakness of single-subject designs is
    a. they are not useful for generating hypotheses that can be tested with larger groups.
    b. they are not helpful in studying rare phenomena.
    c. the results from such designs may not be generalizable to others.
    d. they are susceptible to cohort effects.

11. The state of Vermont tried to anticipate the degree to which middle- and high-school students contemplated suicide. The state collected data from students in 1993, 1995, and 1997. This approach reflects
    a. a cohort study.
    b. a trend study.
    c. a cross-sectional study.
    d. a retrospective study.

Essay Questions

12. What are the advantages of longitudinal designs and cross-sectional designs?

13. How does a panel study differ from a trend study? What are the advantages of each?

14. In the Bond et al. (2001) study on bullying in schools and depression, why could attrition have influenced their results?

15. Why might an ABA design not be appropriate for behavioral (as opposed to drug) treatment for depression?

16. What are the advantages of single-case research?

PEOPLE ARE DIFFERENT: CONSIDERING CULTURAL AND INDIVIDUAL DIFFERENCES IN RESEARCH

CHAPTER OUTLINE

DIFFERENT CULTURAL PERSPECTIVES
What Is Culture?

DEFINING AN INDIVIDUAL'S CULTURE, ETHNICITY, AND RACE
Criteria for Inclusion in a Group
Social Issues and Cultural Research

CROSS-CULTURAL CONCEPTS IN PSYCHOLOGY
Are Psychological Constructs Universal?
Issues in Cross-Cultural Research

CONTROVERSY: DOES CULTURE MAKE A DIFFERENCE IN NEUROLOGICAL DIAGNOSIS?

IS THERE A BIOLOGICAL BASIS FOR RACE?
The Criteria for Race
Current Biological Insights Regarding Race
Historical Error

CONTROVERSY: ARE THERE REALLY DIFFERENT RACES?
Current Controversies

PRACTICAL ISSUES IN CULTURAL RESEARCH
Lack of Appropriate Training Among Researchers

WHY THE CONCEPTS OF CULTURE AND ETHNICITY ARE ESSENTIAL IN RESEARCH
Differences Due to Language and Thought Processes
Differences in Simple and Complex Behaviors
Is Culture-Free Theory Really Free of Culture?
Similarities and Differences within the Same Culture

CULTURAL FACTORS IN MENTAL HEALTH RESEARCH
Content Validity
Translation Problems
Cross-Cultural Norms
Cross-Cultural Diagnoses

SEX AND GENDER: DO MEN AND WOMEN COME FROM DIFFERENT CULTURES?
Stereotypes and Gender-Related Performance

CONTROVERSY: ARE MEN BETTER THAN WOMEN AT MATHEMATICS?

LEARNING OBJECTIVES

- Describe the concept of culture.
- Differentiate the concepts of physical culture and subjective culture.
- Describe the difficulty in applying the concepts of culture, race, and ethnicity in research.
- Explain how affiliation with culture, race, and ethnicity can change across time and situation.
- Explain the strategies researchers use to assign participants to cultural, racial, or ethnic categories.
- Describe the problems that researchers face when they categorize people using stereotypical categories of culture, race, and ethnicity.

■ Provide examples of psychological concepts that were thought to be universal but may have significant cultural components.

■ Differentiate among absolutism, relativism, and universalism.

■ Explain the interpretation paradox in cross-cultural research.

■ Identify four major problems in drawing conclusions based on cross-cultural research.

■ Describe how definitions of race have changed over time.

■ Describe research that attempted to assess intelligence based on brain size.

■ Identify concerns associated with personal characteristics, research considerations, and outcomes when studying people in ethnic groups.

■ Describe how language and thought affect outcomes in cross-cultural research.

■ Explain why researchers need to take into account both similarities and differences across people in a given culture.

■ Identify four methodological considerations associated with mental health research and testing people in different cultures.

■ Explain why content validity is important in using a psychological test in different cultures.

■ Identify the problem of translating test items across cultures and how researchers try to solve it.

■ Describe how cross-cultural norms can affect interpretations of test results.

■ Explain why gender stereotypes can affect the outcome of psychological research.

CHAPTER PREVIEW

Most psychologists would agree that our attitudes and beliefs affect the way we make judgments. When we draw a conclusion about somebody's behavior, our judgments may reflect us as much as the people we observe. That is, we see others in a particular way because of who we are. If we share the same culture as those we study, we may be able to gain insights into why they act as they do. On the other hand, when we observe behaviors of those in other cultures, we may not understand what motivates them.

Understanding the effects of culture on behavior requires detailed knowledge of the person being observed as well as that person's culture, which is not easy. The issues we have to consider are complex. For instance, how do culture, ethnicity, and race affect behavior? The answer is certainly complex. Even though most people firmly believe that there are several easily definable races of people, many scientists have come to the conclusion that the concept of race is a social construction, not a biological fact. According to a great number of anthropologists, sociologists, psychologists, biologists, and geneticists, race is not a particularly useful biological concept. Yet many people believe that it exists.

Even though a concept like race may be scientifically invalid, we can still identify behaviors associated with culture or ethnicity, although there are pitfalls we need to avoid. Research participants are often assigned to categories in simplistic and contradictory ways from one study to another. Fortunately, more researchers are coming to the realization that we need to have good cross-cultural knowledge if we are going to understand people.

Finally, studying differences between women and men poses problems in research. Sometimes, investigators find ways to reinforce pre-existing beliefs by failing to acknowledge what might be considered cultural differences between the sexes. The researchers may believe in myths that are not true, so their research may be flawed.

Throughout this chapter, your beliefs will be challenged, and you will have to deal with controversies that, ultimately, may make you view people differently and change the way you think about studying them.

Different Cultural Perspectives

It would be a mistake to assume that all people think as we do. As a result, we should be cautious in interpreting why people act as they do when these people come from a culture that is different from ours.

For example, Stiles, Gibbons, and Schnellman (1990) asked Mexican and American adolescents to characterize members of the opposite sex. Mexican adolescents relied on stereotypes and talked about internal characteristics. American adolescents were more likely to use physical and sexual descriptors. In addition, the girls who participated in the study tended to make different drawings, depending on their culture. Mexican girls depicted men helping them more than American girls did. If we wanted to study attitudes of Mexican and of American adolescents, we might have a hard time comparing their responses because they would be using different worldviews to generate their responses.

Beyond this, Cohen and Gunz (2002) have documented that people born in Western and Eastern countries have quite different memories of events in their lives. Those from Asia tended to remember events in the first person (e.g., "I did this") when the memories did not involve their being at the center of attention; when they were the center of attention, their memories were in the third person (e.g., "he did this"). People born in the Western world showed memories that were just the opposite, with the center of attention being associated with the first person. The researchers concluded that the differential perspectives on the world actually dictated the way information is processed and the form of subsequent memory.

If the investigators are correct, we can expect people from different cultures to think about things very differently, so if we give them the same task to complete, they may be engaged in quite different mental processes. As such, comparisons about performance may be difficult.

What Is Culture?

Sometimes we think that we understand a concept, but when we try to express our ideas in words, it is very difficult. **Culture** is one such concept. We all know people who act differently than we do because of cultural differences. If somebody asked you to identify differences between your culture and that of another person, you would probably discuss differences in religious beliefs, eating habits, clothing, etc. This is typically what we mean by "culture" (Matsumoto, 1994). At the same time, we have only identified some of the signs associated with cultural differences; we haven't defined culture itself.

Throughout this chapter it will become apparent that our concepts of culture, ethnicity, and race are quite vague and subjective. Unfortunately, the research literature is at times just as confusing. Different investigators use the same term but define it in diverse ways.

Culture.   We can identify two distinct components of culture. Physical culture relates to objects like tools and buildings. Subjective culture, which is of interest to psychologists, refers to such things as familial patterns, language habits, attire, and a wide range of other characteristics that pass from one generation to the next (Betancourt & Lôpez, 1993; Matsumoto, 1994).

Culture—The customs, behaviors, attitudes, and values (Psychological Culture) and the objects and implements (Physical Culture) that can be used to identify and characterize a population.

Other psychologists have defined culture somewhat differently from Matsumoto (1994), involving the notion that culture is not something "out there," but rather that it is a cognitive response a person makes on the basis of his or her interactions with others (Segall, Lonner, & Berry, 1998). For example, it seems unlikely that Americans are overtly conscious of being Americans on a daily basis; this categorization makes sense only when they want to make some

Race—A controversial concept with very limited construct validity about classification of people based on real or imagined biological traits, most often centering on skin color.

Ethnicity—A concept related to a person's identification with a particular group of people, often based on ancestry, country of origin, or religion.

Discussion Questions

1. Give an example of a difference between your own culture and some other culture that you know about with respect to subjective culture.

2. The concepts of race, culture, and ethnicity are not well defined, even in research. What other concepts that may be more readily defined can you think of that might do a better job of predicting people's attitudes and behaviors?

contrast. In their communities, they are simply who they are. Similarly, think about Mexican citizens. People living in Mexico City feel no need to identify themselves as Mexicans or as Hispanics because on a daily basis, it is not a relevant consideration. On the other hand, when people live in a country different from that of their birth, they would likely describe themselves according to place of birth because that information might be relevant to understanding their behavior and because it draws a contrast between them and others.

Race and Ethnicity.   **Race** and **ethnicity** are also difficult concepts. When discussing race, researchers (and people in general) often think of biological characteristics. People who make distinctions this way hope to use an objective, biological means to categorize people.

On the other hand, ethnicity is often thought of as a more subjective concept. A person's ethnicity is associated with affiliation. That is, to what group do people think they belong or what group has affected the way an individual thinks and acts?

It doesn't help researchers that the concept of ethnicity itself is somewhat unclear. For instance, Phinney (1996) noted that "ethnicity is most often thought of as culture. . . . To understand the psychological implications of ethnicity, it is essential to identify the specific cultural characteristics associated with an ethnic group and with the outcomes of interest such as educational achievement or mental health" (p. 920). She pointed out that the cultural characteristics (e.g., attitudes and behaviors) are often used to explain ethnic differences.

Matsumoto (1993) depicted ethnicity differently, suggesting that ethnicity "is defined most often by biological determinants; culture, however, must be defined by sociopsychological factors. . . . Defined in this way, the parameters of culture are 'soft,' and perhaps more difficult to distinguish, than the parameters of ethnicity, which are set in biology and morphological differences" (p. 120). An additional argument is that race is a category imposed by a dominant group, whereas ethnicity is an affiliation that people choose (Markus, 2008).

Complicating all these issues is the fact that in research, people often use culture interchangeably with race, ethnicity, and nationality (Betancourt & Lôpez, 1993). In many studies, people must often indicate race by selecting categories that really encompass ethnicity or nationality, not race. Latinos, for instance, can be White, Black, Asian, American Indian, or any combination thereof. It is pretty clear that researchers have not yet solved even the issues of defining terms, much less behaviors associated with cultural differences.

Finally, before we make sweeping claims about people based on nationality, it would be important to keep in mind that there seems to be no convincing evidence that people within a given nation show marked similarities with respect to personality. McCrae and Terracciano (2006) addressed the question of whether there really are national characteristics. Their data led to the conclusion that "people everywhere find it easy to develop stereotyped ideas of whole nations and agree well enough with each other to believe their views are consensually validated. But while there is some consensus, there is no accuracy. National-character stereotypes are apparently not even exaggerations of real differences: They are fictions" (p. 160).

Defining an Individual's Culture, Ethnicity, and Race

Scientific designations should be based on valid, objective, and stable scientific criteria. The categories researchers use often reflect social and political conditions. For example, in record keeping, the Census Bureau is not trying to be scientific; it is trying to describe the population of the United States. Still, scientific research relies on Census Bureau categories. Berreby (2000) has pointed out that the utility of racial classifications depends in part on how well people define the categories they use.

Further, Rodriguez (2000) pointed out that the concept of race or ethnicity may not help us understand behavior because an individual may fall into different categories, depending on who is doing the assessment. For instance, when the U.S. government collects data on an individual, the Bureau of the Census does not regard Hispanics as constituting a race, whereas federal agencies that deal with civic rights issues do have a separate racial category for Hispanics. Suppose you wanted to carry out a research project to see if people in different racial categories achieve different educational levels. Would your data include a racial category for Hispanics? With governmental categories, you could argue either way, if you consider that the government has sanctioned both approaches. This duality is problematic for scientific research, which relies on objective and stable measurements and classifications.

Another concern in categorizing research participants is that a researcher may use terms that are clear in the context of an investigation but that might be unclear to others. For instance, Selten et al. (2001) examined psychotic disorders among Turkish, Moroccan, and Hindustani people who had migrated to The Netherlands. But Bhui and Bhugra (2001) pointed out that the terms Turkish and Moroccan reflect place of birth, whereas Hindustani refers to religion. Such a mixture of categories can cause confusion in cross-cultural comparisons. Suppose a Turk was a Hindu. Into what category would he or she fall?

Further, how a person identifies with a given ethnic group can change, depending on the particular context and the degree of the person's acculturation and may very well change over the course of the person's life. For instance, Benet-Martinez et al. (2002) discovered that Chinese Americans switch their cultural perspective from Chinese to American in different ways, depending on whether they viewed Chinese and American cultures as consistent or contradictory with one another.

As a result, studying the effect of ethnicity is very difficult: It is hard to define ethnicity precisely and an individual's commitment to a given ethnic group will vary according to the present circumstances.

Criteria for Inclusion in a Group

The criteria for inclusion in a group change over time. For instance, over the years the United States census has classified people into ethnic groups on the basis of what language they spoke, then their last name, then their place of origin, and now, through self-identification.

Asking people to place themselves into categories can itself lead to problems. Self-categorization changes depending on whether people are given a list of groups from which they must choose or can identify their preferred group affiliation on their own. The self-selection also depends on perceived advantages associated with being considered as a member of one group or another (Panter et al., 2009).

Clearly, people classify themselves differently depending on what is at stake (e.g., Phinney, 1996; Panter et al., 2009). For example, Phinney (1996) cited research in which 259 university students self-identified as American Indian or Alaska Native. Only 52 could provide confirmation that they belonged in those categories. If tuition aid depends on ethnic status, people might classify themselves differently. Research often relies on data resulting from these self-classifications.

In addition, as Phinney (1996) pointed out, when we try to categorize people according to ethnicity, the labels we create are not particularly useful when people come from mixed backgrounds. Beyond that, Phinney noted that "a common practice is to interpret empirical results or clinical observations in terms of cultural characteristics that are assumed to exist but that are not directly assessed" (p. 921). That is, researchers make assumptions about behaviors of the groups they are studying, but the researchers often do not check to make sure that their assumptions are valid. According to Phinney, when investigators have taken the time to look at supposedly relevant cultural characteristics, the results have often shown that researchers' assumptions are misguided.

As an example of a difficulty in categorization, consider the Chinese, a group that has recently been studied extensively in cross-cultural psychology. Chang (2000) noted that the Chinese are not easy to characterize because being Chinese can mean an enormous number of things. For one thing, there is no single "race" because of the genetic and anthropological variability among the Chinese, who can count over 50 ethnic minorities encompassed under the overarching term "Chinese." In addition, the diversity in language is so great that you could find two languages labeled "Chinese" that are as different from one another as German is from French. Another consideration is that people from urban and rural areas can have very different cultures, as can people who are either literate or illiterate.

Researchers studying Chinese people living outside China sometimes use the family name as an indicator of being Chinese. This is a problematic strategy. Chang pointed out that the name Lee can be Chinese and has been used to signify Chinese ethnicity, even though Lee is also a Korean and a Vietnamese name. Lee can also be a Western name—there is no evidence that the Confederate General Robert E. Lee was Chinese. Further, the most common Chinese surname, Chang, is also a Korean name.

Sometimes, researchers are even broader in their categorization schemes. Cohen and Gunz (2002), in studying the difference between Eastern and Western thought, simply included a participant in the Eastern category if he or she had been born in Asia. The range of ethnicity across groups is vast. Participants in the Asian group were probably as different from one another as they were from the participants who grew up in North America. In other research, Kim, Atkinson, and Yang (1999) put into one category Asian Indians, Cambodians, Filipinos, Hmong, Japanese, Koreans, and others. This represents a stereotype that all people from Eastern cultures share significant attitudes and behaviors and that they all differ from people in the West.

To add to the confusion, Kim et al. (1999) have suggested that as people from Asian countries become acculturated to the United States, their behaviors change more quickly than their attitudes, which may not change even across generations. So in one sense, they are attitudinally still members of an ethnic group but behaviorally they are not. When we describe people within some arbitrarily determined category, we may be talking about very different types of people as though they were the same, and we may incorrectly decide that a single person is more consistently ethnic than he or she really is.

Because of these complex issues, some psychologists have argued that because of the methodological and conceptual problems associated with categorizing people, it is not useful to regard people from a given category as constituting an intact group. This issue looms large because researchers often do not use empirical assessments to verify that people in a given group actually share important behaviors and attitudes other than race (Helms, Jernigan, & Mascher, 2005). With respect to health-related research, Shields et al. (2005) suggested that researchers report the ethnic and racial makeup of their samples but not use the categories as variables in statistical analysis.

Social Issues and Cultural Research

The way we categorize people has implications for the way we think of social issues. As you can see in Figure 14.1, the National Center for Educational Statistics reported that high school dropout rates for Hispanics are very high (Kaufman et al., 2000). What should we conclude from the fact that Hispanics are nearly seven times more likely to drop out of high school than Americans of Asian descent? This question is too simplistic because

Discussion Questions

1. What problems can arise when investigators doing cultural research use data collected by the government to study people in different racial and cultural categories? Why is it important for researchers to consider the idea that people within any given group are really very heterogeneous?

2. Why is it reasonable to suppose that degree of acculturation is a better predictor of behavior than ethnic background? Give some examples of behaviors and attitudes associated with degree of acculturation.

FIGURE 14.1 *High School Dropout Rates According to Ethnicity/Race in the United States*

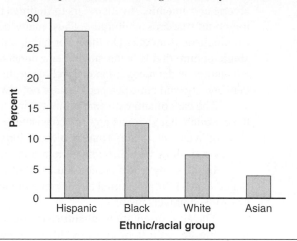

Source: Kaufman et al., 2000

dropout rates for Hispanics drop by two-thirds for families who have been in the United States for two generations or more. Thus, ethnic categories are less important than degree of acculturation.

Rather than concentrating on ethnicity, it might make more sense to talk about other variables, like the number of years people have lived in a given culture, socioeconomic status, fluency in English, nature of one's peers, and so forth (Chiriboga et al., 2007; Watkins, Mortazavi, & Trofimova, 2000).

Yee and colleagues (1993) summarized the problems nicely: They noted that psychologists themselves use common stereotypes and rely on self-identification. The use of stereotypes suffers from four notable problems: It (a) neglects important differences among people in the same group, (b) assumes with no proof that behaviors that differ across groups are based on racial or cultural differences, (c) inappropriately depicts race and other variables as being related, and (d) relies on ideas for which there is no scientific consensus.

Cross-Cultural Concepts in Psychology

Historically, psychologists have not concerned themselves with cultural differences. From the first decades of the 1900s and into the 1960s, most psychologists were behaviorists who thought that organisms were similarly affected by reinforcement contingencies—how often they were rewarded or punished. As a result, it didn't make much difference to psychologists whether they studied rats, pigeons, or people from any background. The causes of behavior were seen as the same universally.

Are Psychological Constructs Universal?

Early cross-cultural researchers imposed their own cultural viewpoints on the behaviors of the people they studied, which meant that they failed to understand the subtleties of other cultures. Such an approach could probably be forgiven because the researchers were opening up a new field of study and knew much less than they thought they did or needed to know for complete understanding of the people they researched. Still, after a while, it became clear that things were not as simple as people had hoped.

Etic— A research finding that appears to be universally true across cultures.

Emic—A research finding that is valid only within a given culture.

Absolutism—In discussions of cultural research, the concept that maintains that behavioral phenomena can be viewed from the same perspective, regardless of the culture in which they appear.

Relativism—In discussions of cultural research, the concept that maintains that behavioral phenomena can be understood only within the context of the culture in which they occur.

Universalism—A moderating view in cultural research that maintains that behavioral phenomena may be based on invariant psychological processes but that each culture will induce different manifestations of those underlying processes.

One of the distinctions that resulted from critical analysis of the research was between an **etic** and an **emic.** An etic refers to findings that result from studies across cultures and that may hold true cross-culturally. Thus, many people might regard the taboo against incest or cannibalism as an etic. On the other hand, an emic refers to a finding that is particular to a single culture that is being studied and understood in local terms. Although these two terms are gaining wider recognition in psychology, they are still controversial because the distinction between etic and emic perspectives are not always clear (Lonner, 1999).

The case of anorexia and bulimia is instructive here. Smith, Spillane, and Annus (2006) have argued that anorexia appears consistently across cultures, but that bulimia is a phenomenon of Western culture. Thus, two conditions that many people regard as having overlap in causes may show very different cultural manifestations.

In the study of different cultures, Berry, Poortinga, Segall, and Dasen (1992, cited in Segall et al., 1998) identified three orientations in cross-cultural psychology: absolutism, relativism, and universalism.

The first orientation, **absolutism** assumes that behavioral phenomena are basically the same, regardless of cultures. In this view, depression will be depression; it does not differ from one locale to another. Should we believe this? Price and Crapo (1999) illustrate the difficulty with accepting the concept of depression as a single, unvarying construct across cultures. For example, the Hopi do not have a single category that corresponds to the Western view of depression; they have five different categories. For them depression as most of us view it would be too broad a label to be therapeutically useful. Further, the hopelessness of major depression would be accepted by some Buddhists as simply being "a good Buddhist" (p. 126). In a Buddhist culture, it would make no sense to describe symptoms of depression (as we know them) as a pathological condition because Buddhists believe that hopelessness is part of the world and that salvation arises, in part, in recognition of this hopelessness.

A second orientation is **relativism.** A relativistic approach stands in contrast to absolutism in that relativists make no attempts to relate psychological constructs across cultures. A researcher with this orientation would undertake only emic research, believing that the phenomena of any culture stands independently from those in any other. According to Segall et al. (1998), few psychologists favor either the extreme of absolutism or of relativism. Most fall between these two poles.

The final orientation is **universalism.** This approach strikes a balance between absolutism and relativism, accepting the idea that there may be universal psychological processes, but that they manifest differently, depending on the particular culture. For example, Segall, Campbell, and Herskovits (1966) found that susceptibility to perceptual illusions was widespread and suggested universal, underlying cognitive processes. At the same time, reactions differed depending on a person's life experience.

According to the absolutist viewpoint, if perceptual illusions are caused by universal sensory processes, we should all experience illusions the same way. But that usually doesn't happen. According to the relativist viewpoint, there could be little or no similarity in perceptions across cultures because perception in this orientation arises only from experience. That, too, doesn't seem very common. According to the universalist perspective, the same internal processes take place but lead to different interpretations because of experience. The truth is likely to fall somewhere between the extreme viewpoints.

Although scientists hope for psychological constructs that are valid across cultures, careful examination of behaviors so far leads us to be careful to avoid falling prey to our own cultural biases. In the Controversy box on culture and neurological diagnosis, we see that something as objective as medical diagnosis is susceptible to cultural influences. The case study provided by Klawans (2000) provides an illustration of cultural problems in diagnosing brain damage. The patient and the physician came from different backgrounds

■ ■ ■ ■ ■

CONTROVERSY
Does Culture Make a Difference in Neurological Diagnosis?

Diagnosing a medical or psychiatric condition resembles the formal research process quite closely. Physicians initially ask enough questions to allow them to form hypotheses about a problem. They then make observations and draw conclusions. If they still don't have enough information to identify the source of a patient's problems, they generate more hypotheses and ask more questions. Finally, the physician comes to a conclusion and treats the patient. In many cases, the ultimate diagnoses are correct, but sometimes they are wrong. This is exactly what happens in research. With luck, we are right most of the time, but research and diagnosing are complicated enough that sometimes we are wrong.

The neurologist Harold Klawans (2000) described a case from the 1970s in which a patient with neurological problems was initially misdiagnosed because of cultural factors. The patient, who had suffered repeated blackouts due to carbon monoxide poisoning in the workplace, was brought to a Chicago hospital.

As part of the diagnostic process, an attending neurologist asked the patient who the mayor of Chicago was. He responded correctly, but was unable to identify any other, previous mayors, asking if there ever had been any other mayors. He was also unable to name the current president or any previous presidents. The patient did not know that President John Kennedy had been assassinated, and had no knowledge of the Vietnam war, which was a very controversial aspect of American culture at the time. This patient was an American who had lived through all of these events, so it was very strange for him not to know such fundamental cultural knowledge.

The neurologist finally asked the patient to identify which of four objects was different from the others: hammer, wood, chisel, wrench. The patient replied that none of them was different; they were all the same. At that point, the doctor concluded that the patient had suffered severe brain damage.

As Klawans discovered through further questioning, though, the patient's memory for some things (like baseball) going back 40 years was very acute. The trouble with the initial diagnosis was that the first doctor had not taken culture into account. The patient, who had grown up in Mississippi in the 1930s, had gone to school for two years and had never learned to read. As a result, the patient's memories rested on what he had experienced directly. He didn't watch the news on television, so it is no surprise that he didn't know about the president, about Vietnam, about politics. None of these things had ever entered his world.

Klawans stated that people who don't read don't classify objects the way that literate people do. The task of categorizing the hammer, wood, chisel, and wrench is a foreign concept to them. It is only relevant to those of us who use written words to designate objects. The ability to read brings a set of skills that we take for granted, like classifying, but that ability is very closely bound to literacy.

If the patient hadn't experienced it himself, he didn't have a memory for an event. Imagine for yourself how much you would know about world events if you didn't read about them or see them on the news. His concept of the world was very different from that of the first doctor. In the end, it was clear that the patient's mental faculties were as sharp as anyone else's. Had Klawans not been attuned to this cultural difference, the patient might have been diagnosed with severe brain damage.

and had radically different points of view, which could pose challenges for adequate diagnosis and treatment.

Issues in Cross-Cultural Research

When researchers pursue cross-cultural research, they can fall prey to certain problems in interpreting their data. Van de Vijver and Leung (2000) have identified four major concerns in research on people from different cultural groups.

1. Although some behavioral differences across cultures reflect important cross-cultural differences in thought and behavior, some differences in behavior are quite superficial and do not relate to important, underlying psychological processes.
2. Sometimes psychological tests legitimately generate different patterns of scores across cultures. There is often a tendency to treat them as artifacts of measurement error, that is, to see the test as deficient rather than as identifying true differences between groups. In other words, when we indeed find cultural differences, it might be tempting to ignore them rather than share unpopular results.

3. Researchers are prone to overgeneralization from their results. That is, differences due to small sample biases or poor measurement instruments may lead researchers to make more of their data than they should.
4. Differences across groups may reflect lack of equivalence across samples. The differences could occur because the samples contain different types of people who differ in critical ways, not because the cultures differ.

These difficulties imply what van de Vijver and Leung (2000) call the **interpretation paradox** of cross-cultural research. Large differences between very diverse cultures are easy to obtain but hard to interpret because the reasons for the differences may be caused by any of a number of multiple factors. On the other hand, small differences between people of similar cultures may be hard to spot, but when observed, are easy to interpret because the groups being assessed share many features, so the reasons for differences stand out and are easy to identify.

Is There a Biological Basis for Race?

Interpretation paradox—In cultural research, the fact that large differences between groups are easy to spot but hard to understand because there are so many factors that could be responsible, whereas small differences are harder to spot but easier to explain.

Psychologists in the United States have studied one particular ethnic group to a great extent, blacks or African Americans. Very often, the research does not appear to center around culture or ethnicity. Rather, investigators cast their studies in terms of race.

You probably imagine a person's race as something that is clearly defined; many people do. The problem lies in the process we use to classify a person. In the United States, we have had a tradition of calling a person "black" or African American if the person has any African ancestry, no matter how remote or how little. This pattern is known colloquially as the **one-drop rule,** also known as **hypodescent.** A person is black if he or she has "one drop of black blood." In Brazil, a person with any Caucasoid features is regarded as "white" (Zuckerman, 1990). The validity of such racial categorization is suspect if a person's race changes simply because he or she enters a different country.

Psychologists continue to use race as a conceptual category in research, despite good arguments for not doing so (e.g., Helms, Jernigan, & Mascher, 2005). For instance, racial categories can reflect researchers' beliefs more than actual characteristics of participants. In addition, in many studies, researchers do not report the operational definitions of race by which they categorize participants. As Helms et al. reported, researchers sometimes classify people of Asian descent as minorities and sometimes as "white," even in the same study. Liang, Li, and Kim (2004) suggested that this multiple categorization occurs in everyday life and may cause stress, independent of the supposed racial category.

One-drop rule (hypodescent)—One means by which a person is racially categorized as a member of a low status group such that if he or she has "one drop" of blood from a given group (i.e., any ancestor, no matter how remote, from that group), the individual is automatically classified as being from that group, used specifically with people of African descent who live in the United States.

The Criteria for Race

Race is clearly a strange concept scientifically. Why does a single ancestor determine race when there are so many ancestors who are ignored? And why does a single black ancestor make a person black, when a single white ancestor does not make a person white? The concept of race in scientific research is troublesome; race-determining characteristics fall on a continuum, but people create all-or-none categories. Whenever you have a continuum, but you try to make discrete categories, you have to make a decision as to where to put the cutoff for inclusion into different categories. Such decisions are arbitrary, and another person could make a different decision that has as much validity (or lack thereof) as yours.

The use of the concept of race, even among the educated, has sometimes been very loose. For instance, *The Mother's Encyclopedia* (1942) discussed rheumatic fever, asserting that "some races who live in New York are especially prone to it, particularly Italians and Jewish people" (p. 1028). Further, in the United States, there used to be a greater belief in the nature of the continuum regarding black and white, even if there was no real scientific basis for it. Historically, an individual with one black grandparent was classified as a quadroon; a person with one black great-grandparent was listed as an octoroon. These "races" were considered as real as any others.

A great many scientists have concurred that race is a social construction, not a natural phenomenon. Anthropologists and some biologists seem to have caught on to this idea some time ago, but some social and behavioral scientists have been slower to adopt this conclusion.

The problem with race as a construct that might help us understand behavior is that individual differences within races overwhelm the biological differences between races. In other words, if you look at the variability between any two people in the same culture, they show much more variability in genetic makeup than do two "average" people with ancestors on different continents.

At the phenotypical level, race is often defined in terms of features like skin color, but also hair type, eye color, and facial features. These turn out to be unreliable markers for race; in fact, they are not correlated with one another, meaning that just because a person shows one "racial" characteristic, it doesn't mean that he or she will show the others (Zuckerman, 1990). In addition, there are people in the so-called Negroid groups who are lighter in skin color than others in the so-called Caucasoid groups.

As you will see in the Controversy box on different races, scientists have identified a number of different problems associated with the use of racial categories in scientific research. There will undoubtedly be continued debate about the topic of race because of its importance as a social concept.

Current Biological Insights Regarding Race

Scientists working on the Human Genome Project, which is an attempt to identify the genetic makeup of human beings, has brought attention to this issue. According to Harold Freeman of North General Hospital in Manhattan, the percentage of genes that reflect differences in external appearances associated with race is about 0.01 percent (Angier, 2000).

Since the emergence of humans in present form, there have been about 7,000 generations. This is not a sufficiently large number to lead to clear differentiation of one group from another, according to geneticists. Further, there has always been mixing of genes of various groups when they come in contact with one another, intermarry, and reproduce. Biological variables may differentiate groups in a general way, but these variables are not, in and of themselves, markers for race because a person from any group could show them. "For instance, Afro-Americans are at a higher risk [for essential hypertension] than Anglo-Americans. From our perspective, what is of scientific interest is not the race of these individuals, but the relationship between the identified biological factors . . . and hypertension" (Betancourt & Lôpez, 1993, p. 631). The biological factors contribute causally to the hypertension; race is a correlational variable.

Still, some psychologists argue that real racial differences exist. They cite the notion that brain sizes, on average, are largest in Asians, middle-sized in whites, and smallest in blacks, a pattern that reflects trends in IQ scores. That is, the claim is that IQ score and brain size are positively correlated. At the same time, Peters (1993) noted that in studies of brain size and IQ, measurement error as small as one millimeter could account for the observed difference across races.

Historical Error

Unfortunately, from the beginning, research that investigated brain size and intelligence suffered from fatal flaws (Gould, 1996). In the 1840s, Samuel George Morton found that whites had the largest brains, Indians were in the middle, and blacks were on the bottom.

CONTROVERSY
Are There Really Different Races?

How many races are there? Many people in the United States would list white, black, Hispanic, Native American, and Asian, believing that these categories are valid, discrete groupings. That is, you are white or you are not; you are black or you are not; etc. Everybody falls into one and only one category.

The truth is not so simple. In reality, there do not seem to be biologically based markers that separate people conveniently and reliably. For example, skin color, which many people use to define inclusion in a racial category, is inconsistent. There are black people who are lighter than white people. Similarly, people of Asian descent span many different skin colors. The same is true for Native Americans and Hispanics. Skin lightness or darkness may be the most obvious trait that people rely on, but any characteristic you select has the same weaknesses.

People are very hard to classify precisely and objectively. One reason is that the differences among people are usually on a continuum. One person has more or less of this or that trait. When you have such continua, any point on the continuum that you use to create categories is going to be arbitrary; another person can justify using a different point.

Once scientists decided that racial differences were interesting, there were always problems defining race. In the 1920s, scientists agreed that there were three European races; in the 1930s, they changed it to 10 European races. At the same time, there was a single African-based racial category. Africa is a big continent (over 11 million square miles); Europe is a small continent (about 4 million square miles). Not surprisingly, Africans show much greater genetic diversity than Europeans do. Why then was there only one African race? The categorization process was based on socially derived beliefs, not scientific measurement.

In addition, if you look at a map, it is not clear where Europe ends and Asia begins. The boundary is arbitrary. Further, if you look at a map, you will see that the line that divides Asia and Africa is also arbitrary. So is the distinction between Asian and African people. By the same token, why should we have any faith that the distinction between Europeans and Asians is real? It is too easy to form stereotypes and consider them to be objective, reliable, and valid. But assigning people to different racial categories based on an arbitrary boundary is questionable. In some ways, it would be similar to identifying people from Ohio and Michigan as being from different races based on an arbitrary politically drawn line.

In terms of psychological research, we see again and again that behaviors and characteristics attributed to race generally have their causes in social or environmental factors. When researchers account for these factors, the effect of "race" generally diminishes or vanishes.

If a fine analysis eliminates effects of "race" on behavior in most of situations that have been studied, a critical thinker might conclude that the remaining differences could well be due to factors that researchers have not yet identified.

Nobody has yet identified scientifically reliable and valid definitions of race based on biology or genetics. As Yee et al. (1993) and others have pointed out, even in scientific research, depictions of race are generally made from a layperson's point of view, with no real scientific backing. Finally, it seems reasonable to believe that when one argument after another falls, it becomes more parsimonious to believe that racial factors per se are irrelevant and that social and economic factors create differences between groups.

As it turns out, his sample of skulls was egregiously poor. He specifically included a large number of Peruvian Inca skulls; these people were small of stature. He had very few Iroquois Indians, whose skulls were large. As a result, the mean skull size of Indians was artificially low.

Morton also decided to eliminate some Caucasian skulls, of Hindus who were small, thereby raising the average of Caucasians. There is no evidence that Morton thought he was doing anything inappropriate, because he kept meticulous records that others could investigate. If he had tried to cheat, he would not have kept such good records or made them public. He assumed that white Europeans had greater intelligence than others; the use of skull and brain size was simply meant to quantify what "everybody knew to be true." So he had little reason to doubt his methodology or his conclusions.

Discussion Questions

1. Could historical mistakes concerning the relationship between race and the measurement of IQ recur today? How?
2. What difficulties arise in using the concept of genetic differences as the source of supposed racial differences?
3. How have society's ideas affected how we have defined race?

Current Controversies

Modern psychologists (e.g., Cernovsky, 2000) have countered the argument about brain size and intelligence with the fact that mean brain size of groups living near the equator is less than that of groups nearer the poles, so that brain size is correlated with geography of one's ancestors and not much else. Besides, women's brains are smaller than men's, even after body size is taken into consideration. There is no evidence that women are less intelligent than men.

Another problem arises when we equate a score on a standardized test with intelligence. An IQ score is just that, a test score. It relates to behaviors that the test makers regard as important, like how well you do in school. It is true that your grades in school will correlate pretty well with your IQ score, but much of that may be due to the fact that IQ scores are based, to a degree, on tasks that are valued in educational settings. Thus, it is no surprise that people who score low on intelligence tests do not do well in school.

Flynn (1999) has refuted a number of arguments that relate IQ and race, concluding that environmental differences explain differences in scores on IQ tests and that genetic (i.e., racial) interpretations, when investigated empirically, lead to conclusions that simply do not make sense. In fact, he has documented and discussed the regular increase in IQ scores across many countries over the past several decades that have emerged in too short a time to be genetically mediated (e.g., Flynn, 2007). There is good reason to believe that the causes are environmental, such as improved nutrition for pregnant women (Lynn, 2009) and increased access to education with better pedagogical practices (Blair et al., 2005). Further, the Flynn effect may have disappeared or reversed itself in some countries (Shayer & Ginsburg, 2009; Teasdale & Owen, 2005), while progressing in other, such as Estonia (Must et al., 2008), again within a time frame too rapid to be genetically based.

The controversy will undoubtedly persist for a long time because the issues remain socially controversial and complex and the arguments multifaceted.

Practical Issues in Cultural Research

Sue (1999) has pointed out some of the major issues in carrying out cross-cultural research. One of them is that many researchers may have difficulty finding participants from different cultural groups. Just like students who have little time for anything other than home life, schoolwork, and extracurricular activities, researchers have limited amounts of time.

The result is that when they plan their own research, they make use of student participants because of availability; it doesn't hurt that the students are also willing, bright, and motivated. The people who volunteer for research are different from people in general and in many colleges may not show much cultural diversity. And even when there is diversity, research samples may include mostly students. The truth is that it would take a considerable amount of time, money, and energy to find the diverse samples that are desirable. Given the practical considerations, researchers generally feel that they have to live with the samples they can access, even if it limits how well their results apply to different groups.

Lack of Appropriate Training Among Researchers

In addition to having access to fairly homogeneous samples, researchers may simply not have the knowledge or training needed to conduct high-quality, cross-cultural research. Fortunately, the Council of National Psychological Associations for the Advancement of Ethnic Minority Interests has developed guidelines published by the American Psychological Association for research with ethnic minority communities (Council of National Associations, 2000). Some of their major points appear in Table 14.1.

Discussion Question

1. Why is it useful to include people from cultural groups you are studying when you plan your study and when you interpret your results?

TABLE 14.1 *Important Considerations Regarding Research with People of Ethnic Groups*

Personal Characteristics
Develop awareness of the culture of the group you study
Become aware of the effects of the culture and oppression and discrimination
Recognize multiple linguistic and communication styles
Recognize the heterogeneity that exists within any simple ethnic label
Identify the degree to which an individual is acculturated

Research Considerations
Recognize cultural assumptions and biases in creating methods and materials
Make sure all measurement instruments make sense from the cultural viewpoint of the group
    you study
Use measurement instruments that are appropriately normed and that have established reliability
    and validity
Determine if the research is culturally relevant to the group you study
Establish appropriate comparison (control) groups
Use adequately translated materials to maximize effectiveness of communication
Conduct a cost/benefit analysis to make sure the research is worth doing

Outcomes
Interpret results within the appropriate cultural context
Consider alternate explanations
Remember that difference does not mean deviance
Request help from community members in interpreting your research results
Increase mainstream outlets for minority research
Recognize the existence of confounding variables like educational level and socioeconomic status

Source: Council of National Psychological Associations, 1999.

These considerations are important in any research project. They just happen to be particularly relevant to research with ethnic minorities. If you keep these points in mind, any research with any population will be better.

Why the Concepts of Culture and Ethnicity Are Essential in Research

After the long discussion about the controversial concepts of race and ethnicity, you may wonder why we should consider it in our research. The reason is that various groups of people differ from one another in many ways. These groups just don't differ in the simplistic ways we normally think. We need to identify what differences appear across groups, as well as what differences occur within groups. We also need to identify factors that cause those differences because group affiliation alone may not be the only, or the most important, reason.

Differences Due to Language and Thought Processes

The importance of culture on psychological processes stands out clearly in a body of research associated with the way people recognize emotions on the faces of people in photographs. For example, Matsumoto, Anguas-Wong, and Martinez (2008) tested native Spanish speakers who were proficient in English either in Spanish or in English. Participants saw photographs and attempted to identify the emotion of the person depicted and to rate the intensity of the emotion. The participants were better at recognizing emotions when tested in English, even though their native language was Spanish. On the other hand, they rated the intensity of the emotions higher when doing it in Spanish. In earlier research, Matsumoto and Assar (1992) tested students in India who were bilingual in English and in Hindi. The students recognized emotions more accurately when they used English than Hindi. According to Matsumoto and Assar, people who speak English come from cultures in which people are used to talking openly about emotions. This cultural effect may lead English speakers to greater recognition and accurate judgment of emotions.

Further support for the importance of language in thought came from research by Marian and Neisser (2000), who demonstrated that bilingual people have easier access to memories when they try to recall those memories using the language they would have used when they initially experienced the event.

Language involves more than different word use. In fact, Ball, Giles, and Hewstone (1984) suggested that in order to learn a second language, you must also learn the culture of that language. You won't understand the language completely unless you know its context. The research by Matsumoto and colleagues reveals that culture may affect the way people think about or express their ideas. If you were conducting research that involved only speakers of English (which is true for the vast majority of psychological research), your conclusions about how people respond to the world around them will be very limited.

Language may also influence thought in other ways. Hedden and colleagues (2002) noted that Chinese speakers have an advantage over English speakers in some numerical tasks because the Chinese words representing numbers are shorter, thus easier to remember. They found no such advantage on a visuo-spatial task involving completing visual patterns. Thus, language may affect not only what you think but also how you think. Cross-cultural research needs to take such differences into account.

Differences in Simple and Complex Behaviors

Even simple responses may differ as a function of culture. When Chinese and American students indicated how often they engaged in certain behaviors, the Chinese participants may have had better memories than American students (Ji, Schwarz, & Nisbett, 2000). The researchers concluded that, as members of a collectivist society, the Chinese are expected to monitor their own behaviors closely. The Americans, on the other hand, did not seem to have as reliable a memory for their behaviors and had to estimate them. Thus, even a simple memory task may lead to fundamentally different ways of responding, depending on your culture.

Not surprisingly, differences in behaviors also occur in more complex situations. For instance, people in China seem to have a different approach to problem solving than people in the Western world. Peng and Nisbett (1999) studied Chinese students and American students in several experiments to see how they responded to contradictory statements in decision making. Chinese students were generally more comfortable accepting two contradictory statements as involving partial truths; American students were more likely to look for a single, logical truth.

These differences reflect fundamentally different views of the world. If you look at the psychological literature in problem solving, you find that there is remarkably little non-Western thought. In problem solving, the emphasis in most research is on logic and rationality that arrives at a single, logically coherent response. Before we claim that such approaches are a good general characterization of problem solving, we should remember that perhaps a billion people (or more) in this world would disagree with our representation of thought and decision making.

It is important to remember that the modes of thought favored in the East and in the West are both useful and valid, but both are incomplete. As Peng and Nisbett (1999) pointed out, the world is complex and contradictory. Thus, we may have to accommodate our thoughts to accept potential contradictions and incomplete knowledge. At the same time, a non-dialectical or Western approach is useful for identifying when a particular argument is better supported by data and for generating useful counterarguments to rebut a possibly flawed argument.

If we want to generate a complete description of the way people think and solve problems, we cannot ignore the fact that our approach to problem solving reflects ways that we are comfortable with, but they are not the only ways that are valid. Knowing about culture helps us know about thought. Ignoring the effects of culture will mean that we have incomplete knowledge about thought and behavior.

Is Culture-Free Theory Really Free of Culture?

The importance of understanding cultural effects on behavior emerges when we look at the studies of how babies attach themselves to parents. Rothbaum and colleagues (2000) described the general tenets of attachment theory and assessed whether the theory is more culturally relevant in the Western hemisphere than elsewhere. This is an important discussion because many psychologists view attachment theory as evolutionarily based, thus free of cultural biases.

Three of the important tenets of attachment are as follows: First, there is a connection between maternal sensitivity and security of attachment. Second, secure children are more socially and emotionally competent than insecure children. Third, infants who show higher levels of adaptation are more likely to explore when they feel secure. These notions seem pretty straightforward. The research on attachment has typically involved middle-class American children. If attachment were strictly a part of evolutionary development, this would not be a problem. However, cultural differences may be important in the behaviors, and the very basis of the theory may be biased toward Western perspectives (Keller, 2008).

As Rothbaum et al. (2000) noted, when parents or teachers identify potentially problematic behavior, the Japanese may identify one set of behaviors as appropriate and a different set as troublesome. The Americans could reverse the pattern. Rothbaum et al. maintain that in order to understand the nature of children's attachment, we have to understand the culture because attachment theory is not as culture-free as psychologists have traditionally believed.

These researchers may raise valid points, but not all psychologists agree. For instance, Chao (2001) suggested that Rothbaum didn't define the term *culture* adequately, equating it with nations. Van Ijzendoorn and Sagi (2001) and Chao also argued that there is too much variability within Japanese and within American cultures for easy generalizations about Japanese people and American people. The disagreements aren't reconciled easily because of the difficulties associated with cultural research.

Similarities and Differences within the Same Culture

People who grow up in the same culture share attitudes, values, and behaviors, but such people are not merely clones of one another. Part of the problem is that people in a group may show similarities on one dimension but not on another. Matsumoto (1993) investigated differences in emotion among Americans of various ethnic groups.

He asked his research participants to identify the emotion displayed in facial photographs and rate its intensity. They also indicated how appropriate a display of the emotion was. He discovered that some differences existed among Asian Americans, blacks, Hispanics, and whites, but the differences were inconsistent. Sometimes the different groups rated emotions in the pictures the same, but sometimes not. For example, Americans of Asian ancestry looked at a given picture and saw less anger than an American of African ancestry. But the Asian Americans saw an equal amount of sadness as African Americans. In addition, African Americans saw more intense emotions generally in pictures of white people than did Asian, Hispanic, or white Americans.

Discussion Questions

1. How can culture affect our memories and our perspectives on emotion?

2. Why would the results of a problem-solving study differ if the researcher recruited Chinese versus American participants? For what kinds of problems would the Chinese show an advantage? the Americans?

3. Use Matsumoto's (1993) research on facial expressions to argue that different groups sometimes show similarities, but sometimes they don't.

This pattern of findings suggests that if we are studying emotions, we could sometimes treat all Americans as more or less similar (e.g., for happiness and sadness), but not all the time (e.g., for fear). Simple research like this can reflect the complexity of cross-cultural studies.

Finally, researchers who assume that people within a given nation share stereotypical traits may be making a significant mistake. As noted before, McCrae and Terracciano (2006) have demonstrated that there is no empirical support for a so-called national culture.

Cultural Factors in Mental Health Research

Psychologists continue to make progress in mental health research, documenting the effectiveness of various therapies for different problems and identifying variables associated with normal and abnormal behavior. As we have recognized the diversified culture in the United States, we have begun to pay attention to the different needs of people of varying backgrounds, although we still know much less than we need to know.

One type of research that clinical psychologists conduct involves assessing the validity of psychological tests across cultural boundaries. If we cannot translate tests into different languages to convey the same ideas as they do in English, we cannot be confident that test results signify the same psychological processes. A poorly translated test will not assess the same thing in both languages. Problems also occur when clinicians try to use a test with minority or immigrant populations when that test is created for and standardized on a white population born in the United States and raised to speak English. In either case, the scores might mean different things.

Chen (2008) has identified four major issues associated with testing people from different cultures. They include issues of (a) translation: Do questions in different languages actually ask the same thing? (b) Construct invariance: Are the concepts the same across cultures? (c) Response styles: Do people in different cultures tend to show the same response patterns? (d) Social desirability: Are there differences in impression management across cultures? Some of these concerns were raised in the context of survey research but are worth mentioning again. Examples of some of the problems appear below.

Content Validity

The process of ensuring that psychological tests serve diverse populations is difficult (Rogler, 1999). Diagnostic and research instruments need to make sense from the viewpoint of those who use them; that is, the tests must show, among other things, **content validity.** The questions should, in expert judgment, relate to what the test assesses. When psychologists create tests, they have to decide what questions to ask. This is where their expert judgment comes in. The problem is that potential patients or clients may not share the same culture as the psychologist, so the patient or client may be answering a different question than the clinician is asking.

Rogler (1999) illustrated this point through a particular question on the Diagnostic Interview Schedule (DIS), which he noted is the most influential test in psychiatric epidemiology. The question asks, "Do you often worry a lot about having clean clothes?" This question might be useful in identifying whether people are overly distressed about unreasonable things. The problem with this question is that it assumes that the person answering it has access to running water. If you have all the water you need, then worrying about clean clothes might be a sign of psychological distress. On the other hand, if you do not have access to running water, laundry facilities, and so forth, such a worry becomes a reasonable preoccupation.

Content validity—The degree to which the material contained in a test relates to the concept being assessed.

As it turns out, many Plains Indians in the United States do not have access to running water. Thus, to respond that they do not worry about clean clothes would probably be more indicative of a problem than if they replied that they do worry. From this point of view, we can see that what might be an appropriate question on the DIS for many of us would be entirely inappropriate for others of us.

Translation Problems

If questions pose difficulties within the same language, imagine what problems arise if we try to translate the test into a different language for use by people whose cultural outlook does not match ours. Rogler (1999) provided another example from the DIS to illustrate the dilemma of creating a faithful translation of a test item into a different language.

He identified the question that reads, "I felt I could not shake off the blues even with help from my family or friends." In trying to translate this apparently simple and straightforward item into Spanish, he encountered great difficulty. In translation, an individual tries to stay as close to the original wording as possible, but there were no suitable Spanish equivalents. One problem here is that in English, "the blues" has a particular meaning that does not survive in a translation to the Spanish word *azul,* the color blue. Rogler also noted that in the United States, we often think that it would be possible, by force of will, to "shake off" an unwanted mood. Is this concept shared by Spanish speakers? If so, what Spanish verb would be appropriate? He wondered whether the word *sacudir* would be a good translation. It means to shake off vigorously like a dog shakes water off its body. He decided that *sacudir* would not be appropriate.

After considerable contemplation, he translated the item by rewording the original English sentence to read "I could not get over feeling sad even with help from my family or friends." He then found it easier to prepare a Spanish version. Normally, a translator tries not to deviate from the original form of an item, but in this case, there was probably no alternative if the translation was to be meaningful. Table 14.2 provides other examples that Rogler generated to illustrate the cultural biases of the DIS.

TABLE 14.2   *Examples Reflecting a Strong Effect of Culture That May Cause Problems Across Cultures*

Example	*Reason for the Problem*
In assessing dissociation, the Dissociative Experience Scale asks about the following: "Some people have the experience of driving a car and suddenly realizing that they don't remember what has happened during all or part of the trip."	The question assumes that the person taking the test takes long car trips. This kind of factual assumption is a problem because people living in the inner city rarely, if ever, drive in places that do not have heavy traffic. As such, an answer to the question will not provide useful information.
Translation of the Clinical Analysis Questionnaire into Spanish.	Thirty-six percent of test items contained grammatical errors and involved direct translation of colloquialisms that made no sense in Spanish. With these translation problems, we could conclude that the questions in the different languages did not have the same meaning.
How does schizophrenia affect decision making among married couples in San Juan, Puerto Rico?	Among the people studied, decision making was not a critical aspect of familial interactions, as it is in the United States. In Puerto Rico, the corresponding dimension was how "men's work" and "women's work" was divided. Knowing about decision making would not help in understanding problems or devising treatments.
Description of symptoms of bipolar disorder in the Amish.	The typical examples that clinicians look for include buying sprees, sexual promiscuity, and reckless driving, which are not applicable to the Amish. Instead, relevant symptoms involve behaviors like excessive use of public telephones, treating livestock too roughly, or giving gifts during the wrong season of the year.

Source: Rogler, 1999.

One useful technique for ensuring comparability of items across languages is **back translation** (Banville, Desrosiers, & Genet-Volet, 2000). In this process, an item is translated from one language to a second. Then a blind translator converts it back to the first language. For example, an item might start in English, be translated into Spanish, then back again into English. If the original version in the first language is equivalent in meaning to the version that has been translated out of, then back into, English, the item is likely to capture the same concepts in both languages.

Cross-Cultural Norms

Back translation—In cross-cultural research, the process by which comparable testing instruments are developed, by translating from an original language to a second language, then back to the first to ensure that the original version and the translation back into that language produce comparable meanings.

Relatively few distress inventories have received scrutiny on a cross-cultural basis; none have involved norms with college students (Cepeda-Benito & Gleaves, 2000). Ironically, although college students form the typical research participant in psychology, the clinical literature seems to underrepresent them.

When researchers have investigated cross-cultural equivalence of inventories, they have revealed a complex picture. For instance, the complete version of the Center for Epidemiologic Studies–Depression scale seems valid for Americans of African, European, and Mexican descent (Aneschensel, Clark, & Frerichs, 1983), although the short version produces differences between Americans of African and European descent (Tran, 1997, cited in Cepeda-Benito & Gleaves, 2000).

In one study, Cepeda-Benito and Gleaves (2000) investigated the generalizability of the Hopkins Symptom Checklist-21 (HSCL-21) across blacks, Hispanics, and whites. This test is a short, 21-item version of a longer, 57-item inventory designed to measure distress. The HSCL-21 shows validity across a wide array of cultural groups, including Italian, Vietnamese, Latino, and European Americans. Cepeda-Benito and Gleaves investigated whether college students of differing backgrounds responded uniquely to it.

They discovered that the HSCL-21 would be an appropriate test of black, Hispanic, and white college students. Given that other research revealed good construct validity of the inventory, one might have a degree of confidence that a clinician might use this test appropriately with students of many ethnic groups.

Cepeda-Benito and Gleaves (2000) were appropriately cautious in stating that their participants may not be representative of other ethnic college populations. Also, it is true that not every American ethnic group was represented in the research, but its generality across the three disparate groups tested provided cautious optimism. Unfortunately, the number of psychological tests that have been normed for varied groups is still uncomfortably small.

Cross-Cultural Diagnoses

One consequence of the lack of information on the validity of psychological tests for minority populations is that the tests might lead to diagnoses that are based more on ethnicity than on problematic behavior. As Iwamasa, Larrabee, and Merritt (2000) have shown, people may be predisposed to classify individuals of different ethnic groups in predetermined ways.

Iwamasa et al. (2000) identified the criteria for personality disorders listed in the Diagnostic and Statistical Manual (DSM; American Psychiatric Association, 1987). In clinical work, mental health workers observe an individual and make note of behaviors that occur. If a person shows a certain, well-specified group of behaviors, he or she may be diagnosed with a particular personality disorder as a result. In Iwamasa et al.'s study, the researchers asked their participants to sort these diagnostic criteria in three different ways: according to their presence in men versus women, by ethnicity, and by self (i.e., is this characteristic of you?). Some of the statements that the participants rated appear in Table 14.3. The participants did

Discussion Questions

1. How does culture affect diagnosis of psychological or psychiatric problems? What effect do biases and assumptions have?

2. Why would it be a problem for diagnosing psychological problems if a clinician simply translated questions on a psychological test on the spot? What could you do if a client or patient was not fluent enough to answer the questions in English?

TABLE 14.3 *Examples of Descriptions from DSM-III-R That Participants Rated as Typical in Men Versus Women, in Different Ethnic Groups, and of the Participants Themselves*

Examples of Description	*Personality Disorder with Which the Description Is Associated*	*Group in Which the "Symptoms" Are Considered Typical*
Has no regard for the truth Has never sustained a totally monogamous relationship for more than one year	Antisocial	African American
Is easily hurt by criticism or disapproval Fears being embarrassed by blushing, crying, or showing signs of anxiety in front of other people	Avoidant	European American
Inappropriate, intense anger or lack of control of anger, e.g., frequent displays of temper, constant anger, recurrent physical fights Chronic feelings of emptiness or boredom	Borderline	European American
Feels devastated or helpless when close relationships end Allows others to make most of his or her important decisions, e.g., where to live, what job to take	Dependent	European American
Is overly concerned with physical attractiveness Is uncomfortable in situations in which he or she is not the center of attention	Histrionic	European American
Reacts to criticism with feelings of rage, shame, or humiliation (even if not expressed) Believes that his or her problems are unique and can be understood only by other special people	Narcissistic	European American
Perfectionism that interferes with task completion, e.g., inability to complete a project because own overly strict standards are not met Inability to discard worn-out or worthless objects even when they have no sentimental value	Obsessive-Compulsive	European American
Expects, without sufficient basis, to be exploited or harmed by others Bears grudges or is unforgiving of insults or slights	Paranoid	African American
Neither desires nor enjoys close relationships, including being part of a family Is indifferent to the praise and criticism of others	Schizoid	Asian American
Odd or eccentric behavior or appearance Inappropriate or constricted affect, e.g., silly, aloof, rarely reciprocates gestures or facial expressions, such as smiles or nods	Schizotypal	Native American

Source: Iwamasa et al., 2000.

not know that they were dealing with clinical diagnostic criteria. Rather, they simply identified their stereotypes of the "normal" behaviors of people of different types.

The results suggest that strong cultural effects could occur in diagnosing personality disorders. The college students' beliefs about normal characteristics of blacks are the same as the criteria used by psychologists and psychiatrists to diagnose antisocial and paranoid personality disorders. Similarly, the students' depiction of the typical behavior of Asian Americans reflects what clinicians look for in people who are schizoid. According to the research results, people of European descent showed a wide range of behaviors associated with different pathologies.

These results suggested that when people think of the behavior of blacks, whites, Asian Americans, and Native Americans, those behaviors are the same ones used by mental health practitioners to diagnose psychological disorders. The problem is not with Americans of various heritages. The problem is with people's biases and assumptions.

If a psychiatrist or clinical psychologist used implicit stereotypes in dealing with different types of patients or clients, it could lead to differential diagnoses for what might be normal behavior.

Iwamasa et al. studied undergraduate volunteers, not clinicians. In addition, the undergraduates did not assign the diagnostic criteria in the same way that clinicians do. Would the results generalize to clinical psychologists and psychiatrists? Given that mental health workers are members of society, with the same biases, we might suspect so, although we don't know. Only when research takes place in a clinical setting will we know how cultural biases affect the ways that practitioners diagnose people. Until this research is conducted, we need to be skeptical that the best decisions are being made.

Sex and Gender: Do Men and Women Come from Different Cultures?

Discussion Questions

1. In what aspects of life could you argue that men and women come from different cultures? In what aspects could you argue that they come from the same culture?

2. What stereotypes can you think of that are associated with people of a culture other than yours? How could these stereotypes play out in these people's lives? What stereotypes might Europeans have of people from the United States that would cause Americans to act differently?

3. Is there any evidence to suggest that stereotypes have an effect on the people who are the victims of those stereotypes? How could you investigate ways to reduce the effects of stereotype threat?

Much has been made of the behavioral differences between men and women. Is it really true that Men Are from Mars and Women Are from Venus (Gray, 1992)? The short answer is that men and women may differ in some ways, but there are more similarities than differences (e.g., Eagly, 2009; Hyde, 2005)

If we regard culture the way that Matsumoto (1994) defined it, as "the set of attitudes, values, beliefs, and behaviors, shared by a group of people, communicated from one generation to the next via language or some other means of communication" (p. 4), we might very well argue that men and women are culturally different in some important ways. In addition, people stereotype men and women differently, just as people stereotype whites and blacks differently.

Iwamasa et al.'s (2000) research on the perception of stereotypically female or male behaviors also shed light on the fact that people have certain expectations about behaviors across the sexes. The investigators found that normal but stereotypically female behavior was associated with certain disorders (e.g., avoidant personality, paranoia) and normal but stereotypically male behavior with others (antisocial personality, schizoid personality).

In the realm of everyday behavior, people often make a big issue of the differences between women and men in math test scores, which are small when they exist at all. Although we don't understand all the factors associated with any differences, there are enough ambiguities that we should be skeptical of biological explanations. Some important issues about gender differences appear in the Controversy box on men, women, and math on page 354.

Stereotypes and Gender-Related Performance

Could stereotypes of women negatively affect their performance in the same way that stereotypes affect the performance of African Americans and Asian Americans (Cheryan & Bodenhausen, 2000; Steele & Aronson, 1995)? According to Inzlicht and Ben-Zeev (2000), when women attempt to solve difficult math problems in the presence of men, they are less successful than when they are in the presence of other women only. These researchers suggest that, in the presence of men, women act out the stereotype of poorer female performance in mathematics, although other investigators have found that stereotype threat occurs mainly in conjunction with anxiety (Delgado & Prieto, 2008).

Moving back to the question of possible cultural differences between men and women, it seems that some psychologists might be comfortable with the idea. Women see themselves as different from men in some respects; men see themselves as different from women in some respects. Knowing what you do about our culture, do you think that these perceived differences revolve around attitudes, beliefs, and behaviors that are passed from one generation to another? If so, they fit generally accepted definitions of cultural differences.

CONTROVERSY
Are Men Better Than Women at Mathematics?

It is a very widely held belief that women have better verbal abilities than men. Conversely, many people believe that men show better mathematical abilities than women do. In fact, among the general public, you don't hear much argument about it. Just take a look at high school math courses: Boys like them and are more likely to enroll in them. On the other hand, girls like poetry and literature and are more willing to enroll in them. Given that most people will gravitate toward things they do better in, doesn't this say something about the relative abilities of boys and girls in math and English?

The patterns of enrollment in math and in English definitely give us important information, but not necessarily the information we think. Maybe ability doesn't have as much to do with enrollment and success in classes as other factors like encouragement and discouragement. Consider the fact that, at one point, talking Barbie dolls complained how hard mathematics is. Is there a message here? Perhaps years of emphasizing that girls don't like math but boys do, and that boys don't like English but girls do takes its toll.

As Caplan and Caplan (1999) have noted, the popular media have reported about male superiority in mathematics. Should we believe these accounts of sex differences in mathematical abilities?

Two decades ago, Benbow and Stanley (1980, 1983) claimed that hormonal differences in math performance may have been responsible for the differences between men and women. As Caplan and Caplan pointed out, however, nobody bothered to measure hormonal levels of the men or women in the research. Thus, the argument that hormones affect performance goes something like this: Men have higher testosterone levels than women. The men scored higher than the women. Thus, higher testosterone levels lead to higher math scores.

Logically, you cannot use two true, but unrelated, statements to prove an argument. There doesn't seem to be any reliable evidence that testosterone levels bear any relationship to math ability.

According to Caplan and Caplan, people are predisposed to believe in male superiority in math. As such, they are likely to accept plausible-sounding arguments ("the difference is hormonal") even though those arguments are not based on research. When people are predisposed to believe in this difference between the sexes, they tend to ignore potentially potent factors like parents' and teachers' expectations, and responses to society's stereotypes.

We also have to take into consideration the dynamics of the testing situation. As Inzlicht and Ben-Zeev (2000) have shown, the context in which women take tests can influence their performance. Women doing math in the presence of men didn't perform as well as when they were in a single-sex environment. Another point to remember is that research has consistently documented female strengths in quantitative courses (e.g., Schram, 1996). Before we accept facile explanations based on questionable theory, we should rely on well-documented information and explanations that research has provided.

Finally, how do we explain the fact that recent research has revealed that the gap in women's and men's scores is narrowing? Are women becoming more masculine? Are men becoming more feminine? Are men's and women's hormonal levels changing? These are generally unlikely explanations. Greater emphasis on female success in math courses, increased encouragement to take math courses, higher motivation levels, and the nature of the testing situation are probably better explanations.

Chapter Summary

In order to understand why people act as they do, we need to understand the cultural context in which those behaviors occur. The effects of culture, race, and ethnicity all surface in our behaviors. The problem that researchers face in considering these contextual questions is that the terms people use every day and even in scientific research are often quite vague. One researcher may refer to ethnicity in describing a behavior, whereas a different researcher may refer to culture in describing the same thing. Because of the problems with definitions, the conclusions that people draw about causes of behavior are sometimes suspect.

One persistent controversy in this area involves the questionable concept of race. There are quite a number of supposed racial categories. The problem is that these categories aren't scientifically defensible. The recent work in genetics indicates that genes are not going to be a useful way of defining races. Still, some scientists maintain that racial categories are useful in their research, even if they cannot define the concept very well.

Because of the complexities of culture, race, and ethnicity, scientific researchers have to work hard to understand the relationship between these constructs and people's behaviors. Research across cultures can be difficult because cultural factors may cause people to understand even simple situations differently. Judgments made by two people from the same cultural background may differ greatly; judgments across cultural boundaries may be nearly impossible to understand without research into those factors. Within the United States, differences between men and women have provided a good deal of controversy, with many questions yet unanswered.

Key Terms

Absolutism	Emic	One-drop rule (hypodescent)
Back translation	Ethnicity	Race
Content validity	Etic	Relativism
Culture	Interpretation paradox	Univeralism

Chapter Review Questions

Multiple Choice Questions

1. The customs, values, and attitudes that can be used to characterize and identify a population refer to
   a. an etic.
   b. an emic.
   c. culture.
   d. relativism.

2. The notion that a person identifies with a particular group of people based on ancestry, religion, or country of origin involves the concept of
   a. ethnicity.
   b. race.
   c. physical culture.
   d. psychological culture.

3. When researchers try to study potential differences across racial and ethnic groups, the categories they use
   a. now rely on well-specified biological and genetic differences.
   b. generally overlap with religious categories, making comparisons difficult.
   c. are unchanging for a single individual over that person's lifespan.
   d. often rely on governmental rather than scientific criteria.

4. When researchers have studied differences between Hispanic and Anglo residents of the United States,
   a. the research shows few reliable differences between the groups.
   b. the research relies on categories recognized by behavioral scientists.
   c. the research often ignores the differences among people within each group itself.
   d. the research typically uses categorization data from several decades ago, so the results are questionable.

5. The virtually universal taboo against cannibalism would be regarded by researchers as
   a. a universal construct.
   b. a hypothetical construct.
   c. an etic.
   d. an emic.

6. The concept that internal, psychological processes may be universal but that they are expressed differently across cultures is associated with
   a. absolutism.
   b. etics.
   c. universalism.
   d. ethnic constructs.

7. The concept of race is controversial scientifically because
   a. the social history of the races has always been troublesome.
   b. the genetic differences between some races is larger than it is between other races.
   c. depending on the categorization process used, an individual could be placed in different racial categories.
   d. scientists have not been able to determine exactly where the different races fall on the racial continuum.

8. When interpreting the results of cultural research on immigrants to a country, investigators should note that
   a. the differences across cultural groups are usually much larger than the differences within groups.
   b. developing test norms for a new culture is often costly and is not worth the cost most of the time because the norms change slowly.
   c. understanding the degree of acculturation of participants is critical to interpreting results.
   d. it is most useful to develop a single interpretation of research results and to avoid the complication of seeking alternate explanations.

9. Matsumoto and Assar (1992) tested participants who spoke English and Hindi on their abilities to recognize emotions of people in photographs. They concluded that
   a. the participants were engaged in the same types of mental processing regardless of language.
   b. the participants' thought processes were more conducive to thinking about emotions when they spoke English.
   c. speakers of English had less willingness to deal with the emotions depicted in the photographs.
   d. the same ideas and emotions are expressed easily in either language.

10. If American research participants were asked to identify the emotion in a facial photograph and rate its intensity, the results might be hard to interpret because
    a. there is little agreement on what behaviors are associated with different emotions.
    b. Americans of different cultural backgrounds show similar responses to some emotions but different responses to others.
    c. people often label the emotion depicted in a photograph very differently and with little consistency.
    d. people from different parts of the country label emotions in consistently different ways.

11. When a test is successfully back translated, it
    a. can be retranslated into virtually any new language.
    b. retains the same meaning in the initial language and the language into which it is translated.
    c. will have validity with respect to cross-cultural norms.
    d. cannot be forward translated afterward.

12. Iwamasa et al. (2000) studied differences in stereotypical female and male behaviors and found that
    a. there are really few consistent differences in behaviors across genders, even though many people perceive differences.
    b. the differences in math and verbal performances between women and men are consistently large.
    c. the stereotypes about male and female differences are true for most high school and college students.
    d. stereotypically female behaviors were associated with certain disorders and stereotypically male behaviors were associated with other disorders.

13. In the discussions of female-male differences in math ability, researchers
    a. are reluctant to publish studies showing female superiority.
    b. measured hormonal differences between women and men and found that the hormones played a part in the higher scores of men.
    c. discovered that if women are tested with men, the women use the situation competitively to raise their math performance.
    d. have reported that the differences between sexes is, on average, small and is getting smaller.

Essay Questions

14. Why is it so hard to distinguish among the effects of culture, race, and ethnicity in our research?

15. Why should we differentiate between etics and emics in our explanations of behavior?

16. Why are culture, race, and ethnicity hypothetical constructs? In what sense are they useful and in what sense are they limited?

17. What are some difficulties that scientists have had in categorizing people by race and in defining race?

18. Why is content validity a critical concept to consider in conducting research on tests administered by mental health workers when working with people from different backgrounds and cultures?

WRITING A RESEARCH REPORT

Most research reports in psychology appearing in journals have a standard format, which is specified in the *Publication Manual of the American Psychological Association* (6th ed.). The use of a consistent style makes it easier for readers to know where to find information in the paper. In addition, once writers learn the basics of APA style, it can be easier to write up a report because it is clear where to put various kinds of information.

In general, APA style papers have the following components in this order:

- Title Page
- Abstract
- Introduction
- Methods
- Results
- Discussion
- References
- Tables
- Figures

Occasionally, there are deviations from this listing. For instance, if a manuscript reports on two or more studies, the author might combine the Results and Discussion section for each study rather than creating two sections. Then there might be a General Discussion after the final study. Once you learn the basic format and after you read a large number of published journal articles, you may find it fairly easy to decide how to modify a manuscript if you need to. Following APA style isn't difficult, but you have to pay attention to a lot of small details. The hardest part of formatting is keeping track of those details.

As with any writing you do, it is important to communicate well. The former editor of the journal *Teaching of Psychology,* Charles Brewer, has commented that writers should strive for "clarity, conciseness, and felicity of expression." This means that you should be clear in making your points; you should use economy in your writing, keeping it as short as you can while still getting your message across; and you should write so that your readers doesn't have to fight their way through a tangled thicket of words to get your point.

Each section of your report will answer certain questions for your reader. For instance, if readers want to know the topic of your research, they know to look in the introduction. If they are asking what you found when you analyzed your data, they know to look in the results section. If they would like to use your ideas and conduct their own research, they know to look in the methodology section to find out how you carried out your study.

This appendix is designed to help you learn appropriate use of APA style in producing your own paper. It will also be useful in giving you guidance on writing style. When it comes to the content, you will have to develop that on your own. Remember that this guide to APA style only highlights the material in the *Publication Manual of the American Psychological Association* that you can use for writing a basic paper. There are some style guidelines that we have not included here because they are relatively rare, like how to cite a newspaper editorial that has no stated author. The information in this appendix will be useful for creating a basic APA-formatted manuscript. There are many other details in the publication manual itself.

Formatting Your Manuscript

There are a few general considerations involved in formatting an APA-style manuscript. To begin with, you should set your margins at one inch on the top, bottom, and sides. Then leave them that way. In addition, everything in the manuscript should be double-spaced. Set your word processor's line spacing at double-spaced. Then leave it that way. (If you are using complex equations, you might need triple spacing, but that is about the only exception to double-spacing.) If you are using Word® as your word processor, you should disable the feature that inserts a small amount of extra space between paragraphs. (Under *Paragraph > Indents and Spacing*, or under *Paragraph > Spacing*, depending on your version of Word, check the box that specifies no space between paragraphs.)

Another aspect of APA style is that every page should feature the running head in the upper left corner and the page number in the upper right-hand corner. The best way to display the running head and to paginate appropriately is with your word processor's function for creating a page header. By using the header function, you guarantee that this information appears where it needs to on every page. If you type in the header and the page number manually, any time you add or eliminate material in your manuscript, the header and page number will wind up in the wrong place.

When you are typing your manuscript, you will create several different sections (e.g., introduction, methods, results, discussion). Do not begin a new section on a new page. As a rule, just continue to type, using normal double-spacing between lines. There are several exceptions to this; they are explained below.

In addition, you have to create headings for each section. There are different levels of headings, depending on the complexity of your manuscript. For most single-study manuscripts, you will use two different types of headings.

When you finish typing the main body of the manuscript and the references, you then add any tables that you want to include. The tables do not appear on the pages with the normal text. They are put at the end, right after the references. Each table goes on a separate page. Following the tables are the figures, one to a page. Graphs, charts, and pictures are all classified as figures.

Figure A.1 shows the general format of a single-study manuscript. Remember that this is a primer on APA style. There are other guidelines that are relevant to more complex manuscripts than you are likely to produce. You can refer to the *Publication Manual* for those details. You can also learn from reading and referring to journal articles that have been published.

FIGURE A-1 *General Outline of an APA-style Paper*

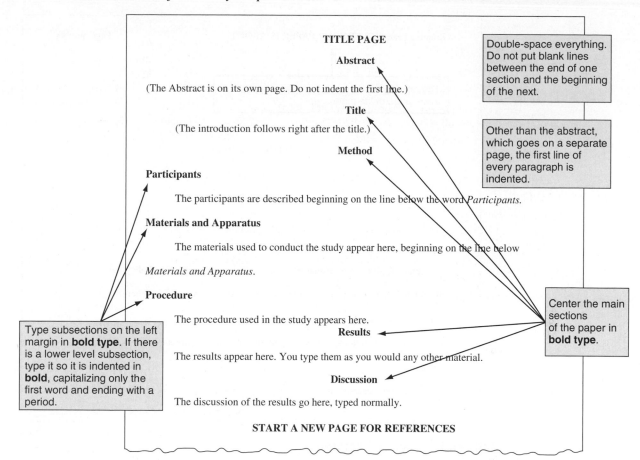

Title Page

The title page is pretty simple to construct, but it is important to include all the information that is required. You can see the general format in Figure A.2. There are three main components of the title page: the running head and page number on one line, followed by the title and author information, then any author's notes.

Running Head

The running head is like an abbreviated title. It should explain the general nature of your project. It is limited to a maximum of 50 characters (i.e., letters and spaces). If your full title is "Study habits of college students over four years," an abbreviated title for the running head could be *STUDENT STUDY HABITS.* (It should be in capital letters.)

FIGURE A-2 *Format of the Title Page in APA Style*

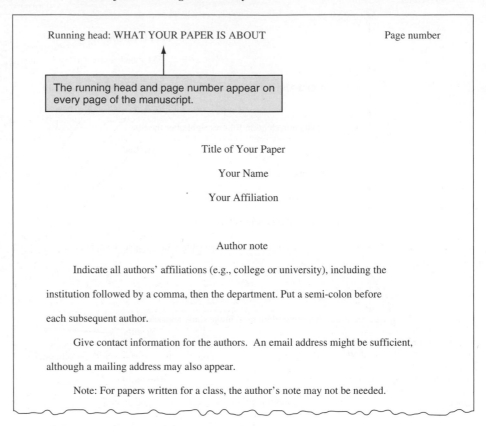

Title and Author Information

The title of the paper should clue the reader into the nature of your project. The recommended length is 10 to 12 words. Your name and your affiliation, which will be your school (unless your instructor tells you otherwise for a class paper), appear just below the title of the paper. They let the reader know who you are and where you come from.

Abstract

The abstract is a brief description of the purpose of the project, what methods the author used to address the issues of interest, the results of data collection, and the conclusions and interpretations the author drew. This section gives the reader a general sense of the paper so he or she can decide whether to read the entire paper.

The abstract is typed on its own page, immediately after the title page. It appears as a block. That is, the first line is not indented. The length of an abstract varies by journal, but is typically 150 to 250 words.

Introduction

The introduction section begins with the title of the article you are writing. The word *Introduction* does not appear. So type the title, then begin the introduction itself. As with the rest of your manuscript, use double-spacing, with no extra space between the title and the beginning of the introduction. This section addresses several questions that prepare the reader for the ideas discussed throughout the manuscript:

- What is the general topic of the research article?
- What do we know about this topic from previous research?
- What are you trying to demonstrate in your research?
- What are your hypotheses?

The introduction sets the stage for the development of all ideas that follow. When you write the introduction, you explain what we already know about the topic addressed in the paper. You describe previous research and talk about the ideas others have developed. Then you present your own ideas, the ones that your research focuses on. There should be a logical connection between the issues you raise about previous research and the project you are introducing. That is, how does the previous work help lead to your ideas?

You are likely to make your first mention of the work of previous researchers in the introduction. There is a general format for referring to that work. When you cite a published journal article, you typically use the authors' last names and indicate the year of publication or presentation of their work. (It is rare that you use authors' initials, first names, or institutional affiliations when you write.) As you see in Figure A.3, you might mention names in the text per se or in parentheses. The APA *Publication Manual* describes the conventions in detail for citing authors. The highlights are in Figure A.3.

FIGURE A-3 *Reference Formats for Citing Work in a Manuscript in APA Style*

The first time you mention a reference, list the last names of all the authors, unless there are more than six. Put the year of publication in parentheses. A period to end the sentence goes after the parentheses.

If you wanted to discuss whether people equate sex and death, you could refer to the research by Goldenberg, Pyszczynski, McCoy, Greenberg, and Solomon (1999). They provided evidence about the sex-death link. Or you could cite the research questioning the effectiveness of the so-called "three strikes" laws that mandate lengthy prison sentences (Stolzenberg & D'Alessio, 1997)

If your first citation of a work appears in parentheses, give the last names of all authors unless there are more than six. Use an ampersand—&— instead of the word *and* before the final author's name.

The second time you refer to work done by three or more authors, cite only the first author. So when mentioning the work linking sex and death by Goldenberg et al. (1999), you use the first author's last name and the Latin abbreviation *et al.*, which stands for *and others* (but you do not use italics). The year goes in parentheses. If you refer to work by two authors, you cite them both any time you mention them, such as the work on prison sentences (Stolzenberg & Dalessio, 1997). If you mention work done by six authors or more, like the work by Stoloff et al. (2010), you include only the first author's name, even the first time you cite it.

If a work has six or more authors, list only the first author's last name, followed by the designation *et al.* (but not in italics). You do this even the first time you mention it.

Method

This section of the manuscript contains several subparts. Each one is pretty much self-contained. The purpose of the method section is to let the reader know how you actually carried out your project. There should be enough detail so another person could read your words and reproduce your study in nearly identical form.

You should present only those details that would be relevant to the purpose and outcome of the study. It isn't always clear what to include, but you have to make your best judgment. For instance, the size, shape, and location of the room in which you conducted your study would not normally be very important. But if the room turned out to be very crowded, it might have affected your results. Or if there was a lot of noisy traffic outside the room, the participants' behaviors might have been affected. You have to decide which details are important and which can be left out.

The different segments of the method section describe who took part, what materials and implements were important in carrying out the study, and the procedure used to complete the research.

Participants

In this subsection, you tell the reader who participated in the study, how many people (or rats, mice, pigeons, etc.) were involved, and the demographics of your sample (e.g., age, ethnicity, educational level, or other details as appropriate). The topics that give your reader appropriate information about your participants include the following:

- How many humans or nonhumans were studied?
- If there were nonhuman animals, what kind were they?
- If there were people, what were their characteristics (e.g., average and range of age, gender, race or ethnicity, were they volunteers or were they paid, etc.)?

Apparatus and Materials

The basic issues in this subsection involve what you needed to carry out your study. Sometimes you have used machines, computers, or other instrumentation. Much psychological research also requires materials that participants read, learn, memorize, and so on. When you have created your own apparatus, you should describe it in great detail. If you used a commercially available apparatus, you can simply mention the type of apparatus (with make and model), the company that provided it, and any other relevant details that would be useful for somebody who might want to replicate your study or simply to understand your approach. Important information about materials and apparatus include:

- How many and what kind of stimuli, questions, etc. were used?
- What instrumentation, if any, was used to present material to participants and to record their responses?

Procedure

This subsection addresses the issue of what the participants actually did during the research session. The details here should give a complete account of what your participants did from the time the study began until the debriefing was done. You do not need to give details about what you did prior to the session or afterward; if this information is important for some reason, it is probably more appropriate to connect with the apparatus and materials. The important elements of the procedure are as follows:

- After the participants arrived, what did they do? What was the sequence of tasks in which they engaged? How long did it take?
- What did the experimenters do as they interacted with participants?

Results

In this section, you give a verbal description of your results, accompanied by appropriate quantitative information (e.g., means and standard deviations, statistical analyses). It is often difficult for a reader to understand your results if you simply list all of them without describing them. A long series of numbers (e.g., means of the groups), for instance, can be hard for a reader to comprehend without some narrative to accompany them. The critical questions in the results section include the following:

- What were patterns of behaviors among participants?
- Did behaviors differ when groups were compared?
- What types of behaviors are predictable in the different testing conditions?
- Were there predictable relationships among variables?
- What were the results of any statistical tests?

Your results section can also include tables and figures. Sometimes a table or a figure can present important information much more simply than you can describe it in words. When that is the case, make good use of tables and figures. At the same time, try to avoid using tables and figures that contain very little information. You probably don't want to use a graph, for example, if you have only two group means to compare.

In detailing your results, make sure that you give enough of a verbal description so the reader has a good idea of what you found. If you only present numerical information, the reader may have difficulty understanding which results were most important and how they related to one another. When you supplement your writing with tables and figures, you can often get your point across very effectively. Tables allow you to present exact values for your data, whereas figures (which may require the reader to estimate numerical values) allow the reader to get an overall picture of the pattern of results.

Tables.   Tables can present data very effectively and efficiently. They are relatively easy to create with the Tables function in your word processing program. Figure A.4 outlines some of the main components and the format of a table.

At times, tables can get quite complex, especially when there are many groups being compared or when researchers use complex statistical analyses. The basic format is pretty simple, though. The table consists of a label that gives enough information to the readers so they don't have to refer back to the text to comprehend the contents of the table. The table also contains data, often organized by conditions or groups. Sometimes, mean values appear in the margins of the tables, the so-called marginal means. In some cases, tables may not contain numbers, but involve only words and text. This type of table follows the same general principles as numeric tables.

FIGURE A-4 *Format of a Table in APA Style*

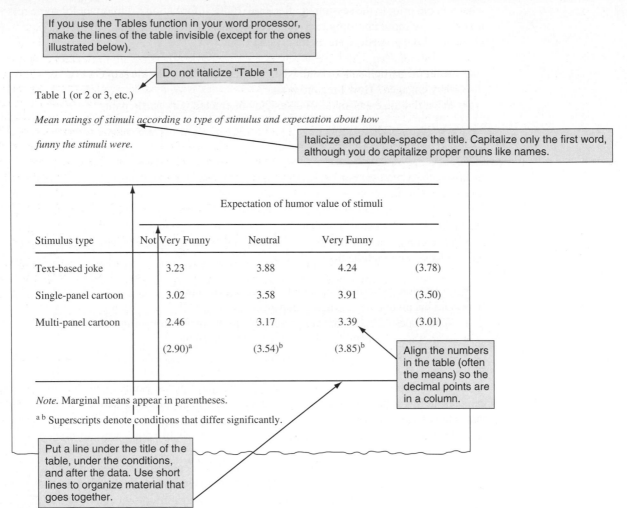

Figures.   Graphs and charts used to be difficult to construct when an author had to draw them by hand. Currently, however, data analysis software and spreadsheets permit easy construction of graphs. It is important to remember that when you use graphic presentations, you should make sure that they convey the information you want in a manner that is easy for the reader to comprehend. As noted before, graphs should not contain too little information because they would be a waste of space in a journal. On the other hand, graphs should not be too cluttered. It takes some practice in creating effective visual presentations; you can learn how to construct them by looking at published figures to see which ones are effective and which are not.

The main types of figures used in research articles are line graphs, bar graphs, and scatter diagrams. Line graphs show the relation between two quantitative variables. Bar graphs are often used to represent relations among categorical variables. Scatter diagrams usually reflect correlational analyses. Figures A.5 and A.6 provide examples of line graphs that look slightly different, but that convey the same information. The two graphs show that the depiction can look different depending on which independent variable you label on the X-axis and which variable you indicate by different kinds of lines within the graph.

FIGURE A-5 *Example of a Line Graph in APA Style*

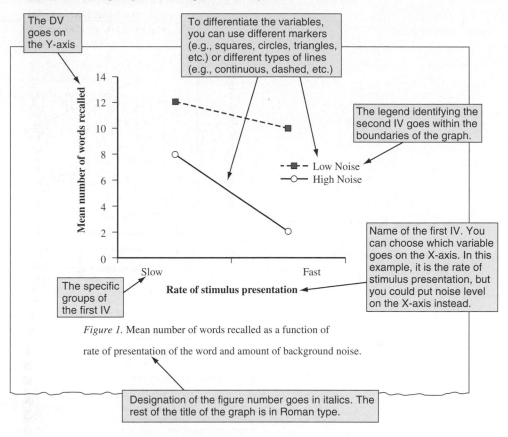

Figure 1. Mean number of words recalled as a function of
rate of presentation of the word and amount of background noise.

Figure A.5 places the first variable, Rate of Presentation, on the X-axis and the second variable, Noise Level, within the graph, represented by different lines. Figure A.6 places Noise Level on the X-axis and Rate of Presentation within the graph.

You can represent your data in bar graphs. Typically, bar graphs represent categorical data, but the example in Figure A.7 is based on the same continuous data we've been working with in these examples. You can see that the visual representation of the bar graph shows the same pattern that you saw in Figure A.5.

If you have completed a correlational analysis, you might want to present a scatter diagram that reveals the relation between two variables. The basic format of this type of figure is the same as for line graphs and bar graphs. The type of information in a scatter diagram is different in an important way, though. Unlike line and bar graphs, which present data at the level of groups, a scatter diagram includes data points from each individual on two variables being measured.

In a scatter diagram, if the overall pattern of data is circular, there is little correspondence between the measurements on the two variables. If all points in the scatter diagram were to fall on a single line, there would be a perfect correspondence between measurements on the two variables. In psychological research, because of the complexity of people's behaviors, the relationships are far from perfect, and scatter diagrams tend to be more cigar-shaped. Figure A.8 shows a scatter diagram for a correlation of .71.

FIGURE A-6   *Line Graph Presenting the Same Information as in Figure A-5 but with the Variables on Different Axes Compared to Figure A-5*

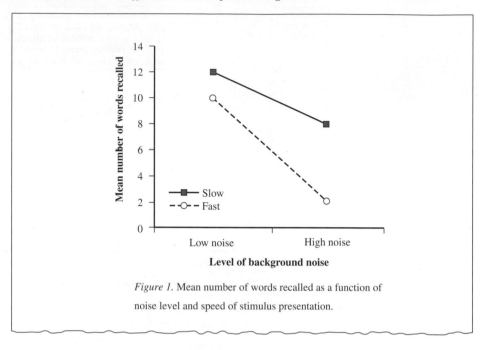

FIGURE A-7   *Example of a Bar Graph in APA Style*

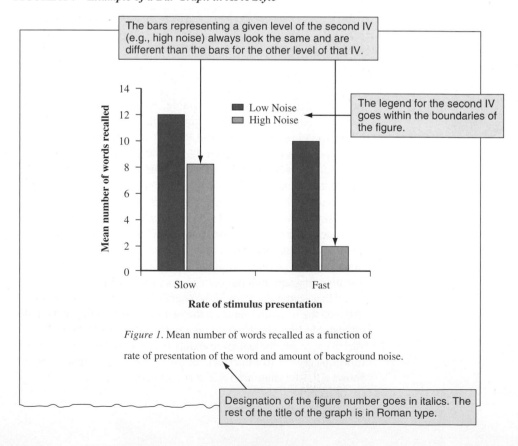

FIGURE A-8   *Example of a Scatter Diagram in APA Style Showing a Correlation Coefficient of .71*

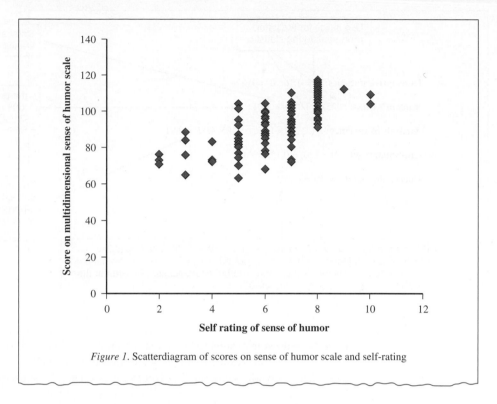

Figure 1. Scatterdiagram of scores on sense of humor scale and self-rating

Statistical Results.   The statistics that you are most likely to use in your research report are the analysis of variance, the Student's *t*-test, the Pearson product-moment correlation, and the chi-square test. When you type your research results, you need to follow specific guidelines about including necessary information. Figure A.9 gives the formatting for these tests.

Discussion

After you tell the reader what has happened, you need to spend some time explaining why it happened. The results section is simply a description of the results, without much explanation. By contrast, the discussion offers you the opportunity to explain why your results occurred as they did and why they are important to the psychological community.

When you discuss your findings, it is important to relate them to the ideas you presented in your introduction section. The introduction set the stage for the research, so your reader will expect you to show why those ideas are important to your results. This is the section of the manuscript that allows you to draw inferences about important psychological processes that are taking place among your participants. It is perfectly appropriate for you to speculate on the meaning of your data. If others disagree, they can always do their own research to provide for support their ideas. When you speculate, you should give the logic behind your arguments. Otherwise, you are only giving an opinion, not logical speculation. The discussion section addresses the following questions:

- What do the results mean?
- What explanations can you develop for why the participants responded as they did?
- What psychological processes help you explain participants' responses?
- What questions have not been answered fully and what are the limitations to your research?

FIGURE A-9 *Format for Presenting Statistical Results in APA Style*

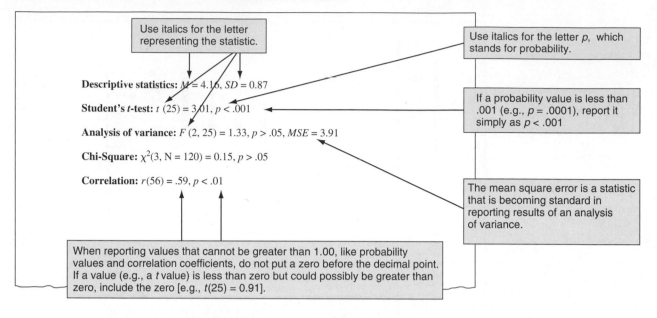

- How do your results relate to the research cited in the introduction?
- How do your results relate to other kinds of research?
- What new ideas emerge that you could evaluate in a subsequent experiment?

References

The reference section includes the full citation for any work that you referred to in your writing. This section is only for works cited in your paper; it is not a general bibliography related to your topic. The rule is that if something was referred to in the manuscript, it belongs here; if a work was not mentioned in your writing, it does not belong here.

The reference section is actually fairly easy to create because you know exactly what the section must contain. The only difficulty is making sure that you use the correct format in the citation. You may be familiar with styles other than APA's, like MLA (from the Modern Language Association) or the Chicago style. They are considerably different from APA style. Fortunately, in your manuscripts, you are likely to use only a few of the many types of sources available, so it is easy to become familiar with the rules for citing references. Examples appear in Table A.1.

The most common sources are journal articles, books and book chapters, presentations at conferences, and electronic resources. Each of these can come in several different varieties, so you will have to make sure that you are following the APA guidelines exactly. For details on the less common types of references, you can consult the *Publication Manual of the American Psychological Association.* There are also numerous websites that provide help. The technical information about the citations tells the reader:

- What research was cited in the report (e.g., work published in journals or other written sources, research presentations, personal communications)?
- Where was the information made public?

TABLE A-1   *Common APA-style Reference Formats*

Use the *hanging indent* feature of your word processor to indent lines after the first one.

Journal articles

Journals usually come out multiple times each year. Do not indicate which issue it is unless the journal starts each issue numbered with Page 1. Most scientific journals continue their pagination across issues, so the only Page 1 is the first page of the first issue in a given year or volume.

General format:

Lastname, Initials of first author, Lastname, Initials of second author, & lastname, Initials of third author. (Year of publication). Title of article. *Name of Journal in Italics, Volume Number in Italics,* page numbers. doi number. Retrieved from <URL>.

If you retrieved a publication from an online source, at the end of the citation indicate *Retrieved from* <URL>. Give the web address (i.e., the URL) (but not in italics and not with pointy brackets). If the material could be changed or updated, give the date you retrieved it: *Retrieved December 1, 2010 from* <URL>. Otherwise, do not include the date your retrieved it.

Example of a journal article with one author:

Braaten, R. F. (2010). Song recognition in zebra finches: Are there sensitive periods for song memorization? *Learning and Motivation, 41,* 202–212. doi:10.1016/j.lmot.2010.04.005

With more than seven authors, list the first six, followed by a comma and three periods (. . .), ending with the name of the final author. Unfortunately for Aaron Del Re and Timothy Baardseth, the seventh and eighth authors, their names will not appear in the citation. If there are seven authors, list them all.

Example of a journal article with multiple authors:

Gangestad, S. W., Thornhill, R., & Garver-Apgar, C. E. (2010). Fertility in the cycle predicts women's interest in sexual opportunism. *Evolution and Human Behavior, 31,* 400–411. doi:10.1016/j.evolhumbehav.2010.05.003

Separate authors' names with a comma after the person's initials. Before the final author's name, use a comma and an ampersand—&—which means *and*.

Example of a journal article with more than seven authors:

Wampold, B. E., Imel, Z. E., Laska, K. M., Benish, S., Miller, S. D., Flückiger, C., . . . & Budge, S. (2010). Determining what works in the treatment of PTSD. *Clinical Psychology Review, 30,* 923–933. doi:10.1016/j.cpr.2010.06.005

Books and book chapters

General format:

Lastname, Initials of first author, & Lastname, Initials of all other authors. (Year of publication). *Title of book in italics* (Edition number not in italics). City and State/Country: Publisher's name.

Books that have been revised come out in different editions. For such books, indicate the version, that is, which edition it is.

Only the first word of the title is capitalized. It appears in italics.

Example of book with one author:

Stanovich, K. E. (2004). *How to think straight about psychology* (7th ed.). Boston, MA: Allyn & Bacon.

*Use a comma and an ampersand—&—before the name of the final author.

*If the title of the work has a colon, capitalize only the first word after the colon.

Example of book with two authors:

Beins, B. C., & Beins, A. M. (2008). *Effective writing in psychology: Papers, posters, and presentations.* Malden, MA: Blackwell.

(continued)

TABLE A-1 Continued

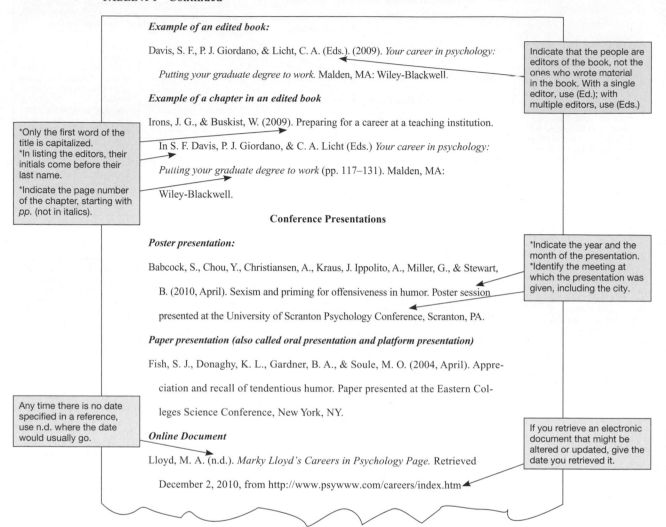

Example of an edited book:

Davis, S. F., P. J. Giordano, & Licht, C. A. (Eds.). (2009). *Your career in psychology:*

    Putting your graduate degree to work. Malden, MA: Wiley-Blackwell.

Indicate that the people are editors of the book, not the ones who wrote material in the book. With a single editor, use (Ed.); with multiple editors, use (Eds.)

Example of a chapter in an edited book

Irons, J. G., & Buskist, W. (2009). Preparing for a career at a teaching institution.

    In S. F. Davis, P. J. Giordano, & C. A. Licht (Eds.) *Your career in psychology:*

    Putting your graduate degree to work (pp. 117–131). Malden, MA:

    Wiley-Blackwell.

*Only the first word of the title is capitalized.
*In listing the editors, their initials come before their last name.
*Indicate the page number of the chapter, starting with *pp.* (not in italics).

Conference Presentations

Poster presentation:

Babcock, S., Chou, Y., Christiansen, A., Kraus, J. Ippolito, A., Miller, G., & Stewart,

    B. (2010, April). Sexism and priming for offensiveness in humor. Poster session

    presented at the University of Scranton Psychology Conference, Scranton, PA.

*Indicate the year and the month of the presentation.
*Identify the meeting at which the presentation was given, including the city.

Paper presentation (also called oral presentation and platform presentation)

Fish, S. J., Donaghy, K. L., Gardner, B. A., & Soule, M. O. (2004, April). Appre-

    ciation and recall of tendentious humor. Paper presented at the Eastern Col-

    leges Science Conference, New York, NY.

Any time there is no date specified in a reference, use n.d. where the date would usually go.

Online Document

Lloyd, M. A. (n.d.). *Marky Lloyd's Careers in Psychology Page.* Retrieved

    December 2, 2010, from http://www.psywww.com/careers/index.htm

If you retrieve an electronic document that might be altered or updated, give the date you retrieved it.

Writing Style

As the *Publication Manual of the American Psychological Association* points out, scientific writing is different from fiction or other creative writing. Scientific writing benefits from clear and direct communication, whereas creative writing benefits from the creation of ambiguity, abrupt changes in perspective, and other literary devices. When you write a research report, you should concentrate on making your point clearly, avoiding prose that doesn't contribute to the logic of your arguments.

This section presents some common problems in writing that you should note. Much of your writing to this point has probably been more literary than scientific, so you might have to unlearn some habits that you have developed.

Precision of Expression

When you write, avoid using more words than you need and avoid words that are more technical than necessary. Sometimes communication is better when you use a technical term because it has a specific meaning that the term transmits very efficiently. On the other hand, when you use complex wording to describe a simple situation, the reader can get confused. Using impressive terminology may not help you get your point across.

Just as you should avoid being too technical, you have to make sure that you are not too informal in your language. If an experiment has some methodological flaws, for example, and the results might be confounded, you should not make vague statements like *The methodological flaws skewed the results* because the word *skew* could mean just about anything. You would want to be more specific, suggesting that *The methodological flaws led to higher mean scores in Groups A and B,* or something equally explanatory. Or if your participants engaged in a behavior in some circumstances, you should specify how often the behavior occurred; ill-defined statements like *most of the time* do not communicate as precisely as you want in a research report. Writing is a skill that you need to develop. Keep in mind that if you fail to communicate, the problem is with you most of the time, not with your reader.

Another grammatical feature that leads to problems is the use of passive voice verbs (e.g., *they were asked to move* instead of *I asked them to move*). For one thing, such verbs make for dull prose. Another problem is that passive voice verbs lead to lack of clarity. That is, to say that *The participants were given the materials* means that you are not telling your reader who did the giving. When you use passive voice verbs, the actor is often hidden. In some cases, it is important to know who completed the action. In virtually all cases, active voice verbs make your prose livelier.

Avoiding Biased Language

When you describe or refer to people in your writing, it is important to use language that gets your point across but also shows sensitivity to the individuals and groups to which you refer. For example, sexist language can be problematic. If you make a statement that *The pioneers, their wives, and their children who settled the western states experienced hardships we cannot even imagine,* you are showing bias in your language. The implication is that the men were the pioneers, whereas the women and children were not.

Another type of bias that we see less than we used to regarding the sexes is the use of the word *man* to refer to people in general. The convention of using *man* to refer to people also led to the use of male pronouns (i.e., *his, him*) when the meaning supposedly included women. This change has led to the use of plural pronouns in referring to a single person (e.g., *A student can be rude when they use their cell phones in class*). Although this has gained acceptance in speech, it is not appropriate in formal writing because if you use a pronoun to refer to *a student,* the pronoun must be singular. One solution is to use plural nouns (e.g., *students*) so the use of plural pronouns is grammatically consistent. The use of *he or she, his or her,* or other double pronouns can also solve the problem if you use a singular noun. If you used either *he* or *she* to refer to all people, it could confuse the reader because if you write something like *When a student engages in prosocial behavior, she helps other people,* it implies that your statement is limited to females.

A further issue regarding pronouns involves the use of first person pronouns (e.g., *I* or *we*). Many students have learned to avoid using the personal pronoun *I*. Teachers have said to use passive voice verbs or to use *we* in their writing when they mean only a single person, that is, themselves. According to APA style, it is appropriate to use *I* when referring to yourself. This usage makes it clear that you are talking about yourself, a single person, rather than a group. Using *I* also avoids the use of passive voice verbs, which you should keep to an absolute minimum.

Another issue involves sensitivity to diverse groups, particularly with respect to the labeling of those groups. It is impossible to state a set of unchanging rules because the terms we use to denote people in various groups change. It may not be possible to satisfy everybody in every group, but you should be aware of the terms at any particular time are appropriate for describing people in different groups. Incidentally, if you use the words *Black* and *White* as racial or ethnic terms, these words should be capitalized. If you use *Black* to refer to a group, do not compare the group to *European Americans;* rather, use *Black* and *White* in combination or *African American* and *European American.*

Recently, authorities on writing have concluded that it is not appropriate to refer to people as though a single characteristic defined them completely. For example, in discussing people with handicaps, you should avoid calling them *the handicapped* because such a term implies that the handicap is perhaps their most significant characteristic. Noting that they are either *handicapped people* or *people with handicaps* highlights the fact that they are, first and foremost, people. Similarly, referring to *depressives* or *the depressed* hides the fact that people with depression show other important characteristics that are unrelated to depression. People are more complex than a single attribute.

For a task as difficult as writing well, these few rules will not suffice by themselves. But they provide a good start. For best results, you should consult with good writers, refer to writing manuals, read well-written reports, and revise your own work extensively. If you combine these approaches with diligence in creating your own prose, your ability to communicate your ideas will develop nicely.

On the following pages, you will see an example of an APA-style paper. It is likely to resemble the papers you will be writing, although specific details of your paper may differ.

EXPECTATIONS ABOUT HUMOR   1

Running head: HUMOR EXPECTATIONS AND HUMOR RATINGS 1

Expectations about Humor Affect Ratings:

A Generalizable Effect with Social Implications

Bernard C. Beins, Caitlin McCarthy, Marci Rigge,

Brittany Rigoli, and Stephine Sawyer

Ithaca College

Author Note

Bernard C. Beins, Psychology Department, Ithaca College; Caitlin McCarthy, Psychology Department, Ithaca College; Marci Rigge, Psychology Department, Ithaca College; Brittany Rigoli, Psychology Department, Ithaca College; Stephine Sawyer, Psychology Department, Ithaca College.

Use the header function in your word processor to insert the title of the paper in the upper left corner of each page. If the title is long, limit it to about 50 characters.

The abstract is typed as a single block with no indentation. The abstract appears on its own page.

Abstract

Previous research has revealed that when participants expect jokes to be either funny or not funny, joke ratings conform to expectations. In our study, we generated expectations in participants about stimuli they would be rating. Their expectations affected joke ratings. The findings reinforce the idea that people use context rather than an objective metric for assessing humor. Visual and verbal humor were susceptible to expectation, suggesting that the effect is a generalized response to humorous stimuli. The results have implications for social issues, such as responses to the offensive humor surrounding comments by radio personality Don Imus.

If you are the sole author, do not use a plural pronoun like *our* or *we.* If you use a singular pronoun, use *I* or *me.*

Expectations about Humor Affect Ratings:

A Generalizable Effect with Social Implications

Funniness has no objective metric. Individual differences and varied

contexts affect people's views of stimuli and the extent to which they see

jokes and cartoons as being funny. On a general level, some of the so-called

Big Five personality traits are associated with humor appreciation (Benfante

& Beins, 2007). On an individual level, specific factors are important. Ryan

and Kanjorski (1998) found that participants who were more accepting of

violence found sexist humor more enjoyable than participants who were less

accepting. Similarly, participants with more traditional views of women's

roles enjoyed sexist humor more than participants with progressive views of

women's roles (Moore, Griffiths, & Payne, 1987).

In addition to personality traits, context also impacts humor

appreciation. In previous research (Wimer & Beins, in press), when

participants expected verbal jokes to be either not very funny or very funny,

the ratings of those jokes conformed with expectations. That is, the purported

---

Start the introduction with the title of the paper. Do NOT use the word *Introduction* to start the section

Names of authors within parentheses are separated by commas, with an ampersand (&) before the final author.

When talking about research, use past tense verbs (i.e., *enjoyed* rather than *enjoy*).

Names of authors in the text are separated by commas, with *and* before the final author.

The first time you refer to a study with multiple authors, use all their names if there are five or fewer authors. Subsequently, if there are two authors, always use both their names. When there are three or more authors, just use the first author's name followed by "et al."

context of the joke led participants to view the jokes as consistent with the

context. Furthermore, Wilson, Lisle, Draft, and Wetzel (1989) discovered

similar effects of expectations with cartoons.

In the present study, we expanded the scope of the stimuli to include

jokes, single-panel cartoons and images, and multiple-panel cartoons. Based

on the findings of Wimer and Beins (in press) with jokes and of Wilson et

al. (1989) with cartoons, we hypothesize that participants will conform to

expectations in their ratings of the stimuli.

It is an open question at this point whether participants will react

to the varying types of stimuli in the same way. Single-panel stimuli

have greater immediacy than do jokes that require reading from start

to finish. Multiple-panel cartoons may be midway between the other

two types of stimuli with regard to how much cognitive processing

must take place prior to getting the point of the humor. If participants

develop an overall mindset based on their expectations, they may

show the same pattern of rating for all types of humor, regardless of

cognitive effort required for understanding it. On the other hand, if

EXPECTATIONS ABOUT HUMOR   5

the pattern of elevated or depressed ratings emerges after complete

processing of a stimulus, the single-panel cartoons may show less

effect of expectation.

Method

Participants

We recruited a total of 94 participants from psychology classes.

They volunteered in exchange for extra credit in those classes. Participants

were predominately white (84%), but also included students from various

other groups, including Asian (9.6%), Hispanic (3.2%), and Black (1.1%).

Some students chose the "Other" category (2.1%). The mean age was

19.13 years ($SD = 1.12$).

Materials and Apparatus

The stimuli included 30 stimuli: 10 jokes, 10 single-panel images or

cartoons, and 10 multiple-panel cartoons. We found them on various sites

on the internet. The stimuli were in randomized blocks of three such that

each block had one stimulus of each type. Participants viewed the stimuli

as we projected them onto a screen using PowerPoint.

In a paper reporting a single study, two levels of headings are usually sufficient. The major headings are centered and are in bold with each word beginning with a capital letter. The minor headings are on the left margin and are bold.

The second-level heading is just like the first level except that it is flush left.

Avoid words you really do not need. In this case, it would be better to eliminate *a total of* because it does not add anything to the sentence.

Do not start sentences with numerals. If you have to start a sentence numerically, write out the number. Generally, try to put the number somewhere within the sentence.

If you need a third-level heading, put it in bold, indent it, and capitalize only the first word.

A fourth-level heading is like the third-level heading but is italicized.

A fifth-level heading is like the fourth-level heading, but is italicized and NOT bolded.

    Nature of the stimuli. The 10 jokes involved short stories that were one or two paragraphs in length. They were the kinds of jokes that the research team believed that college students would enjoy.

    The single-panel images included pictures of people or objects appearing in humorous contexts, as opposed to cartoon figures. The multiple-panel cartoons were like those appearing in the comic sections of newpapers.

Procedure

    After completing informed consent forms, the participants learned that previous participants had rated the stimuli and that we wanted to get their ratings. In one group, participants heard, embedded in the general directions, that previous participants had rated the jokes as not very funny. A second group learned that participants had rated the stimuli as very funny. In a control group, they only learned that others had already rated the stimuli. Participants rated the stimuli on a scale of 1 (*Not very funny*) to 7 (*Very funny*).

When you use rating scales, put the verbal anchors within parentheses, in italics.

When presenting statistics, if it uses a Roman letter (e.g., *M* for the mean, *F* for the results of an analysis of variance, or *p* for a probability value), italicize the letter.

When presenting statistics, if it uses a Greek letter, do not italicize the letter.

If you create figures or tables, make sure you refer to them in the text.

Results

As hypothesized, participants conformed to the message they had received about whether the jokes were funny. Participants in the Very Funny group produced the highest mean ratings ($M = 3.85$, $SD = 0.876$), followed by Control participants ($M = 3.54$, $SD = 0.993$), and Not Very Funny participants ($M = 2.90$, $SD = 0.917$). The mean for the Not Very Funny condition was significantly lower than the other two, which did not differ significantly, $F(2, 91) = 11.263$, $p < .001$, $\eta^2 = .198$. The results appear in Figure 1.

The type of stimulus was significant. Participants rated jokes as funniest ($M = 3.79$, $SD = 1.02$), followed by single-panel stimuli ($M = 3.52$, $SD = 1.04$), and multiple-panel cartoons ($M = 3.04$, $SD = 0.98$). All three differed significantly, $F(2, 182) = 40.123$, $p < .001$, $\eta^2 = .306$. The interaction between variables was not significant, $F(4, 182) = 0.141$, $p = .967$.

The results reveal that the effects of priming were the same for a given expectation, regardless of type of stimulus. It made no difference regarding

EXPECTATIONS ABOUT HUMOR   8

ratings whether the participant was assessing a text-based joke, a single-panel

cartoon, or a multi-panel cartoon. These results appear in Table 1.

Discussion

Once again, the results indicate that people are susceptible to context

when they respond to humor. The same stimulus can be seen as very funny or

not very funny, depending on the setup. And the effect seems generalizable:

The same effect emerges, regardless of stimulus type.

This susceptibility to a message has implications for the use of

humor in everyday life. When the radio personality Don Imus made

racially offensive comments on his program, he intended it to be

embedded in a humorous context. That is, he was saying, "This is

funny," with the expectation that the audience would find it so.

As it turned out, although a message can sway people in a particular

direction, people will reject improbable messages about humor (Wimer &

Beins, in press). Furthermore, individual characteristics of a (large) subset

of listeners may lead them to find an attempt at humor to be offensive (e.g.,

Moore et al., 1987; Ryan & Kanjorski, 1998).

Avoid passive voice verbs because you do not know who the actor is. In this example, who can see the stimuli as funny or not? It is the people. So say that *people can see the same stimulus as very funny or not, depending on the setup.*

In the Discussion section, it is a good idea to talk about the research you mentioned in your introduction.

Interestingly, even though people find some humor to be offensive, they may also find it funny (Beins et al., 2005) and may be inclined to repeat it even when they find it offensive (Ryan & Kanjorski, 1998). So for situations like those of Don Imus, he may encounter contradictory responses: Some people may find his statements funny because of expectations, but they may also find them offensive. Those who experience extreme reactions and outrage are probably not likely to find the attempt at humor actually to be funny. But the dynamics of who will find something funny are complicated enough that a potentially offensive statement will lead to a variety of reactions. And, as Wimer and Beins (in press) showed, if the humor is outrageous enough, people will cease to accept the message that it is funny.

The references begin on a separate page. Like everything else in the paper, you should double-space them.

Use the hanging indent function of your word processor to indent lines after the first one in the reference.

For conference presentations, give the month if possible.

Alphabetize your references by the last name of the first author. Do not number the references.

When an article has a doi number, indicate it. Databases like PsycINFO provide it. You can often find it in the article itself.

References

Beins, B. C., Agnitti, J., Baldwin, V., Yarmosky, S., Bubel, A., MacNaughton, K., & Pashka, N. (2005, October). How Expectations Affect Perceptions of Offensive Humor. Poster presented at the annual convention of the New England Psychological Association, New Haven, CT.

Benfante, L., & Beins, B. C. (2007, October). Self-reflection and sense of humor: The Big Five Personality characteristics and humor. Poster presentation at the annual convention of the New England Psychological Association, Danbury, CT.

Moore, T. E., Griffiths, K., & Payne, B. (1987). Gender, attitudes towards women, and the appreciation of sexist humor. *Sex Roles, 16*(9), 521–531. doi:10.1007/BF00292486

Ryan, K. M., & Kanjorski, J. (1998). The enjoyment of sexist humor, rape attitudes, and relationship aggression in college students. *Sex Roles, 38*(10), 743–756. doi:10.1023/A:1018868913615

Wilson, T. D., Lisle, D. J., Kraft, D., & Wetzel, C. G. (1989). Preferences

as expectation-driven inferences: Effects of affective expectations on

affective experience. *Journal of Personality and Social Psychology,*

56, 519–530. doi:10.1037/0022-3514.56.4.519

Wimer, D., & Beins, B. C. (In press). Expectations and perceived humor.

Humor: International Journal of Humor Studies.

If a reference has seven or more authors, indicate the first six, then use three periods (. . .) to indicate authors that you do not list, then list the final author. The final citation will thus have the first six authors (with a comma after the sixth author) then three periods, and the final author of the article.

By citing an article as *in press,* you are giving the reader enough information to track it down when it appears in print.

The actual citation for this reference is as follows:

Wimer, D. J., & Beins, B. C. (2008). Expectations and perceived humor. *Humor: International Journal of Humor Research, 21*(3), 347–363. doi:10.1515/HUMOR.2008.016

Table 1

The table number goes on the first line. The title starts on the next line, in italics. Only the first word of the title is capitalized.

Mean ratings of stimuli according to type of stimulus and expectation about how funny the stimuli were.

Put a horizontal line under the title. Use a shortened horizontal line to group elements that go together. Use a full line above the beginning of the data and at the end of the data. Do not include vertical lines.

Stimulus type	Expectation of humor value of stimuli			
	Not Very Funny	Neutral	Very Funny	
Text-based joke	3.23	3.88	4.24	(3.78)
Single-panel cartoon	3.02	3.58	3.91	(3.50)
Multi-panel cartoon	2.46	3.17	3.39	(3.01)
	$(2.90)^a$	$(3.54)^b$	$(3.85)^b$	

Note. Marginal means appear in parentheses.

$^{a\ b}$ Superscripts denote conditions that differ significantly.

Put any notes below the line at the bottom of the table. The first note is a general note. Second-level notes relate to specific conditions, rows, or columns. Use lowercase superscripts to indicate the relevant areas of the table. If you want to indicate probabilities in the table, put them as third-level notes. Generally, use one asterisk (*) to indicate $p < .05$. two asterisks for $p < .01$, and three asterisks for $p < .001$. Do not indicate significance levels beyond .001.

Make sure the columns are clearly different in appearance so the reader can tell which group they indicate.

Indicate the groups for one independent variable on the X axis and the group for the second independent variable in a convenient space within the graph.

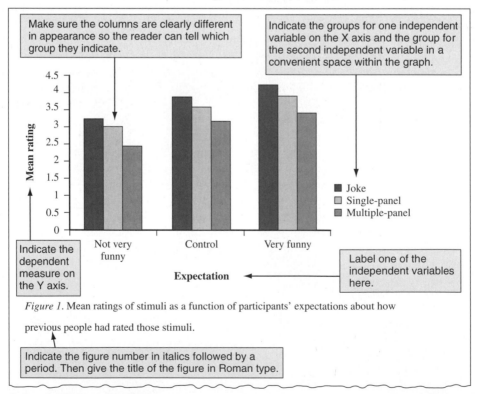

Indicate the dependent measure on the Y axis.

Label one of the independent variables here.

Figure 1. Mean ratings of stimuli as a function of participants' expectations about how previous people had rated those stimuli.

Indicate the figure number in italics followed by a period. Then give the title of the figure in Roman type.

DEVELOPING AN ORAL PRESENTATION

Faculty and students often deliver results of their research at professional meetings. Several opportunities to present work are available at annual national meetings (e.g., American Psychological Association, Association for Psychological Science). In addition to these national venues, opportunities to present your work are available at many regional or local meetings throughout the year. You may also be asked to present your research in class, on campus during a research day, or at a local undergraduate research conference in your state. Regardless of the forum, it is important to develop a plan for presenting your research in a professional way.

Researchers may present their findings during a single session (usually an hour in length), as one member of a panel, or during a poster session. Regardless of the venue, presentations should be clear, concise, and professionally delivered.

It is important to remember that presenting your work orally is different than presenting the work in writing. You should tailor your presentation to meet the needs of a live audience. Remember, people don't want to listen to dry boring facts. Instead, people want to hear interesting information that is directly relevant to their interests. So, for example, if you are presenting results that indicate that positive reinforcement can be useful in helping people to quit smoking, then highlight the broader psychological phenomenon—positive reinforcement—while at the same time keeping the presentation lively and interesting.

Keep the message simple. Your audience is not reading your paper. So, people are not able to easily reference complicated details, and if you provide too much detail, you may lose people. Try to focus on presenting two or three key points. Keep the presentation of these points short, succinct, and direct.

As you are planning your presentation, follow the same general structure of your paper. Introduce your research with an interesting idea. For example, you might begin by presenting the audience with a question like: How can we reduce smoking? Then state your specific hypothesis and the general approach that you used in your study. You can then provide the audience with information about the participants, specific methodology, and results. Keep your presentation broad and don't focus too much on details. Present only the most important results. For example, if you found two or three important outcomes, then focus on those points. And, be sure to leave time to offer conclusions and accept questions from your audience.

Preparing for the Presentation

You usually begin preparing for a professional presentation after completing a research project and writing your paper. So, really you are simply adapting your paper to a different forum. Fortunately, if you use the headings contained in your paper, you already have a general structure for the presentation. Nevertheless, it is important to plan your presentation so that you meet the requirements of the presentation and the time limits that are imposed.

Presenters usually begin their talk with a general introduction of the research topic. One strategy is to begin with an interesting statement, idea, or story. If you are able to engage the audience at the very beginning of your presentation, they are more likely to understand your research. However, it is also important to link the interesting idea to existing research and ultimately to your study. Keep your summary of previous research broad. Don't try to describe every detail from existing studies or you risk losing your audience in the details. Link the key points from the review of the literature to the research that you will be presenting and explicitly state your hypotheses.

After you provide the audience with a general overview of the research topic, you are ready to provide details about how you conducted your study. Begin with a description of your participants. For example, if you surveyed students, you might provide information about the demographics of the sample (e.g., race, gender). This is also the time to describe the materials that you used to conduct your study. For example, if you used a survey, provide the audience with information about the number and type of survey items. It might also be helpful to create a graphic that illustrates the materials that you used in your study. In this portion of the presentation you are trying to provide the audience with a clear picture of what you did in your study.

After creating interest and explaining the procedures, the most important part of your presentation is telling the audience what you found. Because you find the results exciting, it is easy to get caught up in the details of your results. Resist the temptation to present every single piece of data. Present the results simply and directly. For example, if you found that one group performed better than a second group, then convey these findings to the audience. Don't spend too much time reciting specific statistical details. In short, summarize the findings.

You don't want to leave the audience hanging. Plan to offer conclusions that have been derived from your research. Highlight the key findings from your study and relate these findings back to the initial hypotheses. Offer explanations for your results. In other words, if you discovered something unusual, then offer reasons for your findings. Finally, provide your audience with a succinct summary of the key points from your research.

Dealing with Anxiety

Delivering a research presentation to any audience can be intimidating. Regardless of whether this is your first presentation, or one of several presentations, it is scary to stand before colleagues and present your work. The most important step that you can take to make the experience better is to become comfortable with your material. So, if you are presenting results from research that you conducted, think about how you will convey the results, and become comfortable with the ideas.

Regardless of how well you prepare, it is okay to occasionally stumble over a word or an idea. We all stumble from time to time. Think about a recent lecture that your teacher might have given. In all likelihood your teacher had difficulty explaining a concept, or she may have stumbled over a word or idea. In this case the teacher may have restated an idea or repeated a phrase. You can do the same thing if necessary. Try to imagine that you are having a conversation about your ideas and you want to explain your research to a friend. The more comfortable you can become, the better your presentation will be.

Resist the urge to be a perfectionist. It is impossible for you to know everything about a topic. Sometimes you will receive a question that you cannot answer. Not being able to answer one or two questions is okay. Develop a plan for how you will respond to a question that you are not prepared to address. For example, you might indicate that the person asking the question has provided you with some good ideas of things to consider in your future work. Ultimately, you need to emphasize the findings from your study and communicating in a professional, yet comfortable manner will help you to deliver a good presentation.

CREATING A POSTER

Throughout this text we have provided information about how to conduct research and scientifically report results of a study. Developing a well-written manuscript that conveys scientific findings is always an important goal. In addition to writing a manuscript, sometimes researchers present results of a study in a poster session at a professional meeting. These sessions are much like a science fair. Large, movable wallboards or tri-fold poster boards are available for poster display. Attendees are usually walking around, passing posters, and discussing research findings with the authors. In this section we offer practical advice for creating a poster from the research report.

A poster is usually a much more succinct version of the research paper. In general, you should use the APA style guidelines when you develop the poster. However, because of space limitations, your poster will include less information than the paper. So, it is important to create a poster that allows people to quickly identify the key points in your study. Results of the study should be emphasized because people are usually interested in what you found. Specific details are discussed when someone stops to more carefully review your information. In other words, a well-developed poster creates interest and draws people in for further discussion.

Practical Considerations

Technology is continuing to evolve, so opportunities to create interesting posters are expanding. Posters are often produced using one large banner-style printer. Alternatively, a poster is created using PowerPoint© slides and printed on individual sheets. Regardless of how you chose to create your poster, presentation (i.e., PowerPoint) software is useful because templates are often available to help you develop the content.

Usually, the conference organizers impose size restrictions for the poster. In general, you can anticipate having a space that is approximately 4×6 feet for available for the poster. Font size is particularly important because people need to be able to read the poster from several feet away. The title of the poster is usually written in 48-point font, headings in 36-point font, and text is usually produced using an increasing smaller font size. Although visual appeal is important, the content of the poster is much more critical.

A poster typically includes all of the major sections of a paper. So, the title, along with author(s), and affiliation should be a prominent feature that clearly identifies the poster. An abstract, much like that of the paper, is usually the first section of the poster. Remember, the abstract contains the research question or hypotheses, methodology, results, and conclusions. Major sections, derived from your paper (e.g., Method, Results, and Discussion) should also be easily identifiable through the headings. Key references should also be available to the attendees.

Text that appears in each section of the poster is much shorter than the narrative that is contained in a research paper. Posters include short sentences that introduce key points, followed by a bulleted list of items that help to convey the reasons for conducting the research, methodology employed, and major findings. Background information helps the reader to understand the rationale for your research project. So information about prior research should be followed by a brief synopsis of what you planned to investigate, and the hypotheses that guided the research. The method section should include a description of participants, materials or apparatus, and procedures that were used to conduct the study. The results section should include key data directly related to hypotheses, and when relevant, figures and tables. So, if you found large mean differences, then these data should be reported and clearly displayed. Information that lends itself to visual presentation is particularly useful to include in the results section. Finally, the discussion section typically includes an explanation of results, limitations, and implications of the findings.

Creating the Poster in PowerPoint

It is possible to create a single large banner-style poster using a single PowerPoint slide. The first step in creating a large, single sheet, banner-style poster is to use the design tab and select the custom option in the page setup of PowerPoint. Specify the size (e.g., 48×72 inches) for a single slide. PowerPoint automatically creates the slide in the landscape orientation. After you create the slide, you can view the entire slide (poster) or a portion of the slide. The zoom function located in the lower right-hand portion of the page allows you to adjust how much of the slide you are viewing at any given time.

You are now ready to begin adding content to your slide. It is sometimes helpful to begin by adding gridlines. Gridlines allow you to align and center text boxes. First select the view tab, and then simply click on gridlines so they will appear on the slide. Don't worry; you can uncheck the tab before you print so that the gridlines don't appear on your final poster. The gridlines allow you to place text boxes on the slide and to add information to each box to create each section of the poster. Images, graphs, and art can all be added to your poster using the insert options available in PowerPoint. You may have to periodically readjust the view size to get a sense of how the poster (e.g., Abstract, Method, Results) will appear when printed. (Additional information about how to develop the banner poster can also be obtained from a colleague or you can find technical information at the following website: http://www.teachpsych.org/otrp/resources/.)

It is less expensive to create a poster using single slides. When creating individual slides for a poster presentation, it is often desirable to use one of the existing templates available in PowerPoint. These templates are visually appealing and many of the formatting details are preset so that you don't have to worry about centering or justifying your text.

Several layout options are available within each template. For example, bullets, charts, graphs, images, or combinations of these formats can all be placed on a PowerPoint slide. If you are building a slide using a bulleted list, begin by adding a title to the slide. Then insert the list in the preset bullets. Text can also be added by merely typing on the desired information onto each slide.

Graphs and tables can now be easily placed on a slide. Select the layout that allows you to insert an image, graph, or table. Copy the desired element from your manuscript and paste it into the available area of the slide. You may also import an image, but this process is a bit more cumbersome. After you paste the graph or table onto the slide, you can easily increase or decrease the size of the image using the sizing functions available in PowerPoint.

Presenting the Poster

Presenting a poster is one way to convey your research in a professional venue, but without the pressure of speaking to a large group of people. Not only do you have the opportunity to convey your findings, but quite often, a conversation about your research may lead to additional insights and studies.

You should plan to set up your poster a few minutes before the session is officially scheduled to begin. As illustrated in Figure C.1, when placing the poster on the available poster boards, it is important to mount individual pages so that they flow in a logical sequence. For example, people generally read from up to down and left to right. Therefore, each section should be logically placed so that the reader can easily follow your ideas.

Figure C.2 shows the layout of an actual poster presented at a professional conference. As you can see, each section is clearly indicated and the amount of text is not extensive. The text is much less than you would see in a written paper, and, relatively speaking, the amount of space devoted to visual elements (figures in this case) is high. The reduced amount of text can be offset either by handouts with the complete paper or conversations with people at the poster session who are interested in your work.

Presenting a poster can be a very rewarding experience, sometimes resulting in additional ideas for extending your research. Because it is not possible to convey all of the details of a study, it might also be useful to provide people with a brief handout that summarizes your poster. Be sure to include contact information so that if someone is interested in finding out more about your research, they have a way to contact you.

FIGURE C.1   *Example Poster Layout Using Individual Sheets or Banner*

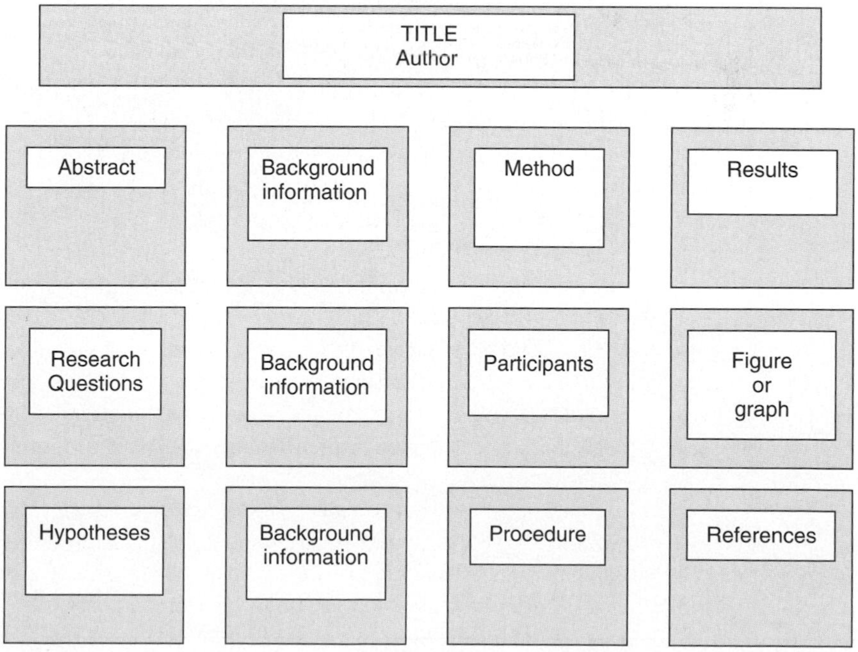

FIGURE C.2   *Example of a Poster Displayed at the Annual Convention of the Eastern Psychological Association*

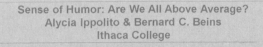
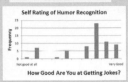

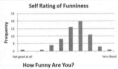

Source: Ippolito & Beins, 2011.

ANSWERS TO CHAPTER REVIEW QUESTIONS

Chapter 1

Answers to Multiple Choice Questions

1. b	**6.** c	**11.** d
2. a	**7.** d	**12.** b
3. d	**8.** a	**13.** d
4. a	**9.** a	**14.** c
5. c	**10.** a	**15.** b

Answers to Essay Questions

16. Identify and describe the four goals of scientific research. Include in your description how the four goals build on one another.
Suggested points:

 a. Description—the process of documenting the existence of behaviors of interest
 b. Prediction—the ability to predict behaviors given knowledge of prior conditions
 c. Explanation—identifying reasons for the occurrence of a behavior
 d. Control—using knowledge of a phenomenon to predict when it will occur and being able to explain the reasons for the behavior in such a way as to control that behavior.

17. Identify and describe the five ways of knowing described by the philosopher Charles Sanders Peirce.

 a. Tenacity (the obvious/intuition)—knowing something because "everybody knows it is true" or because "it is obvious" so that people are comfortable and simply refuse to abandon that knowledge.
 b. Authority—reliance on an expert or authority figure
 c. A priori method—use of deductive logic or logical proof
 d. Experience—use of one's own life as a measure of what is generally true
 e. Scientific approach—reliance on empirical methods that are objective, empirical, public, and replicable

18. How do scientists and pseudoscientists differ with regard to the evidence that they will accept to support their ideas?

 Ideally, scientists continually revise their ideas based on empirically based evidence. In addition, they are willing to develop theories to accommodate new findings, to update their methods to improve on the quality of research, and to question new information critically.

 On the other hand, pseudoscientists rely on flimsy and questionable evidence; they are not willing to question information that supports their ideas. At the same time, they avoid contradictory information that fails to support their ideas. In addition, pseudoscientists show a resistance to change in their ideas, and they are unlikely to seek further development of theory; in fact, they tend to avoid testing their ideas critically.

Chapter 2

Answers to Multiple Choice Questions

1. d	**10.** a	**19.** b
2. a	**11.** a	**20.** b
3. d	**12.** d	**21.** b
4. c	**13.** b	**22.** a
5. d	**14.** a	**23.** a
6. b	**15.** c	**24.** c
7. a	**16.** c	**25.** d
8. c	**17.** b	
9. d	**18.** c	

Answers to Essay Questions

26. Identify the five general principles of APA regarding ethical conduct and what behaviors they pertain to.

    Beneficence and nonmaleficence—Providing help and avoiding harm to those with whom a psychologist acts; being aware of the effects of one's behavior on others

    Fidelity and responsibility—Working to gain the trust of others; upholding professional standards

    Integrity—Acting honestly and truthfully; keeping promises; correcting harmful effects

    Justice—Ensuring access to the benefits of psychology to others on an equal basis; recognizing one's biases; recognizing one's limitations and the boundaries of one's competence

    Respect for people's rights and dignity—Safeguarding the rights of people; respecting cultural and individual differences; avoiding behavior based on stereotypes and biases regarding others

27. What types of research can be exempt from Institutional Review Board (IRB) consideration, according to U.S. federal law?

    Research conducted in established or commonly accepted educational settings, involving normal educational practices, can be exempt from approval, such as the effects of different instructional strategies.

    Research involving the use of educational tests, survey procedures, interview procedures or observation of public behavior. (Surveys and interviews on sensitive or controversial topics may require IRB approval, though.)

    In addition, research involving public officials or political candidates can be exempt from IRB approval.

    Research involving the collection or study of existing, publicly available data, documents, records, pathological specimens, or diagnostic specimens is exempt if the personal identity of those providing the data is protected.

28. When people oppose the use of animal research, what arguments do they produce?

    Some people argue from a practical standpoint, saying that we don't learn very much about people from studying animals, so keeping animals confined to laboratories reduces the quality of the animals' lives and doesn't produce useful research results.

    Other people argue from a moral standpoint, maintaining that we don't have the right to keep animals captive or to treat them inhumanely.

Chapter 3

Answers to Multiple Choice Questions

1. a	**7.** a	**13.** a
2. c	**8.** b	**14.** b
3. b	**9.** a	**15.** a
4. d	**10.** d	**16.** b
5. b	**11.** b	**17.** a
6. c	**12.** b	

Answers to Essay Questions

18. Where on the continuum of formality of ideas will a beginning student's research likely to fall? Explain your answer.

    Students are likely to pose research questions that arise from their own experiences, that is, from less formal points on the continuum. Students' levels of knowledge are going to be less than those of experienced researchers, so students will be less familiar with research to replicate, although after some preliminary study, they might be able to do so. Beginning students are unlikely to come up with significant tests of theory because they are just learning about the content of psychology.

19. Explain how changes in psychology and changes in society have affected psychologists' use of animals in research.

    Some psychologists have speculated that decreases in the amount of animal research has resulted, in part, from a change in theoretical perspectives from behaviorism to cognitivism. Behaviorists were willing to generalize to people from animals; cognitive psychologists less so.

    A second reason is that psychologists have turned their attention to different research questions, ones that are less likely to be answered through animal research. Part of this may be due to the increasing number of women in psychology.

    A third reason is that people, including psychologists, are more sensitive to the ethical issues associated with animal research.

20. Why could it be more profitable for a beginning researcher to do an exact replication, while it would be more profitable for a seasoned researcher to do a conceptual replication?

    Beginning researchers can benefit from learning how to carry out research by following the well-specified procedures of earlier research. This will help them avoid overlooking important potential problems because most of these problems will have been ironed out by the original researchers. Seasoned researchers who can anticipate potential problems can be more confident that they will be able to create well-structured studies that go beyond the original studies.

21. What are the advantages of a literature review of research related to your own investigations?
    a. You can learn what experts in the area are interested in.
    b. You can get clues about how to conduct your own study, avoiding mistakes that might have beset earlier researchers.
    c. You can see how other researchers have defined their concepts and made their measurements.

Chapter 4

Answers to Multiple Choice Questions

1. b	**6.** b	**11.** a
2. a	**7.** d	**12.** b
3. d	**8.** d	**13.** b
4. d	**9.** c	**14.** d
5. c	**10.** c	**15.** a

Answers to Essay Questions

16. Why is applied research often conducted outside a formal laboratory, whereas theoretical research generally takes place in a laboratory?
    Suggested points:
    Applied research very often answers a specific question about behaviors in a natural setting. As such, it may be important to study behaviors in the environments in which they typically occur, rather than in a restricted and somewhat artificial atmosphere of the lab.
    On the other hand, in theoretical research, investigators are frequently interested in the effect of a variable that has a consistent, but small, effect on behavior. In such a situation, it makes sense to eliminate variables that have big effects on behavior that will obscure the effects of variables that have smaller effects. One way to get rid of the larger effects of variables you aren't interested in is to control the environment very carefully, which is easiest to do in a lab.

17. We hope to be able to generalize our research results to people other than those who actually participated in our research. For the typical psychology study, why is it hard to determine the people to whom our research will generalize?
    Suggested points:
    Most psychological research with people involves undergraduate psychology students, the majority of whom are female. So we are likely to be able to generalize to other young, educated women, although it isn't always clear if we can generalize to men or to people younger or older than the female college students. For some measurements, the participants we use may be representative of many other people, but for other measurements (e.g., attitudes), the participants may not be like older or younger people or men, or even female students at other schools or in different parts of the country or in other countries.
    The issue is complicated because, for some measurements, our participants produce very similar results to many other groups (e.g., speed of learning one type

of material versus another), whereas for other measurements (e.g., attitudes toward abortion), participants in a single location may not be like others.

Chapter 5

Answers to Multiple Choice Questions

1. b	**5.** b	**9.** b
2. d	**6.** d	**10.** c
3. a	**7.** c	
4. b	**8.** b	

Answers to Essay Questions

11. The scale of measurement is ratio because the tips were reported as money.

12. The correct scale of measurement for gender is nominal. The scale of measurement for age is ratio.

13. Measures of central tendency that are most important for age are Mean and Median.

14. The demographic characteristics most appropriate for using mode as the central tendency are gender and race.

15. The measure of central tendency most appropriate for use with skewed data is the median.

16. Participants were traditionally aged college students ($M = 22, SD = 2$). The oldest participant was 28 years old and the youngest participant was 18 years old. The ages of the participants appeared to be normally distributed with a Range of 10.

17. The scores in this distribution have a greater range, yet the *SD* is constant. Therefore, it is quite likely that an outlier increased the range, and created a skewed distribution.

Answers to Practice Exercises

18. Ratio level data: $M = 23.7, MDN = 21.5$, Mode $= 21$, Range $= 19, SD = 5.72$.

19. Group: Categorical reported as frequency data (Four people in group 1, three people in group 2, and three people in group 3). DV reported as interval level data, $M = 3.9, MDN = 4$, Bimodal, Modes $= 3$ and 4, Range $= 4, SD = 1.20$.

20.

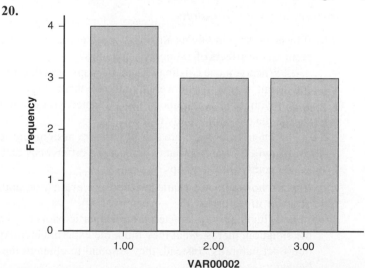

21.

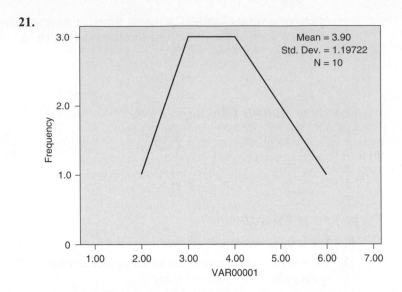

22. The range for each set of data is 4. In fact the standard deviation for the first set of data is actually slightly larger ($SD = 1.62$) than for variable 2 ($SD = 1.33$). It is important to note that the absolute values of the data do not necessarily reflect the size of variability.

Chapter 6

Answers to Multiple Choice Questions

1. c	**7.** d	**13.** c
2. b	**8.** b	**14.** b
3. b	**9.** d	**15.** c
4. b	**10.** b	**16.** d
5. a	**11.** a	
6. d	**12.** c	

Answers to Essay Questions

17. Why is research involving already existing groups rather than randomly assigned groups prone to the effects of extraneous variables?

When you use existing or intact groups, you don't have a guarantee that they are equivalent; that is, if you were to measure them on the DV, they might differ from the start. If you didn't know about this difference, you would mistakenly attribute a difference at the end of the study to the IV.

When groups are created by random assignment, there is less chance that the groups will differ systematically because differences that could be critical are spread out randomly across groups.

18. Explain how demand characteristics and evaluation apprehension affect participant behavior in research.

With demand characteristics, the participants react to the perceived demands of the situation, that is, what they think the experimenter expects of them. As such, they don't act naturally. Instead, they respond to clues in the environment to direct their behaviors.

Evaluation apprehension affects participants as they act differently because they know they are being observed. They may act in a particular way in order to look better in the eyes of the researcher, for instance.

Chapter 7

Answers to Multiple Choice Questions

1. a	**5.** c	**9.** b
2. a	**6.** c	**10.** c
3. b	**7.** b	
4. a	**8.** d	

Answers to Essay Questions

11. The standard deviation provides an index of how far individual scores vary from the mean, whereas the standard error of the mean is an index of how far a sample mean varies from a population mean. In other words, these two values are similar, but the *SD* refers to individual scores and the *SEM* refers to a sample of means.

12. As the sample size increases, the standard error of the mean decreases.

13. The *SEM* for a sample size of 100 is 1 and the *SEM* for a sample size of 25 is 2. The standard error of the mean increases as the sample size decreases.

14. The *z* distribution can be used to locate an individual score at a percentile. The *z* distribution also provides a probability value associated with a single sample (*z* test).

15. The unit normal table contains *z* scores and corresponding probability values. These probability values are easily translated to percentages of the area that is present in the normal distribution.

16. A desirable effect size is a value that indicates a meaningful amount of difference. For example, if we are testing a new drug designed to reduce pain, we would want the amount of pain to be reduced by at least two points (on a scale of one to ten), if we are going to invest money in developing the drug.

17. The single sample *z* test is used when we have a population standard deviation, but we use a *t* test when we don't know the population standard deviation.

18. We use the *t* table to determine if our t statistic is statistically significant.

19. A Type I error is detecting a difference when a difference is not present, or a false positive. So, if I am interested in making sure that I don't miss detecting the use of performance enhancing substances, then I would employ a smaller alpha (e.g., .01) to increase the likelihood that I don't miss any incidents. However, at the same time, I will also be increasing my Type II error. A Type II error is not detecting a difference when a difference is present, or a false negative. If I am interested in making sure that I don't wrongly accuse an athlete of using performance enhancing substances, then I might be more willing to accept a Type II error.

20. I would increase the sample size for my experiment.

Answers to Practice Exercises

21. Kyle's *z* score is $z = .8$. Jeremy's $z = -.8$.

22. A *z* score of 1.89 corresponds to a percentile ranking of 97%.

23. Begin with by calculating *SEM* for each sample.
    a. Sample size of 10 $z = 2.11$
    b. Sample size of 30 $z = 3.65$
    c. Sample size of 40 $z = 4.22$

    As the sample size gets larger, the z score gets larger.
24. Sample size of 50; $z = 4.71$.
    Sample size of 25; $z = 3.33$
25. $t(24) = 2.5$ is statistically significant.

Chapter 8

Answers to Multiple Choice Questions

1. c	**5.** c	**9.** d
2. b	**6.** b	**10.** c
3. d	**7.** d	
4. a	**8.** d	

Answers to Essay Questions

11. The *t* test ratio is really the ratio of explained error variance (difference between means) to error variance.
12. The standard error of the difference between two means reflects an average amount of error variability and is the denominator in calculating the *t* statistic for the independent samples *t* test. The standard error of the difference score reflects the average amount of error variability when calculating the *t* statistic for the related samples *t* test. Both of these values serve as the denominator when calculating the *t* test.
13. The repeated measures *t* test removes the error variability associated with differences between individuals. Thus the repeated measures *t* test contains less error.
14. Confidence intervals provides a reader with an index of the amount of error that is present in the study, relative to the data. For example, if the confidence interval is quite large, the reader would know minor changes in an average score may not result in statistically significant differences.
15. The estimated standard error of the mean difference score is smaller because error differences associated with difference among individuals in a treatment are not present.
16. The repeated measures design will contain less error because error associated with differences among people in two different locations will not be present. Each person will act as their own control.
17. It might be particularly useful to match students on a variable that might otherwise confound results. If we match on a variable of interest, we might extract some error.
18. Matching might be particularly useful if I am working with athletes.
19. It is not possible to conduct a repeated measures study with using a participant variable because the participants fall into only one category. For example, participants are either male or female; similarly, they may be either Type A or Type B personality.
20. Sequence effects occur when the sequence of treatments makes a difference in the outcome. Testing effects of exercise are likely to have a sequence effect. Order effects occur when the addition of treatments together make a difference (cumulative). Testing the effects of caffeine are likely to have an order effect.

Answers to Practice Exercises

21. Use an independent samples *t* test.
22. Result is $t(18) = -4.88$, $p < .05$. In other words, the BB treatment resulted in significantly more weight loss that the EG treatment.
23. Use a repeated measures *t* test.
24. Result is $t(9) = 6.77$, $p < .05$. The results for the memory treatment were significant.
25. Effect size: $d = 2.12$.

Chapter 9

Answers to Multiple Choice Questions

1. c	**5.** a	**9.** b
2. b	**6.** a	**10.** d
3. b	**7.** b	
4. c	**8.** c	

Answers to Essay Questions

11. The denominator represents error or individual differences within treatment. The numerator reflects the variability between treatments.
12. To obtain a significant *F* ratio, it is important to maximize the differences between groups and minimize differences within groups.
13. If there is a great deal of variability in one group and not in another, then homogeneity of variance will not be met.
14. Treatment df are reflected in the numerator and error df are reflected in the denominator. Thus, these degrees of freedom are associated with the ratio for the *F* value.
15. Eta squared provides an index of explained variance.
16. The Repeated Measures ANOVA reduces error variance because each participant acts as their own control across treatments.
17. The Repeated Measures ANOVA contains less error than the Between Groups ANOVA
18. The repeated measures ANOVA has the potential for carry over effects, which may introduce a new type of error into the analysis.

Answers to Practice Exercises

19. Source Table

Source of Variation	SS	df	MS	F
TREATMENT	30	3	10	20
ERROR	18	36	.5	
TOTAL	48	39		

Tukey *HSD*

$$HSD = q\sqrt{\frac{.5}{10}} = q\sqrt{.05} = q(.22) = (3.85)(.22) = .86$$

All of the pairwise comparisons are significant because the mean differences exceed .86 in all cases.

Graph

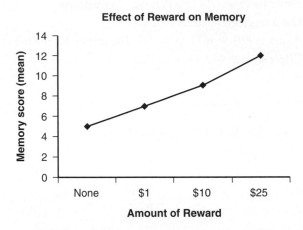

Source Table

Source of Variation	SS	df	MS	F
TREATMENT	40	2	20	16
ERROR	214.11	117	1.83	
Between Subjects	117	39	3	
Within Subjects	97.5	78	1.25	
TOTAL	62	119		

Graph

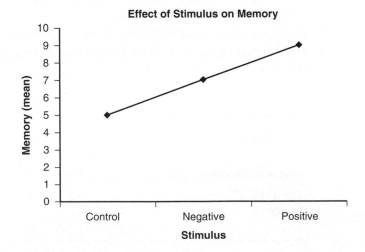

20. $k = 4, N = 50, F(3, 26) = 4.0, p < .05$.
21. $k = 4, N = 5, N = 20, F(3, 12), p < .05$.
22. $k = 5, N = 25$

Chapter 10

Answers to Multiple Choice Questions

1. a	**5.** a	**9.** c
2. d	**6.** c	**10.** c
3. b	**7.** b	
4. b	**8.** d	

Answers to Essay Questions

11. The factorial ANOVA includes more than one IV and the one-way ANOVA includes only one IV.

12. Number of treatment conditions are calculated by multiplying the number of levels of each independent variable.

13. The number of variables present in this design is three. Two levels of the first IV and three levels of the remaining two IVs are present. A total of 12 conditions are present.

14. The advantages include examining multiple variables at the same time. Additionally, when multiple IVs are used, it allows the researcher to examine how multiple levels of one IV may interact with levels of another IV.

15. Calculated F values are compared to tabled F values for the interaction and main effects. If the F calculated value exceeds the F tabled value, the test is statistically significant.

Answers to Practice Exercises

16. Number of treatment levels $= 18$.

17. Number of treatment levels for the second IV $= 3$.

18. Factor A – significant, Factor B – significant, $N = 24$

19. Answer to table questions below. Number of participants $N = 20$.

Source of Variation	SS	df	MS	F
TREATMENT	50			
Factor A (Gender)	10	1	10	4.00
Factor B (Voice)	10	1	10	4.00
A × B	40	1	40	16.00
ERROR	40	16	2.50	
TOTAL	90	19		

20. The main effect for Factor A was not statistically significant, $F(1, 16) = 4.00, p > .05$. The main effect for Factor B was not statistically significant, $F(1, 16) = 4.00, p > .05$. The interaction effect was statistically significant, $F(1, 16) = 16.00, p < .05$.

21. $\omega^2 = \dfrac{SS_{A \times B} - (df_{A \times B}MS_{Error})}{SS_{TOTAL} + MS_{Error}} = \dfrac{40 - (1)(2.50)}{90 + 2.5} = .41$

Chapter 11

Answers to Multiple Choice Questions

1. d	**6.** c	**11.** a
2. c	**7.** c	**12.** c
3. a	**8.** b	**13.** a
4. c	**9.** b	**14.** c
5. b	**10.** c	

Answers to Essay Questions

15. Why do open-ended questions provide more information to survey researchers than closed-ended questions? What drawbacks are associated with open-ended questions? Suggested points:

Open-ended questions allow a respondent to provide the best answer to a question, whereas closed-ended questions force the respondent to choose from a selected set. The open-ended questions may lead to answers that the researcher doesn't anticipate, which could be positive, leading to more valid answers; such answers could be problematic, though, because they are hard to code and summarize when respondents take very different paths to their answers.

16. Identify the seven major problems associated with survey questions about attitudes.

a. The wording of a question can lead a respondent in a particular direction, especially with emotionally sensitive topics.

b. Previous questions have an effect on what kind of information people have in mind when they respond to a later item.

c. The respondents' beliefs about what the interview is supposed to be about will lead them to tailor their responses so as to be more helpful to the surveyor.

d. The sensitivity of an issue is critical to whether and how people respond.

e. The characteristics of the person doing the interview can be important; respondents are more forthcoming with people who are similar to them.

f. It is hard to distinguish between attitudes that have an attitude already held from those that the respondent has just made up.

g. It is hard to differentiate between attitudes that are deeply and shallowly held.

17. Why does the research on how many adolescents smoke reflect the difficulty in creating good survey research?

The research on adolescent smoking is difficult because adolescents span the ages of 12 to 17 years. The younger adolescents are different in physical, psychological, and others ways from the older ones. The younger adolescents were quite unlikely to smoke anything at all. So categorizing all adolescents together may distort the results.

In addition, the definition of what it means to smoke is hard. If an adolescent had had even a puff of a cigarette, it was considered smoking and would be categorized (for some data analysis) the same way as a pack-a-day smoker. Most of the infrequent smokers had less than one cigarette when the smoked.

Depending on how you define adolescents and how you categorize them and depending on how you define smoking can lead to different pictures of who smokes and how much.

18. What two characteristics typify hidden populations?

a. It is impossible to establish exactly who constitutes the population.

b. There are privacy issues associated with the population.

Chapter 12

Answers to Multiple Choice Questions

1. d	**5.** c	**9.** d
2. c	**6.** b	**10.** c
3. b	**7.** d	
4. d	**8.** c	

Answers to Essay Questions

11. A correlational study differs from a correlational analysis in that the type of design determines whether causal inferences can be drawn. A correlation merely provides an index of relationship.

12. The Pearson's correlation is used when both variables contain interval or ratio level data. A Phi coefficient is used when data are both dichotomous. A Spearman correlation coefficient is used when data are ordinal.

13. A correlation coefficient provides an index and direction of relationship between two variables.

14. We cannot make causal statements about correlations unless an experimental method, involving random assignment, has been used.

15. The example should reflect an increase in the values of one variable, with a decrease in the values of a second variable.

16. Correlation can be affected by confounding factors.

17. The purpose of regression is to derive an equation that can be used to predict future behaviors.

18. We use the value of X, together with beta as a slope, to predict the value of Y.

19. A Chi-Square analysis is used with data that are nominal.

20. The Chi-Square Goodness-of-Fit is used with one variable, and the Chi-Square Test-of-Independence is used when two or more variables are present.

Answers to Practice Exercises

21. $r = -.81, p < .005; r^2 = .66$

22.

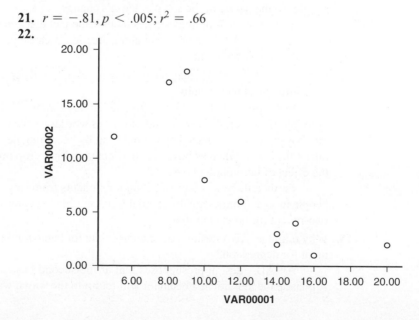

23. $Y = 21.56 + (-1.16)(X)$
     $Y = 21.56 + (-1.16)(5) = 15.76$
24. $\chi^2(3, N = 100) = 26, p < .05$
25. $\chi^2(1, N = 50) = 12.5, p < .05$

	Smile	Frown	Column Total
Men	10(16)	15(9)	25
Women	22(16)	3(9)	25
Row Total	32	18	50

Chapter 13

Answers to Multiple Choice Questions

1. d	**5.** b	**9.** a
2. d	**6.** d	**10.** c
3. c	**7.** d	**11.** b
4. a	**8.** a	

Answers to Essay Questions

12. What are the advantages of longitudinal designs and cross-sectional designs?

   Longitudinal designs permit the study of change in an individual over time, avoiding cohort effects that could confuse change over time in a person with change due to different environments. Cross-sectional designs are quicker to complete, allowing assessment of different populations in a short time period.

13. How does a panel study differ from a trend study? What are the advantages of each?

   A panel study typically involves the study of the same people in successive waves of data collection. A trend study involves studying the same population over time, but not necessarily the same people.

   The advantages of panel studies include the fact that you are studying the same people, so the nature of the sample doesn't change.

   The advantages of trend studies include the fact that you don't have to worry about keeping track of the same people or about attrition because you sample from the population at each measurement.

14. In the Bond et al. (2001) study on bullying in schools and depression, why could attrition have influenced their results?

   In the Bond et al. study, they found that boys showed less depression as a result of bullying. However, the attrition rate for boys was larger than for girls. This might mean that boys who were affected by the bullying by becoming depressed may have dropped out of the study, whereas boys not so affected did not drop out. It would have distorted the effect of bullying on boys.

   Further, there was more attrition for students from single-parent families. Perhaps people in such families are differentially susceptible to depression than are students from two-parent (or other) families.

15. Why might an ABA design not be appropriate for behavioral (as opposed to drug) treatment for depression?

   An ABA design presupposes that at the second baseline phase (i.e., the second A phase), the individual's behavior will return to the way it was before the treatment. In behavioral treatment for depression, if therapy is successful, the person will not return to his or her original depressed state. Thus, an ABA design will not be appropriate.

16. What are the advantages of single-case research?
    a. Single-case research provides a wealth of detail, much more than for a group design, where in-depth information would be too much to evaluate.
    b. Single-case research is also good for studying rare phenomena.
    c. Single-case research can be used for creating and testing research hypotheses.
    d. Single-case research is useful for studying clinical interventions on single people whose specific symptoms are unique.

Chapter 14

Answers to Multiple Choice Questions

1. c	**6.** c	**11.** b
2. a	**7.** c	**12.** d
3. d	**8.** c	**13.** d
4. c	**9.** b	
5. c	**10.** b	

Answers to Essay Questions

14. Why is it so hard to distinguish among the effects of culture, race, and ethnicity in our research?

    People, including psychologists, use the terms culture, race, and ethnicity very imprecisely. One researcher might refer to a person's culture but a second researcher might refer to race or ethnicity in explaining the same behaviors; the researchers might mean the same thing, but they use different terms to refer to the same thing. Or they might really mean different things when they use the terms differently. Unfortunately, there is no consistent agreement about what the terms mean. In addition, the concept of race is problematic because there are not characteristics that we can use to reliably categorize people racially; there will always be confusion because some people resist easy categorization. Many scientists regard race as a social construction rather than as a biological fact.

    It is important to distinguish among them because they can refer to useful construct. For instance, ethnicity is often associated with affiliation (e.g., who do you think you belong with), whereas culture pertains to the objects we use (physical culture) or to behaviors (subjective culture).

15. Why should we differentiate between etics and emics in our explanations of behavior?

    Etics are research results that hold true across cultures; emics are research results pertaining to a single culture. It is important to differentiate between them because we need to pay attention to the fact that behaviors in different societies may have very different causes and explanations.

16. Why are culture, race, and ethnicity hypothetical constructs? In what sense are they useful and in what sense are they limited?

    Culture, race, and ethnicity are hypothetical constructs because they are concepts that psychologists have constructed to help explain and understand behavior. They are hypothetical because we hypothesize that they exist and that they are going to be useful, explanatory concepts.

Sometimes these constructs are helpful because, when measured appropriately, they might be helpful in our understanding of why people in some groups act one way, whereas people in another group act differently. Not everybody in a group acts and thinks the same way, but the hypothetical constructs of culture and ethnicity can give some insights into group processes.

On the other hand, none of these concepts can be precisely defined and measured, which is why we rely on external markers (e.g., skin color) to represent them. These external markers may not really be very helpful in understanding behavior because they are only imperfectly correlated with thought and behavior. People within a given group differ from one another in many ways, so trying to figure out how a single person thinks is not feasible.

17. What are some difficulties that scientists have had in categorizing people by race and in defining race?

   a. Skin color has often been a means by which people are racially categorized. This is unreliable because sometimes people with darker skin will be considered "white" while people with lighter skin will be considered "black."

   b. Race is seen as involving discrete, mutually exclusive categories; a person falls in one and only one category. In reality, the characteristics associated with the categories fall on a continuum, so the cutoff points are arbitrary.

   c. Scientists have not reached consensus about what racial categories there might actually be. There is no set number of racial categories that scientists agree on.

   d. Geographical criteria for race is unreliable because there are many people whose birthplace is not a reliable indicator of their ancestry, which is likely to be mixed in any case.

   e. When scientists did create racial categories, they were based on subjective, nonscientific criteria.

18. Why is content validity a critical concept to consider in conducting research on tests administered by mental health workers when working with people from different backgrounds and cultures?

   Content validity relates to the questions that clinicians ask when working with a client. In order to draw good conclusions, the clinician must ask appropriate questions. What will be appropriate in one setting or with one group may not be useful in another context.

   People with different lifestyles may not share the same perspective, so a simple question might indicate something quite different across groups. Similarly, a certain behavior will reflect normal functioning in one culture, abnormal functioning in a second, and be completely irrelevant in a third. The potential problems are compounded when a clinician wants to translate a question into a different language; there may not be corresponding ideas in different languages.

   In order for test items to be valid for different groups, the concepts have to address the appropriate ideas using appropriate words. Without content validity, answers to individual questions on a test may mislead a clinician entirely.

STATISTICAL TABLES

TABLE E.1 *Significance Values for the Normal Distribution (z)*

Column A contains the z score values
Column B contains the proportion of the distribution in the body
Column C contains the proportion of the distribution in the tail

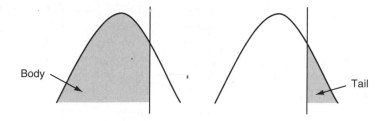

Body →   ← Tail

z score	Proportion in body (P)	Proportion in tail (1-P)	z score	Proportion in body (P)	Proportion in tail (1-P)	z score	Proportion in body (P)	Proportion in tail (1-P)
0	0.5	0.5	0.19	0.5753	0.4247	0.38	0.648	0.352
0.01	0.504	0.496	0.2	0.5793	0.4207	0.39	0.6517	0.3483
0.02	0.508	0.492	0.21	0.5832	0.4168	0.4	0.6554	0.3446
0.03	0.512	0.488	0.22	0.5871	0.4129	0.41	0.6591	0.3409
0.04	0.516	0.484	0.23	0.591	0.409	0.42	0.6628	0.3372
0.05	0.5199	0.4801	0.24	0.5948	0.4052	0.43	0.6664	0.3336
0.06	0.5239	0.4761	0.25	0.5987	0.4013	0.44	0.67	0.33
0.07	0.5279	0.4721	0.26	0.6026	0.3974	0.45	0.6736	0.3264
0.08	0.5319	0.4681	0.27	0.6064	0.3936	0.46	0.6772	0.3228
0.09	0.5359	0.4641	0.28	0.6103	0.3897	0.47	0.6808	0.3192
0.1	0.5398	0.4602	0.29	0.6141	0.3859	0.48	0.6844	0.3156
0.11	0.5438	0.4562	0.3	0.6179	0.3821	0.49	0.6879	0.3121
0.12	0.5478	0.4522	0.31	0.6217	0.3783	0.5	0.6915	0.3085
0.13	0.5517	0.4483	0.32	0.6255	0.3745	0.51	0.695	0.305
0.14	0.5557	0.4443	0.33	0.6293	0.3707	0.52	0.6985	0.3015
0.15	0.5596	0.4404	0.34	0.6331	0.3669	0.53	0.7019	0.2981
0.16	0.5636	0.4364	0.35	0.6368	0.3632	0.54	0.7054	0.2946
0.17	0.5675	0.4325	0.36	0.6406	0.3594	0.55	0.7088	0.2912
0.18	0.5714	0.4286	0.37	0.6443	0.3557	0.56	0.7123	0.2877

(continued)

TABLE E.1   Continued

z score	Proportion in body (P)	Proportion in tail (1-P)	z score	Proportion in body (P)	Proportion in tail (1-P)	z score	Proportion in body (P)	Proportion in tail (1-P)
0.57	0.7157	0.2843	0.98	0.8365	0.1635	1.39	0.9177	0.0823
0.58	0.719	0.281	0.99	0.8389	0.1611	1.4	0.9192	0.0808
0.59	0.7224	0.2776	1	0.8413	0.1587	1.41	0.9207	0.0793
0.6	0.7257	0.2743	1.01	0.8438	0.1562	1.42	0.9222	0.0778
0.61	0.7291	0.2709	1.02	0.8461	0.1539	1.43	0.9236	0.0764
0.62	0.7324	0.2676	1.03	0.8485	0.1515	1.44	0.9251	0.0749
0.63	0.7357	0.2643	1.04	0.8508	0.1492	1.45	0.9265	0.0735
0.64	0.7389	0.2611	1.05	0.8531	0.1469	1.46	0.9279	0.0721
0.65	0.7422	0.2578	1.06	0.8554	0.1446	1.47	0.9292	0.0708
0.66	0.7454	0.2546	1.07	0.8577	0.1423	1.48	0.9306	0.0694
0.67	0.7486	0.2514	1.08	0.8599	0.1401	1.49	0.9319	0.0681
0.68	0.7517	0.2483	1.09	0.8621	0.1379	1.5	0.9332	0.0668
0.69	0.7549	0.2451	1.1	0.8643	0.1357	1.51	0.9345	0.0655
0.7	0.758	0.242	1.11	0.8665	0.1335	1.52	0.9357	0.0643
0.71	0.7611	0.2389	1.12	0.8686	0.1314	1.53	0.937	0.063
0.72	0.7642	0.2358	1.13	0.8708	0.1292	1.54	0.9382	0.0618
0.73	0.7673	0.2327	1.14	0.8729	0.1271	1.55	0.9394	0.0606
0.74	0.7704	0.2296	1.15	0.8749	0.1251	1.56	0.9406	0.0594
0.75	0.7734	0.2266	1.16	0.877	0.123	1.57	0.9418	0.0582
0.76	0.7764	0.2236	1.17	0.879	0.121	1.58	0.9429	0.0571
0.77	0.7794	0.2206	1.18	0.881	0.119	1.59	0.9441	0.0559
0.78	0.7823	0.2177	1.19	0.883	0.117	1.6	0.9452	0.0548
0.79	0.7852	0.2148	1.2	0.8849	0.1151	1.61	0.9463	0.0537
0.8	0.7881	0.2119	1.21	0.8869	0.1131	1.62	0.9474	0.0526
0.81	0.791	0.209	1.22	0.8888	0.1112	1.63	0.9484	0.0516
0.82	0.7939	0.2061	1.23	0.8907	0.1093	1.64	0.9495	0.0505
0.83	0.7967	0.2033	1.24	0.8925	0.1075	1.65	0.9505	0.0495
0.84	0.7995	0.2005	1.25	0.8944	0.1056	1.66	0.9515	0.0485
0.85	0.8023	0.1977	1.26	0.8962	0.1038	1.67	0.9525	0.0475
0.86	0.8051	0.1949	1.27	0.898	0.102	1.68	0.9535	0.0465
0.87	0.8078	0.1922	1.28	0.8997	0.1003	1.69	0.9545	0.0455
0.88	0.8106	0.1894	1.29	0.9015	0.0985	1.7	0.9554	0.0446
0.89	0.8133	0.1867	1.3	0.9032	0.0968	1.71	0.9564	0.0436
0.9	0.8159	0.1841	1.31	0.9049	0.0951	1.72	0.9573	0.0427
0.91	0.8186	0.1814	1.32	0.9066	0.0934	1.73	0.9582	0.0418
0.92	0.8212	0.1788	1.33	0.9082	0.0918	1.74	0.9591	0.0409
0.93	0.8238	0.1762	1.34	0.9099	0.0901	1.75	0.9599	0.0401
0.94	0.8264	0.1736	1.35	0.9115	0.0885	1.76	0.9608	0.0392
0.95	0.8289	0.1711	1.36	0.9131	0.0869	1.77	0.9616	0.0384
0.96	0.8315	0.1685	1.37	0.9147	0.0853	1.78	0.9625	0.0375
0.97	0.834	0.166	1.38	0.9162	0.0838	1.79	0.9633	0.0367

z score	Proportion in body (P)	Proportion in tail (1-P)	z score	Proportion in body (P)	Proportion in tail (1-P)	z score	Proportion in body (P)	Proportion in tail (1-P)
1.8	0.9641	0.0359	2.21	0.9864	0.0136	2.62	0.9956	0.0044
1.81	0.9649	0.0351	2.22	0.9868	0.0132	2.63	0.9957	0.0043
1.82	0.9656	0.0344	2.23	0.9871	0.0129	2.64	0.9959	0.0041
1.83	0.9664	0.0336	2.24	0.9875	0.0125	2.65	0.996	0.004
1.84	0.9671	0.0329	2.25	0.9878	0.0122	2.66	0.9961	0.0039
1.85	0.9678	0.0322	2.26	0.9881	0.0119	2.67	0.9962	0.0038
1.86	0.9686	0.0314	2.27	0.9884	0.0116	2.68	0.9963	0.0037
1.87	0.9693	0.0307	2.28	0.9887	0.0113	2.69	0.9964	0.0036
1.88	0.9699	0.0301	2.29	0.989	0.011	2.7	0.9965	0.0035
1.89	0.9706	0.0294	2.3	0.9893	0.0107	2.71	0.9966	0.0034
1.9	0.9713	0.0287	2.31	0.9896	0.0104	2.72	0.9967	0.0033
1.91	0.9719	0.0281	2.32	0.9898	0.0102	2.73	0.9968	0.0032
1.92	0.9726	0.0274	2.33	0.9901	0.0099	2.74	0.9969	0.0031
1.93	0.9732	0.0268	2.34	0.9904	0.0096	2.75	0.997	0.003
1.94	0.9738	0.0262	2.35	0.9906	0.0094	2.76	0.9971	0.0029
1.95	0.9744	0.0256	2.36	0.9909	0.0091	2.77	0.9972	0.0028
1.96	0.975	0.025	2.37	0.9911	0.0089	2.78	0.9973	0.0027
1.97	0.9756	0.0244	2.38	0.9913	0.0087	2.79	0.9974	0.0026
1.98	0.9761	0.0239	2.39	0.9916	0.0084	2.8	0.9974	0.0026
1.99	0.9767	0.0233	2.4	0.9918	0.0082	2.81	0.9975	0.0025
2	0.9772	0.0228	2.41	0.992	0.008	2.82	0.9976	0.0024
2.01	0.9778	0.0222	2.42	0.9922	0.0078	2.83	0.9977	0.0023
2.02	0.9783	0.0217	2.43	0.9925	0.0075	2.84	0.9977	0.0023
2.03	0.9788	0.0212	2.44	0.9927	0.0073	2.85	0.9978	0.0022
2.04	0.9793	0.0207	2.45	0.9929	0.0071	2.86	0.9979	0.0021
2.05	0.9798	0.0202	2.46	0.9931	0.0069	2.87	0.9979	0.0021
2.06	0.9803	0.0197	2.47	0.9932	0.0068	2.88	0.998	0.002
2.07	0.9808	0.0192	2.48	0.9934	0.0066	2.89	0.9981	0.0019
2.08	0.9812	0.0188	2.49	0.9936	0.0064	2.9	0.9981	0.0019
2.09	0.9817	0.0183	2.5	0.9938	0.0062	2.91	0.9982	0.0018
2.1	0.9821	0.0179	2.51	0.994	0.006	2.92	0.9982	0.0018
2.11	0.9826	0.0174	2.52	0.9941	0.0059	2.93	0.9983	0.0017
2.12	0.983	0.017	2.53	0.9943	0.0057	2.94	0.9984	0.0016
2.13	0.9834	0.0166	2.54	0.9945	0.0055	2.95	0.9984	0.0016
2.14	0.9838	0.0162	2.55	0.9946	0.0054	2.96	0.9985	0.0015
2.15	0.9842	0.0158	2.56	0.9948	0.0052	2.97	0.9985	0.0015
2.16	0.9846	0.0154	2.57	0.9949	0.0051	2.98	0.9986	0.0014
2.17	0.985	0.015	2.58	0.9951	0.0049	2.99	0.9986	0.0014
2.18	0.9854	0.0146	2.59	0.9952	0.0048	3	0.9987	0.0013
2.19	0.9857	0.0143	2.6	0.9953	0.0047	3.01	0.9987	0.0013
2.2	0.9861	0.0139	2.61	0.9955	0.0045	3.02	0.9987	0.0013

(continued)

TABLE E.1   Continued

z score	Proportion in body (P)	Proportion in tail (1-P)	z score	Proportion in body (P)	Proportion in tail (1-P)	z score	Proportion in body (P)	Proportion in tail (1-P)
3.03	0.9988	0.0012	3.36	0.9996	0.0004	3.69	0.9999	1E-04
3.04	0.9988	0.0012	3.37	0.9996	0.0004	3.7	0.9999	1E-04
3.05	0.9989	0.0011	3.38	0.9996	0.0004	3.71	0.9999	1E-04
3.06	0.9989	0.0011	3.39	0.9997	0.0003	3.72	0.9999	1E-04
3.07	0.9989	0.0011	3.4	0.9997	0.0003	3.73	0.9999	1E-04
3.08	0.999	0.001	3.41	0.9997	0.0003	3.74	0.9999	1E-04
3.09	0.999	0.001	3.42	0.9997	0.0003	3.75	0.9999	1E-04
3.1	0.999	0.001	3.43	0.9997	0.0003	3.76	0.9999	1E-04
3.11	0.9991	0.0009	3.44	0.9997	0.0003	3.77	0.9999	1E-04
3.12	0.9991	0.0009	3.45	0.9997	0.0003	3.78	0.9999	1E-04
3.13	0.9991	0.0009	3.46	0.9997	0.0003	3.79	0.9999	1E-04
3.14	0.9992	0.0008	3.47	0.9997	0.0003	3.8	0.9999	1E-04
3.15	0.9992	0.0008	3.48	0.9997	0.0003	3.81	0.9999	1E-04
3.16	0.9992	0.0008	3.49	0.9998	0.0002	3.82	0.9999	1E-04
3.17	0.9992	0.0008	3.5	0.9998	0.0002	3.83	0.9999	1E-04
3.18	0.9993	0.0007	3.51	0.9998	0.0002	3.84	0.9999	1E-04
3.19	0.9993	0.0007	3.52	0.9998	0.0002	3.85	0.9999	1E-04
3.2	0.9993	0.0007	3.53	0.9998	0.0002	3.86	0.9999	1E-04
3.21	0.9993	0.0007	3.54	0.9998	0.0002	3.87	0.9999	1E-04
3.22	0.9994	0.0006	3.55	0.9998	0.0002	3.88	0.9999	1E-04
3.23	0.9994	0.0006	3.56	0.9998	0.0002	3.89	0.9999	1E-04
3.24	0.9994	0.0006	3.57	0.9998	0.0002	3.9	1	0
3.25	0.9994	0.0006	3.58	0.9998	0.0002	3.91	1	0
3.26	0.9994	0.0006	3.59	0.9998	0.0002	3.92	1	0
3.27	0.9995	0.0005	3.6	0.9998	0.0002	3.93	1	0
3.28	0.9995	0.0005	3.61	0.9998	0.0002	3.94	1	0
3.29	0.9995	0.0005	3.62	0.9999	1E-04	3.95	1	0
3.3	0.9995	0.0005	3.63	0.9999	1E-04	3.96	1	0
3.31	0.9995	0.0005	3.64	0.9999	1E-04	3.97	1	0
3.32	0.9995	0.0005	3.65	0.9999	1E-04	3.98	1	0
3.33	0.9996	0.0004	3.66	0.9999	1E-04	3.99	1	0
3.34	0.9996	0.0004	3.67	0.9999	1E-04	4	1	0
3.35	0.9996	0.0004	3.68	0.9999	1E-04			

TABLE E.2   *Significance Values for the t Distribution*

Computed values of t are significant if they are larger than the critical value in the table.

	α Levels for Directional (One-Tailed) Tests				
	.05	**.025**	**.01**	**.005**	**.0005**
α Levels for Nondirectional (Two-Tailed) Tests					
df	**.10**	**.05**	**.02**	**.01**	**.001**
1	6.314	12.706	31.821	63.657	636.619
2	2.920	4.303	6.965	9.925	31.598
3	2.353	3.182	4.541	5.841	12.924
4	2.132	2.776	3.747	4.604	8.610
5	2.015	2.571	3.365	4.032	6.869
6	1.943	2.447	3.143	3.707	5.959
7	1.895	2.365	2.998	3.499	5.408
8	1.860	2.306	2.896	3.355	5.041
9	1.833	2.262	2.821	3.250	4.781
10	1.812	2.228	2.764	3.169	4.587
11	1.796	2.201	2.718	3.106	4.437
12	1.782	2.179	2.681	3.055	4.318
13	1.771	2.160	2.650	3.012	4.221
14	1.761	2.145	2.624	2.977	4.140
15	1.753	2.131	2.602	2.947	4.073
16	1.746	2.120	2.583	2.921	4.015
17	1.740	2.110	2.567	2.898	3.965
18	1.734	2.101	2.552	2.878	3.922
19	1.729	2.093	2.539	2.861	3.883
20	1.725	2.086	2.528	2.845	3.850
21	1.721	2.080	2.518	2.831	3.819
22	1.717	2.074	2.508	2.819	3.792
23	1.714	2.069	2.500	2.807	3.767
24	1.711	2.064	2.492	2.797	3.745
25	1.708	2.060	2.485	2.787	3.725
26	1.706	2.056	2.479	2.779	3.707
27	1.703	2.052	2.473	2.771	3.690
28	1.701	2.048	2.467	2.763	3.674
29	1.699	2.045	2.462	2.756	3.659
30	1.697	2.042	2.457	2.750	3.646
40	1.684	2.021	2.423	2.704	3.551
60	1.671	2.000	2.390	2.660	3.460
120	1.658	1.980	2.358	2.617	3.373
∞	1.645	1.960	2.326	2.576	3.291

© R. A. Fisher and F. Yates (2007). *Statistical Tables for Biological, Agricultural and Medical Research,* reprinted by permission of Pearson Education Limited. Adapted from Table III.

TABLE E.3 *Significance Values for the Analysis of Variance (F test)*

Degrees of freedom for treatments (df$_{between}$) appear in the left column. Degrees of freedom for the error term (df$_{within}$ or df$_{error}$) are across the top. Computed values of *F* are significant if they are larger than the critical value in the table.

Values for $\alpha = .05$ are in normal Roman type

Values for $\alpha = .01$ are in bold type

Values for $\alpha = 0.001$ are in italics

DF for the numerator (DF$_{BETWEEN}$ OR DF$_{TREATMENT}$)									
	1	*2*	*3*	*4*	*5*	*6*	*8*	*12*	*24*

DF for the denominator (DF$_{WITHIN}$ OR DF$_{ERROR}$)										
1	$\alpha = .05$	161.4	199.5	215.7	224.6	230.2	234.0	238.9	243.9	249.0
	$\alpha = .01$	**4052**	**4999**	**5403**	**5625**	**5764**	**5859**	**5982**	**6106**	**6234**
	$\alpha = .001$	*405284*	*500000*	*540379*	*562500*	*576405*	*585937*	*598144*	*610667*	*623497*
2	$\alpha = .05$	18.51	19.00	19.16	19.25	19.30	19.33	19.37	19.41	19.45
	$\alpha = .01$	**98.50**	**99.00**	**99.17**	**99.25**	**99.30**	**99.33**	**99.37**	**99.42**	**99.46**
	$\alpha = .001$	*998.5*	*999.0*	*999.2*	*999.2*	*999.3*	*999.3*	*999.4*	*999.4*	*999.5*
3	$\alpha = .05$	10.13	9.55	9.28	6.12	9.01	8.94	8.84	8.74	8.64
	$\alpha = .01$	**34.12**	**30.82**	**29.46**	**28.71**	**28.24**	**27.91**	**27.49**	**27.05**	**26.60**
	$\alpha = .001$	*167.0*	*148.5*	*141.2*	*137.1*	*134.6*	*132.8*	*130.6*	*128.3*	*125.9*
4	$\alpha = .05$	7.71	6.94	6.59	6.39	6.26	6.16	6.04	5.91	5.77
	$\alpha = .01$	**21.20**	**18.00**	**16.69**	**15.98**	**15.52**	**15.21**	**14.80**	**14.37**	**13.93**
	$\alpha = .001$	*74.14*	*61.25*	*56.18*	*53.44*	*51.71*	*50.53*	*49.00*	*47.41*	*45.77*
5	$\alpha = .05$	6.61	5.79	5.41	5.19	5.05	4.95	4.82	4.68	4.53
	$\alpha = .01$	**16.26**	**13.27**	**12.06**	**11.39**	**10.97**	**10.67**	**10.29**	**9.89**	**9.47**
	$\alpha = .001$	*47.18*	*37.12*	*33.20*	*31.09*	*29.75*	*28.84*	*27.64*	*26.42*	*25.14*
6	$\alpha = .05$	5.99	5.14	4.76	4.53	4.39	4.28	4.15	4.00	3.84
	$\alpha = .01$	**13.74**	**10.92**	**9.78**	**9.15**	**8.75**	**8.47**	**8.10**	**7.72**	**7.31**
	$\alpha = .001$	*35.51*	*27.00*	*23.70*	*21.92*	*20.81*	*20.03*	*19.03*	*17.99*	*16.89*
7	$\alpha = .05$	5.59	4.74	4.35	4.12	3.97	3.87	3.73	3.57	3.41
	$\alpha = .01$	**12.25**	**9.55**	**8.45**	**7.85**	**7.46**	**7.19**	**6.84**	**6.47**	**6.07**
	$\alpha = .001$	*29.25*	*21.69*	*18.77*	*17.19*	*16.21*	*15.52*	*14.63*	*13.71*	*12.73*
8	$\alpha = .05$	5.32	4.46	4.07	3.84	3.69	3.58	3.44	3.28	3.12
	$\alpha = .01$	**11.26**	**8.65**	**7.59**	**7.01**	**6.63**	**6.37**	**6.03**	**5.67**	**5.28**
	$\alpha = .001$	*25.42*	*18.49*	*15.83*	*14.39*	*13.49*	*12.86*	*12.04*	*11.19*	*10.30*
9	$\alpha = .05$	5.12	4.26	3.86	3.63	3.48	3.37	3.23	3.07	2.90
	$\alpha = .01$	**10.56**	**8.02**	**6.99**	**6.42**	**6.06**	**5.80**	**5.47**	**5.11**	**4.73**
	$\alpha = .001$	*22.86*	*16.39*	*13.90*	*12.56*	*11.71*	*11.13*	*10.37*	*9.57*	*8.72*
10	$\alpha = .05$	4.96	4.10	3.71	3.48	3.33	3.22	3.07	2.91	2.74
	$\alpha = .01$	**10.04**	**7.56**	**6.55**	**5.99**	**5.64**	**5.39**	**5.06**	**4.71**	**4.33**
	$\alpha = .001$	*21.04*	*14.91*	*12.55*	*11.28*	*10.48*	*9.92*	*9.20*	*8.45*	*7.64*
11	$\alpha = .05$	4.84	3.98	3.59	3.36	3.20	3.09	2.95	2.79	2.61
	$\alpha = .01$	**9.65**	**7.20**	**6.22**	**5.67**	**5.32**	**5.07**	**4.74**	**4.40**	**4.02**
	$\alpha = .001$	*19.69*	*13.81*	*11.56*	*10.35*	*9.58*	*9.05*	*8.35*	*7.63*	*6.85*
12	$\alpha = .05$	4.75	3.88	3.49	3.26	3.11	3.00	2.85	2.69	2.50
	$\alpha = .01$	**9.33**	**6.93**	**5.95**	**5.41**	**5.06**	**4.82**	**4.50**	**4.16**	**3.78**
	$\alpha = .001$	*18.64*	*12.97*	*10.80*	*9.63*	*8.89*	*8.38*	*7.71*	*7.00*	*6.25*

DF for the numerator (DF_BETWEEN OR DF_TREATMENT)									
	1	2	3	4	5	6	8	12	24
DF for the denominator (DF_WITHIN OR DF_ERROR)									
13 $\alpha = .05$	4.67	3.80	3.41	3.18	3.02	2.92	2.77	2.60	2.42
$\alpha = .01$	9.07	6.70	5.74	5.20	4.86	4.62	4.30	3.96	3.59
$\alpha = .001$	17.81	12.31	10.21	9.07	8.35	7.86	7.21	6.52	5.78
14 $\alpha = .05$	4.60	3.74	3.34	3.11	2.96	2.85	2.70	2.53	2.35
$\alpha = .01$	8.86	6.51	5.56	5.03	4.69	4.46	4.14	3.80	3.43
$\alpha = .001$	17.14	11.78	9.73	8.62	7.92	7.43	6.80	6.13	5.41
15 $\alpha = .05$	4.54	3.68	3.26	3.06	2.90	2.79	2.64	2.48	2.29
$\alpha = .01$	8.68	6.36	5.42	4.89	4.56	4.32	4.00	3.67	3.29
$\alpha = .001$	16.59	11.34	9.34	8.25	7.57	7.09	6.47	5.81	5.10
16 $\alpha = .05$	4.49	3.63	3.24	3.01	2.85	2.74	2.59	2.42	2.24
$\alpha = .01$	8.53	6.23	5.29	4.77	4.44	4.20	3.89	3.55	3.18
$\alpha = .001$	16.12	10.97	9.00	7.94	7.27	6.81	6.19	5.55	4.85
17 $\alpha = .05$	4.45	3.59	3.20	2.96	2.81	2.70	2.55	2.38	2.19
$\alpha = .01$	8.40	6.11	5.18	4.67	4.34	4.10	3.79	3.45	3.08
$\alpha = .001$	15.72	10.66	8.73	7.68	7.02	6.56	5.96	5.32	4.63
18 $\alpha = .05$	4.41	3.55	3.16	2.93	2.77	2.66	2.51	2.34	2.15
$\alpha = .01$	8.28	6.01	5.09	4.58	4.25	4.01	3.71	3.37	3.00
$\alpha = .001$	15.38	10.39	8.49	7.46	6.81	6.35	5.76	5.13	4.45
19 $\alpha = .05$	4.38	3.52	3.13	2.90	2.74	2.63	2.48	2.31	2.11
$\alpha = .01$	8.18	5.93	5.01	4.50	4.17	3.94	3.63	3.30	2.92
$\alpha = .001$	15.08	10.16	8.28	7.26	6.62	6.18	5.59	4.97	4.29
20 $\alpha = .05$	4.35	3.49	3.10	2.87	2.71	2.60	2.45	2.28	2.08
$\alpha = .01$	8.10	5.85	4.94	4.43	4.10	3.87	3.56	3.23	2.86
$\alpha = .001$	14.82	9.95	8.10	7.10	6.46	6.02	5.44	4.82	4.15
21 $\alpha = .05$	4.32	3.47	3.07	2.84	2.68	2.57	2.42	2.25	2.05
$\alpha = .01$	8.02	5.78	4.87	4.37	4.04	3.81	3.51	3.17	2.80
$\alpha = .001$	14.59	9.77	7.94	6.95	6.32	5.88	5.31	4.70	4.03
22 $\alpha = .05$	4.30	3.44	3.05	2.82	2.66	2.55	2.40	2.23	2.03
$\alpha = .01$	7.94	5.72	4.82	4.31	3.99	3.76	3.45	3.12	2.75
$\alpha = .001$	14.38	9.61	7.80	6.81	6.19	5.76	5.19	4.58	3.92
23 $\alpha = .05$	4.28	3.42	3.03	2.80	2.64	2.53	2.38	2.20	2.00
$\alpha = .01$	7.88	5.66	4.76	4.26	3.94	3.71	3.41	3.07	2.70
$\alpha = .001$	14.19	9.47	7.67	6.69	6.08	5.65	5.09	4.48	3.82
24 $\alpha = .05$	4.26	3.40	3.01	2.78	2.62	2.51	2.36	2.18	1.98
$\alpha = .01$	7.82	5.61	4.72	4.22	3.90	3.67	3.36	3.03	2.66
$\alpha = .001$	14.03	9.34	7.55	6.59	5.98	5.55	4.99	4.39	3.74
25 $\alpha = .05$	4.24	3.38	2.99	2.76	2.60	2.49	2.34	2.16	1.96
$\alpha = .01$	7.77	5.57	4.68	4.18	3.86	3.63	3.32	2.99	2.62
$\alpha = .001$	13.88	9.22	7.45	6.49	5.88	5.46	4.91	4.31	3.66
26 $\alpha = .05$	4.22	3.37	2.98	2.74	2.59	2.47	2.32	2.15	1.95
$\alpha = .01$	7.72	5.53	4.64	4.14	3.82	3.59	3.29	2.96	2.58
$\alpha = .001$	13.74	9.12	7.36	6.41	5.80	5.38	4.83	4.24	3.59

(continued)

TABLE E.3 Continued

DF for the numerator (DF$_{BETWEEN}$ OR DF$_{TREATMENT}$)									
	1	2	3	4	5	6	8	12	24
DF for the denominator (DF$_{WITHIN}$ OR DF$_{ERROR}$)									
27 $\alpha = .05$	4.21	3.35	2.96	2.73	2.57	2.46	2.30	2.13	1.93
$\alpha = .01$	**7.68**	**5.49**	**4.60**	**4.11**	**3.78**	**3.56**	**3.26**	**2.93**	**2.55**
$\alpha = .001$	13.61	9.02	7.27	6.33	5.73	5.31	4.76	4.17	3.52
28 $\alpha = .05$	4.20	3.34	2.95	2.71	2.56	2.44	2.29	2.12	1.91
$\alpha = .01$	**7.64**	**5.45**	**4.57**	**4.07**	**3.75**	**3.53**	**3.23**	**2.90**	**2.52**
$\alpha = .001$	13.50	8.93	7.19	6.25	5.66	5.24	4.69	4.11	3.46
29 $\alpha = .05$	4.18	3.33	2.93	2.70	2.54	2.43	2.28	2.10	1.90
$\alpha = .01$	**7.60**	**5.42**	**4.54**	**4.04**	**3.73**	**3.50**	**3.20**	**2.87**	**2.49**
$\alpha = .001$	13.39	8.85	7.12	6.19	5.59	5.18	4.64	4.05	3.41
30 $\alpha = .05$	4.17	3.32	2.92	2.69	2.53	2.42	2.27	2.09	1.89
$\alpha = .01$	**7.56**	**5.39**	**4.51**	**4.02**	**3.70**	**3.47**	**3.17**	**2.84**	**2.47**
$\alpha = .001$	13.29	8.77	7.05	6.12	5.53	5.12	4.58	4.00	3.36
40 $\alpha = .05$	4.08	3.23	2.84	2.61	2.45	2.34	2.18	2.00	1.79
$\alpha = .01$	**7.31**	**5.18**	**4.31**	**3.83**	**3.51**	**3.29**	**2.99**	**2.66**	**2.29**
$\alpha = .001$	12.61	8.25	6.60	5.70	5.13	4.73	4.21	3.64	3.01
60 $\alpha = .05$	4.00	3.15	2.76	2.52	2.37	2.25	2.10	1.92	1.70
$\alpha = .01$	**7.08**	**4.98**	**4.13**	**3.65**	**3.34**	**3.12**	**2.82**	**2.50**	**2.12**
$\alpha = .001$	11.97	7.76	6.17	5.31	4.76	4.37	3.87	3.31	2.69
120 $\alpha = .05$	3.92	3.07	2.68	2.45	2.29	2.17	2.02	1.83	1.61
$\alpha = .01$	**6.85**	**4.79**	**3.95**	**3.48**	**3.17**	**2.66**	**2.34**	**1.95**	
$\alpha = .001$	11.38	7.32	5.79	4.95	4.42	4.04	3.55	3.02	2.40
∞ $\alpha = .05$	3.84	2.99	2.60	2.37	2.21	2.10	1.94	1.75	1.52
$\alpha = .01$	**6.64**	**4.60**	**3.78**	**3.32**	**3.02**	**2.80**	**2.51**	**2.18**	**1.79**
$\alpha = .001$	10.83	6.91	5.42	4.62	4.10	3.74	3.27	2.74	2.13

TABLE E.4   *Significance Values for the Pearson Product–Moment Correlation (r)*

Computed values of r *are significant if they are larger than the value in the table.*

α Levels for Directional (One-Tailed) Tests				
.05	**.025**	**.01**	**.005**	**.0005**
α Levels for Nondirectional (Two-Tailed) Tests				
df **(# pairs − 2)** **.1**	**.05**	**.02**	**.01**	**.001**
1 .9877	.9969	.9995	.9999	.9999988
2 .9000	.9500	.9800	.9900	.9990
3 .8054	.8783	.9343	.9587	.9912
4 .7293	.8114	.8822	.9172	.9741
5 .6694	.7545	.8329	.8745	.9507
6 .6215	.7067	.7887	.8343	.9249
7 .5822	.6664	.7498	.7977	.8982
8 .5494	.6319	.7155	.7646	.8721
9 .5214	.6021	.6851	.7348	.8471
10 .4973	.5760	.6581	.7079	.8233
11 .4762	.5529	.6339	.6835	.8010
12 .4575	.5324	.6120	.6614	.7800
13 .4409	.5139	.5923	.6411	.7603
14 .4259	.4973	.5742	.6226	.7420
15 .4124	.4821	.5577	.6055	.7246
16 .4000	.4683	.5425	.5897	.7084
17 .3887	.4555	.5285	.5751	.6932
18 .3783	.4438	.5155	.5614	.6787
19 .3687	.4329	.5043	.5487	.6652
20 .3598	.4227	.4921	.5368	.6524
25 .3233	.3809	.4451	.4869	.5974
30 .2960	.3494	.4093	.4487	.5541
35 .2746	.3246	.3810	.4182	.5189
40 .2573	.3044	.3578	.3932	.4896
45 .2428	.2875	.3384	.3721	.4648
50 .2306	.2732	.3218	.3541	.4433
60 .2108	.2500	.2948	.3248	.4078
70 .1954	.2319	.2737	.3017	.3799
80 .1829	.2172	.2565	.2830	.3568
90 .1726	.2050	.2422	.2673	.3375
100 .1638	.1946	.2301	.2540	.3211

TABLE E.5 *Significance Values for Chi-Square* (χ^2)

Computed values of χ^2 are significant if they are larger than the value in the table.

	α Levels			
df	.10	.05	.01	.001
1	2.706	3.841	6.635	10.827
2	4.605	5.991	9.210	13.815
3	6.251	7.815	11.345	16.266
4	7.779	9.488	13.277	18.467
5	9.236	11.070	15.086	20.515
6	10.645	12.592	16.812	22.457
7	12.017	14.067	18.475	24.322
8	13.362	15.507	20.090	26.125
9	14.684	16.919	21.666	27.877
10	15.987	18.307	23.209	29.588
11	17.275	19.675	24.725	31.264
12	18.549	21.026	26.217	32.909
13	19.812	22.362	27.688	34.528
14	21.064	23.685	29.141	36.123
15	22.307	24.996	30.578	37.697
16	23.542	26.296	32.000	39.252
17	24.769	27.587	33.409	40.790
18	25.989	28.869	34.805	42.312
19	27.204	30.144	36.191	43.280
20	28.412	31.410	37.566	45.315
21	29.615	32.671	38.932	46.797
22	30.813	33.924	40.289	48.268
23	32.007	35.172	41.638	49.728
24	33.196	36.415	42.980	51.179
25	34.382	37.652	44.314	52.620
26	35.563	38.885	45.642	54.052
27	36.741	40.133	46.963	55.476
28	37.916	41.337	48.278	56.893
29	39.087	42.557	49.588	58.302
30	40.256	43.773	50.892	59.703

TABLE E.6 *The Studentized Range Statistic q (Critical Values for Tukey's HSD)*

MS_w df	α	2	3	4	5	6	7	8	9	10	11
5	.05	3.64	4.60	5.22	5.67	6.03	6.33	6.58	6.80	6.99	7.17
	.01	5.70	6.98	7.80	8.42	8.91	9.32	9.67	9.97	10.24	10.48
6	.05	3.46	4.34	4.90	5.30	5.63	5.90	6.12	6.32	6.49	6.65
	.01	5.24	6.33	7.03	7.56	7.97	8.32	8.61	8.87	9.10	9.30
7	.05	3.34	4.16	4.68	5.06	5.36	5.61	5.82	6.00	6.16	6.30
	.01	4.95	5.92	6.54	7.01	7.37	7.68	7.94	8.17	8.37	8.55
8	.05	3.26	4.04	4.53	4.89	5.17	5.40	5.60	5.77	5.92	6.05
	.01	4.75	5.64	6.20	6.62	6.96	7.24	7.47	7.68	7.86	8.03
9	.05	3.20	3.95	4.41	4.76	5.02	5.24	5.43	5.59	5.74	5.87
	.01	4.60	5.43	5.96	6.35	6.66	6.91	7.13	7.33	7.49	7.65
10	.05	3.15	3.88	4.33	4.65	4.91	5.12	5.30	5.46	5.60	5.72
	.01	4.48	5.27	5.77	6.14	6.43	6.67	6.87	7.05	7.21	7.36
11	.05	3.11	3.82	4.26	4.57	4.82	5.03	5.20	5.35	5.49	5.61
	.01	4.39	5.15	5.62	5.97	6.25	6.48	6.67	6.84	6.99	7.13
12	.05	3.08	3.77	4.20	4.51	4.75	4.95	5.12	5.27	5.39	5.51
	.01	4.32	5.05	5.50	5.84	6.10	6.32	6.51	6.67	6.81	6.94
13	.05	3.06	3.73	4.15	4.45	4.69	4.88	5.05	5.19	5.32	5.43
	.01	4.26	4.96	5.40	5.73	5.98	6.19	6.37	6.53	6.67	6.79
14	.05	3.03	3.70	4.11	4.41	4.64	4.83	4.99	5.13	5.25	5.36
	.01	4.21	4.89	5.32	5.63	5.88	6.08	6.26	6.41	6.54	6.66
15	.05	3.01	3.67	4.08	4.37	4.59	4.78	4.94	5.08	5.20	5.31
	.01	4.17	4.84	5.25	5.56	5.80	5.99	6.16	6.31	6.44	6.55
16	.05	3.00	3.65	4.05	4.33	4.56	4.74	4.90	5.03	5.15	5.26
	.01	4.13	4.79	5.19	5.49	5.72	5.92	6.08	6.22	6.35	6.46
17	.05	2.98	3.63	4.02	4.30	4.52	4.70	4.86	4.99	5.11	5.21
	.01	4.10	4.74	5.14	5.43	5.66	5.85	6.01	6.15	6.27	6.38
18	.05	2.97	3.61	4.00	4.28	4.49	4.67	4.82	4.96	5.07	5.17
	.01	4.07	4.70	5.09	5.38	5.60	5.79	5.94	6.08	6.20	6.31
19	.05	2.96	3.59	3.98	4.25	4.47	4.65	4.79	4.92	5.04	5.14
	.01	4.05	4.67	5.05	5.33	5.55	5.73	5.89	6.02	6.14	6.25
20	.05	2.95	3.58	3.96	4.23	4.45	4.62	4.77	4.90	5.01	5.11
	.01	4.02	4.64	5.02	5.29	5.51	5.69	5.84	5.97	6.09	6.19
24	.05	2.92	3.53	3.90	4.17	4.37	4.54	4.68	4.81	4.92	5.01
	.01	3.96	4.55	4.91	5.17	5.37	5.54	5.69	5.81	5.92	6.02
30	.05	2.89	3.49	3.85	4.10	4.30	4.46	4.60	4.72	4.82	4.92
	.01	3.89	4.45	4.80	5.05	5.24	5.40	5.54	5.65	5.76	5.85
40	.05	2.86	3.44	3.79	4.04	4.23	4.39	4.52	4.63	4.73	4.82
	.01	3.82	4.37	4.70	4.93	5.11	5.26	5.39	5.50	5.60	5.69
60	.05	2.83	3.40	3.74	3.98	4.16	4.31	4.44	4.55	4.65	4.73
	.01	3.76	4.28	4.59	4.82	4.99	5.13	5.25	5.36	5.45	5.53
120	.05	2.80	3.36	3.68	3.92	4.10	4.24	4.36	4.47	4.56	4.64
	.01	3.70	4.20	4.50	4.71	4.87	5.01	5.12	5.21	5.30	5.37
∞	.05	2.77	3.31	3.63	3.86	4.03	4.17	4.29	4.39	4.47	4.55
	.01	3.64	4.12	4.40	4.60	4.76	4.88	4.99	5.08	5.16	5.23

Source: E. S. Pearson and H. O. Hartley, *Biometrika Tables for Statisticians,* Vol. 1, 3rd ed., 1966, Cambridge Press, New York, by permission of the Biometrika Trustees.

REFERENCES

ACHRE Report. (n.d.). Retrieved from www.hss.energy.gov/healthsafety/ohre/roadmap/achre/chap7_2.html

Ackerman, R., & Goldsmith, M. (2008). Control over grain size in memory reporting—with and without satisficing knowledge. *Journal of Experimental Psychology: Learning, Memory, and Cognition, 34*, 1224–1245. doi: 10.1037

Adair, J. G. (1984). The Hawthorne effect: A reconsideration of the methodological artifact. *Journal of Applied Psychology, 69*, 334–345.

Adair, J. G., Dushenko, T. W., & Lindsay, R. C. L. (1985). Ethical regulations and their impact on research practice. *American Psychologist, 40*, 59–72.

Affsprung, E. H. (1998). Assessing for a history of serious depression among first-year college students. *Journal of College Student Psychotherapy, 12*, 61–65.

Alcock, J. (2011). Back from the future: Parapsychology and the Bem affair. Retrieved April 23, 2011, from http://www.csicop.org/specialarticles/show/back_from_the_future

American Psychiatric Association. (1987). *Diagnostic and statistical manual of mental disorders* (3rd ed. revised). Washington, DC: Author.

American Psychological Association. (2002). Ethical principles of psychologists and code of conduct. *American Psychologist, 57*, 1060–1073.

American Psychological Association. (2010). *Publication manual of the American Psychological Association* (6th ed.). Washington, DC: Author.

Anderson, J., & Fienberg, S. E. (2000). Census 2000 controversies. *Chance, 13*(4), 22–30.

Anderson, K. C., & Insel, T. R. (2006). The promise of extinction research for the prevention and treatment of anxiety disorders. *Biological Psychiatry, 60*, 319–321.

Aneschensel, C. S., Clark, V. A., & Frerichs, R. R. (1983). Race, ethnicity, and depression: A confirmatory analysis. *Journal of Personality and Social Psychology, 44*, 385–398.

Angier, N. (2000, August 22). Do races differ? Not really, DNA shows. Retrieved from www.nytimes.com/library/national/science/082200sci-genetics-race.html

Aronson, J., Lustina, M. J., Good, C., Keough, K., Steele, C. M., & Brown, J. (1999). When white men can't do math: Necessary and sufficient factors in stereotype threat. *Journal of Experimental Social Psychology, 35*, 29–46.

Ashcraft, M. H., & Krause, J. A. (2007). Social and behavioral researchers' experiences with their IRBs. *Ethics & Behavior, 17*, 1–17.

Austad, S. N. (2002). A mouse's tale. *Natural History, 111*(3), 64–70.

Avoiding plagiarism, self-plagiarism, and other questionable writing practices: A guide to ethical writing. (2009). Office of Research Integrity. Retrieved December 11, 2009, from http://ori.dhhs.gov/education/products/plagiarism

Azar, B. (2000a, April). Online experiments: Ethically fair or foul? *Monitor on Psychology, 31*, 50–52.

Azar, B. (2000b, April). A web of research. *Monitor on Psychology, 31*, 42–44.

Babbie, E. (1995). *The practice of social research* (7th ed.). Belmont, CA: Wadsworth.

Bachorowski, J-A., & Owren, M. J. (2001). Not all laughs are alike: Voiced but not unvoiced laughter readily elicits positive affect. *Psychological Science, 12,* 252–257.

Baer, M. (2010). The strength-of-weak-ties perspective on creativity: A comprehensive examination and extension. *Journal of Applied Psychology, 95,* 592–601. doi:10.1037/a0018761

Baker, J. P. (2008). Mercury, vaccines, and autism: One controversy, three histories. *American Journal of Public Health, 98,* 244–253. doi:10.2105/AJPH.2007.113159

Ball, P., Giles, H., & Hewstone, M. (1984). Second language acquisition: The intergroup theory with catastrophic dimensions. In H. Tajfel (Ed.), *The social dimension* (Vol. 2, pp. 668–694). Cambridge, UK: Cambridge University Press.

Banville, D., Desrosiers, P., & Genet-Volet, G. (2000). Translating questionnaires and inventories using a cross-cultural translation technique. *Journal of Teaching in Physical Education, 19,* 374–387.

Barchard, K. A., & Williams, J. (2008). Practical advice for conducting ethical online experiments and questionnaires for United States psychologists. *Behavior Research Methods, 40,* 1111–1128. doi:10.3758/BRM.40.4.1111

Baron-Cohen, S., Burt, L., Smith-Laittan, F., Harrison, J., & Bolton, P. (1996). Synaesthesia: Prevalence and familiarity. *Perception, 25,* 1073–1079.

Barreto, R. E., Volpato, G. L., & Pottinger, T. G. (2006). The effect of elevated blood cortisol levels on the extinction of a conditioned stress response in rainbow trout. *Hormones and Behavior, 50,* 484–488.

Bartolic, E. I., Basso, M. R., Schefft, B. K., Glauser, T., & Titanic-Schefft, M. (1999). Effects of experimentally-induced emotional states on frontal lobe cognitive task performance. *Neuropsychologia, 37,* 677–683.

Basha, S. A., & Ushasree, S. (1998). Fear of success across life span. *Journal of Personality & Clinical Studies, 14,* 63–67.

Batson, C. D., Duncan, B., Ackerman, P., Buckley, T., & Birch, K. (1981). Is empathetic emotion a source of altruistic motivation? *Journal of Personality and Social Psychology, 40,* 290–302.

Baumrind, D. (1964). Some thoughts on ethics of research: After reading Milgram's "Behavioral study of obedience." *American Psychologist, 19,* 421–423.

Beach, F. A. (1950). The snark was a boojum. *American Psychologist, 5,* 115–124.

Beck, H. P., Levinson, S., & Irons, G. (2009). Finding Little Albert: A journey to John B. Watson's infant laboratory. *American Psychologist, 64,* 605–614. doi:10.1037/a0017234

Beins, B. C. (2011). Methodological and conceptual issues in cross-cultural research. In K. D. Keith (Ed.), *Cross-Cultural Psychology* (pp. 37–55). Malden, MA: Wiley-Blackwell.

Beins, B. C. (2010, August). Students and psychological research: Fostering scientific literacy. In B. C. Beins (Chair), *Psychology, psychology students, and scientific literacy—implications for teaching.* Symposium presented at the annual convention of the American Psychological Association, San Diego, CA.

Beins, B. C., & Beins, A. M. (2008). *Effective writing in psychology: Papers, posters, and presentations.* Malden, MA: Blackwell.

Bell, G., & Brady, V. (2000). Monetary incentives for sex workers. *International Journal of STD & AIDS, 11,* 483–484.

Bell, N. S., Mangione, T. W., Hemenway, D., Amoroso, P. J., & Jones, B. H. (2000). High injury rates among female Army trainees: A function of gender? *The American Journal of Preventive Medicine, 18*(3) Supplement 1, 141–146.

Bem, D. J. (2011). Feeling the Future: Experimental evidence for anomalous retroactive influences on cognition and affect. *Journal of Personality and Social Psychology, 100,* 407–425.

Benbow, C. P., & Stanley, J. C. (1983). Sex differences in mathematical reasoning ability: More facts. *Science, 222,* 1029–1031. doi:10.1126/science.6648516

Benbow, C. P., & Stanley, J. C. (1980). Sex differences in mathematical ability: Fact or artifact? *Science, 210,* 1262–1264. doi:10.1126/science.7434028

Benet-Martínez, V., Leu, J., Lee, F., & Morris, M. W. (2002). Negotiating biculturalism: Cultural frame switching in biculturals with oppositional versus compatible cultural identities. *Journal of Cross-Cultural Psychology, 33,* 492–516. doi:10.1177/0022022102033005005

Benton, S. A., Robertson, J. M., Tseng, W-C., Newton, F. B., & Benton, S. L. (2003). Changes in counseling center client problems across 13 years. *Professional Psychology: Research and Practice, 34,* 66–72.

Berkowitz, L. (1992). Some thoughts about conservative evaluations of replications. *Personality & Social Psychology Bulletin, 18,* 319–324.

Berreby, D. (2000). Race counts. [Review of *Changing race: Latinos, the census and the history of ethnicity in the United States.*] *The Sciences, 40,* 38–43.

Betancourt, H., & Lôpez, S. R. (1993). The study of culture, ethnicity, and race in American psychology. *American Psychologist, 48,* 629–637.

Bhui, K., & Bhugra, D. (2001). Methodological rigour in cross-cultural research. *The British Journal of Psychiatry, 179,* 269.

Birnbaum, M. H. (1974). Using contextual effects to derive psychophysical scales. *Perception and Psychophysics, 15,* 89–96.

Birnbaum, M. H. (1999). How to show that 9 > 221: Collect judgments in a between-subjects design. *Psychological Methods, 4,* 243–249.

Blair, C., Gamson, D., Thorne, S., & Baker, D. (2005). Rising mean IQ: Cognitive demand of mathematics education for young children, population exposure to formal schooling, and the neurobiology of the prefrontal cortex. *Intelligence, 33,* 93–106. doi:10.1016/j.intell.2004.07.008

Bond, L., Carlin, J. B., Thomas, L., Rubin, K., & Patton, G. (2001). Does bullying cause emotonal problems? A prospective study of young teenagers. *British Medical Journal, 323,* 480–484.

Bowman, L., L., & Anthonysamy, A. (2006). Malaysian and American students' perceptions of research ethics. *College Student Journal, 40,* 11–24.

Bramel, D., & Friend, R. (1981). Hawthorne, the myth of the docile worker, and class bias in psychology. *American Psychologist, 36,* 867–878.

Bray, J. H., Adams, G. J., Getz, J. G., & Baer, P. E. (2001). Developmental, family, and ethnic in influences on adolescent alcohol usage: A growth curve approach. *Journal of Family Psychology, 15,* 301–314.

Brewer, N. T., Hallman, W. K., Fiedler, N., & Kipen, H. M. (2004). Why do people report better health by phone than by mail? *Medical Care, 42,* 875–883. doi:10.1097/01.mlr.0000135817.31355.6b

Bröder, A. (1998). Deception can be acceptable. *American Psychologist, 53,* 805–806.

Bull, R., & Stevens, J. (1980). Effect of unsightly teeth on helping behavior. *Perceptual and Motor Skills, 51,* 438.

Burger, J. M. (2009). Replicating Milgram: Would people still obey today? *American Psychologist, 64,* 1–11.

Burnham, G., Lafta, R., Doocy, S., & Roberts, L. (2006). Mortality after the 2003 invasion of Iraq: A cross-sectional cluster sample survey. *The Lancet, 368,* 1421–1428. doi: 10.1016/50140-6736(06)69491-9

Burtt, H. E. (1920). Sex differences in the effect of discussion. *Journal of Experimental Psychology, 3,* 390–395.

Byrnes, J. P., Miller, D. C., & Schafer, W. D. (1999). Gender differences in risk taking: A meta-analysis. *Psychological Bulletin, 125,* 367–383.

Cai, W-H., Blundell, J., Han, J., Greene, R. W., & Powell, C. M. (2006). Postreactivation glucocorticoids impair recall of established fear memory. *Journal of Neuroscience, 26,* 9560–9566.

Campbell, D. T., & Stanley, J. C. (1966). *Experimental and quasi-experimental designs for research.* Chicago, IL: Rand McNally.

Caplan, P. J., & Caplan, J. B. (1999). *Thinking critically about research on sex and gender* (2nd ed.). New York, NY: Longman.

Carr, S. C., Munro, D., & Bishop, G. D. (1995). Attitude assessment in non-western countries: Critical modifications to likert scaling. *Psychologia, 39,* 55–59.

Carstens, C. B., Haskins, E., & Hounshell, G. W. (1995). Listening to Mozart may not enhance performance on the revised Minnesota paper form board test. *Psychological Reports, 77,* 111–114.

Caruso, K. (2004, September 6). *Joann Mitchell Levy, sixth NYU student to die by suicide in the past year.* Retrieved from www.suicide.org/joann-mitchell-levy-nyu-suicides.html

Case summaries. (2004). Office of Research Integrity Newsletter, *12*(4), 5–7. Retrieved from http://ori.dhhs.gov/documents/newsletters/vol12_no2.pdf

Ceci, S. J., & Bruck, M. (2009). Do IRBs pass the minimal harm test? *Perspectives in Psychological Science, 4,* 28–29.

Cepeda-Benito, A., & Gleaves, D. H. (2000). Cross-ethnic equivalence of the Hopkins Symptom Checklist-21 in European American, African American, and Latino college students. *Cultural Diversity and Ethnic Minority Psychology, 6,* 297–308.

Cernovsky, Z. Z. (2000). On the similarities of American blacks and whites. In B. Slife (Ed.), *Taking sides: Clashing views on controversial psychological issues.* Guilford, CT: Dushkin/McGraw Hill.

Chandra, A., Mosher, W. D., Copen, C., & Sionean, C. (2011, March 3). Sexual behavior, sexual attraction, and sexual identity in the United States: Data from the 2006–2008 national survey of family growth. *National Health Statistics Reports, 36,* 1–36.

Chang, W. C. (2000). In search of the Chinese in all the wrong places! *Journal of Psychology in Chinese Societies, 1,* 125–142.

Chao, R. (2001). Integrating culture and attachment. *American Psychologist, 56,* 822–823.

Charges of fake research hit new high. (2005, July 10). Retrieved from www.msnbc.msn.com/id/8474936/

Chen, F. F. (2008). What happens if we compare chopsticks with forks? The impact of making inappropriate comparisons in cross-cultural research. *Journal of Personality and Social Psychology, 95,* 1005–1018. doi:10.1037/a0013193

Cheryan, S., & Bodenhausen, G. V. (2000). When positive stereotypes threaten intellectual performance: The psychological hazards of "model minority" status. *Psychological Science, 11,* 399–402.

Chiriboga, D. A., Jang, Y., Banks, S., & Kim, G. (2007). Acculturation and its effect on depressive symptom structure in a sample of Mexican American elders. *Hispanic Journal of Behavioral Sciences, 29,* 83–100. doi:10.1177/0739986306295875

Cho, H., & Larose, R. (1999). Privacy issues in internet surveys. *Social Science Computer Review, 17,* 421–434.

Christakis, D. A. (2009). The effects of infant media usage: What do we know and what should we learn? *Acta Paediatrica, 98,* 8–16. doi:10.1111/j.1651-2227.2008.01027.x

Christensen, L. (1988). Deception in psychological research: When is its use justified? *Personality and Social Psychology Bulletin, 14,* 664–675.

CIA–The world factbook–United Kingdom. (2007). Retrieved July 11, 2007, from www.cia.gov/library/publications/the-world-factbook/geos/uk.html

Cialdini, R. B. (1980). Full-cycle social psychology. *Applied Social Psychology Annual, 1,* 21–47.

Cialdini, R. B., Darby, B. L., & Vincent, J. E. (1973). Transgression and altruism: A case for hedonism. *Journal of Experimental Social Psychology, 9,* 502–516.

Clark, D. M., & Teasdale, J. D. (1985). Constraints on the effects of mood on memory. *Journal of Personality and Social Psychology, 52,* 749–758.

Cohen, D., & Gunz, A. (2002). As seen by the other . . . : Perspectives on the self in the memories and emotional perceptions of Easterners and Westerners. *Psychological Science, 13,* 55–59.

Cohen, J. (1988). *Statistical power analysis for the behavioral sciences.* Hillsdale, NJ: Lawrence Erlbaum Associates.

Cohen, S., Alper, C. M., Doyle, W. J., Treanor, J. J., & Turner, R. B. (2006). Positive emotional style predicts resistance to illness after experimental exposure to rhinovirus or influenza A virus. *Psychosomatic Medicine, 68,* 809–915.

Cohen, S., Tyrrell, D. A., & Smith, A. P. (1991). Psychological stress and susceptibility to the common cold. *New England Journal of Medicine, 325,* 606–612.

Coile, D. C., & Miller, N. E. (1984). How radical animal activists try to mislead humane people, *American Psychologist, 39,* 700–701.

Consumers in the 18-to-24 age segment view cell phones as multi-functional accessories; crave advanced features and personalization options. (2007, January 22). Retrieved from http://www.comscore.com/press/release.asp?press=1184

Cook, D. J. (1996). Randomized trials in single subjects: The N of 1 study. *Psychopharmacology Bulletin, 32,* 363–367.

Cook, P. J., & Ludwig, J. (1998). Defensive gun uses: New evidence from a national survey. *Journal of Quantitative Criminology, 14,* 111–131.

Council of National Psychological Associations for the Advancement of Ethnic Minority Interests. (2000). *Guidelines for research in ethnic minority communities.* Washington, DC: American Psychological Association.

Couper, M. P., Kapteyn, A. Schonlau, M., & Winter, J. (2007). Noncoverage and nonresponse in an Internet survey. *Social Science Research, 36,* 131–148.

Cranford, J. A., McCabe, S. E., Boyd, C. J., Slayden, J, Reed, M. B., Ketchie, J. M., Lange, J. E., & Scott, M. S. (2008). Reasons for nonresponse in a web-based survey of alcohol involvement among first-year college students. *Addictive Behaviors, 33,* 206–210. doi:10.1016/j.addbeh.2007.07.008

Crocker, P. R. E. (1993). Sport and exercise psychology and research with individuals with physical disabilities: Using theory to advance knowledge. *Adapted Physical Activity Quarterly, 10,* 324–335.

Croizet, J-C., & Claire, T. (1998). Extending the concept of stereotype and threat to social class: The intellectual underperformance of students from low socioeconomic backgrounds. *Personality & Social Psychology Bulletin, 24,* 588–594.

Cronin, K. L., Fazio, V. C., & Beins, B. C. (1998, April). Mood does not affect the funniness of jokes but jokes affect your mood. Presented at the Thirteenth Annual University of Scranton Psychology Conference, Scranton, PA.

Cunningham, S. (1984). Genovese: 20 years later, few heed a stranger's cries. *Social Action and the Law, 10,* 24–25.

Cytowic, R. E. (1993). *The man who tasted shapes.* New York, NY: G. P. Putnam & Son.

Cytowic, R. E. (1997). Synaesthesia: Phenomenology and neuropsychology—A review of current knowledge. In S. Baron-Cohen & J. E. Harrison (Eds.), *Synaesthesia: Classic and contemporary readings.* Cambridge, MA: Blackwell.

Darley, J. M., & Latané, B. (1968). Bystander intervention in emergencies: Diffusion of responsibility. *Journal of Personality and Social Psychology, 8,* 377–383.

da Veiga, F. A., & Saraiva, C. B. (2003). Age patterns of suicide: Identification and characterization of European clusters and trends. *Crisis: The Journal of Crisis Intervention and Suicide Prevention, 24,* 56–67. doi:10.1027//0227-5910.24.2.5

Davenport, S. M., & Shannon, M. A. (2001). *Using SPSS to solve statistical problems: A self-instruction guide.* Upper Saddle River, NJ: Prentice Hall.

Deci, E. L., & Ryan, R. M. (1985). *Intrinsic motivation and self-determination in human behavior.* New York, NY: Plenum.

Deese, J., & Hulse, S. H. (1967). *The psychology of learning* (3rd ed.). New York: McGraw-Hill.

Delgado, A. R., & Prieto, G. (2008). Stereotype threat as validity threat: The anxiety-sex-threat interaction. *Intelligence, 36,* 635–640. doi:10.1016/j.intell.2008.01.008

Demographics of internet users. (2009). Pew Internet and American Life Project. Retrieved December 17, 2009, from www.pewinternet.org/Trend-Data/Whos-Online.aspx

Demographics of internet users (2007). Pew Internet & American Life Project, February 15–March 7, 2007 Tracking Survey. Retrieved July 17, 2007, from http://www.pewinternet.org/trends/User_Demo_6.15.07.htm

Diener, E., Matthews, R., & Smith, R. E. (1972). Leakage of experimental information to potential future subjects by debriefed subjects. *Journal of Experimental Research in Personality, 6,* 264–267.

Dillman, D. A. (2000). *Mail and Internet surveys: The tailored design method.* New York, NY: Wiley.

Dillman, D. A., Phelps, G., Tortora, R., Swift, K., Kohrell, J., Berck, J., Messer, B. L. (2009). Response rate and measurement differences in mixed-mode surveys using mail, telephone, interactive voice response (IVR) and the Internet. *Social Science Research, 38,* 1–18. doi:10.1016/j.ssresearch.2008.03.007

Dixon, W. A., & Reid, J. K. (2000). Positive life events as a moderator of stress-related depressive symptoms. *Journal of Counseling & Development, 78,* 343–347.

Duncan, S. C., Duncan, T. E., & Strycker, L. A. (2006). Alcohol use from ages 9 to 16: A cohort-sequential latent growth model. *Drug and Alcohol Dependence, 81,* 71–81.

Eagly, A. H. (2009). The his and hers of prosocial behavior: An examination of the social psychology of gender. *American Psychologist, 64,* 644–658. doi:10.1037/0003-066X.64.8.644

Election Polls—Accuracy Record in Presidential Elections (2011). Retrieved May 1, 2011, from http://www.gallup.com/poll/9442/Election-Polls-Accuracy-Record-Presidential-Elections.aspx

Elliott, A. J., & Thrash, T. M. (2004). The intergenerational transmission of fear of failure. *Personality and Social Psychology Bulletin, 30,* 957–971. doi:10.1177/0146167203262024

Elms, A. C. (2009). Obedience lite. *American Psychologist, 64,* 32–36.

Ethical principles of psychologists and code of conduct. (2002). Retrieved from www.apa.org/ETHICS/code2002.html

Exline, J. J., & Lobel, M. (1999). The perils of outperformance: Sensitivity about being the target of a threatening upward comparison. *Psychological Bulletin, 125,* 303–337.

Fairburn, C. G., Welch, S. L., Norman, P. A., O'Connor, B. A., & Doll, H. A. (1996). Bias and bulimia nervosa: How typical are clinical cases? *American Journal of Psychiatry, 153,* 386–391.

Fanelli, D., Innogen, & ISSTI. (2009). How many scientists fabricate and falsify research? *Office of Research Integrity Newsletter, 17*(4), 11. Retrieved from http://ori.dhhs.gov/documents/newsletters/vol17_no4.pdf

Farley, P. (2003, January 21). Young scientist's paper gets him in hot water with colleagues. Retrieved January 23, 2003, from www.boston.com.

Fausto-Sterling, A. (1993). The five sexes: Why male and female are not enough. *The Sciences, 33*(2), 20–25.

Felmingham, K., Kemp, A., Williams, L., Das, P., Hughes, G. Peduto, A., et al. (2007). Changes in anterior cingulate and amygdala after cognitive behavior therapy of posttraumatic stress disorder. *Psychological Science, 18,* 127–129.

Fernandez, E., & Sheffield, J. (1996). Relative contributions of life events versus daily hassles to the frequency and intensity of headaches. *Headache, 36,* 595–602.

Field, A. (2009). *Discovering statistics using SPSS* (3rd ed.). Thousand Oaks, CA: Sage.

Finkel, S. E., Guterbok, T. M., & Borg, M. J. (1991). Race of interviewer effects in a preelection poll: Virginia 1989. *Public Opinion Quarterly, 55,* 313–330.

Fisher, C. (2005). Deception research involving children: Ethical practices and paradoxes. *Ethics & Behavior, 15,* 271–287.

Fisher, C. B., & Fyrberg, D. (1994). Participant partners: College students weigh the costs and benefits of deceptive research. *American Psychologist, 49,* 417–427.

Flynn, J. R. (2007). *What is intelligence? Beyond the Flynn effect.* Cambridge, UK: Cambridge University Press.

Flynn, J. R. (1999). Searching for justice: The discovery of IQ gains over time. *American Psychologist, 54,* 5–20.

Fombonne, R. (2001). Is there an epidemic of autism? *Pediatrics, 107,* 411–412. doi: 10.1542/peds.107.2.411

Francis, L. J., & Jackson, C. J. (1998). The social desirability of toughmindedness: A study among undergraduates. *Irish Journal of Psychology, 19,* 400–403.

Frank, O., & Snijders, T. (1994). Estimating the size of hidden populations using snowball sampling. *Journal of Official Statistics, 10,* 53–67.

French, S., & Stephen, J. (1999). Religiosity and its association with happiness, purpose in life, and self-actualisation. *Mental Health, Religion & Culture, 2,* 117–120.

Friman, P. C., Allen, K. D., Kerwin, M. L. E., & Larzelere, R. (2000). Questionable validity, not vitality. *American Psychologist, 55,* 274–275. doi:10.1037/0003-066X.55.2.274

Furnham, A., & Nederstrom, M. (2010). Ability, demographic and personality predictors of creativity. *Personality and Individual Differences, 48,* 957–961. doi:10.1016/j.paid.2010.02.030

Gaito, J. (1980). Measurement scales and statistics: Resurgence of an old misconception. *Psychological Bulletin, 87,* 564–567.

Gawrylewski, A. (2007). Case reports: Essential or irrelevant? *The Scientist.* Retrieved from www.the-scientist.com/news/home/53192

Gazdella, B. M., Masten, W. G., & Stacks, J. (1998). Students' stress and their learning strategies, test anxiety, and attributions. *College Student Journal, 32,* 416–422.

Gehricke, J.-G., & Shapiro, D. (2000). Reduced facial expression and social context in major depression: Discrepancies between facial muscle activity and self-reported emotion. *Psychiatry Research, 95,* 157–167.

Geier, A. B., Rozin, P., & Doros, G. (2006). Unit bias: A new heuristic that helps explain the effect of portion size on food intake. *Psychological Science, 17,* 521–525. doi:10.1111/j.1467-9280.2006.01738.x

Gendall, P., Hoek, J., & Brennan, M. (1998). The tea bag experiment: More evidence on incentives in mail surveys. *Journal of the Market Research Society, 40,* 347–351.

Generational differences in online activity. (2009). Pew Internet and American Life Project. Retrieved December 17, 2009, from http://pewinternet.org/Infographics/Generational-differences-in-online-activities.aspx

Gladwell, M. (2002, March 13). John Rock's error. *The New Yorker,* 52–63.

Glaze, J. A. (1928). The association value of non-sense syllables. *Journal of Genetic Psychology, 35,* 255–269.

Glueck, W. F., & Jauch, L. R. (1975). Sources of ideas among productive scholars: Implications for administrators. *Journal of Higher Education, 46,* 103–114.

Goldenberg, J. L., Pyszczynski, T., McCoy, S. K., Greenberg, J., & Solomon, S. (1999). Death, sex, love, and neuroticism: Why is sex such a problem? *Journal of Personality and Social Psychology, 77,* 1173–1187.

Goldston, D. B., Molock, S. D., Whitbeck, L. B., Murakami, J. L., Zayas, L. H., & Hall, G. C. N. (2008). Cultural considerations in adolescent suicide prevention and psychosocial treatment. *American Psychologist, 63,* 14–31. doi:10.1037/0003-066X.63.1.14

Goodman-Delahunty, J. (1998). Approaches to gender and the law: Research and applications. *Law and Human Behavior, 22,* 129–143.

Gosling, S. D., Vazire, S., Srivastava, S., & John, O. P. (2004). Should we trust web-based studies? A comparative analysis of six preconceptions about internet questionnaires. *American Psychologist, 59,* 93–104.

Gould, S. J. (1996). *The mismeasure of man* (2nd ed.). New York: W. W. Norton.

Gray, J. (1992). *Men are from Mars, women are from Venus: A practical guide for improving communication and getting what you want in your relationships.* New York, NY: HarperCollins.

Green, C. W., & Reid, D. H. (1999). A behavioral approach to identifying sources of happiness and unhappiness among individuals with profound multiple disabilities. *Behavior Modification, 23,* 280–293.

Grissom, R. J., & Kim, J. J. (2005). *Effect sizes for research.* Mahwah, NJ: Lawrence Erlbaum Associates.

Gruder, C. L., Stumpfhauser, A., & Wyer, R. S. (1977). Improvement in experimental performance as a result of debriefing about deception. *Personality and Social Psychology Bulletin, 3,* 434–437.

Guenedi, A. A., Hussaini, A. A., Obeid, Y. A., Hussain, S., Al-Azri, F., & Al-Adawi, S. (2009). Investigation of the cerebral blood flow of an Omani man with supposed "spirit possession" associated with an altered mental state: A case report. *Journal of Medical Case Reports, 9,* 3:9325. doi:10.1186/1752-1947-3-9325

Gwiazda, J., Ong, E., Held, R., & Thorn, F. (2000). Vision: Myopia and ambient night-time lighting. *Nature, 404,* 144.

Halvari, H., & Kjormo, O. (2000). A structural model of achievement motives, performance approach and avoidance goals and performance among Norwegian Olympic athletes. *Perceptual & Motor Skills, 89,* 997–1022.

Handling misconduct: Case summaries. (2009). Office of Research Integrity. Retrieved December 11, 2009, from http://ori.hhs.gov/misconduct/cases/

Harris, B. (1980). The FBI's files on APA and SPSSI: Description and implications. *American Psychologist, 35,* 1141–1144.

Hawker, D. S. J., & Boulton, M. J. (2000). Twenty years' research on peer victimization and psychosocial maladjustment: A meta-analytic review of cross-sectional studies. *Journal of Child Psychology and Psychiatry, 41,* 441–455.

Hay, C. A., & Bakken, L. (1991). Gifted sixth-grade girls: Similarities and differences in attitudes among gifted girls, non-gifted peers, and their mothers. *Roeper Review, 13,* 158–160.

Hays, W. L. (1988). *Statistics* (4th ed.). Chicago, IL: Holt, Rinehart, and Winston.

Hayslip, B., McCoy-Roberts, L., & Pavur, R. (1998–99). Selective attrition effects in bereavement research: A three-year longitudinal analysis. *Omega, 38,* 21–35.

Headden, S. (1997, December 8). The junk mail deluge. *U.S. News & World Report,* 42–48.

Heckathorn, D. D. (1997). Respondent-driven sampling: A new approach to the study of hidden populations. *Social Problems, 44,* 174–199.

Hedden, T., Park, D. C., Nisbett, R., Ji, L. J., Jing, Q., & Jiao, S. (2002). Cultural variation in verbal versus spatial neuropsychological function across the lifespan. *Neuropsychology, 16,* 65–73.

Heerwegh, D. (2009). Mode differences between face-to-face and web surveys: An experimental investigation of data quality and social desirability effects. *International Journal of Public Opinion Research, 21,* 111–121. doi:10.1093/ijpor/edn054

Helms, J. E., Jernigan, M., & Mascher, J. (2005). The meaning of race in psychology and how to change it: A methodological perspective. *American Psychologist, 60,* 27–36.

Hemenway, D. (1997). The myth of millions of annual self-defense gun uses: A case study of survey overestimates of rare events. *Chance, 10,* 6–10.

Heron, J., Golding, J., & ALSPAC Study Team. (2004). Thimerosal exposure in infants and developmental disorders: A prospective cohort study in the United Kingdom does not support a causal association. *Pediatrics, 114,* 577–583. doi: 10.1542/peds.2003-1176-L

Hertz-Picciotto, I., Green, P. G., Delwiche, L., Hansen, R., Walker, C., & Pessah, I. N. (2009). Blood mercury concentrations in CHARGE study: Children with and without autism. *Environmental Health Perspectives*. Retrieved December 10, 2009, from http://ehp.niehs.nih.gov/members/2009/0900736/0900736.pdf doi: 10.1289/ehp.0900736

Heuer, H., Spijkers, W., Kiesswetter, E., & Schmidtke, V. (1998). Effects of sleep loss, time of day, and extended mental work on implicit and explicit learning of sequences. *Journal of Experimental Psychology: Applied, 4,* 139–162.

High accuracy found in 2000 elections. (2001, Jan. 4). *St. Petersburg Times,* 3A.

Hilts, P. J., & Stolberg, S. G. (1999, May 13). Ethical lapses at Duke halt dozens of human experiments. *New York Times.* Retrieved from www.nytimes.com/yr/mo/day/news/national/science/sci-duke-research.html

Holahan, C. K., & Sears, R. R. (1995). *The gifted group in later maturity.* Stanford, CA: Stanford University Press.

Holmes, J. D. (2010, August). Is Scientific Literacy Compatible with Student Interests? Implications for Teaching. In B. C. Beins (Chair), Psychology, Psychology Students, and Scientific Literacy: Implications for Teaching. Symposium presented at the annual convention of the American Psychological Association, San Diego, CA.

Holmes, J. D., Beins, B. C., & Lynn, A. (2007, June). Student views of psychology as a science: Findings and implications. Presented at the Eastern Conference on the Teaching of Psychology, Staunton, VA.

Holmes, T. H., & Rahe, R. H. (1967). The social readjustment rating scale. *Journal of Psychosomatic Research, 11,* 213–218.

Hong, Y., & Chiu, C. (1991). Reduction of socially desirable responses in attitude assessment through the enlightenment effect. *Journal of Social Psychology, 131,* 585–587.

Horvitz, D., Koshland, D., Rubin, D. Gollin, A., Sawyer, T., & Tanbur, J. M. (1995). Pseudo-opinion polls: SLOP or useful data? *Chance, 8,* 16–25.

Howell, D. C. (2007). *Statistical methods for psychology* (6th ed.). Belmont, CA: Wadsworth.

Hrycaiko, D., & Martin, G. L. (1999). Applied research studies with single-subject designs: Why so few? *Journal of Applied Sport Psychology, 8,* 183–199.

Humphreys, K. (2009). Responding to the psychological impact of war on the Iraqi people and U.S. veterans: Mixing icing, praying for cake. *American Psychologist, 64,* 712–723. doi: 10.1037/0003-066X.64.8.712

Hyde, J. S. (2005). The gender similarities hypothesis. *American Psychologist, 60,* 581–592. doi:10.1037/0003-066X.60.6.581

Ideland, M. (2009). Different views on ethics: How animal ethics is situated in a committee culture. *Journal of Medical Ethics, 35,* 258–261. doi:10.1136/jme.2008.026989

Inzlicht, M., & Ben-Zeev, T. (2000). A threatening intellectual environment: Why females are susceptible to experiencing problem-solving deficits in the presence of males. *Psychological Science, 11,* 365–371.

Ioannidis, J. P. A. (2005). Why most published research findings are false. *PLoS Medicine, 2,* e124, 696–701. Retrieved from http://www.plosmedicine.org

Ippolito, A. & Beins, B. C. (2011, March). Sense of humor: Are we all above average? Poster presentation at the annual convention of the Eastern Psychological Association, Cambridge, MA.

Iwamasa, G. Y., Larrabee, A. L., & Merritt, R. D. (2000). Are personality disorder criteria ethnically biased? A card-sort analysis. *Cultural Diversity and Ethnic Minority Psychology, 6,* 284–296.

Jenni, D. A., & Jenni, M. A. (1976). Carrying behavior in humans: Analysis of sex differences. *Science, 194,* 859–860.

Jennings, C. (2000, May/June). [Letter to the editor.] *The Sciences, 40*(3), 5.

Ji, L.J., Schwarz, N., & Nisbett, R. E. (2000). Culture, autobiographical memory, and behavioral frequency reports: Measurement issues in cross-cultural studies. *Personality and Social Psychology Bulletin, 26,* 585–593.

Johnson, T. P., Fendrich, M., Shaligram, C., Garcy, A., & Gillespie, S. (2000). An evaluation of the effects of interviewer charcteristics in an RDD telephone survey of drug use. *Journal of Drug Issues, 30,* 77–102.

Jones, H. E., & Contrad, H. S. (1933). The growth and decline of intelligence: A study of a homogeneous group between the ages of ten and sixty. *Genetic Psychology Monographs, 13,* 223–298.

Judd, C. M., Smith, E. R., & Kidder, L. H. (1991). *Research methods in social relations.* Fort Worth, TX: Holt, Rinehart, & Winston.

Juhnke, R., Barmann, B., Cunningham, M., & Smith, E. (1987). Effects of attractiveness and nature of request on helping behavior. *Journal of Social Psychology, 127,* 317–322.

Kaneto, H. (1997). Learning/memory processes under stress conditions. *Behavioural Brain Research, 83,* 71–74.

Kaplan, C. D., Korf, D., & Sterk, C. (1987). Temporal and social contexts of heroin-using populations: An illustration of the snowball sampling technique. *Journal of Nervous and Mental Disease, 175,* 566–574.

Kasof, J. (1993). Sex bias in the naming of the stimulus person. *Psychological Bulletin, 113,* 140–163.

Katsev, R., Edelsack, L., Steinmetz, G., Walker, T., & Wright, R. (1978). The effect of reprimanding transgression on subsequent helping behavior: Two field experiments. *Personality and Social Psychology Bulletin, 4,* 326–329.

Kaufman, P., Kwon, J. Y., Klein, S., & Chapman, C. D. (2000). *Dropout rates in the United States: 1999.* Washington, DC: National Center for Educational Statistics.

Kaur, M., Liguori, A., Lang, W., Rapp, S. R., Fleischer, A. B., & Feldman, S. R. (2006). Induction of withdrawal-like symptoms in a small randomized, controlled trial of opioid blockade in frequent tanners. *Journal of the American Academy of Dermatology, 54,* 709–711.

Kazdin, A. E. (1998). *Research design in clinical psychology* (3rd ed.). Boston, MA: Allyn & Bacon.

Keith-Spiegel, P., & Koocher, G. P. (2005). The IRB paradox: Could the protectors also encourage deceit? *Ethics & Behavior, 15,* 339–349.

Keller, H. (2008). Attachment—past and present. But what about the future? *Integrative Psychological & Behavioral Science, 42,* 406–415. doi:10.1007/s12124-008-9080-9

Keller, J. (2007). Stereotype threat in classroom settings: The interactive effect of domain identification, task difficulty and stereotype threat on female students' maths performance. *British Journal of Educational Psychology, 77,* 323–338.

Kennedy, D., & Norman, C. (2005, July 1). What don't we know? *Science, 309,* 75.   doi:10.1126/science.309.5731.75

Kiecker, P., & Nelson, J. E. (1996). Do interviewers follow telephone survey instructions? *Journal of the Market Research Society, 38,* 161–176.

Kim, B. S. K., Atkinson, D. R., & Yang, P. H. (1999). The Asian Values Scale: Development, factor analysis, validation, and reliability. *Journal of Counseling Psychology, 46,* 342–352.

Kim, G., Chiriboga, D. A., & Jang, Y. (2009). Cultural equivalence in depressive symptoms in older White, Black, and Mexican-American adults. *Journal of the American Geriatrics Society, 57,* 790–796. doi:10.1111/j.1532-5415.2009.02188.x

King, M. F., & Bruner, G. C. (2000). Social desirability bias: A neglected aspect of validity testing. *Psychology and Marketing, 17,* 79–103.

Kirnan, J. P., Alfieri, J. A., Bragger, J. D., & Harris, R. S. (2009). An investigation of stereotype threat in employment tests. *Journal of Applied Social Psychology, 39,* 359–388. doi: 10.1111/j.1559-1816.2008.00442.x

Klawans, H. L. (2000). *Defending the cavewoman and other tales of evolutionary neurology.* New York, NY: W. W. Norton.

Kleck, G., & Gertz, M. (1995). Armed resistence to crime: The prevalence and nature of self-defense with a gun. *Journal of Criminal Law and Criminology, 86,* 150–187.

Korn, J. H. (1998). The reality of deception. *American Psychologist, 53,* 805.

Kovar, M. G. (2000). Four million adolescents smoke: Or do they? *Chance, 13,* 10–14.

Kozulin, A. (1999). Profiles of immigrant students' cognitive performance on Raven's Progressive Matrices. *Perceptual & Motor Skills, 87,* 1311–1314.

Krantz, J. H., & Dalal, R. (2000). Validity of web-based psychological research. In M. H. Birnbaum (Ed.), *Psychological experiments on the internet* (pp. 35–60). San Diego, CA: Academic Press.

Kravitz, R. L., Franks, P. Feldman, M. D., Gerrity, M., Byrne, C., Tierney, W. M., & Sampson, M. (2010). Editorial peer reviewers' recommendations at a general medical journal: Are they reliable and do editors care? *PLoS ONE, 5*(4): e10072 doi: 10.1371/journal.pone.0010072

Krishnan, A., & Sweeney, C. J. (1998). Gender differences in fear of success imagery and other achievement-related background variables among medical students. *Sex Roles, 39,* 299–310.

Krosnick, J. A., Holbrook, A. L., Sberent, M. K., Carson, R. T., Hanemann, W. M., Kopp, R. J., et al. (2002). The impact of "no opinion" response options on data quality: Non-attitude reduction or an invitation to satisfice. *Public Opinion Quarterly, 66,* 371–403.

Krosnick, J. A. (1999). Survey research. *Annual Review of Psychology, 50,* 537–567.

Kumari, R. (1995). Relation of sex role attitudes and self esteem to fear of success among college women. *Psychological Studies, 40,* 82–86.

La Greca, A. M., & Silverman, W. K. (2009). Treatment and prevention of posttraumatic stress reactions in children and adolescents exposed to disasters and terrorism: What is the evidence? *Child Development Perspectives, 3,* 4–10. doi:10.1111/j.1750-8606.2008.00069.x

La Greca, A. M., Silverman, W. K., Vernberg, E. M., & Prinstein, M. J. (1996). Symptoms of posttraumatic stress in children after Hurricane Andrew: A prospective study. *Journal of Counseling and Clinical Psychology, 64,* 712–723.

Laidler, J. R. (2004). The "Refrigerator Mother" hypothesis of autism. Retrieved December 10, 2009, from www.autism-watch.org/causes/rm.shtml

Lang, F. R., & Heckhausen, J. (2001). Perceived control over development and subjective well-being: Differential benefits across adulthood. *Journal of Personality and Social Psychology, 81,* 509–523.

Langer, E., Pirson, M., & Delizonna, L. (2010). The mindlessness of social comparisons. *Psychology of Aesthetics, Creativity, and the Arts, 4,* 68–74. doi:10.1037/a0017318

Latané, B., & Darley, J. M. (1970). *The unresponsive bystander: Why doesn't he help?* New York: Appleton-Century-Crofts.

Lavender, J. M., & Anderson, D. A. (2009). Effect of perceived anonymity in assessments of eating disordered behaviors and attitudes. *International Journal of Eating Disorders, 42,* 546–551. doi:10.1002/eat.20645

Lawson, C. (1995). Research participation as a contract. *Ethics and Behavior, 5,* 205–215.

Lee, Y-T., & Ottati, V. (1995). Perceived in-group homogeneity as a function of group membership salience and stereotype threat. *Personality & Social Psychology Bulletin, 21,* 610–619.

Lehman, D. R., Lempert, R. O., & Nisbett, R. E. (1988). The effects of graduate training on reasoning: Formal discipline and thinking about everyday-life events. *American Psychologist, 43,* 431–442.

Leirer, V. O., Yesavage, J. A., & Morrow, D. G. (1991). Marijuana carry-over effects on aircraft pilot performance. *Aviation, Space, and Environmental Medicine, 62,* 221–227.

Leonhard, C., Gastfriend, D. R., Tuffy, L. J., Neill, J., & Plough, A. (1997). The effect of anonymous vs nonanonymous rating conditions on patient satisfaction and motivation ratings in a population of substance abuse patients. *Alcoholism: Clinical and Experimental Research, 21,* 627–630.

Lewis, C. A., McCollam, P., & Joseph, S. (2000). Convergent validity of the Depression-Happiness Scale with the Bradburn Affect Balance Scale. *Social Behavior & Personality, 28,* 579–584.

Liang, C. T. H., Li, L. C., & Kim, B. S. K. (2004). The Asian American Racism-Related Stress Inventory: Development, factor analysis, reliability, and validity. *Journal of Counseling Psychology, 51,* 103–114.

Lifton, R. J. (1986). *The Nazi doctors: Medical killing and the psychology of genocide.* New York, NY: Basic Books.

Liston, C., & Kagan, J. (2002). Memory enhancement in early childhood. *Nature, 419,* 896.

Loftus, E. F. (1975). Leading questions and the eyewitness report. *Cognitive Psychology, 7,* 560–572.

Loftus, E. F. (1997). Memories for a past that never was. *Current Directions in Psychological Science, 6,* 60–65.

Loftus, E. F. (2003, January). Illusions of memory. Presented at the National Institute on the Teaching of Psychology. St. Petersburg Beach, FL.

Lonner, W. J. (1999). Helfrich's "principle of triarchic resonance": A commentary on yet another perspective on the ongoing and tenacious etic-emic debate. *Culture & Psychology, 5,* 173–181.

López-Muñoz, F., & Álamo, C. (2009). Psychotropic drug research in Nazi Germany: The triumph of the principle of malfeasance. *Acta Neuropsychiatrica, 21,* 50–53. doi:10.1111/j.1601-5215.2008.00338.x

Lord, F. M. (1953). On the statistical treatment of football numbers. *American Psychologist, 8,* 750–751.

Luria, A. R. (1968). *The mind of a mnemonist.* New York, NY: Basic Books.

Lynch, D. J., McGrady, A., Alvarez, E., & Forman, J. (2005). Recent life changes and medical utilization in an academic family practice. *Journal of Nervous and Mental Disease, 193,* 633–635. doi:10.1097/01.nmd.0000177778.27069.77

Lynn, R. (2009). What has caused the Flynn effect? Secular increases in the development quotients of infants. *Intelligence, 37,* 16–24. doi:10.1016/j.intell.2008.07.008

MacGeorge, E. L., Samter, W., Feng, B., Gillihan, S. J., & Graves, A. R. (2004). Stress, social support, and health among college students after September 11, 2001. *Journal of College Student Development, 45,* 655–670.

Macias, S. (2010, August). Psychology 101: The Most "Scientific" of all Sciences? In B. C. Beins (Chair), Psychology, Psychology Students, and Scientific Literacy: Implications for Teaching. Symposium presented at the annual convention of the American Psychological Association, San Diego, CA.

Malmo, R. B., Boag, T. J., & Smith, A. A. (1957). Physiological study of personal interaction. *Psychosomatic Medicine, 19,* 105–119.

Mandel, E. (2007). Gender, machiavellianism, study major, and fear of success. *Polish Psychological Bulletin, 38,* 40–49.

Manning, R., Levine, M., & Collins, A. (2007). The Kitty Genovese murder and the social psychology of helping: The parable of the 38 witnesses. *American Psychologist, 62,* 555–562. doi:10.1037/0003-066X.62.6.555

Manucia, G. K., Baumann, D. J., & Cialdini, R. B. (1984). Mood influences on helping: Direct effects or side effects? *Journal of Personality and Social Psychology, 46,* 357–364.

Marans, D. G. (1988). Addressing researcher practitioner and subject needs: A debriefing-disclosure procedure. *American Psychologist, 43,* 826–828.

Marian, V., & Neisser, E. (2000). Language-dependent recall of autobiographical memories. *Journal of Experimental Psychology: General, 129,* 361–368.

Markus, H. R. (2008). Pride, prejudice, and ambivalence: Toward a unified theory of race and ethnicity. *American Psychologist, 63,* 651–670. doi:10.1037/0003-066X.63.8.651

Martin, G. N. (2000). There's more neuroscience. *American Psychologist, 55,* 275–276. doi:10.1037/0003-066X.55.2.275

Martinez-Ebers, V. (1997). Using monetary incentives with hard-to-reach populations in panel surveys. *International Journal of Public Opinion Research, 9,* 77–86.

Martinson, B. C., Anderson, M. S., & de Vries, R. (2005). Scientists behaving badly. *Nature, 435*(7043), 737–738. doi:10.1038/435737a

Matsumoto, D., Anguas-Wong, A. M., & Martinez, E. (2008). Priming effects of language on emotion judgments in Spanish-English bilinguals. *Journal of Cross-Cultural Psychology, 39,* 335–342. doi:10.1177/0022022108315489

Matsumoto, D. (1993). Ethnic differences in affect intensity, emotion judgments, display rule attitudes, and self-reported emotional expression in an American sample. *Motivation and Emotion, 17,* 107–123.

Matsumoto, D. (1994). *Cultural influences on research methods and statistics.* Pacific Grove, CA: Brooks/Cole.

Matsumoto, D., & Assar, M. (1992). The effects of language on judgments of universal facial expressions of emotion. *Journal of Nonverbal Behavior, 16,* 85–99.

Matthews, G. A., & Dickinson, A. M. (2000). Effects of alternative activities on time allocated to task performance under different percentages of incentive pay. *Journal of Organizational Behavior Management, 20,* 3–27.

Mazzoni, G. A., & Loftus, E. F. (1998). Dream interpretation can change beliefs about the past. *Psychotherapy, 35,* 177–187.

McAuliffe, W. E., Geller, S., LaBrie, R., Paletz, S., & Fournier, E. (1998). Are telephone surveys suitable for studying substance abuse? Cost, administration, coverage and response rate issues. *Journal of Drug Issues, 28,* 455–481.

McCabe, S. E. (2004). Comparison of web and mail surveys in collecting illicit drug use data: A randomized experiment. *Journal of Drug Education, 34,* 61–72. doi:10.2190/4HEY-VWXL-DVR3-HAKV

McCoy, T. P., Ip, E. H., Blocker, J. N., Champion, H., Rhodes, S. D., Wagoner, K. G., Mitra, A., & Wolfson, M. (2009). Attrition bias in a U.S. internet survey of alcohol use among college freshmen. *Journal of Studies on Alcohol and Drugs, 70,* 606–614.

McCrae, R. R., & Terracciano, A. (2006). National character and personality. *Current Directions in Psychological Science, 15*(4), 156–161. doi:10.1111/j.1467-8721.2006.00427.x

McCrea, S. M., Hirt, E. R., & Milner, B. J. (2008). She works hard for the money: Valuing effort underlies gender differences in behavioral self-handicapping. *Journal of Experimental Social Psychology, 44,* 292–311. doi:10.1016/j.jesp.2007.05.006

McGlone, M. S., & Aronson, J. (2007). Forewarning and forearming stereotype-threatened students. *Communication Education, 56,* 119–133.

McGuire, W. J. (1983). A contextualist theory of knowledge: Its implications for innovation and reform in psychological research. In L. Berkowitz (Ed.), *Advances in experimental social psychology* (Vol. 16). Orlando, FL: Academic Press.

McMorris, B. J., Petrie, R. S., Catalano, R. F., Fleming, C. B., Haggerty, K. P., & Abbott, R. D. (2009). Use of web and in-person survey modes to gather data from young adults on sex and drug use: An evaluation of cost, time, and survey error based on a randomized mixed-mode design. *Evaluation Review, 33*, 138–158. doi:10.1177/0193841X08326463

Melnik, T. A., Baker, C. T., Adams, M. L., O'Dowd, K., Mokdad, A. H., Brown, D. W., et al. (2002). Psychological and emotional effects of the September 11 attacks on the World Trade Center—Connecticut, New Jersey, and New York, 2001. *Mortality and Morbidity Weekly Report, 51,* 784–786.

Mendoza, M. (2005). Allegations of fake research hit new high. Yahoo News. Retrieved from www.news.yahoo.com

Meston, C. M., Heiman, J. R., Trapnell, P. D., & Paulhus, D. L. (1998). Social desirable responding and sexuality self-reports. *Journal of Sex Research, 35,* 148–157.

Milgram, R. M., & Davidovich, N. (2010). Creative thinking and lecturer effectiveness in higher education. *International Journal of Creativity & Problem Solving, 20*, 7–14.

Milgram, S. (1963). Behavioral study of obedience. *Journal of Abnormal and Social Psychology, 67,* 371–378.

Milgram, S. (1964). Issues in the study of obedience: A reply to Baumrind. *American Psychologist, 19,* 848–852.

Milgram, S. (1974). *Obedience to authority: An experimental view.* New York, NY: Harper & Row.

Miller, A. G. (2009). Reflections on "Replicating Milgram" (Burger, 2009). *American Psychologist, 64*, 20–27.

Miller, J. D. (2007a, February). The public understanding of science in Europe and the United States. Presented at the annual meeting of the American Association for the Advancement of Science, San Francisco, CA.

Miller, J. D. (2007b, February). Civic scientific literacy across the life cycle. Presented at the annual meeting of the American Association for the Advancement of Science, San Francisco, CA.

Miller, M. A., & Rahe, R. H. (1997). Life changes scaling for the 1990s. *Journal of Psychosomatic Research, 43,* 279–292.

Miller, N. (1985). The value of behavioral research on animals. *American Psychologist, 40,* 423–440.

Miller, R. S. (1995). On the nature of embarrassability: Shyness, social evaluation, and social skill. *Journal of Personality, 63,* 315–339.

Mills, C. G., Boteler, E. H., & Oliver, G. K. (1999). Digit synaesthesia: A case study using a stroop-type test. *Cognitive Neuropsychology, 16,* 181–191.

Miracle, A. D., Brace, M. F., Huyck, K. D., Singler, S. A., & Wellman, C. L. (2006). Chronic stress impairs recall of extinction of conditioned fear. *Neurobiology of Learning and Memory, 85,* 213–218.

Mishra, L. K., & Singh, A. P. (2010). Creative behaviour questionnaire: Assessing the ability of managers to produce creative ideas. *Journal of the Indian Academy of Applied Psychology, 36*, 115–121.

Mobile web audience already one-fifth the size of PC-based internet audience in the U.K. (2007, May 14). Retrieved from www.comscore.com/press/release.asp?press=1432

Modern Language Association of America. (1995). *MLA handbook for writers of research papers* (4th ed.). New York: Author.

Mohr, D. C., Goodkin, D. E., Bacchetti, P., Boudewyn, A. C., Huang, L., Marrietta, P., Cheuk, W., & Dee, B. (2000). Psychological stress and the subsequent appearance of new brain MRI lesions in MS. *Neurology, 55,* 55–61.

Mook, D. G. (1983). In defense of external invalidity. *American Psychologist, 38,* 379–387.

Moonesinghe, R., Khoury, M. J., & Janssens, A. C. J. W. (2007). Most published research findings are false—but a little replication goes a long way. *PLoS Medicine, 4,* e28, 218–221.

Moore, D. W. (2005) Three in four Americans believe in paranormal. Gallup News Service. Retrieved from http://home.sandiego.edu/~baber/logic/gallup.html

Moore, D. W. (1992). *The superpollsters: How they measure and manipulate public opinion in America.* New York, NY: Four Walls Eight Windows.

Morris, J. S., Scott, S. K., & Dolan, R. J. (1999). Saying it with feeling: Neural responses to emotional vocalizations. *Neuropsychologia, 37,* 1155–1163.

Müller, F. R. (2000, May/June). [Letter to the editor.] *The Sciences, 40,* 5.

Münsterberg, H. (1914). *Psychology and social sanity.* New York, NY: Doubleday, Page, & Co.

Murphy, K. R., & Myors, B. (2004). *Statistical power analysis: A simple and general model for traditional and modern hypothesis tests.* Mahwah, NJ: Lawrence Erlbaum Associates.

Must, O., te Nijenhuis, J., Must, A., & van Vianen, A. E. M. (2009). Comparability of IQ scores over time. *Intelligence, 37,* 25–33. doi:10.1016/j.intell.2008.05.002

Muzzatti, B., & Agnoli, F. (2007). Gender and mathematics: Attitudes and stereotype threat susceptibility in Italian children. *Developmental Psychology, 43,* 747–759.

Nasrallah, M., Carmel, D., & Lavie, N. (2009). Murder, she wrote: Enhanced sensitivity to negative word valence. *Emotion, 9,* 609–618. doi:10.1037/a0016305

Neumann, D. L., & Kitlertsirivatana, E. (2010). Exposure to a novel context after extinction causes a renewal of extinguished conditioned responses: Implications for the treatment of fear. *Behaviour Research and Therapy, 48,* 565–570. doi:10.1016/j.brat.2010.03.002

Newman, J., Rosenbach, J. H., Burns, K. L., Latimer, B. C., Matocha, H. R., & Vogt, E. E. (1995). An experimental test of "the Mozart effect": Does listening to his music improve spatial ability? *Perceptual and Motor Skills, 81,* 1379–1387.

The NIMH Multisite HIV Prevention Trial: Reducing HIV sexual risk behavior (1988). *Science, 280,* 1889–1894.

Nisbet, M. (1998). New poll points to increases in paranormal belief. *Skeptical Inquirer, 22*(5), 9.

Norenzayan, A., & Schwarz, N. (1999). Telling what they want to know: Participants tailor causal attributions to researchers' interests. *European Journal of Social Psychology, 29,* 1011–1020.

North, C. S., Nixon, S. J., Shariat, S., Mallonee, S., McMillen, J. C., Spitznagel, E. L., & Smith, E. M. (1999). Psychiatric disorders among survivors of the Oklahoma City bombing. *Journal of the American Medical Association, 282,* 755–762.

Novi, M. J., & Meinster, M. O. (2000). Achievement in a relational context: preferences and influences in female adolescents. *Career Development Quarterly, 49,* 73–84.

Nunnally, J. C. (1978). *Psychometric theory* (2nd ed.). New York, NY: McGraw-Hill.

O'Muircheartaigh, C., Krosnick, J. A., & Helic, A. (2000). Middle alternatives, acquiesence, and the quality of questionnaire data. Working paper, Harris School, University of Chicago.

Office of Research Integrity: Handling misconduct. (nd). Retrieved from http://ori.dhhs.gov/html/misconduct/casesummaries.asp\#1

Office of Research Integrity Annual Report 2007. (2008). Retrieved from http://ori.dhhs.gov/documents/annual_reports/ori_annual_report_2007.pdf

Office of Research Integrity Annual Report 2006. (2007). Retrieved from http://ori.dhhs.gov/documents/annual_reports/ori_annual_report_2006.pdf

Office of Research Integrity Annual Report 2005. (2006). Retrieved from http://ori.dhhs.gov/documents/annual_reports/ori_annual_report_2005.pdf

Office of Research Integrity Annual Report 2004. (2005). Retrieved from http://ori.dhhs.gov/documents/annual_reports/ori_annual_report_2004.pdf

Office of Research Integrity Annual Report 2003. (2004). Retrieved from http://ori.dhhs.gov/documents/annual_reports/ori_annual_report_2003.pdf

Office of Research Integrity Annual Report 2002. (2003). Retrieved from http://ori.dhhs.gov/documents/annual_reports/ori_annual_report_2002.pdf

Office of Research Integrity Annual Report 2001. (2002). Retrieved from http://ori.dhhs.gov/documents/annual_reports/ori_annual_report_2001.pdf

Ogden, C. L., Fryar, C. D., Carroll, M. D., & Flegal, K. M. (2004). Mean body, height, weight and body mass index: United States 1960–2002. Retrieved from the Centers for Disease Control http://www.cdc.gov/nchs/data/ad/ad347.pdf

Olmsted, D. (2009, July 27). Olmsted on autism: Mercury mayhem. *Age of Autism.* Retrieved December 10, 2009, from www.ageofautism.com/2009/07/olmsted-on-autism-mercury-mayhem.html

Omer, S. B., Salmon, D. A., Orenstein, W. A., deHart, M. P., & Halsey, N. (2009). Vaccine refusal, mandatory immunization, and the risks of vaccine-preventable diseases. *New England Journal of Medicine, 360,* 1981–1988. Retrieved from http://content.nejm.org/cgi/reprint/360/19/1981.pdf

Orne, M. T. (1962). On the social psychology of the psychological experiment: With particular reference to demand characteristics and their implications. *American Psychologist, 17,* 776–783.

Orne, M. T., & Scheibe, K. T. (1962). The contribution of nondeprivation factors in the production of sensory deprivation effects. *Journal of Abnormal and Social Psychology, 68,* 3–12.

Ornstein, R., & Sobel, D. (1987). *The healing brain.* New York, NY: Simon and Schuster.

Ortmann, A., & Hertwig, R. (1997). Is deception acceptable? *American Psychologist, 52,* 746–747.

Osofsky, H. J., Osofsky, J. D., Kronenberg, M., Brennan, A., & Hansel, T. C. (2009). Posttraumatic stress symptoms in children after Hurricane Katrina: Predicting the need for mental health services. *American Journal of Orthopsychiatry, 79,* 212–220. doi:10.1037/a0016179

Oyserman, D., Coon, H. M., & Kemmelmeier, M. (2002). Rethinking individualism and collectivism: Evaluation of theoretical assumptions and meta-analyses. *Psychological Bulletin, 128,* 3–72. doi:10.1037/0033-2909.128.1.3

Paasche-Orlow, M. K., Taylor, A. A., & Barncati, F. L. (2003). Readability standards for informed-consent forms as compared with actual readability. *New England Journal of Medicine, 348,* 721–726.

Panter, A. T., Daye, C. E., Allen, W. R., Wightman, L. F., & Deo, M. E. (2009). It matters how and when you ask: Self-reported race/ethnicity of incoming law students. *Cultural Diversity and Ethnic Minority Psychology, 15,* 51–66. doi:10.1037/a0013377

Park, R. L. (2003). The seven warning signs of bogus science. *Chronicle of Higher Education, 49*(21), B20. Retrieved from www.chronicle.com/free/v49/i21/21b02001.htm

Paschall, M. J., & Freisthler, B. (2003). Does heavy drinking affect academic performance in college? Findings from a prospective study of high achievers. *Journal of Studies on Alcohol, 64,* 515–519.

Paschall, M. J., Bersamin, M., & Flewelling, R. L. (2005). Racial/Ethnic differences in the association between college attendance and heavy alcohol use: A national study. *Journal of Studies on Alcohol, 66*(2), 266–274.

Peirce, C. S. (1877). The fixation of belief. *Popular Science Monthly, 12,* 1–15. Retrieved from www .peirce.org/writings/p107.html

Peng, K., & Nisbett, R. E. (1999). Culture, dialectics, and reasoning about contradiction. *American Psychologist, 54,* 741–754.

Peters, M. (1993). Still no convincing evidence of a relation between brain size and intelligence in humans. *Canadian Journal of Experimental Psychology, 47,* 751–756.

Phinney, J. S. (1996). When we talk about American ethnic groups, what do we mean? *American Psychologist, 51,* 918–927.

Plous, S. (1996a). Attitudes toward the use of animals in psychological research and education. *American Psychologist, 51,* 1167–1180.

Plous, S. (1996b). Attitudes toward the use of animals in psychological research and education: Results from a national survey of psychology majors. *Psychological Science, 7,* 352–358.

Powell, M. C., & Fazio, R. H. (1984). Attitude accessibility as a function of repeated attitudinal expression. *Personality and Social Psychology Bulletin, 10,* 139–148.

Presser, S., & Stinson, L. (1998). Data collection mode and social desirability bias in self-reported religious attendance. *American Sociological Review, 63,* 137–145.

Price, W. F., & Crapo, R. H. (1999). *Cross-cultural perspectives in introductory psychology* (3rd ed.). Pacific Grove, CA: Brooks/Cole Wadsworth.

Quinn, G. E., Shin, C. H., Maguire, M. G., & Stone, R. A. (1999). Myopia and ambient lighting at night. *Nature, 399,* 113–114.

Quraishi, M. (2008). Researching Muslim prisoners. *International Journal of Social Research Methodology: Theory & Practice, 11,* 453–467. doi:10.1080/13645570701622199

Radford, B. (1998). Survey finds 70% of women, 48% of men believe in paranormal. *Skeptical Inquirer, 22*(2), 8.

Radner, D., & Radner, M. (1982). *Science and unreason.* Belmont, CA: Wadsworth.

Rampey, B. D., Dion, G. S., & Donahue, P. L. (2009). The Nation's Report Card: Trends in Academic Progress in Reading and Mathematics 2008. Retrieved from http://nces.ed.gov/nationsreportcard/pubs/main2008/2009479.asp

Rasinski, K. A. (1989). The effect of question wording on public support for government spending. *Public Opinion Quarterly, 53,* 388–394.

Rauch, S. L., Shin, L. M., & Phelps, E. A. (2006). Neurocircuitry Models of posttraumatic stress disorder and extinction: Human neuroimaging research-past, present, and future. *Biological Psychiatry, 60,* 376–382.

Rauscher, F. H., Shaw, G. L., Gordon, L. (1998). Key components of the Mozart effect. *Perceptual and Motor Skills, 86,* 835–841.

Rauscher, F. H., Shaw, G. L., & Ky, K. N. (1993). Music and spatial task performance. *Nature, 365,* 611.

Rauscher, F. H., Shaw, G. L., & Ky, K. N. (1995). Listening to Mozart enhances spatial-temporal reasoning: Towards a neurophysiological basis. *Neuroscience Letters, 185,* 44–47.

Ray, J. J. (1990). Acquiescence and problems with forced-choice scales. *Journal of Social Psychology, 130,* 397–399.

Recarte, M. A., & Nunes, L. M. (2000). Effects of verbal and spatial-imagery tasks on eye fixations while driving. *Journal of Experimental Psychology: Applied, 6,* 31–43.

Renner, M. J., Mackin, R. S. (1998). A life stress instrument for classroom use. *Teaching of Psychology, 25,* 46–48.

Research ethics and the medical profession. Report of the Advisory Committee on Human Radiation Experiments. (1996). *Journal of the American Medical Association, 276,* 403–409.

Reynolds, P. D. (1982). *Ethics and social science research.* Englewood Cliffs, NJ: Prentice-Hall.

Rheumatic fever and heart disease. (1942). In *The Mother's Encyclopedia* (Vol. 5, pp. 1028–1029). New York, NY: The Parents Institute.

Rieps, U-D. (2010). Design and formatting in internet-based research. In S. D. Gosling & J. A. Johnson (Eds.), *Advanced methods for conducting online behavioral research* (pp. 29–43). Washington, DC: American Psychological Association.

Ring, K., Wallston, K., & Corey, M. (1970). Mode of debriefing as a factor affecting subjective reaction to a Milgram-type obedience experiment: An ethical inquiry. *Representative Research in Social Psychology, 1,* 67–88.

Robins, R. W., Gosling, S. D., & Craik, K. H. (1999). An empirical analysis of trends in psychology. *American Psychologist, 54,* 117–128.

Rockwood, T. H., Sangster, R. L., & Dillman, D. A. (1997). The effect of response categories on survey questionnaires: Context and mode effects. *Sociological Methods and Research, 26,* 118–140.

Rodriguez, C. E. (2000). *Changing race: Latinos, the census and the history of ethnicity in the United States.* New York: New York University Press.

Rogler, L. H. (1999). Methodological sources of cultural insensitivity in mental health research. *American Psychologist, 54,* 424–433.

Rosenthal, R. (1979). The "file drawer problem" and tolerance for null results. *Psychological Bulletin, 86,* 638–641.

Rosenthal, R. (2003). Covert communication in laboratories, classrooms, and the truly real world. *Current Directions in Psychological Science, 12,* 151–154. doi:10.1111/1467-8721.t01-1-01250

Rosenthal, R., & Fode, K. L. (1966). Three experiments in experimenter bias. *Psychological Reports, 12,* 491–511.

Rosenthal, R. & Rosnow, R. L. (1975). *The volunteer subject.* New York, NY: Wiley.

Rosnow, R. L., & Rosenthal, R. (1997). *People studying people: Artifacts and ethics in behavioral research.* New York, NY: W. H. Freeman.

Ross, L. M., Hall, B. A., & Heater, S. L. (1998). Why are occupational therapists not doing more replication research? *The American Journal of Occupational Therapy, 52,* 234–235.

Rothbaum, F., Weisz, J., Pott, M., Kiyake, K., & Morelli, G. (2000). Attachment and culture: Security in the United States and Japan. *American Psychologist, 55,* 1093–1104.

Rothman, D. J. (1994, Jan. 9). Government guinea pigs. *New York Times,* Section 4, 23.

Rothman, M. (1996). Fear of success among business students. *Psychological Reports, 78,* 863–869.

Rozin, P. (2007). Exploring the landscape of modern academic psychology: Finding and filling the holes. *American Psychologist, 62,* 754–766. doi:10.1037/0003-066X.62.8.754

Rozin, P. (2006). Domain denigration and process preference in academic psychology. *Perspectives on Psychological Science, 1,* 365–376. doi:10.1111/j.1745-6916.2006.00021.x

Rubin, Z. (1985). Deceiving ourselves about deception: Comment on Smith and Richardson's "Amelioration of deception and harm in psychological research." *Journal of Personality and Social Psychology, 48,* 252–253.

Ryff, C. D. (1989). Happiness is everything, or is it? Explorations on the meaning of psychological well-being. *Journal of Personality and Social Psychology, 57,* 1069–1081.

Salsburg, D. (2001). *The lady tasting tea: How statistics revolutionized science in the twentieth century.* New York, NY: W. H. Freeman.

Satisfaction with local schools. (2005). Survey Research Unit School of Public Affairs Baruch College/ CUNY. Retrieved from http://etownpanel.com/results.htm

Schaie, K. W. (1992). The impact of methodological changes in gerontology. *International Journal of Aging and Human Development, 35,* 19–29.

Schaie, K. W. (2000). The impact of longitudinal studies on understanding development from young adulthood to old age. *International Journal of Behavioral Development, 24,* 257–266.

Scharrer, E. (2001). Men, muscles, and machismo: The relationship between television violence exposure and aggression and hostility in the presence of hypermasculinity. *Media Psychology, 3,* 159–188.

Schechter, R., & Grether, J. K. (2008). Continuing increases in autism reported to California's developmental services system: Mercury in retrograde. *Archives of General Psychiatry, 65,* 19–24. doi:10.1001/archgenpsychiatry.2007.1

Schillewaert, N., Langerak, F., & Duhamel, T. (1998). Non-probability sampling for WWW surveys: A comparison of methods. *Journal of the Market Research Society, 40,* 307–322.

Schram, C. M. (1996). A meta-analysis of gender differences in applied statistics achievement. *Journal of Educational and Behavioral Statistics, 21,* 55–70.

Schuller, R. A., & Cripps, J. (1998). Expert evidence pertaining to battered women: The impact of gender of expert and timing of testimony. *Law and Human Behavior, 22,* 17–31.

Schulz, D., Buddenberg, T., & Huston, J. P. (2007). Extinction-induced "despair" in the water maze, exploratory behavior and fear: Effects of chronic antidepressant treatment. *Neurobiology of Learning and Memory, 87,* 624–634.

Schwarz, N. (1999). Self-reports: How the questions shape the answers. *American Psychologist, 54,* 93–105.

Schwarz, N., Hippler, H. J., Deutsch, B., & Strack, F. (1985). Response categories: Effects on behavioral reports and comparative judgments. *Public Opinion Quarterly, 49,* 388–395.

Scriven, M., & Paul, R. (2007). Defining critical thinking. Retrieved March 19, 2008, from http://www.criticalthinking.org/aboutCT/define_critical_thinking.cfm

Scientists should adopt codes of ethics, scientist-bioethicist says. (2007, February 5). Retrieved from www.sciencedaily.com/releases/2007/02/070201144615.htm

Sechrist, G. B., & Stangor, C. (2001). Perceived consensus influences intergroup behavior and stereotype accessibility. *Journal of Personality and Social Psychology, 80,* 645–654.

Segall, M. H., Campbell, D. T., & Herskovits, M. J. (1966). *The influence of culture on visual perception.* Indianapolis, IN: Bobbs-Merrill.

Segall, M. H., Lonner, W. J., & Berry, J. W. (1998). Cross-cultural psychology as a scholarly discipline: On the flowering of culture in behavioral research. *American Psychologist, 53,* 1101–1110.

Selten, J.-P., Veen, N., Feller, W., Blom, J. D., Schols, D., Camoenië, W., Oolders, J., van der Velden, M., Hoek, H. W., Rivero, V. M., van der Graaf, Y., & Kahn, R. (2001). Incidence of psychotic disorders in immigrant groups to the Netherlands. *British Journal of Psychiatry, 178,* 367–372. doi:10.1192/bjp.178.4.367

Shannon, E. R., Neibling, B. C., & Heckert, T. M. (1999). Sources of stress among college students. *College Student Journal, 33,* 312–317.

Shayer, M., & Ginsburg, D. (2009). Thirty years on—a large anti-Flynn effect? (II): 13-and 14-year-olds. Piagetian tests of formal operations norms 1976–2006/7. *British Journal of Educational Psychology, 79,* 409–418. doi:10.1348/978185408X383123

Sherer, M., Maddux, J. E., Mercandante, B., Prentice-Dunn, S., Jacobs, B., & Rogers, R. W. (1982). The Self-Efficacy Scale: Construction and validation. *Psychological Reports, 51,* 663–671.

Shields, A. E., Fortun, M., Hammonds, E. M., King, P. A., Lerman, C., Rapp, R., & Sullivan, P. F. (2005). The use of race variables in genetic studies of complex traits and the goal of reducing health disparities: A transdisciplinary perspective. *American Psychologist, 60,* 77–103. doi:10.1037/0003-066X.60.1.77

Shih, T-H., & Fan, X. (2008). Comparing response rates from Web and mail surveys: A meta-analysis. *Field Methods, 20,* 249–271. doi:10.1177/1525822X08317085

Shulruf, B., Hattie, J., & Dixon, R. (2008). Factors affecting responses to Likert type questionnaires: Introduction of the ImpExp, a new comprehensive model. *Social Psychology of Education, 11,* 59–78. doi:10.1007/s11218-007-9035-x

Shute, N. (2011). More young people scorning sex, study finds. Retrieved May 1, 2011, from http://www .npr.org/blogs/health/2011/03/03/134235838/more-young-people-scorning-sex-study-finds

Sieber, J. E. (2009). Evidence-based ethical problem solving. *Perspectives in Psychological Science, 4,* 26–27.

Siegel, S., & Castellan, N. J. (1988). *Nonparametric statistics for the behavioral sciences.* New York: McGraw-Hill.

Silver, N. (2008, November 6). The popular vote. Retrieved May 1, 2011, from http://www.fivethirtyeight .com/

Singer, B., & Benassi, V. A. (1981, Winter). Fooling some of the people all of the time. *Skeptical Inquirer, 5,* 17–24.

Singer, E., Von Thurn, D. R., & Miller, E. R. (1995). Confidentiality assurances and survey response: A review of the experimental literature. *Public Opinion Quarterly, 59,* 266–277.

Singh, S. (1999). *The code book: The evolution of secrecy from Mary Queen of Scots to quantum cryptography.* New York, NY: Doubleday.

Smith, G. T., Spillane, N. S., & Annus, A. M. (2006). Implications of an emerging integration of universal and culturally specific psychologies. Perspectives on *Psychological Science, 1,* 211–233. doi:10.1111/j.1745-6916.2006.00013.x

Smith, P. C. (2007). Assessing students' research ideas. In D. S. Dunn, R. A. Smith, & B. C. Beins (Eds.), *Best practices for teaching statistics and research methods in the behavioral sciences* (pp. 59–70). Mahwah, NJ: Lawrence Erlbaum Associates.

Soliday, E., & Stanton, A. L. (1995). Deceived versus nondeceived participants' perceptions of scientific and applied psychology. *Ethics and Behavior, 5,* 87–104.

Soliman, F., Glass, C. E., Bath, K. G., Levita, L., Jones, R. M., Pattwell, S. S., Casey, B. J. (2010). *Science Express Reports.* A genetic variant BDNF polymorphism alters extinction learning in both mouse and human. Published online 14 January 2010. doi:10.1126/science.1181886

Spear, J. H. (2007). Prominent schools or other active specialties? A fresh look at some trends in psychology. *Review of General Psychology, 11,* 363–380. doi:10.1037/1089-2680.11.4.363

Spencer, S. J., Steele, C. M., & Quinn, D. M. (1999). Stereotype threat and women's math performance. *Journal of Experimental Social Psychology, 35,* 4–28.

Steele, C. M., & Aronson, J. (1995). Stereotype threat and the intellectual test performance of African Americans. *Journal of Personality and Social Psychology, 69,* 797–811.

Steinberg, N., Tooney, N., Sutton, C., & Denmark, F. (2000, May/June). [Letter to the editor]. *The Sciences, 40,* 3.

Stevens, S. S. (1951). *Handbook of experimental psychology.* New York: Wiley.

Stigler, S. M. (1986). *The history of statistics: The measurement of uncertainty before 1900.* Cambridge, MA: The Belknap Press of Harvard University Press.

Stiles, D. A., Gibbons, J. L., & Schnellman, J. D. (1990). Opposite-sex ideal in the U.S.A. and Mexico as perceived by young adolescents. *Journal of Cross-Cultural Psychology, 21,* 180–199.

Stokes, S. J., & Bikman, L. (1974). The effect of the physical attractiveness and role of the helper on help seeking. *Journal of Applied Social Psychology, 4,* 286–294.

Straus, M. A., Sugarman, D. B., & Giles-Sims, J. (1997). Spanking by parents and subsequent antisocial behavior of children. *Archives of Pediatrics and Adolescent Medicine, 151,* 761–767.

Strohmetz, D. B., & Moore, M. P. (2003, March). Impact of a tattoo on a helping request. Poster presented at the annual convention of the Eastern Psychological Association, Baltimore, MD.

Sue, S. (1999). Science, ethnicity, and bias: Where have we gone wrong? *American Psychologist, 54,* 1070–1077.

Takooshian, H., & O'Connor, P. J. (1984). When apathy leads to tragedy: Two Fordham professors examine "Bad Samaritanism." *Social Action and the Law, 10,* 26–27.

Tang-Martínez, Z., & Mechanic, M. (2000, May/June). [Letter to the editor.] *The Sciences, 40,* 5–6.

Teasdale, T. W., & Owen, D. R. (2005). A long-term rise and recent decline in intelligence test performance: The Flynn effect in reverse. *Personality and Individual Differences, 39,* 837–843. doi:10.1016/j.paid.2005.01.029

Teeter, P. A., & Smith, P. L. (1989). Cognitive processing strategies for normal and LD children: A comparison of the K-ABC and microcomputer experiments. *Archives of Clinical Neuropsychology, 4,* 45–61.

Thompson, W. F., Schellenberg, E. G., & Husain, G. (2001). Arousal, mood, and the Mozart effect. *Psychological Science, 12,* 248–251.

Thornhill, R., & Palmer, C. T. (2000). Why men rape. *The Sciences, 40,* 30–36.

Todd, J. L., & Worell, J. (2000). Resilience in low-income, employed, African-American women. *Psychology of Women Quarterly, 24,* 119–128.

Todorov, A. (2000). Context effects in national health surveys: Effects of preceding questions on reporting serious difficulty seeing and legal blindness. *Public Opinion Quarterly, 64,* 65–76.

Toepoel, V., Das, M., & Van Soest, A. (2009). Design of web questionnaires: The effects of the number of items per screen. *Field Methods, 21,* 200–213. doi:10.1177/1525822X08330261

Tolin, D. F., Maltby, N., Diefenbach, G. J., Hannan, S. E., & Worhunsky, B. S. (2004). Cognitive-behavioral therapy for medication nonresponders with obsessive-compulsive disorder: A wait-list controlled open trial. *Journal of Clinical Psychiatry, 65,* 922–931.

Traugott, M. W. (2005). The accuracy of the national preelection polls in the 2004 presidential election. *Public Opinion Quarterly, 69,* 642–654. doi:10.1093/poq/nfi061

Tsouderos, R., & Callahan, P. (2009, December 7). Autism: Kids put at risk. *Los Angeles Times*. Retrieved December 10, 2009, from www.latimes.com

Underwood, B. J., & Freund, J. S. (1970). Word frequency and short-term recognition memory. *American Journal of Psychology, 83,* 343–351.

Uriell, Z. A., & Dudley, C. M. (2009). Sensitive topics: Are there modal differences? *Computers in Human Behavior, 25,* 76–87. doi:10.1016

Use of the internet for conducting opinion and marketing research: Ethical guidelines (2000). Retrieved from http://www.mra-net.org/resources/documents/internet_ethics_guidelines.pdf

Vadillo, M. A., Bárcena, R., & Matute, H. (2006). The internet as a research tool in the study of associative learning: An example from overshadowing. *Behavioural Processes, 73,* 36–40.

van de Vijver, F. J. R., & Leung, K. (2000). Methodological issues in psychological research on culture. *Journal of Cross-Cultural Psychology. Special Issue: Millennium, 31,* 33–51. doi:10.1177/0022022100031001004

van Ijzendoorn, M. H., & Sagi, A. (2001). Cultural blindness or selective inattention? *American Psychologist, 56,* 824–825.

VanVolkinburg, G. A. (1998). Restaurant server posture related to add-on scales. *Journal of Psychological Inquiry, 3,* 11–13.

Varvel, S. A., Wise, L. E., Niyuhire, F., Cravatt, B. F., & Lichtman, A. H. (2007). Inhibition of fatty-acid amide hydrolase accelerates acquisition and extinction rates in a spatial memory task. *Neuropsychopharmacology, 32,* 1032–1041.

Vasquez, D. (2009, April 7). All wired up but not so happy about it. Media Life. Retrieved from http://www.medialifemagazine.com/artman2/publish/New_media_23/All_wired_up_but_not_so_happy_about_it.asp

Velleman, P. F., & Wilkinson, L. (1993). Nominal, ordinal, interval, and ratio typologies are misleading. *The American Statistician, 47,* 65–72.

Velten, E. (1968). A laboratory task for induction of mood states. *Behavior Research and Therapy, 6,* 473–482.

Velten, E., Jr. (1997). A laboratory task for induction of mood states. In S. Rachman (Ed.), *Best of behavior research and therapy* (pp. 73–82). New York: Pergamon/Elsevier Science.

The 1997 Vermont Youth Risk Behavior Survey: Statewide Report (1997). Retrieved August 3, 2007, from http://healthvermont.gov/pubs/yrbs/yrbs_1997.pdf

The 2001 Vermont Youth Risk Behavior Survey: Statewide Report (2001). Retrieved August 3, 2007, from http://healthvermont.gov/pubs/yrbs/yrbs_2001.pdf

The 2005 Vermont Youth Risk Behavior Survey: Statewide Report (2005). Retrieved from http://healthvermont.gov/pubs/yrbs/yrbs_2005.pdf

The 2009 Vermont Youth Risk Behavior Survey: Statewide Report. (2009). Retrieved from www.ruralpartnerships.org/storage/2009-.1126/science.11818862009%20VT%20YRBS.pdf

Vispoel, W. P. (2000). Computerized versus paper-and-pencil assessment of self-concept: Score comparability and respondent preferences. *Measurement and Evaluation in Counseling and Development, 33,* 130–143.

Vispoel, W. P., & Forte Fast, E. E. (2000). Response biases and their relation to sex differences in multiple domains of self-concept. *Applied Measurement in Education, 13,* 79–97.

Wadman, M. (2005). One in three scientists confesses to having sinned. *Nature, 435,* 718–719.

Wakefield's article linking MMR vaccine and autism was fraudulent (2011, January 5). *BMJ, 342:*c7452 doi: 10.1136/bmj.c7452

Waldo, C. R., Berdahl, J. L., & Fitzgerald, L. F. (1998). Are men sexually harassed? If so, by whom? *Law and Human Behavior, 22,* 59–79.

Wallace, W. P., Sawyer, T. J., & Robertson, L. C. (1979). Distractors in recall, distractor-free recognition, and the word-frequency effect. *American Journal of Psychology, 91,* 295–304.

Walsh, M., Hickey, C., & Duffy, J. (1999). Influence of item content and stereotype situation on gender differences in mathematical problem solving. *Sex Roles, 41,* 219–240.

Walsh, W. B. (1976). Disclosure of deception by debriefed subjects: Another look. *Psychological Reports, 38,* 783–786.

Wang, P. S., Gruber, M. J., Powers, R. E., Schoenbaum, M., Speier, A. H., Wells, K. B., & Kessler, R. C. (2007). Mental health service use among Hurricane Katrina survivors in the eight months after the disaster. *Psychiatric Services, 58,* 1403–1411. doi:10.1176/appi.ps.58.11.1403

Wann, D. L., & Wilson, A. M. (1999). Relationship between aesthetic motivation and preferences for aggressive and nonaggressive sports. *Perceptual & Motor Skills, 89,* 931–934.

Watkins, D., Mortazavi, S., & Trofimova, I. (2000). Independent and interdependent conceptions of self: An investigation of age, gender, and culture differences in importance and satisfaction ratings. *Cross-Cultural Research: The Journal of Comparative Social Science, 34,* 113–134.

Watson, J. B., & Rayner, R. (1920). Conditioned emotional reactions. *Journal of Experimental Psychology, 3,* 1–14. doi:10.1037/h0069608

Watson, J. B., & Rayner, R. (2000). Conditioned emotional reactions. *American Psychologist, 55,* 313–317. doi:10.1037/0003-066X.55.3.313

Wentland, E. J., & Smith, K. W. (1993). *Survey responses: An evaluation of their validity.* Boston, MA: Academic Press.

Westen, D. (1998). The scientific legacy of Sigmund Freud: Toward a psychodynamically informed psychological science. *Psychological Bulletin, 124,* 333–371.

What is plagiarism? (2010). Retrieved December 11, 2009, from http://wps.prenhall.com/hss_understand_plagiarism_1/0,6622,427065-,00.html

Wilkinson, L., & the Task Force on Statistical Inference. (1999). Statistical methods in psychology journals: Guidelines and explanations. *American Psychologist, 54,* 594–604.

Willimack, D. K., Schuman, H., Pennell, B-E, & Kepkowski, J. M. (1995). Effects of a prepaid nonmonetary incentive on response rates and response quality in a face-to-face survey. *Public Opinion Quarterly, 59,* 78–92.

Wilson, D. W. (1978). Helping behavior and physical attractiveness. *Journal of Social Psychology, 104,* 313–314.

Wimer, D. J., & Beins, B. C. (2000, August). Is this joke funny? Only if we say it is. Presented at the annual convention of the American Psychological Association. Washington, DC.

Wimer, D. J., & Beins, B. C. (2008). Expectations and perceived humor. *Humor: International Journal of Humor Studies, 21,* 347–363. doi:10.1515/HUMOR.2008.016

Winer, B. J., Brown, D. R., & Michels, K. M. (1991). Statistical principles in experimental design (3rd ed.). Boston: McGraw-Hill.

Winkielman, P., Knäuper, B., & Schwarz, N. (1998). Looking back at anger: Reference periods change the interpretation of (emotion) frequency questions. *Journal of Personality and Social Psychology, 75,* 719–728.

Wrzesniewski, A., Rozin, P., & Bennett, G. (2003). Working, playing, and eating: Making the most of most moments. In C. L. M. Keyes, & J. Haidt (Eds.), *Flourishing: Positive psychology and the life well-lived* (pp. 185–204). Washington, DC: American Psychological Association.

Wrzesniewski, A., McCauley, C. R., Rozin, P., & Schwartz, B. (1997). Jobs, careers and callings: A tripartite categorization of people's relations to their work. *Journal of Research in Personality, 31,* 21–33. doi:10.1006/jrpe.1997.2162

Wutzke, S. E., Conigrave, K. M., Kogler, B. E., Saunders, J. B., & Hall, W. D. (2000). Longitudinal research: Methods for maximizing subject follow-up. *Drug and Alcohol Review, 19,* 159–163.

Yee, A. H., Fairchild, H. H., Weizmann, F., & Wyatt, G. E. (1993). Addressing psychology's problem with race. *American Psychologist, 48,* 1132–1140.

York, J., Nicholson, T., Minors, P., & Duncan, D. F. (1998). Stressful life events and loss of hair among adult women: A case-control study. *Psychological Reports, 82,* 1044–1046.

Zadnik, K., Jones, L. A., Irvin, B. C., Kleinstein, R. N., Manny, R. E., Shin, J. A., & Mutti, D. O. (2000). Vision: Myopia and ambient night-time lighting. *Nature, 404,* 143–144.

Zajonc, R. B. (1965). Social facilitation. *Science, 149,* 269–274.

Zeller, S., Lazovich, D., Forster, J., & Widome, R. (2006). Do adolescent indoor tanners exhibit dependency? *Journal of the American Academy of Dermatology, 54,* 589–596.

Zettle, R. D., & Houghton, L. L. (1998). The relationship between mathematics and social desirability as a function of gender. *College Student Journal, 32,* 81–86.

Zimbardo, P. G. (1972). On the ethics of intervention in human psychological research: With special reference to the Stanford prison experiment. *Cognition, 2,* 243–256.

Zimmerman, F. J., Christakis, D. A., & Meltzoff, A. N. (2007). Associations between media viewing and language development in children under age 2 years. *Journal of Pediatrics, 151,* 364–368. doi:10.1016/j.jpeds.2007.04.071

Zuckerman, M. (1990). Some dubious premises in research and theory on racial differences. *American Psychologist, 45,* 1297–1303.

Zusne, L., & Jones, W. H. (1989). *Anomalistic psychology: A study of magical thinking* (2nd ed.). Hillsdale, NJ: Lawrence Erlbaum Associates.

2010 census: Census bureau should take action to improve the credibility and accuracy of its cost estimate for the decennial census (2008). Retrieved January 20, 2010, from http://www.usatoday.com/news/nation/census/2010-08-10-census10_ST_N.htm

AUTHOR INDEX

ACHRE report, 26
Ackerman, R., 274
Adair, J. G., 38, 143
Adams, G. J., 318
Affsprung, H. H., 131
Agnolik, F., 143
Álamo, C., 25
Alcock, J., 15
Allen, K. D., 56
ALSPAC Study Team, 17
Anderson, D. A., 262
Anderson, J., 261
Anderson, K. C., 97
Anderson, M. S., 27, 28
Aneschensel, C. S., 351
Angier, N., 343
Anguas-Wong, A. M., 346
Annus, A. M., 340
Anthonysamy, A., 41
Aronson, J., 143, 144, 353
Ashcraft, M. H., 35
Assar, M., 347, 356
Atkinson, D. R., 338
Austad, S. N., 134
Azar, B., 43, 65

Babbie, E., 98
Bachorowski, J. A., 237
Baer, M., 83
Baer, P. E., 318
Baker, J., 17
Bakken, L., 141
Ball, P., 347
Banks, S., 263
Banville, D., 351
Bárcena, R., 65
Barchard, K. A., 43

Barncati, F. L., 35
Baron-Cohen, S., 329
Barreto, R. E., 97
Bartolic, E. I., 86
Basha, S. A., 141
Basso, M. R., 86
Batson, C. D., 7
Baumann, D. J., 7
Baumrind, D., 36, 37
Beach, F. A., 43
Beins, A. M., 27, 74
Beins, B. C., 13, 27, 74, 86, 205
Bell, G., 85, 86
Bell, N. S., 137
Bem, D., 15
Benassi, V. A., 14
Benbow, C. P., 354
Benet-Martinez, V., 337
Bennett, G., 57
Benton, S. A., 97, 131
Ben-Zeev, T., 353, 354
Berdahl, J. L., 60
Berkowitz, L., 94
Berreby, D., 336
Berry, J. W., 335
Bersamin, M., 322
Betancourt, H., 335, 336, 343
Bhugra, D., 337
Bhui, K., 337
Bikman, L., 9
Birnbaum, M. H., 193, 194
Bishop, G. D., 13
Blair, C., 345
Bodenhausen, G. V., 353
Bond, L., 320, 321, 322, 332
Borg, M. J., 268
Boteler, E. H., 328, 329

Boulton, M. J., 320
Bowman, L. L., 41
Brady, V., 85, 86
Bramel, D., 143
Bray, J. H., 318
Brennan, M., 64
Brewer, N. T., 274
Bröder, A., 39
Brown, D. R., 215
Bruck, M., 35
Bruner, G. C., 272
Buddenberg, T., 97
Bull, R., 8
Burger, J. M., 36
Burnham, G., 99
Burtt, H., 12
Buxtun, P., 26
Byrnes, J. P., 141

Cai, W.-H., 97
Callahan, P., 17
Campbell, D. T., 136, 340
Caplan, J. B., 354
Caplan, P. J., 354
Carmel, D., 93
Carr, S. C., 13
Carstens, C. B., 70
Caruso, K., 315
Castellan, N. J., 299
Ceci, S. J., 35
Cepeta-Benito, A., 351
Cernovsky, Z. Z., 345
Chandra, A., 271
Chang, W. C., 338
Chao, R., 348
Chen, F. F., 349
Cheryan, S., 353

441

Chiriboga, D. A., 263, 339
Chiu, C., 272
Cho, H., 64
Christakis, D. A., 2
Christensen, L., 39, 41
Cialdini, R. B., 7
Claire, T., 143
Clark, D. M., 7
Clark, V. A., 351
Cohen, D., 335, 338
Cohen, J., 186
Cohen, S., 87
Coile, D. C., 44, 45, 49
Collins, A., 7
Conrad, H. S., 314
Cook, D. J., 326
Cook, P. J., 266
Coon, H. M., 263
Copen, C., 271
Corey, M., 37
Couper, M. P., 65
Craik, K. H., 55
Cranford, J. A., 62
Crapo, R. H., 13, 340
Cripps, J., 60
Crocker, P. R. E., 58
Croizet, J-C., 143
Cronin, K., 86
Cunningham, S., 7
Cytowic, R. E., 328, 329, 330

Dalal, R., 65
Darby, B. L., 7
Darley, J. M., 7
Das, M., 263
Davenport, S. M., 197
Davidovich, N., 83
de Vries, R., 27, 28
Deci, E. L., 57
Deese, J., 93
Delgado, A. R., 353
Delizonna, L., 83
Desrosiers, P., 351
Dickinson, A. M., 86
Diener, E., 40
Dillman, D. A., 63, 266, 268
Dion, G. S., 319
Dixon, R., 270
Dixon, W. A., 86, 131
Dolan, R. J., 86
Donahue, P. L., 319
Doros, G., 58
Dudley, C. M., 272
Duffy, J., 143

Duhamel, T., 63
Duncan, S. C., 318
Duncan, T. E., 318
Dushenko, T. W., 38

Eagly, A. H., 353
Elliott, A. J., 141
Elms, A. C., 36
Exline, J. J., 141

Fairburn, C. G., 99
Fan, X., 61
Fanelli, D., 28
Farley, P., 27
Fazio, R. H., 269
Fazio, V., 86
Felmingham, K., 97
Fernandez, E., 84
Field, A., 215
Fienberg, J., 261
Finkel, S. E., 268
Fisher, C. B., 39
Fisher, C., 41, 42
Fitzgerald, L. F., 60
Flewelling, R. L., 322
Flynn, J. R., 345
Fode, K. L., 140, 144
Fomnbonne, R., 17
Forte Fast, E. E., 263, 272
Francis, L. J., 272
Frank, O., 277
Freisthler, B., 322
French, S., 86
Frerichs, R. R., 351
Freund, J. S., 92
Friend, R., 143
Friman, P. C., 56
Fryberg, C., 39
Fryberg, D., 41, 42
Furnham, A., 83

Gaito, J., 107
Gawrylewski, A., 89, 328
Gazdella, B. M., 90
Gehricke, J-G., 86
Geier, A. B., 58
Gendall, P., 64
Genet-Volet, G., 351
Gertz, M., 53, 266
Getz, J. G., 318
Gibbons, J. L., 335
Giles, H., 347
Giles-Sims, J., 284
Ginsburg, D., 345

Gladwell, M., 52
Glauser, T., 86
Glaze, J. A., 90
Gleaves, D. H., 351
Glueck, W. F., 54
Goldenberg, J. L., 54
Golding, J., 17
Goldsmith, M., 274
Goldston, D. B., 315
Goodman-Delahunty, J., 59, 60
Gordon, L., 70
Gosling, S. D., 55, 61
Gould, S. J., 343
Gray, J., 353
Green, C. W., 86
Grether, J. K., 17
Grissom, R. J., 166, 216
Gruder, C. L., 40
Guenedi, A. A., 89
Gunz, A., 335, 338
Guterbok, T. M., 268
Gwiazda, J., 140

Hall, B. A., 68
Hall, G. C. N., 315
Halvari, H., 86
Harris, B., 11
Hartwig, R., 41
Haskell, E., 70
Hattie, J., 270
Hawker, D. S. J., 320
Hay, C. A., 141
Hays, W. L., 108, 111, 116, 150, 158, 167, 184, 216
Hayslip, B., 322
Headden, S., 259
Heater, S. L., 68
Heckathorn, D. D., 276-277
Heckert, T. M., 131
Heckhausen, J., 288
Hedden, T., 347
Heerwegh, D., 263
Helic, J. A., 274
Helms, J. E., 338, 342
Hemenway, D., 53, 266
Heron, J., 17
Herskovits, J. C., 340
Hertz-Picciotto, J., 17
Heuer, H., 90
Hewstone, M., 347
Hickey, C., 143
Hilts, P. J., 27
Hirt, E. R., 141
Hoek, J., 64

Holahan, C. K., 320
Holmes, J. D., 13
Holmes, T. H., 83, 84, 85
Hong, Y., 272
Horvitz, D., 276
Houghton, L. L., 272
Hounshell, G. W., 70
Howell, D. C., 109, 207, 284
Hrycaiko, D., 327
Hulse, S. H., 93
Humphreys, K., 2
Husain, G., 70
Huston, J. P., 97
Hyde, J. S., 353

Ideland, M., 44
Innogen, 28
Insel, T. R., 97
Inzlicht, M., 354, 354
Ioannidis, J. P. A., 9
ISSTI, 28
Iwamasa, G. Y., 42, 351, 353, 356

Jackson, C. J., 272
Jang, Y., 263
Janssens, A. C. J. W., 9
Jauch, L. R., 54
Jenni, D. A., 298
Jenni, M. A., 298
Jennings, C., 11
Jernigan, M., 338, 342
Ji, N. L., 347
Johnson, T. P., 271
Jones, H. E., 314
Jones, W. H., 15
Joseph, S., 86
Judd, C. M., 98, 321
Juhnke, R., 8

Kagan, J., 27, 46
Kaneto, H., 87
Kaplan, C. D., 276
Kasoff, J., 141
Katsev, R., 7
Kaufman, P., 338
Kaur, M., 2
Kazdin, A. E., 238
Keith-Spiegel, P., 35
Keller, H., 348
Keller, J., 143
Kemmelmeier, M., 263
Kerwin, M. L. E., 56
Khoury, M. J., 9
Kidder, L. K., 98, 321

Kiecker, P., 142
Kim, B. S. K., 338, 342
Kim, G., 263
Kim, J. J., 166
King, M. F., 272
Kirk, R., 295
Kirnan, J. P., 144
Kitlertsirivatana, E., 326
Kjormo, O., 86
Klawans, H. L., 340, 341
Kleck, G., 53, 266
Knäuper, B., 266
Koocher, G. P., 35
Korf, D., 276
Korn, J. H., 41
Kovar, M. G., 270
Krantz, J. H., 65
Krause, J. A., 35
Kravitz, R., 10
Krishnan, A., 141
Krosnick, J. A., 264, 272, 273, 274, 275
Kumari, R., 141
Ky, L., 68

La Greca, A. M., 10, 321, 323
Laidler, J. R., 17
Lang, F. R., 288, 289
Langer, E., 83
Langerak, F., 63
LaRose, R., 64
Larrabee, A. L., 42, 351
Larzelere, R., 56
Latané, B., 7
Lavender, J. M., 262
Lavie, N., 93
Lawson, C., 41
Lee, Y-T., 143
Lehman, D. R., 13
Leirer, V. O., 194
Lempert, R. O., 13
Leonhard, C., 271
Leung, K., 341–342
Levine, M., 7
Lewis, C. A., 86
Li, L. C., 342
Liang, C. T. H., 342
Lifton, R. J., 25
Lindsay, R. C. L., 38
Liston, R. J., 27, 46
Lobel, M., 141
Loftus, E. F., 140, 142
Lonner, W. J., 335, 340
López, S. R., 335, 336, 343
López-Muñoz, F., 25

Lord, F. M., 107
Ludwig, J., 266
Lynch, D. J., 84
Lynn, A., 13
Lynn, R., 345

Maascher, J., 338
MacGeorge, E. L., 97
Macias, S., 13
Mackin, R. S., 85
Mandel, E., 141
Manning, R., 7
Manucia, G. K., 7
Marans, D. G., 40
Marian, V., 347
Markus, H. R., 336
Martin, G. L., 327
Martin, G. N., 56
Martinez, E., 346
Martinez-Ebers, V., 64
Martinson, B. C., 27, 28
Mascher, J., 342
Masten, W. G., 90
Matsumoto, D., 13, 335, 336, 346, 347, 348, 353 356
Matthews, G. A., 86
Matthews, R., 40
Matute, H., 65
Mazzoni, G. A., 140
McAuliffe, W. E., 271
McCabe, S. E., 43
McCollam, P., 86
McCoy, W. K., 322
McCoy-Roberts, L., 322
McCrae, R. R., 336, 349
McGlone, M. S., 143
McGuire, W. J., 58, 59
McGuire, W. J., 79
McRae, R. R., 141
Mechanic, M., 11
Meinster, M. O., 85, 86
Melnik, T. A., 97
Meltzoff, A. N., 2
Mendoza, M., 27
Merit, R. D., 42
Merritt, R. D., 351
Meston, C. M., 272
Michels, K. M., 215
Milgram, R. M., 83
Milgram, S., 24, 36, 37, 38, 45, 47, 48
Miller, A. G., 36
Miller, D. C., 141
Miller, E. R., 262
Miller, J. D., 13

Miller, M. A., 87
Miller, N. E., 44, 45, 49
Miller, R. S., 41
Mills, C. G., 328, 329
Milner, B. J., 141
Miracle, A. D., 97
Mishra, L. K., 83
Mohr, D. C., 84
Molock, S. D., 315
Mook, D. G., 134-135
Moonesinghe, R., 9
Moore, D. W., 14, 258
Moore, M. P., 85
Morris, J. S., 86
Morrow, D. G., 194
Mortazavi, S., 339
Mosher, W. D., 271
Müller, F. R., 11
Munro, D., 13
Münsterberg, H., 12, 13
Murakami, J. L., 315
Murphy, K. R., 154, 186
Muzzati, B., 143
Myors, B., 154

Nasrallah, M., 93
Nederstrom, M., 83
Neibling, B. C., 131
Neisser, U., 347
Nelson, J. E., 142
Neumann, D. L., 326
Newman, J., 70
Nisbet, M., 14
Nisbett, R. E., 13, 347
Norenzayan, A., 268
North, C. S., 2
Novi, M. J., 85, 86
Nunes, L. M., 99
Nunnally, J. C., 108

O'Connor, P. J., 7
O'Muircheartaigh, C., 274
Ogden, C. L., 112
Oliver, G. K., 328, 329
Olmstead, D., 17
Omer, S. B., 17
Orne, M. T., 39, 143, 147
Ornstein, R., 84
Ortmann, A., 41
Osofsky, H. J., 10
Ottati, V., 143
Owen, D. R., 345
Owen, M. J., 237
Oyserman, D., 263

Paasche-Orlow, M. K., 35
Palmer, C. T., 11
Panter, A. T., 337
Park, R., 15
Paschall, M. J., 322
Pavur, R., 322
Peirce, C. S., 7-8
Peng, K., 347
Peters, M., 343
Phelps, E. A., 97
Phinney, J. S., 336, 337
Pirson, M., 83
Plous, S., 44, 45, 55, 93
Pottinger, T. G., 97
Powell, M. C., 269
Presser, S., 272
Price, W. F., 13, 340
Prieto, G., 353

Quinn, D. M., 143
Quinn, G. E., 139–140
Qurashi, M., 41

Radford, B., 14
Radner, D., 15
Radner, M., 15
Rahe, R. H., 83, 84, 85, 87
Rampey, B. D., 319
Randi, J., 14
Rasinski, K. A., 268
Rauch, S. L., 97
Rauscher, F. H., 68, 70
Ray, J. J., 272
Recarte, M. A., 99
Reid, D. H., 86
Reid, J. K., 86, 131
Renner, M. J., 85
Reynolds, P. D., 34
Rieps, U-D., 67
Ring, K., 37
Robertson, L. C., 92
Robins, R. W., 55
Rockwood, T. H., 266
Rodriguez, C. E., 336
Rogler, L. H., 42, 349, 350
Rosenthal, R., 9, 94,
    140, 143
Rosnow, R. L., 94, 143
Ross, L. M., 68
Rothbaum, F., 348
Rothman, D. J., 26
Rothman, M., 141
Rozin, P., 56, 57, 58
Rubin, Z., 40

Ryan, R. M., 57
Ryff, C. D., 293

Sagi, A., 348
Salsburg, D., 151, 206
Sangster, R. L., 266
Sawyer, T. J., 92
Schafer, W. D., 141
Schaie, K. W., 312, 313, 314, 317
Scharrer, E., 284
Schechter, R., 17
Schefft, B. K., 86
Scheibe, K. T., 143, 147
Schellenberg, E. G., 70
Schillewaert, N., 63, 64
Schnellman, J. D., 335
Schram, C. M., 354
Schuller, R. A., 60
Schulz, D., 97
Schwarz, N., 266, 268, 269, 347
Scott, S. K., 86
Sears, R. R., 320
Segall, M. H., 335, 340
Selten, J-P., 337
Shannon, E. R., 131
Shannon, M. A., 197
Shapiro, D., 86
Shaw, G. L., 68
Shayer, M., 345
Sheffiend, J., 84
Shields, A. E., 338
Shih, T-H., 61
Shin, L. M., 97
Shulruf, B., 270, 271
Shute, N., 271
Sieber, J. E., 35
Siegel, S., 299
Silver, N., 260
Silverman, W. K., 10
Singer, B., 14
Singer, E., 262
Singh, A. P., 83
Singh, S., 11
Sionean, C., 271
Smith, A. P., 87
Smith, E. R., 98, 321
Smith, G. T., 340
Smith, K. W., 266, 321
Smith, P. C., 59
Smith, R. E., 40
Smith, T. L., 86
Snijders, T., 277
Sobel, D., 84
Soliday, E., 39

Soliman, F., 134
Spear, J. H., 56
Spencer, S. J., 143
Spillane, N. S., 340
Stacks, J., 90
Stanley, J. C., 136, 354
Stanton, A. L., 39
Steele, C. M., 143, 144, 353
Steinberg, N., 11
Stephen, J., 86
Sterk, C., 276
Sternberg, R. S., 54
Stevens, J., 8
Stevens, S. S., 107
Stigler, S. M., 106
Stiles, D. A., 335
Stinson, L., 272
Stokes, S. J., 9
Stolberg, S. G., 27
Straus, M. A., 284
Strohmetz, D. B., 85
Strycker, L. A., 318
Stumpfhauser, A., 40
Sue, S., 345
Sugarman, D. B., 284
Sweeney, C. J., 141

Takooshian, H., 7
Tang-Martinez, Z., 11
Taylor, A. A., 35
Teasdale, J. D., 7
Teasdale, T. W., 345
Teeter, P. A., 86
Terracciano, A., 336, 349
Thompson, W. F., 70

Thornhill, R., 11
Thrash, T. M., 141
Titanic-Schefft, M., 86
Todd, J. L., 293
Todorov, A., 266
Toepoel, V., 263
Tolin, D. F., 178
Traugott, M. W., 260
Trofimova, I., 339
Tsouderos, R., 17
Tyrell, D. A., 87

Underwood, B. J., 92
Uriell, Z. A., 272
Ushasree, S., 141

Vadillo, M. A., 65
Van de Vijver, F. J. R., 341-342
Van Ijzendoorn, M. H., 348
Van Soest, A., 263
van Volkinburg, G. A., 107
Varvel, S. A., 97
Vasquez, D., 63
Velleman, P. F., 107
Velten, E., 86, 86
Vincent, J. E., 7
Vispoel, W. P., 61, 263, 272
Volpato, G. L., 97
Von Thurn, D. R., 262

Wadman, M., 27, 28
Waldo, C. R., 60
Wallace, W. P., 92
Wallston, K., 37

Walsh, M., 143
Walsh, W. B., 40
Wang, P. S., 323
Wann, D. L., 86
Watkins, D., 339
Wentland, E. J., 266, 321
Westen, D., 5
Whitbeck, L. B., 315
Wilkinson, L., 76, 107
Williams, J., 43
Willimack, D. K., 64
Wilson, A. M., 86
Wilson, D. W., 8
Wimer, D. J., 205, 207, 215, 216, 222
Winkielman, P., 266
Worell, J., 293
Wrzesniewski, A., 57
Wundt, W., 27
Wutzke, S. E., 324, 331
Wyer, R. S., 40

Yang, P. H., 338
Yee, A. H., 339, 344
Yesavage, J. A., 194
York, J., 84

Zadnik, K., 140
Zajonc, R. B., 88
Zayas, L. H., 315
Zeller, S., 2
Zettle, R. D., 272
Zimbardo, P. G., 24
Zimmerman, F. J., 2
Zusne, L., 15

A priori method, 7
ABA design, 325–26
ABAB design, 325, 326
Absolutism, 340
Abstract, 74
Accuracy of surveys, 260
Acquiescence, 273
Active deception, 39
Adolescent smoking, 270
Advantages of repeated measures designs, 192–95
Advantages to Internet research, 64–65
Advertising ethics, 31
American Psychological Association, 29–32
Animal research (ethics), 43–45
Anonymity, 32, 261
ANOVA, 204–17
    assumptions of ANOVA, 205–207
    effect size, 216–17
    Error Variance, 211–12
    Eta squared, 217
    F statistic, 212–14
    homogeneity of variance, 206
    Hartley *F* Max test, 206
    Levene's test of equality of variances, 206
    Omega squared, 217
    post hoc analyses, 214–17
    Scheffé test, 216
    Source Table, 209
    Total variance, 208–209
    Treatment variance, 209–11
    Tukey *HSD* test, 215–16
APA, 29–32
Apparatus section in a research report, 75, 76
Applied research, 88
Archival research, 90, 91
Aspirational goals, 29
Assessment (ethics), 31
Attitude questions, 268–69

Attrition, 321–24
Attrition threat, 137, 139
Authority, 7
Autism, 17

Back translation, 351
Bar chart, 121
Basic research, 88
Behaviorism, 55
Beneficence, 29, 30
Between groups ANOVA, 205–17
Biological basis for race, 342–45
Biosocial effects, 144
Bivariate correlation, 282
Blind study, 142–43
Bogus science, 15–18
Boundaries of competence, 31

Carry-over effects, 195
Case study, 89–90, 91, 328–29
Causal ambiguity, 132
Cause-effect relationships, 131–32
Census, 259
Chain-referral methods, 276
Chain-referral sampling, 100
Characteristics of pseudoscience, 16
Chi-Square goodness of fit, 295–98
Chi-Square test of independence, 298–300
Chronically accessible memories, 268
Closed-ended question, 264
Cluster sampling, 99
Coercion, 32
Cognitive revolution, 55–56
Cohort effects, 314
Cohort sequential design, 317–18
Cohort study, 316–17
Common themes in longitudinal research, 312–13
Concerns about attitude surveys, 268–69

Confidence intervals, 185, 190–91
Confidentiality, 31, 32, 261
Confound, 138–41
Construct validity, 68
Content validity, 349–50
Continuous data, 120
Continuum of research ideas, 53–55
Control, 4, 6
Control group, 135
Convenience sampling, 99
Correlational analyses, 282–91
   coefficient of determination, 291
   linear relationship, 283
   outlier, 287
   negative correlation, 289
   Pearson's r, 284–87
   positive correlation, 289
   restriction of range, 288
   significance, 290
   size of correlation, 288–89
Correlational research, 88–89, 91
Correlational studies, 282
Cost-benefit analysis, 36
Counterbalancing, 195–96
Covariance rule, 131
Cover story, 39, 142
Cramer's V, 300–301
Criteria for inclusion into a group, 337–38
Cross-cultural concepts in research, 342
Cross-cultural diagnoses, 351–52
Cross-cultural norms, 351
Cross-sectional research, 313–14
Cross-sectional versus longitudinal research, 313–14
Cross-sequential design, 317–18
Culture, 335–36
Culture and neurological diagnosis, 341
Culture and science, 10–13
Culture-free theory, 348

Data driven, 9
Date range search, 72
Debriefing, 26, 39, 40
Deception, 38–42
Decreases in animal research, 55
Degrees of freedom, 167–68
Dehoaxing, 39, 40
Demand characteristics, 143
Demographics of Internet users, 62
Description, 4–5
Descriptive statistics, 106–107
Descriptor search, 72
Desensitization, 39, 40
Determining the causes of behavior, 131–36
Determining the research setting, 88

Differences due to language and thought, 346–47
Different races, 344
Discrete data, 120
Discussion section in a research report, 75, 77
Double blind study, 142–43

Effect size, 155, 165–66
   Cohen's d, 186–87, 191
   Eta squared, 217
   Omega squared, 227
Electronic databases, 71
Emic, 340
Empirical approach, 9
Enforceable rules, 29–30
Estimated standard error of the mean difference
     score, 189
Ethical guidelines, 29
Ethical guidelines for Internet research, 262
Ethical standards, 29–32
Ethnicity, 336
Etic, 340
Evaluating if-then statements, 38
Evaluation apprehension, 143
Experiment, 130–31
Experimental analysis of behavior, 325
Experimental control, 136–41
Experimental group, 135
Experimental realism, 145
Experimental research, 89, 91
Experimenter bias, 144
Experimenter effects, 142
Explanation, 4, 6–7
External validity, 134–35
Extraneous variable, 138–41

Fabrication of data, 27
Factorial ANOVA, 236–52
   assumptions of factorial ANOVA, 237–38
   F statistic, 247–48
   factorial design, 236
   effect size, 251
   Error variance, 245–47
   interaction effect, 248–49
   main effects, 249–50
   post hoc analyses, 250–51
   Total variance, 239
   Treatment variance, 240–45
Falsifiability, 5–6
Falsification of data, 27
Fear of success, 141
Fidelity, 29, 30
Finding hidden populations, 276–77
Formal sources of research ideas, 53–55
Frequency polygon, 124

Gender stereotypes, 353–54
Generalization, 97

Hawthorne effect, 143–44
Hidden populations, 276–77
Histogram, 121
History threat, 137, 139
Human relations, 31
Hypodescent, 342
Hypothesis testing, 151–53
    Alternative (Research) Hypothesis, 151–52
    Null Hypothesis, 151–52
    steps in hypothesis testing, 164–65
Hypothetical construct, 83, 86

Impression management, 272
Independent samples *t* test, 180–84
Inferential statistics, 151
Informal sources of research ideas, 53–55
Informed consent, 26, 32
Institutional Review Board (IRB), 30, 34–35, 36
Instrumentation threat, 137–38, 139
Integrity, 29, 30
Internal validity, 132–34
Internal validity rule, 132
Internet research, 59–66, 67
    ethics, 42–43
Interpretation paradox, 342
Introduction section in a research report, 75–76
IRB. *See* Institutional Review Board (IRB)
Issues in cross-cultural research, 341–42
Issues in longitudinal research, 320–24

Judgmental sampling, 100
Junk science, 18
Justice, 29, 30

Key informant sampling, 276
Keyword search, 72
Kurtosis, 118

Limitations of repeated measures designs, 195–96
Literature review, 68–74
Literature search, 86–87
Longitudinal research, 90, 91, 312–24

Matched pairs, 195
Materials section in a research report, 75, 76
Maturation threat, 137, 139
Mean difference score, 188
Measures of central tendency, 109–11
    mean, 110–11
    median, 110
    mode, 109–10

Measures of Variability, 113–18
    range, 114
    standard deviation, 114–18
    variance, 117–18
Memory questions, 265–68
Method section in a research report, 75, 76
Misunderstandings about single-case research, 327–28
Mode of survey data collection, 271–72
Mortality threat, 137, 139
Mozart effect, 70
Mundane realism, 145

N of 1 Randomized Clinical Trial (RCT), 326
Natural pairs, 195
Naturalistic observation, 39
Nature of participants, 94
Nazis, 25, 38
Negatively skewed, 112–13
Neuroscience, 56, 57
Nondifferentiation, 275
Nonmaleficence, 29, 30
Non-parametric test, 295
Nonprobability sampling, 99–100
Nonsampling error, 99
Normal distribution, 111, 118, 156–57
Nuremburg Code, 33

Obedience research, 35–38
Objective, 8–9
Observational research, 88, 91
Office of Research Integrity (ORI), 28
One-drop rule, 342
Open-ended question, 264
Operational definition, 83, 86
Optimizing, 273–75
Order effects, 195
ORI, 28

Panel study, 318, 320
Parameters, 117
Parametric assumptions, 184
Participant effects, 142–43
Participant section in a research report, 75, 76
Passive deception, 39
Peer review, 10, 69–70
Physical culture, 335
Physical harm, 26
Placebo group, 135
Plagiarism, 27, 32
Pooled variance, 181
Population, 93, 260
Positively skewed, 112
Power, 154
Practical issues in cultural research, 345–46

Prediction, 4, 6
Primary source, 73
Privacy, 31
Probability sampling, 97–99
Probability theory, 150–51
Problems with Internet research, 65–66
Procedure section in a research report, 75, 76
Prospective study, 321
Pseudoscience, 14–15
Psychological harm, 26
Psychosocial effects, 144
PsycINFO, 71–73
   search options, 72
Public, 10
Publishing (ethics), 31
Purposive sampling, 100

Qualitative research, 90, 91
Quasi-experimental research, 89, 91
Questionnaire research, 91
Quota sampling, 100

Race, 336–38
Radiation in food, 26
Random assignment, 132–34, 178
Reading a journal article, 74–77
Realism in research, 144–45
Record-keeping ethics, 31
Reference section in a research report, 75, 77
Regression, 291–93
   line of best fit, 291
   multiple regression, 293–95
   regression equation, 292
Relativism, 340
Repeated Measures ANOVA, 220–28
   assumptions of repeated measures ANOVA, 221–22
   effect size, 227–28
   Error variance, 223–26
   F statistic, 226–27
   Omega squared, 227
   post hoc analyses, 227
   Total variance, 222–23
   Treatment variance, 223
Repeated (related) measures *t* test, 187–90
Replicability, 9–10
Replication, 66, 68, 70
Representative sample, 93
Research setting, 88
Resolving ethical issues, 31
Respect for people's rights and dignity, 29, 30
Respondent motivation, 64
Respondent-driven sampling, 276–77
Response bias, 270–75
Response rates to online surveys, 63–64

Responsibility, 29, 30
Results section in a research report, 75, 76–77
Retrospective study, 320–21
Role playing, 39

Sample, 93
Sample size, 94, 96
Sampling distributions, 157–59
Sampling frame, 263
Sampling issues, 275–77
Satisficing, 264, 273–75
Scales of Measurement, 106–109
   interval scale, 108
   nominal scale, 107
   ordinal scale, 108
   ratio scale, 108–109
Science and culture, 10–13
Scientific approach, 7
Scientific literacy, 13–18
Secondary source, 73
Selection threat, 137, 139
Self-deception positivity, 272
Self-selected sample, 275
Sensitive issues, 271–72
Sequence effects, 195
Sigma, 117
Significance testing, 162–63, 180
Similarities within cultures, 348–49
Simple random sampling, 98
Simulation, 39
Single blind study, 143
Single-case designs, 325–28
Single sample *t* test, 166–71
Single sample *z* test, 162
Single-subject experimentation, 324–25
Skewness, 112–13
Snowball sampling, 276
Social desirability, 272–73
Social desirability bias, 272
Social Readjustment Rating Scale (SRRS), 84
Spontaneously occurring events, 58
SPSS
   correlation, 301–302
   descriptive statistics, 119–25
   regression, 302
   Chi-Square, 302–306
   single sample *t* test, 171–73
   independent samples *t* test, 196–97
   related samples *t* test, 197–99
   repeated measures ANOVA, 228–31
   independent samples ANOVA, 217–20
   factorial ANOVA, 252–53
Standard error of the difference between two means, 181
Standard error of the mean (*SEM*), 159–61

Statistical regression threat, 138, 139
Stratified random sampling, 98
Strengths of single-participant designs, 326–27
Subjective culture, 335
Suicidal ideation, 315–16
Sum of Squares, 114–15
Survey, 258–59
Survey rescarch, 91
Synesthesia, 329–330
Syphilis, 25–26
Systematic sampling, 98

Targeted sampling, 276
Teaching (ethics), 31
Telescoping, 266
Temporal precedence rule, 131–32
Temporarily accessible memories, 268
Tenacity, 7
Terror management theory, 54
Tertiary source, 73–74
Testing threat, 138, 139
Tests of theory, 38
Theoretical research, 88
Therapy (ethics), 31
Thesaurus (PsycINFO), 73

Threats to internal validity, 136–38
Training supervision (ethics), 31
Translation problems, 350–51
Trend study, 314–16, 319
Tuskegee study, 25–26
Type I error (alpha), 66, 67, 153
Type II error, 66, 67, 154–55

U.S. Census, 261
Unanswered questions, 3
Unethical research practices, 25–29
Universalism, 340
Using previous research, 38

Validity, 66
Validity of everyday beliefs, 58
Variable, 83, 86
Varieties of longitudinal research, 314–24
Verifiability, 9–10
Voluntary participation, 26

Weaknesses of single-participant designs, 327
Whole-body radiation, 26
Withdrawal designs, 325–26
Women as jurors, 12